CZ.5.11

CZ.5.11

THE VICTORIA HISTORY
OF THE
COUNTIES OF ENGLAND

———

A HISTORY OF
MIDDLESEX

VOLUME VIII

THE VICTORIA HISTORY
OF THE
COUNTIES OF ENGLAND

EDITED BY C. R. ELRINGTON

THE UNIVERSITY OF LONDON
INSTITUTE OF
HISTORICAL RESEARCH

Oxford University Press, Walton Street, Oxford OX2 6DP
London New York Toronto
Delhi Bombay Calcutta Madras Karachi
Kuala Lumpur Singapore Hong Kong Tokyo
Nairobi Dar es Salaam Cape Town
Melbourne Auckland

and associated companies in
Beirut Berlin Ibadan Mexico City Nicosia

Oxford is a trade mark of Oxford University Press

Published in the United States by
Oxford University Press, New York

Printed in Great Britain
at the University Press, Oxford
by David Stanford
Printer to the University

INSCRIBED TO THE

MEMORY OF HER LATE MAJESTY

QUEEN VICTORIA

WHO GRACIOUSLY GAVE THE TITLE TO

AND ACCEPTED THE DEDICATION

OF THIS HISTORY

A HISTORY OF THE COUNTY OF MIDDLESEX

EDITED BY T. F. T. BAKER

VOLUME VIII

ISLINGTON AND
STOKE NEWINGTON PARISHES

PUBLISHED FOR

THE INSTITUTE OF HISTORICAL RESEARCH

BY

OXFORD UNIVERSITY PRESS

1985

Distributed by Oxford University Press until 1 January 1988
thereafter by Dawsons of Pall Mall

CONTENTS OF VOLUME EIGHT

LIST OF ILLUSTRATIONS

For permission to reproduce material in their possession, thanks are rendered to: City of London, Guildhall Library; the Greater London Council Photographic Library; London Borough of Hackney, Library Service, Archives Department; London Borough of Islington, Libraries Department; the National Monuments Record (N.M.R.) of the Royal Commission on Historical Monuments (England). The coats of arms were drawn by Patricia A. Tattersfield.

Plates between pages 124 and 125

LIST OF ILLUSTRATIONS

LIST OF ILLUSTRATIONS

LIST OF MAPS

All the maps except those on pages 12–13, 16, and 150 were drawn by K. J. Wass of the Department of Geography, University College, London, from drafts prepared by T. F. T. Baker, D. K. Bolton, and P. E. C. Croot.

EDITORIAL NOTE

THE present volume is the first to have been compiled for a Committee that was formed in 1979 to continue and complete the Middlesex History. The compilation of the earlier volumes, with the exception of Volume Two, was financed and supervised by the Middlesex Victoria County History Council, which represented the Local Authorities whose areas had remained within the administrative county of Middlesex until 1965. When that Council finished its task with the preparation of Volume Seven, which was published in 1982, there remained to be written the history of the part of the ancient county which lay within the area under the London County Council between 1889 and 1965. The seven London Boroughs whose areas made up that part of the ancient county had agreed jointly to provide for the V.C.H. volumes covering what may be called inner Middlesex. In 1980 the Committee which they set up for the purpose, under the chairmanship of Dr. David Avery, took on the financial support and supervision of the Middlesex V.C.H. editorial staff, which has remained unchanged since 1978. The University of London gratefully acknowledges the support of the Committee and the generosity of the London Boroughs which it represents.

The work of the Committee's predecessor is described in a booklet, *The Middlesex Victoria County History Council, 1955–84*, which also lists the contents of the first seven volumes of the Middlesex History. The structure and aims of the Victoria History as a whole are outlined in the *General Introduction* (1970).

Those who have provided information for the present volume or commented on parts of the text are named in the footnotes, and they are sincerely thanked for their help. Particular mention must be made here of the valuable contributions of Mr. H. V. Borley and Mr. R. M. Robbins, C.B.E., who read the sections of the text dealing with communications, of Mr. J. C. Connell, who read the article on Islington, and of Miss J. Dailey and Mr. D. Mander and their respective staff, who read the article on Stoke Newington.

MIDDLESEX
VICTORIA COUNTY HISTORY
COMMITTEE

As at 1 April 1985

Chairman

DAVID AVERY, ESQ.

Representatives of the following Local Authorities

London Boroughs

Camden   Islington
Hackney   Kensington and Chelsea
Hammersmith and Fulham   Tower Hamlets
                 Westminster

The Greater London Council

Representatives of

The London and Middlesex Archaeological Society
The Institute of Historical Research

Co-opted Members

I. W. DAVIES, ESQ.
MISS HERMIONE HOBHOUSE, M.B.E.

Hon. Secretary: R. G. SURRIDGE, ESQ.
Hon. Treasurer: MELVYN BARNES, ESQ.

CLASSES OF DOCUMENTS
IN THE PUBLIC RECORD OFFICE
USED IN THIS VOLUME
WITH THEIR CLASS NUMBERS

Chancery

	Proceedings	
C 1	Early	
C 2	Series I	
C 3	Series II	
C 5	Six Clerks Series, Bridges	
C 6		Collins
C 7		Hamilton
C 8		Mitford
C 9		Reynardson
C 10		Whittington
C 43	Rolls Chapel Series	
C 54	Close Rolls	
C 66	Patent Rolls	
C 78	Decree Rolls	
C 93	Proceedings of Commissioners of Charitable Uses, Inquisitions, and Decrees	
	Inquisitions post mortem	
C 133	Series I, Edw. I	
C 138	Hen. V	
C 142	Series II	
C 143	Inquisitions ad quod damnum	
C 260	Chancery Files (Tower and Rolls Chapel), Recorda	

Court of Common Pleas

CP 25(1)	Feet of Fines, Series I
CP 25(2)	Series II

Exchequer, King's Remembrancer

E 134	Depositions taken by Commission
E 178	Special Commissions of Inquiry
E 179	Subsidy Rolls, etc.
E 211	Ancient Deeds, Series DD

Exchequer, Augmentation Office

E 303	Conventual Leases
E 304	Conveyances of Crown Lands
E 309	Enrolments of Leases
E 310	Particulars for Leases
E 315	Miscellaneous Books
E 317	Parliamentary Surveys
E 318	Particulars for Grants of Crown Lands
E 320	Particulars for the Sale of the Estates of Charles I
E 326	Ancient Deeds, Series B

Exchequer, Lord Treasurer's Remembrancer's and Pipe Offices

E 367	Particulars and Warrants for Leases

Ministry of Education

ED 3	Educational Returns, London
ED 7	Public Elementary Schools, Preliminary Statements
ED 14	London General Files
ED 15	Private Schools not recognized for Grant or Efficiency, Returns
ED 16	Supply Files

Registry of Friendly Societies

FS 1	Rules and Amendments, Series I
FS 2	Indexes to Rules and Amendments, Series I

Home Office

HO 107	Population Returns
HO 129	Ecclesiastical Returns

Board of Inland Revenue

IR 18	Tithe Files
IR 29	Tithe Apportionments
IR 30	Tithe Maps
IR 58	District Valuation Books

Justices Itinerant, Assize and Gaol Delivery Justices, etc.

JUST 1	Eyre Rolls, Assize Rolls, etc.

Exchequer, Office of the Auditors of the Land Revenue

LR 2	Miscellaneous Books
LR 14	Ancient Deeds, Series E

Ministry of Agriculture, Fisheries, and Food

MAF 9	Deeds and Awards of Enfranchisement
MAF 20	Manor Files
MAF 68	Agricultural Returns: Parish Summaries

Ministry of Health

MH 12	Poor Law Union Papers
MH 13	Correspondence

Maps and Plans

MPE, MPF	Maps and plans taken from various classes

LIST OF CLASSES OF DOCUMENTS

SELECT LIST OF
CLASSES OF DOCUMENTS IN THE
GREATER LONDON RECORD OFFICE
USED IN THIS VOLUME
WITH THEIR CLASS NUMBERS

A/CSC	Corporation of the Sons of the Clergy, estate records
AR/BA	Architect's Records, Building Acts
Cal. Mdx. Rec.	Calendar of Sessions Records, 1607–12
Cal. Mdx. Sess. Bks.	Calendar of Sessions Books, 1638–1752
Is. B.G.	Islington Board of Guardians, records
M83/BAR	Manorial Records, Barnsbury
M83/NB	Manorial Records, Newington Barrow
MBO	Metropolitan Building Office, records
MBW	Metropolitan Board of Works, records
MR/LV	Licensed Victuallers' Lists
MR/TH	Hearth Tax Assessments
P83/MRY	Parish Records, St. Mary, Islington
P94/MRY	Parish Records, St. Mary, Stoke Newington

NOTE ON ABBREVIATIONS

Among the abbreviations and short titles used the following may require elucidation, in addition to those noted in the Victoria History's *Handbook for Editors and Authors* (1970):

Abstract of Ct. Rolls	W. M. Marcham, 'Abstract of Court Rolls' of Stoke Newington, 1675–1882. Transcript in HAD (see below)
B.L.	British Library (used in references to documents transferred from the British Museum)
Bacon, *Atlas of Lond.* (1886)	*Ordnance Atlas of London and Suburbs*, ed. G. W. Bacon (1886)
Baker's plan	*Islington and its Environs*, drawn by E. Baker and engraved by B. Baker, 1793; revised edns. 1805, 1817. In Islington libr.
Booth, *Life and Labour*	C. Booth, *Life and Labour of the People in London* (17 vols. revised edn. 1902–3). Survey begun 1886
C.C.C.	Council for the Care of Churches (formerly Council for Places of Worship)
Calamy Revised	*Calamy Revised*, ed. A. G. Matthews (1934)
Clarke, *Lond. Chs.*	B. F. L. Clarke, *Parish Churches of London* (1966)
Colvin, *Brit. Architects*	H. Colvin, *Biographical Dictionary of British Architects, 1600–1840* (1978)
Coull, *Islington*	T. Coull, *History and Traditions of Islington* (1861)
Cromwell, *Islington*	T. K. Cromwell, *Walks through Islington* (1835)
Cruchley's New Plan (1829)	[G. F.] *Cruchley's New Plan of London and its Environs* (1829)
Dent's plan (1806)	'Survey of the Parish of St. Mary, Islington', by R. Dent, 1805–6; also MS. reference book. In Islington libr.
Draft Index to par. ledger I	Draft index to Stoke Newington parish ledger I, 1779–81 (HAD P/M/CW 10)
Ft. of F. Lond. & Mdx.	*Calendar to the Feet of Fines for London and Middlesex*, ed. W. J. Hardy and W. Page (2 vols. 1892–3)
Foot, *Agric. of Mdx.*	P. Foot, *General View of the Agriculture of the County of Middlesex* (1794)
Freshfield, *Communion Plate*	E. Freshfield, *Communion Plate of the Parish Churches in the County of London* (1895)
G.L.C.	Greater London Council
G.L.R.O.	Greater London Record Office. Contains the collection of the former Middlesex Record Office (M.R.O.)
Guide for assessors of par. 1781–2	Included in Draft Index to par. ledger I (see above)
Guildhall MSS.	City of London, Guildhall Library. Contains registers of wills of the commissary court of London (London division) (MS. 9171), bishops' registers (MS. 9531), diocesan administrative records (MSS. 9532–9560), court rolls and books of Stoke Newington (MS. 14233), and records transferred by the Church Commissioners and from St. Paul's cathedral library
HA and HAD	Hackney Archives Department, Rose Lipman Library, De Beauvoir Road. Contains many records, including cuttings and illustrations, transferred from S.N.L. (see below) since 1982
Hackney dist. bd. of wks. *Ann. Rep.*	Hackney district board of works, *Annual Reports*, with those of surveyors and medical officer of health, 1856–94 (HAD J/BW/24–34)
Hackney dist. bd. of wks., Min. bk.	Hackney district board of works, Minute books, 1855–94 (HAD J/BW/1–22)
Hennessy, *Novum Rep.*	G. Hennessy, *Novum Repertorium Ecclesiasticum Parochiale Londinense* (1894)
Hist. Lond. Transport	T. C. Barker and M. Robbins, *History of London Transport* (2 vols. 1975)
Hist. Mon. Com. *W. Lond.*	Royal Commission on Historical Monuments, *Inventory of the Historical Monuments in London*, ii, *West London* (H.M.S.O. 1925)

Islington libr.	London Borough of Islington, Central Library, Fieldway Cresent. Contains vestry records from the 17th century and later local government records
L.B.	London Borough
L.C.C.	London County Council
L.C.C. *Lond. Statistics*	L.C.C. *London Statistics* (26 vols. 1905–6 to 1936–8, beginning with vol. xvi). Followed by ibid. new series (2 vols. 1945–54 and 1947–56) and by further new series from 1957
Lewis, *Islington*	S. Lewis, *History and Topography of the Parish of St. Mary, Islington* (1842), including plan surveyed by R. Creighton and engraved by J. Dower, 1841
Lysons, *Environs*	D. Lysons, *Environs of London* (4 vols. 1792–6 and Supplement 1811)
M.B.	Metropolitan Borough
M.B.W.	Metropolitan Board of Works
M.L.R.	Middlesex Land Registry. The enrolments, indexes, and registers are at the Greater London Record Office
Mackeson's Guide	C. Mackeson, *Guide to the Churches of London* (1866 and later edns.)
Marcham, Digest	W. M. Marcham, 'Digest of court rolls and other records' of Stoke Newington. Transcript in HAD (see above)
Mdx. County Rec.	*Middlesex County Records* [1550–1688], ed. J. C. Jeaffreson (4 vols. 1886–92)
Mdx. County Rec. Sess. Bks. 1689–1709	*Middlesex County Records, Calendar of the Sessions Books 1689 to 1709*, ed. W. J. Hardy (1905)
Mdx. Sess. Rec.	*Calendar to the Sessions Records* [1612–18], ed. W. le Hardy (4 vols. 1935–41)
Middleton, *View*	J. Middleton, *View of the Agriculture of Middlesex* (1798)
Mudie-Smith, *Rel. Life*	R. Mudie-Smith, *Religious Life of London* (1904)
Nelson, *Islington*	J. Nelson, *History and Antiquities of the Parish of Islington* (1811, 3rd edn. 1829), including plan by H. Warner, 1735
New Lond. Life and Labour	H. Llewellyn Smith and others, *New Survey of London Life and Labour* (9 vols. 1930–5). Survey undertaken 1928
Newcourt, *Rep.*	R. Newcourt, *Repertorium Ecclesiasticum Parochiale Londinense* (2 vols. 1708–10)
Norden, *Spec. Brit.*	J. Norden, *Speculum Britanniae: Middlesex* (facsimile edn. 1971)
P. N. Mdx. (E.P.N.S.)	*Place-Names of Middlesex* (English Place-Name Society, vol. xviii, 1942)
Pevsner, *Lond.* ii	N. Pevsner, *Buildings of England: London except the Cities of London and Westminster* (1952)
Plan [*c.* 1853]	'Plan of the Parish of St. Mary, Islington,' engraved by J. Dower [*c.* 1853]. In Islington libr.
Portrait of Lond. Suburb, 1844	*Portrait of a London Suburb, 1844* (catalogue of Hugh Evelyn exhibition of Shepherd watercolours, 1982)
Ref. bk. to Wadmore map (1813)	Reference book (HAD M 3899) to map by J. Wadmore, 1813, to accompany Prebendary of Stoke Newington's Estate Act, 1814. The map is lost but the frontispiece in Robinson, *Stoke Newington*, is based on it, without the numbers
Rep. on Bridges in Mdx.	*Report of the Committee of Magistrates Appointed to make Enquiry respecting the Public Bridges in the County of Middlesex* (1826). Copy in G.L.R.O.
Rep. Com. Eccl. Revenues	*Report of the Commissioners Appointed to Inquire into the Ecclesiastical Revenues of England and Wales* [67], H.C. (1835), xxii
Rep. Cttee. on Returns by Over-seers, 1776	*Report of the Select Committee on Returns by Overseers of the Poor 1776*, H.C., 1st ser. ix
Robinson, *Stoke Newington*	W. Robinson, *History and Antiquities of the Parish of Stoke Newington* (1820)
Rocque, *Map of Lond.* (1741–5)	J. Rocque, *Exact survey of the cities of London, Westminster, and the borough of Southwark, and the country near ten miles around* (1746, facsimile edn. 1971)

S.N.L.	Stoke Newington Library, Church Street. The local collection has been transferred since 1982 to HAD (see above), but the library's references have been retained in this volume
Stoke Newington B.C. mins.	Stoke Newington borough council, Minute books, 1900–64 (HAD SN/C/2–63)
Stoke Newington vestry, *Ann. Rep.*	Stoke Newington vestry, *Annual Reports*, with those of the surveyors and medical officer of health, 1894–1900 (HAD M/V/9–14)
T.L.M.A.S.	Transactions of the London and Middlesex Archaeological Society (1856 to date). Consecutive numbers are used for the whole series, although vols. vii–xvii (1905–54) appeared as N.S. i–xi
Thorne, *Environs*	J. Thorne, *Handbook to the Environs of London* (1876) [alphabetically arranged in two parts]
Tithe (1848)	Indexed TS. copy of Stoke Newington tithe award, 1848 (HAD book catalogue 912)
Tomlins, *Islington*	T. E. Tomlins, *Perambulation of Islington* (1858)
Vestry mins.	Minute books of the parish of St. Mary, Stoke Newington, 1681–1743 (HAD P/M/1), 1784–1895 (HAD P/M/3–7)
Walker Revised	*Walker Revised*, ed. A. G. Matthews (1948)

OSSULSTONE HUNDRED

(continued)

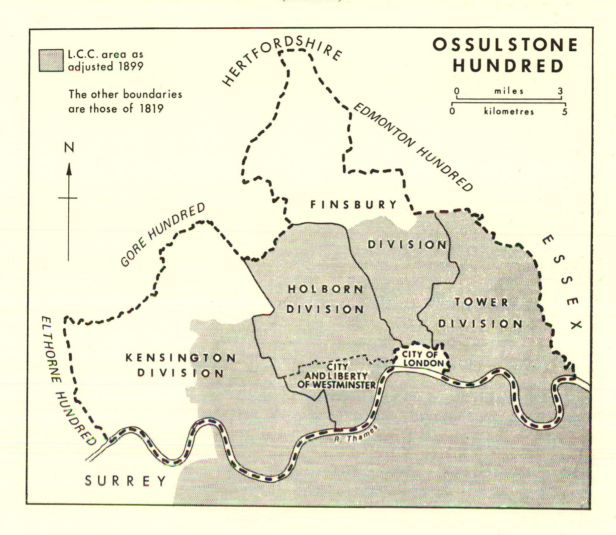

FINSBURY DIVISION (INNER PART)

ISLINGTON

ISLINGTON,[1] whose high street lay at the first milestone from the City of London, was known in the 17th and 18th centuries as a salubrious pleasure resort, and by the last quarter of the 20th century parts of it had recaptured their mid 19th-century reputation for gentility. It has also been distinguished by ideological fervour, religious in the 19th century, political in the 20th. The parish stretched 5.2 km. north-west to south-east along the line of the Great North Road, and 3.6 km. across at its widest point. It was bounded by St.

Pancras on the west, Hornsey on the north and north-east, Stoke Newington and Hackney on the east, Shoreditch on the south-east, and St. Luke's and Clerkenwell on the south. Its area was 3,033 a. in 1805 and 1848;[2] following the Metropolis Management Act, 1855, Islington became a civil metropolitan parish within the area of the Metropolitan Board of Works, with minor boundary changes bringing its area to 3,127 a. in 1861. Under the London Government Act, 1899, it became the metropolitan borough of

[1] The article was written in 1983.
[2] Dent's plan and ref. bk., in Islington libr.; P.R.O., IR 29/21/33.

1

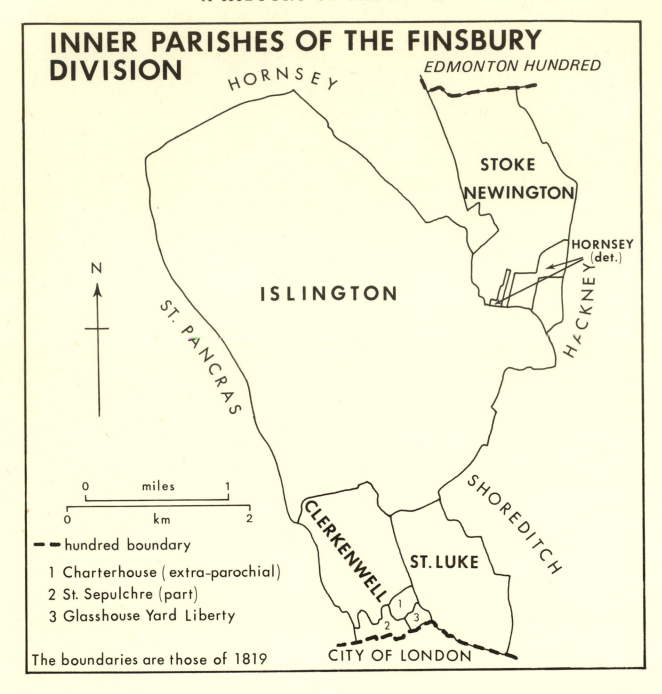

INNER PARISHES OF THE FINSBURY DIVISION

EDMONTON HUNDRED

HORNSEY

STOKE NEWINGTON

HORNSEY (det.)

ISLINGTON

ST. PANCRAS

HACKNEY

N

0 — miles — 1
0 — km — 2

- - hundred boundary

1 Charterhouse (extra-parochial)
2 St. Sepulchre (part)
3 Glasshouse Yard Liberty

The boundaries are those of 1819

SHOREDITCH

CLERKENWELL

ST. LUKE

CITY OF LONDON

Islington with 3,091 a., exchanging land with all the neighbouring parishes.[3] From 1965 it formed the major part of the London Borough of Islington, the remainder having been the metropolitan borough of Finsbury (parishes of Clerkenwell and St. Luke's, Old Street). Besides Islington town, part of which lies in Clerkenwell, the parish included hamlets at Upper and Lower Holloway, Ring Cross, Highbury, with most of Newington Green, and part of Kingsland.

Islington lies mainly on London Clay, except for the extreme north part of the parish on Highgate hill and along Hornsey Lane which lies on Claygate Beds with Bagshot sand on the summit.[4]

In most of the eastern and southern parts the clay is overlaid with river terrace gravels and brickearth: Boyn Hill gravel covers the south-west quarter, Taplow gravel the south-east corner, where the brickearth has been removed, and brickearth most of the eastern side.

The parish rises from 20 m. in the south-east to 100 m. in the north-west, with noticeable inclines near Copenhagen fields and at Highbury, and Highgate hill climbs steeply to the ridge along which Hornsey Lane marks the northern boundary. Lanes marked the western and most of the north-eastern boundaries; the south and east boundaries were manorial ones.

[3] *Census*, 1861, 1901; G.L.R.O., Is. B.G. 247/2.
[4] Para. based on Geol. Surv. Map 6″, drift, Lond. sheets V. NW., II. SW. (1920 edn.).

Hackney brook rises at Holloway near Mercers Road, running south to cross Holloway Road near Tufnell Park Road and then continuing to Lowman Road, where it turns north-east and runs along Gillespie Road to leave the parish at Mountgrove Road.[5] In 1613 the New River was completed, meandering in and out of the parish at Blackstock Road and Green Lanes, and re-entering farther down Green Lanes to run south and south-east through Canonbury, under Essex Road in a culvert, along Colebrooke Row, and out of the parish near the junction of City Road and Goswell Road to the river head just south of the Angel. Where the river crossed Hackney brook and Gipsy Lane (later Mountgrove Road) it was carried 17 ft. above the brook and lane in a trough, constructed in 1618, and came to be known as the boarded river. The river remained open until the Colebrooke Row stretch was culverted in 1861, the stretch south of Green Lanes in 1868–70, and from Douglas Road to the Thatched House inn in 1892–3; in 1946 the river ended at Stoke Newington. Thereafter much of the course of the river in Islington became ornamental water.[6]

COMMUNICATIONS. It was believed that a Roman road from Cripplegate to St. Albans ran through Islington along the line of Prebend Street and Highbury Grove to Stroud Green,[7] possibly following an earlier track,[8] but no firm evidence has been found. Two roads linking Islington with London were known as 'streets' c. 1170[9] and the northern part of Essex Road was called Seveney Street in the 16th century,[10] perhaps indicating a Roman origin.[11] The continuation of Essex Road to Newington Green connected it with Green Lanes, also thought to be ancient.[12] The continuations of the 12th-century routes from London, St. John Street from west Smithfield and Goswell Street from Aldersgate, joined just before entering Islington near the Angel. It is therefore likely that the Great North Road, of which Aldersgate was the start, also existed at that time, running along Upper Street into Holloway Road. Before the 14th century it was thought to have left the parish northward along Tallington or Tollington Lane (also called Devil's Lane and later Hornsey Road) to Crouch End, but by 1300 the route had become as important as Ermine Street and was so impassable that a new road was made up Highgate Hill; the bishop was claiming a toll by 1318

and inhabitants of Islington were granted pavage to repair the road up the hill in 1380.[13] The name Holwey was used for the district around the road by 1307.[14] A road known as the Back Road, later Liverpool Road, ran from High Street to Ring Cross bypassing Upper Street by the late 16th century,[15] and connecting with lanes across the western part of the parish. It was particularly useful for large herds of cattle bound for Smithfield market, which were penned overnight in layers along its length.[16]

Another probably ancient route was the lane from Battle or Bradford Bridge (King's Cross) to Highgate recorded in 1492.[17] The lower part was called Longhedge lane in 1504[18] and Longwich lane in the late 16th century,[19] but Maid or Maiden Lane in 1735,[20] the name it was known by in the 19th century until it became York Road (later Way), Brecknock Road, and Dartmouth Park Hill. Rocque, however, called it the Black Lane, probably an error for Black Dog Lane, in 1746,[21] while an estate plan of 1758 called it the lane from Battle Bridge to the Black Dog, Highgate,[22] a tavern that stood on the site of St. Joseph's. Plans of Barnsbury demesnes called it Back Lane in 1727 and Maiden Lane in 1755.[23] Maiden Lane, however, seems to have originally been applied to the road that ran from Upper Holloway southward parallel to the boundary route, with links to Kentish Town, Copenhagen House, Lower Holloway, and the Back Road. Although the route had dwindled into mere field lanes by the 19th century, it was probably much more important in the medieval period or earlier, apparently having been the main route from Gray's Inn and Clerkenwell to High Barnet, running from Longwich Lane to Tollington Lane.[24] In 1467 sums were bequeathed for the repair of Mayde Lane and the highway from the foot of Mayde Lane to the parish church, which must have been Holloway Road. Bequests in 1494 and 1497 for repairing the highway and two bridges between Ring Cross and Maiden Lane Cross also suggest that Maiden Lane joined Holloway Road.[25] Another name for the road was Hagbush Lane, used in 1676,[26] 1735,[27] and 1746, but parts were also called Copenhagen Lane and Maiden Lane in 1746.[28] Maiden Lane was used in a plan of 1758,[29] and Mead Lane was the name of the link to the three-mile stone in Holloway Road in 1727 and 1820.[30]

Lower Street and Lower Road (later Essex Road) continued to Ball's Pond, to Newington Green, and to Kingsland, where it joined Ermine

[5] Geol. Surv. Map 6″, sheet II. SW.
[6] M. Cosh, New River (Islington libraries, 1982); Plan of Islington (c. 1853), in Islington libr.; inf. from Mr. J. C. Connell.
[7] I. D. Margary, Roman Rds. in Britain (1967), 201; Inner Lond. Archaeology Unit, Archaeology of Islington [after 1974].
[8] W. F. Grimes, Excavation of Roman and Medieval Lond. (1968), 43–4.
[9] Deed cited in Tomlins, Islington, 18.
[10] P.R.O., SC 6/Hen. VIII/2396, m. 94.
[11] Margary, Roman Rds. 26.
[12] Below, Stoke Newington.
[13] J. T. Coppock and H. C. Prince, Gtr. Lond. (1964), 54; V.C.H. Mdx. vi. 103. Inf. based on Norden, who does not give his source.
[14] P.N. Mdx. (E.P.N.S.), 126.

[15] B.L. Maps 186.h.2. (12).
[16] Below, econ., agrarian; other est. (Drapers).
[17] P.R.O., E 303/8/Lond. no. 134.
[18] Ibid. E 315/104, f. 186.
[19] Tomlins, Islington, 30.
[20] Ibid. 12.
[21] Rocque, Map of Lond. (1741–5).
[22] G.L.R.O., A/CSC/3161/B.
[23] G.L.R.O., map dept., 627 JI 1727, 626 JI 1755.
[24] Tomlins, Islington, 30.
[25] Guildhall MSS. 9171/6, f. 16; 8, ff. 77, 194v.
[26] P.R.O., C 6/79/47.
[27] Nelson, Islington (1829), plan (1735).
[28] Rocque, Map of Lond. (1741–5).
[29] G.L.R.O., A/CSC/3161/B.
[30] G.L.R.O., map dept., 627 JI 1727; Tomlins, Islington, 26.

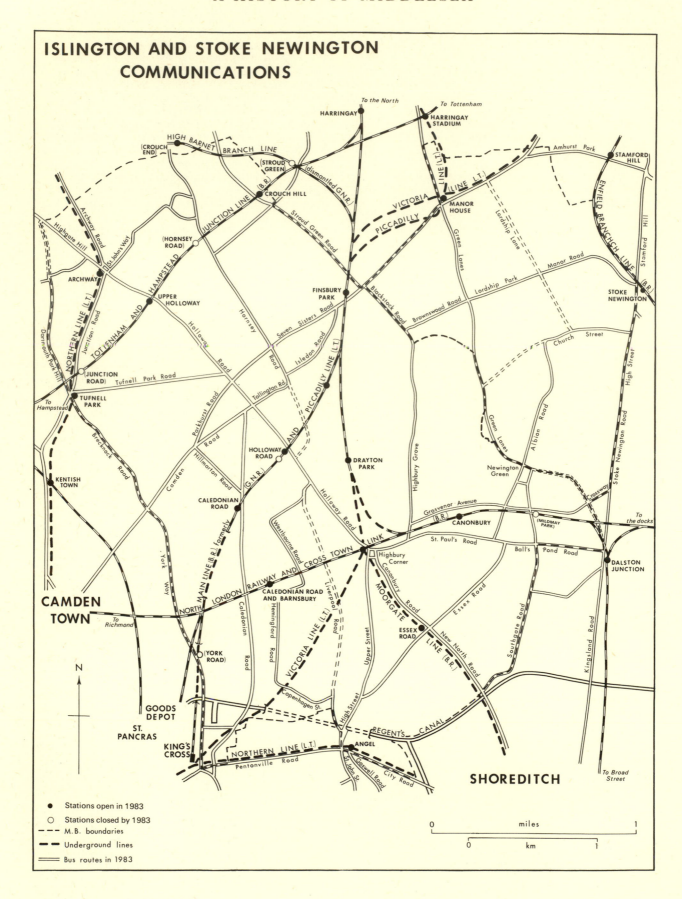

ISLINGTON AND STOKE NEWINGTON COMMUNICATIONS

Legend:
- ● Stations open in 1983
- ○ Stations closed by 1983
- – – – M.B. boundaries
- ▬ ▬ Underground lines
- ═══ Bus routes in 1983

0 miles 1
0 km 1

Street. It was a highway in 1582 when money was left for its repair.[31] Other local roads were Heame or Hame Lane, so called in the early 17th century,[32] which ran from Tollington Lane towards Brownswood until the 19th century when it was replaced by Seven Sisters Road. Hopping Lane linked Holloway Road and Ball's Pond by the 1540s,[33] and a lane from Hopping Lane to Highbury Barn and on past Highbury woods to Stroud Green, in use by 1692,[34] was later called Highbury Grove and Highbury Vale. From the fields east of the town Frog Lane ran from Lower Road to the parish boundary at City Gardens and thence to Old Street.[35] Along the eastern boundary lay another lane from Ball's Pond Road to Hoxton, including the strip of land called Islington common in 1817.[36] The lane was called Long Acre in 1532[37] and Hyde Lane in 1554,[38] and parts were taken into Southgate Road in the 19th century.

By the late 17th century all the roads were in bad condition; statute labour was not adequate, even with assistance from the pockets of the surveyors, and additional rates were levied on the parish by the Middlesex justices.[39] William Heron's trust, administered by the Clothworkers' Company of London, provided £8 a year from the late 16th century towards repairing the highway from Highgate to Clerkenwell and the road from Highgate through Kentish Town to Battle Bridge.[40]

An Act of 1716 set up the Islington turnpike trust, also known as the Hampstead and Highgate trust. In 1735 it controlled 6½ miles of road in the parish, covering the modern Islington High Street, Upper Street, Holloway, Liverpool, Essex, and Ball's Pond roads and Highgate Hill. The trust, with the Marylebone turnpike trust, also became responsible for the New Road (Marylebone, Euston, and Pentonville roads) built from Paddington to the Angel between 1756 and 1775. The continuation from the Angel to Finsbury Square, called City Road, was built in 1761. Parts of both roads touched Islington on its southern boundary. In the early 19th century four new turnpike roads were built in the parish. Two were to improve the Great North Road: Archway Road, built in 1813 to bypass Highgate Hill; New North Road, authorized in 1813 and built by 1823 to bypass the town and lead more directly to the City. Two were to improve communications with London's west end. Caledonian Road, originally the Chalk Road but renamed after the Caledonian asylum, was built in 1826 to provide a direct cut from the area west of the City to Holloway Road via Battle Bridge. Camden Road and Seven Sisters Road was the last of the major through routes, from Camden Town to Tottenham. Begun in 1825, it had reached Holloway when the Metropolitan turnpike trust was created in 1826 and Tottenham by 1834.[41]

The Great North Road remained a major route for goods being carried to the docks, and to the channel ports via the Blackwall tunnel. Archway Road was widened to a dual carriageway over the site of Whittington College in the early 1970s,[42] leaving Archway tavern and the Methodist central hall on a traffic island. In addition, the middle section of Holloway Road was widened to four and six lanes, but congestion persisted at either end, while the heavy lorries using the route, which sliced the parish diagonally in two, blighted trade and damaged old buildings along the narrower stretches. Hopping Lane, renamed St. Paul's Road in the 19th century, linked Holloway Road and Dalston, and also carried heavy goods traffic using East London routes.

Small bridges crossed tributaries of Hackney brook at Heame Lane, Tollington Lane, Ring Cross, and London fields in 1614-16[43] and 1735.[44] The parish was responsible in 1692 for mending the bridge in Heame Lane,[45] possibly the one known as Prestbourne bridge in 1540.[46] None of the bridges was mentioned in 1826, by which time the streams were probably culverted. Three bridges crossed the New River, at Green Lanes, Ball's Pond Lane (St. Paul's Road), and City Road, all maintained by the New River Co. Bridges over the canal at Maiden Lane and Frog Lane and the tunnel were maintained by the Regent's Canal Co.[47]

Long-distance coaches used the Great North Road in the 18th century and by the 1790s two local stage coaches ran return journeys every hour: Chilton's coach to the Royal Exchange and George Jenks's to the Exchange and Temple Bar. A carrier ran a daily return service between the Angel in Wells's Row (Highbury Corner) and the Flower Pot, Bishopsgate.[48] By 1816 a local short-stage service of three coaches daily made return journeys between London and Holloway.[49] In 1825 eleven coaches making 53 return journeys a day terminated at Islington, with four more at Highgate making 10 return journeys.[50] The first omnibus service was operated by George Shillibeer in 1829 along the New Road past the Angel to the Bank. Thereafter services increased so rapidly that in 1838-9, besides 55 vehicles using the New Road, 42 omnibuses served Islington. From Islington 15 ran to Kennington Gate, two to the Elephant and Castle, and one to Albany Road (possibly Southwark); from Holloway 19 ran to the City and two to Charing Cross; two ran from Highgate to the Bank, and another from

[31] P.R.O., PROB 11/65 (P.C.C. 9 Rowe, will of Wm. Rickthorne).
[32] Guildhall MS. 3460/1; P.R.O., C 8/422/53.
[33] P.R.O., E 315/230, p. 89.
[34] P.R.O., C 8/436/98.
[35] Nelson, *Islington* (1829), plan (1735).
[36] Baker's plan (1817).
[37] P.R.O., SC 6/Hen. VIII/2396, m. 94.
[38] Guildhall MS. (formerly St. Paul's MS. C (Dean's Reg., Sampson), ff. 304v-5).
[39] Tomlins, *Islington*, 32; P.R.O., C 10/285/34.
[40] Below, charities.
[41] *Rep. Sel. Cttee. on Met. Turnpike Rds.* H.C. 355, pp. 177-90 (1825), v; C. A. A. Clarke, 'Turnpike Trusts of Islington and Marylebone from 1700 to 1825' (Lond. Univ. M.A. thesis, 1955); *V.C.H. Mdx.* vi. 103; 52 Geo. III, c. 154; *P.N. Mdx.* (E.P.N.S.), p. xxxiv; Coppock and Prince, *Gtr. Lond.* 53-6. Rec. of trust are in Islington libr.
[42] *V.C.H. Mdx.* vi. 103.
[43] Guildhall MS. 3460/1.
[44] Nelson, *Islington*, plan (1735).
[45] Islington libr., vestry min. bk. 1662-1708, 246.
[46] P.R.O., SC 6/Hen. VIII/2402, m. 4.
[47] *Rep. on Bridges in Mdx.* 141.
[48] *Univ. British Dir.* (1791-7), iii. 434.
[49] *V.C.H. Mdx.* vi. 106.
[50] *Hist. Lond. Transport*, i. 391.

Highbury Barn to the Royal Exchange.[51] In the next two decades builders in Islington and Holloway, whose success depended on good transport to the City, promoted omnibus services.[52] E. & J. Wilson of Holloway ran the largest fleet in the parish with 11 vehicles in 1839, and 48, operating from Highbury to the City, in 1856, when their fleet was sold to the Compagnie Générale des Omnibus de Londres (from 1858 the London General Omnibus Co.). Other vehicles sold to the L.G.O.C. were 19 from Islington to Chelsea, 10 running from Barnsbury Park to Kennington, 2 from Islington to Kennington, and 2 from Caledonian Road to Pimlico. Omnibuses also ran from Hornsey Rise to the Post Office and to Sloane Square, and from Archway tavern to Westminster. Vehicles from Tottenham to Oxford Street passed along Ball's Pond Road, and the eastern part of the parish was also served by fleets operating through Dalston to the City.[53]

The first tramway in Islington was opened in 1871 by the North Metropolitan Tramways Co. from the Nag's Head, Holloway Road, to the Angel via both Upper Street and Liverpool Road, and on to Finsbury Square.[54] It was extended to Archway tavern and Finsbury Park in 1872, when the company opened another line from Dalston to Islington Green via Ball's Pond and Essex roads. London Street Tramways extended their routes from Camden Town to the Nag's Head in 1872 and from Kentish Town to Archway tavern in 1875. Other routes opened were from City Road along Southgate Road to Newington Green and Riversdale Road in 1874, from King's Cross to the Nag's Head along Caledonian Road in 1878, and from Highbury Corner to Old Street along New North Road in 1879. An electric tram service from Highbury station along Upper Street to the Angel and on to Rosebery Avenue was started in 1906 and extended in 1907 along Holloway Road to Archway tavern; in 1908 through services ran from Highbury to Tower Bridge via Westminster and the Elephant and Castle, and from Highbury to Kennington Gate.[55]

Motor buses had superseded horse buses on the L.G.O.C.'s routes from Highbury Barn and Barnsbury by 1911.[56] Trolleybuses replaced trams from 1938,[57] and were in turn replaced by buses in 1961.[58]

An extension of the Paddington branch of the Grand Junction canal, under a separate company and the name Regent's canal, was authorized by Act of 1812 to run from near the Paddington basin to the Thames at Limehouse.[59] The section from Camden Town to the Thames was the last to be opened, in 1820, and included the 960-yd. Islington tunnel between Muriel Street and Colebrooke Row.[60] The City Road basin, on the parish boundary, came to supersede the Paddington basin as a distribution point for London. Although the canal was intended to link the Thames with the Midlands, local transport became much more important, particularly in carrying coal: in 1835 one-fifth of all coal imported into London entered the canal, mostly for local use. Building materials also formed much of the tonnage, which more than doubled between 1823 and 1832. The growing trade attracted building along the canal: privately owned basins included Horsfall basin, near York Way, opened in 1825, with warehouses, depots, and businesses nearby. After the opening of the London & Birmingham Railway in 1838 transhipment helped to maintain the tonnage carried by water, particularly coal for the gasworks and timber, and to defeat schemes in the 1850s and 1880s to convert the canal to a railway. Most trade was local, however, by the early 20th century, the Midlands traffic having been largely lost to rail. In 1929 the Regent's and Grand Junction canals joined in a new Grand Union Canal Co., which was transferred to the British Transport Commission in 1948. Commercial craft belonged only to private carriers after 1963, when the canal passed to the British Waterways Board. Locally the canal became important both for boating and for waterside walks.

The East & West India Docks & Birmingham Junction Railway was incorporated in 1846 to construct a line between the London and North Western's goods station at Camden Town and the West India docks. The section from Highbury to Bow Junction was opened in 1850 and in addition a 15-minute through passenger service started between Islington and Fenchurch Street via Bow. Although it followed a roundabout route to the City, the service was both quick and cheap and catered for a large residential area, cutting across the middle of the parish. Known as the North London Railway from 1853, it opened a line to its own City terminus at Broad Street in 1865, and services to Fenchurch Street ceased after 1868.[61] The line ran in a cutting from Caledonian Road to Dalston, so preserving the middle-class character of the area nearby. Stations serving Islington and opened in 1850 were Islington (called Highbury from 1872) at Highbury Corner, and Kingsland in Hackney, just north of the present Dalston Junction which replaced it in 1865.[62] Caledonian Road was opened in 1852, replaced a little eastward by Barnsbury in 1870 (renamed Caledonian Road and Barnsbury from 1893), which from 1855 was much used as access to the Metropolitan market; the N.L.R. also built a cattle terminal at Maiden Lane in 1854 in expectation of the market.[63] Newington Road and Ball's Pond was opened in 1858 but replaced a little westward by Canonbury in 1870, when the lines were quadrupled. By the 1870s the neighbourhood had been built over and a further

[51] *Hist. Lond. Transport*, i. 398–401.
[52] R. Glass and others, *Lond., Aspects of Change* (1964), 35.
[53] *Hist. Lond. Transport*, i. 404–5, 411; L.T.E. *Lond. General: Story of Lond. Bus, 1856–1956*, 68–70.
[54] Para. based on *Hist. Lond. Transport*, i. 185.
[55] Ibid. ii. 94–5; below, plate 7.
[56] *Hist. Lond. Transport*, ii. 169.
[57] Ibid. ii. 300–1.
[58] Inf. from Mr. R. M. Robbins.

[59] Para. based on C. Hadfield, *Canals of E. Midlands* (1970), 127–34, 231–7, 240, 247.
[60] Plate 1.
[61] *Hist. Lond. Transport*, i. 51; R. M. Robbins, *North Lond. Rly.* (1974), 1–4.
[62] Robbins, *N.L.R.* 11–12, 28.
[63] Ibid. 12; E. Course, *Lond. Rlys.* (1962), 241; H. P. White, *Gtr. Lond.* (Regional Hist. of Rlys. of Gt. Britain, iii, 1963), 77.

station, Mildmay Park, was opened in 1880. Another, Maiden Lane, was added on the western boundary of the parish in 1887.[64]

The last stretch of the Great Northern Railway's line under Copenhagen fields to its temporary terminal at Maiden Lane was opened in 1850, but did little to link Islington with central London until suburban stations served the northern half of the parish. Holloway and Caledonian Road was opened for passengers for London in 1852 and full service in 1856, and Seven Sisters Road in 1861, the latter merely two wooden platforms in a predominantly rural area. After the through connexion between King's Cross and the City was opened by the Metropolitan Railway in 1863, suburban passenger traffic was expected to increase. A footbridge and waiting-shed were added at Seven Sisters Road in 1868 and a waiting-room and covered platforms in 1869, when the name was changed to Finsbury Park. The G.N.R. opened the Canonbury spur for goods in 1874, linking its line with the N.L.R., and the latter ran passenger services to the G.N.R.'s suburban stations from 1875, giving passengers from Finsbury Park and beyond an alternative route to the City.[65]

The heavy suburban passenger traffic caused the G.N.R. to build a new tunnel under Copenhagen fields, opened 1886, and led eventually to the development of two underground lines serving Islington.[66] The G.N. & City Railway built a line from Finsbury Park to a City terminus at Finsbury Pavement (Moorgate). Projected in 1891, it was opened in 1904 with intermediate stations at Drayton Park, Highbury, and Essex Road, and later became the Highbury branch of the Northern line. The Great Northern, Piccadilly & Brompton Railway opened a line, later the Piccadilly line, in 1906 between Finsbury Park and Hammersmith via London's west end, with stations at Gillespie Road (renamed Arsenal (Highbury Hill) 1932), Holloway Road, Caledonian Road, and York Road (corner of York Way and Bingfield Street). A third underground line, later the Northern Line, opened in 1907 by the Charing Cross, Euston & Hampstead Railway, linked the north-western extremity of the parish with London's west end, with stations at Highgate and Tufnell Park; Highgate station was successively renamed Archway (Highgate) in 1939, Highgate (Archway) in 1941, and Archway in 1947.[67]

North Islington also had a passenger service over the Tottenham & Hampstead Junction line, which was opened in 1868 and ran from the Lea Valley line via Crouch Hill to Highgate Road in St. Pancras. The Great Eastern Railway ran a passenger service to Fenchurch Street via Strat-ford, but closed it in 1870 because the route was circuitous and only at Holloway were there many residents. The Midland Railway started suburban trains between Moorgate Street and Crouch Hill in 1870, with additional stations at Hornsey Road (opened 1872), Upper Holloway, and Junction Road (1872). Because the service was good the district served by the line became completely built up between 1870 and 1882.[68] Although just outside the parish, the City & South London, later the Northern, line gave southern Islington a useful service to Moorgate, with stations at the Angel from 1901, at City Road from 1901 to 1922, and at King's Cross from 1907.[69]

The Underground stations reduced local use of the earlier lines and led to some closures.[70] Most of the passenger traffic at the G.N.R.'s Holloway Road station was lost to the Piccadilly line's station nearby from 1906, until the former finally closed in 1915.[71] The N.L.R.'s Mildmay Park station closed in 1934, after a period of limited opening times, because residents worked in local industry rather than in the City.[72] The N.L.R.'s Maiden Lane station closed in 1916 as a wartime measure and did not reopen. The Piccadilly line's York Road station closed in 1932, probably because of social changes, and Junction Road and Hornsey Road stations both closed in 1943.[73]

From the 1960s Islington became increasingly popular with middle-class commuters to central London. The Highbury branch of the Northern line, transferred to British Rail in 1976, and London Transport's Northern and Piccadilly lines, linked most parts with the City or the west end, and from 1968 the Victoria line[74] gave a quicker link between Finsbury Park, Highbury, King's Cross, and the west end. The N.L.R., although threatened with closure in the 1960s[75] and early 1980s, continued to run trains to the City besides forming part of a crosstown link promoted in the early 1980s. The two remaining stations on the former Tottenham & Hampstead Junction line, at Crouch Hill and Upper Holloway, were part of the Gospel Oak to Barking crosstown line from 1981, but both that line[76] and the N.L.R. line were possibly more important as part of the freight routes through the capital than for local services. The Great Northern line from the Second World War became more important locally for freight than for passengers, with goods and coal depots at Highbury Vale, Clarence Yard, and Finsbury Park (East Goods Sidings) that attracted businesses and warehouses. Clarence Yard and East Goods Sidings were closed in 1960 and Highbury Vale in 1971. The G.N.R. Canonbury line was still used in 1983 for through freight trains.[77]

[64] Robbins, *N.L.R.* 12.

[65] C. H. Grinling, *Hist. of Gt. Northern Rly.* (1966), 89, 203, 257–8, 303; White, *Gtr. Lond.* 79; Course, *Lond. Rlys.* 242; inf. from Mr. R. M. Robbins.

[66] Grinling, *G.N.R.* 379; White, *Gtr. Lond.* 103.

[67] A. E. Bennett and H. V. Borley, *Lond. Transport Rlys.* (1963), 10–11, 13–14, 19, 24, 26–7; *Hist. Lond. Transport,* ii. 112.

[68] White, *Gtr. Lond.* 150–2; *Hist. Lond. Transport,* i. 131, 349; Course, *Lond. Rlys.* 243.

[69] Bennett and Borley, *Lond. Transport,* 10; inf. from Mr. H. V. Borley.

[70] White, *Gtr. Lond.* 152.

[71] Course, *Lond. Rlys.* 229, 242.   [72] Ibid. 240, 243.

[73] Ibid. 243.

[74] *Hist. Lond. Transport,* ii. 347; inf. from Mr. R. M. Robbins.

[75] Robbins, *N.L.R.* 29.

[76] White, *Gtr. Lond.* 151–2.

[77] Inf. from Mr. H. V. Borley.

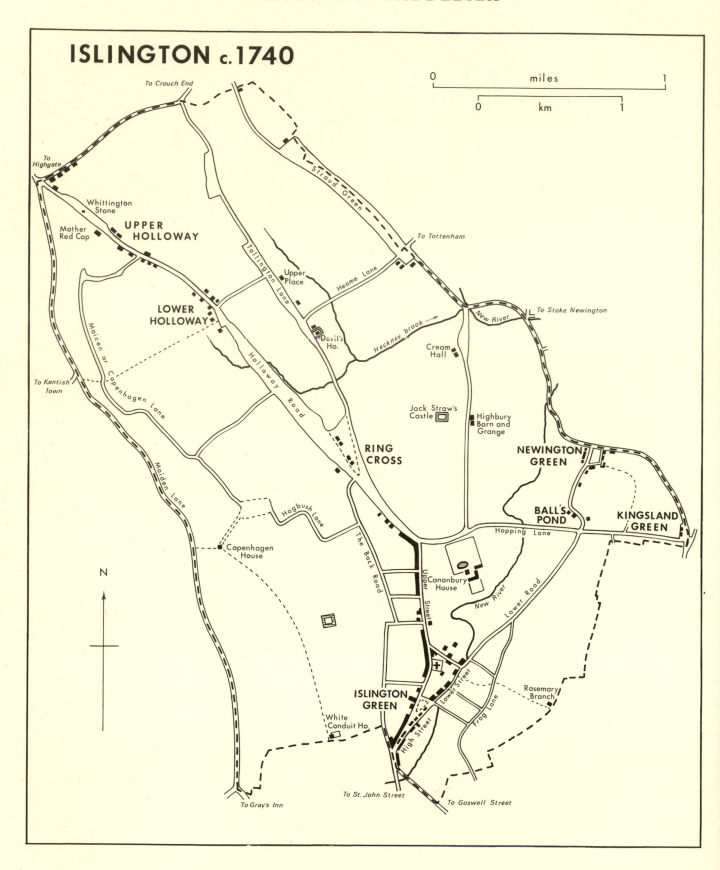

ISLINGTON c.1740

To Crouch End
To Highgate
Whittington Stone
Mother Red Cap
UPPER HOLLOWAY
Stroud Green
To Tottenham
Upper Place
Heame Lane
Tollington Lane
LOWER HOLLOWAY
Devil's Ho.
Hackney brook
Cream Hall
New River
To Stoke Newington
Maiden or Copenhagen Lane
Holloway Road
To Kentish Town
Jack Straw's Castle
Highbury Barn and Grange
NEWINGTON GREEN
RING CROSS
BALL'S POND
KINGSLAND GREEN
Maiden Lane
Hagbush Lane
Hopping Lane
The Back Road
Copenhagen House
Canonbury House
New River
Upper Street
Lower Road
N
ISLINGTON GREEN
White Conduit Ho.
High Street
Lower Street
Frog Lane
Rosemary Branch
To Gray's Inn
To St. John Street
To Goswell Street

GROWTH. Neolithic implements have been found at Islington, besides Roman pottery and coins,[78] but the two Roman gravestones discovered in the 18th and 19th centuries were probably imports rather than evidence of settlement.[79] The moated site west of Barnsbury Square probably marks a medieval manor house and not a Roman camp as popularly believed.[80] Settlements at Islington and Tollington supplied two men each to man a ship c. 1000,[81] when they were called Gislandune, 'Gisla's hill or down', and Tollandune, 'Tolla's hill'. Gislandune gradually changed to Iseldon, which continued in use well into the 17th century. Forms approximating to Islington, recorded from 1464, were not common until the mid 16th century.[82] The settlements were on the estates of the bishop of London and the chapter of St. Paul's, who held most of the land before the Conquest. In 1086 there were 27 men enumerated on the Islington estates, and another 29 men on estates of the bishop that probably lay in Islington, including the Berners holding.[83] Islington and Tollington were members of the hundred in 1086, but Tollington was not listed later and probably ceased to be of any significance,[84] although it was still the location of a few tenements in the early 16th century.[85] The names of other settlements appeared only in the 13th and 14th centuries, relating to manors rather than hamlets: *Bernersbury*, *Neweton Berewe* or *Heybury*, and *Canonesbury*.[86]

Several moated sites indicate substantial medieval houses. Barnsbury manor house, by 1297 probably on the site west of Barnsbury Square, was not mentioned after 1388.[87] The site on the west side of Holloway Road, opposite Manor Gardens, part of the Barnsbury manor farm in the 18th century, originally belonged to a freeholder of Barnsbury manor.[88] The moated house belonging to the prior of the hospital of St. John of Jerusalem at Highbury had been built by 1338 but was destroyed in 1381.[89] A fourth moat existed in Tollington Lane just south of Heame Lane, which in 1611 was occupied by the Devil's house, formerly called Lower Place, and a copyhold tenement of the manor of Highbury.[90] Other substantial houses existed at Canonbury and at Cutlers, probably the site of Copenhagen House, by 1373.[91] Freehold messuages were changing hands in the late 13th century.[92] It is probable that customary tenements then existed on their 16th-century sites and that they were

concentrated at road junctions as in the 18th century, at Upper and Lower Holloway, Ring Cross, Tollington Lane, and Newington Green, in addition to Islington High Street. One or two were probably inns serving the Great North Road, although no evidence exists for them before the 16th century.

In 1548 there were 440 communicants in Islington,[93] where the small village with its hamlets was known principally for its inns, which often harboured recusants and fugitives, and for fields which were used for illicit prayer meetings, counterfeiting coins, training militia, fighting duels, and archery and other sport.[94] Its proximity to London and Westminster, with rural surroundings, attracted rich and eminent residents. In the 15th century several citizens or their widows died in Islington. Thomas Cromwell lived at Canonbury in the 1530s,[95] Henry Percy, earl of Northumberland (d. 1537), lived at Newington Green 1536–7;[96] the countess of Lennox was writing from Islington in 1571,[97] and Edward, Lord Windsor, had left goods in the parish in 1576.[98] The town was also a convenient lodging for those who wanted to stay unobtrusively in touch with the court and parliament.[99] In the later 17th century it acquired popularity following the exploitation of Islington Spa (Clerkenwell), opposite Sadler's Wells, as a resort. Many visitors lodged in Islington itself, and during the 18th century the parish was one of those which became popular as a retreat from the metropolis.[1] Even Samuel Johnson recognized the benefit of Islington's air as part of his visits to the vicar, Mr. Strahan.[2]

The number of houses in Islington, estimated at 325 in 1708,[3] rose to 937 in 1732,[4] 1,060 in 1788, 1,200 in 1793,[5] and 1,745 in 1801 when the population was 10,212.[6] The late 18th century brought an increase in the range of services and trades in the town catering for the better-off, with 11 hairdressers, a Staffordshire-warehouse, a tea and muslin warehouse, a wine merchant, and a toy shop.[7] Terraces along the main roads and some streets behind them were built for middle-class residents, attracted by the air or the nearness of London, so that by 1819 Islington was said to be chiefly composed of the dwellings of retired citizens and others connected with the metropolis. It retained an air of antiquity, however, from its many old buildings: once the residences of prominent people, they had generally been converted into shops and inns.[8]

[78] M. Sharpe, *Mdx. in British, Roman and Saxon Times* (1932), 2, 113.
[79] *V.C.H. Mdx.* i. 72.
[80] *T.L.M.A.S.* i. 321–3; *V.C.H. Mdx.* ii. 8.
[81] A. J. Robertson, *Anglo-Saxon Charters*, 145, 389.
[82] *P.N. Mdx.* (E.P.N.S.), 124, 126.
[83] *V.C.H. Mdx.* i. 120, 122, 126, 129.
[84] Ibid. vi. 1–2.
[85] P.R.O., SC 6/Hen. VIII/2402, m. 4.
[86] *P.N. Mdx.* (E.P.N.S.), 125.
[87] Below, manors.
[88] Below, other est. (Brewhouse).
[89] Below, manors.
[90] Nelson, *Islington* (1829), 136.
[91] Below, manors (Canonbury); other est. (Cutlers).
[92] e.g. P.R.O., CP 25(1)/148/36.
[93] *Lond. and Mdx. Chantry Certificates* (Lond. Rec. Soc. xvi), 62.
[94] e.g. Hist. MSS. Com. 24, *12th Rep. IV, Rutland*, i,

p. 419; ibid. 6, *7th Rep.* p. 538a; ibid. 75, *Downshire*, ii, p. 185; *Cal. Pat.* 1560–3, 24.
[95] Below, manors (Canonbury).
[96] *L. & P. Hen. VIII*, x, p. 356; xi, pp. 66, 181–2, 215, 217; xii (1), pp. 336, 482, 484, 520, 541, 557.
[97] *Cal. S.P. Dom.* 1547–80, 428.
[98] Hist. MSS. Com. 55, *Var. Coll.* ii, p. 298.
[99] e.g. *Cal. S.P. Dom.* 1637–8, 130, 162.
[1] Hist. MSS. Com. 29, *14th Rep. II, Portland*, iii, pp. 341, 415; ibid. 29, *15th Rep. IV, Portland*, iv, p. 34; ibid. 7, *8th Rep. III*, p. 9a.
[2] *Boswell's Life of Johnson*, ed. G. B. Hill and L. F. Powell (1934), iv. 271, 416.
[3] E. Hatton, *New View of Lond.* (1708), 380.
[4] Company of Par. Clerks, *New Remarks on Lond.* (1732), 235.
[5] Nelson, *Islington* (1829), 9.   [6] *Census*, 1801.
[7] *Univ. Brit. Dir.* (1791–7), iii. 437–40.
[8] J. Dugdale, *New Brit. Traveller* (1819), iii. 504.

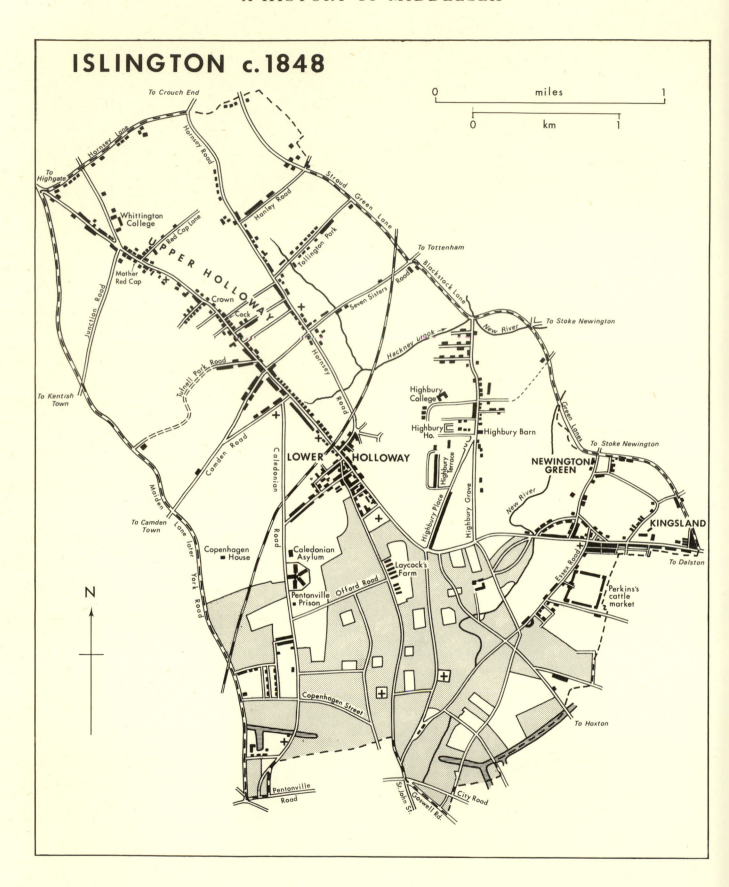

ISLINGTON c.1848

The 19th century saw a rapid but erratic spread of building to cover the entire parish. The increase in population was large up to the 1860s: the decades of heaviest increase were 1841–51 with 71 per cent, 1821–31 with 67 per cent, and 1851–61 with 63 per cent, and the other decades each had an increase of *c.* 49 per cent. After 1861 growth slowed considerably, to 38 per cent and 32 per cent respectively in the next two decades, and to 13 per cent and 5 per cent in the 1880s and 1890s.[9] The population growth was attributed solely to the increase in building in 1831.[10] The number of houses rose by 80 per cent between 1821 and 1831, 33 per cent between 1831 and 1841, 62 per cent between 1841 and 1851, and 50 per cent between 1851 and 1861. Although it still rose by 35 per cent in the next decade, it fell from 22 per cent in the 1870s to 9 and 1 per cent respectively in the last two decades of the century.[11]

The spread of building from the 1830s can be attributed to the introduction of omnibuses which allowed clerks and artisans to join merchants and professional men in living farther from their employment.[12] The decline of the southern half of Islington as a genteel suburb was as sudden as its rise, when better housing was built farther north at Highbury, Tollington Park, and Tufnell Park from the 1860s. Middle-class Jews settled in Barnsbury from *c.* 1840 but by the time that a synagogue was opened for them in 1868, migration had already turned towards Highbury.[13] The poor were also moving in, displaced by clearances, especially for railway yards at the termini; from Somers Town many very poor people settled in badly built streets near Tufnell Park, so reducing its attraction for the better-off.[14] In the 1890s the northern part of the parish began to lose its middle-class residents to outer Middlesex, and large houses fell into multi-occupation. By 1903 Islington appeared 'dreary and depressing', with the largest population of all the London boroughs, very little open space, and above average overcrowding. Few well-to-do people remained, except in Highbury and Canonbury, and houses in spacious grounds had been replaced by crowded terraces to accommodate an influx of the working class.[15] The borough attracted a shifting population, especially in the south near King's Cross, Caledonian Road, and Upper Street.

By 1921 Islington's housing was less overcrowded than it had been in 1911, although nearly 20 per cent of its families still lived with more than two persons to a room.[16] In 1931 the housing stock served a different population than the one for which it had been built, as the table shows. Dwellings with 3 to 5 rooms included most of the municipal flats. Municipal housing, however, made little impact before the Second World War. The Revd. Donald Coggan, a curate in the mid 1930s, thought that Islington reflected a dismal decade, with drab streets and ill kept, overcrowded tenement buildings, where conditions were grim.[17]

Change was more rapid after the Second World War, when bombed sites could be used for new municipal housing, although it took time merely to replace the 3,200 houses destroyed in the war.[18] Between 1921 and 1939 the borough had built 1,682 homes and the L.C.C. 1,951. By 1958 the borough had built 3,378 homes since 1946 and by 1962 the L.C.C. had provided 2,834. Slum clearance was undertaken but in 1967 of the London boroughs Islington still had the most multi-occupied dwellings, representing 59 per cent of the total, and the most households, 77 per cent of the total number, lacking such basic amenities as their own stove, sink, bath, and W.C. It was London's most densely populated M.B. in 1951, being very short of public open space, and in 1968 its density at 70 persons per acre (including Finsbury) far exceeded its neighbours Hackney at 52 and Camden at 45. The borough council continued an intensive programme of clearance for new housing estates and reserved some of the land for open spaces, which increased from 60 a. in 1958 to 107 a. in 1971.

TABLE: OCCUPANCY OF DWELLINGS, 1931

Dwellings with:	Percentage of total dwellings	Percentage of dwellings occupied by:		
		1 family	2 fams.	3 or more fams.
9 rooms or more	18	12	18	70
6 to 8 rooms	51	17	40	43
3 to 5 rooms	25	77	19	4
1 to 2 rooms	6	99	1	—

Source: Census, 1931.

[9] *Census*, 1801–1901.
[10] Ibid. 1831.
[11] Based on ibid. 1821–1901.
[12] D. J. Olsen, *Growth of Victorian Lond.* (1979), 190–1.
[13] V. D. Lipman, 'Rise of Jewish Suburbia', *Jewish Hist. Soc. of Eng.* xxi. 85–6.
[14] Olsen, *Victorian Lond.* 283.
[15] Mudie-Smith, *Rel. Life*, 135.
[16] *Census*, 1921.
[17] D. Coggan, *Convictions* (1975), 18.
[18] Para. based on Islington M.B. *Evidence to Royal Com. on Local Govt. in Gtr. Lond.* (1958), 1–2, 10; Islington L.B. *Homes for Islington* (1967), 4–5; Islington Fabian Soc. *Living in Islington* [1968]; Islington L.B. *Our Changing Islington* (1971), 9.

1844

1877

1904

ISLINGTON: EVOLUTION OF SETTLEMENT, 1844–1904

From the 1960s Islington, particularly the south part, was also changed by its revived popularity with middle-class families, which bought leasehold or freehold houses and rehabilitated them. The trend was intensified by estate agents and speculators, and in Canonbury and Barnsbury working-class tenants were forced or encouraged to leave desirable terraces. Conservation areas were formed and traffic schemes put into operation.[19] The subsequent rise in property values made it profitable to rehabilitate less favoured streets also. The council continued to clear for rehousing, however, until prolonged resistance to the clearance of part of Upper Holloway caused it to change to rehabilitation for the benefit of sitting tenants.[20] Financial constraints from the late 1970s also favoured rehabilitation.

The population was 10,212 in 1801 and rose steadily, to 22,417 in 1821, 37,316 in 1831, 95,329 in 1851, and 155,341 in 1861. Thereafter the rate of growth declined, and the population was 213,778 in 1871, 282,865 in 1881, 319,143 in 1891 and 335,238 in 1901. It fell to 327,403 in 1911, rose again slightly to 330,737 in 1921, but fell again to 321,795 in 1931, 235,632 in 1951, and 228,833 in 1961. In 1971, after reorganization as Islington L.B., the population of 16 wards was 228,384.

ISLINGTON TOWN. The earliest firm evidence for the main settlement is a sketch-map of *c.* 1590, showing rows of houses lining the wide main road.[21] From the junction of the roads from St. John's Street and Aldersgate, building on the west side, which lay in Clerkenwell parish up to the Back Road, was continuous as far as Islington green, apart from the junction with the Back Road, and on the east was continuous almost to the green with a few detached buildings beyond. On the south side of the green were a pond and the parish cage. Two buildings on the east side were inns, as were seven on the west side, including the southernmost building with a gateway beside it, probably the later Angel inn. The

---

[19] Below, Barnsbury.
[20] Below, Holloway.

[21] B.L. Maps, 186. h. 2. (12), photocopy of plan in Hatfield MSS.

13

main road, later called Islington High Street, divided at the green, the western fork to Islington church and Holloway becoming known as Upper Street, the eastern fork leading behind the church to Newington becoming Lower Street and eventually Essex Road.[22]

Inns clearly contributed to Islington's growth: in 1553 there were 15 licensed victuallers in Islington, as distinct from Holloway.[23] Most of the inns and other buildings along the main roads were copyholds of Barnsbury, Highbury, Canonbury, and the Prebend manors; medieval buildings, called homestalls, therefore, had probably stood on those sites.[24] By 1601 the town included houses on the site of Hedgerow, in Upper Street, occupied by a collarmaker, a vintner, a glazier, a shoemaker, a tailor, a wheelwright, and a weaver. By 1630 the site had c. 11 houses, including the Nag's Head and Blackhorse inns, still the homes of trades- and craftsmen.[25] Some copyholds in Upper and Lower streets north of Islington green served Londoners and gentlemen as country houses and in the late 18th century appeared to have been built or improved in the 16th and early 17th centuries. One of the earliest known was the Fowlers' house, a copyhold of Canonbury manor on the north side of Cross Street (later nos. 40-2). Thomas Fowler, who married Alice Heron or Herne of Islington, died there in 1556, probably in the house where his descendants were living in 1588 and where stained glass included the arms of Fowler and of Heron. The timber framed and plaster house had first-floor plaster ceilings of 1595, with decoration similar to some at Canonbury House. At the end of the garden a small brick building, probably a summerhouse or porter's lodge known later as Queen Elizabeth's Lodge, bore the arms of Fowler, esquire, on one side and those of Sir Thomas Fowler, Bt., with the date 1655 on another.[26] A house where Sir Thomas Fisher, Bt., died in 1636[27] was taxed on 30 hearths, the greatest number in the parish in 1662.[28] It was probably the house on the east side of Lower Street opposite Cross Street, copyhold of the Prebend manor, occupied by Sir Richard Fisher, in 1690, when the garden, enlarged to include the site of 2 cottages and parts of neighbouring holdings, stretched back to Frog Lane. Thought to date from the earlier 17th century and reputed in 1690 to have cost £4,000 to build, the house in the early 19th century was of brick, refaced in Roman cement, and contained the arms of the Fisher and Fowler baronetcies. Nearby were five other houses, let by Fisher.[29]

Between the churchyard and Lower Street a large copyhold house belonged to the Draper family in the early 17th century and was sold by Sir Thomas Draper, Bt., in 1662 to James Cardrow. In 1687 the house had a great hall and wainscotted rooms and shutters, some decorated in an earlier manner. There were a fishpond, gardens, and orchards, including house or priory garden, with a sun and moon dial on a pedestal and ornamental flower pots.[30]

Ward's or King John's Place in Lower Street, between Greenman's Lane and Paradise Place, was a large irregular timber framed and plaster building, with coats of arms carved and in stained glass.[31] Sir Robert Ducie, Bt. (d. 1634), lord mayor of London, may have lived there. The initials HD over the main entrance probably commemorated his youngest son Sir Hugh (d. c. 1678), whose son Sir William Ducie, Bt. (d. ?1691), also lived in Islington.[32] Another house of the early 17th century stood in Upper Street where Theberton Road later joined it; it was the residence of Sir John Miller by 1624 until 1639, and had windows with his arms, carved chimney pieces, and ornamented plaster ceilings. By 1725 it had become the Pied Bull inn.[33] Another, on the east side of Lower Street near Boon's Lane, was in the Prebend manor, and contained a chimney piece with the initials IM. It was a timber framed and plaster house of three projecting storeys, the central projection forming a porch and the entrance flanked by caryatids; the interior had panelled oak wainscotting and ornamented plaster ceilings. By 1725 it had become the Queen's Head inn.[34]

Several similar houses in Upper and Lower streets presumably had wealthy owners in the 16th and 17th centuries. By the late 17th century, however, such houses were being let, often as inns. The Fowlers' house was let with 6 a. by Sir Richard Fisher in 1673 to David Davies, who covenanted to build three substantial houses on the southern part of the grounds, probably fronting Lower Street. The houses were completed and Davies was also to rebuild the mansion if he should pull it down; he does not appear to have done so, although by the early 19th century it had been refronted in brick.[35] By 1690 the Fowlers' estate, on both sides of the eastern end of Cross Street, included in addition to the great house, a house and 3-a. field, the Dog and Partridge inn which probably became the Thatched House by 1765,[36] and c. 14 other houses and a barn.[37] In 1790 the great house was called Queen Elizabeth's House and had been divided into two, having formerly been a boarding school.[38] The Drapers' house was let from 1666 to a tenant, who sublet the north and south ends. The coach house, with stables, yard and orchard, was let separately in 1668 and walled off, and the coach house was turned into a double fronted house.[39] Ward's Place served several uses in the 18th century: Dr.

[22] Plate 2.
[23] G.L.R.O., MR/LV1, m. 7 and d.
[24] Below, manors; other est. (Christ's Hosp.); see map of manors.
[25] Guildhall MS. 12958/3.
[26] P.R.O., PROB 11/38 (P.C.C. 10 Ketchyn, will of T. Fowler); Lewis, Islington, 165; Nelson, Islington (1829), 258-60.
[27] G.E.C. Baronetage, ii. 30.
[28] P.R.O., E 179/252/32, p. 26.
[29] Ibid. C 7/597/81; Nelson, Islington (1829), 356; below, plate 5.

[30] P.R.O., C 6/259/11; G.E.C. Baronetage, iii. 35.
[31] Plate 4.
[32] G.E.C. Baronetage, ii. 77; Nelson, Islington (1829), 188-91.
[33] Nelson, Islington (1829), 117-23; G.L.R.O., MR/LV4/51.
[34] Guildhall MS. 11816B, pp. 113-14; Nelson, Islington (1829), 349-51; G.L.R.O., MR/LV4/49; below, plate 8.
[35] P.R.O., C 10/500/19, 24; Nelson, Islington (1829), 259.
[36] G.L.R.O., MR/LV8/40.
[37] P.R.O., C 7/597/81.
[38] M.L.R. 1790/9/397.
[39] P.R.O., C 7/58/60.

Robert Poole's smallpox hospital by 1740, parish workhouse in 1758, a meeting place for seceders from Lower Street chapel in the 1760s, and at some time a soap factory, before being divided into separate tenements.[40]

While the larger houses lost their wealthy residents, the steady growth in middle-class houses began. Building was usually in short rows, often named after the builder or financer. A large old house in Upper Street on the southern corner of Cross Street was replaced by Rufford's Buildings in 1688, built by Nicholas Rufford who had already built another set of Rufford's Buildings in 1685 on the eastern side of High Street next to an inn later called the Blue Coat Boy.[41] The row of houses on the west side of Upper Street was known as the Hedgerow by 1668. Other rows by 1732 included Oddy's Buildings, Chad's Row, Yeates Row, and Pierpont's Buildings and Rents on the eastern side of High Street, where John Pierpont had acquired land in 1718.[42] Some detached houses were also built. The vicarage house near the Pied Bull was built or rebuilt in the late 17th century and another house built on its grounds.[43] Farther along Upper Street, north of Cut Throat Lane (later Barnsbury Street) was another detached house, built in 1716 and 1719 and occupied by Jacob Harvey in 1735.[44]

By 1735 the area of the town was closely built up along the main roads.[45] The west side of High Street, in Clerkenwell parish, and its continuation as Upper Street were almost completely built up to the lower end of Holloway Road, where Wells's Row stood approximately on the site of Highbury Corner. The row was probably built by John Wells, brickmaker, who was letting new houses there from 1722[46] and had kilns on land to the west. The east side of High Street and its continuation as Lower Street were more open, with farm land around Pierponts Row, but Lower Street was almost filled as far as Greenman's Lane and building was beginning in the lanes running south-east.[47] Between Upper and Lower streets as far as Cross Street there were also many buildings along the main frontages, and facing the green on the north was a terrace called Old Paradise Row. On the east side of High Street south of the green stood some almshouses and another small group of houses, with a narrow passage between them and the fields behind.[48]

In the 18th century Islington's popularity as a resort was shown by the increased number of inns, many with skittle grounds,[49] and more houses were built for residents and tradesmen. Rosoman's Buildings, 13 houses facing the green and stretching from River Lane (later St. Peter's Street) southward, were built on land belonging to Thomas Rosoman of Clerkenwell between 1758 and 1768, mostly by himself. The Three Tuns inn at the corner of River Lane was replaced by Rosoman with four houses between 1764 and 1769.[50] In the same period part of the grounds of the Fowlers' house was built over. Thatched House Row was built on the Lower Street frontage between 1758 and 1762, and behind it Astey's Buildings and Pleasant Row were built facing each other across the New River by John Astey between c. 1761 and 1764. Houses were also being built on the south side of Cross Street by 1767, the first group being finished in 1771 and the remainder of the 17 houses occupied by 1779. Most were built by Benjamin Williams and John Davis, Islington carpenters, and have pedimented Doric doorcases, although nos. 23, 33, and 35 have later doorcases imitating those of the Adams in the Adelphi.[51] Five old timber houses at the Hedgerow were replaced by brick ones in 1779 by Thomas Nowell, who also took a lease of land behind and by 1785 had completed a row called Nowell's Buildings, fronting the Back Road.[52] Camden Street, leading south-east from the green, was being built between 1760 and 1768 on land leased by Thomas Rosoman to Brass Crosby,[53] and at the west end Cumberland Row was built from 1767 in the passage behind the buildings in High Street,[54] later called Camden Passage. A little to the south Pullins Row was built in the late 18th century on a field belonging to Pullin's dairy farm fronting High Street. By the 1790s buildings continued northward along Upper Street to Holloway Road on the west side and to Canonbury Lane on the east, and along Lower Street to the New River and the junction with Frog Lane.[55] In Upper Street opposite Cross Street, Dr. William Pitcairn (1711–91) started a botanical garden of c. 4 a. attached to his house; for a while after his death it contained many rare plants and trees.[56] The area between Upper and Lower streets was still largely open behind the main road frontages, part being St. Mary's churchyard and Jones's burial ground.[57] North of Cross Street the Tufnell family still had open ground near the Fowlers' house, for which building agreements were made by Robert Cannon in 1808 and, following Cannon's bankruptcy, by John Morgan in 1810. Much of the site, stretching north to Hawes Street, was built over by 1817, leaving the old house with some garden behind.[58]

Growth in the 19th century mainly took the form of rebuilding and changes in use.[59] Commercial premises increased to serve a rapidly rising population, and many of the old houses in Lower Street were replaced by rows of shops. Ward's Place was demolished c. 1800, the Queen's

[40] Nelson, *Islington* (1829), 191.
[41] Ibid. 258; P.R.O., MAF 20/136.
[42] Co. of Par. Clerks, *New Remarks on Lond.* (1732), 235; M.L.R. index.
[43] Below, churches.
[44] Nelson, *Islington* (1829), 113–14.
[45] Para. based on Nelson, *Islington*, plan (1735).
[46] e.g. M.L.R. 1722/4/249, 258.
[47] Below, growth, SE. Islington.
[48] See parish map c. 1740, p. 8.
[49] Below, social.
[50] G.L.C., Historic Bldgs. Div., ISL 38.

[51] Ibid. ISL 17; J. Summerson, *Georgian Lond.* (1962), 314.
[52] Guildhall MS. 12958/1, 4.   [53] M.L.R. 1768/1/510.
[54] Tomlins, *Islington*, 192.
[55] Baker's plan (1793).
[56] Nelson, *Islington* (1829), 115; Cromwell, *Islington*, 288–9.
[57] Below, prot. nonconf. (Islington chapel).
[58] Islington libr., deeds box III/3; Baker's plan (1817); P.R.O., IR 30/21/33.
[59] For bldg. on open areas adjoining the town, see below, Canonbury, SE. Islington, Barnsbury.

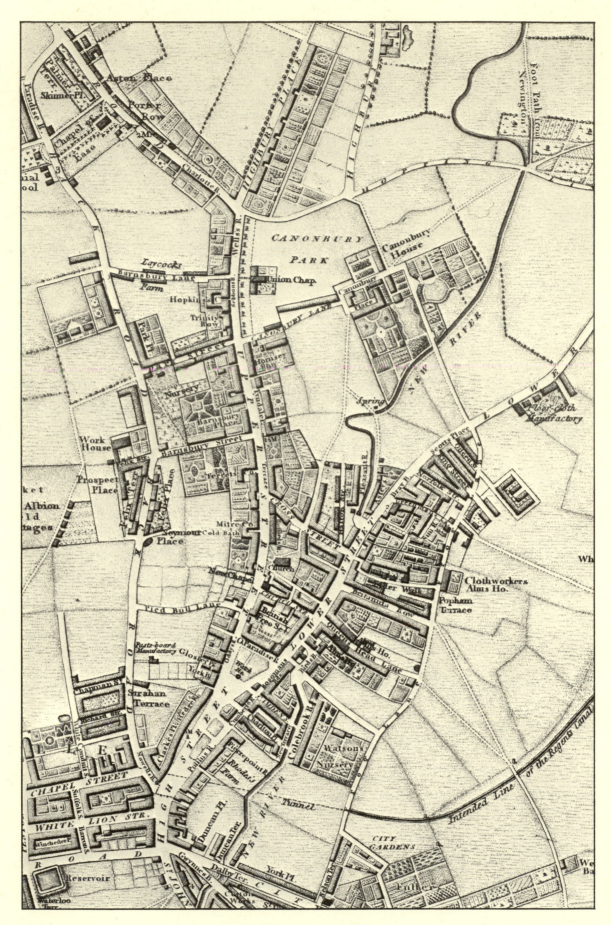

ISLINGTON TOWN IN 1817

16

Head in 1829, and Fisher's House, to make way for Pickering Place and the houses behind, in 1845. The Fowlers' house, nos. 40-2 Cross Street, was demolished in 1850 and the site used for a Baptist chapel.[60] The galleried Angel inn at the corner of High Street and Pentonville Road was rebuilt in 1819 as a coaching hotel. Barnsbury Place in Upper Street had been built before 1811, on the garden of Harvey's house, and land behind was taken for the Church Missionary College, designed by William Brooks and built in 1824.[61] In 1837 the Literary and Scientific Institution, designed by Gough & Roumieu, was built in Wellington Street (later Almeida Road).[62] The strip of land on the east side of High Street south of Islington green, partially built on in the mid 18th century, was filled with more small houses and shops facing both High Street and Camden passage behind: Phelps Cottage was built in Pullins Row in 1838 and at the south end new buildings included a large one used as a bazaar and then by 1858 as an upholsterer's showroom.[63] A little southward the Philharmonic Hall (Grand theatre) was built in 1860.[64] On the opposite side of the main road the first part of the Agricultural Hall was opened in 1861 for the Royal Smithfield Show, on a site that stretched back to Liverpool Road.[65]

The provision of working-class housing brought major changes after 1860. By the 1840s the town's population was mainly poor, living in overcrowded and decaying courts and yards off the main roads. Many of the courts had been the yards attached to inns: Swan, George, Wheatsheaf, and Rose and Crown yards were some of them, mostly at the lower end of the town. Some houses in Swan Yard were lodging houses for tramps, with cellars used for sleeping in 1848; five years later they were still filthy, as were similar courts.[66] From 1865 efforts were made to replace the worst slums with working-class dwellings. The first block was by the Peabody Trust in Greenman's Lane (Greenman Street) in 1865, designed by H. A. Darbishire in a 'crushingly unattractive vaguely Italianate' style that became standard on its estates.[67] The medical officer for Islington visited the parish's 110 courts and alleys in 1874 and reported on three particularly bad areas: eight courts east of High Street between Duncan Street and City Road, including Swan Yard and Rose and Crown Court, with 78 houses unfit for habitation; Little Pierponts Row in Camden Passage between Duncan Street and Charlton Crescent, with 8 houses; and 25 courts and buildings east of Essex Road between Greenman Street and Britannia Row, with 219 houses.[68] In the third area Quinn's

Buildings was built in Popham Street in 1876 apparently by a philanthropic body,[69] but all three districts were submitted to the M.B.W. under the Artisans' and Labourers' Dwelling Act, 1875, for clearance.[70]

The first scheme was for the south-east High Street area in 1877. It was to rehouse 515 people and 32 inhabitants of lodging houses, living on either side of the Philharmonic theatre in five blocks of four or five storeys accommodating at least 556 people in 138 tenements. In 1880 part of Blackhorse Yard and nos. 48 and 50 High Street were included in the scheme.[71] The sites were sold to the Improved Industrial Dwellings Co., whose ultimate accommodation for 798 on c. 1 a.[72] probably included the six-storeyed Myddelton Flats, built in 1882 beside the theatre.[73] The area off Essex Road followed in 1878, where 1,796 people were to be displaced from c. 250 houses over c. 5 a. between Britannia Row and the south side of Peabody Square (Greenman Street), 3,422 were to be housed, and a new street was to be formed in the line of Anglers Gardens; the site was sold to the Peabody trustees and others.[74] Both schemes were delayed by legal problems and the refusal of occupants in High Street to leave or pay rent, until government sanction was obtained to remove them. Many then moved to Elder Walk in the second area, where they again refused to recognize the M.B.W. as landlord. In 1881, however, the High Street site and the first part of the Essex Road site, Britannia Row, were cleared; the remainder was cleared in 1882.[75] The five parts of the Essex Road site were all sold by 1884, when building had begun over the whole area.[76] Edinburgh, Cornwall, and Queen's cottages, in Popham Street, were probably built by one of the bodies who bought the sites. They were designed by a Mr. Worley and built in 1889, a fortress-like block with turrets, where the interior courtyards had open staircases and galleries.[77] Ultimately there were on the High Street site four blocks near High Street and six near City Road, and on the Essex Road site there were five blocks for 510 people north of Dibden Street, fifteen between Dibden and Pickering streets for 556 people, four between Pickering and Popham streets for 2,000, and fourteen blocks between Popham Street and Britannia Row for 800.[78]

Another important change was the widening of Upper Street, between the green and the Unitarian church on the east side and between Waterloo Terrace and Barnsbury Street on the west. Property on both sides was bought by the M.B.W. and cleared, including the weatherboarded Fox public house, by the green, Islington dispensary, and Islington chapel, which were

[60] Nelson, *Islington* (1829), 188; Tomlins, *Islington*, 115, 193-4.
[61] S. Lewis, *Islington As It Was* (1854), 56; Colvin, *Brit. Architects*, 144; Nelson, *Islington* (1829), 113-14.
[62] Below, social.
[63] G.L.R.O., P83/MRY1/546; Lewis, *Islington*, plan; Tomlins, *Islington*, 91.
[64] Below, social.
[65] Ibid.
[66] G.L.R.O., P83/MRY1/721; MRY1/747/14; P.R.O., MAF 20/12, no. 182.
[67] Pevsner, *Lond.* ii. 237.
[68] M.O.H. *Ann. Rep.* (1874-5), 27, 42.
[69] *Ind. Mons. Gtr. Lond.* (1969), 37; Pevsner, *Lond.* ii. 237.

[70] *Rep. of M.B.W. 1876*, H.C. 225, p. 607 (1877), lxiii.
[71] Ibid.; ibid. *1877*, H.C. 213, pp. 468, 528 (1878), lxv; *Lond. Statutes*, i. 531, 577.
[72] L.C.C. *Housing of Working Classes in Lond.* (1913), 146.
[73] Datestone.
[74] *Lond. Statutes*, i. 546-7; L.C.C. *Housing of Working Classes*, 146; *Rep. of M.B.W. 1878*, H.C. 230, pp. 454, 509 (1878-9), lxi.
[75] *Rep. of M.B.W. 1880*, H.C. 240, pp. 330, 405 (1881), lxxix; *1881*, H.C. 188, pp. 329, 402-3 (1882), lix; *1882*, H.C. 169, p. 574 (1883), lix.
[76] Ibid. *1884*, H.C. 186, p. 847 (1884-5), lxvii.
[77] *Ind. Mons. Gtr. Lond.* 37; Pevsner, *Lond.* ii. 237.
[78] *Rep. of M.B.W. 1885*, H.C. 170, p. 474 (1886), lvii.

all rebuilt farther back. Bodies were removed from the front part of the churchyard to Finchley cemetery, and new railings set up. Some artisans' houses were demolished, displacing 140 people, and a site was set aside in 1887 in Waterloo Terrace for flats to take 178.[79] The widened Upper Street was reopened early in 1888 and the remaining land auctioned, in 17 plots between the green and Church Street and in 22 between Church Street and the vestry hall (Florence Street), and filled with substantial terraces of shops. Land adjoining the churchyard was sold for a new vicarage.[80]

In 1892 the vestry was allowed to displace 190 people in Norfolk Square, which lay on the south side of Shepperton Street near Popham Road and covered ½ a.; the area had been considered unhealthy since 1880 but it was not considered practical to rebuild.[81] Islington generally had little appeal to the middle class: the terraced houses in streets off the main roads were no longer in single-family occupation but let as rooms. When the impoverished author portrayed in *New Grub Street*, published in 1891, took a lodging off Upper Street, his fastidious wife could not be expected to join him there.[82] Although Islington was not fashionable as a residence, High Street and Upper Street became a smart shopping area from the mid 19th century, rivalling Brompton Road, with many drapers, outfitters, and jewellers; in 1881 it was the 'classic ground' for trousseau shopping, and was particularly noted for underclothes.[83] Most of the 18th century buildings along the Hedgerow and Upper Street were given imposing shop fronts[84] and in 1899 the Angel inn was rebuilt as a hotel, designed by Eedle & Meyers in pale terracotta stone with a corner cupola;[85] it became a Lyons cornerhouse restaurant from 1921 to 1959.[86]

After the First World War more attempts were made to provide working-class housing. The Church Missionary Society sold its college in Upper Street in 1917 and the building was replaced with Suttons model dwellings,[87] but most schemes were municipal and were concentrated between Upper Street and New North Road.[88] Halton Mansions on the east side of Halton Road was the first state-aided scheme in Islington, built in 1922–3 with 168 flats in 3 four-storeyed blocks. It was followed in 1926 by Tyndale Mansions with 102 flats, north and south of the new town hall, and in 1934 Wakelin House, 109 dwellings in a five-storeyed block, was built on the west side of Sebbon Street. A private estate was built in 1936–7 by the Compton Housing Association between Canonbury Road and Sable Street, with 153 dwellings in five-storeyed blocks, similar to council developments. The estate, Compton Flats, was later acquired by

the council and renovated between 1967 and 1975.

After the Second World War, Canonbury Court was built in 1948 between Sebbon Street and Halton Road, blocking off Shillingford Street. The site of c. 4 a. had been acquired from the Northampton estate and 132 flats in 7 four-storeyed blocks were built. An additional block was built in Florence Street in 1960, and in 1967 the estate had 141 dwellings. Barratt House was built near Compton Flats in 1953 with 22 dwellings, and Hume Court in 1960 near Hawes Street with 36 dwellings. An area off High Street between Camden Passage and Colebrooke Row, known as Camden Walk, was replaced with 50 flats 1967–9 known as Colinsdale, and a smaller scheme in Queen's Head Street 1968–70 involved the rehabilitation of nos. 57–63 (odd) Queen's Head Street and nos. 13–15 Cruden Street, an L-shaped block of decayed terraced houses, to provide 5 houses, 2 flats, and 2 maisonettes. The council rehabilitated or rebuilt similar small groups of houses, and private schemes were also carried out. Major rebuilding was done behind the east side of Essex Road as part of the Popham Road estates.[89] In 1983 houses in Melville Street were cleared, including the Essex Road frontage.

Large-scale changes were made to High Street in the early 1980s. Most of the buildings on the east side from Duncan Street almost to City Road, and including the Grand theatre and Myddelton Flats, with all the land behind east to the rear of Duncan Terrace, were cleared for a large office block. In 1983 some shops on the opposite side of the main road in the Hedgerow had been demolished for rebuilding, with Parkfield Street behind. Plans to demolish the old Lyons Corner House, which had been used as an annexe to City University after 1959, to make way for road improvements were resisted and after renovation the building became the London branch of the Co-operative Bank c. 1982. In 1983 shops at the south end of High Street were in poor condition and those remaining on the east side empty and due for demolition. North of the new office block however, some 18th-century houses remained near Duncan Street, nos. 80 and 84–94 High Street being mid 18th-century, as did Phelps Cottage of 1838. The rest of Camden Passage consisted of shops, many selling antiques for which it had become widely known. London Transport's former transformer station between Upper and High streets was converted into an antique mall c. 1980. Some houses on the site of Rosoman's Buildings at the corner of St. Peter's Street were rebuilt in their original style for private sale c. 1981. Two small modern townhouse developments a little to the north in Essex Road were also private. Most of both Essex Road

[79] *Rep. of M.B.W. 1882,* H.C. 169, p. 559 (1883), lix; *1885,* H.C. 170, p. 374 (1886), lvii; *1886,* H.C. 157, pp. 469, 563 (1887), lxxi; *1887,* H.C. 159, pp. 566, 671 (1888), lxxxvii.

[80] Ibid. *1888,* H.C. 326, p. 823 (1889), lxvi.

[81] Ibid. *1880,* H.C. 240, p. 329 (1881), lxxix; L.C.C. *Housing of Working Classes,* 149.

[82] G. R. Gissing, *New Grub Street.*

[83] A. Adburgham, *Shops and Shopping 1800–1914* (1964), 151; C. Harris, *Islington* (1974), 184.

[84] Islington Soc. *Upper Street Survey* (1980).

[85] Pevsner, *Lond.* ii. 238.

[86] Inf. from Mr. J. C. Connell.

[87] J. Rooker, *Reminiscences of One Hundred Years' Work for C.M.S. in Islington* (1927), pp. 6–7.

[88] Rest of para. and the next based on 'Wakelin/Halton Local Area Study', Islington Planning Dept., 1974, vol. i, pp. 11, 13, 15, 21; Islington M.B. *Completion Ceremony— Canonbury Ct. Sebbon St. 1948*; Islington L.B. *Homes for Islington* (1967), pp. 7–8, plan; Islington L.B. *Our Changing Islington* (1971), 5; Islington L.B. *Queen's Head St./Curden St. Rehabilitation Scheme.*

[89] Below, SE. Islington.

and Upper Street, however, was commercial, providing shopping, services, and take-away food for a working-class population and wine bars, expensive restaurants, and specialist shops for new middle-class residents and visitors.

CANONBURY covered the area from behind Cross Street north to St. Paul's Road. Until the 18th century the only buildings were at Canonbury House, which existed in 1373.[90] By 1730 Canonbury tavern had been built[91] to the north-east of the house, where its tea-gardens shared in Islington's popularity as a resort.

In 1763 2 a. given to Hornsey parish for the Draper charity[92] were leased for 99 years and assigned to Thomas Bird, who by 1768 had built 10 houses fronting Upper Street, known later as Hornsey Row, and 8 on the south side of Canonbury Lane.[93] From c. 1770 John Dawes replaced the south range of Canonbury House with new houses and the west range with a villa; the east range was divided into three dwellings. More houses were built on the south side in the late 18th century.[94] In Upper Street just south of Hornsey Row another small group of houses called Tyndale Place was built c. 1792.[95]

In 1803 Lord Northampton made a building agreement with Henry Leroux of Stoke Newington for a large area fronting Upper Street, Canonbury Lane, and Hopping Lane.[96] Compton Terrace, on the east side of Upper Street, was started by 1806 when the first Union chapel, a two-storeyed building with a central pediment, and two houses had been completed and leased to Leroux,[97] but only the chapel and four houses existed in 1817.[98] An agreement was made in 1805 for Canonbury Square,[99] where Leroux let plots on the north side in 1808.[1] He went bankrupt in 1809 and was living in the square in 1810,[2] but no further work was apparently done to complete it. By 1817 the north side had been finished with the houses on the north side of Canonbury Lane.[3] In 1819 and 1822 Henry Flower and Samuel Kell agreed to complete Compton Terrace, and leases were granted on the houses in 1821 and 1827–31.[4]

New North Road, cut from Highbury Corner across Canonbury Square to Lower Road c. 1820,[5] had a small mews at the northern end by 1829.[6] In 1821 agreements were made with Richard Laycock for the houses on the south and east sides of the square, together with the ground south of it between Sebbon Street and Alwyne Villas and from New North Road to Canonbury Street south-east of the New River. Leases were granted for the south side of the square in 1821, and for houses in the other streets between 1821 and 1826, but none of the streets was apparently completed

in 1829, and no houses stood west of New North Road or in Sebbon Street. Large three- and four-storeyed terraces were built in the square and along New North Road, where Albion and Union terraces stood in 1829. Houses in the other streets were smaller and many were in a cottage style. Canonbury Terrace, on the west side of the street later called Alwyne Villas, had a datestone of 1824, but only a few houses were recorded in 1829. Willow Terrace (later Canonbury Grove) and Northampton and Canonbury streets were also incomplete, but land between them fronting Lower Road had been built up.[7]

In 1837 Charles Havor Hill agreed to build on Canonbury Park North and South and in Grange Road,[8] but only a very few pairs stood at the south-west end of Canonbury Park South by 1841. West of New North Road, however, Halton Street had been extended northward by 1841 to join the main road, and terraces built on either side at the north end and on the east side farther south. Canonbury Grove and the adjoining streets had been completed by 1841, and north of the square the few houses of Compton Place had been built. A small terrace was built in Lower Road opposite John Perkins's market, far from other houses in Canonbury.[9]

During the 1840s Canonbury Park North and South were laid out with semi-detached villas, whose gardens on the south side stretched to the New River, and by 1849 a few had also been completed in Grange Road; most of the leases were granted by 1850. Canonbury tavern was demolished in 1846 and the site with adjoining land was built over with St. Mary's Grove by 1849 and Compton Road, started soon afterwards; leases were granted between 1847 and 1853. Several small local builders were involved, including E. Conquest, William Aspland, King & Co., William Timewell, P. Donnelly, J. Rashbrook, and George Frasi.[10]

In 1847 James Wagstaff made a building agreement for the land between Alwyne Villas and the gardens of Canonbury Park South, which included the 16th-century garden and summer-houses of Canonbury House. There he built the villas on the east side of Alwyne Villas, in Alwyne Road and Place, and Willow Bridge Road. The earliest houses were nos. 2 and 4 Alwyne Villas, described as 'cottage villas', and nos. 1–4 Alwyne Road, all leased to him in 1848. Nos. 6–16 Alwyne Villas followed in 1849 and leases of the remaining houses gradually up to 1860.[11]

By the early 1850s more villas had been built, on the south side of St. Paul's Road between Grange Road and Canonbury Park, and on the remaining fields south-east of the New River.[12] Behind Douglas Road, with its villas facing the

[90] Below, manors.
[91] G.L.R.O., MR/LV5/21.
[92] V.C.H. Mdx. vi. 200.
[93] G.L.C., Hist. Bldgs. Div., ISL 48.
[94] Below, manors.
[95] Nelson, Islington (1829), 255.
[96] G.L.C., Hist. Bldgs. Div., ISL 6.
[97] P.R.O., C 54/15980, no. 20.
[98] Nelson, Islington (1829), 254; Baker's plan (1817).
[99] G.L.C., Hist. Bldgs. Div., ISL 6.
[1] Islington libr., deed 255.
[2] G.L.C., Hist. Bldgs. Div., ISL 6.

[3] Baker's plan (1817).
[4] G.L.C., Hist. Bldgs. Div., ISL 6.
[5] Above, communications.
[6] Cruchley's New Plan (1829).
[7] G.L.C., Hist. Bldgs. Div., ISL 6; Cruchley's New Plan (1829).
[8] G.L.C., Hist. Bldgs. Div., ISL 6.
[9] Lewis, Islington, plan (1841).
[10] P.R.O., IR 30/21/33; G.L.C., Hist. Bldgs. Div., ISL 6.
[11] G.L.C., Hist. Bldgs. Div., ISL 6, 13.
[12] Para. based on Plan of Islington [c. 1853]; Stanford, Libr. Map of Lond. (1862 edn. with additions to 1865).

river, Marquess, Clephane, Ashby, and Quadrant roads had been partially built up by the early 1850s and completed before 1865, with Marquess Grove as infilling behind the church. Villas were also built on the north-east side of Canonbury Street, with St. Matthew's church at the southern end. Building was also carried out fronting St. Paul's Road as far as the church, and along Lower Road (later Essex Road): Canonbury Villas between Canonbury Street and Ashby Road, Spencer Terrace between Ashby and Clephane roads, and more villas and terraces up to the church. In 1857 C. H. Hill agreed to build in Alwyne Square, filling the land between Canonbury Park North and St. Paul's Road, where the houses by 1865 were known as Canonbury Park Square.[13]

The remaining land of the Canonbury demesne, west of Halton Street, was also built over. Sebbon and Spencer streets adjoined Halton Street by the 1850s and Sable Street, just south of Canonbury Square, had been built up by 1865.[14]

Changes were slight until after the Second World War, the only extensive rebuilding being between Upper Street and Halton Road.[15] Most of the residential areas of Canonbury kept a high social status and in 1929 were in the lowest category of overcrowding with less than one person to a room. The block between New North Road and Compton Road north of Canonbury Square was in the middle category of 1.25 to 1.50 persons to a room, and both the terraced block between New North Road and Canonbury Street, near Essex Road, and the area between New North Road and Upper Street, south of Canonbury Square, had 1 to 1.25 persons.[16] The L.C.C. had completed 80 flats in Northampton Street near Essex Road, in the most overcrowded area, by 1937 and increased them to 116 flats by 1967.[17]

Canonbury Square and Place had several residents prominent in literary and artistic spheres between and after the World Wars, including Evelyn Waugh in 1928, Vanessa Bell and Duncan Grant, and Eric Blair (George Orwell) 1944-5.[18] The new owners of part of the estate from 1952, Oriel Property Trust, stopped reletting to local tenants and began to rehabilitate Canonbury Square and its neighbourhood hoping to attract middle-class tenants. By 1961 Canonbury, the first area in Islington to be gentrified, had a higher concentration of professional and managerial residents than the rest of the borough.[19]

The council built several estates in Canonbury after the Second World War.[20] Near St. Paul's Road, Dixon Clark Court, with 60 dwellings in 1967, was built in Compton Road, and Elizabeth Kenny House, with 36 dwellings, near Grange Road. Three new estates joined the L.C.C.'s

estate in a badly overcrowded area: Eric Fletcher Court, with 75 dwellings in 1967, in Canonbury Street, Sickert Court, with 238 dwellings nearby on the site of Quadrant Road, and Ashby House, with 35 dwellings, a little farther along Essex Road. The area between those flats and Essex Road was planted with grass and trees. A little farther north-east the Douglas estate between Clephane and Douglas roads had 239 dwellings in 1959. Soon afterwards the council undertook one of its largest and most successful schemes, the Marquess estate, on 28 a. that included Douglas, Marquess, and Clephane roads, fronting St. Paul's Road and Essex Road as far south as Ashby Grove. Designed by Darbourne & Darke, it provided 1,200 flats and maisonettes of dark red brick, in a landscaped setting which included part of the New River Walk. The area was closed to through traffic, maisonettes at ground level had their own gardens, and upper levels were reached by a ramp. Completed in 1976, the estate has been praised as an example of municipal housing and planning.[21]

SOUTH-EAST ISLINGTON, east of High Street and Essex Road, in the 17th century was open land: in the northern part large freehold fields, and in the southern mainly copyhold land of tenements which lined High Street and Lower Street, as the part of Essex Road between Islington green and Cross Street was then known.[22] Frog Lane crossed the southern part from the boundary with St. Luke's to join the continuation of Lower Street north of the town, known as Lower Road, and, as the town grew, lanes and footpaths were made from Lower Street to Frog Lane. In 1735 they were River or Water Lane (later St. Peter's Street), also mentioned in 1717,[23] Boons, Almshouse, or Queen's Head Lane, Elder Walk, and Gunter's, Curriers, or Greenman's Lane.[24] Midway along the north side of Queen's Head Lane stood ten almshouses of the Clothworkers' Company of London, built c. 1658 with funds from John Heath (d. 1641).[25] Away from the town, the only building known to have existed in the early 18th century was the Rosemary Branch inn, at the parish boundary by 1716.[26]

In the early 18th century a pair of two-storeyed cottages (later nos. 56-7 Colebrooke Row) with attics and linked doorways was built on the south side of the New River near River Lane, probably c. 1717 when the site with the surrounding Hattersfield[27] was sold to Walter Burton, who built a brewhouse and brick kilns there. Another pair (later nos. 58-9 and much altered), possibly of the same date, stood at right angles facing south. Bricks and tiles were made there in the

[13] G.L.C., Hist. Bldgs. Div., ISL 6.
[14] Plan [c. 1853]; Stanford, *Map* (1865).
[15] Above, Islington town, for rebldg. in 20th cent. of area SW. of New North Rd.
[16] *New Lond. Life and Labour*, iv, maps.
[17] L.C.C. *Lond. Housing* (1937); Islington L.B. *Homes for Islington* (1967), map.
[18] P. Zwart, *Islington: Hist. and Guide* (1973), 97; C. Harris, *Islington* (1974), 192-3.
[19] J. Pitt, *Gentrification in Islington* [1977], 7-8.
[20] Para. based on *Homes for Islington* (1967), map; Isling-

ton L.B. 'Estate Properties in Permanent Management' (TS. list 1980 in Islington libr.).
[21] C. McKean and T. Jestico, *Guide to Modern Bldgs. in Lond. 1965-75*, 44; Islington L.B. *Canonbury Marquess Rd. Housing Dev. Area* (n.d.), in Islington libr.
[22] Above, Islington town.
[23] M.L.R. 1717/3/238-9.
[24] Nelson, *Islington*, plan (1735); Tomlins, *Islington*, 12-13 (1735 survey).
[25] P.R.O., C 7/452/94.
[26] G.L.R.O., MR/LV3/3.
[27] Below, other est.

1730s and the field became known as Tile kiln field.[28] In 1725 there were three inns in Frog Lane: the Chequer, Flower Pot, and Fox and Cub.[29] Frog Hall, an inn recorded in 1735 and 1746 which had a sign of a plough drawn by frogs,[30] was not licensed by that name, which may have been a local nickname. In 1765 the inns in the Lane were the Rose, Barley Mow, Plough, and Angel (the last possibly the Angler).[31] A few other buildings stood near Frog Lane in 1735, in the lanes off Lower Street. Greenman's Lane had buildings at the Lower Street end, and others stood at the east end of Elder Walk and near the almshouses in Queen's Head Lane.[32] The Rosemary Branch inn seems to have closed between 1730 and 1751, and a white lead factory with two large windmills occupied the site by 1786, but a new Rosemary Branch was also built there in 1783.[33]

Domestic building increased from the 1760s. Bird's Buildings (later nos. 60–5 Colebrooke Row) were built on the north side of River Lane in 1767, and the houses originally called Colebrooke Row were said to have been built in 1768, becoming nos. 55 to 41, although nos. 54–5, much altered, may have been older. They are three-storeyed with attics, and had pedimented Doric doorcases; three were given an extra storey. Nos. 40 to 37 (later demolished) may have been built at the same time or c. 1775 with nos. 36 to 34, and the row ended on the south where the junction with the later Gerrard Road lies.[34] The last house at the southern end, then no. 1 Colebrooke Row, was originally the Colebrooke Arms but became a girls' and by 1828 a boys' school. A white plaster house behind the row was occupied for some years by William Woodfall (1746–1803), parliamentary reporter. At the north end of the row one of the houses facing south was the Revd. John Rule's school in the 1760s and 1770s and next to it were the Castle inn and tea-gardens.[35] The land on the east side of Colebrooke Row was let to William and James Watson as a nursery garden in 1770.[36]

In 1770 the Clothworkers' Company built eight almshouses on the south side of Frog Lane opposite Elder Walk, to replace those at Whitefriars founded by Margaret, countess of Kent, c. 1538 for widows of freemen of the company.[37] Building between Frog Lane and Lower Street increased in the later 18th century. Britannia Row had been constructed between the two roads by 1773[38] and was well built up by the 1790s.[39] Two houses were built in Queen's Head Lane c. 1786,[40] and the Davis almshouses on the south

side in 1794.[41] Anglers Gardens and Paradise Place, which had at least 31 small houses in 1798, ran from Frog Lane between Elder Walk and Greenman's Lane.[42] In the early 19th century Greenman's Lane contained a factory belonging to Thomas Wontner & Sons, hatters, employing 40–50 people, and in 1808 Wontner built a family house on the north side of the lane.[43] Farther north in the angle between Frog Lane and Lower Road stood a dairy farm bought in 1774 by Thomas Scott, who in 1791 also bought a large tract between Frog Lane and the Rosemary Branch, on which he began building from the Lower Street end.[44] By 1806 the terraced houses of Scotts Place fronted Lower Street and the land as far as Frog Lane was filled by Norfolk, King, and Queen streets.[45] By 1817 the streets had been extended a little way south-east of Frog Lane and some building had begun, while Popham Street, between Elder Walk and Britannia Row, had been built with small terraced houses and Popham Terrace fronted Frog Lane.[46] In the 1820s the small houses off Frog Lane near Elder Walk were occupied by artisans, many of them in watchmaking and similar trades, while Britannia Row had factories for cut glass and watch-springs.[47] In Lower Road a little north-east of the junction with Frog Lane a floor-cloth factory had been built between 1806 and 1817, with a few detached and terraced houses just beyond it, including Barossa Lodge, with a verandah, and a pair of stuccoed villas (later nos. 296–8 Essex Road). The factory, probably of 1812, was a stuccoed three- or four-storeyed building, in a plain Grecian style on the ground floor with Ionic pilasters from the first floor up.[48]

Farther south, near the New River building also increased after 1760. Campden or Camden Street was made between Islington green and the New River and houses were being built there in 1768.[49] By the 1790s a small farmyard stood at the New River end[50] and possibly one or two houses, which may have included the detached six-roomed stuccoed cottage occupied by Charles Lamb in 1823. More building by the New River began when the architect James Taylor (c. 1765–1846) built New Terrace (later nos. 50–8 Duncan Terrace) on the west bank in 1791, extending it (as the later nos. 46–9 Duncan Terrace) south of Charlton Place and completing it by 1794.[51] The terrace was also called Colebrooke Terrace c. 1830.[52] Taylor built Charlton Place, between Cumberland Row in High Street and the river, from 1790 to 1795, with a curved south side called Charlton Crescent.[53]

[28] M.L.R. 1717/3/238–9; 1727/3/183–4; J. Summerson, *Georgian Lond.* (1962), 314; G.L.C., Historic Bldgs. Div., ISL 10.
[29] G.L.R.O., MR/LV4/49.
[30] Nelson, *Islington*, 357, plan (1735); Rocque, *Map of Lond.* (1741–5), sheet 6.
[31] G.L.R.O., MR/LV8/40.
[32] Nelson, *Islington*, plan (1735).
[33] Below, social.
[34] G.L.C., Historic Bldgs. Div., ISL 10; Summerson, *Georgian Lond.* 314.
[35] Nelson, *Islington* (1829), 194–5.
[36] M.L.R. 1774/3/497.
[37] *6th Rep. Com. Char.* H.C. 12, p. 217 (1822), ix.
[38] M.L.R. 1773/3/155.
[39] Baker's plan (1793).

[40] M.L.R. 1786/1/604.
[41] Below, charities.
[42] M.L.R. 1798/3/660.
[43] Nelson, *Islington* (1829), 186; Islington L.B. *Tibberton Sq. 1839–1979* (1979, booklet in Islington libr.).
[44] Below, other est. (Hides).
[45] Dent's plan (1806).
[46] Baker's plan (1817).
[47] Nelson, *Islington* (1829), 186, 357.
[48] Baker's plan (1817); Summerson, *Georgian Lond.* 314; Pevsner, *Lond.* ii. 235.
[49] M.L.R. 1768/1/97–9, 158, 511.
[50] Nelson, *Islington* (1829), 197.
[51] Colvin, *Brit. Architects*, 813; datestone.
[52] Cromwell, *Islington*, 177.
[53] Colvin, *Brit. Architects*, 813; datestone.

City Road crossed the southern tip of the parish from 1761,[54] and by the late 18th century an area on the boundary called City Gardens contained several small houses with some ground attached, many let to Londoners as country cottages or retirement homes.[55] Later, however, the area deteriorated and in 1846 it had a very 'degraded' population.[56] From *c.* 1800 speculative building began in and near City Road. Nelson Terrace between the road and City Gardens was completed by 1802,[57] while City Road itself acquired two imposing terraces. Dalby Terrace on the south was built in 1803 by Mr. Dalby, a manufacturer, on a common formerly used for executions and prize fighting; the house at its west end faced west to the New River with a double bow-windowed front, and was occupied by Dalby, who sought to move a footpath to the farther side of the river.[58] York Place, opposite Dalby Terrace between the New River and Nelson Terrace, may have been built slightly earlier. Building also began along the New River from City Road northward. The first houses in Duncan Terrace (probably nos. 1–10) had been built by 1817, as had River Terrace on the opposite side, where the later nos. 1–3 Colebrooke Row and the corner house were built first.[59] The rest of the district was still open, and the field behind the original Colebrooke Row had become Watson's nursery.[60]

By 1829 both the Regent's canal and New North Road had been completed through the district, the latter along King Street, with Shepperton Street crossing it diagonally to the Rosemary Branch. In Lower Road, Annett's Crescent (later nos. 246–90 Essex Road) was built in 1819 between Frog Lane and the floor-cloth factory, with three-storeyed stuccoed houses with attics, basements, and unusual balconies, designed by William Burnell Hué.[61] Thomas Scott built terraces between King and Rotherfield streets, while at the south-east end of Rotherfield Street at the junction with Sherborne Street the later nos. 22–38 (even) Rotherfield Street formed an ornate stuccoed terrace: its Corinthian pilasters and other decorations were unrelated to those on later building nearby, which was mainly two-storeyed linked pairs, and were more in keeping with Annett's Crescent in Essex Road with which it may have formed part of an earlier building scheme.[62] Farther south the new Windsor Street between Lower Street and Frog Lane was built up,[63] and Thomas Wontner built the 24 houses of Tibberton Square on his own garden between 1823 and 1828.[64] At the northern end of the district, by Ball's Pond Road, the glebe estate was built over *c.* 1822 by Philip Dorset Goepel, with Strahan Place facing Ball's Pond Road, Glebe Terrace facing the Lower Road, and

Dorset (later Dove), Orchard (later Wakeham), and Henshall streets.[65] Islington cattle market was built between 1833 and 1836 south of the glebe estate[66] and by 1841 Northchurch Road had been laid along its south side, with a small row, Prospect Place, at the south-east corner. By the same date, more building had gone up in Shepperton Street, almost completed on the north side of South (later Basire) Street, and on adjoining parts of New North Road.[67]

In the southern part of the district, Duncan Terrace was extended in the 1830s, probably in two stages, nos. 11–21 and 22–32, reaching Duncan Street by 1839. Duncan Street was laid from Pullins Row in High Street to the New River *c.* 1834, when the Catholic Apostolic church was built on the north side, and by 1839 the South Islington Proprietary school stood at the street's north-east corner.[68] The Roman Catholic church in Duncan Terrace was completed in 1843 and the houses on either side, nos. 33–9 and 40–5, were under way in 1841 and completed by 1851.[69] In River Terrace the Presbyterian church was built 1834,[70] when the land behind was still brickfields, but James Rhodes had laid out Sudeley and Alfred (later Elia) streets and Vincent Terrace by 1837 and Gordon (later Quick) Street in 1838. A few houses in Elia Street, which ran to the river beside the Scotch church, had been completed by 1838, 22 by 1839, and the rest in 1841. Four and seven houses were completed in Vincent Terrace and Sudeley Street respectively in 1839, Sudeley Street being completed in 1842. Rhodes used at least three builders, William Beckingham, John Wilson, and Thomas Allen,[71] and probably also built the short terrace facing the river between Elia Street and Vincent Terrace (later nos. 13–19 Colebrooke Row), completed by 1841.[72] Gerrard Street was formed in 1841 by agreement between Rhodes and Thomas Cubitt,[73] who owned the former Watson's nursery which he had used for brickmaking from the 1820s. Cubitt gave the site for St. Peter's church and schools, built in 1834 and 1839 respectively, and between 1837 and 1841 built six houses fronting River Lane (later nos. 18–28 St. Peter's Street), between the later Danbury and Grantbridge streets.[74] By 1841 River Lane, renamed St. Peter's Street, had been extended from Frog Lane across the canal, and a small row of houses stood in the fields by the canal. In the 1840s both sides of St. Peter's Street were being built up, as were the small streets leading off near the canal: Clarence and Hanover streets (later Burgh Street and the lower end of Noel Road), the south-east side of Danbury Street, most of which were built on James Rhodes's land,[75] and the short streets between

[54] Above, communications.
[55] Nelson, *Islington* (1829), 215; M.L.R. 1786/5/138.
[56] *Lond. City Mission Mag.* xi (1846), 210.
[57] G.L.C., Historic Bldgs. Div., ISL 11.
[58] Islington libr., vestry min. bk. 1777–1811, f. 153; Nelson, *Islington* (1829), 217.
[59] Summerson, *Georgian Lond.* 314; Baker's plan (1817).
[60] Baker's plan (1817).
[61] Colvin, *Brit. Architects*, 438; below, plate 18.
[62] See proposed street layout in *Cruchley's New Plan* (1829).
[63] *Cruchley's New Plan* (1829).
[64] Islington L.B. *Tibberton Sq.*

[65] Ch. Com., deed 250661.
[66] Below, econ., markets.
[67] Lewis, *Islington*, plan (1841).
[68] *Cruchley's New Plan* (1829); P.R.O., C 54/15673, no. 12; C 54/14229, no. 27.
[69] Lewis, *Islington*, plan (1841); P.R.O., HO 107/10/2/2; below, Rom. Cathm.
[70] Below, prot. nonconf.
[71] G.L.C., Historic Bldgs. Div., ISL 11.
[72] Lewis, *Islington*, plan (1841).
[73] P.R.O., C 54/12520, no. 2.
[74] H. Hobhouse, *Thos. Cubitt: Master Builder* (1971), 353–4.
[75] Ch. Com., file 14508.

Rheidol Terrace and the canal as far as the Clothworkers' land.[76]

Cubitt sold the three pieces of land fronting Gerrard Road to Rhodes in 1843, and that road's three-storeyed terraced houses, with basements and stuccoed ground floors, had been completed by 1848.[77] The rest of Cubitt's land between Gerrard Road and St. Peter's Street was let to local builders. William Timewell took a block at the north end of Devonia Road opposite St. Peter's church in 1845 and the rest of the west side and the equivalent sites on the east side in a small grant of 1847 and a larger one of 1850. In 1850 he also received the west side of part of Frog Lane (later Danbury Street). The west and east sides of Grantbridge Street, originally called Oxford and Cambridge terraces, were let in 1852 to Joseph Berdoe, who sublet to William Quilter in 1856 and 1857, except a small parcel on the east side let directly to Quilter in 1857.[78] By the early 1850s, Noel Road had also been laid out and terraced houses built on the canal side.[79]

The Clothworkers' Company, with c. 60 a. between New North Road and St. Peter's Street, laid out its estate for building from 1846, together with the Church Commissioners, who owned a small adjoining estate.[80] A small area north-east of New North Road near the canal was the first to be leased by the company, in 1846 to Richard Field, a printer and commission agent, but only the part fronting the main road was built on at that time. Nos. 138–76 (even) New North Road were built for Field by Messrs. Robson & Estall and William Bear, and the carcases were completed in 1846 and 1847. Land farther north along the road was taken by Richard Elcom, a victualler, and in 1846–7 Bear built nos. 180–90, originally called Elcom Terrace, and nos. 192–202, Bear Place. Field also took the block bounded by Prebend Street, Coleman Fields, and Basire Street, where terraced houses built by Charles Haswell and Elias Treby were ready in 1848, and he assigned the adjoining block bounded by Prebend Street, Coleman Fields, and Bishop Street to Richard Noakes Field, who built it up in the 1850s. On the other side of the estate, the block bounded by St. Peter's Street, Rheidol Terrace, and Cruden Street as far as the backs of houses in Queen's Head Lane, with provision for 14 semi-detached and 74 terraced houses,[81] was taken by James and Thomas Ward and built up by James Ward and sublessees. Leases for nos. 7–21 St. Peter's Street, pairs of stuccoed villas originally called Angell Terrace after the Clothworkers' surveyor, Samuel Angell, who probably laid out the estate, were granted in 1848 and for the rest of the block from 1848 to 1852.

Most of the Clothworkers' estate was taken by Henry Rydon, probably in 1847 when he agreed for the Church Commissioners' estate bounded by Linton Street, Arlington Square, New North Road, and the canal. Building began on the south-west side of New North Road but proceeded fairly evenly between 1847 and 1852 over the whole area, which was bounded by New North Road, the canal, St. Paul's Street, Union Square, and Bevan Street. Work also proceeded on the adjoining block bounded by St. Paul's, Prebend, Canon, and Rector streets, and on a plot originally taken by R. N. Field and sublet to Rydon in 1850, bounded by St. Paul's and Prebend streets and Coleman Fields. In all Rydon built 95 houses on the Church Commissioners' land and 240 on the Clothworkers'. Few of his builders were responsible for more than a handful of contiguous houses: W. T. Catling built half the west side of Arlington Square and John Hill most of the east side.

Other builders included Edward Rowland, Thomas Evans, Job Palmer, and John Hebb, who also took land on their own account. In 1851–2 Rowland and Evans took leases direct from the Clothworkers for houses which they had built in Wilton Square and Wilton Villas, and John Hebb took part of the block between Coleman Fields, Prebend, Basire, and St. Paul's streets, building all the houses north-eastward from no. 84 Prebend Street and no. 26 St. Paul's Street. Job Palmer and John Morgan took separate leases of houses in the block bounded by Coleman Fields and St. Paul's, Canon, and Prebend streets. St. Philip's church and schools were built in Arlington Square in 1855, on land reserved by the Church Commissioners, and the Clothworkers' almshouses in Frog Lane, on an island site between Popham Road and Bishop Street, may have been rebuilt at about that date or c. 1872, when part of the site was used for St. James's church; they were rebuilt as two-storeyed blocks in Jacobean style with a gabled first storey.[82] The last part of the estate to be built up was the Packington charity land. James Rhodes agreed for brickmaking and building over 15 years, and only one lease was made before 1859, although the south-eastern end of the estate was built up or under construction by the mid 1850s. Five houses in Essex Road were demolished after 1856, when John Hebb took over the building, to make way for the north-western end of Packington Street, and more houses were completed in 1859 after the agreement had been assigned to John Jay. Jay assigned the land in 1859 to Hebb, who built up most of the estate, comprising Packington, Dame, and the south-west side of Ann streets, and Arlington Street was extended south-westward. Hebb acted as contractor for several builders, who ceremonially thanked him on completion of the work in 1861.

The northern part of the district was the last to be completed. Rotherfield Street was built up between 1841 and 1848, and the streets up to the south-west side of Halliford Street and south side of Downham Road had also been built up by 1848, together with the land along Essex Road as far as the market. The remaining land on either side of the market was building ground and brickfields.[83] By the mid 1850s the market had closed,[84] and a terrace called Lansdown Cottages

[76] Lewis, *Islington*, plan (1841); P.R.O., IR 30/21/33.
[77] Hobhouse, *Cubitt*, 354; P.R.O., IR 30/21/33.
[78] Hobhouse, *Cubitt*, 354–6.
[79] Plan [c. 1853].
[80] Following three paras. based on G.L.C., Historic Bldgs.
Div., ISL 20.
[81] B.L. prints, Crace Colln. portfolio XV, no. 62.
[82] G.L.C., Historic Bldgs. Div., almshos. file.
[83] Lewis, *Islington*, plan (1841); P.R.O., IR 30/21/33.
[84] Plan [c. 1853].

bordered Essex Road between Northchurch Road and Wakeham Street. All the space between Halliford Street and Wakeham Street was built over by 1865, except the east end of Baxter and Mitchison roads,[85] mainly with houses of three storeys and basements in terraces, fours, or pairs, but with houses of two storeys and basements in Baxter, Mitchison, and part of the north side of Ockendon roads.

The parts of south-east Islington adjoining the town suffered, like the town, from overcrowding.[86] Elsewhere the area was mixed, although with the rest of Islington it suffered a social decline from the late 19th century. In 1929 there were two patches of the severest overcrowding, over 1.75 persons to a room, north and south of Popham Street, with three of 1.50 to 1.75 persons to a room, between Shepperton Road and Downham Road, between Tibberton Square and Windsor Street, and between St. Peter's and Dame streets near the canal. The blocks between Packington Street and Queen's Head Lane, and between Devonia Road, Rheidol Terrace, and the canal, had a middle density of 1.25 to 1.50 persons, and the area between Ockendon and Northchurch roads had the lowest, with less than one person to a room; the remainder had a density of 1 to 1.25 persons.[87]

War-time bombing and the need to relieve overcrowding led to the clearance of several large sites. Bentham Court, designed by E. C. P. Monson,[88] was built in 1949 between Rotherfield Street and New North Road, with 134 flats in 3 four-storeyed blocks, the one facing Essex Road having shops on the ground floor, and included a new public house on the corner of Ecclesbourne Road. Farther east Rotherfield Court and Southgate Court had 52 and 26 flats respectively, and McIndoe Court nearby had 40 flats. On the south-west side of New North Road Parke Court was built with 39 dwellings between Shepperton Road and Basire Street, while Baring Court and Arbon Court with 30 and 22 flats were built near the canal. Farther south Cluse Court with 156 flats was built near where St. Peter's Street crosses the canal, and Hermitage House with 24 flats replaced part of the 18th-century Colebrooke Row at the corner of Gerrard Road.[89] Among private post-war building, the London Parochial Charities trustees in 1949 completed Isleden House, on c. 1 a. of the Packington charity land in Prebend Street. Intended to show how old people could live in a populous district, it provided 74 flats for 211, with an administration block and with medical and other services.[90]

From the late 1960s further housing schemes were undertaken. The G.L.C. built Widford House fronting Colebrooke Row and running back along the south side of Elia Street. The borough council in 1967 had begun 153 new dwellings in Popham Street,[91] and in the 1970s cleared a large area in Popham Road adjoining Parker Court. Rebuilding around Rotherfield Street was also extended along the north side of New North Road c. 1980. The largest and most controversial scheme was on the Packington estate, where 12 a. at the south end of Packington Street were cleared for 538 flats in large blocks, after a long fight to have the original houses renovated.[92]

Renovation by the council became more common in the 1970s and, with a high demand by owner-occupiers, the 19th-century housing stock was gradually being rehabilitated in 1983. At the northern end of the district the former glebe estate, whose shallow terraces had been far below standard in 1936,[93] had largely been rebuilt with factories after the Second World War, and St. Paul's school was replaced with private housing c. 1980. In 1983 the streets between Ball's Pond and New North roads were largely unaltered, except by the council housing mentioned above, but the white lead mills at the Rosemary Branch and some small streets behind had been cleared for a park, almost the only open space for children in the district. In New North Road most of the houses had become small shops and were decayed in 1983, owing mainly to heavy traffic, although some renovation was under way and several houses remained. Both sides of the road between Shepperton and Essex roads had been replaced by council housing. South-west of New North Road the part of the Clothworkers' estate developed by Henry Rydon was largely unchanged, with its spacious streets. Most of the area north-west of Popham Road had been rebuilt, however, and few original houses remained. South-west of St. Peter's Street was also largely unaltered, with houses among the most expensive in Islington, particularly along the canal. Many had been converted into maisonettes, either privately or by the council, while the large terraces along City Road were almost entirely in commercial use.

BARNSBURY and KING'S CROSS, covering the whole of the parish west of the settlement along Upper Street and south of the N.L.R. line, was mainly built over in the earlier 19th century. The only medieval building recorded was Barnsbury manor house,[94] which was probably not inhabited after the 14th century, although its moated site remained until the 19th century; no other early sites have been identified. The extreme south-western corner of the parish was part of a settlement called Battle Bridge, on the boundary with St. Pancras, where lived a miller punished for sedition in the 1550s and Cliffe, a cobbler said to have written *The Cobblers Book*, printed in 1589, denying the Church of England.[95] A chapel was built near the south end of Maiden Lane in the 1770s and a few small houses existed by the end of the century, inhabited in 1810 mainly by shopkeepers and artisans and labourers. The area was made unattractive by its proximity to the Fleet river and the trades that had gathered there,

[85] Stanford, *Libr. Map of Lond.* (1862 edn. with additions to 1865).
[86] Above, Islington town.
[87] *New Lond. Life and Labour*, iv, maps.
[88] Inf. from Mr. J. C. Connell, correcting Pevsner, *Lond.* ii. 237.
[89] Islington L.B. *Homes for Islington* (1967).
[90] Trustees of Lond. Parochial Chars. *Isleden Ho.* (1951).
[91] *Homes for Islington* (1967).
[92] Ibid.; P. Zwart, *Islington: Hist. and Guide* (1973), 116.
[93] M. Fitzgerald, *Church as Landlord* (1937), 58–60.
[94] Below, manors.
[95] Nelson, *Islington* (1829), 72.

including a pottery, a paint manufacturer, and a bone collector. Tile kilns were operating farther north along Maiden Lane,[96] while the building of the Horsfall basin on the canal in 1825[97] drew more trade, especially in heavy building materials. Farther east at the conduit house near the Back Road on the boundary were the tea-gardens called the White Conduit House, opened in the 1730s but possibly with an earlier forerunner, since there had been a bowling green beside the conduit in the 1650s.[98] In 1777 the parish workhouse was built half-way up the Back Road,[99] but speculative building did not follow until nearer the end of the century.

The first such building took place in the Back Road, as individual landowners sought to take advantage of a demand stimulated by the building of Pentonville, in Clerkenwell. Park Place, a small terrace at the junction of Islington Park Street, is dated 1790.[1] Opposite on Nathaniel Bishop's Barnfield estate, building also began around that date. Although 3½ a. fronting the Back Road had been reserved for building in 1718,[2] no houses were recorded in the 1740s.[3] In 1810 there were cottages on land included in a building agreement. Five houses, already built on ½ a. excluded from the agreement,[4] probably formed the beginning of Barnsbury Terrace, on the Back Road above the lane later known as Barnsbury Park. Farther south, on the glebe estate between the Back Road and White Conduit gardens, the rector granted leases to Richard Chapman on completed houses in Strahan Terrace, fronting Liverpool Road, and in the streets running back to White Conduit Street, later Mantell, Ritchie, and Batchelor streets, in 1808, 1810 and 1813, and on Elizabeth Terrace in Cloudesley Place in 1819.[5] Just north of the workhouse Morgan's Place (nos. 281–5 Liverpool Road) was under way by 1817[6] and completed in 1818,[7] and south of the workhouse houses in Felix Place on the east side of Liverpool Road were let by the builder, George Pocock, in 1805;[8] the terraces opposite, called Felix Street, Prospect Place, and Felix Terrace, had also been completed by 1817.[9] West of the houses were 9 a. called Great and Little Bowling Alley fields, which George Thornhill let to Christopher Bartholomew in 1789. Bartholomew farmed them until 1794 and was succeeded by a cowkeeper, who occupied the land in 1808, when the fields were used for cricket and other sports.[10] There was one house there in 1803, later known as Oldfield's dairy, and by 1817 Thomas Oldfield, who had taken over the lease, had built four more houses known as Albion Cottages in what became Thornhill Road, one of them being a tea-house.[11]

By 1817 two streets linking the Back Road with Upper Street had terraced building: Park Street was almost completely lined, but Barnsbury Street had only a little building on the north side. The rest of the area between the two north–south routes was mostly still fields. Laycock's large dairy farm was at the north end, a paste-board factory had been built towards the south opposite the later Cloudesley Place, and between Park and Barnsbury streets lay a large nursery.[12] From the 1820s some of Islington's most attractive estates were laid out, in a metropolitan style: spacious squares were linked by unified terraces with regular façades, in contrast with the monotonous terraces that were to cover much of the parish.

The trustees of the 16-a. Stonefields charity estate, which adjoined the glebe estate, obtained an Act to grant building leases in 1811,[13] but building began only in the 1820s. Parcels were let in 1824 to John Emmett, Dorset Goepel, Philip Langhorn, David Sage, and Richard Chapman;[14] Cloudesley Square formed the centre, and the estate included a terrace facing Cloudesley Road and Cloudesley Terrace in Liverpool Road, the latter built by Emmett and completed by 1829.[15] Holy Trinity church was built 1826–9 in the middle of the square, and the parish school in 1830[16] at the top of Cloudesley Street, which was not completed until 1839, by Louis England, a local timber merchant.[17] Building continued in the 1820s on the Barnfield estate under an agreement with Robert Clarke, with villas on the north side of Barnsbury Park, and two cottages at the east end of the south side were built in 1821. Park Terrace, fronting Liverpool Road, was built in 1822 stretching both sides of Brooksby Street.[18] Leases were granted to Samuel Dallman for houses in Barnsbury Terrace in 1824 (nos. 341–5 Liverpool Road) and 1826 (nos. 329–39). Dallman also built nos. 44–6 Bewdley Street, leased in 1824, while houses at the corner of Bewdley Street and Thornhill Road, part of Minerva Terrace, were leased in 1830 to Louis England and included one which became the King William IV. Clarke took the remainder of the estate for building in 1830; the rest of the south side of Barnsbury Park was leased in 1833–5 and the rest of Bewdley Street 1836–7.[19] Land on the west side of the estate was let to John Huskisson in 1832, and by 1834 Mountfort House, on part of the moated manor-house site, was ready for letting.[20]

In the south-western part of the parish, George Thornhill had let large areas on brickmaking agreements from 1808, and in 1823 he began making building leases for 3½ a. south of the canal, including Southampton (later Calshot) Street

[96] Ibid. 71, 73.
[97] C. Hadfield, *Canals of E. Midlands*, 133.
[98] M. Cosh, *Hist. Walk Through Barnsbury* (1981), 2; below, social.
[99] Below, local govt.
[1] Datestone reset on remaining bldg.
[2] Below, other est.
[3] Rocque, *Map of Lond.* (1741–5), sheet 6.
[4] 55 Geo. III, c. 64 (Private).
[5] Ch. Com., deed 25066 I.
[6] Baker's plan (1817).
[7] Datestone.
[8] Islington libr., index of deeds.

[9] Baker's plan (1817).
[10] Hunts. R.O., Thornhill MSS., deeds 148/2/824, 831 (N.R.A. Rep. 16298).
[11] G.L.C., Hist. Bldgs. Div., ISL 61; Baker's plan (1817).
[12] Baker's plan (1817).
[13] Below, charities; plate 18.
[14] Lewis, *Islington*, 126.
[15] Nelson, *Islington* (1829), 295.
[16] Below, churches; educ.
[17] G.L.C., Hist. Bldgs. Div., ISL 5.
[18] Datestone; Plan [c. 1853].
[19] G.L.C., Hist. Bldgs. Div., ISL 5.
[20] Ibid.; Cromwell, *Islington*, 396.

and Thornhill Street (later Wynford Road). Land was reserved for Thornhill Bridge Place north of the canal in 1827, and on the east side of his estate Gainford Terrace in Richmond Avenue, near Thornhill Road, was built c. 1829. He also put capital into the making of Caledonian Road in 1826, which furthered growth in the western part of the parish.[21] The laying out of the estate was mainly supervised by Joseph Kay (d. 1847), who took over in 1813 from Henry Richardson, who had also been originally involved in the Barnfield estate.[22] Other building was started from 1827 at the east end of Copenhagen Street, where c. 25 houses were completed by 1833,[23] and at Cooks field between Park and Barnsbury streets, where Thomas Cubitt laid out c. 5 a. behind the Church Missionary College. He marked out College Cross, where he laid sewers, and c. 1827 built two or three pattern houses in College Cross and in Manchester Terrace fronting Liverpool Road, but sublet the other plots to local builders. Few were let until after a building recession and most of the agreements were made in 1833–4. By c. 1835 only the north end of Manchester Terrace and three houses in the middle (nos. 10–12) had been built, with houses on the south side of Park Street and four at the south end of College Street (later Cross).[24]

Just south of Cubitt's land, between Barnsbury and Theberton streets, building on Thomas Milner Gibson's estate also started in the 1820s.[25] Leases were granted for houses in Moon Street in 1824, near the Pied Bull and in Studd Street at the east end of Theberton Street, and for the White Horse and houses at the west end in 1825. Leases for houses on the south side of Theberton Street followed, 1827–33, and on the north side, 1835–7. The south side of Gibson Square, a continuation of the south side of Theberton Street, was let in 1829, the west side in 1833–4, the north in 1834–5, and the east in 1835–6. The 22 houses in Trinidad Place fronting Liverpool Road were completed from 1830 to 1835. The proprietary school and the chapel and school on the south side of Barnsbury Street, east and west of the street into Milner Square, were completed in 1831 and 1835 respectively. Milner Square was started in 1827[26] but houses on the east side were not leased until 1840 and although building on the west side had been agreed with William Spencer Dove, work had not started in 1846, when Gibson's estate was enfranchised, and was completed only in the 1850s. Leases were granted to jobbing builders or their nominees and the most important leaseholders in 1846, and therefore builders of the estate, were Louis England with 60 houses, William Spencer Dove with 44 houses, some workshops, and building land in Milner Square, Thomas Gardiner with 18, and Charles Weston Anderson with 15 and the Pied Bull inn. Their holdings were scattered and only

Dove held leases of an entire run of houses, in Milner Square. The construction of a terrace by several builders with a handful of plots each, the method used for most building in the 19th century, is often evident in the façades, despite a uniform elevation and plan.

Just as building seems to have been slow on the Gibson estate, with 13 years between agreement and lease for a house in Milner Square for example, so the recession affected work on the Thornhill estate, where the main building started only from the late 1830s.[27] Agreements for Hemingford Terrace at the south end of Hemingford Road and for land on the south side of Richmond Avenue at its east end were made by Thornhill in 1838 and 1840 with William Dennis and George Price, partners who also agreed in 1838 with Henry Rhodes, surveyor for the Coxe family's Denmark estate, to build 10 houses in Denmark Terrace and 17 in Denmark Street, allowing a plot for the British school in 1840. Dennis and Price also agreed in 1841 for a large plot west of Caledonian Road, from Copenhagen Street probably to the N.L.R., and in 1841 agreed with Thornhill for the land between Hemingford and Caledonian roads on either side of Richmond Avenue, subletting some plots. The Drapers' Company's estate between Stonefields and Barnfield was also laid out from 1839, after several attempts to interest builders from 1824. Thomas and Richard Carpenter, cattle salesmen, took a short lease in 1831, but in 1839 Richard took a building lease of most of Lonsdale Square and a few plots in Barnsbury Street on the north side of the estate and of St. George's Terrace on the south. His son R. C. Carpenter, the church architect, was appointed to design the square. Six other builders took leases on the estate: Louis England had nearly all of Barnsbury Street and a few plots in St. George's Terrace; T. Pearson and S. Phillips had a few plots each in the square, and three builders had two each in St. George's Terrace. Barnsbury Street (nos. 73–111 (odd), 28–62 (even)) was ready first, in 1840, followed by St. George's Terrace (later nos. 91–107, 111–125 (odd) Richmond Avenue) by 1841, and the square was completed in 1845.[28] In addition Malvern Terrace and the east end of Albion (later Ripplevale) Grove were built 1839–41, the latter being completed in the mid 1840s, and Belitha Villas were built as Italianate pairs c. 1845.[29]

In 1841 the area between Liverpool and Thornhill roads was filling rapidly but the rest of Barnsbury was largely empty. Cloudesley Square and its adjoining streets were almost filled, as were Barnsbury Park and neighbouring streets on the Barnfield estate. East of Liverpool Road only Gibson Square, Theberton Road, and College Cross were filled, leaving cow layers north of Park Street and some land around the Gibson estate still open. West of Thornhill Road the area

[21] Hunts. R.O., Thornhill MSS., deeds 148/2/834–48 (N.R.A. Rep. 16298); G.L.C., Hist. Bldgs. Div., ISL 4; Cosh, *Barnsbury*, 19.   [22] Colvin, *Brit. Architects*, 480.

[23] G.L.C., Hist. Bldgs. Div., ISL 30.

[24] H. Hobhouse, *Thos. Cubitt: Master Builder* (1971), 56–7, 346–8.

[25] Para. based on P.R.O., MAF 9/163, no. 159, Schedule of leases on Gibson's est. Leases were granted on completion

of bldg.

[26] D. Braithwaite, *Building in the Blood* (1981), 113.

[27] Para. based on MS. vol. 'Thornhill, Caledonian and Denmark ests.', rec. of Dennis & Price, in Islington libr.

[28] C. Speaight, *R. C. Carpenter and Lonsdale Sq.* (1979); Pevsner, *Lond.* ii. 263; G.L.C., Hist. Bldgs. Div., ISL 5.

[29] G.L.C., Hist. Bldgs. Div., ISL 5; Cosh, *Barnsbury*, 17, 21.

nearest the road and between Richmond Avenue and Pentonville was nearly all built over, as was a patch between the canal and the Clerkenwell boundary east of Caledonian Road. West of Caledonian Road what seem to have been detached or semi-detached villas and cottages were built in Bemerton, Lyon, and Gifford streets, and in Buckingham (later Boadicea) Street c. 1845 near the canal, with terraces between the latter and Caledonian Road, besides a small terrace on the south side of Randell's Road.[30]

By the mid 1850s the rest of Barnsbury was almost completely filled.[31] West of Caledonian Road the detached villas planned or built in Bemerton Street were replaced by terraces, except in Sutton Gardens west of Upper Bemerton Street, which was laid out with detached or semi-detached houses. The street plan between Sutton Gardens and Maiden Lane was altered by the G.N.R. line's cutting and tunnel, which separated from the rest of the parish a small portion built over by c. 1853 and the site of Stroud Vale Artisan dwellings in 1879.[32] Apart from Randell's 4-a. tile field and kilns in Maiden Lane, the area north of the canal was filled with terraces by c. 1853, while south of the canal some streets of houses were built to join the factories and warehouses, including Keystone Crescent west of Caledonian Road, and 30 houses in Albion (later Balfe) Street built by 1847 by George Crane.[33] In 1862 the banks of the canal had many tall factory chimneys, but Caledonian Road north of the canal was still lined with its 'genteel suburban terraces', each with little front gardens.[34]

Thornhill Square[35] was being laid out in 1848 with its adjacent streets, and St. Andrew's church in the centre of the crescent was completed in 1854. Barnsbury Square was laid out with semi-detached villas between Mountfort House and Thornhill Road and in Mountfort Crescent north of the house. On the south side Mountfort Terrace was built and some villas were also built behind the house; all were completed by 1848. South of Barnsbury Square, land that had been a nursery in 1848[36] was the site of Richmond Crescent and Terrace on the north side of Richmond Avenue and a continuation of Ripplevale Grove by c. 1853, but the central portion of Lofting Road was finished only in the 1860s. Open space also remained towards Upper Street. Part, just south of Theberton Street, was used for the London Fever hospital, built in 1849 with ground for expansion behind. Farther south King Edward and Paradise (later Parkfield) streets were built with small terraced houses, but some open ground remained behind the terraces lining Liverpool Road, while north of Park Street the cow layers kept open most of the ground as far as the N.L.R.

Thereafter, the only major additions in the area were buildings on the site of Randell's tile field and Sutton Gardens in the 1870s. York Way board school was built on the west side of the tile field in 1874,[37] with small terraced houses in Delhi and Outram streets behind. Houses in East Street, later a continuation of Gifford Street, made way for Gifford Street board school at the north end in 1877,[38] with five-storeyed blocks of model working-class dwellings called Beaconsfield Buildings built south of the school in 1878-9 by the Victoria Dwellings Association to a design of Charles Barry the younger.[39]

The houses in the squares, in major roads such as Caledonian, Liverpool, Hemingford, and Richmond roads, and in other groups such as Barnsbury Park, Richmond Crescent, and Albion Grove, were middle-class: substantial three- or four-storeyed terraces with basements and attics, or detached and semi-detached villas, generally stuccoed with bay windows. The lesser streets had two- or three-storeyed houses for the lower middle class and artisans. The social status of many streets soon declined. Three quarters of the occupants of Denmark Terrace, for example, were middle-class in 1841, but only a third in 1851.[40] The squares maintained their status longest, being self-contained and often cut off from the rest of the neighbourhood by gates; in some cases, such as Lonsdale Square, the leases stipulated single-family occupation.[41] West of Caledonian Road the tile kilns and pollution from industries at Belle Isle in the early 1850s exasperated householders who had moved there for fresh air and perhaps accounted for a particularly quick decline. Problems were exacerbated by poor drainage. Houses in Great and Little William streets suffered from damp basements and sewage oozing through the walls; farther east an open sewer behind Mountfort Terrace and Lofting Road complained of in 1848 was still a health hazard in 1853. In Storey Street piles of builders' rubbish prevented it from being paved for several years after the houses were occupied. Many of the defects, not unique to Barnsbury, were the result of quick growth and discouraged from staying those who could afford to move farther away. The occupants of most of the large terraced houses fronting Caledonian Road, between Lyon and Copenhagen streets, changed from private residents to tradesmen and craftsmen between the beginning and middle of the 1850s.

After the area was built up there were few major changes until the Second World War. Some houses made way for schools: in Everilda Street for St. Thomas's school in 1866, in Vittoria Place in 1879, between Edward Square and Buckingham Street in 1887, and between Batchelor and Ritchie streets in 1891. Public buildings included the imposing Agricultural Hall, built in 1861-2 between Liverpool Road and Upper Street.[42] The Great Northern hospital moved in 1864 to Pembroke Villa, Caledonian Road, which had been occupied by George Price,

[30] Lewis, *Islington*, plan (1841).
[31] Following two paras. based on Plan [c. 1853].
[32] *P.O. Dir. Lond.* (1879).
[33] G.L.C., Hist. Bldgs. Div., ISL 33.
[34] H. Mayhew and J. Binny, *Criminal Prisons of Lond.* (1862), 113.
[35] Plate 17.
[36] P.R.O., IR 30/21/33.
[37] Below, educ.
[38] Ibid.
[39] *Ind. Mons. Gtr. Lond.* (1969), 37; below, plate 20.
[40] D. W. Jones, 'Suburbanisation of SW. Islington 1820-50' (Lond. Univ. unpub. M.Sc. course paper, 1978), p. D6.
[41] Ibid. p. C11.
[42] Below, social.

the builder, in 1844. It took over the neighbouring Twyford Villa, once the home of William Dennis, and adjoining houses until by 1867 the hospital occupied the whole block between Stanmore and Twyford streets, where it remained until 1888. The buildings were replaced by Caledonian Road baths in 1892. Not far away a branch library was built in 1907 by the western exit from Thornhill Square. Open land beside Laycock's dairy and cow layers was taken in 1883 for the four blocks of model dwellings at the junction of Station and Liverpool roads, called Liverpool Buildings, as well as a board school in Station Road in 1885, and the L.G.O.C.'s factory extending either side of Laycock Street by 1886.[43] Factories were built on part of Laycock's yard by 1908 and part was sold for Laycock Street school, built 1915.[44] Laycock Mansions were built nearby in 1926.[45] At the junction with Liverpool Road the Samuel Lewis Trust built five blocks of dwellings between 1910 and 1914.[46] More artisans' dwellings were built in 1902 at the corner of Thornhill Road and Barnsbury by the East End Dwellings Co. and called Thornhill Houses.[47]

Municipal housing began in the area shortly before the Second World War with the L.C.C.'s $4\frac{1}{2}$-a. Barnsbury estate near Pentonville, begun in 1936[48] to relieve serious overcrowding. In 1931 Denmark Street and Terrace, Beaconsfield Buildings, the area between Station Road and Laycock Street, and a small area on the south side of Park Street were the most overcrowded, with 1.75 or more persons to a usable room. Streets north of Bingfield Street, around King's Cross, south of Copenhagen Street, near Barnsbury Road and Richmond Avenue, and the Samuel Lewis Buildings had 1.50 to 1.75 persons; the rest of the area west of Caledonian Road, between Liverpool and Hemingford roads south of Richmond Avenue had 1.25 to 1.50 persons, and other parts of the district had 1 to 1.25, except Ripplevale Grove and Richmond Crescent and some mainly commercial parts, which had under 1 person to a room. By contrast in Tufnell Park and Highbury the density was almost everywhere under 1 person to a room.[49]

Bombing during the Second World War destroyed many houses, particularly north of Copenhagen Street and west of Caledonian Road, and the borough council began large-scale rebuilding.[50] York Way Court on the north side of the canal between York Way and Boadicea Street was completed in 1947, with 293 flats and maisonettes in 14 four-storeyed blocks, followed by Naish Court on the opposite side of Copenhagen Street with 212 flats and maisonettes. The rest of the area west of Caledonian Road was nearly all rebuilt over the next 30 years, as the L.C.C.'s (later G.L.C.'s) Bemerton estate. Caithness House and Orkney House were built in the

early 1960s, followed by blocks at the north and south ends of the estate, the latter including a fire station and cinema. The estate was completed with blocks near Stanmore Street behind the Caledonian Road baths, which were also rebuilt. Beaconsfield Buildings was acquired by the G.L.C. in 1966; the 383 flats, known as one of the worst slums in the area and nicknamed the Crumbles, were cleared over seven years from 1967. The site became Bingfield park and an adventure playground, with the Crumbles play castle put up in 1975 by children and architectural students and described as an adventurous example of local self-help.[51] The Barnsbury estate was also extended in several phases to fill the area between Barnsbury and Caledonian roads south of Copenhagen Street, while to the north the streets between Barnsbury Road and Matilda Street were cleared to form much needed open space.

From the 1960s further changes were effected when young professional people began to renovate the run-down 'late Georgian' houses.[52] The Barnsbury Association was formed in 1964 by new middle-class residents and produced a scheme for closing much of the area to through traffic. When the Barnsbury conservation area was created in 1965 such a scheme was introduced at considerable expense and was bitterly criticized for putting all through traffic along streets that remained working-class. At the same time house prices in Barnsbury rose more sharply than elsewhere: in 1972 the average price was more than three times the average in 1966, and following the designation of Barnsbury as a General Improvement Area in 1972 it immediately rose to four times. The result was that property speculators and estate agents put pressure on unprotected tenants, mostly coloured immigrants in furnished rooms, to move out; sitting tenants were offered money or alternative accommodation, or threatened with court action. Many went into temporary accommodation until rehoused by the council, or into run-down areas such as Westbourne Road and Upper Holloway,[53] and many families had long-standing connexions with the area broken. The G.L.C. was involved in renovating houses in Cloudesley Place that were intended for working-class tenants, but the costs made the rents too high, and the G.L.C. withdrew for the same reason from a similar joint venture with an offshoot of the Barnsbury Association. By the early 1970s the remaining tenants had begun to resist eviction, and property companies found it less profitable to undertake protracted struggles to clear them. One company sold its holdings to Islington council in 1973, which over the next four years bought and renovated many houses for existing tenants wherever possible. The traffic scheme was modified. The gentrification of Barnsbury achieved

[43] Inf. from Mr. J. C. Connell; Bacon, *Atlas of Lond.* (1886).
[44] P.R.O., IR 58/42942, nos. 1–8.
[45] Inf. from Mr. J. C. Connell.
[46] P.R.O., IR 58/42942, no. 13; Pevsner, *Lond.* ii. 237.
[47] Datestone.
[48] L.C.C. *Lond. Housing* (1937), 259.
[49] *New Lond. Life and Labour*, iv, maps 1.

[50] Para. based on *Thornhill Urban Trail* (Teachers' Notes 1977), 1; Islington L.B. *Homes for Islington* (1967).
[51] C. McKean and T. Jestico, *Guide to Modern Bldgs. in Lond. 1965–75*, 79.
[52] Following two paras. based on *New Statesman*, 27 Nov. 1970; A. Power, 'A Battle Lost: Barnsbury 1972' (TS. Nov. 1972 in Islington libr.); J. Pitt, *Gentrification in Islington* [1977].
[53] Below, Holloway.

fame as the subject of articles in national journals, and affected local politics in the 1980s, when new middle-class residents radicalized the local Labour party and contributed to the formation of a local S.D.P. branch.[54]

In 1983 Barnsbury retained many buildings of the earlier 19th century in unified squares and terraces, making it attractive to current taste. The part between Milner Square and Thornhill Square was almost all filled with the original houses, or with open space where they had been cleared, and became a Conservation Area. Apart from the few surviving villas around Barnsbury Square, most of the houses are stuccoed and in the restrained classical style once common throughout London, but two of the squares stand out architecturally. Milner Square, attributed to Roumieu & Gough but probably more by Roumieu, has been seen as a negation of harmonious classical proportions, with strong vertical lines on the four-storeyed façades emphasized by tall narrow windows.[55] Described as architecture 'of the most sinister description', which 'it is possible to visit . . . many times and still not be absolutely certain that you have seen it anywhere but in an unhappy dream',[56] the square's grim aspect has been somewhat relieved by renovation. Lonsdale Square, by R. C. Carpenter, is radically different from surrounding houses, and described as 'Stucco Tudor'.[57] The asymmetrical three-storeyed houses, with basements and sharply gabled attics, have Tudor-style doorways and window dressings. South of Copenhagen Street and west of Caledonian Road almost all the older houses have been replaced by large council estates, with some industry near the canal. North of Lofting Road the buildings are more mixed, with new blocks of flats, maisonettes, and town houses keeping the same scale as older houses, and several shops and small businesses, especially around Liverpool and Thornhill roads.

HOLLOWAY and TOLLINGTON. Tollington was a settlement c. 1000, when it was to provide two men for a ship.[58] The manor or estate there in 1086 had nine tenants,[59] whose farmsteads were probably near the junction of Heame Lane and Tollington Lane (later that of Seven Sisters and Hornsey roads), since a moated farmhouse lay on the south side of the junction.[60] Another settlement grew up nearby at Stroud Green, mentioned in 1407.[61] In 1540 twelve tenants at Tollington and Stroud were part of the manor of Highbury,[62] and from the early 15th century some of the tenants were Londoners.[63] One tenement was Barton's farm in Tollington Lane in 1557.[64] Al-

though Tollington remained in use as a place name to the end of the 17th century,[65] it was superseded by Holloway and the hamlet had ceased to have a separate identity by the 18th century.

The stretch of the Great North Road through North Islington was known as the Holloway by 1307,[66] giving its name to the district and attracting settlement. By the mid 15th century it was the residence of copyholders and craftsmen and had several inns. A medieval moated farmhouse stood about half-way along the road near the junction with the later Tufnell Park Road,[67] and tenants of St. John's and St. Mary's, Clerkenwell, gave Holloway as their residence.[68] By the 17th century and probably earlier, settlement was concentrated at three junctions of the high road with local roads:[69] Upper Holloway at the upper end of the original Maiden Lane (also called Hagbush Lane), near the later Junction Road and Archway tavern, Lower Holloway at Roffe's Lane, and Ring Cross at Tollington Lane. From the 1820s the name Ring Cross was dropped and the area became Lower Holloway, while Upper Holloway was used for the whole area down to Camden Road.[70] The leper hospital of St. Anthony was built in fields half-way up the west side of Highgate Hill in 1473, marked with a wayside cross which later became the site of the Whittington stone.[71] By the 1550s settlement in Holloway included three licensed alehouses.[72] The account of later growth is divided between Lower Holloway, the area bounded by Camden Road, the parish boundary on the west, and the N.L.R., including building on the north-east side of Holloway Road at Ring Cross, and Upper Holloway, the northern end of the parish from Camden Road on the west and the G.N.R. on the east.

Lower Holloway. The junction of Hornsey and Holloway roads was known as Ring Cross by 1494,[73] and had early settlement. Lower or Nether Holloway was recorded in 1553.[74] The only medieval dwelling known to have existed away from the high road was called Cutlers in 1373 and was probably the site of Copenhagen House, so named by 1695.[75] A house in 'Maid Lane' inhabited by Stephen Rolfe in 1467[76] may also have been in that part of the parish rather than farther north in Upper Holloway. In 1766–7 Joseph Pocock and Daniel Harrison built Paradise Row, a terrace of 31 houses, near the north end of the Back Road; far from other building at Pentonville and built long before Barnsbury was begun, it remained isolated until c. 1800.[77] Individual villas and small terraces appeared in Holloway Road towards the end of the 18th century: by 1805 Ring Cross was linked with

[54] *Observer*, 21 Feb. 1982, p. 9.
[55] Pevsner, *Lond.* ii. 236.
[56] J. Summerson, *Georgian Lond.* (1962), 283.
[57] Pevsner, *Lond.* ii. 236.
[58] Robertson, *Anglo-Saxon Charters*, 145.
[59] *V.C.H. Mdx.* i. 129.
[60] Below.
[61] *P.N. Mdx.* (E.P.N.S.), 124.
[62] Below, manors (Highbury).
[63] e.g. P.R.O., PROB 11/2A (P.C.C. 27 Marche, will of John Woodhouse); PROB 11/9 (P.C.C. 8 Dogett, will of Hen. Green).
[64] Guildhall MS. 9171/13, f. 106v.
[65] *P.N. Mdx.* (E.P.N.S.), 126.
[66] Ibid.
[67] Below, other est. (Brewhouse).
[68] Below, manors (St. John's); other est. (St. Mary's).
[69] See parish map c. 1740, p. 8; above, communications.
[70] *Cruchley's New Plan* (1829) and later plans.
[71] Below, pub. svces.
[72] Below, social.
[73] Guildhall MS. 9171/8, f. 77.
[74] *P.N. Mdx.* (E.P.N.S.), 126.
[75] Below, other est.
[76] Guildhall MS. 9171/6, f. 16.
[77] G.L.C., Hist. Bldgs. Div., ISL 31.

Lower Holloway by building along the north-east side of Holloway Road, and with Upper Street by buildings on both sides,[78] with continual additions and infilling. On the south-west side of Ring Cross, George Pocock built several small streets on land belonging to Lord Northampton including George's Place and Cornwall Place c. 1800 and Independent Place, adjoining the latter, c. 1806.[79] A water-proofing factory was at the bottom of Hornsey Road by 1801;[80] the nonconformist Holloway chapel was built in 1804,[81] with Holloway Place next to it. After land on the north-east side of the high road near Highbury Crescent was enfranchised in 1806, several houses were built, such as no. 72 Holloway Road in 1812, and houses to the south built by the mason and sculptor John Atkinson.[82] By 1811 growth was such that the chapel of ease, completed 1814, was sited there between Holloway and the back roads,[83] and the new parochial schools were built in the Back Road opposite the chapel grounds in 1815.[84]

Another small settlement grew up on the western boundary of the parish, at Belle Isle, Maiden Lane. Buildings existed there in 1793[85] and by 1829 several industries, mainly noxious, had been established, such as horse-slaughtering and the making of cart grease, varnish, and chimney pots.[86] Just to the north Copenhagen House had become a resort for Londoners, amid fields which were used by Sunday strollers and for political meetings in the 1790s.[87]

Growth in the western part of the parish was stimulated by the building in 1826 of a road from Holloway Road at Camden Road to King's Cross, but little of it was residential until the 1840s. The road was later named Caledonian Road after the Royal Caledonian asylum, built in 1827–8 on a 2-a. site in Copenhagen fields east of the road, to replace premises in Hatton Garden. The asylum had been incorporated in 1815 as a charity to support and educate the children of Scottish servicemen killed or wounded in action and of poor Scots living in London. The building was designed by George Tappen in Greek revival style, with a central portico based on that of Philip of Macedon's temple at Delos, and was enlarged in 1844. It opened with 40 boys in 1828, increased to 56 by 1835, and from 1845 girls also were admitted. The school was recognized under the Elementary School Act in 1871, when 63 boys and 40 girls lived there under the auspices of the Established Church of Scotland. The children's Highland dress in Royal Stewart tartan attracted much attention in the neighbourhood, where the asylum remained until 1903.[88]

In 1826 Thomas Cubitt bought 24 a. of Copenhagen fields, all except 1 a. on the east side of the new road, stretching from the asylum to Offord Road. The land was probably bought for brick-making, to supply Cubitt's building work in Bloomsbury, and the area had brickfields belonging to other large London contractors. He sold 6–9 a. to the government in 1839 as the site for Pentonville prison.[89] A model prison, designed by Sir Charles Barry in accordance with plans made by Lieut.-Col. J. Jebb for a reformed system of separate confinement, was built 1840–2 in the form of five radiating blocks, with 520 cells, and gatehouses covering $6\frac{3}{4}$ a. south of the Caledonian asylum. Originally intended for short-term prisoners, by 1848 the prison was receiving the insane for long stays and more exercise facilities had to be introduced.[90] In 1851 it housed 533 adult male prisoners and 44 staff.[91] Cubitt used the rest of his land for bricks until 1851, selling a strip at the south end for the N.L.R. line in 1848 and more land to the railway in 1857.[92]

Meanwhile building was starting to spread westward from Holloway Road. By 1829 Palmer Place and Street and Madras Place had been built between Holloway Road and Paradise Row; Paradise House stood on the north side of the schools in the Back Road, by now renamed Liverpool Road, with the beginning of Bride Street on the south side. North from Park Street South (the middle section of Offord Road), houses had been built in York Place (later St. Clement Street) and Barnsbury Grove. Farther along Holloway Road, Cornwall Place and George's Place (later George's Road) had been continued westward, as Eden Grove and the Grove, with terraced and detached houses to join Caledonian Road.[93] St. James's church was built in Victoria (later Chillingworth) Road in 1837–8 and the district schools in George's Road in 1838.[94] By 1841 the area between Palmer Place and Victoria Road had been partially built up, more infilling had taken place north of Victoria Road, and the stretch of Holloway Road from Holloway chapel to Camden Road had been filled by a long terrace, set back from the road, called Loraine Place. More building had gone up south of the schools and chapel of ease, where Albion and Union (later Furlong and Orleston) roads had been laid out and a few semi-detached villas built. West of Liverpool Road the area south of the schools and Sheringham Road was covered with detached houses westward to Westbourne Road, and Bride Street was also extended almost to Roman Way, although building was still slight.[95]

West of Caledonian Road, Belle Isle had grown to have a population of 185 c. 1842. Between it and the road, three or four streets formed Experimental Gardens or Frenchman's colony or Island. The settlement had been established shortly before 1842 by Peter Henry Joseph Baume, who

[78] Dent's plan (1806).
[79] Colvin, *Brit. Architects*, 649 n.; Islington libr., deed 266.
[80] Nelson, *Islington* (1811), 84.
[81] Below, prot. nonconf.
[82] G.L.C., Hist. Bldgs. Div., ISL 18.
[83] Below, churches.   [84] Below, educ.
[85] Baker's plan (1793).
[86] Nelson, *Islington* (1829), 74.
[87] Below, social.
[88] Colvin, *Brit. Architects*, 807; P.R.O., ED 7/82; ED 3/4; K. Carson, 'Royal Caledonians', *Temple Mag.* [1900–1],

119–26 (in Islington libr.).
[89] H. Hobhouse, *Thos. Cubitt: Master Builder* (1971), 345–6, 357–8.
[90] Colvin, *Brit. Architects*, 91; H. Mayhew and J. Binny, *Criminal Prisons of Lond.* (1862), 113–16; S. Lewis, *Islington As It Was* (1854), 60; below, plate 28.
[91] P.R.O., HO 107/10/1/70.
[92] Hobhouse, *Cubitt*, 358–60.
[93] *Cruchley's New Plan* (1829).
[94] Below, churches; educ.
[95] Lewis, *Islington*, plan (1841).

had intended it as a community formed on the principles of Robert Owen.[96] Baume let small plots on which poor people could build and himself built cottages for sale or letting. Missionaries opened a school in a cottage there in 1839 with Sunday services, to counteract the influence of the 'infidel Frenchman'; the services soon failed but the school had c. 70 children in 1846. On Sunday the colony had swings and roundabouts in use, which attracted passers by.[97] In 1851 it was inhabited by 48 families of craftsmen and labourers,[98] but the buildings had apparently disappeared by c. 1853.[99]

In 1848 the sanitary inspectors found that both Belle Isle and Experimental Gardens had filthy cottages, with open drains, and that most residents kept pigs.[1] In the 1840s the area was further disturbed by the G.N.R. line, which, although it crossed Copenhagen fields in a tunnel for most of the way, came out into a cutting on the west side of the Gardens, and from the early 1850s the N.L.R. line ran on the south side of Belle Isle and the Gardens. By c. 1853 the cottages were being replaced by terraces. The industries at Belle Isle remained a blight on residential growth, a source of worry to medical officers, and an eyesore. In 1853 a passenger on the N.L.R. complained to the government's Board of Health of a knacker's yard which not only produced a stench but subjected travellers to the view of parts of dead horses.[2] The area west of Caledonian Road was further affected by the sale c. 1852 of Copenhagen House and 72 a. to the Corporation of London, which demolished the house and built the Metropolitan Cattle Market on 30 a., opened in 1855.[3] Drovers' lodgings, five public houses, and two hotels were put up around the market, and the Corporation built a block of working-class dwellings c. 1865.[4]

In the 1850s building began on Cubitt's land, but the railway, prison, and market made poor neighbours and houses had to be designed for artisans and clerks rather than the wealthier residents catered for south of Offord Road. The 1 a. on the west side of Caledonian Road was leased in 1853 to Henry Law, who built the 14 houses in Arthur Terrace fronting Caledonian Road (nos. 353–79 odd), with a workshop added to the first house and a stable yard at the back.[5] Law continued Arthur Terrace on the opposite side of Caledonian Road with seven houses (? nos. 418–406 even) in the block between Market (later Wheelwright) and Cumberland (later Ponder) streets in 1856.[6] In 1853 Thompson and Crosswell started building south of the prison with the City of Rome public house and some houses at the east end of both streets, but the south side of Market Street was completed only in 1863 and the north side of Cumberland Street in 1866, the

south side being sold to the railway.[7] In the same period building joined Roman Road to the streets spreading westward from Holloway Road. Some houses in Roman Road were occupied in 1858,[8] and in 1860 leases were granted for houses built by William Dennis behind the Caledonian asylum and in three new streets linking Roman and Westbourne roads.[9] In Hollingsworth Road a little farther east Mrs. Mary Tealby started a temporary home for lost dogs in stables behind nos. 15 and 16, raising funds from friends. After her death in 1865 the home was carried on by a committee which included her brother the Revd. Edward Bates. Although ridiculed by press and public, the home received benefactions and by 1869 was admitting an average of 850 dogs a month, with c. 200 kept there at any one time. Complaints about the noise in a residential area prompted a move in 1871 to more suitable premises, where the enterprise became the Battersea Dogs' Home.[10]

The remaining open land north of the market was built over in the 1860s and early 1870s. Penn Road, with St. Luke's church and the houses behind Camden Road, was built in the 1860s, as was the south-west side of Hillmarton Road,[11] but the angle between Hillmarton and Caledonian roads was filled a little later. Hungerford Road was partially built up by 1862, from either end, and more houses there were leased in 1873.[12] The houses between Camden Road and the market, influenced by the proximity to Tufnell Park, were substantial terraced and detached buildings.

Further growth took the form of infilling and additions to the industrial premises near the market, until some rebuilding was done by local authorities. The district was not uniform in character and some middle-class streets near Camden Road contrasted with the market area and pockets of severe overcrowding. A ragged school was needed for Holloway by 1846, housed in Brand Street off Hornsey Road,[13] where the houses had to be limed and cleansed in 1849, when one family was sleeping on a damp floor and three others had to be supplied with bedsteads,[14] and the area nearby centred on Queensland Road was found to be poor and of very low moral character at the end of the century. The same was true of the area around St. James's and Wellington streets, while in Belle Isle the inhabitants, although not among the poorest, were rough.[15] In 1929 four areas of Lower Holloway were in the second highest category of overcrowding with 1.50 to 1.75 persons to a room: between Eden Grove and Sheringham Road, between Liverpool and Wellington roads, between Blundell and Brewery roads, south of the market, and in Queensland Road and along Drayton Park

[96] Ibid. 393; plan (1841).
[97] *Lond. City Mission Mag.* xi (1846), 212.
[98] P.R.O., HO 107/10/1/52.
[99] Plan [c. 1853].
[1] G.L.R.O., P83/MRY1/727.
[2] P.R.O., MH 13/261, no. 5631/53.
[3] Hobhouse, *Cubitt,* 359; below, plate 22.
[4] L.C.C. *Lond. Housing* (1937), 183; Islington L.B. *Homes for Islington* (1967), 7.
[5] Hobhouse, *Cubitt,* 358–60.
[6] Islington libr., deed 418.

[7] Hobhouse, *Cubitt,* 359–60.
[8] *D.N.B.* s.v. W. H. Stowell.
[9] Islington libr., MS. vol. 'Thornhill, Caledonian and Denmark ests.', rec. of Dennis & Price, Bldrs.
[10] *Dogs' Home Battersea 1860–1960* (cent. booklet in Islington libr.).
[11] O.S. Map 6", Mdx. XII. SW. (1863–9 edn.).
[12] Islington libr., deeds index.
[13] Lewis, *Islington As It Was,* 82.
[14] G.L.R.O., P83/MRY1/720.
[15] C. Booth, *Life and Labour,* 1st ser. (1), 249–50.

to the railway line. The area west of Liverpool Road and housing at the Metropolitan market had 1.25 to 1.50 persons, while the least crowded areas, with less than 1 person to a room, were Furlong Road and Crane Grove near St. Mary Magdalene's and between Camden and Hungerford roads and either side of Hillmarton Road. The remainder had a density of 1 to 1.25.[16]

The L.C.C. undertook much rehousing. In 1901 it bought the 2-a. Caledonian asylum and after the occupants had moved out in 1903 replaced the building with 5 five-storeyed blocks containing 272 flats around a garden, designed by a Mr. Riley and completed in 1906.[17] The L.C.C. also rebuilt two of the worse areas at Brand Street and George's Road, known together as the Ring Cross estate and completed in 1928. At Brand Street two blocks with shops fronting Hornsey Road called Branston and Rollit houses were built to house 292 people, and Rollit Street was laid out to replace Brand Street. The cleared site extended from Hornsey Road to the Northern Polytechnic, built in Holloway Road in 1896, and the east end of the site was used for an extension to the polytechnic.[18] The north side of George's Road around Hartnoll Street was rebuilt in 1929 with Radford House, five-storeyed blocks containing 111 flats, and the smaller four-storeyed Hartnoll House with 24 flats for cheaper letting to slum tenants. A garden was laid out in 1930, and c. 1 a. in the south-west corner was used for Hope Street (Ring Cross) primary school and Barnsbury Central school for boys, opened 1931.[19] Between 1934 and 1942 the L.C.C. also built 6 five-storeyed blocks on the site of Loraine Place, Holloway Road.[20]

The greatest changes took place after the Second World War, at the cattle market, and at Westbourne Road. The Corporation of London sold Corporation Buildings to the borough council in 1935 and the 28-a. site of the Metropolitan market to the L.C.C. after the market's closure in 1939. The 'flea market' known as the Caledonian market which had also been held there moved to Bermondsey Square, Bermondsey (Surr.).[21] The G.L.C. and Islington L.B. cleared Corporation Buildings and various halls and sheds from 1965, leaving the central clock tower as a landmark. Caledonian Market estate, with 271 dwellings designed by Farber & Bartholomew, was built c. 1967[22] on the south side of the road and west of the clock tower; open space was left both around the tower and south of Market Road, where public gardens and sports grounds included an astro-turf football pitch first used in 1971.[23] Two blocks of eleven-storeyed flats were also built between Rowstock Gardens and Camden Road, with some four-storeyed blocks of masionettes. In the 1970s two- and three-storeyed flats and houses were built east of

the clock tower grounds and an eight- and a four-storeyed block farther east on the south side of North Road, the rest of the road being filled with industrial premises. The other large scheme involved clearing a decayed area between Bride Street and George's Road, where housing problems had been made worse by families displaced from Barnsbury seeking cheap private accommodation; the area was compared unfavourably with the worst city ghettoes in the U.S.A.[24] In the 1970s the housing between Roman Way and Westbourne Road was replaced by two-storeyed houses and open spaces, with some roads closed to traffic, and old houses retained on the outskirts were gradually rehabilitated.

In 1983 Lower Holloway bore a mixed aspect. Although the market area was largely housing and open space, to the south and east were mainly industrial and commercial premises. Nineteenth-century houses remained south of Camden Road, where many had been converted into flats, and around Arundel Square and south of St. Mary Magdalene's church, where rehabilitation had preserved some attractive streets. The central part of the district, west of Liverpool Road, had been largely rebuilt, and a spacious park had greatly improved residential amenities. The changes there, however, contrasted with the stretch of Caledonian Road between the G.N.R. and N.L.R. Once the focal point for local shops, businesses, and entertainments, it has a mixture of new and decayed buildings, and a general air of disuse that reveals local economic decline.

Upper Holloway. By the late 16th century a gentleman's residence, probably a former farmhouse, stood at the foot of Highgate Hill, occupied in the early 17th century by Christopher Wase and later by the Masters and Blount families. A small house next to it was sold by the Blounts in the mid 17th century.[25] The Mother Red Cap inn stood almost opposite on the west side of the high road by the 1630s, when it seems to have been the haunt of prostitutes.[26] A little south of the Mother Red Cap was another inn by the 1680s, later known as the Horse and Groom.[27] Fields separated the hamlet from the next settlement south along the high road, at the junction with Roffe's or Cock Lane (later Tollington Way), where at least one inn, the Crown, stood in the early 17th century. Opposite the entrance to the lane by the early 18th century stood the Half Moon, noted for its Holloway cheesecakes.[28] A little farther south was the moated site of the Brewhouse estate.[29] In the early 18th century a house was built there, known later as the manor farm and part of the Barnsbury demesne.[30]

By the 1740s houses stood on both sides of the high road in Upper Holloway at the junction with the original Maiden Lane, and in Lower Holloway at the junction with Roffe's Lane, with a few

[16] *New Lond. Life and Labour*, iv, maps 1.
[17] L.C.C. *Housing of Working Classes in Lond.* (1913), 78, 153; Pevsner, *Lond.* ii. 239.
[18] Below, educ.
[19] L.C.C. *Housing 1928-30* (1931), 69-70.
[20] *P.O. Dir. Lond.* (1934, 1942).
[21] P. Zwart, *Islington: Hist. and Guide* (1973), 156-8.
[22] L.C.C. *Lond. Housing* (1937), 183; *Homes for Islington* (1967), 7-8.
[23] Inf. from Mr. J. C. Connell.
[24] *New Statesman*, 27 Nov. 1970.
[25] Below, other est.
[26] Corymbaeus (*pseud.*), *Barnabae Itinerarium* (1638 edn.), 2nd part.
[27] Below, other est. (Palmer).
[28] Nelson, *Islington* (1811), 83-4, 103.
[29] Below, other est.
[30] Below, manors.

more at the three-mile stone, approximately at the later Camden Road junction.[31] A settlement also grew up on the slope at the extreme northern limit of the parish, with the Black Dog at the later corner of Dartmouth Park Hill and Highgate Hill and a scattering of houses along Hornsey Lane at the Highgate end. A few buildings also stood at Mount Pleasant, where the road from Crouch End to Stroud Green entered the parish, and at the Green itself. Another settlement had been formed in Tollington Lane above and below Heame Lane, including the copyhold moated farmhouse called Lower Place or the Devil's House, which stood there in the 16th century and was an inn in 1721.[32]

Little change occurred in the settlement pattern until the 1820s. In the hamlets, consisting mainly of farmhouses, inns, and craftsmen's shops, new houses were built and older ones improved. On the north-east side of the high road at Upper Holloway some ancient houses in 1811 were thought to have once been occupied by gentry.[33] One was probably the 17th-century Blounts' house, which seems to have stood just south of the later St. John's Way and was probably the house owned by Mr. Dickenson in 1806.[34] Another was owned by Robert William Sievier, sculptor and inventor (d. 1865), in 1848, on the south corner of Red Cap Lane (later Elthorne Road). Sievier, who invented several manufacturing processes, probably built the india-rubber works that stood at the end of his land by 1841. He also carried out experiments in electric telegraphy there. The house was called Old Manor House in 1851, probably because part was ancient, but it had been doubled in size, with a new front that included a bas-relief by Sievier; it was demolished in 1897.[35] In 1820 Hornsey Road was still said to be the haunt of footpads.[36] By that date, however, new buildings were beginning to fill in the frontages along Holloway Road south of Lower Holloway, with small terraces and cottage-style houses built mainly for Londoners as 'retiring villas'.[37] In Upper Holloway the Mercers' Company of London built Whittington College in 1822 on the east side of Archway Road (opened 1813) to replace the almshouses in St. Michael's Paternoster (London), founded by Richard Whittington in 1424. The site was chosen to be as near the Whittington stone as possible. The two-storeyed building stood on three sides of a courtyard, with a chapel in the middle of the central block, and was designed in an early Gothic style by George Smith (d. 1869), surveyor to the Company. It contained two-roomed houses for 30 almswomen who were relatives of company members. Gardens were laid out around the building, which was faced with Portland cement in 1830, and an extra bedroom was added to each house in 1877.[38]

Besides the old inns, the Mother Red Cap and the Horse and Groom, the Archway tavern had been built in the angle between Archway Road and Highgate Hill, while a few small terraces were appearing on the hill, including Bedford Place opposite the Whittington stone and Whittington Place and Gordon Place slightly higher on the west side. A little south of the Horse and Groom St. John's church was built in 1828 but still had fields on three sides. Hornsey Road had attracted even more building and by 1829 was filled with villas and cottages from Heame Lane to the new Hanley Road, with another isolated group half-way to Hornsey Lane. Tollington Park had also been laid out and a few villas built at the west end.[39]

The western part of Upper Holloway being still free of building, the Corporation of London bought 10 a. or more for a cemetery during the cholera epidemic of 1832 and held c. 27 a. on the north side of Camden Road in 1848.[40] Between 1849 and 1852 its house of correction for all classes of convicted criminals was built on 8 a. there. Designed by J. B. Bunning, the prison was notable for its front and gateway, a copy of Warwick Castle, built in Kentish rag with Caen stone dressings. It had accommodation in 4 three-storeyed wings for 288 men, in one wing for 56 women, and one wing for 56 juveniles.[41] The prison was taken over by the government in 1878 and used only for women from c. 1903.[42] As Holloway prison, it became well known for the imprisonment of suffragettes, for internments during the Second World War, and for executions. Upper Holloway also attracted a few industrial works, which brought strong objections from landowners and residents. A printers' ink factory was ordered to close in 1827, reopened, again closed in 1838, and had started up once more in 1853.[43] Brickmaking and lack of sewers were other nuisances that grew worse as building spread.[44]

A noticeable increase in building began in Upper Holloway in the 1840s. The Sons of the Clergy granted building leases for land around the Horse and Groom in 1842, and St. John's Park was partially laid out.[45] Leases were granted in Hanley Road c. 1840, and by 1849 Hanley Road and Tollington Park were about half filled, mainly with terraces. Nos. 96–108 Tollington Park, attributed to Gough & Roumieu, were partly built 1839–40.[46] Houses were also being built in Seven Sisters Road, which had replaced Heame Lane, and in roads leading off Holloway Road, between Parkhurst and Camden roads, and at the east end of Tufnell Park Road.[47]

[31] Para. based on Rocque, *Map of Lond.* (1741–5), sheet 5.
[32] Below, other est.; G.L.R.O., MR/LV3/90.
[33] Nelson, *Islington* (1811), 83.
[34] Dent's plan (1806); below, other est.
[35] *D.N.B.*; Gunnis, *Dict. Brit. Sculptors*, 351–2; Lewis, *Islington*, plan (1841); *N. & Q.* 9th. ser. i. 81; P.R.O., HO 107/10/2/11.
[36] *One Hundred Years in Hornsey Rd. 1821–1921* (cent. booklet of Hornsey Rd. Wes. mission, in Islington libr.), 5.
[37] Nelson, *Islington* (1811), 84; *Cruchley's New Plan* (1829).
[38] J. Imray, *Char. of Ric. Whittington* (1968), 49, 52, 77–9, 81–2; Colvin, *Brit. Architects*, 753; H. Hobhouse, *Lost Lond.* (1971), 147.
[39] *Cruchley's New Plan* (1829).
[40] P.R.O., IR 29/21/33.
[41] Mayhew and Binny, *Criminal Prisons of Lond.* 533–8; Hobhouse, *Lost Lond.* 154; below, plate 29.
[42] Zwart, *Islington: Hist. and Guide*, 164–5; inf. from Mr. J. C. Connell.
[43] P.R.O., MH 13/261, no. 3393/53.
[44] Ibid. MH 13/261, nos. 3063/53, 6008/49.
[45] Below, other est. (Palmer).
[46] G.L.C., Hist. Bldgs. Div., ISL 12.
[47] Lewis, *Islington*, plan (1841); P.R.O., IR 30/21/33, tithe map 1848.

Building was still fairly scattered and many of the houses were detached villas with spacious grounds.

Denser building began in the 1850s, especially east of Holloway Road where 110 houses were under construction at one time in 1851, as opposed to only 18 on the west side; 65 were being built in Cottenham Road (later Sussex Way) and the adjoining streets were also being started.[48] Long Lands estate, east of Hornsey Road, was bought by the St. Pancras, Marylebone and Paddington Freehold Land Society, and sold off in plots in 1851; the provisional street names, Reform, Franchise, Liberty, and Freehold, reflected the society's aim to create more voters, but were soon changed, to Alsen, Andover, Victor, and Durham roads.[49] The society also owned the Seven Sisters Road estate east of Long Lands, comprising Campbell (later Whadcoat) Road and the west side of Nightingale (Fonthill) Road, on which plots were sold off from 1857.[50] It had another estate on the west side of Holloway Road, where Hampden, Cromwell, and Rupert streets were laid out by the mid 1850s; two houses in Hampden Road were completed in 1855.[51] Other land societies were also laying out estates in Islington in the 1850s. The National Freehold Land Society had a small estate off Hornsey Rise just north of Hanley Road including Lambton and Grenville roads, and the Birkbeck Freehold Land Society laid out an area south of St. John's Road (later Way). North of St. John's Road a small area called St. John's Ville, immediately east of Whittington College, was under construction in the early 1850s, although only two of the planned streets were built by 1860. Farther west on Highgate Hill, where terraces lined the main road, Salisbury and Brunswick roads were built. The smallpox hospital was built in 1850 and St. Joseph's retreat in 1858. A few terraces appeared in Junction Road and St. John's Park, and roads were being laid across the estate of the Sons of the Clergy and land adjoining belonging to the Hargrave family. West of the prison Hilldrop Crescent and neighbouring streets were added to the substantial terraces and semi-detached villas that had been built along Camden Road and Brecknock Road. Just to the north the demesne land of the Tufnell estate had been set aside as Tufnell Park, with two roads (Carleton and Tufnell Park roads) lined with villas and with open space between the roads. By c. 1853, however, only the Lodge and a few houses at the junction of Carleton and Brecknock roads had been built.[52]

Not only were estates being built with much open space between them, but building was far from rapid or consistent even where a street plan had been laid down. Most of the streets started in the 1850s were not completed until the 1870s or 1880s, and in the 1890s early villas were replaced

by terraces.[53] Sales of most of the St. Pancras Freehold Land Society's plots singly, or at not more than four to a person,[54] also made building progress erratic and had important social consequences, of which Campbell Road became the extreme example. Work started there in the 1860s but in 1871 only 63 houses out of the final 104 were ready, with 16 more under way; the rest were finished slowly during the 1870s. While the street was unfinished it remained unpaved and unlighted and was used for rubbish, with the result that poorer tenants moved into the six-roomed houses intended for clerks and social decline set in from the start.[55] Many of Islington's roughest streets in the 1930s had experienced the same early history: Rupert Road, another St. Pancras Freehold Land Society street, George's Road in Lower Holloway, and Bemerton Road and its adjoining streets in Barnsbury.[56]

Although much infilling remained to be completed, by the late 1860s land north of the G.N.R. and Holloway Road as far as the Tottenham and Hampstead line had few open areas, the principal ones being south of Hanley Road, land adjoining the G.N.R., most of which soon became the railway company's goods and coal yards, and land north and west of the City workhouse, built c. 1860 in Cornwallis Road.[57] Two of the smaller spaces were nursery grounds. Other parts of North Islington were less densely built over but apart from Tufnell Park and the fields around it, and those around Islington workhouse in St. John's Way, open ground was scattered in small parcels. Houses with large gardens were being divided: the Hollies east of Crouch Hill was sold off in 20 plots as Holly Park from 1864–7.[58] Progress was made on the Hargrave estate.[59]

Building in Tufnell Park had started around St. George's church and been extended in Carleton Road, the scheme for a park having been abandoned and the whole area being gradually laid out for building.[60] Houses here were still substantial villas similar to those in Tollington Park and Hanley Road, and demand for them was apparently not as high as for lower middle-class terraces, which by the 1860s predominated among the finished houses. Several institutions acquired healthy sites on the higher ground at the northern end of the parish. St. Mary's workhouse school had been built in Hornsey Road in 1853, and the new workhouse called Islington Institution in St. John's Road in 1865.[61] The Alexandra orphanage for infants, a charity to house and educate children up to the age of 8, was built on 3½ a. between Hazelville and Sunnyside roads. In 1871, when 101 children were receiving school instruction and another 11 were in the nursery, the orphanage was described as very interesting and well conducted.[62] The Aged Pilgrims Friend Society built a home for 120 pensioners at the northern corner of St. John's Road and Hazelville

48 P.R.O., HO 107/10/2/13.
49 Islington libr., deed 887.
50 Ibid. deeds 3663–71.
51 G.L.R.O., Acc. 1417/26.
52 Plan [c. 1853].
53 e.g. Tollington Pk. and adjoining streets: G.L.C., Hist. Bldgs. Div., ISL 12.
54 Islington libr., deeds 3663–71.
55 Hist. Workshop, viii. 4–5.
56 Above, Barnsbury.
57 Later Islington workho.: below, local govt., bd. of guardians. Called West London union workhouse on O.S. Map 6″, Mdx. XII. SW. (1863–9 edn.).
58 Islington libr., deed 3286.
59 O.S. Map 6″, Mdx. XII. SW. (1863–9 edn.).
60 Ibid.
61 Below, local govt., bd. of guardians.
62 P.R.O., C 54/16806, no. 2; ED 3/4.

Road in 1870. The two-storeyed building was designed by F. Boreham in Tudor Gothic style around a large courtyard with chapel, hall, and committee rooms.[63] Holborn union built its infirmary on 2¾ a. on the west side of Archway Road between 1875 and 1885.[64]

From the 1870s the remaining land was filled and existing streets were completed, until by the mid 1890s the only open spaces were the grounds of the institutions, two sports grounds, and the gardens of a few large houses, especially along Hornsey Lane. Most of the building was in crowded terraces[65] of the 1870s and early 1880s. By 1886 Tufnell Park was partly filled: Carleton Road was lined with detached and semi-detached houses, but open ground remained in Anson, Hugo, and Dalmeny roads, west and north of All Saints' church. Campdale Road had been laid but not built up and to its west the land had become a sports field by the 1890s. Mercers Road, on land belonging to the Mercers' Company, was partially built up. Pemberton Road terminated in land which also became a sports ground, and the south side of Hargrave Road was still open in 1886. Between Highgate Hill and Archway Road building had started in Despard and Bismarck roads, north of Holborn infirmary. On the east side of Archway Road the large houses, White-hall and Alpha Villas, stood on Hornsey Lane but between them and Whittington College and Miranda Road the land was still open in 1886. Building had started in Cheverton, Dresden, and Ashmount roads, with some detached houses in Hazelville Road and the still mainly empty Sunnyside Road. In the north-east corner of the parish Holly Park had been completed with detached houses, and on the boundary Mount Pleasant House, standing in the 1860s, had been replaced by terraces that belonged more to Crouch End than Upper Holloway, as a G.N.R. branch line cut them off from the rest of Crouch Hill. Some detached houses stood on the north side of Warltersville Road, but on the south side Warltersville House still had much open land behind it in the 1890s. Roads like Hanley Road and Tollington Park, started in the 1840s, were finished by the mid 1890s, but some large villas on the south side of Tollington Park were replaced by small terraced houses in Birnam Road in the late 1890s.[66]

The latest estate was Whitehall Park, designed by R. W. Hill and begun in 1889, Whitehall Park and Gladsmuir Road being completed in 1891, Cressida Road in 1892, and Harberton Road in 1893.[67] The original house, Whitehall, was not sold for building until 1910, when it included land on three sides through which Fitzwarren Avenue had been laid in a crescent around the south side with an exit into Whitehall Park.[68] Some building took place soon after the sale, but many houses were not built until the period between the World Wars. Many small infillings

included six houses in College Gardens, which were built between nos. 4 and 6 Carleton Road c. 1900 in the grounds of the former Queen's College private school.[69]

Growth nearby brought changes to Holloway Road, as a centre for commerce and services. Tradesmen and craftsmen had lived along the road since it was first recorded, and with the spread of building the range of activities increased, particularly along the east side.[70] Towards the end of the 19th century the stretch of Holloway Road north-west of the G.N.R. line became an important shopping area with some substantial firms all on the east side, including (from south to north) Jones Bros., linendrapers (nos. 348–66), Beale's, refreshment contractors and confectioners (nos. 370–4), Thomas Usher, tailors (nos. 376–80), Ephraim Hart & Co., house furnishers (nos. 404–6, 416–20), and B. Davies, fancy drapers (nos. 426–34). The west side of the road remained mainly residential from Loraine Place to Mercers Road, with a concentration of doctors and dentists between Camden and Parkhurst roads in 1902. At Upper Holloway small tradesmen were on both sides of the road and increased as houses were converted to shops or other commercial uses. The few large private houses were also replaced at that period. Grove House made way for the Great Northern hospital in the 1880s and the Sieviers' house for commercial premises in 1897. The Blounts' house, possibly called Elm Lodge, and some neighbouring detached houses had been replaced by Giesbach Road and shops fronting the high road by 1894.[71]

Although Tufnell Park and Tollington Park retained well-to-do residents, Upper Holloway in the 1890s was mainly the home of clerks and artisans, served by an army of small tradesmen and characterized in *The Diary of a Nobody* by Mr. Pooter, who strove to maintain a front of gentility.[72] Some streets, however, had a rougher population, including Campbell Road, known familiarly as the Bunk or Campbell Bunk, with the reputation from the 1890s to the Second World War of being the worst street in North London. Its social decline stemmed from the way in which it had been built up[73] but was hastened from the early 1880s, when a large building intended as a public house was registered as a common lodging house for 90 men. Many houses were sold because of difficulties in repaying mortgages and several also became lodging houses, which drew a rough and shifting population, whereupon most respectable residents left. Soon an address there became a bar to decent employment, however menial, and brought condemnation on anyone suspected of a crime. Residents in the 1890s did casual work or were thieves or prostitutes, and roughness was increased by London slum clearances from the 1870s, many people coming from the courts around the Angel.

[63] G.L.C., Hist. Bldgs. Div., almsho. file.
[64] *Ret. of Pauper Hosps. and Schs.*, H.C. 313, p. 64 (1884–5), lxvii.
[65] Para. based on Bacon, *Atlas of Lond.* (1886); O.S. Map 6″, Mdx. XII. SW. (1894–6 edn.).
[66] G.L.C., Hist. Bldgs. Div., ISL 12.
[67] Ibid. ISL 37; below, plate 16.

[68] Hornsey libr., Potter Colln. 6/91.
[69] 'College Gdns. Story' (TS. 1967 in Islington libr.).
[70] Based on *P.O. Dir. Lond.* (1858, 1902).
[71] O.S. Map 6″, Mdx. XII. SW. (1894–6 edn.).
[72] G. and W. Grossmith, *Diary of a Nobody* (1892).
[73] Above.

Although it did not look like a slum, having standard three-storeyed houses with area railings lining a wide street, 30 per cent of its households were overcrowded in the 1930s, compared with 7.5 per cent for Islington as a whole, and on average more than 11 people shared each six-roomed house. Like similar streets in the parish and elsewhere in London, Campbell Road had its own subculture with a vocabulary formed from 19th-century thieves' and costers' slang that was unknown to the neighbouring streets. The street also represented working-class independence, a freedom secretly envied by many, so that the demise of the road was later widely regretted even by some who had regarded it with horror.[74]

Communities in streets like Campbell Road were eventually dispersed by the spread of local authority housing, which limited tenants' freedom by curtailing their economic activities. Such housing was, however, badly needed: in 1929 parts of Campbell and Playford roads and Poole Park had the worst overcrowding with over 1.75 persons to a room; the rest of those streets and those around Wedmore Street and north of Rupert Road had 1.50 to 1.75 persons, and Rupert Road, Fonthill Road to Stroud Green Road, Andover Road, and the area between Hornsey and Cornwallis roads all had between 1.25 and 1.50 persons to a room.[75] In Upper Holloway the first municipal housing was in Wedmore Street, where the L.C.C. bought eight semi-detached houses with land at the rear in 1901 as a site for Wessex Buildings, with accommodation for 1,050 in three blocks, two completed in 1904 and one in 1905.[76] Little municipal building was done until after the First World War, when several sites were bought by the L.C.C. for people displaced by slum clearance. The site of 16 houses and a small factory adjoining Wessex Buildings was bought and 2 five-storeyed blocks were built c. 1931 with 46 dwellings, while 8 of the houses which fronted Wedmore Street were kept.[77] Hornsey Rise estate between Hazelville and Sunnyside roads was completed in 1928 on the site of the Alexandra orphanage, which in 1913 was Shoreditch's additional workhouse; three large three-sided blocks of flats were built,[78] which were modernized c. 1980. By 1937 the L.C.C. had also completed 253 dwellings in Wedmore Street and 170 in Andover Street, and started others in Tufnell Park Road and Hilldrop Road. The borough council also built several estates, especially in the northern extremity where there were houses with large gardens and other parcels of vacant land. Manchester Mansions, off Hornsey Lane, was opened in 1921, and Hornsey Lane estate in 1939. Farther east were Warltersville Mansions (opened 1926), the Highlands (1934) on the east side of Crouch Hill, Blythe Mansions (1937) near Hornsey Rise, Hillrise Mansions (1932) and off Hornsey Rise, Coleman Mansions, Crouch Hill

(1937), and Leyden Mansions (1931) on the south side of Warltersville Road.[79]

Several other municipal estates were built, mostly between Hanley Road and Seven Sisters Road or between Hornsey and Holloway roads.[80] By 1967 the borough had 27 estates of 20 or more dwellings in the area, with 12 more in progress, and the G.L.C. owned 5 estates and 4 housing schemes and sites. After the Second World War Campbell Road (renamed Whadcoat Road in the 1930s) was one of the first streets to be demolished, with some surrounding streets, and it was removed entirely to provide the site for flats at Haddon Court in the 1950s and for Clifton Court and the Six Acres estate in the 1960s. The latter was opened in 1969, and provided 356 family flats and maisonettes in 7 four-storeyed blocks and a six- and a twelve-storeyed block. It covered c. 9 a., included a Y.M.C.A. building and a home for retired people, and was interspersed with open spaces and games areas.[81] The estate joined the council's estate on the east, while the area west of Durham Road was also rebuilt by the G.L.C. in the 1970s as the Alsen Road estate with over 1,000 houses, stretching to Hornsey Road and joining an older L.C.C. estate in Andover Road. Between Isledon Road and the G.N.R. line another large clearance was made for the council's Harvist estate, with 432 flats in tower blocks surrounded by open space, completed in 1970. At the junction of Tollington and Hornsey roads the Sobell indoor sports centre was completed in 1973.[82]

The area between Hornsey and Holloway roads was also largely rebuilt by the council from the 1950s. Bennett Court near Seven Sisters Road, Shaw and Landseer Courts just north of Tollington Way, and Simmons House, Sussex Close, and Oakdale Court near Kingsdown Road were completed by 1967. Further estates were started in the 1960s, in Salterton Road near Bennett Court, and along Sussex Way at Bavaria Road near Simmons House.[83] The second was completed in 1979 and Bavaria and Simmons House together provided 206 houses, flats, and maisonnettes fronting Hornsey Road and running back to Sussex Way, having replaced run-down houses, shops, and small factories.[84] Farther north, between Fairbridge Road and St. John's Way, the G.L.C. cleared c. 30 a. in the early 1970s for over 1,500 homes[85] in a mainly traffic-free complex, with open space and some old buildings such as the school in Duncombe Road. At its clearance the area had become one of the worst examples of urban decay in London and the subject of a book on social problems.[86] Adjoining areas were also cleared: the Aged Pilgrims asylum and part of the former workhouse were demolished and housing was built at the Hazelville and Cheverton Road frontages, while the west side of the site was taken for a garden, play area, and the Caxton House com-

[74] Hist. Workshop, viii. 4–5.
[75] New Lond. Life and Labour, iv, maps 1.
[76] L.C.C. Housing of Working Classes in Lond. (1913), 78.
[77] L.C.C. Housing 1928–30 (1931), 100, 103.
[78] Ibid. 91; L.C.C. Municipal Map of Lond. (1913).
[79] Islington L.B. Northern Estates Planning Study (draft report 1977), map 3; Homes for Islington (1967), map.
[80] Para. based on Homes for Islington, map.
[81] Islington L.B. Six Acres Estate (opening prog. 1969 in Islington libr.).
[82] Below, social.   [83] Homes for Islington, map.
[84] Bavaria Rd. Estate Tenants' Handbk. [1979] (in Islington libr.).   [85] Homes for Islington, map.
[86] J. Rowland, Community Decay (1973).

munity centre, opened in 1976. A large area at the junction of Hazelville Road and Hornsey Rise was cleared and part became an adventure playground, to ameliorate the serious lack of leisure facilities. Additional council estates were built near Hornsey Lane: Redwood Court in 1968, the New Orleans estate in 1972–4, and more flats at Warltersville Mansions in 1972–3.[87] A major clearance was also carried out on the west side of Highgate Hill in the 1970s. New blocks were added to the Whittington hospital and the area south of the hospital as far as Junction Road was cleared for housing, with a large office block and new shops and Underground station at the corner of Junction Road and Highgate Hill. Rebuilding was extended westward in the late 1970s to Bickerton Road.

The south-west part of the district, in Tufnell Park and Camden Road, where housing had not been allowed to decay so far, was not rebuilt to the same extent. L.C.C. estates in Tufnell Park Road and Hilldrop Road were planned in 1936[88] but probably not completed until c. 1950, and borough council estates had been added near both of them by 1967. The borough council also demolished houses at the junction of Anson, Carleton, and Brecknock roads c. 1948[89] and built the Brecknock Road estate with 226 dwellings in the 1950s. The G.L.C. and Islington L.B. in the 1970s added to their Hilldrop estates,[90] which together covered a wide area on the north side of Camden Road west of Holloway prison; one of the blocks, Margaret Bondfield House, replaced the semi-detached house in Hilldrop Crescent where Dr. Crippen had lived.[91] The prison was also rebuilt over several years from 1972 to provide medical and psychiatric facilities for the whole women's prison service, with accommodation for prisoners and staff on a new ground plan,[92] that eventually involved demolishing the Gothic gateway, despite widespread protests. The Corporation of London, which had retained adjoining land, also rebuilt its estate between Parkhurst and Camden roads in the 1970s.

Widespread clearance, although it removed substandard dwellings, also destroyed sounder houses and disrupted communities, since many families were not rehoused nearby. As a result in Upper Holloway, the area most affected by council rebuilding, a working-class residents' association, formed to resist further demolition, in 1975 saved over 200 houses in Charteris Road off Tollington Park, after a campaign that involved M.P.s, government ministers, and the national media. Despite evidence that rehabilitation was cheaper than rebuilding, Islington L.B. for some time refused to reverse its decision and finally did so by one vote. Thereafter, however, the council rapidly rehabilitated houses and the Charteris Neighbourhood Tenants' Co-operative was formed to manage and allot them.[93]

The co-operative was one of several tenants' management groups, modelled on the Holloway Tenant Co-operative, formed in 1972 and possibly the first of its kind in England.[94] It was started by three community workers at a time of intense property speculation and displacement, to convert dilapidated houses that were not included in the council's schemes and offer them preferably to the sitting tenants. The co-operative took over houses bought and converted by the Circle 33 housing trust and eventually became a registered housing association.[95] The original founders withdrew, leaving the local tenants to manage the co-operative. It represented a radical change after a hundred years of working-class housing in Islington, from provision in accord with middle-class ideas to decisions made by the tenants themselves.

The co-operative was one of several groups, including housing associations and Holloway Housing Aid Centre, participating in the North Islington Housing Rights Project, also set up in 1972 and funded by Shelter, to avert the problems that gentrification had brought in Barnsbury. Its main aim was to improve five areas in north-east Islington, containing 2,000 substandard homes, by rehabilitation and forming tenants' co-operatives. Existing tenants were to be rehoused in the same street or immediate neighbourhood,[96] to avoid the effects of rehabilitation in Barnsbury which had created a bigger housing problem elsewhere.

In 1983 Upper Holloway presented a very mixed appearance, with different types of housing, commerce, and small industry. Holloway Road and the adjoining part of Seven Sisters Road formed the largest commercial area; it had a major department store and several large chain stores and supermarkets, while retaining many smaller specialist and food shops, besides some street stalls, and served much of North London. Spreading out from the central commercial area around the Nag's Head junction were more small shops, often run-down and catering for ethnic minorities. Such shops could be found along Seven Sisters Road towards Finsbury Park, along Hornsey Road as far as Hornsey Rise, along Holloway Road as far as Archway tavern, and along Junction Road. The shopping area of Upper Holloway Road and Junction Road had once been important but offered only a limited provision after the closing of the Co-operative department store c. 1980. Despite schemes to separate industry from housing, many scattered small workshops remained where 19th-century buildings still stood.

HIGHBURY received its name from the situation of the manor house of Newington Barrow, on a hill surrounded by the demesne. The name came to be used for the district extending roughly

[87] *Northern Est. Planning Study* (draft rep. 1977).
[88] L.C.C. *Lond. Housing* (1937).
[89] 'College Gdns. Story', 16–17.
[90] Islington L.B. 'Estate Properties in Permanent Management' (TS. list 1980 in Islington libr.).
[91] Zwart, *Islington: Hist. and Guide*, 167.
[92] 'Holloway Redevelopment', Prison Dept., Home Office (TS. 1972 in Islington libr.).

[93] N. Islington Housing Rights Project, *Street by Street: Improvement and Tenant Control in Islington* (1976).
[94] Similar scheme started in Liverpool at about the same time.
[95] A. Power, *Holloway Tenant Co-operative: Five Years On* (1977); *Facts and Figures About Holloway Tenant Co-operative* (1979).
[96] N. Islington Housing Rights Project, *Street by Street*.

southward from the parish boundary to High-bury Corner and westward from the New River to Drayton Park, but before the 18th century the only settlement was at the Hospitallers' manor house and grange, recorded in 1338. After the house had been destroyed in 1381, the grange and barn remained on the east side of the track that ran south to Hopping Lane roughly on the later line of Highbury Park and Highbury Grove. The moated site of the house, known as Jack Straw's castle, remained empty west of the track until 1781. In 1611 only the grange and barn were mentioned but in 1692 Highbury house and farm adjoined the barn.[97] A farmhouse, called Cream Hall by 1745,[98] was built at the south-east corner of Highbury wood between 1692 and 1718, and may have replaced an earlier house near Stroud Green which was called Cream Hall in 1718.[99]

Residential growth began in the 1770s when John Dawes, who had bought much of the demesne and former woods,[1] granted leases in 1774–9 for the 39 houses of Highbury Place, built by John Spiller, a speculative builder of Southwark, under an agreement of 1773.[2] The originality of the design of the houses has been attributed to the architect James Spiller.[3] In 1781 Dawes built Highbury House on the moated site.[4] The central portion of Highbury Terrace was dated 1789;[5] nos. 1–16 had been built by 1794, with land reserved for extension at the north end,[6] where by 1829 there were 22 houses of different sizes by several builders.[7] North-east of the terrace stood Highbury Hill House, designed for the physician William Saunders by Daniel Asher Alexander c. 1790 and later occupied by Joseph Wilson.[8] By 1805 Highbury Lodge had been built on Dawes's land at the north end of Highbury Terrace and adjoining Saunders's grounds.[9]

In 1794 the hamlet consisted of Highbury House and Highbury Hill House, Highbury Barn, a resort and tea-gardens, and the two terraces of Highbury Terrace and Place. The land behind Highbury Place was divided into leasehold meadows and gardens of c. 2 a. each, with outbuildings and a nursery; the land facing it and behind Highbury Terrace was similarly leased, mainly to the residents. South of Highbury Place and along Holloway Road was a nursery, while the larger meadows on the west side of Dawes's estate were let together for grazing. On the east side of Highbury Grove, not part of Dawes's estate, stood a nonconformist chapel.[10] Residents in the 1820s were merchants and other prosperous City men,[11] who saw Highbury as separate from the rest of Islington, with gates closing off the private road past Highbury Place

from Holloway Road. In 1820 the inhabitants tried in vain to obtain their own lighting and watching Act, instead of contributing to the parish rate.[12]

By c. 1817 further substantial detached houses stood on the east side of Highbury Grove between Highbury Barn and the chapel,[13] which itself became a dwelling house after the congregation had moved to Union chapel in 1806.[14] North of the Barn, Highbury Park House and a smaller house almost opposite had been built by 1814.[15] In 1820 Thomas Cubitt took c. 12 a. between Highbury Barn and the footpath to Stoke Newington, on which he built moderate sized but elegant villas. Ten houses, mostly by Cubitt, faced west to Highbury Park and eight had been leased by 1825. Behind them, plots were laid along Highbury Grange; those on the north side were subcontracted to Samuel and Charles Cleaver and two were ready for leasing in 1821. At least one on the south side, no. 4, was built by John Bentley to whom it was leased in 1825. The remaining plots went quickly and the houses were finished by 1832.[16] Highbury Park led northward past Cream Hall into Highbury Vale, where building was also under way in 1824 in the later Hurlock and Elwood streets, which had been part of the Cream Hall or Highbury woods estate and sold to William Bennett, a London silversmith, in 1819.[17] Trustees acquired another parcel of the estate, on the north side of a private road later called Aubert Park, for the dissenters' Highbury College, designed by John Davies in Ionic style and built in 1825–6. The grounds of c. 5 a. extended north-west behind the college; 1½ a. on the east side was added in 1835 and a smaller plot on the west side in 1854 when the college had become a training school for school-masters. The buildings and grounds covered 7 a. in 1866, when it became an Anglican theological college.[18]

By 1829 some building fronted Holloway Road west of Highbury Place, although the land behind was still fields. Highbury Park had been extended northward with more villas between the New-ington footpath (later site of Kelross Road) and Highbury Park House. Opposite Cubitt's villas Park Terrace of 20 uniform houses had been started by 1829[19] and completed by 1841. The private road past Highbury College was con-tinued south as Highbury Park West (later Hamilton Park West) and a few semi-detached stuccoed villas had been built on the west side by 1841, while farther north Highbury Vale was filling on the west side and building had started in Park Place (later Conewood Street).[20] In 1844 land south of Highbury Terrace was laid out for

[97] Below, manors (Highbury).
[98] Rocque, *Map of Lond.* (1741–5).
[99] Below, other est. (Highbury woods).
[1] Below, manors (Highbury).
[2] Colvin, *Brit. Architects*, 772; M.L.R. 1774/4/127.
[3] Pevsner, *Lond.* ii. 239.
[4] Below, manors.
[5] Datestone.
[6] Islington libr., deed 558 and plan.
[7] Nelson, *Islington* (1829), 172–3.
[8] Ibid. 173; Colvin, *Brit. Architects*, 65.
[9] Baker's plan (1805); P.R.O., IR 30/21/33.
[10] Islington libr., deed 558.
[11] Nelson, *Islington* (1829), 169, 173.

[12] Islington libr., vestry min. bk. 1812–24, 228, 236, 247–8.
[13] Baker's plan (1817).
[14] Below, prot. nonconf.
[15] Islington libr., deed 3148.
[16] H. Hobhouse, *Thos. Cubitt: Master Builder* (1971), 38–40; Colvin, *Brit. Architects*, 243; Islington libr., deed 3490.
[17] Islington libr., deed 372; G.L.R.O., P83/MRY1/390.
[18] Colvin, *Brit. Architects*, 253; G. C. B. Davies, *Men for the Ministry* (1963), 24; P.R.O., C 54/10711, no. 9; C 54/11240, no. 9; C 54/13998, no. 4; C 54/14682, no. 6; below, churches; prot. nonconf.; plate 23.
[19] *Cruchley's New Plan* (1829).
[20] Lewis, *Islington*, plan (1841).

Highbury Crescent by James Wagstaff and James Goodbody; nos. 19–25 were let to Goodbody in 1846. The houses were pairs of large Italianate villas, with rich and varied decorations in stucco.[21] By 1848 villas on the south side of Highbury Crescent West (later Fieldway Crescent) ran down to Holloway Road, and Christ Church was opened in 1848 at the top of Highbury Grove to serve the rapidly growing suburb.[22]

Highbury New Park was one of two estates laid out in the 1850s, being developed from 1851 by Henry Rydon on former land of Francis Maseres, which had passed to Robert and William Fellowes.[23] Three houses fronting Highbury Grove south of Aberdeen Park were leased in 1851 and Park Road (later Highbury New Park), Grosvenor Road (later Avenue), Highbury Quadrant, Paradise Road (later Collins Road on the line of the Stoke Newington footpath), and Beresford Terrace were laid out. A road later called Petherton Road was planned for the east side of the New River along a footpath from St. Paul's Road to Green Lanes.[24] Land at the junction of Highbury Grove and Park Road was sold to the Church Missionary Society, which opened its children's home there in 1853.[25] By 1852 six houses had been built at the west end of Grosvenor Road, 7 in Highbury Grove, Rydon's home Pyrland House in Park Road, and about 6 at the extreme northern end of the estate near Green Lanes. By the mid 1850s about 20 houses had been built at the southern end of Park Road and by 1860 43 houses stood at that end and 33 at the northern, leaving a large central stretch unbuilt, and 12 in Grosvenor Road. Eight houses in Beresford Terrace were completed in 1859. Fourteen large houses were built fronting Green Lanes between 1854 and 1864 in addition to the house at the corner of Paradise Road, which had been built between 1829 and 1841.[26] The imposing detached and semi-detached houses on the estate, built by various sublessees, were designed by Charles Hambridge in mixed Italo-Romanesque styles. In wide streets with spacious gardens, they were apparently in great demand in the 1850s.

Aberdeen Park was also laid out at that time. Owned in 1848 by George Morrice, it was a compact block on the east side of Highbury Grove just south of Highbury Barn. Large detached and semi-detached villas in Italian style were built by the mid 1850s facing Highbury Grove and on the south side of Aberdeen Park, a private road running eastward, which was later extended roughly in a square to fill the shape of Morrice's estate.[27] St. Saviour's church was built fronting the eastern side of the extension in 1866, at the expense of the Revd. W. D. Morrice,[28] but

many plots on that part of the estate remained vacant in the 1890s.[29]

By the mid 1850s building was in progress elsewhere in Highbury. Land belonging to Highbury House and to Highbury Hill House was being laid out: the road later known as Highbury Hill was made from Christ Church, running north of Highbury Hill House, and some substantial villas were built on the north side near the church and on the south side west of Highbury Hill House. Leigh Road was laid west and south of Highbury House and some building began at the east end, while a terrace was built fronting east to Highbury Park. Hamilton Park on the north side of the House was also laid out and two terraces were built on the central portion. A row of semi-detached villas was built at the south end of Highbury Grove facing the Highbury New Park estate.[30] At the same time building was starting north of Highbury, along Blackstock Lane. Ambler Road and the north-eastern end of Monsell Road, then called King's Road, were laid out in the 1840s, but although a couple of older cottages stood near the junction with Seven Sisters Road in 1848, only one building stood in Ambler Road and none in King's Road.[31] By the mid 1850s there were a few terraced houses and cottages on the west side of Blackstock Road and north side of King's Road,[32] to which some terraces fronting Seven Sisters Road and the newly formed St. Thomas's Road were added in the 1860s.[33] Land between the N.L.R. and St. Paul's Road was also being filled with terraces in the 1850s, and Alma Terrace at the corner of St. Paul's Road and Highbury Grove (later nos. 214–22 even, St. Paul's Road) was built in 1854–5 with houses and shops.[34]

Highbury Hill Park, later Drayton Park, was offered for building leases between 1855 and 1865. One of the last unbuilt estates, it formed the western boundary of Highbury from Hackney brook almost to Holloway Road. The road, later called Drayton Park, running the length of the estate and joining Holloway Road, was constructed in the early 1850s and a link with Hornsey Road called Benwell Road was built with terraces.[35] The estate was intended to have detached and semi-detached villas, but the few houses of the 1860s at the Holloway Road end were more modest terraced houses than elsewhere in Highbury, probably because of the proximity to Ring Cross. A new road later called Bryantwood Road, between Drayton Park and Benwell Road, also had a few terraced houses of that period, twelve of which on the north side were let to Charles Bryantwood in 1868.[36] The G.N.R.'s Canonbury spur line, opened in 1874[37] close to the west side of Drayton Park, prevented

[21] G.L.C., Historic Bldgs. Div., ISL 6, 32.
[22] P.R.O., IR 30/21/33.
[23] Below, other est. (Maseres). Inf. on Highbury New Pk. based on J. Smallshaw, *Hen. Rydon and Highbury New Pk. Estate* (n.d., privately printed, supplied by author); *Lond. Jnl.* vii (1) (1981), 29–44.
[24] For bldg. in Petherton Rd. and eastern part of est. see below, Newington Green.
[25] S. Lewis, *Islington As It Was* (1854), 57; below, churches.
[26] *Cruchley's New Plan* (1829); Lewis, *Islington*, plan (1841).

[27] Plan [c. 1853]; O.S. Map 6″, Mdx. XII. SW. (1863–9 edn.).
[28] Below, churches.
[29] O.S. Maps 6″, Mdx. XII. SW. (1863–9, 1894–6 edns.).
[30] Plan [c. 1853].   [31] P.R.O., IR 30/21/33.
[32] Plan [c. 1853].
[33] O.S. Map 6″, Mdx. XII. SW. (1863–9 edn.).
[34] G.L.R.O., Acc. 1417/25–6, 31.
[35] Plan [c. 1853].
[36] G.L.R.O., map. dept., 3276 JI [c. 1865]; O.S. Map 6″, Mdx. XII. SW. (1863–9 edn.); Islington libr., deeds 853, 851.
[37] Above, communications.

building on that side of the road and led to the opposite side being filled with terraces.

The type of house built elsewhere in Highbury also changed. In the 1860s building had continued in the roads already laid down: the two arms of Highbury Quadrant were almost filled with *c*. 45 detached and semi-detached villas similar to the rest of the estate, and Highbury Hill and the roads around Highbury House were also filling rapidly with large houses.[38] In the 1870s, however, the building of such villas ended, probably because demand ceased but possibly because of a greater financial return from closely packed houses. In the central part of Highbury New Park, land intended for a crescent opposite St. Augustine's church was built over in 1873–7 with terraces fronting Highbury New Park and lining Balfour and Stradbroke roads behind, which joined Highbury Grange. More terrraces by 1877 linked Highbury Quadrant with Riversdale Road.[39] Land on either side of Highbury Hill north of Aubert Park was let for building in 1878 and terraced houses were put up,[40] and in the late 1870s and the 1880s more building was carried out in St. Thomas's Road and adjoining streets.[41]

By the mid 1890s there was little land left, apart from the 25½-a. Highbury Fields bought for a public park in 1885,[42] and the spaces that had been left in earlier periods had been filled with small streets of terraces. Such areas comprised the remaining land north of Gillespie Road, between Riversdale and Mountgrove roads, between the Quadrant and Highbury Grange, the area west of the spur railway line, and east of Highbury Place.[43] Few of the important houses remained in their former state. Highbury House had lost almost all its grounds; Highbury Hill House and its grounds became a school in 1894;[44] Cream Hall made way for Legard Road and St. John's church in the early 1880s.[45] South of St. John's the detached Loxford House, built in the 1850s, still had large grounds; Highbury College, renamed St. John's Hall, also retained its grounds, and much of the Aberdeen Park estate was still open.[46]

The 20th century saw no major changes in Highbury's appearance until after the Second World War, although there were minor changes, often connected with the area's social character. Before 1914 Highbury still contained well-to-do residents[47] and houses in streets such as Highbury New Park and Highbury Hill were normally occupied by single families, but by 1930 most had been subdivided or taken for schools or institutions,[48] and the Highbury Athenaeum became a film studio in the late 1930s.[49] An example was no. 150 Highbury New Park, which in 1936 had

two flats on the ground floor with a shared bathroom, one flat and two bed-sitting rooms on the first floor, and one flat with a balcony on the second floor; its detached stable block, which had been converted into a caretaker's cottage in 1914, was a garage with a flat over it, let separately and with its own garden.[50] Despite multi-occupation, overcrowding was not a problem in Highbury as a whole, which had few of the very poor. Almost all the area was in the lowest category of occupancy in 1929, with under one person to a room, except the Monsell, Gillespie, and Conewood area, with between 1 and 1.25 persons to a room, and a strip along Drayton Park, with the second highest category at 1.50 to 1.75 persons.[51]

Change in use affected the larger and older buildings, and encouraged infilling. The most significant change took place in 1913, when part of the grounds of St. John's Hall was leased to Woolwich Arsenal football club.[52] The subsequent success of Arsenal made Highbury nationally known, although it drew crowds which had a depressing effect on nearby housing. The remaining older houses also disappeared in the period between the World Wars. Highbury Hill House was demolished *c*. 1928 and school buildings were put up in the grounds.[53] Highbury House followed in 1938 and formed the site of Eton House flats, built by the Old Etonian Housing Association in 1939.[54] Loxford House was sold to the National Children's Home, whose chief offices moved there in 1925 from the Leysian Mission, City Road; additions, including a family centre, were built behind the house.[55] In Highbury New Park the grounds of Pyrland House became the site of Holmcote Gardens in 1926.[56] Several villas in Highbury Park and on the south side of Highbury Grange were replaced by the four-storeyed blocks of Addington Mansions in 1922.[57] Avenell Road Mansions was built in 1930.[58] Many small works and businesses appeared in major roads such as Highbury Grove and Gillespie Road, and also in quieter ones such as Highbury Terrace and Place, which, like other once select streets, had few private residents left.[59]

After the Second World War large-scale rebuilding in parts of Highbury replaced bombed buildings and provided new municipal housing. The Blackstock estate in Hurlock Street was planned in 1936 and 3 five-storeyed blocks were completed before or after the Second World War, with a fourth added later. Eight four- and five-storeyed blocks of flats and maisonnettes had been built by 1967 on the north side of Grosvenor Avenue stretching to Highbury New Park, which also contained several other blocks, both municipal and private. The largest area to be rebuilt

[38] O.S. Map 6″, Mdx. XII. SW. (1863–9 edn.).
[39] Smallshaw, *Highbury New Pk. Est.* 7–8.
[40] Islington libr., deed 403.
[41] Ibid. deeds index.
[42] Below, pub. svces.
[43] O.S. Map 6″, Mdx. XII. SW. (1894–6 edn.).
[44] Below, educ., pub. schs.
[45] Below, manors.
[46] O.S. Map 6″, Mdx. XII. SW. (1894–6 edn.).
[47] Mudie-Smith, *Rel. Life*, 135.
[48] *P.O. Dir. Lond.* (1902 and later edns.).
[49] Below, econ., industry.
[50] Islington libr., deeds 4212, 4215.

[51] *New Lond. Life and Labour*, iv, maps 1.
[52] Below, social.   [53] Below, educ., pub. schs.
[54] P. Zwart, *Islington: Hist. and Guide* (1973), 140; inf. from Mr. J. C. Connell.
[55] *Nat. Children's Home 1869–1969* (booklet in Islington libr.); 'Thank you St. John's' (TS. booklet in Islington libr.); inf. from Mr. J. S. Ellis.
[56] Smallshaw, *Highbury New Pk. Est.*, 8.
[57] O.S. Map 6″, Mdx. XII. SE. & SW. (1938); inf. from Mr. J. C. Connell.
[58] Islington L.B. 'Estate Properties in Permanent Management' (TS. list 1980 in Islington libr.).
[59] *P.O. Dir. Lond.* (1927 and later edns.).

was where the Quadrant estate, 611 dwellings in 40 four- and five-storeyed blocks, was built by the L.C.C. between Collins Road and Green Lanes and between the two arms of Highbury Quadrant. Opened in 1954, the estate developed the use of low-rise blocks in conjunction with terraced housing. St. John's Hall was badly bombed and the college did not return after the war, the buildings being replaced by Aubert Court with 100 dwellings. Most municipal estates were smaller, with *c.* 50 dwellings or less.[60]

In the early 1980s Highbury still appeared an attractive suburb, where new buildings matched the scale of their neighbours and many stood in wide tree-lined streets. On the east side Highbury New Park, the south side of Grosvenor Avenue, and Aberdeen Park have many of their original villas, interspersed with small blocks of flats. Highbury Grove and its continuation as Highbury Park suffer from traffic and the latter has also become a shopping street. Two of Cubitt's Highbury Park villas, nos. 54 and 56, still stand, as does Park Terrace opposite, while Addington Mansions was renovated by the borough council and renamed Taverner Square and Peckitt Square in 1982.[61] On the west side Highbury Place, Highbury Terrace, and Highbury Crescent survive around the trees of Highbury Fields. No. 1 Highbury Place was the studio of Walter Sickert from 1927 to 1934[62] and no. 25 was the boyhood home of Joseph Chamberlain from 1845 to 1854.[63] A few large villas also remain in Highbury Hill, mostly divided into flats as elsewhere in Highbury. Farther west near Drayton Park many two- and three-storeyed terraced houses remain but others have been demolished or converted into business premises or shops, while the North London polytechnic has rebuilt part of the south side of Benwell Road. The northern part of the area is the most changed and resembles the neighbouring parts of Upper Holloway, with large council estates, modest terraced houses, and many commercial premises, especially in Gillespie and Blackstock roads.

NEWINGTON GREEN and KINGSLAND comprise the eastern extremity of the parish, jutting into Hackney, and include the south side of Ball's Pond Road from Kingsland to Southgate Road and the whole area north of Ball's Pond and St. Paul's roads east of the New River. At Kingsland by the 18th century a small green on the west side of the main road (Ermine Street) lay in Islington at the junction of the roads to Newington Green (Boleyn Road) and to Islington (Ball's Pond Road). South of the latter were Kingsland leper hospital and chapel, founded in 1280; the hospital

lay in Hackney, but the parish boundary ran southward through the north door of the chapel, which was considered part of Islington.[64] On the west side of Kingsland green a copyhold farm of Highbury manor, held by a London merchant, stood in the mid 16th century.[65] In 1664 the Islington part of Kingsland had 7 households, two with 6 and one with 7 hearths, and four not chargeable.[66]

Newington Green was probably also a medieval settlement, as many free and copyhold tenements of Highbury manor were there in the late 15th century.[67] The north side of the green lay in Stoke Newington, the remainder in Islington. By 1445 prosperous Londoners lived in the hamlet, where many owned copyhold property in the early 16th century.[68] Other residents included Henry Percy, earl of Northumberland (d. 1537), 1536-7.[69] A timber-framed building which stood at the north-east corner of the green until the late 18th century was probably 16th-century, forming four sides of a courtyard and containing gilded and painted wainscotting. By the late 18th century, when it was demolished, it was called Bishop's Place and was divided into tenements occupied by poor people.[70] By 1611 a large house on the south side of the green, probably of at least six bays with three storeys and with ornate ceilings, was occupied by Alderman William Halliday, who may have built it. It was later called Mildmay House and then Eagle House, nos. 9-10 Newington Green.[71]

In 1664 Newington Green had 27 taxable households, and 5 not chargeable. Eight of the houses had between 10 and 16 hearths, and 14 had 5 to 9 hearths.[72] The 17th century brought more building, including the replacement of large houses by several smaller. In 1658 a copyhold house, gardens, orchards, and outhouses on the west side of the green, belonging to Hugh Thomas, were replaced by a terrace of 4 three-storeyed brick houses,[73] later nos. 52-5 Newington Green, with gabled fronts, brick pilasters on the upper storeys, and recessed blank arches to the first floor windows.[74] The Halliday (Mildmay) estate, with four houses in addition to the main house in 1622,[75] had about seven dwellings in 1649, besides the main house.[76] In 1673 four houses on the estate, which lay mainly south and south-east of the green, were let on repairing leases and some very old houses were sold for improvement.[77] At the north-east corner of the green probably six houses were built by the 1690s beside a farmhouse belonging to Joan Miller in 1663.[78] A house on the west side next to no. 55 had 13 hearths in 1664 when it was occupied by Thomas Lavender.[79] Sir Thomas Halton, Bt.,

[60] Islington L.B. *Homes for Islington* (1967); L.C.C. *Lond. Housing* (1937); 'Thank you St. John's'; G.L.C. *Home Sweet Home* (1976), 52.
[61] Inf. from Mr. J. C. Connell. [62] Plaque.
[63] L.C.C. *Indication of Hos. of Historical Interest in Lond.* pt. 44 [1915], 5, 7.
[64] *V.C.H. Mdx.* i. 210; Tomlins, *Islington*, 211. Full treatment of Kingsland reserved for Hackney.
[65] P.R.O., C 3/52/9.
[66] G.L.R.O., MR/TH/1, mm. 31d.-32.
[67] G.L.R.O., P83/MRY1/NB.
[68] M. Fitch, *Index to Testamentary Rec. in Consistory Ct. of Lond.* i. 165; Guildhall MS. 9171/10, f. 290.
[69] Above.
[70] Nelson, *Islington* (1829), 175.
[71] 20th-cent. photo. in *Changing Face of Newington Green* (Factory community centre, 1977), 46; below, other est. (Mildmay).
[72] G.L.R.O., MR/TH/1, mm. 31d.-32.
[73] P.R.O., C 5/193/84; G.L.C., Hist. Bldgs. Div., ISL 40.
[74] Pevsner, *Lond.* ii. 432.
[75] Guildhall MS. 3460/2.
[76] P.R.O., C 5/2/50.
[77] Ibid. C 6/287/49.
[78] Ibid. C 6/323/10; ibid. E 179/252/32, p. 32.
[79] Ibid. E 179/252/32, p. 33.

was living there by 1717 and died at Newington Green in 1726.[80] In addition to having rich residents, the hamlet was popular with nonconformists, several of whom kept academies there from 1665.[81]

In the early 18th century Kingsland green, much smaller than Newington green, was similarly lined with houses.[82] A few had also been built away from the two greens, with a small cluster near Essex Road, called Ball's Pond.[83] Near the large pond, used for shooting, was an inn called the Boarded House and known by the sign of the Salutation, from which John Ball had issued his own tokens probably in the later 17th century.[84] A Thomas Ball had lived at or near the green in 1645 and Anne Ball occupied a house in the area with 16 hearths in 1663.[85] On the west side of Newington Road, near its bend, stood the two Virginia Houses by 1735.[86] About half way along the road on its east side stood an inn called the Weavers Arms by 1725 and probably by 1716.[87] A little farther north, behind Mildmay House, the Spring Gardens inn had been built by 1725 and was known as Spring Gardens coffee house by 1765.[88] East of the green, the Coach and Horses stood by 1721 in the lane which later took its name.[89] By 1725 more houses had been built on the north side of nos. 52–5 Newington Green, including nos. 44 and 45 to which Samuel Wright was admitted in 1727 and 1725 respectively[90] and which marked the green's junction with Green Lanes in 1735.[91] In 1740 the Mildmay estate included three brick houses, one very old, together with another used as a stable, and one, at the south-east corner of the green by the passage to Kingsland, formerly called the workhouse and since converted into a dwelling.[92] The green itself was railed in 1742.[93]

Residents of Newington Green in the 18th century included ministers of the Unitarian chapel, built on the north side of the green in Stoke Newington in 1708.[94] Robert Whithear, minister 1732–6, lived at no. 55 in 1736, and Dr. Richard Price, 1758–91, at no. 54 from 1758 to 1783.[95] The large house nearby, formerly occupied by Sir Thomas Halton, was the home of Samuel Harris, an East India merchant, followed by his daughter Mary and son-in-law Daniel Radford. The Radfords' daughter Mary and her husband Thomas Rogers lived from 1760 to 1767 at no. 52, which was probably where Samuel Rogers, the poet, was born in 1763. The Rogers family moved in 1767 to Radford's house, into which in 1767 Thomas Rogers (d. 1793) incorporated the adjoining no. 55. The large house was rebuilt or refronted in the 18th century and was sold by Samuel Rogers in 1797.[96] A little to the

south a farmhouse, later known as Dells Farm, was built between 1753 and 1793 on land belonging to Peter Maseres.[97]

By the end of the 18th century building had become relatively dense in the three settlements of Newington Green, Kingsland, and Ball's Pond, but it had not spread very far. Ball's Pond in particular had several new houses. The Virginia Houses had been replaced by a terrace, and another terrace with a crescent at its centre was built on the east side of Newington Road at the south end c. 1791.[98] Behind the crescent a lane led from Newington Road into Ball's Pond Road, cutting off the corner, and Prospect Row had been built on its north-east side. Houses had begun to spread eastward from Newington Green along Coach and Horses Lane; they probably formed what was later called Keppel Row.[99]

By 1817 the south side of Ball's Pond Road was lined with two- and three-storeyed terraces, including Brunswick Place dated 1812, Bellevue Terrace, and Union Row at the east end on the parish boundary. Much of the land was still fields but there were also nurseries: Barr's at Ball's Pond, Dassington's at Kingsland, and a third on the south side of Mildmay House on the site of Spring Gardens.[1] Building continued in the 1830s, with Pleasant Row in Coach and Horses Lane (later Matthias Road) east of Keppel Row and Maberly Terrace in a gap on the south side of Ball's Pond Road.[2]

On the north side of the road several groups of almshouses[3] were built in the 1830s and 1840s. The earliest on the south-east side of King Henry's Walk, was designed for the Tylers' and Bricklayers' Company by William Grellier in a Gothic style: eight houses were completed in 1835 and a north block with four houses was added in 1838–9.[4] The Metropolitan Benefit Societies, founded in 1829, built their asylum in 1836 on the south side of the Tylers' Company's, fronting Ball's Pond Road. The two-storeyed building of buff and grey brick and stone dressings was designed by S. H. Ridley in Tudor Gothic style, with 14 small houses and a central hall around three sides of a large courtyard; the hall was rebuilt in 1930–1.[5] William Lee's and John Peck's almshouses, belonging to the Dyers' Company of London, moved from Bethnal Green and were built in 1840–1 in King Henry's Walk, north of the Tylers' almshouses. The two-storeyed symmetrical block of brick with stone dressings was designed by S. S. Teulon in a Gothic style, with niches and four-centred arches, to include 10 houses and a central hall or chapel. In 1850–2 Teulon added north-east and south-west blocks of 8 houses each, to rehouse Tyr-

[80] G.L.C., Hist. Bldgs. Div., ISL 40; below, manors (Barnsbury).
[81] Below, educ., priv. schs.
[82] Nelson, *Islington* (1829), plan (1735).
[83] M.L.R. 1753/2/447; see parish map c. 1740.
[84] Nelson, *Islington* (1829), 179, plate XIV.
[85] P.R.O., E 179/253/13; E 179/252/32, p. 33.
[86] Nelson, *Islington* (1829), plan (1735).
[87] G.L.R.O., MR/LV3/3, 4/48.
[88] Ibid. MR/LV4/48, 8/40.
[89] Ibid. MR/LV3/90.
[90] G.L.C., Hist. Bldgs. Div., ISL 40.
[91] Nelson, *Islington* (1829), plan (1735).
[92] M.L.R. 1750/2/48.

[93] Lewis, *Islington*, 311.
[94] Below, Stoke Newington, prot. nonconf.
[95] G.L.C., Hist. Bldgs. Div., ISL 40.
[96] Ibid.; A. J. Shirren, *Sam. Rogers* (priv. printed, 1963, unpag.); *Changing Face of Newington Green*, 12.
[97] Below, other est. (Maseres).
[98] M.L.R. 1791/4/218.   [99] Baker's plan (1793).
[1] Ibid. (1817).
[2] Lewis, *Islington*, plan (1841); 1805 map with (undated) addns. in *Changing Face of Newington Green*, 7.
[3] Para. based on G.L.C., Hist. Bldgs. Div., almshos. files.
[4] Colvin, *Brit. Architects*, 365; W. G. Bell, *Tylers' and Bricklayers' Co.* (1938), 56–7.
[5] Datestone; Pevsner, *Lond.* ii. 236.

whitt's and West's almshouses. The Cutlers' Company of London built 12 almshouses c. 1840 on the east side of the Metropolitan Benefit asylum, in what became nos. 1–12 Cutler's Terrace, a two-storeyed symmetrical block in a Gothic style.[6] The Bookbinders' Provident Institution, founded 1830, was built in 1843 in Ball's Pond Road at the corner between the Metropolitan Benefit asylum and King Henry's Walk, with the building around three sides of a courtyard.[7] By 1841 a few buildings had also appeared on the north-west side of King Henry's Walk, and Mildmay Place had been built where the walk joined the extension of Boleyn Road.[8]

Building also began in the 1830s farther west on the north side of St. Paul's Road, where the marquess of Northampton owned 19 a. of nursery ground. St. Paul's Terrace, nos. 14–100 St. Paul's Road, was built by 1837 with four storeys and basements. The row was broken by St. Paul's Place, linking St. Paul's Road with Newington Green Road, and Northampton Park was laid from the north end of St. Paul's Place in an arc to join St. Paul's Road. A gap between no. 14 St. Paul's Road and no. 4, a Gothic cottage of c. 1830, was not filled until the 1850s. By 1841 St. Paul's Place was similar to St. Paul's Terrace, and Northampton Grove was nearly filled with pairs of two-storeyed Italianate villas. Bingham Street off St. Paul's Place had been built up by 1843 with smaller two-storeyed houses without basements, and a short row, nos. 8–13, of three-bayed houses.[9]

In the next decade new roads were laid across the Mildmay estate and building increased in the south and east parts of the area.[10] By the mid 1850s Mildmay Park from Newington Green to Ball's Pond Road was lined with pairs of substantial stuccoed houses of three storeys, with side porches and basements. Mildmay Street was partially built up and the lines of Mildmay Grove North and South had been laid out on either side of the N.L.R. line, which was completed through the district in 1850. In the north-east corner of the parish some small streets were built up with terraces between King Henry Street and Boleyn Road, and extended a little west and north of King Henry Street as Arundel Street, Suffolk Place, and Arundel Grove. The houses were probably all working-class like those in Arundel Grove, two-storeyed, plain, with only one first-floor window in the front, and opening straight on to the street.[11] South of the N.L.R. line King's (later Kingsbury), Canterbury, and Stanley roads were laid out with terraces between the almshouses and Kingsland, and houses were also built fronting Ball's Pond Road. The old chapel at Kingsland was demolished in 1846 and the Star and Garter built there, still straddling the boundary.[12]

In the 1860s building was extended over most of the Mildmay estate, which was sold in lots in 1859,[13] and spread west of Newington Green Road.[14] Mildmay Grove was built up on both sides with three-storeyed stuccoed terraces with porticos and basements. Mildmay Road had similar terraces, except east of King Henry Street where Mildmay Villas contained two-storeyed pairs with basements, side porches, and stuccoed pilasters.[15] Infilling had taken place between John (later St. Jude's) Street and the N.L.R. line, with a terrace of two-storeyed houses opening straight on to the street but with some stucco decoration,[16] in addition to a few three-storeyed houses; more terraces were built between the almshouses and Kingsland, principally at the southern end of Kingsbury Road, and in Hawthorn Street and Bishops Grove. Three-storeyed terraces had been built by 1865 in King Henry's Walk and Ball's Pond Road on the edge of the Bookbinders' asylum site, and on the north-west side of King Henry's Walk pairs and terraces were built similar to those in Mildmay Road. Between Mildmay Road and Mildmay Grove North, Wolsey Road and Queen Margaret's Grove were built with two-storeyed houses with basements and stuccoed dressings, while behind the north side of Mildmay Road the small terraces of Woodville Grove were built, together with the southern end of Woodville Road. Northward the ground was still open as far as the houses in Matthias Road. A station was opened in 1858 on the east side of Newington Green Road. Between that road and the New River, south of the N.L.R. line, the whole area had been covered by 1865: Northampton Grove at the eastern end of Northampton Road had two-storeyed terraced houses with stucco dressings by 1862,[17] and a cul-de-sac on the west side of Douglas Road North (later Wallace Road) filled the space to the New River by 1865.

Most of the land north of the N.L.R. line and east of the New River belonged to the Maseres estate,[18] and was bought in 1852 by Henry Rydon, who began laying out Highbury New Park.[19] The land east of the river, which included Dells farm, was mainly brickfields until 1862, when Rydon began to lay it out, extending Grosvenor Road (later Avenue) eastward across the New River to Newington Green Road, and similarly extending Beresford Terrace as Beresford Road, which incorporated Dells Farm on its north side as no. 18. Petherton Road was also laid out, with the New River as an open stream down the middle.[20] By 1865 a few terraced houses stood at the east end of Grosvenor Road, on both sides, and Beresford Road, on the south side, with new terraces of shops fronting Newington Green Road between the railway and Beresford Road.[21] In 1859 Rydon also bought c. 6 a. of the Mildmay estate straddling the New River near Green Lanes, and the house and grounds of 4¾ a., later

[6] P.R.O., C 54/12064, no. 8; C 54/12475, no. 11.
[7] Ibid. C 54/12072, no. 13.
[8] Lewis, *Islington*, plan (1841).
[9] G.L.C., Hist. Bldgs. Div., ISL 6; Lewis, *Islington*, plan (1841).
[10] Para. based on Plan [c. 1853]. The plan has some inaccuracies for the Mildmay area.
[11] Plate 12. [12] Tomlins, *Islington*, 212.
[13] J. Smallshaw, *Hen. Rydon and Highbury New Pk. Est.* 6.

[14] Para. based on Stanford, *Libr. Map of Lond.* (1862 edn. with additions to 1865).
[15] Photo. in *Changing Face of Newington Green*, 45.
[16] Photo. in ibid. 29.
[17] Smallshaw, *Highbury New Pk. Est.* 15.
[18] Below, other est.
[19] Above, Highbury.
[20] Smallshaw, *Highbury New Pk. Est.* 5, 10, 15.
[21] Stanford (1865).

called Gloucester House, that had belonged to Samuel Rogers.[22]

Building continued on Rydon's estate throughout the 1860s and 1870s.[23] Two terraces of shops were built at the south-west and south-east junctions of Grosvenor and Wallace roads in 1867 and 1868 respectively, and houses were built between the junction and the eastern end of Grosvenor Road by 1870; the houses were three-storeyed stuccoed terraces with basements, more modest than those at the Highbury end. The N.L.R. station was moved from Newington Road to Wallace Road in 1870,[24] and houses on the north side of Grosvenor Road west of Wallace Road were built as far as the New River by 1872, although the south side was not completed until 1880. Beresford Road was completed in 1871, and the terraced shops between Beresford and Ferntower roads were built in 1868. Building in Ferntower and Pyrland roads began in 1869, and 28 houses in the former were occupied in 1874, with the rest completed c. 1877. The first houses were in a classical style similar to those in Grosvenor Road, but after 1874 the style was changed to an ornate Gothic. Building began at the southern end of Petherton Road in 1870 and nos. 2–10 (even), a terrace of large double-fronted houses, was completed by 1872. On the west side no. 1 was detached and nearby houses were also well spaced. The eastern side was completed by 1880, with shops at the northern end by the junction with Green Lanes, and most of the western side was filled by 1882. The striking width of the road, with the New River down the centre, was accentuated by the stuccoed Gothic terraces, of three-storeys with attics and basements. Leconfield and Poet's roads were laid out in 1873; in 1877 Leconfield Road was nearly filled with two-storeyed terraces with basements, and Poet's Road was built up between Petherton and Leconfield roads.

The grounds behind Mildmay House along the rear of Mildmay Grove North remained open until 1869, when the Mildmay Mission built its conference hall, followed by the adjoining Deaconess House in 1871. Mildmay Memorial hospital was built in the compound in 1883 and Mildmay House, nos. 9–10 Newington Green, was taken over in 1885 for the nurses.[25] The green itself was bought by Islington vestry and laid out as a park after complaints in 1874 about its condition.[26]

In the 1880s the few remaining spaces were filled. Poet's Road was extended to Ferntower Road by I. Edmondson and a terrace on the north side built by 1883. The rest was soon built up and Dalston synagogue was added in 1885. Edmondson also added shops to the ground floors of two of the four 17th-century houses at the green (nos. 52–5) c. 1880–2, and the other two were adapted for commercial use. He replaced Gloucester

House with a terrace of shops, nos. 56–61 Newington Green and nos. 2–10 Ferntower Road, in 1882–3.[27] Monte Cristo House, a four-storeyed building at the north-west corner of the green and possibly the former home of Samuel Wright, was for sale in 1889, when its extensive grounds bounded by Green Lanes were one of the last empty sites in a populous district.[28] By 1886 the open land east of the green was filled with Matthias Road board school, opened in 1884, and Mayville and Woodville roads, stuccoed two-storeyed terraces in a Gothic style; Docwra's Buildings had been built between Mildmay Park and King Henry's Walk.[29] By 1900 many buildings around the green were shops, and there were clusters of small shops in Matthias Road, Mildmay Park, King Henry's Walk, Newington Green Road, and Mayville Street.

As elsewhere in Islington, social changes took place in the 20th century. The houses along the principal roads had been built for middle-class residents, for whom an additional station had been opened on the east side of Mildmay Park in 1880. In 1934 the station closed because residents worked mainly in local industry.[30] Most houses were divided but overcrowding in 1929 was not as bad as in some parts of the parish. The Mildmay Mission buildings and the west and south sides of the green had less than one person to a room, and most of the remainder of the district had only 1 to 1.25 persons; the areas from Mildmay Street to Ball's Pond Road and from King Henry Street to Boleyn Road were in the middle range, with 1.25 to 1.50.[31]

Between 1934 and 1942 Dells Farm was replaced by Beresford Lodge, a block of flats, and another block, Mildmay Court, was built at the corner of Mildmay Park and Mildmay Grove.[32] Three sets of almshouses were closed: the Bookbinders' in 1927, the Tylers' and Bricklayers' in 1937, and the Dyers' in 1938.[33] Major changes, however, came only after the Second World War, when widespread bomb damage made room for council housing.

The L.C.C.'s Mayville estate was begun with Congrieve House and Patmore House in Matthias Road, Campion House, Southwell House, and Meredith House in Boleyn Road, and Webster House in King Henry Street, all built between 1947 and 1952. In the 1960s Mayville Street, Arundel Grove, Woodville Road, and the villas at the east end of Mildmay Road made way for blocks including the twelve-storeyed Conrad House, Neptune House, Brontë House, and Beckford House. The estate had 352 dwellings in 1967, with another 173 planned in King Henry Street, and in 1983 comprised almost the whole area bounded by Matthias, Boleyn, and Mildmay roads and Newington Green school.[34] On a bombed site in Kingsbury Road the four-storeyed blocks of Kerridge Court were built by the

[22] Smallshaw, *Highbury New Pk. Est.* 6.
[23] Para. based on ibid. 10–12.
[24] Above, communications.
[25] Below, pub. svces.; undenom. missions.
[26] *The Times*, 14 July 1874, 9f.
[27] Smallshaw, *Highbury New Pk. Est.* 11; below, Judaism.
[28] S.N.L. 60.5, Sales Partics. LC 1637.
[29] Below, educ., pub. schs.; photo. in *Changing Face of*

Newington Green, 44; Bacon, *Atlas of Lond.* (1886).
[30] Above, communications.
[31] *New Lond. Life and Labour*, iv, maps 1.
[32] *P.O. Dir. Lond.* (1934, 1942).
[33] G.L.C., Historic Bldgs. Div., almhos. files.
[34] *P.O. Dir. Lond.* (1947 and later edns.); *Changing Face of Newington Green*, 43–5; Islington L.B. *Homes for Islington* (1967), map.

L.C.C. between 1947 and 1952; they had 130 dwellings by 1967, when 2.4 a. nearby at Cutler's Terrace, Bishop's Grove, and Hawthorne Street were being filled with 77 dwellings by Islington council. In King Henry's Walk, the Dyers' and Tylers' sites were rebuilt with Tudor Court between 1952 and 1959 and the Bookbinders' site was taken for a Roman Catholic church in 1964. The G.L.C. had built a home for the handicapped on the south-west side of Tudor Court by 1975.[35]

A bombed site in Poet's Road was used for Masefield Court between 1952 and 1959, and New River Court was built nearby in Petherton Road.[36] On the opposite side of the road Petherton House was built between 1947 and 1952. Another bombed site, in Queen Margaret's Grove, was rebuilt with Wells Court between 1952 and 1959, and Queen Margaret Court between 1959 and 1964. The Mildmay conference centre was replaced by Besant Court between 1952 and 1959, with 70 dwellings in eleven-storeyed and five-storeyed blocks. The former Mildmay House and adjoining buildings were demolished and the seven-storeyed Hathersage House was built between 1964 and 1975 fronting Newington Green. Farther south near Ball's Pond Road several sites were cleared in the 1960s. In Newington Green Road several blocks of John Kennedy Court had been built by 1975, one on the west side north of the junction with Bingham Street, the others on the east side at the junction with Mildmay Avenue and Street. The rest of the area between those flats and Mildmay Park was also rebuilt, with a library and the thirteen-storeyed Haliday House. On the east side of Mildmay Park, Pennefather House and other flats were built in the late 1970s.

Although some smaller sites were also filled by new buildings, from the 1970s more effort was spent on rehabilitation. Housing action areas were declared to the east and west of Newington Green Road, where many of the three-storeyed terraces were converted to flats. The borough council drew up a plan for the Mildmay area after consultation with the residents.[37]

In 1983 most of the buildings at Newington Green were in commercial use, including the four 17th-century houses (nos. 52–5) on the west side that survived behind single-storeyed shop fronts. At the north-east corner nos. 31 and 32 form an early 19th-century three-storeyed pair, possibly part of a larger group. No. 30, two-storeyed with attics and stucco dressings, is joined to nos. 29 and 28, a three-storeyed pair with bows on two floors and pilasters, late 19th-century or a refronting of an earlier house. The Weavers Arms in Newington Green Road, probably rebuilt as a square detached house in the early 19th century, is set back from the road and has a single-storeyed addition in front. An older house survives in Matthias Road at no. 67, three-

storeyed and with a bow window on the first floor, possibly early 19th-century and derelict in 1981. South of Matthias Road only a few of the original houses remain in King Henry Street, whose south side is intact. Farther south, in King Henry's Walk there are two pairs of villas, with side porches and pilaster strips, similar to those demolished in Mildmay Road.

To the east the area around St. Jude Street was being partially demolished and partially rehabilitated c. 1980. The least altered street is Mildmay Grove, where all the houses are 19th-century, although many have lost their porticos. The area between Newington Green and Petherton roads is also substantially as built. South of the N.L.R. line very few 19th-century houses remain, except in small clusters in Newington Green Road or Mildmay Park, and there is a mixture of residential and commercial use. The houses around St. Paul's Place and Road are exceptional, belonging more with Canonbury than Newington Green. On the east side of Newington Green Road near the south end a few small houses, part of the late 18th-century crescent, were converted from shops back to dwellings c. 1980. There are still many shops and small businesses, notably motor works and showrooms.

SOCIAL AND CULTURAL ACTIVITIES.
Fifteen victuallers were licensed for Islington (excluding the Clerkenwell side of High Street) in 1553 and three for Holloway.[38] Many inns were copyholds and probably existed before the earliest records in the 16th century. The Red Lion, on the east side of High Street in Highbury manor, was mentioned in the 1540s and 1583,[39] and the George, on the west side in the manor of St. John's, Clerkenwell, in 1539.[40] The Fleur de Lis existed c. 1588, renamed the Cockatrice by 1618, on the east side of High Street.[41] The Talbot existed in 1570, the King's Head in 1594, and the Bear in 1599.[42] In the late 16th century High Street was lined with inns from the junction of Goswell Road and the St. John's Street road almost to the green, with six on the Clerkenwell side, one at the corner of the Back Road and Upper Street, and two on the east side.[43] The first building on the west side of High Street, on the site of the Angel, was shown as an inn in the late 16th century, although the first known reference was in 1614; it was formerly a messuage called Sheepcote and let by St. John's, Clerkenwell. Additional building was done c. 1638.[44] The freehold Horse's Head or Nag's Head stood near the southern end of Upper Street in 1601 and 1704.[45] The Bull's Head, renamed the Griffen by 1602 and the King's Arms by 1612, stood on the east side of High Street, together with the Rose and Crown, mentioned in 1602, 1612, and 1648.[46] The Castle stood on the south side of Cross

[35] Homes for Islington, 13; P.O. Dir. Lond. (1947 and later edns.).
[36] Para. based on P.O. Dir. Lond. (1947 and later edns.).
[37] Changing Face of Newington Green, 47; Islington L.B. Mildmay Local Area Study (1976).
[38] G.L.R.O., MR/LV1, mm. 7 7d., 11.
[39] P.R.O., C 1/1242/23; ibid. REQ 2/65/95.
[40] Ibid. SC 6/Hen. VIII/2402, m. 4.

[41] Ibid. REQ 2/100/32; B.L. Add. MS. 15556, f. 173.
[42] P.R.O., C 3/105/66; C 3/243/99; C 2/Eliz. I/P 8/38.
[43] B.L. Maps 186.h.2. (12).
[44] Ibid.; P.R.O., SC 6/Hen. VIII/2402, m. 4; ibid. C 142/343, no. 136; Cal. S.P. Dom. 1638–9, 262.
[45] Guildhall MSS. 12958/3, 4.
[46] Islington libr., MS. vol. of Abstract of deeds, p. 65; Guildhall MS. 3460/1; Cal. S.P. Dom. 1648–9, 174.

Street, near Upper Street, by 1610 and in 1683, but was demolished by 1788.[47] The Swan lay on the east side of High Street near another George by 1618 and in 1693.[48] The Saracen's Head also stood on that side by 1617, and was rebuilt or altered in 1618.[49] Other 17th-century inns included the Cock in 1614,[50] the Blue Boar in 1619 and again in 1632,[51] the Black Horse near the Nag's Head in 1630,[52] the Prince's Arms, the Bull, and the George on the east side of High Street in 1628 and 1632,[53] the latter forming part of the site of Rufford's Buildings by 1682,[54] the Maidenhead in 1638,[55] the Falcon, formerly the Dolphin, in 1651 and 1667, the Spread Eagle in 1651,[56] the Red Lion in 1653 and the White Lion in 1673, both on the west side of High Street,[57] the Crown in 1659,[58] the Holy Lamb in 1665,[59] the Bluebell, the Queen's Arms, and the Black Bear in 1668 and 1674,[60] the Three Cups in 1678,[61] the White Horse in Canonbury manor in 1691,[62] the White Horse, Lower Holloway, in 1700,[63] and the Eagle and Child, formerly the Green Dragon, in 1709.[64] The inn at Holloway mentioned by Samuel Pepys in 1661 as the Sign of the Woman with cakes in one hand and a pot of ale in the other was the Mother Red Cap, Upper Holloway,[65] which existed in the 1630s.[66]

Identification of later inns with those mentioned above is uncertain. In 1716 there were 56 alehouse keepers[67] and in 1721 inns included the Rosemary Branch, the King's Head, Upper Street, the Coach and Horses, Newington Green, and the Devil's or Duval's House, Tollington Lane.[68] In 1725 there were c. 100 inns and beershops in the parish selling spirits, especially gin. In addition to the many inns in Upper and Lower streets, there were the Rosemary Branch, three inns in Frog Lane, four near Newington Green, one at Kingsland, three near Stroud Green, one at the end of Hornsey Lane, two in Tollington Lane, two on Highgate Hill, three at Upper Holloway, two at Holloway, one at Ring Cross, five in Lower Holloway, and White Conduit house.[69] In 1765 there were 60 licensed victuallers, which excluded keepers of beershops.[70]

By the 18th century many inns had become resorts for Londoners, with tea-gardens in addition to earlier bowling greens and skittle gardens, and, in the 19th century, music and dancing. A few of them are described below.

White Conduit House tavern may have existed by the 1650s, when there was a bowling green near the Charterhouse conduit head.[71] Tea-gardens opened there in 1730, and had a circular fishpond, several tree-lined walks with boxes cut into the hedge, two large tea-rooms, and several smaller ones. It attracted respectable Londoners rather than fashionable society. Cricket was played in an adjoining field and in 1824 a bandstand was set up and bowls and archery were introduced. Balloon ascents took place from 1824 to 1844, and firework displays and fêtes were held there in what was advertised as the New Vauxhall. In 1828 the old house was replaced by the Apollo Room, for dancing, tea, and billiards. An outdoor orchestra and small theatre were added. The resort gradually declined in appeal and respectability, although variety acts continued to be presented until the building was demolished in 1849 and the site built over. A public house called the White Conduit House was built on part of the site.[72]

In 1704 the occupier of the sign of the Last near the Nag's Head, Upper Street, put out tables in an adjoining field and permitted archery and other pastimes, which drew a large clientele. By 1748 the Star and Garter, possibly the same inn, rented a skittle ground in the field.[73]

The King's Head tavern, Upper Street, opposite the parish church, was said to have been built c. 1543 and had a Dutch pin ground. The inn was replaced c. 1864 by one standing farther back.[74] In the late 1970s and 1980s it was widely known for theatrical performances at the back of the ground floor bar, some of which later transferred to West End theatres.

Highbury Barn tavern and tea-gardens originated as a small house selling cakes and ale c. 1740, becoming a tavern with tea-gardens under a Mr. Willoughby, who laid out a bowling green and trap and ball ground. The barn was used for assemblies and for large trade and society dinners in the 19th century. It developed into a dancing resort from 1856 and the proprietor Edward Giovannelli in 1865 built the Royal Alexandra theatre with a capacity of 1,900 on part of his grounds, together with a dining hall and dancing platform. Residents' opposition led to the licence being refused and its popularity quickly declined. The theatre closed in 1871 and the gardens were built over by 1883.[75]

Copenhagen House had become a tavern and tea-gardens by 1753, with skittles, Dutch pins, a fives court, and a cricket field. Set on a hillside with extensive views towards London, it was a popular place for Sunday strollers. It acquired a rougher reputation c. 1816, with bulldog fights

[47] P.R.O., C 2/Jas. I/N 2/62; C 8/282/7; G.L.R.O., P83/MRY1/157/1, 158/15.
[48] B.L. Add. MS. 15556, f. 173.
[49] Guildhall MS. 3460/2; P.R.O., C 3/326/47.
[50] G.L.R.O., P83/MRY1/133, f. 4.
[51] P.R.O., C 3/299/34; C 8/74/4.
[52] Guildhall MS. 12958/3.
[53] P.R.O., C 8/74/4.
[54] M.L.R. 1725/5/100; above, growth (Islington town).
[55] Cal. S.P. Dom. 1637-8, 324.
[56] P.R.O., C 8/185/102.
[57] Ibid. C 8/349/161.
[58] Ibid. C 7/452/94.
[59] Guildhall MS. 12958/3.
[60] P.R.O., C 7/492/44; C 5/575/102.
[61] Ibid. C 5/535/86.
[62] Ibid. C 7/329/59.
[63] Ibid. C 6/319/24.
[64] Ibid. C 10/518/2.
[65] Diary of Sam. Pepys, ed. Latham and Matthews, ii. 184.
[66] Above, growth, Upper Holloway.
[67] G.L.R.O., MR/LV3/3.
[68] Ibid. MR/LV3/90.
[69] Ibid. MR/LV4/40-62.
[70] Ibid. MR/LV8/40.
[71] Shown on Wenceslas Hollar's View of the New River Head.
[72] Guildhall MS. 474A; M. Cosh, Barnsbury, 2, 4; E. Beresford Chancellor, Pleasure Haunts of Lond. (1925), 375-8.
[73] Guildhall MSS. 12958/1, 4.
[74] Guildhall MS. 474A.
[75] Ibid.; D. Howard, Lond. Theatres (1970), 7; Chancellor, Pleasure Haunts, 380; below, plate 6.

and bull-baiting, but tea drinking revived from 1816 to 1830. It closed in 1853 to make way for the Metropolitan market.[76]

Other taverns noted for their tea-gardens in the 18th century included the Devil's House, Tollington Lane; the Mother Red Cap, Upper Holloway, with bowling green, quoits, and skittle ground; the Horse and Groom, Upper Holloway; the Crown, formerly the Angel and then Wilkes's Head, Holloway, with a skittle ground; Canonbury House tavern; Spring Gardens, Newington Green; and the Castle inn tea-gardens, Colebrooke Row.[77] The Rosemary Branch tavern, built 1783, had besides its concert room and tea-gardens a pond of nearly 1 a., where boats could be hired. The gardens were used for balloon ascents, rope dancing, and fireworks, and there was an equestrian theatre which burned down in 1853. The tavern was licensed for music and dancing until 1887, when it was closed because of safety requirements.[78]

In the mid 19th century many public houses were licensed for music and dancing, often with a small music hall on the first floor, but many had to close under safety regulations introduced in 1878.[79] Among the longest surviving were the Alma, 29 Alma Street, New North Road, licensed from 1856 to c. 1922, with two concert rooms holding 300, reduced to 100 after safety alterations;[80] the Offord Arms, no. 388 Caledonian Road, licensed 1854–90;[81] the Baxter Arms, no. 30 Baxter Road, licensed 1868–89;[82] the Island Queen, Noel Road, licensed 1857–89[83] and noteworthy in the 1970s for its Victorian interior adorned with two gigantic papier-maché representations of topical figures suspended from the ceiling. In all about 20 public houses and halls had music licenses in 1863, 24 in 1888.[84]

The best known of the music halls, evolving into a variety theatre, was the one usually known as Collins's music hall. It began as the Lansdowne tavern, in Paradise Row, Islington Green, where by 1846 the landlord put customers who wanted to sing, and later paid performers, in a separate room. The inn was bought in 1862 by Samuel Thomas Collins Vagg, a well known music hall artist, who opened it as the Lansdowne music hall with a capacity of 600 behind the public house. In 1897 the whole building was rebuilt as a theatre with a capacity of 1,800, an interior in the style of Louis XIV, and 10 bars. Called Islington Hippodrome during the First World War, it was a repertory theatre until 1932, a variety theatre following music-hall traditions from 1932 to 1937, and then a repertory theatre again. After the Second World War attendances dwindled and the quality of the shows declined. After a fire in 1958 the building was sold to

Andersons, timber merchants, and demolished in 1963. At the music hall's height between 92 and 162 acts were put on each evening and performers who started there included Marie Lloyd, George Robey, Harry Lauder, Harry Tate, George Formby, Vesta Tilley, Tommy Trinder, Gracie Fields, Tommy Handley, and Norman Wisdom.[85]

The Grand theatre on the east side of High Street opened in 1860 as the Philharmonic hall designed by Finch, Hill & Paraire with a capacity of 1,500. Alterations were made in 1870 with a new stage and promenade and the seating reduced to 758. From 1871 light French operas and can-can girls attracted a fashionable male audience. The hall burned down in 1882 and reopened in 1883 as the Grand theatre, designed by Frank Matcham. That burned down in 1887, was rebuilt in 1888 with a capacity of c. 3,000, and again burned in 1900, whereupon a fourth building was erected, also designed by Matcham. From 1908 it was called the Empire, Islington, from 1912 the Islington Palace, and from 1918 the Islington Empire. It was an ABC cinema from 1933, called the Empire with 1,029 seats, and closed in 1962.[86] The Victorian classical façade was finally demolished in 1981.

The Tavistock Repertory Co., which started as an amateur company in Tavistock Place, Bloomsbury, part of the Mary Ward Settlement, moved to Canonbury in 1952, converting King Edward's Hall into a theatre and using Canonbury tower as box office and rehearsal rooms. The professional company put on a full season of plays in 1983.[87]

The Little Angel theatre, Dagmar Passage, behind the parish church, was run by John Wright as a permanent puppet theatre from 1961, in the former temperance hall of Henry Ansell.[88]

Anna Scher's children's theatre, nos. 70–2 Barnsbury Road, began as a school drama club in 1968, expanded and in 1970 moved into a community hall, and in 1976 acquired its own theatre and office in Barnsbury Road. The theatre's aim was to develop children's artistic abilities through mime, dance, stage technique, and backstage work. Membership was limited to c. 500, with a waiting list of over 1,000 in 1978, divided into three groups for those aged 6 to 22 years, and a young professional group. The theatre also ran courses in drama.[89]

St. George's Elizabethan theatre, Tufnell Park Road, was founded in the former St. George's church in 1970 after a four-year campaign by George Murcell and others. The church's plan allowed Shakespeare's plays to be presented in an Elizabethan-style playhouse. It was also intended to give young actors a classical training and to

---

[76] Guildhall MS. 474A; Chancellor, *Pleasure Haunts*, 378–80.

[77] Guildhall MS. 474A; Chancellor, *Pleasure Haunts*, 374, 378; P.R.O., MAF 20/111; W. Wroth, *Lond. Pleasure Gdns.* (1896), 172.

[78] Guildhall MS. 474A; Howard, *Lond. Theatres*, 199; *Rep. of M.B.W. 1885*, H.C. 170, p. 437 (1886), lvii.

[79] Howard, *Lond. Theatres*, passim.

[80] Ibid. 11; *Rep. of M.B.W. 1885*, p. 434.

[81] Howard, *Lond. Theatres*, 161.

[82] Ibid. 20.   [83] Ibid. 121.

[84] G.L.R.O., MR/LMD/25/4; LMD 29/5A.

[85] Howard, *Lond. Theatres*, 49; TS. notes on Collins's Music Hall (1959, in Islington libr.); *Rep. of M.B.W. 1885*, p. 435; Zwart, *Islington: Hist. and Guide*, 104.

[86] Howard, *Lond. Theatres*, 121–2; *Rep. of M.B.W. 1883*, H.C. 186, pp. 357–8 (1884), lxviii; *1887*, H.C. 159, p. 629 (1888), lxxxvii; M. A. F. Webb, *Lond. Suburban Cinemas 1946–80* (priv. printed).

[87] Zwart, *Islington: Hist. and Guide*, 95; inf. from theatre co.

[88] Zwart, *Islington: Hist. and Guide*, 101, 103; below.

[89] Anna Scher Chldn.'s Theatre Ltd. *Ann. Rep.* (1978, 1979).

serve local needs, producing plays on the schools' syllabus.[90]

The Royal Agricultural Hall was built by a company formed by the Smithfield Club, which needed a better site for its annual show. The Agricultural Hall Co., formed in 1860, chose William Dixon's cattle layers in Liverpool Road, where the first hall, designed by Frederick Peck and covering nearly 2 a., was opened in 1862. The hall was 75 ft. high and its arched glass roof had a span of 125 ft., with wide galleries all round it. The Minor hall, behind it at the Upper Street end, was renamed St. Mary's hall in 1867. The pig hall was added on the south side of the entrance in 1867, land was bought at the corner of Upper and Berners streets in 1880 and used for further enlargements in 1881-2, and more room was made for implement manufacturers from 1883. Permission was granted in 1884 for 'Royal' to be used in the title. In 1895 the company bought land on the north side of St. Mary's hall and built a new Minor hall, for more pigs and sheep, and introduced slaughter classes. In 1907 the new Minor hall was extended and renamed Gilbey hall, in the early 1920s the main hall gallery was extended, and in 1925 a new entrance hall was built. The Methodist chapel in Barford Street was bought c. 1930 and made way for a new annexe in 1932, called New hall. Although the building was primarily for the annual Smithfield show, held in December, it was popular for many other purposes: dog shows, dairy shows, circuses, musical recitals, the North London Working Classes Industrial Exhibition (1864), grand balls, military tournaments, revivalist meetings, a bull-fight (stopped by the R.S.P.C.A.), six-day marathon walking, and cycling races. By the beginning of the 20th century it was the principal exhibition centre for London. St. Mary's hall was licensed as a music hall, as were Berner's hall and Prince's Saloon until 1888, also within the complex. St. Mary's hall was renamed the Empire music hall and refurbished internally in 1895. It was licensed as a cinema in 1908, was renamed Islington Palace in 1912, and was entirely rebuilt in 1914. By 1918 it was the Blue Hall cinema and in 1946 it became the Gaumont, seating 1,303, which closed in 1963 and was used for bingo until 1975. The rest of the Royal Agricultural Hall had been requisitioned during the Second World War and the G.P.O.'s Mount Pleasant sorting office moved there in 1943. The Smithfield show did not return there after the war and the overseas parcels office remained until 1971. Demolition was prevented because of the building's architectural importance, and Islington L.B. bought the site in 1976. Schemes for its use were under consideration in 1983.[91]

The Parkhurst theatre, no. 401 Holloway Road, was opened 1890 as a hall for 400 and was rebuilt

in 1898. It closed as a theatre in 1909 and was used as a cinema about that time. Fights at whist-drives in the early 1930s led to its closure. The Holloway Empire, no. 564 Holloway Road, was opened in 1899 by Moss Empires as the Empire Theatre of Varieties, designed by W. G. R. Sprague, with a capacity of 1,210. It was licensed as a cinema in 1923, closed in 1938, and remained empty until sold for demolition in 1953. The Marlborough theatre, no. 383 Holloway Road, was designed by Frank Matcham to hold 2,612 and opened in 1903. Plays and operettas were presented until 1916, when it was used for variety shows. It was a cinema by 1919, closed in 1957, and was demolished in 1962 to make way for Marlborough House, used by the Polytechnic of North London in 1983.[92] The Finsbury Park Empire, between St. Thomas's and Prah roads, was opened in 1910 by Moss Empires, with a capacity of c. 2,000. It closed in 1960 and was demolished.[93]

The Screen-on-the-Green cinema, no. 83 Upper Street, opened as the Picture Theatre in 1911 and closed in 1914. It reopened in 1915 as the Empress and closed in 1950, but opened again as the Rex in 1951, when it seated 514. It closed in 1970 and was reopened as the Screen-on-the-Green with 293 seats, an independent club cinema, with showings of new and old films. The Carlton, no. 161 Essex Road, opened in 1930 with an unusual neo-Egyptian front and seated 2,248. It was called the ABC cinema in 1962 and closed in 1972, becoming a Mecca Bingo theatre.[94] The Odeon cinema, Upper Street, seating 1,138, occupied the former vestry hall in 1946 until it closed in 1961. The site became a petrol station.[95] The Angel cinema, no. 7 High Street, seated 1,457 and was renamed the Odeon in 1963. It was derelict in 1980. The Victoria, an independent cinema at nos. 272-80 New North Road, seated 731 and closed in 1957.[96] The Imperial Picture Theatre was built at no. 2 Holloway Road in 1913, renamed Highbury Imperial Picture Theatre by 1924, and Highbury Picture Theatre by 1931. It closed in 1959 and was replaced by a petrol station.[97] The Coronet cinema, at the corner of Holloway and Loraine roads, was called the Savoy in 1947 and became the ABC between 1964 and 1975. It closed in 1983.[98] The Gaumont cinema, at the corner of Holloway and Tufnell Park roads, became the Odeon between 1959 and 1964,[99] and was still presenting general release films in 1983.

The Islington Literary and Scientific Society was established in 1833 and first met in Mr. Edgeworth's academy, Upper Street. Its object was to spread knowledge through lectures, discussions, and experiments, politics and theology being forbidden. A building was erected in 1837 in Wellington (later Almeida) Street, designed by

90 St. George's Elizabethan Theatre Ltd. *Manifesto* (TS. 1970, in Islington libr.); *Consecration of St. Geo.'s Ch.* (booklet 1975).
91 E. Powell, *Hist. of Smithfield Club* (1902), 10-12, 17-18, 21, 24, 45; *Ind. Mons. Gtr. Lond.* (1969), 36; E. Ledster, *Royal Agric. Hall* ([c. 1976] in Islington libr.); Webb, *Lond. Sub. Cinemas*; Howard, *Lond. Theatres*, 123; *Rep. of M.B.W. 1888*, H.C. 326, p. 820 (1889), lxvi; inf. from Islington L.B. and Mr. J. C. Connell.
92 Howard, *Lond. Theatres*, 116, 149, 171; notes on exhibi-

tion 'Holloway in Pictures', Islington libr.; Pevsner, *Lond.* ii. 238; inf. from Mr. J. C. Connell.
93 Howard, *Lond. Theatres*, 84.
94 Webb, *Lond. Sub. Cinemas*; inf. from Mr. J. C. Connell.
95 Ibid.; Islington M.B. *Illus. Guide to Hsg. and Local Govt. Exhib.* (1946), 7.
96 Webb, *Lond. Sub. Cinemas*.
97 Inf. from Mr. J. C. Connell.
98 Ibid.; *P.O. Dir. Lond.* (1947 and later edns.).
99 *P.O. Dir. Lond.* (1959 and later edns.).

Roumieu & Gough in a Grecian style and faced in Roman cement. It included a library, with 3,300 volumes in 1839, reading room, museum, laboratory, and lecture theatre seating 500. Membership was 430 in 1839 and 561 in 1841, and the subscription was 2 guineas a year. The library was sold off in 1872 and the building sold or leased in 1874 to the Wellington Club, which occupied it until 1886.[1] In 1885 the hall was used for concerts, balls, and public meetings.[2] The Salvation Army bought the building in 1890, renamed it Wellington Castle barracks, and remained there until 1955.[3] After serving as a factory and showroom for Beck's British Carnival Novelties for a few years from 1956, it remained empty until in 1978 a campaign began to turn it into a theatre. A public appeal was launched in 1981 and a festival of avant-garde theatre and music was held there and at other Islington venues in 1982. The aim was ultimately to present a full nine-month season of experimental theatre, including productions from abroad.[4]

The Athenaeum, Camden Road, was built in 1871 at the junction of Camden and Parkhurst roads, after appeals for a literary and scientific institution for the area. The building of brick and terracotta was designd by F. R. Meeson in an Italianate style. It contained meeting halls, libraries, and a hall for theatrical and musical performances, seating 600. It was later taken over by Beale's, the caterers, as the Athenaeum hall. In 1912 and 1915 it housed an orchestral society and music teachers, and was used for concerts, and after the Second World War rehearsals were held there by Donald Wolfit's Advance Players Association. In 1955 the building was demolished and the site used for a petrol station.[5]

The Highbury Athenaeum, no. 96A Highbury New Park, was opened in 1882 as a literary or scientific club, and the building was also licensed for music 1882-9, having a concert hall on the ground floor holding 1,060, and a music hall above.[6] It closed c. 1920, and the building was acquired by the Rank film company in the late 1930s to make second features to train young directors and actors. Associated with it was a charm school for young actresses. The studio closed c. 1950,[7] and the building was taken over to make I.T.V. programmes for a few years. It was demolished in 1963 and replaced by flats.

The Islington Athenaeum was opened at no. 107 Upper Street in 1847 to provide weekly winter lectures on religion, history, and natural sciences.[8] It failed after c. 6 years and the property was sold in 1854. The building was licensed 1852-60 for music as Baker's Rooms.[9]

Myddelton hall, at the corner of Upper and Wellington streets, was founded in 1875 and used for bazaars and other local functions.[10]

The Bishop Wilson Memorial hall was opened on the site of Islington chapel in Church Street by 1886. It was replaced by a new memorial hall on the north side of the churchyard in 1890,[11] which in turn was replaced by a new hall and community centre nearby in 1975-7.[12]

The fields around Copenhagen House were used for meetings of the London Corresponding Society from 1795 when Robert Orchard, a member of the society, was the inn's landlord. Meetings were said to draw as many as 40,000, and one held in November 1795 attended by John Gale Jones, democratic politician and surgeon, was caricatured by Gillray.[13] The fields were used again in 1834, for a mass rally of trades unionists in support of the Tolpuddle martyrs.[14]

In 1792 Alexander Aubert was chairman of a society to suppress sedition, and in 1797 he was appointed lieutenant-colonel commandant of the new Loyal Islington Volunteers. The force, one regiment of infantry and one of cavalry commanded by Capt. J. P. Anderdon, attracted gentlemen from surrounding parishes and soon had over 300 members. A dispute between some officers and Aubert led to its being disbanded in 1801.[15] In 1803 fresh threats of invasion led to the formation of a volunteer corps of c. 300, led by Mr. Wheelwright of Highbury and drilled by Mr. Dickson in Cooks field, Upper Street. It was disbanded in 1806 because of insufficient funds.[16]

The 1st City of London Volunteer Engineers, formed in 1861, had drill rooms at Bird's Buildings, Islington Green (3rd Company), a house in Copenhagen Street in 1869 for the 4th Company, no. 68 Colebrooke Row for the 5th Company, and rooms in Theberton Street for the 6th Company, also in 1869. In 1877 their headquarters moved from the Barbican to no. 68 Colebrooke Row. In 1881 the corps numbered 761, and no. 2 Barnsbury Park, with a large garden, was rented as headquarters and drill rooms for all the companies. In 1897 no. 1 Barnsbury Road, formerly Barnsbury Park Collegiate School, was also rented. The corps became part of the Territorial Association in 1908. In 1913 nos. 1 and 2 Barnsbury Park were demolished and a new headquarters built at the Offord Road end of the site. The units moved to Finchley in 1961.[17]

Residents formed the Islington Soup Society in 1799 to sell cheap food and coal to the poor. A committee of 65 was to manage a shop and solicit subscriptions, a shed in Cadds Row was offered as a soup kitchen, and £350 was collected in three days. At the end of 1801 further collection was thought unnecessary and in 1805 the society was

[1] Islington Antiquarian and Historical Soc. paper read 1933 (in Islington libr.); T. Claxton, *Hints to Mechanics* (1839), 223; G.L.R.O., Historic Bldgs. Div., ISL 1.
[2] *Rep. of M.B.W. 1885*, H.C. 170, p. 438 (1886), lvii.
[3] G.L.R.O., Historic Bldgs. Div., ISL 1.
[4] *New Standard*, 13 May 1981; *Observer*, 23 May 1982.
[5] Pevsner, *Lond*. ii. 239; docs. found in fndn. stone of Athenaeum, and Note on its Hist., in Islington libr.; Howard, *Lond. Theatres*, 16.
[6] Para. based on notes by K. Sugden in Islington Archaeology & Hist. Soc. newsletter (Nov. 1981); *Rep. of M.B.W. 1882*, H.C. 169, p. 535 (1883), lix; Howard, *Lond. Theatres*, 16.
[7] A. Wood, *Mr. Rank* (1952), 172, 263.

[8] Athenaeum, 1st Ann. Rep. 1848, in Islington libr.
[9] Howard, *Lond. Theatres*, 17.
[10] *Holloway and Islington Jnl*. 15 Dec. 1972.
[11] Bacon, *Atlas of Lond*. (1886); G.L.R.O., P83/MRY1/110; *D.N.B.* s.v. D. Wilson.
[12] Inf. on St. Mary's ch., in Islington libr.
[13] Chancellor, *Pleasure Haunts*, 378-80; *D.N.B.* s.v. J. G. Jones.
[14] Islington M.B. *Illus. Guide to Hsg. and Local Govt. Exhib.* (1946), 6.
[15] Nelson, *Islington* (1829), 142-4.
[16] Ibid. 113, 144-5.
[17] *Hist. of 353 (Lond.) Medium Regt. R.A. (T.A.) 1861-1961* (in Islington libr.).

wound up.[18] The Islington Friendly Clothing Society was formed in 1816 to enable the poor to buy clothes at half the cost of the materials. Subscribers increased rapidly in 1818, a depository was formed at no. 8 Barnsbury Street, and the society may still have been running in 1854.[19] The Female Association was instituted in 1816 for visiting and relieving sick poor in their homes, in association with Islington chapel. In 1819 relief was recommended for 51 cases, consisting of 178 individuals.[20] The Charity Organisation Society, Islington committee, was formed c. 1868 to help the sick poor, and provide bedding and clothes for large families. The office was at no. 17 Compton Terrace, and a second was opened at no. 365 Camden Road. In 1946 it became known as the Family Welfare Organisation, to help those whose family life was endangered by hardship. In the 1960s the organization was running local Citizens' Advice Bureaux.[21]

A Working Man's Institute savings bank was started in 1858 and continued to 1873 or later.[22]

Henry Ansell purchased a hall in Church Passage, Cross Street, before 1910 and founded the first temperance society in Islington, called the Islington Working Men's Total Abstinence Society.[23] The hall became the Little Angel puppet theatre in 1961.[24]

The Caxton House settlement was started in 1944 to relieve the poverty of the Pooles Park area. The Presbyterian mission hall at no. 59 Andover Road was rented as club rooms, youth clubs were started, and a settlement house was opened at no. 112 Fonthill Road.[25] The Caxton House community centre was built in St. John's Way in 1976.[26]

The Islington Bus Co. was started in 1972 in Manor Gardens as a charity funded through the council and the I.L.E.A. to help local groups. It came to support c. 300 groups, giving regular help with matters such as printing, and in 1976–7 moved to Palmer Place. The organization ran a brightly painted double-decker bus that was used during weekdays as a play-school and could be booked in the evenings by any Islington group for transport, or for a meeting, crèche, or exhibition. Toys and equipment were also provided on loan.[27]

The 'Angel of Islington', a canal boat based at City Road basin, was financed by Islington L.B., the I.L.E.A., and local fund-raising, and was operated by Islington Narrow Boat Association as a charity. Schools and local groups could hire it for day or week-end cruises.[28]

Londoners' rights to use Finsbury fields for archery and other sports appear to have extended to fields in the south-east of Islington, where the Artillery Company of London re-established its archery marks in the 1780s.[29] The Royal Toxophilite Society, established 1780, was at Highbury 1820–5.[30] Fields around Canonbury were popular for dog-fighting and duck-hunting in the 1820s.[31]

The first Islington cricket club held matches in a field near White Conduit House c. 1780. In the early 19th century the Albion cricket field was well known and the Albion club played there until 1834, when it moved to Copenhagen House.[32] The Middlesex County cricket team had its first permanent ground at Islington in 1863 but moved to Lillie Bridge in 1869.[33]

Woolwich Arsenal F.C. moved to Highbury in 1913, renting part of the grounds of St. John's Theological College. The east side of the ground had covered seats, but the rest was uncovered and for standing only, with a huge bank on the west, terraced to the top and called Spion Kop, until a new west stand with an imposing entrance was built in the 1930s. The team was voted into the First Division for the 1919–20 season and, under Herbert Chapman as manager, achieved national standing between 1925 and 1934. It came top of the league three times and won the F.A. Cup in 1929–30, and Chapman succeeded in having the name of the nearby Underground station changed from Gillespie Road to Arsenal. In the 45 seasons between 1919 and 1971 Arsenal won the League eight times and the F.A. Cup four times. Although their most successful period was the 1930s, their outstanding achievement was in 1970–1 when they became only the second team in the 20th century to win both the League and the F.A. Cup, and in 1972 they received the freedom of Islington.[34]

Sports facilities were greatly improved in 1973 with the building of the Michael Sobell Sports Centre, Hornsey Road, using £1,100,000 given by Sir Michael Sobell, a retired industrialist and member of the Variety Club, for a sports and social centre in a deprived area of London. Designed by W. D. Laming of R. Seifert & Partners, the several halls cater for about 30 activities, including archery, ski practice, and smallbore rifle and pistol shooting. The main arena has retractable seating for 1,800 spectators and there is also a hall for health classes, ballet practice, and drama, besides a discothéque, ice rink, restaurant, bar, and meeting rooms.[35]

Highbury Terrace had its own residents' association between 1812 and 1834.[36] The Islington and North London Art Union was formed in 1842, the subscribers drawing lots for works of art which had been displayed at the Royal Academy, British Institute, or Society of British Artists during the year. The committee decided on the number and value of the paintings when

[18] Islington libr., Islington Soup Soc. min. bk.
[19] Lewis, *Islington As It Was*, 85; *Rep. and Reg. of Islington Friendly Clothing Soc.* (1819, in Islington libr.).
[20] *Third Rep. of the Female Assoc.* (in Islington libr.).
[21] Charity Organisation Soc. *Ann. Rep.* (1943–4 and later edns., in Islington libr.).
[22] G.L.R.O., P83/MRY1/364, 368.
[23] *Life and Hist. of Hen. Ansell* [pamphlet c. 1910], in Islington libr. [24] Above.
[25] Caxton Ho. *Ann. Rep.* (1944, 1945).
[26] C. McKean and T. Jestico, *Guide to Mod. Bldgs. in Lond.* (1976), 79.

[27] Islington Bus Co. *Ann. Rep.* (1976–7, 1979–80).
[28] 'Angel of Islington', notes in Islington libr.
[29] Nelson, *Islington* (1829), 20–8; P.R.O., C 8/86/255.
[30] *V.C.H. Mdx.* ii. 286.
[31] Islington libr., Lamp and Watch min. bk. 1806–24.
[32] Guildhall MS. 474A.
[33] *V.C.H. Mdx.* ii. 270.
[34] D. Brown, *Arsenal Story* (1972), 24, 29, 31, 33, 130–3; Islington L.B. *Official Guide 1977–8*, 36.
[35] Islington L.B. *Official Guide 1977–8*, 36; McKean and Jestico, *Guide to Mod. Bldgs. in Lond.* 80.
[36] Min. bk. in Islington libr.

the number of ½-guinea subscriptions were known. In the first year there were 20 prizes valued from 3 guineas to £50.[37]

Freemasons set up an Islington Lodge, no. 1471, in Florence Street school rooms in 1874, and later that year at the Cock tavern, Highbury. The lodge had 85 members during its first decade. In 1905 the meetings were moved to the Abercorn Rooms, Bishopsgate.[38]

The Highbury Microscopical and Scientific Society met from 1880 until 1887.[39] The Holly Park Protection Association existed from 1878 to 1890.[40] The Highbury Quadrant Literary Association was founded by the 1870s and survived in 1910–11, presenting varied lectures, preceded by organ recitals, twice or thrice a month in winter.[41] The Islington Camera Club was founded in 1947, meeting at Manor Gardens branch library, and gathered 100 members in its early years. It declined from 1961 but survived in 1969.[42]

Among periodicals produced in the parish were the *Islington Popular Library of Religious Knowledge*, published weekly in 1832; the *Islington Magazine* or *Holloway, Highgate, Highbury and Canonbury Journal of Literature, Science and Fine Arts*, published monthly in 1838; the *Islington Athenaeum*, a weekly literary periodical in 1853; the *North London Magazine*, published monthly in 1866; *Momus or The Islington Journal of Wit, Humour, and Sentiment*, published monthly in 1858; the *Islington*, a monthly journal published 1876–9; and the *Canonbury Amateur Magazine*, published monthly in 1884. The *Islington, Highbury, and Holloway General Advertiser* was published monthly by F. A. Ford 1850–4 and offered free of charge.[43]

Of the local newspapers that survived for 12 months or more, the earliest was also the longest lived. The *Islington Gazette* first appeared on 20 September 1856, founded by William Trounce who also founded the *Islington Directory* in 1852. It appeared twice a week from 1865, but was published five days a week in 1881 owing to demand.[44] In 1901 it was renamed the *Islington Daily Gazette & North London Tribune* and in 1918 the *Daily Gazette*, reverting to the *Islington Gazette* in 1926. The *Islington Times* was started in 1857, renamed the *Islington Times and Finchley, Highgate, Hornsey and Holloway Herald* in 1871, and continued as the *Islington Times and Finsbury Advertiser* 1872–4. The *North London News* was published weekly from 1860 to 1865 and continued as the *North London News & Borough of Finsbury Gazette* until 1895. The *Canonbury & Highbury Advertiser* was published from c. 1872 until 1888, when it was continued as the *Weekly Recorder*, published from Hackney. The *Holloway Press* began in 1872, was renamed the *North Metropolitan and Holloway Press* in 1875, and became the *Holloway Press* in 1880, the *Islington*

& Holloway Press in 1923, and the *North London Press* from 1942. Separate editions for Islington and Camden were published 1948–9 and 1964–71, after which the paper was continued as both the *Holloway & Islington Journal* and the *Camden Journal*, the former being discontinued in 1974. The *Islington News* started in 1877 and was renamed the *Islington News and Hornsey Gazette* in 1897, continuing until 1919. The *Holloway Advertizer* was published 1822–87. The *Arrow* was published monthly from 1887, being renamed the *Northern Arrow* in 1888; it was discontinued in 1890. The *Northern Light and Islington Star* was published from 1889, renamed the *Northern Light* from 1891 and ceasing in 1893. The *Londoner (North Islington Edition)* was published from 1894 and continued in 1896 as the *(Islington) Londoner* until 1897, when it was renamed the *Londoner—Edition for Islington*, but it ceased publication that year. The *Islington Post* was started in 1899 and continued at least to 1908. The *Islington Guardian & North London Observer* was started a few years before 1914, and in 1919 was renamed the *Islington Guardian, North London Observer and Weekly News and Chronicle* until 1924 when it became the *Islington Guardian & Hackney News, North London Observer and Weekly News and Chronicle*. In 1975 it was incorporated with *Islington Chronicle and Finsbury Weekly News*. The *North London Advertizer* was published from 1908 at least to 1910.[45]

MANORS. The manor of *BARNSBURY*, earlier called *BERNERSBURY* or *ISELDON BERNERS*, originated in 5 hides held by Hugh de Berners from the bishop of London in 1086, which before 1066 had been equally divided between Sired, canon of St. Paul's, and the canons as demesne.[46] Although the 5 hides were said to be in the vill of Stepney, they were clearly in Islington, where lords called Ralph de Berners made grants before 1176 and 1253[47] and where tenants were suitors of the Stepney view of frankpledge in the 14th century.[48] Sir William Berners held lands in Islington before 1220, when his widow Beatrice claimed from William's son Sir Ralph Berners, of Berners Roding (Essex), a third of her husband's free lands in Islington,[49] and Sir Ralph was summoned to acquit the service which William had owed the bishop for a free tenement there.[50] It was probably his son Sir Ralph who held ½ knight's fee in Islington in 1242–3.[51] The latter's son, also Sir Ralph de Berners (d. 1297), of West Horsley (Surr.), custodian of the Tower of London, held at his death the manor of Iseldon of the bishop for ½ knight's fee, rent, and suit at the bishop's three-weekly court at Bishop's Stortford Castle. The manor consisted of a

[37] Rep. in Islington libr.
[38] A. E. Hunt and W. N. Edwards, *Short Hist. of Islington Lodge No. 1471* [1974], 5, 12, 20, 31.
[39] Min. bk. in Islington libr.
[40] Min. bk. in Islington libr.
[41] Programme of lectures in Islington libr.
[42] R. Whyte, 'Islington Camera Club: First Twenty-One Yrs.' (TS. 1969, in Islington libr.).
[43] Issues in Islington libr.
[44] *Islington Gaz.* 21 Sept. 1956.
[45] B.L. newspaper index.
[46] *V.C.H. Mdx.* i. 120.
[47] E. A. Webb, *Rec. of St. Barts., Smithfield* (1921), i. 342.
[48] P.R.O., SC 2/191/60, m. 16.
[49] P.R.O., CP 25(1)/282/8, no. 8. Inf. on Berners fam. from *Chron. Jocelin de Brakelonda* (Camd. Soc. [1st ser.]), 144–5; Manning and Bray, *Surr.* iii. 37.
[50] *Cur. Reg. R.* viii. 299.   [51] *Bk. of Fees*, ii. 899.

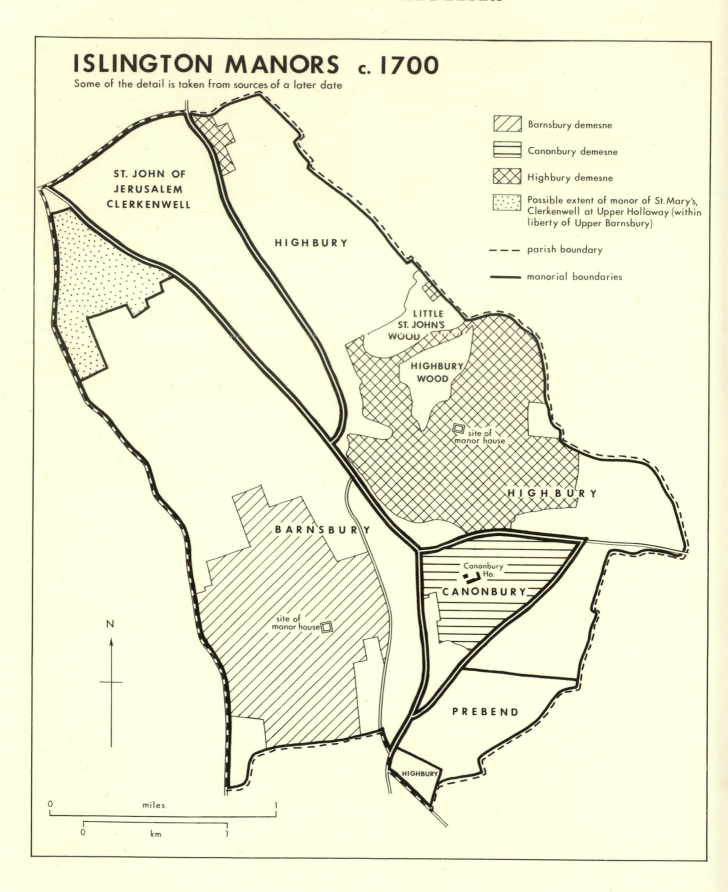

ISLINGTON MANORS c. 1700

Some of the detail is taken from sources of a later date

Barnsbury demesne

Canonbury demesne

Highbury demesne

Possible extent of manor of St. Mary's, Clerkenwell at Upper Holloway (within liberty of Upper Barnsbury)

parish boundary

manorial boundaries

ST. JOHN OF JERUSALEM CLERKENWELL

HIGHBURY

LITTLE ST. JOHN'S WOOD

HIGHBURY WOOD

site of manor house

HIGHBURY

BARNSBURY

Canonbury Ho.

CANONBURY

site of manor house

N

PREBEND

HIGHBURY

0   miles   1

0   km   1

capital messuage, 185 a., rents of assize from free tenants, a foreign rent of a pair of gilt spurs from the tenement of Sir Thomas de Meuse of East Smithfield, rents and works from 48 customary tenants, and perquisites of court.[52] The manor descended to Sir Ralph's son Sir Edmund and in 1303 was settled on him and his wife Amice.[53] Edmund still held the $\frac{1}{2}$ knight's fee in 1316;[54] on the death of Amice it descended to Edmund's son John (d. c. 1341).[55] By 1353 John's son Sir John Berners (d. 1361) held the fee, formerly held by his mother Elizabeth.[56]

After Sir John's death John Chichester, alderman of London, was in possession for eight years, followed by John de Kingsford. Both held by unknown title, while John Berners's son James was a minor,[57] and in 1375 the manor was taken into the king's hands until it could be rightly disposed of.[58] Sir James Berners was in possession by 1386 but forfeited the manor on his impeachment in 1388.[59] The manor, then consisting of a ruined messuage, 243 a., rents, and works,[60] was granted in 1389 to John Innocent and John Nottingham, the king's clerks, for ten years, paying 20 marks a year.[61] In 1391, however, it was found that the wardship of James's son and heir Richard should go to the bishop, reserving to the Crown the fee simple when the entail should end.[62] In 1405–6 the manor, said to be held in chief, was settled on Richard Berners (d. 1412) and his wife Isabel.[63] Richard's widow Philippa (d. 1421) and her husband Sir Thomas Lewknor held a third of the manor as her dower, while the bishop held the rest as guardian of Margery, Richard's daughter and heir,[64] although there was confusion over who was overlord and the two-thirds were granted temporarily to the king's nominees in 1418 with other Berners lands. In 1421 the whole estate passed to Margery, by then wife of John Ferriby, and it was confirmed that it was not held of the king.[65]

In 1428 the $\frac{1}{2}$ knight's fee was held by John Ferriby,[66] and Margery and John conveyed the manor to feoffees in 1435.[67] After Ferriby died without issue in 1441, Margery married Sir John Bourchier, Lord Berners (d. 1474), and the manor was settled on their heirs.[68] At Margery's death in 1475 it passed to her grandson John Bourchier, Lord Berners (d. 1533),[69] who in 1502 sold it to Sir Reynold Bray (d. 1503).[70] Bray left his lands to his nephew Edmund Bray,[71] but in a settle-

ment of 1510 Barnsbury was among lands allotted to Sir Reynold's niece Margery (d. 1539), wife of Sir William (later Lord) Sandys.[72] In 1539 Lord Sandys and his son Thomas, Margery's heir, sold the manor, valued at £30 p.a., to Robert Fowler, vice-treasurer of Calais,[73] whose cousin and heir William Fowler of Steeping Parva (Lincs.) in 1542 sold it to Thomas Fowler, water-bailiff of Calais and merchant of the Staple.[74] Thomas (d. 1556) left the manor to his son Edmund but he left to his widow Alice in addition to her dower his house at Islington[75] for life and any profits from the manor beyond £60 a year granted to Edmund in 1552.[76] Alice was alive in 1560, when Edmund died leaving his infant son Thomas as heir.[77] Thomas (Kt. 1603, d. 1625) settled the manor, except for three parcels, on his widow Dorothy for life, with remainder to his son Sir Thomas (Kt. 1603, Bt. 1628, d. 1656).[78]

In 1646 Sir Thomas purchased from parliament the bishop's interest in the manor and $\frac{1}{2}$ knight's fee, which included a small rent, fines, wards, and the rights to the courts leet and view of frankpledge.[79] The rights do not seem to have reverted to the bishop in 1660. In 1656 the manor descended to his eldest daughter Sarah, widow of Sir Thomas Fisher.[80] After her death c. 1666 the manor passed to her eldest son Sir Thomas Fisher, Bt. (d. 1670), to his son Sir Thomas (d. 1671), and then to Sarah's second son Sir Richard Fisher, Bt. (d. 1707).[81] As Richard had no children his lands passed to Sir Thomas Halton, Bt. (d. 1726), son of his sister Ursula, and then to Sir Thomas's son Sir William (d. 1754),[82] who left the manor in trust for his godson and kinsman William Tufnell.[83] William, who took the surname Jolliffe on inheriting another estate,[84] was succeeded in 1797 by his brother George Tufnell, M.P. (d. 1798), and then by George's eldest son William (d. 1809).[85] Part of the demesne was settled on William's wife Mary Carleton in 1804.[86] William's eldest son the politician Henry Tufnell died in 1854 leaving an infant son Henry Archibald Tufnell (d. 1898).[87] H. A. Tufnell was succeeded by Lieut.-Col. Edward Tufnell (d. 1909), whose widow Ellen Bertha retained a life tenancy in part of the manor[88] and whose trustees were the lords in 1925, when the court books ended.[89] Descent of the manor is not traced after 1925.

The manor house was mentioned in 1297 and

[52] P.R.O., C 133/79, no. 10.
[53] Cal. Pat. 1388–92, 443.
[54] P.R.O., E 315/45, no. 77.
[55] Cal. Pat. 1388–92, 443, wrongly naming John as Ralph.
[56] Feud. Aids, iii. 376, 383.
[57] Cal. Inq. p.m. xiv, pp. 255–6.
[58] Cal. Fine R. 1369–77, 318.
[59] Cal. Inq. Misc. v, p. 15; Cal. Pat. 1385–9, 548; M. McKisack, Fourteenth Cent. (1959), 458.
[60] Cal. Inq. Misc. v, pp. 15–16.
[61] Cal. Fine R. 1383–91, 283.
[62] Cal. Pat. 1388–92, 443; Cal. Close, 1389–92, 405–7.
[63] P.R.O., CP 25(1)/290/60, no. 99.
[64] Ibid. C 138/25, no. 8.
[65] Cal. Close, 1419–22, 2, 240; P.R.O., C 138/56, no. 24.
[66] Feud. Aids, iii. 383, wrongly naming John as Thomas.
[67] P.R.O., CP 25(1)/292/68, no. 176.
[68] Ibid. CP 25(1)/293/70, no. 264.
[69] Complete Peerage, ii. 153.
[70] Cal. Close, 1500–1509, 80–1; P.R.O., CP 25(1)/152/101, no. 83.

[71] N. H. Nicolas, Testamenta Vetusta, ii. 447.
[72] P.R.O., CP 25(2)/51/358/Mich. 2 Hen. VIII; Complete Peerage, xi. 441.
[73] P.R.O., C 54/421, no. 52.
[74] Herald and Genealogist, vii. 559; P.R.O., CP 25(2)/27/184/East. 34 Hen. VIII. Relationship of Thos. and Wm. unknown.   [75] Below, other est.
[76] P.R.O., PROB 11/38 (P.C.C. 10 Ketchyn); ibid. C 142/127, no. 21.   [77] Ibid. C 43/6, no. 64; C 142/127, no. 21.
[78] Ibid. CP 25(2)/324/20 Jas. I. Mich.; C 142/429, no. 114.
[79] G.L.R.O., M83/BAR/135.
[80] Herald and Genealogist, vii. 560; G.E.C. Baronetage, ii. 30.   [81] G.E.C. Baronetage, ii. 30–1.
[82] Ibid. ii. 31 n., 199.   [83] G.L.R.O., M83/BAR/124.
[84] F. W. Steer, Sam. Tufnell of Langleys, 1682–1759, 52.
[85] Burke, Commoners, ii. 183.
[86] G.L.R.O., M83/BAR/139.
[87] P.R.O., MAF 20/12, no. 175, copy of Tufnell's Estate Act, 1862; D.N.B.
[88] P.R.O., MAF 9/163, no. 23713.
[89] G.L.R.O., M83/BAR/20.

was ruinous in 1388.[90] There is no evidence that the lords lived in the parish before Thomas Fowler (d. 1556):[91] the Fowler and Fisher families had mansions near Lower Street which were copyholds of other manors.[92] The manor house probably occupied the moated site that lay on what was later the west side of Barnsbury Square until the 1820s, and was sold with other demesne in the 17th century. Sales of demesne were made in the 1550s and between 1654 and 1678,[93] which probably accounted for all the original demesne. The lord's land, however, was increased by a freehold estate called the Brewhouse and some copyhold that came to the Fishers in the early 17th century,[94] and was thereafter known as Barnsbury demesne. It consisted of a messuage and c. 50 a. in 1637,[95] with 55 a. of copyhold,[96] but was 136 a. in 1755,[97] possibly through additions of copyhold, and c. 120 a. in 1822 and 1862, when Private Acts enabled the Tufnell trustees to make building leases;[98] it forms the site of Tufnell Park. The estate included a moat on the south side of Holloway Road near the later Tufnell Park Road, which was let to John Warminger, carpenter, in 1725 with the messuage which Warminger had recently built within the moat.[99] That house, or another adjoining the moat, was known as the manor farm or house in the 19th century and formed part of the demesne farm in 1804, 1822, and 1862. The house adjoining the moat was occupied by Manor House school in 1851.[1]

The manor of *CANONBURY* originated in property given to the prior and convent of St. Bartholomew, Smithfield. Ralph de Berners granted 10s. rent in Islington before 1176 and a later Ralph granted a manor out of his land there, first mentioned in 1253.[2] In 1306 the estate of c. 277 a. was called the manor of Iseldon, valued at £7 19s. 8½d. and held of Sir Edmund de Berners for ⅛ knight's fee and 4s., and paying 2s. 9¾d. to the overlord, the bishop of London. The manor consisted of demesne, one free tenant, 18 customary holdings, and a mill.[3] In addition in 1334 Henry the Hayward of West Smithfield and Roger Creton, clerk, were licensed to grant a house and 110 a. in Islington and Kentish Town,[4] which was probably the estate known as the manor of Cutlers.[5] In 1349 Edmund of Grimsby was licensed to give land which included 3 a. in Islington.[6]

After the Dissolution Canonbury manor[7] with Cutlers was granted in fee to Thomas Cromwell,

earl of Essex, the lessee by 1529, and it escheated on his attainder in 1540.[8] An annuity of £20 from the manor was granted to Anne of Cleves in 1541, and in 1547 the lands and lordship of Canonbury, excluding some demesne, were granted to John Dudley, Lord Lisle, later duke of Northumberland.[9] He exchanged the manor with the king in 1550 but in another exchange in 1552 received the manor house and part of the demesne,[10] which returned to the Crown on his attainder in 1553. Queen Mary granted the house and demesne for life in 1553 to Sir David Brooke and his wife Catherine, formerly the queen's wet-nurse, but in 1557 granted the manor and the reversion of the house and demesne to Thomas, Lord Wentworth, to hold in chief as $\frac{1}{40}$ knight's fee.[11] Wentworth sold Canonbury manor and Cutlers to John Spencer, later lord mayor, in 1570.[12] Spencer (Kt. 1595, d. 1610) was succeeded by his daughter Elizabeth, wife of William, Lord Compton, later earl of Northampton (d. 1630).[13] Lady Northampton died in possession in 1632 and was succeeded by her son Spencer Compton, earl of Northampton (d. 1643),[14] a royalist[15] whose sequestered estates were among those charged with payments to the Elector Palatine in 1645. Spencer's son James, earl of Northampton (d. 1681), and the dowager countess redeemed the estates by payment of fines from 1650.[16] The manor thereafter descended with the earldom as part of the Northampton settled estates, passing to James's son George (d. 1727), to the latter's sons James (d. 1754) and George (d. 1758), to their nephew Charles (d. 1763), and to Charles's brother Spencer (d. 1796), who was succeeded by his son Charles (d. 1828), created marquess of Northampton in 1812. It then descended to his son Spencer Joshua Alwyne (d. 1851), to Spencer's son Charles (d. 1877), to Charles's brother William (d. 1897), to William's son William George Spencer Scott (d. 1913), and to the latter's son William Bingham (d. 1978).[17] The Northampton trustees had sold the estate to property companies, Western Ground Rents and the Oriel Property Trust, by 1954.[18]

Thomas Cromwell held a lease of the manor house by 1532 and occupied it from 1533 to 1535 or later.[19] William Rickthorne had a lease of the house from 1565 for 31 years and died there in 1582; his widow Anne married Sir Arthur Atye, occupant in the 1590s.[20] From 1599 Sir John Spencer and the Comptons lived there inter-

[90] P.R.O., C 133/79, no. 10; *Cal. Inq. Misc.* v, pp. 15–16.
[91] P.R.O., PROB 11/38 (P.C.C. 10 Ketchyn).
[92] Below, other est.   [93] Below, econ.
[94] Below, other est.   [95] P.R.O., C 142/543, no. 28.
[96] G.L.R.O., M83/BAR/21.
[97] Ibid. map dept. 626 JI 1755.
[98] P.R.O., MAF 20/12, nos. 175, 183.
[99] M.L.R. 1725/5/466.
[1] P.R.O., MAF 20/12, no. 175; ibid. HO 107/1499/10/1/59; Nelson, *Islington* (1829), 99.
[2] Webb, *Rec. of St. Barts.* i. 102, 341; *Cartae Antiquae R.* (Pipe R. Soc. N.S. xxiii), pp. 14–15.
[3] Webb, *Rec. of St. Barts.* 342–3, 447.
[4] P.R.O., C 143/227/17.
[5] Below, other est.   [6] *Cal. Pat.* 1348–50, 270.
[7] *Valor Eccl.* (Rec. Com.), i. 407–8.
[8] *L. & P. Hen. VIII*, iv (3), p. 2574; P.R.O., SC 6/Hen. VIII/2396, m. 121.

[9] P.R.O., E 318/box 38/2042; *Cal. Pat.* 1547–8, 252.
[10] *Cal. Pat.* 1549–51, 364; 1550–3, 369–70; P.R.O., E 318/box 32/1820.
[11] *Cal. Pat.* 1553–4, 268; 1555–7, 442.
[12] P.R.O., CP 25(2)/171/Mich. 12–13 Eliz. I.
[13] Shaw, *Knights*, ii. 91; P.R.O., C 142/318, no. 165.
[14] P.R.O., C 142/490, no. 189.
[15] *D.N.B.*
[16] *Acts and Ords. of Interr.* ed. Firth and Rait, i. 784; *Cal. Cttee. for Compounding*, ii. 1248.
[17] *Complete Peerage*, ix. 677–89; *Who Was Who* (1980).
[18] *Official Opening of New River Walk 1954* (brochure in Islington libr.).
[19] *L. & P. Hen. VIII*, v, p. 557; vi, p. 245; ix, pp. 20, 30, 263.
[20] P.R.O., PROB 11/65 (P.C.C. 9 Rowe, will of Wm. Rickthorne); PROB 11/66 (P.C.C. 18 Butts, will of Anne Atye); Tomlins, *Islington*, 195.

mittently.[21] The house was let from 1617 to 1625 to Francis Bacon, Viscount St. Alban, Lord Chancellor,[22] who may have used it himself, and from 1625 to Thomas Coventry, later Lord Coventry, Lord Keeper, who lived there until his death in 1640. His widow, daughter, and son-in-law Anthony Ashley Cooper, later earl of Shaftesbury (d. 1683), remained there until 1641.[23] The Comptons were at Canonbury in 1653 when the eldest son of James, earl of Northampton, was born there, and in 1662 when another son died there.[24] However, by 1661 parts of the building were leased separately to Arthur Dove and Edward Ellis, as Canonbury House, which was the south range, and Turret House, which was the east range, so called from a bell-turret in the middle of the roof.[25] Ralph Suckley occupied a dwelling there with nine hearths in 1663.[26] William Feilding, earl of Denbigh, died at Canonbury in 1685.[27] Parts of the building were let on 21-year leases in 1727: Canonbury House, on the south side, was let in two parts, each with some garden.[28] Parts were let as lodgings, advertised in 1757 as furnished or unfurnished apartments with a good garden, summer house and coach house, and access to an excellent cold bath. Residents included Samuel Humphreys, librettist of Handel's oratorios, who died at Canonbury House in 1736, Ephraim Chambers the encyclopaedist, who died there in 1740, Oliver Goldsmith at Turret House from 1762 to 1764, Henry Woodfall the printer and journalist who had rooms in Canonbury House, the Speaker Arthur Onslow, the publisher John Newbery, and the poet Christopher Smart.[29] The tower continued to be let as rooms until c. 1840, when it became the residence of Lord Northampton's bailiff.[30] It was afterwards rented by the Islington C. of E. Young Men's Society, followed by the Canonbury Constitutional Club from 1887 to 1907. After restoration in 1907-8 it became part of a social club for the Canonbury tenants.[31] It was leased to the Tavistock Repertory Theatre Co. in 1952 and formed its box office and rehearsal rooms in 1983.[32]

The manor house was presumably the messuage called Canonbury in 1373, which had been part of the grant of Ralph de Berners.[33] William Bolton, prior of St. Bartholomew's 1509-32, is said to have built a new house,[34] and a reset doorway bearing his rebus survives in the central (east) range. That house was probably conventionally arranged around at least one courtyard and its plan was preserved in later rebuildings. Thomas Cromwell was paying for work on the house by early 1533,[35] and a reset datestone of 1556 suggests that further work was done for Thomas, Lord Wentworth. However, it is not until the period of Sir John Spencer's ownership that substantial parts of the surviving buildings can be dated. During his time the house probably had two courtyards, although it is possible that neither was completely enclosed, and the main axis was east-west.[36] Much of the central range survives, although greatly altered, and it has on the first floor a long gallery with an elaborately moulded plaster ceiling bearing the date 1599. At its south end the gallery abuts the main south range. Although ostensibly of various dates in the 18th and early 19th centuries, the range incorporates parts of an earlier building which formed the north side of a walled garden with late 16th-century octagonal summer houses at its southern corners.[37] At the north-west corner of the surviving buildings is a tall brick stair turret of the later 16th century. Against its south side the short wing, which has elaborately panelled rooms of the early 17th century on its upper floors, formerly extended towards the end of the south range but appears to have been separated from it by 1735. By the earlier 18th century the house was a cluster of detached buildings, with the walled garden serving the main house and a larger park of 16 a. on the north side. Within the park were an avenue and canal, presumably of the late 17th or early 18th century and associated with the occupants of the tower or the buildings on the site of the Canonbury tavern, itself built at the south-east corner of the park by 1735.[38] The east end of the south range was partly refaced in the early 18th century and the central section was rebuilt or remodelled c. 1770 by John Dawes, who was erecting buildings there in 1767; the bell-tower on Turret House (the east range) was removed and the building divided into three substantial houses.[39] The west end of the range was rebuilt early in the 19th century; the vicarage house on the site of the west range is of c. 1820. In the early and mid 19th century the garden and the park were divided into building plots, the two summer houses being preserved as adjuncts to no. 4 Alwyne Villas and no. 7 Alwyne Road. In 1907 the tower was extensively restored and King Edward hall built on the east side for the Canonbury tenants;[40] the hall was let with the tower to the Tavistock Repertory Co. in 1952 and was used as the theatre in 1983.

The origin of the manor of *ISLINGTON PREBEND* is uncertain. The canons of St. Paul's were assessed on 4 hides in Islington in 1086[41] but only a small part, if any, went to form the prebendal estate. The prebendal lands may

[21] Tomlins, *Islington*, 195; H. W. Fincham, *Historical Account of Canonbury Tower* (1908), 25; below.
[22] Tomlins, *Islington*, 112.
[23] Ibid.; *D.N.B.* s.v. Coventry, Cooper; Hist. MSS. Com. 78, *Hastings*, ii, p. 71; *Cal. S.P. Dom.* 1631-3, 1633-4, 1637, 1637-8, *passim* (documents dated at Canonbury Ho.).
[24] *Complete Peerage*, ix. 683.
[25] Tomlins, *Islington*, 114 n.
[26] P.R.O., E 179/252/32, p. 26.
[27] *Complete Peerage*, iv. 180.
[28] M.L.R. 1727/5/73-6.
[29] Fincham, *Canonbury Tower*, 32; Tomlins, *Islington*, 196; C. Harris, *Islington* (1974), 61-4.
[30] Tomlins, *Islington*, 196.
[31] Fincham, *Canonbury Tower*, 32.
[32] Inf. from Theatre Co.
[33] *Cal. Inq. Misc.* iii, p. 340.
[34] Tomlins, *Islington*, 194.
[35] *L. & P. Hen. VIII*, vi, p. 372.
[36] For ground plan and detailed description see Hist. Mon. Com. *W. Lond.* 64-7; *Country Life*, lix. 630.
[37] Plate 3.
[38] Nelson, *Islington*, plan (1735).
[39] M.L.R. 1767/5/290; 1771/3/437-8; Fincham, *Canonbury Tower*, 25; Pevsner, *Lond.* ii. 232.
[40] Fincham, *Canonbury Tower*, 37-8.
[41] *V.C.H. Mdx.* i. 122. St. Paul's later acquired Iveney and the Minor Canons' est. at Holloway: below, other est.

have been given by Derman, a prominent citizen of London,[42] who in 1086 was assessed on ½ hide in Islington, formerly held by Algar.[43] Derman gave land to the church when his son Algar, the first known prebendary of Islington, became a canon before 1104;[44] there is no direct evidence that the land was in Islington, but the prebendal land separated the two parts of Newington Barrow or Highbury manor, which was held by Derman's descendants.[45] In 1649, when it was sequestrated, the manor consisted of rents from 13 customary tenants, holding 46 houses and 98 a. There may also have been freehold tenants, as in 1720. There was no demesne or manor house.[46] The manor was sold in 1650 to Maurice Gethin, merchant tailor of London,[47] who was probably among the customary tenants in 1649, but it reverted to the prebendary in 1660. It was transferred to the Ecclesiastical Commissioners in 1845, when it consisted of manorial rights, quitrents, and five old houses built on the waste and forfeited to the lord. Most of the quitrents came from small dwellings built along Essex Road and adjoining lanes by copyholders. Enfranchisements under the Copyhold Act were made from 1844 and were the subject of a scheme in 1846, and compensations for extinguishing manorial rights continued until 1940.[48] The commissioners received 4½ a. in 1845 in return for enfranchisement.[49] The land was let to Henry Rydon in 1847 with a building agreement, and was built over with c. 95 houses by 1850; it is bounded by New North Road, Luiton Street, Arlington Square, and the Regent's canal, and included St. Philip's church and school.[50]

The manor of NEWINGTON BARROW or HIGHBURY was formed from lands granted to the priory and hospital of St. John of Jerusalem, Clerkenwell, in 1270–1 by Alice, daughter of Thomas of Barrow and granddaughter of Bertram of Barrow who had given land to the priory of St. Mary, Clerkenwell, and was the grandson of Derman of London.[51] Alice's grant consisted of a house, mill, and 220 a. in Newington and Islington subject to 7 marks, which Alice gave to St. Mary's, Clerkenwell.[52] The estate formed the Hospitallers' *camera* of Newington in 1338, with the manor and 2 carucates of land, and was leased to the bishop of Lincoln,[53] reverting to the priory by 1348.[54] In 1540 the manor consisted of rents from 12 customary tenants holding 281 a. at Tollington and Stroud, 8 tenants holding 62 a. at

Islington, 13 tenants holding 75 a. at Newington Green, and rents of demesne pastures.[55] It covered the whole area contained by the northern and eastern parish boundaries and the later Hornsey, Holloway, and St. Paul's roads, and most of the parish east of Essex Road and High Street.[56] The manor passed to the Crown at the Dissolution and under Henry VIII's will passed to Princess Mary in 1548.[57] In 1558 it was restored to the Hospitallers[58] but reverted to the Crown when the order was again dissolved under Elizabeth I.[59]

In 1610–11 the manor and rents were granted to Henry, Prince of Wales, and in 1616–17 to Charles, Prince of Wales.[60] In 1627 the manor was valued as part of the estates to be conveyed to trustees to secure the Crown's loans from the City, but was apparently not among the lands sold.[61] The king conveyed it to Sir Allen Apsley in 1629 with other property, in payment of debts incurred by Apsley as victualler of the navy and lieutenant of the Tower of London. Apsley conveyed the estates to feoffees to pay his debts, and seems to have sold the manor to Thomas Austen of London, cheesemonger, who was lord by 1632. In 1639 Apsley's creditors complained that Austen should have conveyed the manor to them. In 1662 Apsley's son Sir Allen tried to recover it from Austen's grandson Thomas who in 1670 successfully opposed a Bill to recover it for the Crown.[62] The manor passed after 1683 to Thomas Austen's son John (Bt. 1714),[63] who in 1725 sold it to James Colebrooke (d. 1752),[64] joining with Colebrooke in the sale of demesne to Peter Abraham Maseres in 1732.[65] Colebrooke's youngest son George was lord in 1761, inherited a baronetcy from his elder brother, and was bankrupted in 1773,[66] whereupon Highbury Barn, the site of the manor house, and the rest of the demesne were sold to John Dawes.[67] The lordship, consisting only of manorial rights and quitrents, was sold in 1791 to Jonathan Eade (d. 1811),[68] passing to his son Joseph and by 1835 to the latter's nephews and trustees Samuel and Francis Pett.[69] By 1855 the manor belonged to Benjamin Badger of Rotherham (Yorks.) (d. 1861). In 1856 it was put up for sale, presumably without success, for Badger's trustees had not yet sold it in 1877.[70] Most copyholds had been enfranchised by the 1850s and a few were enfranchised in 1876 and 1877.[71] The manor has not been traced later.

The whole manor was leased to the bishop of

[42] *Early Charters of St. Paul's* (Camden 3rd ser. lviii), p. xxii n.
[43] *V.C.H. Mdx.* i. 129.
[44] *Domesday Studies*, ii (1891), 556; Le Neve, *Fasti, 1066–1300*, *St. Paul's, Lond.* 57.
[45] Below.
[46] Guildhall MS. (formerly St. Paul's MS. CA 8, Prebendal Surveys, vol. ii, ff. 171–4); ibid. MS. 11231.
[47] P.R.O., C 54/3536, no. 19.
[48] Ch. Com. files 3504, 14508; Guildhall MS. 14233/21.
[49] P.R.O., C 54/13813, no. 1.
[50] G.L.C., Hist. Bldgs. div. files.
[51] *The Ancestor*, ii (1902), 58–61.
[52] P.R.O., CP 25(1)/147/20, no. 493; CP 25(1)/147/24, no. 491.
[53] *Knights Hospitallers in Eng.* (Camd. Soc. [1st ser.]), 126.
[54] P.R.O., SC 11/805.
[55] P.R.O., SC 6/Hen. VIII/2402, m. 11.
[56] G.L.R.O., maps dept., 3274 JI 1854.
[57] *Cal. Pat.* 1548–9, 21.

[58] Ibid. 1557–8, 314.
[59] P.R.O., E 315/202, f. 17.
[60] Ibid. C 66/1879; C 66/2099.
[61] Corp. of Lond. R.O., RCE rentals box 1.18.
[62] P.R.O., C 5/41/3; C 8/74/4; Hist. MSS. Com. 7, *8th Rep. I*, p. 148b; *Cal. S.P. Dom.* 1639, 101, 218; 1670, 101; Tomlins, *Islington*, 124 n.
[63] G.E.C. *Complete Baronetage*, v. 21.
[64] P.R.O., CP 25(2)/1037/12 Geo. I Mich.; CP 25(2)/1164/2 Geo. II Trin.
[65] Below.
[66] G.E.C. *Complete Baronetage*, v. 116; B.L. Add. MS. 15556, f. 176.
[67] Below for Dawes's and other ests. derived from demesne.
[68] Nelson, *Islington* (1829), 138–9.
[69] Cromwell, *Islington*, 24; Tomlins, *Islington*, 124.
[70] P.R.O., MAF 20/136, no. 2052; G.L.R.O., map dept., 3274 JI 1854.
[71] P.R.O., MAF 20/136, no. 2052; Tomlins, *Islington*, 125.

Lincoln for life c. 1338,[72] and from 1540 the Crown made various leases of the manor, the demesnes, and the woods; in the 18th century most of the demesne was sold.[73]

The manor house at Highbury existed by 1338.[74] A substantial stone building used as a country residence by the priors of the hospital of St. John of Jerusalem, it was destroyed in 1381 by the followers of Jack Straw in hatred of the prior Sir Robert Hales, who was also Treasurer, and its moated site was popularly known thereafter as Jack Straw's castle.[75] The house does not appear to have been rebuilt. A grange existing in 1541, with a walled yard, garden, and pasture called Castlehill,[76] was probably the building called Highbury Barn in 1611, on the east side of the castle yard. The moated enclosure was then called Highbury castle, but the house which had stood there had been in ruins for as long as anyone could remember.[77] The barn was the only group of buildings on the site in 1718; it consisted of a range on three sides of a courtyard, with a detached building beside it,[78] and included a farmhouse occupied by John Harrison, farmer of the demesne, in 1692 and known then as Highbury House and later as Highbury Farm.[79] The later Highbury House was built by John Dawes in 1781 on the site of Jack Straw's castle.[80] Highbury Barn became a well known tea-gardens and resort in the 18th century. Its gardens were built over by 1883.[81]

The Knights Hospitallers held various parcels in Islington and Clerkenwell in addition to Highbury manor, including customary and free lands at Upper Holloway for rent and services.[82] Those lands, together with free rents in other parishes, were known by 1624 as the manor of ST. JOHN OF JERUSALEM or ST. JOHN'S, CLERKENWELL,[83] although no manor was recorded before that date. The remainder of their land consisted of three fields called Commandery Mantells in Clerkenwell parish and fields called Woodmansfield, Sheepcroft, and Lambartcroft said to be in Islington but lying near the later Angel in Clerkenwell, which was known then as Sheepcote and also belonged to the hospital.[84] The origin of the lands in Holloway is uncertain. The hospital had been founded c. 1144 with grants of land from Jordan de Briset and his wife Muriel de Munteni.[85] Jordan was the grandson of Brian, identified as the man whose wife held 5 hides of the bishop of London in the vill of Stepney in 1086, which may have included

the land granted by Jordan.[86] In the reign of Henry VI, however, the prior of the hospital held ½ knight's fee formerly William de Vere's,[87] so the Holloway property, detached from the rest of the hospital's lands, may have been acquired from that source. After the Dissolution the Holloway land remained with the Crown until 1624, when it was granted at fee farm to Robert Dixon and William Walley and included in the manor of Clerkenwell alias St. John's, Clerkenwell, and the freehold thereafter descended as part of that manor.[88] In 1539 the Holloway estate consisted of 19 customary rents and customary works for 8 holdings.[89] The copyholds were enfranchised from 1854.[90] The customary holdings formed several substantial estates, some of which are treated below.

The manor of TOLLINGTON, consisting of two hides, was held by Ranulf, brother of Ilger, from the king in 1086, and had formerly been held by Edwin, vassal of King Edward.[91] Nothing further is known of the manor, but the priories of St. John of Jerusalem and of St. Mary, Clerkenwell, both received grants of land at Tollington.[92] Free and customary land held by Robert Foster from St. John's was said to be the manor of Tollington in the 1530s,[93] when it seems likely that the manor had become subsumed into the manor of Highbury. The copyhold estate called Upper Place or Tollington farm[94] may have had a connexion with the manor.

OTHER ESTATES. The estate of ST. MARY'S priory, Clerkenwell, originated in grants, first of 1152 × 1162 from Bertram of Barrow, who gave 80 a. in Islington comprising 40 a. of Newington lordship lying in the Hide, on the north side of the Prebend manor, 20 a. in Newington in Danebottom, near the modern St. Paul's Road, and 20 a. in Tollington,[95] secondly of 1173 × 1189 from Muriel de Munteni, wife of the priory's founder Jordan de Briset, comprising her tenant Wigar Kitte and his land, part of her dowry,[96] thirdly of 1193 × 1196 from the same Muriel of Ravenildes croft in Newington,[97] and fourthly of 1270-1 from Alice of Barrow, coheir of Thomas son of Bertram of Barrow, comprising 7 marks' rent payable from lands in the manor of Newington.[98]

By 1491 the priory's lands in Islington consisted of rents for Great Weryng and Little Weryng fields, Hide field, Hopping field and 2 a.

[72] Knights Hospitallers in Eng. 126.
[73] Below, econ.
[74] Knights Hospitallers in Eng. 126.
[75] Nelson, Islington (1829), 133.
[76] P.R.O., E 315/191, f. 144.
[77] Nelson, Islington (1829), 135; G.L.R.O., MA/DCP/63.
[78] G.L.R.O., MA/DCP/63.
[79] P.R.O., C 8/436/98.
[80] Below, other est.
[81] P. Zwart, Islington: Hist. and Guide, 148; above, social.
[82] P.R.O., SC 6/Hen. VIII/2402, m. 4 and d.
[83] Tomlins, Islington, 127; P.R.O., C 2/Jas. I, F 13/4. Descent of manor reserved for treatment under Clerkenwell. See also other est., St. Mary's, Clerkenwell.
[84] P.R.O., E 318/box 23/1258; E 134/22 Jas. I Hil. 6; SC 6/Hen. VIII/2402. Treatment of the fields is reserved for Clerkenwell. For the Angel see above, social, inns.
[85] Genealogists' Mag. ix. 585-7.

[86] V.C.H. Mdx. i. 120; S. J. Madge, Early Rec. of Harringay (1938), 92-3.
[87] Nelson, Islington (1829), 60.
[88] Tomlins, Islington, 127.
[89] P.R.O., SC 6/Hen. VIII/2402, m. 4 and d.
[90] P.R.O., MAF 20/111, nos. 1651, 1652; MAF 9/185.
[91] V.C.H. Mdx. i. 129.
[92] Above; below, other est. (St. Mary's).
[93] P.R.O., C 1/854/12-13.   [94] Below, other est.
[95] Cartulary of St. Mary Clerkenwell (Camd. 3rd ser. lxxi), nos. 160, 161, 162; V.C.H. Mdx. i. 171; above, manors (Highbury). Newington, meaning the lordship, is not to be confused with the parish of Stoke Newington. Location of lands identified from later sources.
[96] Cart. Clerkenwell, nos. 83-5, 87, 90; Genealogist's Mag. ix. 586-7.
[97] Cart. Clerkenwell, no. 73.
[98] P.R.O., CP 25(1)/147/24, no. 491.

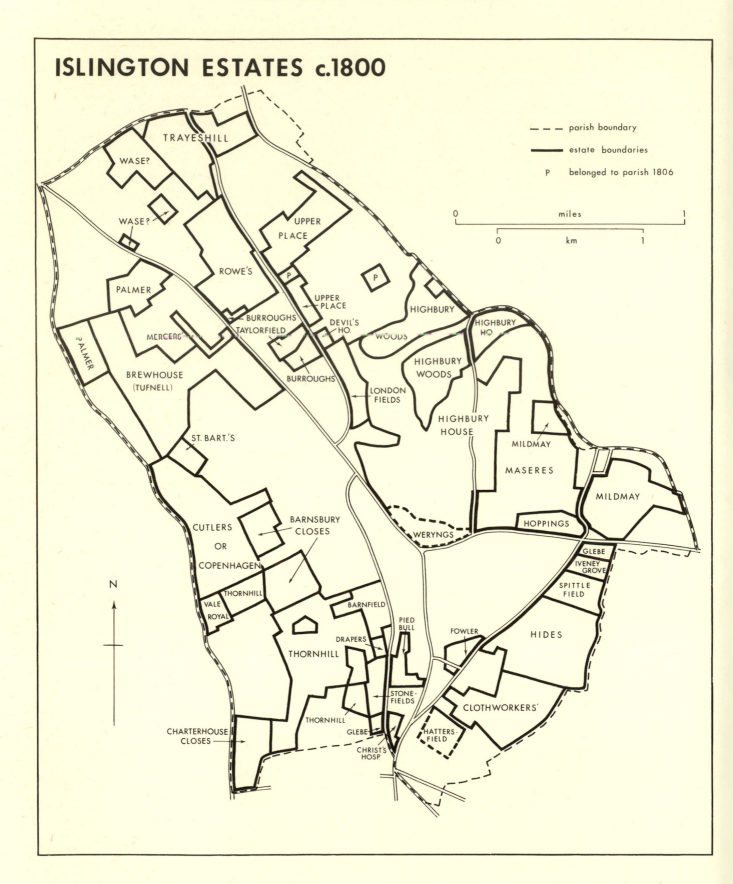

ISLINGTON ESTATES c.1800

- - - parish boundary
——— estate boundaries
P   belonged to parish 1806

0   miles   1
0   km   1

TRAYESHILL

WASE?

WASE?

UPPER PLACE

P

P

ROWE'S

PALMER

UPPER PLACE

HIGHBURY

HIGHBURY HO.

PALMER

MERCERS'

TAYLORFIELD

BURROUGHS

DEVIL'S HO.

WOODS

HIGHBURY WOODS

BREWHOUSE (TUFNELL)

BURROUGHS

LONDON FIELDS

HIGHBURY HOUSE

ST. BART.'S

MILDMAY

MASERES

MILDMAY

CUTLERS OR COPENHAGEN

BARNSBURY CLOSES

HOPPINGS

WERYNGS

GLEBE

IVENEY GROVE

N

THORNHILL

VALE ROYAL

BARNFIELD

SPITTLE FIELD

PIED BULL

FOWLER

HIDES

DRAPERS

THORNHILL

STONE-FIELDS

CLOTHWORKERS'

THORNHILL

GLEBE

HATTERS-FIELD

CHARTERHOUSE CLOSES

CHRIST'S HOSP.

near Wenlocksbarn, rents of assize and six hens at Holloway, rent from land at Highbury held by the Hospitallers and three small rents for land in Islington township and Tollington.[99] In 1535 its lands were valued for rents in Islington at £15 5s. and in Holloway at £1 14s. 2d.[1] After the Dissolution, the customary rents seem to have remained with the manor of St. Mary's, later St. James's, Clerkenwell,[2] for tenements in Upper Holloway said later to cover 110 a.[3] The larger parcels called Hoppings, Weryngs, and Hides, were let by the Crown and sold in fee (below).

HOPPINGS or HOPPING FIELD was a pasture let to a tenant in 1490.[4] The priory leased it in 1538 to John Avery, a royal servant,[5] to whom the Crown granted it in 1540 for life.[6] Avery's lease was surrendered in 1567 by Walter Myers, a court official, who purchased a new 21-year lease.[7] A lease in reversion was granted in 1573 to Christopher Edmondes and another in 1589 to Richard Lilley, for the use of John Maye and John Monday.[8] In 1611 the freehold was said to belong to William, Lord Compton,[9] and it thereafter remained with the earls, later marquesses, of Northampton, as part of their Canonbury estate.[10] In 1806 it consisted of 11 a. on the north side of St. Paul's Road between Newington Green Road and the New River, and was used for a nursery.[11] From the 1830s it formed the site of St. Paul's Terrace, St. Paul's Place, Northampton Park, and Compton Street.

WERYNGS and HIDES were let by St. Mary's, Clerkenwell, in 1490[12] and 1526.[13] After the Dissolution they were granted to John Cocks for 40 years, the Hides consisting of three closes totalling 40 a. and Great and Little Weryng of two closes totalling 20 a.[14] In 1544 Cocks was granted both parcels in fee and shortly afterwards licensed to alienate them to Richard Callard and William Hayes.[15] In 1556 William Hayes was licensed to alienate the estate to John Clerke,[16] husband of Elizabeth, who was Callard's daughter and Hayes's mother. Clerke died in 1557 having settled it on himself and his wife. Weryngs was thereafter to descend to Henry Iden and his heirs and the Hides to Iden for life, before passing to Edward and William Wroth, Elizabeth's sons from her marriage to John Wroth.[17] After Iden's death in 1568 the two parcels therefore descended separately.

In 1575 William Wroth was licensed to alienate the Hides to his cousins Robert and Thomas Wroth.[18] In 1613, however, the estate was settled by Michael Griggs and his son-in-law John Miller, later knighted, on the Millers and their heirs. After Miller's death in 1639 it passed to his widow Mary, who later married first Thomas Wilks and then one Brewer and died in 1673. She was succeeded by John, eldest son of her eldest son Michael (d. 1644).[19] In 1717 Edmund, son and heir of possibly the same John Miller of Marsworth (Bucks.), sold 10 a. of Great Hides, 7½ a. called Newmans field, united with the 10 a., and 8 a., part of the Hides, to Stephen Beckingham, who conveyed the property to trustees in 1729.[20] In 1791 a Stephen Beckingham and his wife Dorothy sold the parcels to Thomas Scott.[21] Another 8 a. of the Hides, called Tippins field, south of Great Hides, was conveyed to Sir George Colebrooke, Bt., in 1769 by John Richardson and others, and sold by Colebrooke to Thomas Scott in 1774.[22] Scott also purchased some copyhold houses in Lower Street (later Essex Road) with c. 15 a., held of Highbury manor,[23] and the Rosemary Branch inn and 4 a. formerly part of the Hides,[24] and began building terraces at the Essex Road side. In 1806 he had c. 16 a. mainly built over and 55 a. between Essex Road and the parish boundary used for brick-making, together roughly covering the area of the Hides[25] and including land around the Rosemary Branch.[26] The estate was held by Mrs. Scott in 1849 and the Scott family continued to build over it in the next two decades.[27]

Weryngs was held by Henry Iden in 1568. He left most of his lands, undivided, between George Hayes, Elizabeth (probably née Hayes) wife of John Iremonger, and William Wroth,[28] but in 1571 Iden's cousins and next heirs, John Gilbert and Joan Rydon or Rygdon, were licensed to alienate a third of Weryngs to Sir Thomas and William Wroth.[29] Sir Thomas died seised of the third in 1573, leaving it to William Wroth, son of his brother John.[30] In 1575 William alienated it with the Hides to his cousins Robert and Thomas Wroth, possibly only in trust.[31] In 1587 he granted to John Iremonger and his wife 15 messuages and 38 a. of land in Islington, Shoreditch, and St. Giles without Cripplegate,[32] probably part of the Iden inheritance, and may have received their share of Weryngs in exchange, as in 1593 Great Weryngs was said to be the inheritance of William Wroth.[33] William died in 1614 without children; Weryngs was left to his wife Mary for life and then to William, son of his first cousin Richard Wroth of Standen (Herts.).[34]

[99] Ibid. SC 6/Hen. VII/396.
[1] Valor Eccl. (Rec. Com.), i. 395.
[2] Reserved for treatment under Clerkenwell.
[3] W. J. Pinks, Hist. Clerkenwell, 17.
[4] P.R.O., SC 6/Hen. VII/396.
[5] Ibid. E 309/Box 3/9 Eliz. I/3, no. 10.
[6] L. & P. Hen. VIII, xv, p. 541.
[7] P.R.O., E 309/Box 3/9 Eliz. I/3, no. 10.
[8] Ibid. E 310/40/3, no. 255; E 310/41/17, no. 756.
[9] Tomlins, Islington, 209.
[10] Above, manors.   [11] Tomlins, Islington, 114.
[12] P.R.O., SC 6/Hen. VII/396.
[13] Ibid. SC 6/Hen. VIII/2118.
[14] Ibid. E 318/Box 8/295.
[15] L. & P. Hen. VIII, xix(1), pp. 43, 284.
[16] Cal. Pat. 1555-7, 414.
[17] Ibid. 1557-8, 342; for the relationships see below (London Fields est.).

[18] P.R.O., C 66/1126, m. 9.
[19] Ibid. C 142/777, no. 92; G.L.R.O., M83/BAR/1; BAR/26.
[20] M.L.R. 1717/4/248-9; 1729/5/50-1.
[21] Ibid. 1790/5/137; 1791/5/394.
[22] Ibid. 1769/2/1-4; 1774/4/347-9.
[23] Ibid. 1774/4/346-8.
[24] Ibid. 1776/2/305.
[25] Islington libr., Dent's plan and ref. bk. (1806).
[26] Ibid., Mobbs' Claim to Wenlock Est. (pamphlet).
[27] P.R.O., IR 29/21/33; above, growth, SE. Islington.
[28] P.R.O., C 142/155, no. 147.
[29] Ibid. C 66/1069, m. 15.
[30] Ibid. C 142/171, no. 97.
[31] Ibid. C 66/1126, m. 9.
[32] Ibid. CP 25(2)/172/29-30 Eliz. I. Mich.
[33] Ibid. REQ 2/210/123; REQ 2/100/32.
[34] Ibid. C 142/357, no. 64.

Its descent thereafter is unknown until 1714, when William Knight and others sold the two closes called Great and Little Weryngs, said to contain 15 a., to Henry Walker of London, brewer.[35] They were in the possession of Mrs. Walker of White Cross Street, London, in 1747[36] and of the Revd. William Nicolls of St. Giles without Cripplegate and his eldest son William Henry Nicolls, later rector of Stoke Newington, by 1760. Rose and Mary Nicolls, cousins and heirs of Samuel the brother of W. H. Nicolls, sold the estate to Robert Mackreth for the use of John Dawes in 1773.[37] The land seems to have lain on the north side of the modern St. Paul's Road between Highbury Grove and Highbury Place, forming part of the site of the terrace and gardens in the latter street, and was thus built over from 1773.

IVENEY or *SEVENEY*, later Eden Grove and Spittle fields, was a freehold parcel within the manor of Highbury, bounded roughly by Essex Road, Orchard Grove, Southgate Street, and Northchurch Road. Thomas of Stortford, precentor of St. Paul's, granted 1 mark a year from his lands at Iveney c. 1239 to the clerks of the choir of St. Paul's; if his tenant should die without heirs, the land itself should revert to St. Paul's and the clerks.[38] In 1254 Thomas's son William quitclaimed to Peter of Newport, archdeacon of London, all his right in his father's tenement at Iveney.[39] By 1261 Peter had granted a field on the south side of the messuage there to the hospital of St. Mary without Bishopsgate in free and perpetual alms for making beds for the sick from straw from the field and bread and gruel from the corn, the hospital paying 6s. 8d. a year to the clerks of St. Paul's choir.[40] The field, said in the Middle Ages to be 14 a. and by 1540 to be 20¼ a. became known as the Spittle fields and descended separately from the rest of Iveney.[41] It passed to the Crown at the Dissolution and in 1553 was granted to William, earl of Pembroke, and William Clerke in free socage.[42] By 1569 it was held by Sir Thomas Leigh (d. 1572), who settled it on his widow Alice and their heirs,[43] and in 1627 by Christopher Hewer and his son Thomas, who held it in 1633 at his death.[44] Its later ownership is uncertain but from its location it appears to have been the 19¼ a. called Great Hides in 1812, which had been settled in 1712, when it was estimated at 21 a., by Richard Sutton, vintner, of London (d. c. 1725) on his wife Anne for life and on his daughters Anne, wife of Thomas Yates, D.D., Elizabeth, wife of

William Booth, and Katharine, wife of Tomlinson Busby.[45] A third of the land formed part of the marriage settlements of the Revd. Richard Sutton Yates (d. 1789) in 1760, and of his son the Revd. Richard William Yates. The whole estate was held by R. W. Yates's widow Hester in 1806, and in 1812 the trustees obtained an Act to grant building leases,[46] but in the 1830s the land formed the site of John Perkins's cattle market.[47]

The rest of Iveney, called Iveney or Eden Grove, which included a house,[48] remained with St. Paul's and was occasionally described as a manor. The house was not recorded after 1383.[49] In 1535 it was leased at a reserved rent of 23s. 4d., as it continued to be, generally for 21 years.[50] In 1649 it consisted of a 6-a. meadow and was valued at £9 a year. Parliament sold it to the leaseholder Thomas Webb of Islington, but it reverted to St. Paul's at the Restoration and was let on the old terms until c. 1811, when Robert Cannon was granted a building lease.[51] It was held by Elisha Ambler and used as a brickfield in 1849[52] and was built over in the 1850s.[53]

The *VALE ROYAL* estate originated in 11 a. in Islington conveyed in 1274–5 to Richard of Hethersett by Gervin, son of Peter the otter-hunter (*lutrarius*), and Denise his wife.[54] Richard granted land and rent to the abbey of Vale Royal (Ches.) in 1299, including 12 a. in Islington held of the heirs of Ralph de Berners.[55] The abbey still held the land, a pasture near St. Pancras church on the east side of Longhedge Lane (later York Way), at the Dissolution.[56] In 1574 the land was claimed as concealed and granted in fee to John and William Marsh, but by 1580 John had sold it.[57] Vale Royal close was owned by Mary, widow of Robert Wood, and Roger Wood in 1673.[58] In 1806 the estate, 10½ a. called Bellfield or Vale Royal, was owned by Samuel Brandon and formed the site of a pottery and a hartshorn factory; it was called Belle Isle in the 19th century.[59]

The estate called *CUTLERS*, reputed to be a manor in the 16th century,[60] may have originated in land held by Adam de Basing (d. 1262), who had received land from William of Haselbech, held of Walter Cardon, clerk, and formerly part of the fee of William de Berners.[61] Basing also received three grants of land in Islington abutting the land of St. John's hospital, Clerkenwell, from William Peacock, son of Peter Freeman.[62] Basing granted land, tenements, and a windmill in Islington and neighbouring parishes to his daughter Avice and her husband William de Hadestok,[63] whose daughter Joan was the mother

[35] M.L.R. 1714/6/43.
[36] G.L.R.O., MA/DCP/63, map.
[37] M.L.R. 1760/2/324–5; 1773/2/141.
[38] Tomlins, *Islington*, 129–30.
[39] Guildhall MS. (formerly St. Paul's, Red box A 36/1014).
[40] Ibid. 36/1015; Tomlins, *Islington*, 130.
[41] Tomlins, *Islington*, 130; P.R.O., SC 6/Hen. VIII/2396, m. 94.
[42] P.R.O., E 318/Box 33/1860; *Cal. Pat.* 1553, 175.
[43] *Abstract of Inq. p.m. for Lond.* iii. 328, 332.
[44] P.R.O., C 142/491, no. 23.
[45] M.L.R. 1725/6/77.
[46] 52 Geo. III, c. 94 (Local and Personal); Dent's plan and ref. bk. (1806).
[47] Below, econ. (markets); P.R.O., IR 30/21/33.
[48] Tomlins, *Islington*, 130.
[49] Guildhall MS. (formerly St. Paul's, Red box A 36/1018).

[50] Ibid. A 36/1017, 1018, A 40/1444; *Valor Eccl.* (Rec. Com.), i. 360.
[51] Guildhall MS. (formerly St. Paul's, CA 10, Prebendal Ests. vol. iv, f. 29); Lysons, *Environs* (Suppl.), 207.
[52] P.R.O., IR 29/21/33.
[53] Above, growth, SE. Islington.
[54] P.R.O., CP 25(1)/148/25, no. 25.
[55] Ibid. C 143/29, no. 4; *Cal. Pat. 1292–1301*, 437.
[56] P.R.O., E 315/104, f. 186.
[57] Ibid. C 2/Eliz. I/P 10/23.
[58] Ibid. C 6/259/56; C 8/349/161.
[59] Dent's plan and ref. bk. (1806).
[60] e.g. *L. & P. Hen. VIII*, v, p. 576; ibid. xvii, p. 265; P.R.O., LR 14/862.
[61] P.R.O., E 326/4356.
[62] *Cat. Anct. D.* i, B 1508, B 1511, B 1521.
[63] Ibid. ii, B 2364.

of Henry Bedyk.[64] By 1334 Henry the hayward, of West Smithfield, and Roger Creton, clerk, held 52 a. from Henry Bedyk. They granted the estate to St. Bartholomew's priory, together with a house and 50 a. of land and 4 a. of meadow held from the priory and 4 a. held from John de Berners.[65] In 1373 the house was called Cotelers.[66] The land lay near Maiden Lane and was often described as in Kentish Town but within Islington parish. The fee remained with St. Bartholomew's until the Dissolution, when it passed to the Crown.

Cutlers, consisting of Great, Middle, and Little Cutlers, Barnfield or Housefield, and Ridymere, was included in the grant of Canonbury to Thomas Cromwell and in grants of both estates to John, duke of Northumberland, to Sir David Brooke and his wife, and to Lord Wentworth,[67] during which time the fields had been let to a London innholder.[68] Wentworth sold Cutlers with Canonbury to Sir John Spencer, and it then passed with Canonbury until 1650 when James, earl of Northampton (d. 1681), sold Great Cutlers, Little Cutlers, and Barn close, with a little close adjoining Cutlers, to Robert Wood of Kingston-upon-Thames (Surr.).[69] Wood's widow Mary, his nephew Roger, and Sir Richard Wiseman sold them to Thomas Batson of London in 1673.[70] In 1786 the estate was held by Elizabeth Batson of Barnsbury, widow, and was known as Copenhagen farm; its 124½ a. included Barnfield, and 2½ a. called Catts acre which lay in St. Pancras parish[71] and had been part of the lands sold by Northampton.[72] In 1806 the 120-a. estate was said to be held by a Mr. Leader,[73] possibly a trustee as it belonged to Robert Batson in 1820[74] and to Alfred Batson in 1849.[75] He sold Copenhagen House and 72 a. for the Metropolitan market c. 1852,[76] and in 1856 left the rest of his Islington estate to trustees, who included another Alfred Batson.[77]

St. Bartholomew's priory had granted a lease of Cutlers with Canonbury to Giles Heron by 1530; he had assigned most of the two estates by 1532 to Thomas Cromwell, who secured new leases,[78] but apparently retained 24 a., let to an undertenant, which passed to the Crown when Heron was attainted on the fall of his father-in-law Sir Thomas More. The Crown let that parcel for 21 years in 1542,[79] but the lease had passed by 1582 to the lessee of Canonbury and Cutlers,[80] with whom it remained. Sir John Spencer and

Lord Compton let the property, to innholders of London and Clerkenwell,[81] and it was also let on long leases in 1786 and 1805.[82] The house mentioned in 1334 and 1373 was not recorded later but was perhaps commemorated in the name Barnfield or Housefield in 1530.[83] In 1786 Barnfield (17½ a.) lay next to Copenhagen Farm,[84] which may have stood on or near the older site. The house existed in 1695, and was a tavern and tea-garden by 1753. It became a resort for Londoners until replaced by the Metropolitan market.[85]

Robert de Ferrers granted an estate in 1377 to Sir Robert Knolles and his wife Constance and others, including land in Islington.[86] In 1380 the reversion on the death of Robert and Constance was granted to the London Charterhouse.[87] The land may have been the croft called Twenty Acres in the south-west extremity of the parish by York Way, let by the Charterhouse to a London innholder in 1492 for 35 years.[88] In 1673 *CHARTERHOUSE* closes (23 a.) belonged to Mary, widow of Robert Wood, and his nephew Roger Wood.[89] Later ownership is uncertain but the estate seems to have been the 23¾ a. formerly part of Henry Penton's estate and owned by William Horsfall in 1806.[90]

Henry Frowyk sold 34½ a. in Islington to Sir John Elrington, treasurer of the king's household, in 1480.[91] They descended to Sir John's son Simon,[92] whose son Thomas inherited 17 a. in Islington and had died by 1529.[93] A later Thomas Elrington and his wife Beatrice sold 12 a. in the close called *HATTERSFIELD*, later *TILE-KILNFIELD*, to William Tooker, grocer of London, in 1551.[94] In 1613 the close, of 10 a. with 2 a. called Buttfield divided from it by the New River, was part of the lands settled on John Miller and his wife Mary. Mary inherited it in 1639 and on her death in 1673 it passed to her grandson John.[95] In 1717 Edmund Miller sold the 10 a. close to Walter Burton, glazier,[96] who built a brewhouse and brick kilns on part before selling it to James Colebrooke in 1727.[97] It passed to Sir George Colebrooke, who in 1766 let a strip on the west side as the site of Colebrooke Row, putting a bridge over the New River and a road through the field.[98] More building leases were granted in Colebrooke Row in 1776.[99] The property was probably sold after Colebrooke's bankruptcy in 1773.[1] John Eddington owned 5½ a. formerly Watson's nursery in 1806, which

[64] *V.C.H. Mdx.* vi. 56–7.
[65] P.R.O., C 143/227, no. 17.
[66] *Cal. Inq. Misc.* iii, p. 340.
[67] Above, manors, Canonbury.
[68] Guildhall MS. 9171/15, f. 273v.
[69] P.R.O., C 9/11/179.
[70] Ibid. C 7/513/16.
[71] M.L.R. 1786/3/91.   [72] P.R.O., C 9/11/179.
[73] Dent's ref. bk. (1806).
[74] G.L.R.O., M83/BAR/7, p. 154.
[75] P.R.O., IR 29/21/33.
[76] Above, growth, Lower Holloway.
[77] P.R.O., C 54/15880, no. 5.
[78] *L. & P. Hen. VIII,* v, pp. 557, 576; P.R.O., SP 2/M, no. 16.
[79] P.R.O., SC 12/11/21; ibid. LR 14/862; ibid. E 315/230, p. 1.
[80] Ibid. PROB 11/65 (P.C.C. 9 Rowe, will of Wm. Rickthorne).
[81] Islington libr., deed III/5; Tomlins, *Islington,* 113 n.

[82] M.L.R. 1786/3/91; Dent's ref. bk. (1806).
[83] P.R.O., LR 14/862.
[84] M.L.R. 1786/3/91.
[85] Ibid.; Nelson, *Islington* (1829), 74; above, social.
[86] *Cal. Close,* 1377–81, 109.
[87] *Cal. Pat.* 1377–81, 549.
[88] P.R.O., E 303/8, Lond. no. 134.
[89] Ibid. C 6/259/56; C 8/349/161.
[90] Dent's plan and ref. bk. (1806).
[91] P.R.O., CP 25(1)/152/98, no. 77.
[92] Ibid. C 1/125/58–60.
[93] Ibid. C 1/546/52.
[94] Ibid. CP 25(2)/61/475/East. 5 Ed. VI, no. 6.
[95] Ibid. C 142/777, no. 92; G.L.R.O., M83/BAR/26; above (Hides).
[96] M.L.R. 1717/4/238–9, 248–9.
[97] Ibid. 1727/3/183–4.
[98] Ibid. 1768/6/345, 431–5.
[99] Ibid. 1776/3/242, 505, 583.
[1] G.E.C. *Baronetage,* v. 116.

was sold in 1827 to Thomas Cubitt, who built a few houses facing St. Peter Street and sold a strip on the south side to James Rhodes in 1843, letting the rest to local builders in the 1850s.[2] Another part of Hattersfield between the New River and High Street and containing 3 a. was sold by Gerard Noel Noel in 1810 to Samuel Rhodes,[3] whose family built over the property in the 1830s.[4]

Robert Foster held over 120 a. of copyhold at Tollington and Stroud in 1539, parts of 12 homestalls in Highbury manor, and 7 other copyhold parcels at Holloway in the manor of St. John's, Clerkenwell, besides unspecified freeholds.[5] Richard Callard c. 1542 bought from Foster 22 a. of freehold known as *LONDON FIELDS* and later as the *HARVIST* estate,[6] in addition to other land and houses some of which are described below. Callard and his descendants, the Hayes and Wroth families, also held Weryngs, Hides, and leases of parts of the Canonbury and Highbury demesnes.[7] Callard (d. 1544) settled his land on Thomas Hayes and his wife Elizabeth, Callard's daughter and heir.[8] Elizabeth was mother of William and Elizabeth Hayes and possibly of George Hayes. She married secondly John Wroth (d. 1556),[9] brother of Sir Thomas Wroth, lessee of Highbury demesne, by whom she had two sons Edward and William, and thirdly John Clerke (d. 1557), son of her father's second wife Anne by Sir John Clerke.[10] Clerke left some lands to Henry Iden to bring up Edward and William Wroth,[11] perhaps including London fields which Iden held at his death in 1568, when most of his land was to be shared equally between George Hayes, Elizabeth Iremonger (probably *née* Hayes), and William Wroth, and their heirs.[12] John and Elizabeth Iremonger and William and Mary Wroth made an agreement c. 1586, which probably divided the estate.[13] In 1586 the Iremongers and William Wroth sold London fields, said to be 20 a., to John Kitchin and his son Anthony. In 1601 Anthony Kitchin sold the property to Roger Bellow of London, brewer, who immediately sold it to Edward Harvist, also a brewer.[14] In 1610 Harvist left the two closes to the Brewers' Company of London in trust for the highway from Tyburn to Edgware; the trust was not observed, which led to litigation in 1811.[15] The estate covered 21¾ a. in 1806,[16] but by 1849 the Brewers' Company held 18 a., the rest having been sold to the G.N.R. Co. for its main line,[17] and hoped to build on it. The estate was vested, however, in the Commissioners of the Metropolitan Turnpike Roads North of the Thames

under the Metropolitan Roads (Harvist Estate) Act, 1855, to enable building leases to be granted. Lying on the east side of Hornsey Road, between Ashburton Grove and Isledon Road, it was mainly built over in the 1860s.[18]

COWLEYS, a freehold parcel of 12 a. of meadow and 2 a. of wood at Stroud, was among the lands left by Henry Iden and shared by Callard's descendants.[19] In 1612 Sir James Pemberton sold it to Anthony Ashe and his wife Elizabeth, with a house and 8 a. at Stroud Green and 10 a. of copyhold called Sanders Down. In 1624 Elizabeth Ashe conveyed the estate to Francis Bickley, who sold it in 1629 to William Brooke, who left it in his will of 1645 to Richard Mayor. In 1666 Mayor's widow Jane and his five daughters sold the house and 8 a. to Mary Guilliam.[20] By 1687 the remaining land was shared between the daughters or their heirs, Catherine wife of John Winterflood, Dinah wife of John Speight, Elizabeth, Mary wife of William Bateman, and Thomas son of Mary Winspear.[21] A fifth share in Cowleys was sold in 1712 by Edward Umfreville to Mary Sheffield, widow,[22] and in 1765 three fifths of both fields were Thomas Winspear's.[23] The whole of Cowleys and Sanders Down was apparently sold in 1765 to Thomas Cogan, who enfranchised Sanders Down in 1769.[24] Later ownership of the property is unknown.

UPPER PLACE was a copyhold house in Tollington, held of Highbury manor with 17 a. called Gentsfield and Barnfield and 1 a.; it belonged to William Wroth at his death in 1614, when the house was divided.[25] The estate was probably Wroth's customary land called Tollington farm, which he had been licensed to let in 1602. John Iremonger, however, had left rents from the farm of Tollington in 1605 to his son Henry, and John's daughter-in-law Marie Fell was entitled to £8 a year dower from the same property.[26] Wroth's widow Mary in 1615 married Richard Colton, who was admitted for her life. On Mary's death in 1630 Arthur Loane was admitted under a surrender to his parents' use by Henry Iremonger, son of John and William Wroth's nephew and legatee. In 1663 Arthur settled 17 a. called Gentsfield and Barnfield and another 1 a. on himself and his son Nathaniel, whose own son Arthur was admitted in 1691 and was succeeded in 1694 by a younger brother John. John (d. 1702) left his land in trust for his daughters Meliora and Maria, but Joshua Draper, one of the trustes, was admitted under a mortgage. In 1720 Maria Loane settled the estate on her

[2] Dent's plan (1806); above, growth, SE. Islington.
[3] P.R.O., C 54/15673, no. 12.
[4] Above, growth, SE. Islington.
[5] P.R.O., SC 6/Hen. VIII/2402, mm. 4, 11; ibid. C 1/854/12.
[6] Ibid. CP 25(2)/27/184/34 Hen. VIII Mich. no. 41; Guildhall MS. 5510.
[7] Above, manors; other est.
[8] P.R.O., PROB 11/30 (P.C.C. 14 Pynnyng); Guildhall MS. 5510.
[9] P.R.O., PROB 11/39 (P.C.C. 4 Wrastley).
[10] Ibid. PROB 11/30 (P.C.C. 14 Pynnyng).
[11] Ibid. PROB 11/39 (P.C.C. 27 Wrastley).
[12] Ibid. C 142/155, no. 147; PROB 11/50 (P.C.C. 25 Babington); above (Weryngs).
[13] P.R.O., CP 25(2)/172/29–30 Eliz. I Mich.

[14] Guildhall MS. 5510.
[15] C. A. A. Clarke, 'Turnpike Trusts of Islington and Marylebone from 1700–1825' (TS. 1955 in Islington libr.).
[16] Dent's plan and ref. bk. (1806).
[17] P.R.O., IR 29/21/33.
[18] Guildhall MSS. 18382; 18,430; Islington libr., deeds 3316–24. [19] P.R.O., C 142/155, no. 147.
[20] Islington libr., deeds index.
[21] Ibid.; P.R.O., C 8/229/131.
[22] M.L.R. 1712/3/93–4.
[23] Islington libr., deeds index.
[24] M.L.R. 1765/5/200–1; 1769/2/84–5.
[25] Para. based on MS. vol. of Abstracts of Deeds, manors of St. John's and Barnsbury, pp. 9–12, 24–8, in Islington libr.; Islington libr., deed 886.
[26] P.R.O., PROB 11/106 (P.C.C. 61 Hayes).

intended marriage with Thomas Huxley, but Draper still held it under the mortgage at his death in 1741, when his interest passed to his nephew Richard Draper. In 1751 Richard surrendered his interest to Meliora, wife of John Shaw, and Susan Huxley, and they immediately sold it to John Gwilt. In 1774 the estate, a house and 20 a. lying east of Hornsey Road near the later Tollington Park, passed to trustees under Gwilt's will. In 1806 it was called Torrington [*sic*] farm and said to be owned by the Revd. Robert Gwilt, who held land amounting in all to 62½ a.,[27] but Edward Gwilt held Upper Place in 1802 and 1808 after the death of the trustees. By 1849 the estate was divided between several owners, including Robert Gwilt who held only 3½ a., and building had started on the land.[28]

Customary land in Highbury manor called *TRAYESHILL*, consisting of 45 a. in Tollington Lane with 12 a. more at the lower end of Trayeshill, was held by William Wroth in 1602. At his death in 1614 Wroth also had a house and 20 a. near Holloway Road,[29] which, with the 12 a., he left to his wife Mary and her heirs and she surrendered to her own use for life and then to her brother John Sammes. Trayeshill was left to Mary for life, and then to Wroth's nephew Thomas Iremonger, who was admitted on Mary's death in 1630. Thomas left the land, with copyholds in Lower Street and in Barnsbury manor, to his nephew William Iremonger, who was admitted between 1650 and 1655. William conveyed the property in 1655 to Henry Man, after mortgaging it to Henry's father Edmund, who soon acquired it and left it in 1657 to his daughter Elizabeth Gardiner. Elizabeth, who had later married Francis Fowke, died in 1706. One of her daughters, Elizabeth Dee (*née* Gardiner) acquired a moiety from Zachariah Gibson, husband of the other daughter Mary Fowke, and died in possession in 1729, leaving her copyhold land to her cousin Thomas Gearing to pay legacies. Gearing died in 1730, whereupon his brother Joshua Gearing immediately surrendered the estate to Mary, wife of Henry Samuel Eyre. In 1750 Mary Eyre was succeeded by her brother and sister Jacob and Sarah Harvey and her husband. Eyre and Jacob Harvey surrenderd the estate, which included a brick house built *c.* 1750 near Hornsey Lane, to Jacob's second son William, who sold it to Sarah Nicoll in 1763; the estate was then 63 a., of which 48 a. including Trayeshill on the west side of Tollington Lane were copyhold and the rest on the east side of the lane freehold. She was succeeded in 1766 by her kinsman John Osborn (d. 1800), under whose will Trayeshill was left in trust for his daughter-in-law Dorothy Osborn for life and then to his eldest grandson John Osborn, followed by his second grandson James. In 1806 Osborn's trustees held a house and 65¼ a., and the

freehold land on the east side of Tollington Lane included *c.* 12 a. that had been an isolated parcel of the demesne of Highbury manor in 1718. In 1849 the Revd. Thomas Jenkins held the estate, which by then excluded the *c.* 12 a. Later ownership has not been traced.

John Iremonger (d. 1605) left a customary house with garden and orchard near Tollington and 8 a. in two closes to his granddaughter Elizabeth Fell. Nathaniel Loane died in possession in 1627, when his son Arthur succeeded him.[30] The property then descended with Upper Place (above) until 1705, when it was surrendered to Elizabeth Burroughs, who was licensed to pull down the house. On Elizabeth's death in 1743 the *BURROUGHS* estate, consisting of a toft where the house had stood, 8 a., and 1 a., was shared by her grandsons, Thomas, William, and Charles, who surrendered their shares to John Highmore's use. On Highmore's death in 1759 his nephew Thomas Burroughs was admitted. Thomas died in 1781 leaving the estate in Holloway to Nathaniel Highmore for life, followed by his niece Mary, wife of John Strong. Highmore died in 1790, when Mary was admitted, and in 1793 the Strongs surrendered the estate to Robert Lepper. Lepper held 15¾ a. in 1806,[31] and on his death in 1812 it passed to his daughter Esther, wife of Robert Enkel or Inkle, who held the estate in 1849.[32] The land, a small part of which lay by the later Tollington Way, the rest just south of Seven Sisters Road, was built over in the 1870s.

LOWER PLACE, also known as *DEVIL'S HOUSE* by 1586,[33] was a freehold house with a garden, orchard, and moat, and lay on the east side of Tollington Lane, a little south of Heame Lane and north of London Fields. In 1569 Henry Iden died in possession of the house, which was among the estates shared by Richard Callard's descendants. In 1611 it was included in a survey of Highbury manor.[34] Its later ownership was not recorded until 1849, when 1¾ a. with buildings belonged to Mrs. Scott, who also owned the Hides.[35]

The minor canons of St. Paul's held a close as copyhold of St. John's manor, Clerkenwell, in 1539 called *TAYLORFIELD* or *BELL-FIELD*.[36] In 1639 the close was 10 a. stretching from Holloway Road to Tollington Lane. Parliament sold it in 1649 to Andrew Bunnion[37] but it reverted to the canons at the Restoration. In the 1820s 1¼ a. was taken for Seven Sisters Road, and the dean and chapter held the remaining 8¾ a.[38] Building leases were granted from 1846 and the estate was built over by the 1860s.[39]

FOWLER'S copyhold, held by Thomas Fowler at his death in 1556, included a house and garden which his widow Alice occupied in 1560.[40] It was probably the house on the north side of Cross Street in Canonbury manor occupied by

[27] Dent's plan and ref. bk. (1806).
[28] P.R.O., IR 29/21/33; IR 30/21/33.
[29] Para. based on Abstracts of Deeds, pp. 9–21; P.R.O., IR 29/21/33; IR 30/21/33; M.L.R. 1774/3/58; G.L.R.O., MA/DCP/63; Dent's plan and ref. bk. (1806).
[30] Para. based on Abstracts of Deeds, pp. 31–8.
[31] Dent's plan (1806).
[32] P.R.O., IR 29/21/33.   [33] Guildhall MS. 5510.
[34] P.R.O., C 142/155, no. 147; Nelson, *Islington* (1829), 136.

[35] P.R.O., IR 29/21/33.
[36] P.R.O., SC 6/Hen. VIII/2402, m. 4.
[37] Guildhall Libr., St. Paul's MSS., Preb. surveys CA 8, vol. ii, ff. 219–21.
[38] Above, communications; P.R.O., IR 30/21/33.
[39] Guildhall Libr., Ch. Com. file III, deeds; P.R.O., HO 107/10/2/10; Ch. Com. S 2, surveys, pp. 422–4.
[40] P.R.O., PROB 11/38 (P.C.C. 10 Ketchyn); ibid. C 142/127, no. 21.

his descendants in 1588. On the death of Sir Thomas Fowler in 1656 the estate probably passed to his daughter Sarah, widow of Sir Thomas Fisher,[41] as it was held by her son Sir Richard Fisher in 1690, when it consisted of the house, a farmhouse and 3 a., the Dog and Partridge inn, a barn, two fields, and c. 14 houses.[42] After Sir Richard's death in 1707 the estate passed to Sir Thomas Halton (d. 1726) and then Sir William Halton (d. 1754), who left it in trust for William Tufnell to be followed by George Tufnell Foster.[43] Its descent thereafter was the same as that of Barnsbury manor,[44] and the estate was still held by the Tufnell trustees in 1862, by which time the land had been built over, fronting Cross and Lower streets and forming Little Cross and Halton streets and Pleasant and Astey's rows.[45]

FISHER'S estate in Lower Street may have belonged in part to Sir Thomas Fisher (d. 1636), but the house later known as Fisher's House with its land was acquired by Sir Richard Fisher in 1680 from Henry Proctor and consisted of a house, garden, and small plot of land, copyhold of Highbury manor,[46] and five houses with 2 a., copyhold of the Prebend manor.[47] After his death the Prebend copyhold, which included Sir Richard's residence, passed under his will to his wife Browne Fisher for life, then in 1740 to Mary, wife of his kinsman Richard Halton for life, then in 1748 to Thomas, the son of Mary's son George in tail male. He surrendered the estate to a trustee during his life.[48] In 1765 Thomas was presumed to have died while abroad and his son William was admitted.[49] As Sir William he surrendered the estate to James Hayes in 1786, who left it to Edward Rowland Pickering, admitted in 1827. It was enfranchised in 1844, having been built over with Pickering Place and other small houses, stretching to Frog Lane.[50] The Highbury copyhold seems to have passed with the Fowler estate. Sir William Halton (d. 1754) was admitted in 1733 and left the copyhold, which included the coachhouse and stables used with Fisher's House, to his aunt Mary Halton for life, and after to George Tufnell Foster. The Tufnell family still held the premises in 1851,[51] but the later ownership has not been traced.

Anne, widow of Sir John Packington, by will of 1559 left to the Clothworkers' Company of London the profits of a copyhold house and land in the Prebend manor, £16 16s. 9d. a year, for charitable purposes. The Company also acquired an adjoining 34 a., which became confused with the Packington land[52] and may have included land said in 1659 to have once belonged to

Henry Swinnerton, followed by John Cruth.[53] In 1649 the Company paid an annual quitrent of £1 13s. 9d. to the prebendary and a fine of £11 1s. 8d. every 20 years.[54] In 1659 the CLOTH-WORKERS' estate included the Crown inn in Boon's Lane and another building near it, c. 50 a., and the Clothworkers' ten almshouses.[55] In the late 18th century the estate was 57¾ a., excluding the two sets of almshouses and other houses in Lower Street, most of it between Frog Lane and the parish boundary.[56] In 1819 2¾ a. were taken by the Regent's Canal Co. In 1827 an arbitrary division of the charity land from the corporate land was made. The Company gave the lords of the manor, the Ecclesiastical Commissioners, 2 a. for enfranchisement in 1845.[57] Building on the estate began soon afterwards and was finished by the early 1860s.[58] The charity estate was taken for Packington and Dame streets; the corporate land lay north-east up to New North Road, with a small block in St. Peter's Street.

HIGHBURY WOODS or CREAM HALL estate was formed from Highbury wood and Little St. John's wood, which were part of the manor of Highbury and had belonged to the hospital of St. John of Jerusalem until the Dissolution.[59] The Crown let the two woods, estimated at 33 a. each to William Dodington for 21 years in 1570.[60] Leases in reversion for 21 years were granted in 1583 to Matthew Martin, the holder in 1604, and in 1590 to James Harden, one of the queen's musicians.[61] In 1594 a lease was granted to Sir John Fortescue for 60 years from 1625 at the same rents, reserving great trees and oaks.[62] Sir John sold it to Sir John Spencer and it passed in turn to William Halliday, then in 1623 to his widow Susanna, who left her leaseholds to her younger daughter Anne Halliday (d. 1657), wife of Sir Henry Mildmay.[63] Anne left the leaseholds in trust for her son William Mildmay, who was still the beneficiary in 1681.[64] In 1651 the fee simple of Highbury wood, estimated at 43½ a., and Little St. John's wood, estimated at 35 a., had been sold to Henry Mildmay, second son of Sir Henry, and Richard Clutterbuck of London, merchant,[65] but it was repossessed by the Crown at the Restoration, and a lease for 31 years from 1685 on the same terms as Fortescue's was granted in 1670 to Thomas Windham on the nomination of his wife Elizabeth, who had helped Charles II to escape after the battle of Worcester.[66]

In 1685 Windham assigned his lease to Anthony Guidott of Lincoln's Inn, whose nephew and namesake was granted a new lease for 31 years from 1714.[67] A lease in reversion was granted in

[41] Above, growth, Islington town.
[42] P.R.O., C 7/597/81.
[43] G.L.R.O., M83/BAR/124; G.L.R.O. maps dept. 7007 JI 1721.
[44] Above, manors (Barnsbury), for Fisher's descendants.
[45] P.R.O., MAF 20/12, no. 183; above, growth.
[46] G.L.R.O., M83/BAR/143-4.
[47] Guildhall MS. 14225/1A, p. 114.
[48] Ibid., pp. 114-18.
[49] Ibid. 2, pp. 28-9, 50, 70.　　[50] P.R.O., MAF 20/110.
[51] G.L.R.O., M83/BAR/124, 147, 151.
[52] P.R.O., C 54/13813, no. 1.
[53] Ibid. C 7/452/94.
[54] Guildhall MS. 11816B, pp. 113-14.
[55] P.R.O., C 7/452/94.

[56] G.L.R.O. maps dept., J ISL 7496, 'plan of Islington estates', 1788-96. For almshos., above, growth, SE. Islington.
[57] P.R.O., C 54/13813, no. 1.
[58] Above, growth, SE. Islington.　　[59] Above, manors.
[60] P.R.O., E 310/38/237, no. 8; Cal. Pat. 1569-92, 81.
[61] P.R.O., LR 2/259, f. 13v.; ibid. E 310/41/18, nos. 847, 855.　　　　　　　　　　　　[62] Ibid. C 66/1415, m. 25.
[63] Ibid. E 317/Mdx. 45, pp. 1-3; ibid. PROB 11/195 (P.C.C. 20 Twisse); C 5/2/50.
[64] Ibid. PROB 11/263, f. 127; ibid. C 7/225/30.
[65] Ibid. E 304/4/L.41; E 320/L.41.
[66] Cal. S.P. Dom. 1668-9, 323; 1670, 143.
[67] Cal. Treas. Bks. 1710, 388; 1714, 215; P.R.O., E 367/3908.

1735 to Anthony's widow Alice and William Guidott for 21 years from 1745, and another in 1759 to Alice Guidott for 23 years from 1767.[68] In 1775 her executor sold her interest in the two woods to John Dawes, who in 1776 secured a new lease of 31 years.[69] Dawes's son John sold the lease in 1789 to Isaac Walker, together with 45 a. of Highbury demesne and the lease of London Fields. In 1798 Walker assigned the house built on the estate called Cream Hall and $45\frac{1}{2}$ a. formerly Highbury wood to Alexander Aubert.[70] A lease of the $45\frac{1}{2}$ a. was granted by the Crown to John Bentley in 1807 at the nomination of Aubert's executrix, for 28 years, and the freehold was sold in 1818 to Jesse Gregson in trust for Robert Felton of Highbury House, who already held a mortgage of Bentley's lease. Felton died bankrupt in 1818 and his estate was sold in 1819. Part was acquired for building in 1824.[71] Highbury wood lay between the south end of the later Blackstock Road and Highbury Hill and included the site of Arsenal F.C. ground. A new lease of Little St. John's wood was made to John or James Walker for a term expiring in 1836, when the freehold was auctioned in ten lots to nine purchasers.[72] The wood, bounded on the north-east by the later Blackstock Road, formed the site of Ambler and Monsell roads and the G.N.R. sidings.

The farmhouse later known as Cream Hall was built by the Guidott family at the south-east corner of Highbury wood, probably c. 1716 when Guidott received permission to convert the woods to pasture,[73] as there was no mention of a house in 1692.[74] Although that house was called Cream Hall in 1746[75] and 1775,[76] it was known as Mrs. Guidott's new farm in 1718 and 1719, when Cream Hall was the name given to a house at Stroud Green.[77] The later Cream Hall may therefore have been rebuilt to replace the earlier house. It was a private dwelling by the early 19th century and was still a villa residence in the 1850s and 1860s, but was sold for building by the early 1880s, forming the site of Legard Road.[78]

Christopher Wase bought a capital messuage and seven closes in Upper Holloway containing c. 50 a. in 1622 from William Daniell, all copyhold of the manor of St. John's, Clerkenwell;[79] the house and four closes of c. 45 a. had been held by Humphrey Harbury (d. 1560) and by his widow Alice (also surnamed Hancock) c. 1570.[80] Wase died in 1643 in possession of the estate, where he apparently lived, besides half of the

manor of St. John's.[81] His widow Judith held *WASE'S* estate for life; she had married William Martin, clerk, by 1649 and was dead by 1675.[82] A Chancery order of that year confirmed an agreement of 1656 between Wase's two daughters whereby 5 a. adjoining Hornsey Lane went, with the half of St. John's manor, to George Masters, who had married Wase's daughter Judith, and all the other lands in Middlesex went to the other daughter Hester (d. 1678) and her husband Sir Henry Blount (d. 1682), the traveller, and then in succession to their second son Charles (d. 1693), the deist,[83] to Charles's eldest son Lt.-Col. Henry Blount (d. 1704), and Henry's brother Charles (d. 1729). A sister Hester, wife of Sir Harry Tyrrell,[84] sold the property in 1732, possibly to Watkinson Wildman and his wife Susanna,[85] who paid rates on it until 1766.[86] Later ownership is uncertain, although the house and land probably formed the 48-a. estate belonging to Edward Dickenson in 1806.[87]

The Blount family also owned two closes called *BARNFIELD* or Barnsbury or Moat field, of $6\frac{1}{2}$ a., and *PONDFIELD* of $20\frac{1}{4}$ a., with its spring, which were part of the demesnes of Barnsbury manor in 1556, when they were let by Edmund Fowler,[88] and included the site of the manor house.[89] Barnfield was among lands settled by Sir Thomas Fowler on his son Thomas in 1601, who probably settled both fields on his daughter Sarah Fisher in 1640.[90] The two fields were probably included in sales of demesne made from 1654 to 1675.[91] By 1678 they were held by Charles Blount (d. 1693), having perhaps been his father's.[92] Charles's son Charles sold them in 1714 to Stephen Terry, cursitor of Chancery.[93] By 1718, $3\frac{1}{2}$ a. on the north-east side, adjoining the Back Road, were set aside for building.[94] The estate passed through Stephen's nephew Richard Terry to Richard's son Stephen, who in 1768 sold it to Nathaniel Bishop (d. 1790), who settled it in 1783 on his son Nathaniel.[95] In 1806 the property consisted of a cottage, $5\frac{1}{2}$ a. and a gravel pit, the $20\frac{1}{2}$ a. Workhouse and Moat fields thrown into one, and a row of houses on $1\frac{1}{4}$ a.[96] The younger Nathaniel (d. 1836)[97] agreed in 1810 with Robert Clarke and Henry Richardson, surveyor to the adjoining Thornhill estate, for a building lease on part of his land, and after their bankruptcy in 1813 obtained an Act in 1815 to enable him to carry out building.[98] The whole estate was built over by 1849,[99] stretching from the Back Road north of the workhouse to Caledonian Road over the later Barnsbury Square.

[68] P.R.O., E 367/6962; ibid. E 367/5079.
[69] M.L.R. 1775/5/282; P.R.O., E 367/5718.
[70] M.L.R. 1789/4/185, 156, 158; 1798/3/489.
[71] G.L.R.O., P83/MRY1/390.
[72] Tomlins, *Islington*, 121–2.
[73] *Cal. Treas. Bks.* 1706, 215.   [74] P.R.O., C 8/436/98.
[75] Rocque, *Map of Lond.* (1741–5).
[76] P.R.O., MPE 472.
[77] G.L.R.O., MA/DCP/63; P.R.O., MPF 375.
[78] Nelson, *Islington* (1829), 150; Tomlins, *Islington*, 198; 'Thank you St. John's' (TS. booklet in Islington libr.).
[79] G.L.R.O., Q/HAL/166.
[80] Guildhall MS. 9171/15, f. 41; P.R.O., C 3/134/40.
[81] P.R.O., C 142/778, no. 108.
[82] *Cal. Cttee. for Compounding*, iii. 2015; G.L.R.O., Q/HAL/167, 168.
[83] G.L.R.O., Q/HAL/170–80; *D.N.B.*

[84] G.L.R.O., Q/HAL/185, 187; Clutterbuck, *Hist. Herts.* i. 211.
[85] M.L.R. 1732/1/84–6.
[86] Islington libr., par. rate bks.
[87] Dent's plan and ref. bk. (1806). An Edw. Dickenson was the husband of Wildman's gt. niece.
[88] P.R.O., C 142/127, no. 21; M.L.R. 1718/5/160.
[89] Above, manors, Barnsbury.
[90] Hunts. R.O., Thornhill MSS., deeds 148/2/783, 784 (N.R.A. Rep. 16298).
[91] Above, manors, Barnsbury.
[92] P.R.O., C 10/410/49.
[93] M.L.R. 1715/5/18.
[94] M.L.R. 1718/5/160.
[95] M.L.R. 1768/1/414–15; 55 Geo. III, c. 64 (Private).
[96] Dent's ref. bk. (1806).   [97] Lewis, *Islington*, 235.
[98] 55 Geo. III, c. 64 (Private).   [99] P.R.O., IR 30/21/33.

In 1587 Jasper Cholmondley died in possession of a capital messuage called the *BREWHOUSE*, with outhouses and 42 a. in Nether Holloway and two closes of 4¾ a. in Islington, all held of Barnsbury manor in free socage. He also held copyhold in various manors.[1] A third of the property passed for life to his widow Margaret, who married William Wootton, and the rest to Cholmondley's eldest son John (d. *c.* 1590), who conveyed it to Thomas Buskel and Richard Cholmondley to pay debts.[2] In 1607 Jasper's son William surrendered 55 a. of his father's copyhold of Barnsbury manor to Thomas Fisher of London,[3] and the freehold estate may have been conveyed at the same time as in 1619 the property was held by Susan, widow of Thomas Fisher, and her son Sir Thomas Fisher (d. 1636), being settled on his wife Sarah.[4] After Sarah inherited the manor of Barnsbury from her father in 1656, the Brewhouse and Fisher's other land became part of the Barnsbury demesnes, known as manor farm.[5]

The *CHRIST'S HOSPITAL* estate originated in a freehold sold by Richard Martin of Islington to John Yorke, brewer of London, and his wife Ellen in 1601. It consisted of a capital messuage known as the Horsehead or Nag's Head, formerly called Gower hawe, a close of 3½ a., and six houses occupied by craftsmen, all on the west side of Upper Street at its junction with the Back Road, and 6 a. called Gosseyfield, on the west side of the Back Road.[6] Yorke (d. 1612) left all his free and copyhold lands to Ellen and then to his son William for life, followed by William's four sons.[7] In 1630 the three surviving sons, John, William, and Samuel, divided their property in Islington and elsewhere: John Yorke received Gosseyfield,[8] William received four houses including the Black Horse and Ringcross field of 5 a., and Samuel received the Nag's Head and an adjoining close, which included ½ a. of copyhold of Barnsbury manor.[9] In 1638 Samuel Yorke sold the Nag's Head, two houses formerly part of it, and the close adjoining to Richard Atkinson, cordwainer of London, whose family had occupied the inn since 1601.[10] Atkinson sold the inn and freehold land to John Browne in 1649,[11] who left it by will proved 1663 to Christ's Hospital towards the maintenance of three scholars at Christ's College and three at Emmanuel College, Cambridge.[12] The ½ a. copyhold, to which Atkinson's four daughters were admitted on his death in 1651, was surrendered to Christ's Hospital in 1662 and enfranchised in 1664,[13] when the close adjoining the inn was

known as Park field.[14] By 1745 there were five wooden tenements fronting Upper Street and three old brick tenements fronting the Back Road.[15] The Hospital also bought houses in 1786 from Thomas Clarke, which included one at the corner of Upper Street and the Back Road.[16] Christ's Hospital's open land was built over in the 1850s with Paradise (later Parkfield) Street.[17] By 1806 the Hospital also owned 6¾ a. in Holloway, described as the site of Skinners Place next to the chapel of ease and a field near Ring Cross.[18]

Gosseyfield, the 6 a. allotted to John Yorke in 1630, was sold following his bankruptcy to John Walter (d. 1656) in 1638.[19] The land passed to Walter's daughter Ann, wife of Walter Mills, and in 1690 she conveyed it to the Draper's Company of London to help maintain its almshouse charities founded by her father. The *DRAPERS*' estate, of 6½ a. in 1806, was let for grazing and fattening cattle on their way to Smithfield until 1839, when it was let for building as the site of Lonsdale Square and the adjacent streets. The Company sold the estate in 1954.

The *MILDMAY* estate originated in a copyhold of Newington Barrow manor. William Halliday or Holliday (d. 1623), alderman of London, held it by 1611 and surrendered it to uses in 1622.[20] He had a capital messuage at Newington Green with a 2-a. orchard and garden enclosed with a brick wall and 44 a. occupied by himself, together with three tenements or cottages, a house with a walled garden and orchard, and *c.* 19 a. The chief house was of at least six bays and probably three storeys; the first floor had oak wainscotting, a decorated plaster ceiling with the initials of James I, and carved chimneypieces, including one with Halliday's arms.[21] In 1623 the estate passed to Halliday's widow Susanna (d. 1646)[22] who later married Robert Rich, earl of Warwick (d. 1658),[23] and the Newington Green estate may have been that which was damaged by soldiers in 1643.[24] By will dated 1645 Susanna left her copyhold to her daughter Margaret Halliday, wife of Sir Edward Hungerford.[25] Margaret (d. 1673) left her copyhold to Henry Mildmay, second son of her sister Anne and Sir Henry, in tail male.[26] Mildmay broke the entail and sold some decayed houses.[27]

After Henry's death in 1704, the estate passed to Letitia (d. 1749), daughter of Henry's son Halliday (d. 1696), and she married a cousin, Humphrey Hervey Mildmay (d. 1761), in 1706. Their son Carew (d. 1768) left the estate to his eldest daughter Jane (d. 1857), whose husband Sir Henry Paulet St. John, Bt. (d. 1808), added

---

[1] P.R.O., C 142/219, no. 88.
[2] Ibid. REQ 2/129/8.
[3] G.L.R.O., M83/BAR/21.
[4] P.R.O., C 142/543, no. 28.
[5] Above, manors, Barnsbury.
[6] Guildhall MS. 12958/3.
[7] Ibid. 2.
[8] Below (Drapers').
[9] Guildhall MS. 12958/3.
[10] Ibid. 1.
[11] Ibid. 4.
[12] Ibid. 2.
[13] Ibid. 1.
[14] Ibid. 4.
[15] Ibid. 1; 5.
[16] P.R.O., C 5/157/25; Guildhall MSS. 12958/4; 1.

[17] Above, growth, Barnsbury.
[18] Nelson, *Islington* (1811), 54; Baker's plan (1817).
[19] Para. based on Drapers' Hall, Walter's trust, deeds D 29, 34, 52, 93, 98, and Estate Cttee. Mins. xv. 15; W. Archer-Thomson, *Drapers' Co.: Hist. of Co.'s Properties and Trusts* (1939–40), i. 249–50; ii. 167, 171.
[20] Nelson, *Islington* (1829), 174; Guildhall MS. 3460/2.
[21] Nelson, *Islington* (1829), 175; 20th-cent. photo. in *Changing Face of Newington Green* (Factory Community Centre 1977), 46.
[22] Guildhall MS. 3460/2; P.R.O., C 5/2/50.
[23] Nelson, *Islington* (1829), 175.
[24] *Cal. S. P. Dom.* 1641–3, 441–2.
[25] P.R.O., PROB 11/195 (P.C.C. 20 Twisse); ibid. C 5/2/50.
[26] Ibid. PROB 11/342, f. 58.   [27] Ibid. C 6/287/49.

the name of Mildmay in 1790.[28] The estate covered 64½ a. in 1806.[29] Lady St. John Mildmay obtained an Act in 1827 to allow her to grant building leases,[30] but little building was done until the 1850s and most of the estate was sold in lots in 1859.[31] The main house had been divided in two by the early 19th century, with one part occupied by Mildmay House boarding school.[32] It was later taken over by the Mildmay Mission as a nurses' home[33] and was demolished c. 1960.[34]

John Banks gave some land on the west side of Holloway Road to the Mercers' Company of London in 1619.[35] The *MERCERS'* estate was 6¾ a. in 1806,[36] and Mercers' Road was built on it in the 1860s.[37] The Mercers' Company also bought land in 1823 on the east side of Archway Road from the Highgate Archway Co., as a site for Whittington college, and bought land opposite the college in 1838. The college housed almswomen until 1966, when it moved to East Grinstead (Suss.) and the site was sold for road widening.[38] A small public garden was laid out on part of the site in the 1970s.

Sir John Miller (d. 1639) bought a house and 14 a., copyhold of Barnsbury manor, from Thomas Sanderson by 1624, and used the house as his residence. He left the estate to his second son John, who was to pay an annuity to another son and who was admitted in 1640. In 1642 John's elder brother Michael surrendered the estate to James Ravenscroft, on condition that Ravenscroft pay the annuity for John. In 1646 Ravenscroft surrendered the estate to the use of his son James and the latter's wife Mary, to use it as security for the payment of legacies to Mary's daughters Elizabeth and Judith, left by their father Theophilus Fletcher. The daughters were admitted to the estate in 1649.[39] Judith, who married Henry Dew, held the estate in 1668, and by 1675 it had passed to her son Henry Dew.[40] By 1727, the house, called the Pied Bull inn, was held by William Westbrook who surrendered it to Thomas Milner, and Milner also held the 14 a. at his death in 1733, when his son Thomas was admitted. In 1798 a kinsman Thomas Milner Gibson was admitted to the *PIED BULL* estate and on his death in 1814 it passed to his son Thomas Gibson.[41] Gibson built over the estate from 1825 to 1842, with Gibson and Milner squares and the adjacent streets, and enfranchised the estate in 1846.[42]

A large copyhold estate at Holloway in the manor of St. John's, Clerkenwell, was held by Thomas Rowe in 1625.[43] *ROWE'S* estate consisted of 50¾ a. drawn from various holdings. By will dated 1624 Rowe left his copyholds to his eldest son John, who was admitted in 1625. John,

by will dated 1657, left his Islington estate to his nephew Thomas Darrell or Dorrill (d. 1700) for life. Henry and William Darrell succeeded in 1701 and immediately conveyed the estate to George Jarvis (d. 1718), who sold a house in Lower Holloway to Elias Moreton in 1717. The rest of Jarvis's estate, including in 1715 a farm-house, 2 barns, 9 fields of c. 60 a., 2 little tenements, and the Plough (later the Crown) in Lower Holloway, was bought in 1720 by Lascelles Metcalfe (d. 1741) and passed to his son Lascelles, who died in 1781 leaving his estate, 57 a. besides 5 a. of copyhold of Highbury manor, to John Harman to pay legacies. Harman left the copyhold by will proved 1817 to his sons Jeremiah, Edward, and Henry to sell as they wished, and Henry was admitted in 1819 as trustee. Seven lots were sold in 1822, when copyholds totalling 31¾ a. and the freehold Further and Hither Dock fields totalling c. 6 a. fronting Hornsey Road were bought by William Mayor.[44] In 1838 the estate was mortgaged to James Peachey, who was listed in 1849 as owning 33¼ a.;[45] the copyhold was enfranchised in 1854. In 1855 Richard Anstead Simmons bought 10½ a. for building and c. 23 a. were conveyed outright by Mayor to Peachey; both blocks were soon built over, from Kingsdown Road to just south of Elthorne Road.[46] Of the rest of Metcalfe's estate, the Crown and 6¾ a. were owned by Charles Bligh in 1849, and 15½ a. were owned by Lord Northampton.[47]

The Revd. James Palmer, vicar of St. Bride's, Fleet Street, had bought a copyhold house and 47 a. at Upper Holloway in the manor of St. Mary's, Clerkenwell, by 1637, and by will published in 1659 left the estate to trustees who were to continue his payments of £5 a year each to 20 widows of orthodox clergymen.[48] In 1693 the trustees conveyed the *PALMER* estate to the governors of the Charity for the Relief of Poor Widows and Children of Clergymen, later known as the Corporation of the Sons of the Clergy, who held the estate until 1972. Most of it was then sold to the Peabody Trust.[49] In 1684 the house, fronting Holloway Road, was the Castle and Falcon inn (later the Horse and Groom),[50] and in 1715 fields totalling 50½ a. stretched westward from the inn to the parish boundary.[51] About 1 a. was given for the site of St. John's church and school in 1827 and the rest was enfranchised in 1846.[52] Building leases were granted from the early 1840s, most of them in the 1850s.[53]

Sir Thomas Fowler in 1639 granted to Richard Corbett, husband of his daughter Jane, *BARNSBURY CLOSES*, part of the demesnes of Barnsbury, in trust for Corbett's sons Thomas and Rowland. The closes consisted of Upper, Lower,

[28] Burke, *Peerage* (1904); M.L.R. 1750/2/48.
[29] Dent's plan and ref. bk. (1806).
[30] P.R.O., C 54/15039, no. 11; 7 & 8 Geo. IV, c. 52 (Private).
[31] Above, growth, Newington Green.
[32] Nelson, *Islington* (1829), 175.
[33] Below, undenom. missions.
[34] Above, growth, Newington Green.
[35] J. Imray, *Char. of Ric. Whittington* (1968), 77.
[36] Dent's ref. bk. (1806).
[37] O.S. Map 6", Mdx. XII. SW. (1863–9 edn.).
[38] Imray, *Char. of Ric. Whittington*, 77–8, 106.
[39] G.L.R.O., M83/BAR/1, 23.
[40] P.R.O., C 5/436/64; C 5/471/100.

[41] G.L.R.O., M83/BAR/2, 7, p. 54.
[42] P.R.O., MAF 9/163, no. 159.
[43] Para. based on MS. vol. of Abstracts of Deeds, pp. 39–44; G.L.R.O., F/PEY/26, 27.
[44] Islington libr., deed 516.
[45] P.R.O., IR 29/21/33.
[46] Islington libr., deed 528 with plan; deed 524.
[47] P.R.O., IR 29/21/33.
[48] G.L.R.O., A/CSC/2628.
[49] Ibid. CSC/3161/o.
[50] Ibid. CSC/2632, 2653, 2657–8.
[51] Ibid. CSC/2648, 3161/B.
[52] P.R.O., C 54/15906, no. 12.
[53] G.L.R.O., A/CSC/3161/G; 2660; 2684–2700B.

and Hither Barnsbury, altered to two closes by 1651, and totalling 15 a., and Clayfield of 3 a. In 1662 the property was held by Rowland Corbett, with two other parcels of land of 24 a., and in 1686 it was being let by Richard Corbett,[54] who died between 1689 and 1696. Richard's widow Elizabeth and son William mortgaged the estate for terms of 500 years and 1,000 years in 1710 and 1716 respectively and as a result the beneficial ownership seems to have been acquired by Richard Orton in 1717,[55] and to have passed by his will dated 1728 to his son William, who assigned his interest in 1737 to his sister Sarah (d. 1780). It then passed to another sister Ann (d. 1786), wife of John Little;[56] she left it to her son Richard, who left it to his five daughters by will proved 1796. In 1826 the daughters and their husbands sold 19 a. of their 43 a. to John Thomas Pocock, who had agreed to sell it to Richard Chapman, the builder. Land owned by the Littles near the Back Road was said to have been sold to Thomas Cubitt by 1840 but all the open land between Pentonville Prison and the Back Road belonged to Pocock's son Samuel in 1849.[57] The Littles' estate lay between Hagbush Lane (roughly Sheringham Road) and Offord Road and took in the site of Westbourne Road. J. T. Pocock also acquired adjoining property, including WATERPIT or BENTLEY'S field which had provided the site of the parochial school in 1814.[58]

The THORNHILL estate originated in the sale of demesne of Barnsbury manor in 1654 to Thomas Arnold, George Arnold, and Edward Anthony, including Bowling Alley fields and totalling 65¼ a.[59] In 1656 the two closes called Maiden Knowles, 17¼ a. near Copenhagen House, were added and in 1670 Anthony confirmed them to George Arnold as Thomas Arnold's heir. By 1720 the estate was owned by Cuthbert Routh, who sold Bowling Alley fields and Maiden Knowles to Thomas Thornhill, subject to a rent charge of £26 to the Haberdashers' Company of London. The rest of the Arnolds' estate was Thornhill's by 1767, when he conveyed it all to his brother George (d. 1827). The estate covered 88 a. in 1806.[60] From 1808 Thornhill made building agreements, which were continued by his son George (d. 1852) and grandson George (d. 1875), until the whole estate had been built over.[61] The freehold of part remained in the Thornhill family, being vested in trustees after the death of Noel Thornhill in 1955, and tenants were seeking to buy freeholds in 1968.[62]

Michael Davison by will dated 1676 left a freehold house and land in Upper Holloway to the parish of St. Benet Sherehog for the upkeep of his tomb.[63] By 1862 the ST. BENET estate was the site of Euston Place, Holloway Road, and the house was called Union Cottage, Hercules Terrace.[64]

The MASERES or HIGHBURY NEW PARK estate originated in the sale of 135 a. of demesne of Highbury manor to Peter Abraham Maseres in 1732,[65] to which were added 4 a. of enfranchised copyhold between the demesne and Newington Green Road in 1753.[66] A farmhouse, later called Dells Farm, was built on the 4 a. by 1793. The estate passed to Peter's elder son Francis Maseres (1731–1824), mathematician and historian,[67] and he held 139¼ a. in 1806, 120 a. in 1822.[68] Francis left the estate to his friend the Revd. Robert Fellowes (1771–1847), philanthropist,[69] who left it to his sons Robert and William.[70] In 1849 the estate was 118½ a.[71] and in 1852 it was transferred to Henry Rydon, who built over it.[72]

The HIGHBURY HOUSE estate was formed from 247 a. of the demesne of Highbury manor sold to John Dawes in 1773.[73] Dawes, who had also bought adjoining lands consisting of the freehold Weryngs and the leases of Highbury woods and of London Fields,[74] laid out Highbury Place and Terrace and built Highbury House in 1781 on the site of the ruined manor house of Highbury, adding extensive pleasure gardens.[75] After his death in 1788 his son John (d. 1822) sold most of the property to pay his father's debts,[76] retaining 92 a. in 1794, of which c. 10 a. had not been demesne.[77] Under the will of the younger John, the remainder of the estate, which was 62 a. in 1849,[78] passed to trustees for Henry Dawes, who was succeeded as beneficial owner by Charles William Dawes, who retained some freehold in 1885, principally the sites of Highbury Place, Terrace, and Crescent and part of Highbury Grove.[79]

After the death of the elder John Dawes, Highbury House was sold to William Devaynes, M.P., and then by 1797 to the astronomer Alexander Aubert (d. 1805), who built an observatory of three storeys, where there was a reflecting telescope said to be the largest made by James Short. Other additions by Aubert included the placing of a clock from St. Peter-le-Poer, Broad Street, in a turret nearby, and the filling of the moat except in front of the house. In 1805 the house with 74 a. was sold to John Bentley, who walled a large part of the grounds, which included a plantation of tobacco in 1809 and were noted as productive

[54] Islington libr., deeds box I/2–8.
[55] M.L.R. 1710/3/78–80; Guildhall MS. 19224/436, file 5.
[56] Rest of para. based on Guildhall MS. 19224/436, file 5.
[57] P.R.O., IR 29/21/33.
[58] Ibid. C 54/9473, no. 13.
[59] Para. based on Hunts. R.O., Cal. of Thornhill MSS. (N.R.A. Rep. 16298); Islington libr., deeds 928, 930.
[60] Dent's plan and ref. bk. (1806).
[61] Above, growth, Barnsbury.
[62] Islington libr. Thornhill Estate Assoc. Memoranda (1968).
[63] Guildhall MS. 849.
[64] Ibid. MS. 7631.
[65] M.L.R. 1732/1/54–5.
[66] M.L.R. 1753/2/447; Baker's plan (1793).

[67] D.N.B.
[68] Dent's plan and ref. bk. (1806); G.L.R.O., MA/DCP/62.
[69] D.N.B.
[70] J. Smallshaw, Hen. Rydon and Highbury New Pk. Est. 4 (booklet from author).
[71] P.R.O., IR 29/21/33.
[72] Above, growth, Highbury.
[73] M.L.R. 1773/3/287–8.
[74] Above.
[75] Univ. Brit. Dir. iii (1791–7), 442.
[76] M.L.R. 1789/4/69, 156, 329.
[77] Islington libr., deed 558.
[78] P.R.O., IR 29/21/33.
[79] Islington libr., deeds 328, 558.

gardens in 1810. The government was said to use the observatory regularly.[80] Bentley was succeeded by Robert Felton in 1815, followed by Mr. Knight, a distiller, and John Gostling, the owner in 1835.[81] The rest of the moat was filled in 1855,[82] and the grounds were built over by the late 1860s. The house was demolished in 1938 and Eton House, Leigh Road, built on the site. Part of the servants' wing survived behind Christ Church hall, Leigh Road, in 1973.[83]

St. Bartholomew's Hospital in 1806 owned 6¾ a. called *BAKER'S* field, of unknown origin. It lay between Camden Road and Tufnell Park in 1849 and was built over with St. Bartholomew's Road (later Dalmeny Avenue) from the mid 1850s.[84]

ECONOMIC HISTORY. AGRARIAN HISTORY. In 1086 there were 12 hides and 1 virgate in cultivation, roughly half the acreage of Islington, including the land which Hugh de Berners held of the bishop, which was probably in the parish. There were six holdings, varying widely in size. Berners held 5 hides and 1 virgate with land for 4 ploughteams, of which one was in demesne and the rest held by villeins. One villein held ½ hide, six bordars shared 3 virgates, two bordars shared ½ virgate, and three cottars shared 2½ a. There was meadow to support 4 teams, and woodland for 150 pigs.[85] The canons of St. Paul's had two holdings of 2 hides each. On one there was arable for 1½ team but only 1 team was kept. Three villeins held 1 virgate, and there was common pasture for their cattle. The other holding had land for 2½ teams and was held from the canons by 4 villeins; there were also 4 bordars and 13 cottars.[86] Ranulf held Tollington, consisting of 2 hides with land for 2 teams. One hide was in demesne with 1 team, but the villeins had 2 teams. Five villeins each held ½ virgate, two bordars held 9 a., and there was a cottar and a serf. There was pasture for the cattle and woodland for 60 pigs. The two holdings were ½ hide each, with land for half a team. Derman's holding had one villein,[87] and Gilbert's holding had one villein and one bordar.[88]

By the early 14th century Islington was divided between five manors, three wholly within the parish and two mainly in Clerkenwell. Neither of the two Clerkenwell manors had demesne land in Islington. Barnsbury had 180 a. of arable and 5 a. of meadow in demesne in 1297, when the 48 customary tenants owed annual works at haymaking and harvest.[89] In 1388 the lord still had demesne in hand with 123 a. of arable, of which 30 a. were

fallow that year, 100 a. of pasture, and 20 a. of meadow. He had 28 a. of corn and 60 a. of oats under crop and kept 39 cows, a bull, four stots, and six steers.[90] The manor had roughly equal amounts of arable and pasture in 1502 with a smaller proportion of meadow.[91] By the mid 16th century at least 134 a. of demesne were leased out.[92] Sales and grants of demesne were made in the 1550s and in 1639 (18 a.), 1654 (65 a.), 1656 (17 a.), 1667 (118 a.), 1675 (18 a.), and by 1678 (27 a.),[93] which included the site of the manor house and probably accounted for all the demesne.

Canonbury manor was nearly all demesne in 1306. The 18 customary holdings consisted of only 17 houses and 12¼ a. of land, while the demesne in hand was 157½ a. of arable, 3¾ a. of meadow besides a close near the manor house, 30 a. of sheep pastures, and 4 a. of grazing around the arable fields for tethered horses and cattle. A 20-a. field called Randulffesfeld was let to Richard de la Pyry.[94] William Yon had a lease of all or part of Canonbury and Cutlers in 1467.[95] By 1529 Thomas Cromwell held a lease of the manor and demesne from the prior of St. Bartholomew's.[96] In 1540 the mansion, garden, dovecot, and six closes of more than 25 a. nearby were let to farm, and eleven other parcels of demesne were let to named tenants; no demesne was apparently in hand.[97] William Rickthorne held some or all of the demesne with his lease of Canonbury House from 1565 and by his will of 1582 made subleases for the rest of his 31-year term of c. 30 a., included three closes of little Cutlers and one close of Fulplasshes.[98] The lease of the mansion to Sir Francis Bacon also included c. 70 a. of demesne.[99] In the 1650s Lord Northampton was leasing out parcels which accounted for most of the land held with the house in the 1540s.[1] The demesne continued to be let, mainly to local tenants, until built over from c. 1800.[2]

Highbury manor had a large proportion of arable to meadow, pasture, and wood in 1338,[3] and the lord had corn and grass growing there in 1380.[4] Only 34 a. out of 300 a. demesne were specified as arable in the 1530s when the land and the grange were leased to Thomas Cromwell.[5] In 1541 the farm of the demesne was let by the Crown for 21 years to Sir Thomas Wroth (d. 1573), through the agency of his father-in-law Sir Richard Rich. New leases were obtained by Wroth in 1562[6] and 1572 for 21 years,[7] by his six sons in 1585 to run until 1605,[8] and in reversion by Sir John Fortescue, Chancellor of the Exchequer, in 1594 for 60 years.[9] The lease had

[80] Nelson, *Islington* (1811), 138–40; *D.N.B.* s.v. Aubert.
[81] Cromwell, *Islington*, 302.
[82] Tomlins, *Islington*, 176.
[83] Zwart, *Islington: Hist. and Guide*, 140.
[84] Nelson, *Islington* (1811), 54; P.R.O., IR 30/21/33; Plan [c. 1853].
[85] *V.C.H. Mdx.* i. 120.
[86] Ibid. 122.
[87] Ibid. 129.
[88] Ibid. 126.
[89] P.R.O., C 133/79, no. 10.
[90] *Cal. Inq. Misc.* v, pp. 15–16.
[91] P.R.O., CP 25(1)/152/101, no. 83.
[92] Ibid. C 142/127, no. 21.
[93] Islington libr., deeds 928, 930; P.R.O., C 6/178/83; C 6/312/16; C 6/83/95; above, other est. (Barnfield, Barnsbury Closes, Thornhill).

[94] Webb, *Rec. of St. Barts.* i. 447–9.
[95] Guildhall MS. 9171/6, f. 30v.
[96] *L. & P. Hen. VIII*, iv (3), p. 2574.
[97] B.L. Harl. Roll I. 15.
[98] P.R.O., PROB 11/65 (P.C.C. 9 Rowe).
[99] Tomlins, *Islington*, 113 n., 114 n.
[1] Islington libr., deeds box 1.
[2] Above, growth, Canonbury.
[3] *Knights Hospitallers in Eng.* (Camden Soc. [1st ser.] lxv), 126.
[4] *Cal. Pat.* 1377–81, 567.
[5] P.R.O., E 315/191, f. 144.
[6] Ibid. E 310/19/90, nos. 27, 33; *D.N.B.*
[7] *Cal. Pat.* 1566–72, 463.
[8] P.R.O., C 66/1260, m. 33.
[9] Ibid. C 66/1415, m. 25.

been assigned to Lord Compton by 1611 when he held 426 a.,[10] and came to William Halliday, who was succeeded by his wife Susanna in 1623. She assigned it to trustees in 1625 and left it to her daughter Anne (d. 1657), wife of Sir Henry Mildmay, and Anne left the lease in trust for her son William Mildmay.[11] The lease presumably expired in 1665 and the lord, Thomas Austen, let 138 a. for 30 years in 1669[12] and probably other parcels on similar leases. Two other parcels of demesne were leased separately in the 16th century, Dambottom or Danesbottom (12 a.) and Longmead (19 a.). Leases of 21 years were granted in 1541 to Sir Henry Knyvett, of the king's household, in 1560 to Thomas, duke of Norfolk, to run from 1562, and in 1568 to Robert Wiseman, gentleman pensioner, from the end of Norfolk's lease.[13] These were probably the two meadows of $32\frac{3}{4}$ a. held by Sir Nicholas Coote in 1611 on a lease dated 1588,[14] and a lease for 60 years for the land was granted in 1610–11 to an unknown lessee.[15] By 1718 they were in the hands of the lord of the manor again, and they were included in the sale of the manor and demesnes. The demesne in 1718 covered c. 380 a. excluding Highbury woods.[16] Sales of demesne were made in 1732 to Peter Abraham Maseres (135 a.) and in 1773 to John Dawes (247 a.).[17] Customary land accounted for at least 418 a. in 1540, of which 281 a. were at Tollington and Stroud, 62 a. in Islington, and 75 a. at Newington Green.[18] In 1611 the manor included $414\frac{3}{4}$ a. of copyhold, $113\frac{3}{4}$ a. held by eight freeholders, and 459 a. demesne.[19]

There is no evidence that Islington had open arable fields, but there were parcels of common land such as Newington green, Kingsland green, and Islington green, which were manorial waste. A small area called Islington common in 1817[20] probably originated as Hyde Lane.[21] In the 17th and 18th centuries a field in the south-east corner of the parish was called the common field of Islington but by 1618 it had been inclosed and divided among copyholders of Highbury,[22] and in the 19th century was the site of City Gardens.[23] It may have been part of the 'common fields about Islington, Hoxton and Shoreditch' where in 1513 Londoners destroyed new hedges and ditches, in order to regain access for archery and other pastimes.[24] The fields were evidently open pastures, in view of their use for sports. Much customary land in Islington, Holloway, and Tollington apparently had been turned into inclosures which had more than one tenant and

varied land use.[25] In the early 16th century arable and pasture existed within the same closes of Cutlers estate and Highbury demesne.[26]

Winter wheat was growing in the 1380s;[27] in 1420 an inhabitant bequeathed cows, pigs, sheep, ewes, a horse and harness, and 6 a. of crops.[28] In 1542 John England, a leading parishioner, bequeathed 15 cows, timber, two dung carts, two other carts with two plough-horses, five oxen, and a yoke and chains.[29] By the 16th century, however, the proximity of London had made grazing important and by 1556 there had been several conversions to pasture of land that had been in tillage for four years in the previous 40. Among local residents Thomas Turvyn was presented for 7 a. at Stroud Green, Thomas Caysar for 30 a., Christopher Newton of Holloway for 6 a., Mistress Wrothe for 30 a. at Highbury, and Lionel Biggins for 40 a.; Londoners included Robert Barton for 16 a. at Tollington, George Deeping for 31 a. at Holloway, the London innholder leasing Trayeshill for 80 a., and one Martin, an innkeeper, for 16 a. at Holloway.[30] London butchers leased large pastures to fatten cattle before slaughter,[31] and John Parnell, a London draper, who had moved to Newington Green, in 1537 was owed by one tenant a fortnight's grazing for 11 beasts at 3d. each per week.[32] The earl of Rutland was renting a close at Islington in 1554 for oxen and sheep.[33] Deals involving horses and hay were also important in the 17th century and it was still common for both innkeepers and farmers to buy cattle for fattening in the 1690s.[34]

Walter Burton bought cows in Oxfordshire and elsewhere c. 1710 and 1720 for himself and his brother-in-law John Radcliffe, who kept them in a shed in Islington. They also obtained grain, besides dung and night-soil for their meadows.[35] Islington, a major source of London's milk supply, was one of the parishes to which special attention was given during an epidemic of cattle distemper (Rinderpest) in 1714. When the disease abated after $2\frac{1}{2}$ months, 667 cows had been destroyed and 550 saved:[36] John Radcliffe had lost 12 cows out of 200, a Mr. Rufford 62 out of 72, and Samuel Pullin 38 out of 87.[37] In the mid 18th century several small grass farms in Upper and Lower streets and Holloway had herds of 20–100 cows.[38] Stock was bought at local markets, such as Islington or Barnet, or on commission in Yorkshire in batches of 10–20. The large cattle were called Holderness but many came from farther north, such as Durham or the

[10] Nelson, *Islington* (1829), 134–6, citing a survey of 1611 now lost.
[11] P.R.O., C 10/13/116; ibid. PROB 11/195 (P.C.C. 20 Twisse); PROB 11/263, f. 127. [12] Ibid. C 5/610/181.
[13] *L. & P. Hen. VIII*, xvii, p. 704; P.R.O., E 310/19/90, no. 33(b); *Cal. Pat.* 1558–60, 278; 1566–9, 266.
[14] Nelson, *Islington* (1829), 136.
[15] Corp. of Lond. R.O., RCE rentals box 1.18.
[16] G.L.R.O., MA/DCP/63.
[17] M.L.R. 1732/1/54–5; 1733/3/287/8.
[18] P.R.O., SC 6/Hen. VIII/2402, m. 11.
[19] Nelson, *Islington* (1829), 136.
[20] Baker's plan (1817).
[21] Above, communications.
[22] B.L. Add. MS. 15556, f. 173.
[23] Location ascertained from B.L. Add. MS. 15556, f. 173, and Dent's plan and ref. bk. (1806).

[24] Holinshed, *Chronicle* (1808), iii. 399.
[25] P.R.O., SC 6/Hen. VIII/2402, mm. 4, 11.
[26] Ibid. E 315/113, ff. 169–80; E 315/191, f. 144.
[27] *Public Wks. in Med. Law*, ii (Selden Soc. xl), 79–80.
[28] Guildhall MS. 9171/3, f. 69.
[29] P.R.O., PROB 11/29 (P.C.C. 25 Spert).
[30] Bodl. MS. Eng. Hist. c. 318, ff. 5–6v.
[31] K. G. T. McDonnell, *Modern Lond. Suburbs* (1978), 61.
[32] P.R.O., PROB 11/27 (P.C.C. 13 Dyngeley).
[33] Hist. MSS. Com. 24, *Rutland*, iv, p. 376.
[34] Inf. from Dr. Peter Edwards; P.R.O., C 7/180/100; C/7/338/11.
[35] P.R.O., E 134/10 Geo. II/Mich. 10 and 16.
[36] *Cal. Treas. Bks.* 1714–15, 82; *Cal. Treas. Bks. and Papers*, 1714–19, pt. 1, 31–4.
[37] M.O.H. *Ann. Rep.* (1865), 10.
[38] Nelson, *Islington* (1811), 106.

North Riding.[39] Very few cows were bred by the keepers; calves were generally sold at birth and the cows fattened after 4 to 7 years' milking. Milking was done by retailers, who contracted for a certain number of cows. The cowkeeper needed only 5 or 6 men to tend 300 cows. The cows were fed grain twice a day even in summer in addition to grass, and also ate turnips, hay, and other supplements. Cowkeepers' meadows were mown two or three times each summer from early May onwards and heavily dressed with manure, to obtain a soft, grassy hay. Demand for milk fell in the summer, when the milk was rich and much was used for butter, the buttermilk being fed to pigs.[40]

By c. 1810 many small dairy farms had been replaced by the concerns of Richard Laycock and Samuel Rhodes, who alone held extensive land or farmstock in Islington. Both men needed large acreages for hay and pasture. Rhodes's farm adjoined Pullins Row in High Street and had formerly belonged to Samuel Pullin who had kept 300–400 cows. Rhodes's stock varied from 400 to 600, the greatest number being kept in winter, and he made several thousand loads of hay which c. 1829 were stacked near Colebrooke Terrace.[41]

Laycock, whose farm lay on both sides of the lane later called Laycock Street, occupied more than 500 a. in Islington, with land at Enfield, and in addition to his farmstead used premises in Hornsey Road to stack hay. He kept 600–700 cows and also more than 100 heavy horses with carts for carrying turnips, potatoes, and grains, mainly for cattle-feed. His premises extended from Upper Street to Liverpool Road and included loose boxes, stables, barns, cowhouses, crop storehouses, grain pits, blacksmiths', wheelwrights', and carpenters' shops, timber yard and sawpits, nos. 4–11 Sebbon's Buildings fronting Upper Street, which included his own residence, the Angel and Crown inn, and six small houses called Moulder's Row at the Liverpool Road end. On the west side of Liverpool Road he owned houses and some building land used as sheep pens in 1835. By that date much of his income came from his covered cattle lairs (often spelt layers), used for keeping animals overnight on their way to Smithfield market. The lairs had been built by the 1820s to hold several thousand bullocks and sheep, and were more advantageous than lairage in the open pens used elsewhere along Liverpool Road. Laycock died in 1834 after 40 years in business, and both he and Rhodes had turned much of their land first to brickmaking and then to building.[42]

In 1841 the occupier of Laycock's farm had six cowsheds, each with 64 cows, pens with 5,000 sheep, and other buildings spread over 16 a., in addition to two or three farms farther from London.[43] There were still some small cow-keepers in the 1840s. A Mr. Briggs had premises at the back of Clifton Place, Holloway Road, where his cows were brought to calve; George Smith had a cow yard and kept 19 cows behind Claremont Row, Barnsbury Mews; a Mr. Vorley had cattle lairs in Upper Holloway in 1849 and he too had turned to brickmaking on some of his land by 1853; a Mr. Dunham, of Gray's Inn Lane, had fields next to the Mother Red Cap inn and in Hornsey Road, where he spread dung.[44] In 1857 there were 54 separate establishments, equally divided between west and east Islington, containing a total of 924 cows. The two chief cowkeepers had 293 and 119 cows respectively, the remainder from 2 to 46. Space, ventilation, and cleanliness were inadequate: only about half the cows received from the country by the largest keeper escaped lung disease during the first two months in sheds and most had to be sold for slaughter. Two very unhealthy sheds were removed, from George's Place and from Lower Road. Licensing was introduced in 1862, for 69 cowhouses then and 71 in 1864.[45]

In 1865 cattle plague started in Mrs. Nicholls's sheds in Liverpool Road (probably the former Laycock's farm) and spread quickly around London. Within three months the number of cows had fallen from 1,317 in 71 licensed cow-sheds to 314 in 45, many beasts having been sent away for safety. By the end of the year 625 cows had died, leaving 274 in the parish.[46] In 1866 there were 61 licensed cowkeepers with 474 cows. The plague discouraged cowkeeping and produced new arrangements for the public supply of milk.[47] In 1866–7 there were still six infected premises.[48] In 1870 there were 33 licensed cow-keepers with 56 sheds, which were carefully checked, and 67 milk-sellers.[49] In 1878 there were 62 sheds licensed for 1,054 cows but not full, and in 1879 there were only 54 sheds.[50]

Incomplete records from 1867 suggest that between 1870, when there was still one agricultural occupier with more than 50 a., and 1885 the number of stock-keepers fell slightly while the number of cows increased, but by 1895 no stock was recorded.[51] A great many pigs were kept, in small numbers, by the poor in areas such as Belle Isle, Britannia Row, Duddy's Rents, and other alleys off Lower Street. Larger piggeries were common, especially around Brandon Street and Belle Isle, where there were six with more than 20 pigs each c. 1855.[52]

NURSERIES AND MARKET GARDENS. From 1668 to c. 1682 part of the grounds of Draper's house near the churchyard was planted with fruit trees and herbs, and the lessee, Catherine Comondall, supported herself by selling the fruit.[53] Andrew Butter leased 1¼ a. on the north side of Church Lane in 1692, where he cultivated fruit trees and other plants and where his landlord built a house

[39] Foot, *Agric. of Mdx.* 82, 89.
[40] Middleton, *View*, 225, 329–36.
[41] Nelson, *Islington* (1829), 108–9, 208–13.
[42] Ibid. 111–12; sale partics. of cattle layers of late Mr. Laycock, 1835, in Islington libr.; Cromwell, *Islington*, 297.
[43] Islington Antiquarian and Hist. Soc., paper read c. 1940 (in Islington libr.).
[44] G.L.R.O., P83/MRY1/721, 730, 747.
[45] M.O.H. *Ann. Rep.* (1857), 14; (1860), 10; (1862), 6; (1864), 19.
[46] Ibid. (1865), 10–13.
[47] Ibid. (1866), 18.
[48] *Rep. M.B.W. 1866–7*, H.C. 45 (1867–8), lviii. 133–4.
[49] M.O.H. *Ann. Rep.* (1870), 14, 17.
[50] Ibid. (1878), 18; (1879), 15.
[51] P.R.O., MAF 68/250, 706, 991, 1333, 1561.
[52] G.L.R.O., P83/MRY1/721; 729; 747/14, 16; M.O.H. *Ann. Rep.* (1856), 12.
[53] P.R.O., C 7/58/60.

for him.[54] Part of the grounds of a large house was let to another gardener, together with a greenhouse, in 1727.[55] In the 18th and early 19th centuries there were several well known nurseries and botanical gardens, some started by amateurs such as Dr. Pitcairn.[56] William Redmond advertised a fine auricula called Triumph in 1756, and in 1810 Mr. Gabell of City Gardens was charging 6d. to inspect his tulips.[57]

William Watson founded a nursery behind Colebrooke Row by 1770, when he and his brother James took a lease of 6 a. of Hattersfield from Sir George Colebrooke, building on it a hothouse and greenhouse.[58] The nursery, a specialist one, in 1771 took part in a great exchange of exotic plants with the Chelsea Physic Garden. The firm became William & James Watson in 1776, but in 1785 James assigned his share of the lease to his brother. Another brother, Thomas, took over at William's death in 1792, and in 1798 was the first person to bring into flower the Pontic azalea, recently sent from the Crimea. The nursery closed in 1824[59] and the land was later sold to Thomas Cubitt.[60]

A nursery of 19 a. on the west side of Kingsland green was run by Lewis & Co. in 1786. Robert Mackie joined in 1787, and the firm of Lewis & Mackie was described in 1797 as a 'patent nursery manufactory'. Thomas Bassington took it over from 1800 but part of his land was taken for brickmaking and building, and by 1810 he had only 8 a. George Henry Bassington had succeeded by 1822 and George Hockley Bunney, a partner from 1824, ran the nursery from 1826 until it closed in 1844. Bunney, who specialized in fuchsias and orchids, was one of the hybridizers of the fuchsia in the 1830s and also had premises at Bedford Conservatories, Covent Garden, by 1833.[61]

A nursery was founded in 1791 by Thomas Barr at Ball's Pond, on the west side of Newington Green Road. It increased in 1798 and covered over c. 11 a., formerly Hopping field, in 1806. Samuel Brooks, Barr's partner from 1819, later took over the nursery, which in 1822 had a good reputation and sent plant collectors to distant countries. Brooks left for Chicago in 1832 and the land was used for building.[62]

Andrew Hogarth was a nurseryman in Lower Street in 1797. His nursery may have been taken over c. 1800 by Henry John & Co., of the Seed and Root Warehouse, opposite the Thatched House inn.[63]

Cooksfield, on the west side of Upper Street between Park and Barnsbury streets, covering 5½ a., became a nursery in 1806 run by a Mr. Townsend, who also rented 2 a. in Frog Lane. George Smith took over after 1810 and remained until the land was built over c. 1827 by Thomas

Cubitt. In 1827 Smith made an agreement with Cubitt for no. 11 Manchester Terrace, Liverpool Road, and all the land behind not required for domestic gardens, and on it he built a large conservatory, where he still exhibited plants in 1835.[64] Smith had a market garden of c. 3 a. on the north side of Richmond Avenue in 1848.[65]

WOODS. In 1086 Hugh de Berners had woodland for 150 pigs, yielding 3s. 6d., and at Tollington woodland for 60 pigs yielded 5s.[66] No wood was mentioned at Barnsbury in the Middle Ages, but many holdings in the northern part of the parish included standing timber. Copyhold at Holloway belonging to John Kitchin in the 1580s had at least 200 mature trees,[67] and copyholders could still fell many in the 18th century: 40 on one holding in 1716 and 80 on another in 1778, both in Holloway.[68] There was still wood and underwood at Yveney or Seveney Grove, on the east side of the later Essex Road near Ball's Pond, in 1430 when the dean and chapter let it to John Hert of Islington and others, with permission to fell the trees, plough and sow the land and to fill in all ditches except that enclosing the grove.[69] By the 16th century, however, Highbury alone retained land set aside as woodland, divided into Highbury wood, just north of the manor grange, and Little St. John's wood farther north-west. Each was said to contain 33 a. in 1569, from which 2 a. were to be set aside for hedging and fencing. Highbury wood had 31 a. of underwood, partly c. 19 years old and partly c. 10 years old but spoiled by livestock owing to the keeper's negligence. St. John's wood had 1 a. of waste without any timber and 30 a. set with underwood c. 12 and 8 years old, also very spoiled. The woods were to be let, reserving to the Crown all standing timber and oak saplings, and the young wood was to be protected for seven years after felling.[70] However, in 1605 it was found that the keeper had let the herbage and allowed stray cattle to damage young growth; within the last three years between 40 and 80 oaks had been felled, between 250 and 500 young trees shrouded, leaving only three or four boughs, and c. 300 loads of timber had been made from oak saplings.[71] There were 371 mature trees by 1650, when Highbury wood was estimated to be 43½ a. and St. John's 35 a. Part of Highbury had recently been grubbed up; if all the wood were to be converted to tillage, the annual value would be £59 13s. 4d. instead of £4 11s. 8d.[72] By 1710 only 25 a. of coppice were left, with no mature trees, and in 1716 the lessee was licensed to grub them up.[73]

MILLS. Hugh de Berners had a mill worth 66s. 8d. in 1086.[74] In 1271 land at Highbury given to the hospital of St. John of Jerusalem included

[54] P.R.O., C 10/240/5.
[55] M.L.R. 1727/5/129.
[56] Above, growth, Islington town.
[57] Nelson, *Islington* (1811), 112.
[58] M.L.R. 1774/3/497.
[59] Ibid. 1786/1/123; *T.L.M.A.S.* xxiv. 185; xxvi. 300.
[60] Below, other est. (Hattersfield).
[61] *T.L.M.A.S.* xxiv. 185; xxvi. 300; Nelson, *Islington* (1811), 112.
[62] *T.L.M.A.S.* xxiv. 185; below, other est. (Hopping field).
[63] *T.L.M.A.S.* xxiv. 185; xxvi. 300.

[64] Nelson, *Islington* (1811), 112; (1829), 113; Hobhouse, *Thos. Cubitt*, 56–7, 347; Cromwell, *Islington*, 348.
[65] P.R.O., IR 30/21/33.
[66] *V.C.H. Mdx.* i. 120.   [67] P.R.O., REQ 2/276/24.
[68] Above, other est. (Iremonger, Rowe).
[69] Guildhall MS. (formerly St. Paul's, Red box A 40/1444).
[70] P.R.O., E 310/38/237, no. 8.
[71] Ibid. E 178/4158.
[72] Ibid. E 317/Mdx. 45, pp. 1–3.
[73] *Cal. Treas. Bks.* 1710, 388; 1716, pt. 2, 599.
[74] *V.C.H. Mdx.* i. 120.

a mill.[75] The manor of Canonbury included a windmill valued at 40s. a year in 1306.[76] No later record of a cornmill in the parish has been found.

MARKETS. Sales of fat bullocks were made at Islington in the 1790s a day or so before Smithfield's weekly market.[77] John Perkins built a large cattle market on the east side of Lower Road under an Act of 1835, completed in 1836, but traders preferred Smithfield and his venture failed in 1837, being used for lairage only thereafter. His market was bought by speculators c. 1847 and reopened in 1849 but had closed by the early 1850s, when the land was laid out for building.[78] The Corporation of London bought a site in Copenhagen Fields for a metropolitan market to replace Smithfield for the sale of live animals. Designed by the City's architect J. B. Bunning, the market was opened in 1855 and covered at least 30 a., mostly with stalls for 7,000 cattle, 3,500 sheep, 1,500 calves, and 900 pigs. The central tower contained a telegraph office and 12 banks. Five taverns were built, one at each corner of the market and the fifth on the opposite side of York Way for the drovers and butchers; two hotels, the City Arms and the Queen's Arms, became tenement dwellings by 1873, and the Drovers' hall was added in 1873. The market later became more general, selling a range of goods until 1939, when the market closed.[79]

TRADE AND INDUSTRY. Early occupations included those of carter in 1352,[80] baker in 1404,[81] smith in 1410,[82] currier in 1445,[83] courser in 1462,[84] drover and labourer in 1465,[85] and loriner in 1474.[86] At the end of the 16th century there was a wide range of tradesmen and craftsmen in the town: collar-maker, vintner, glazier, shoe-maker, tailor, wheelwright, weaver,[87] tanner,[88] and brewer.[89] Some brewers had their own inns but others, such as Francis Marsh in 1624, supplied innkeepers.[90] There was a confectioner in 1667.[91]

Digging clay was permitted to Henry Frowyk on land on the Prebend manor in the 1340s.[92] A field in the same area, straddling the footpath from Islington to Finsbury, was being dug for bricks in the 1590s, and again in 1633 by Francis Tredway, who interfered with the City's archery practice.[93] By c. 1580 Islington's brick-kilns were said to be a resort of rogues and vagabonds.[94] In

1668 a licence was given to dig brick and tile earth on 4 a. behind the Swan inn, High Street, and 1¾ a. in the common field adjoining,[95] all in the area of Tredway's operation. An Islington brick-maker rented 2 a. on the boundary with Shoreditch in 1673, paying 6d. for every thousand bricks made, and was said to have made up to 1,700,000 bricks during the first summer.[96] Another agreement covered 20 a. in 1691, with permission to make bricks during the first ten years; by 1692 c. 1½ a. had been dug up 4 yards deep.[97] Land on the Woods' estate including Vale Royal, Charterhouse Closes, and Commandery Mantels (Clerkenwell) was dug for clay and gravel in the 1680s.[98] Hattersfield, by River Lane (St. Peter's Street), had brick-kilns in 1727 and 1735 and was often called Tilekilnfield, and in 1735 there were also brick-kilns between Wells's Row (Highbury Corner) and the Back Road.[99] Thomas Bird used the field behind Bird's Buildings for brickmaking in 1769.[1] Thereafter, until Islington was completely built up, kilns were a common sight, as building plots were used first for brickburning.[2] In addition to temporary brickburning, two tilemaking firms were long established in Maiden Lane. Adams's tilekilns or a predecessor was at Belle Isle by 1810, making garden and chimney pots.[3] In 1829 the premises included 8 a. for tilemaking and brickburning, a large kiln in operation, a smaller one temporarily used as a storehouse, and sheds and cottages.[4] It was still a pottery in 1865 but had been taken over for Tylor's instrument factory by 1870.[5] Farther south in Maiden Lane were Randell's tilekilns, which moved from Bagnigge Wells Road, Clerkenwell, in 1828[6] and whose site was taken for building in the 1860s.[7]

A wide range of industries existed from the late 18th century. At the Rosemary Branch a windmill for grinding white lead was built in 1786 by Samuel Walker & Co., ironmakers of Rotherham (Yorks.), and a second beside it in 1792, the factory being managed by Walker, Maltby & Co. of Upper Thames Street. By 1829 the firm was called Maltby, Parkers, & Co., and the factory employed 30-40 people.[8] A 20 h.p. steam engine powered the mills by 1835, when the firm was T. and C. Maltby & Co., employing c. 50; two thirds of the workforce were women, reputedly less injured by the process used than men.[9] The works were still there in 1865.[10] In the early 19th

[75] P.R.O., CP 25(1)/147/24, no. 493.
[76] Webb, *Rec. of St. Barts.* i. 449.
[77] Middleton, *View*, 414.
[78] C. F. Green, *Smithfield and Islington Markets* (1847, pamphlet in Islington libr.); Tomlins, *Islington*, 205 n.; 5 & 6 Wm. IV, c. 111 (Local and Personal); *Plan* (c. 1853); inf. from Mr. J. C. Connell.
[79] H. Hobhouse, *Lost. Lond.* (1971), 186; *Ind. Mons. Gtr. Lond.* (1969), 36; inf. from Mr. J. C. Connell; above, growth, Holloway, for later hist. of site.
[80] *Cal. Pat.* 1350-4, 296.
[81] Guildhall MS. 9171/2, f. 52.
[82] *Cal. Close*, 1409-13, 58.
[83] Fitch, *Index to Test. Rec. in Com. Ct. of Lond.* i. 165.
[84] *Cal. Pat.* 1461-7, 3.   [85] Ibid. 318, 344.
[86] *Cal. Close*, 1468-76, 343.
[87] Guildhall MS. 12958/3.
[88] P.R.O., PROB 11/112 (P.C.C. 86 Windebanck, will of John Denicum).
[89] Ibid. PROB 11/102 (P.C.C. 63 Bolein, will of Wm. Senior).

[90] P.R.O., REQ 2/309/11.
[91] Lewis, *Islington*, 306.
[92] *Cal. Close*, 1346-9, 411.
[93] P.R.O., MPF 221; ibid. C 8/86/255.
[94] Nelson, *Islington* (1829), 112.
[95] B.L. Add. MS. 15556, f. 173.
[96] P.R.O., C 7/591/94.
[97] Ibid. C 7/102/84; C 8/434/2.   [98] Ibid. C 6/259/56.
[99] Above, other est.; Nelson, *Islington* (1829), plan (1735).
[1] M.L.R. 1769/2/262.
[2] e.g. Nelson, *Islington* (1811), 111.   [3] Ibid. 74.
[4] G.L.R.O., P83/MRY1/596.
[5] Stanford, *Libr. Map of Lond.* (1862 edn. with additions to 1865); below.
[6] Cromwell, *Islington*, 153.
[7] Stanford, *Libr. Map of Lond.* (1862 edn. with additions to 1865).
[8] Nelson, *Islington* (1829), 183.
[9] Cromwell, *Islington*, 109.
[10] Stanford, *Libr. Map of Lond.* (1862 edn. with additions to 1865).

century Thomas Wontner & Sons, hatters, of the Minories, had a large factory in Greenman's Lane, where 40–50 men and women sorted beaver, seal, and other skins, and R. Kear had a smaller fur factory in Lower Street opposite the Thatched House. Nearby in Britannia Row were Messrs. Bull & Smith, makers of cut-glass, and a factory making watch-springs.[11] Farther north along Lower Road a floor-cloth factory was built c. 1812 and belonged to Samuel Ridley in 1829.[12] Lower Street also had premises used in the 18th century for rectifying spirits to make gin and for soap-making.[13] A patent for water-proofing of 1801 was acquired by Elizabeth Duke & Co. which built a factory at the south end of Hornsey Road and mainly produced water-proofed clothing for the army but also treated ships' sails and other canvas articles. The business declined after the Napoleonic Wars and passed to Ingram & Lermitt, who let the premises to a Mr. Jones, who converted it to a dye-house. The building was demolished c. 1833.[14]

Pasteboard manufacturers equipped with horse-mills were located in Islington in 1808 and 1816. The second of those belonged to Thomas Creswick and lay near the southern end of the Back Road.[15]

Several industries, including noxious ones, were established in Maiden Lane by the early 19th century, before there were many residents nearby. At Battle Bridge in 1829 there was a varnish factory that had formerly been a pottery, a factory making patent yellow paint belonging to Mr. Scheldt, and premises for boiling bones for sale to manufacturers of knife handles or buttons and to farmers.[16] At the south end of Maiden Lane the factory of Rood, Heal, & Co., feather dressers, of Compton Street, Soho, existed in 1811 and 1829. The premises of R. P. Smith, Vaux, & Bell, making stone-blue and mustard, were there in 1811 but unoccupied by 1829. An ale and table-beer brewery in 1811 was probably the brewhouse used for vinegar-making in 1829. Farther north at Belle Isle were Warner's coach and cart grease factory, Margett's chemical laboratory (Parkes's in 1829), a large varnish factory belonging to Wallis & Sons of Long Acre, Adams's tilekilns, a soap-boiling house unoccupied by 1811, and premises for slaughtering horses.[17] Those or similar industries were still carried on in the 1850s, when they had become a health hazard to occupants of new houses. The manufacture of varnish and enamel black, various japanning processes, and the boiling of linseed oil were extensive industries at Belle Isle in 1856, with about 10 factories. The largest belonged to Messrs. Wilkinson & J. S. C. Heywood in Caledonia Place, who had patented a method of condensing the vapours in order to render such manufactures inoffensive. Another varnish factory was owned by a Mr. Schweizer. Two large

factories making blood manure closed c. 1856 and in 1857. Fat melting and gut-scraping for sausage skins were particularly noxious, as were the boiling-houses, three of which were attached to knackers. A fourth, recently moved to Brandon Street from Cow Cross during the Clerkenwell improvements, received condemned meat from City markets and was so offensive that its owners were summoned before the magistrates three times in the year, to little effect. There were 100 slaughterhouses licensed in 1857, 49 in the west side of the parish and 51 in the east, rising to 109 in 1860. Many of those in the western half were concentrated around the Metropolitan market, which included land for abattoirs. Licensing helped to control health risks: a slaughterhouse in Brandon Street that was habitually used for diseased cattle was refused a licence and forced to close.[18]

In 1868 there were complaints about Fretwell's manure works and Turner's varnish factory at Belle Isle, and japanning works at Ball's Pond. Turner's closed in 1870 and two other varnish-makers, Hatfield's and Wallis & Co., were warned to discontinue. Another, Jensen & Nicholson, had recently closed in 1869. Two more, Harman & Price and Mr. Naylor's, closed in 1876–7, leaving only one varnish factory, which did not create a nuisance.[19] The emery works of Acton & Borman were reported a danger to their workers' health in 1869. In 1872 Belle Isle had 38 establishments, 13 fewer than in 1868, and none a threat to health. In 1878 it had 32 factories or yards, including horse-slaughterers and piggeries.[20]

A lamp-black and printers' ink factory was built c. 1827 in Hornsey Road, nearly opposite Hanley Road, by Thomas Davison, a printer of Whitefriars Street. It was burned down three times before 1833, and between 1833 and 1835 a steam-engine was put in to replace horse-power. Complaints were made about the factory by local builders in 1827 and again in 1838. The business was sold to Shackell & Edwards by 1853, when their ink-making brought more complaints, and in 1869 the vapours constituted a nuisance.[21] In 1932 the factory had to be restored after an explosion.[22]

An india rubber factory was established c. 1830 by Messrs. Cornish & Sievier in Upper Holloway on the south side of Red Cap Lane, to make elastic webs for belts, braces, and similar articles. In 1837 the firm was incorporated as the London Caoutchouc Co. The factory employed c. 100 people and used steam-driven machinery.[23]

John Webb started a mineral and soda-water factory at Lamb's Cottage, Colebrooke Row, c. 1830, using steam power. It still existed in 1861.[24]

In 1831 there were 4,874 families supported by trade and manufacture, compared with 320 by agriculture and 3,381 others. Manufacturing of

[11] Nelson, *Islington* (1829), 186, 357.
[12] Ibid. 186; above, growth, SE. Islington; below, plate 18.
[13] Nelson, *Islington* (1829), 186, 191.
[14] Cromwell, *Islington*, 342–3.
[15] A. H. Shorter, *Paper Mills and Paper Makers in Eng. 1495–1800* (Paper Publs. Soc. vi), 62; Baker's plan (1817).
[16] Nelson, *Islington* (1829), 71.
[17] Nelson, *Islington* (1811, 1829), 73–4.
[18] M.O.H. *Ann. Rep.* (1856), 11–13; (1857), 13, 15; (1860),

10; (1864), 20.
[19] Ibid. (1868), 11–12; (1869), 9; (1870), 19; (1876–7), 27.
[20] Ibid. (1869), 9; (1872), 25; (1878), 24.
[21] Cromwell, *Islington*, 339; P.R.O., MH 13/261, no. 3393/53; M.O.H. *Ann. Rep.* (1869), 9.
[22] D. Braithwaite, *Building in the Blood* (1981), 137.
[23] Lewis, *Islington*, 279, plan; *V.C.H. Mdx.* v. 337.
[24] Coull, *Islington*, 116.

products such as white lead, varnish, horsehair, and soap engaged 174 men, excluding labourers, while 3,366 were in retail trade or handicrafts and 2,124 were wholesale merchants, bankers, capitalists, and professional men. The labourers employed by those three groups were 1,335.[25]

The most important industry in the 19th century was building, with its allied trades. A great many small local builders, some of them mentioned above, did the building in Islington;[26] a few of them emerged as large firms. Dove Brothers began with William Spencer Dove (1793–1869) who came from Sunbury and started as a jobbing builder and carpenter in St. Luke's and Islington in 1824, doing redecoration and such work as minor repairs to the church. From the late 1820s he was building houses, especially on the Milner-Gibson estate. His first major commission was the Islington Literary and Scientific Society's premises, Almeida Street, completed 1837, and in 1839 he began work on St. Stephen's, New North Road, the first of many churches built by his firm. In the 1840s Dove also continued as a shop-fitter, joiner, plasterer, and painter. In 1852 his sons formed the Dove Bros. partnership under the supervision of their father. They rented from their father the recently built premises at Moon and Studd streets which became their offices and yard, which in the 1870s had stabling for 12 horses, workshops, stone cutters, a mortar mill, and two steam engines. In 1881 they leased property in the City, where Tokenhouse Buildings was built to provide an office, but they kept their yard in Barnsbury, moving in 1901 to Cloudesley Place. The firm became a limited liability company in 1905, and the last member of the Dove family retired from it in 1970. Between 1858 and 1900 it built 130 churches, but from the 1870s it diversified with civil engineering contracts, besides constructing public buildings, shops, offices, and houses, becoming a major contractor, with a high reputation. Commissions eventually came from all over London, but much early work was done in Islington, where entire buildings included 15 Anglican churches and some nonconformist chapels.[27]

Less widely known builders included in the 1860s Hill of Charlton Place, which later became part of Higgs & Hill.[28] Thurman & White originated when John Thurman, a plumber and glazier, came from Shepton Mallet (Som.) in 1851 and leased premises in Canonbury Road. His daughter Elizabeth married John White, an oilman and colourman of Stoke Newington. The firm, which became a limited company in 1922, was chosen as contractor for the building of King Edward's Hall at Canonbury Place and the renovation of Canonbury Tower in 1907–8. It engaged in a wide range of building all over London and opened branches at Walworth (Surr.) and Hornsey Road.[29]

C. P. Roberts & Co. was founded by Charles Philip Roberts, born in Islington in 1846, who set up as a builder and decorator in Alma Road in 1868. From carrying out small works he gradually took plots on building leases, letting each completed house before starting the next. His house and yard were in Alma Road and the adjoining no. 138 St. Paul's Road was the office. By 1884 he had converted a building at no. 36 Tyssen Street, Dalston Lane, Hackney, into a works yard, keeping his office at St. Paul's Road. In 1886 he became bankrupt for two years, regaining prosperity by rebuilding many of the area's poorly built houses. By the early 20th century the firm was carrying out new works all over London, many for the L.C.C. Roberts's son Charles Ernest took over in 1907, and in 1929 the company moved its offices to High Holborn. Building work in Islington included the Central library and Archway Central Methodist Hall.[30]

Connected with the building industry was C. F. Anderson & Son, founded by Charles Frederick Anderson, who set up as a timber dealer in 1863, renting part of the former Jones's burial ground near Islington green. Anderson built a house in front of his yard, no. 13 Essex Road, and was assisted by his reputation among builders as a good judge of timber. By the mid 1870s he had become a wholesale timber merchant, and had taken over the grounds of no. 68 Colebrooke Row as additional storage. Anderson's son William Frederick took over the business on his father's death in 1899. The firm also occupied nos. 9, 11, and 19 Essex Road by 1901, and in 1902 opened a branch in Southgate. In 1904 it bought houses in Paradise Court adjoining the yard, and opened a glass and ironmongery department at no. 19 Essex Road, a new frontage being built when the road was widened for trams. Andersons was one of a few London firms to sell plywood before the First World War. It also specialized in supplying large quantities of timber to the film studios in Poole Street (Shoreditch) and, from the late 1920s, Elstree studios, where up to 800 sets a year were built. A two-storeyed warehouse was built in Paradise Court in the 1920s. In 1929 the firm became the distributor for new manufactured building boards, being instrumental in opening up markets in Britain for them, and no. 3 St. Peter's Street was leased in 1934 and converted into a wallboard warehouse. Additional premises were acquired during the Second World War and a sawmill was built there. Business in wallboards increased in the 1930s, especially for government building contractors, and in 1937 the firm bought the leasehold of Harris wharf in Graham Street, fronting the City Road basin, for storage. The adjoining City wharf was acquired and rebuilt in 1955. After a fire in 1958 the timber yard was rebuilt, incorporating the former Collins's music hall which had also been badly damaged.[31]

Islington lay in the Victorian manufacturing belt of London, which was based mainly on small workshops, often specializing in one stage of production and grouped in districts serving one

[25] P.R.O., MH 12/7366.
[26] Above, growth.
[27] Braithwaite, *Bldg. in the Blood, passim.*
[28] Ibid. 30.
[29] *Thurman & White: A Name Written in Bricks and Mortar, 1851–1951.*
[30] *The Ho. that Roberts Built: C. P. Roberts & Co. 1868–1968* (booklet).
[31] A. Muir, *Andersons of Islington* (1963).

another. Precision engineering in light metals, with jewellery, and precious metals, was concentrated in an area from Clerkenwell to Barnsbury and Holloway, and by the mid 20th century had diversified into a variety of engineering and metal trades.[32]

John Tylor & Sons, who made water-metering instruments from 1787, built a 150-ft. tower in 1870 at their factory, formerly Adams's tilekilns, Belle Isle, which gave a constant known water pressure by which they could test the instruments. By 1967 the factory had been taken over by Ebonite Container Co. (Mfg.), which used the tower as a boiler flue in making plastic accumulator boxes.[33]

William Hill & Son, organ-builders, had a factory in York Road, which was rebuilt in 1882, and built an organ for Westminster Abbey in 1884. They amalgamated with Norman & Beard of Norwich in 1916, continuing to use the York Road factory until it was bombed in 1943.[34] Bryceson Bros., also organ-builders, were carrying on business from St. Thomas's hall, Highbury, in 1911.[35]

A. C. Cossor was founded in 1896 in Farringdon Road, Clerkenwell, making scientific glassware. In 1918 the firm moved to larger premises in Highbury called Aberdeen works, extended in 1927 with no. 22 Highbury Grove as offices and with the nearby balloon factory of the Spencer brothers, well known aeronauts, as an annexe called Melody works. Bulk production of valves and later of radios was undertaken, providing home construction kits that were easier to use than the old crystal sets. A large three-storeyed factory was built in 1929 in front of the parent factory and more land was bought near Melody works. In the early 1930s the firm developed cathode ray tubes for television, the first television receivers, and the world's first radar receiver. A five-storeyed factory replaced several old houses and gardens in Highbury Grove in 1935, with space for 1,000 additional radio workers, and a front administration block in 1936.[36] The firm moved to Harlow (Essex) in 1958.[37]

Key & Whiting, a bookbinding firm founded in 1799, moved from Harecourt chapel, Aldersgate, to a three-storeyed purpose-built factory in Canonbury in 1904, where it remained in 1949.[38]

Stephens's Ink in 1892 opened a purpose-built factory in Gillespie Road, designed by Michael Stephens and modelled on a Venetian palace, with an illuminated chimney.[39] The firm moved c. 1965 to a former dairy at the corner of Drayton Park and Martineau Road, and the old factory was demolished in 1972.[40]

Beale's, confectioners and bakers, was founded in 1769 by a master baker John Beale, who opened a shop in Oxford Street. Edward Beale, his nephew, started his own business in 1829 at no. 45 Popham Street, Islington, and taught his own nephew William Beale, who in 1861 started his own small business at Highgate Hill, moving to Holloway Road in 1866. In 1889 an imposing four-storeyed building in Holloway Road was built on the sites of nos. 370, 372, 374 Holloway Road and nos. 2, 2a, 4, 6, 8, 10 Tollington Road, designed by F. Wallen in Gothic Revival style in red brick with stone and mosaic decoration. By the end of the century the firm was delivering to 2,000 families a day, with 15 horses and vans for deliveries and 15 horses and 10 vans for the catering department. There were banqueting rooms at the Athenaeum, Camden Road, and Assembly Rooms, Holloway Road. By 1969, however, their building, a Holloway landmark, was out of date. The offices moved to Southgate and the building was replaced by a branch of Sainsbury's supermarkets.[41]

Jones Brothers' department store was founded by William Jones, who had come to London in 1867 and worked as a draper's apprentice until he and his brother John opened a small shop in Holloway. Their building was enlarged several times and by the 1890s included warehouses, workshops, stabling for 50 horses, and accommodation for assistants above the shop. In 1927 the store became one of the Selfridge Provincial Stores, and in 1940 it was bought by the John Lewis Partnership.[42] In 1983 it was the only department store serving the area.

W. H. Hayden, wholesale stationers, founded in 1829 in Paternoster Row, London, moved to no. 52 Holloway Road in 1971. In 1972 it built Digby House and employed c. 70.[43]

In 1956 Islington produced a range of metal manufactures, ink, radios, electric batteries, paint, pianos, laboratory and scientific equipment, cricket bats, tennis racquets, and cattle and poultry food.[44] By the 1970s, however, employment in manufacturing had declined in Islington, possibly by more than the national average of 30 per cent for 1965–76. Many small workshops were closed when their areas were rebuilt because they could not afford relocation. Small industrial premises were still closely intermingled with 19th-century housing, but planners tried to keep industry in zones, principally around the former Metropolitan market, Belle Isle, and King's Cross.[45]

LOCAL GOVERNMENT. MANORIAL GOVERNMENT.

In 1294 the dean and chapter of St. Paul's claimed view of frankpledge, the assize of bread and of ale, infangthief, outfangthief, goods of felons, waifs, strays, tumbril, pillory, and gallows in their manor of Islington. The bishop of London claimed similar rights for

[32] Gtr. Lond. ed. Coppock and Prince, 226–7.
[33] A. Wilson, Lond.'s Industrial Heritage (1967), 60–2.
[34] V.C.H. Mdx. ii. 190–1; vi. 156; Braithwaite, Bldg. in the Blood, 123. [35] V.C.H. Mdx. ii. 193.
[36] Half a Cent. of Progress: A. C. Cossor [1947].
[37] Inf. from Mr. J. C. Connell.
[38] Key & Whiting: The Years Between: 1799–1949.
[39] Ind. Mons. Gtr. Lond. (1969), 36.
[40] Inf. from Mr. J. C. Connell.
[41] Beale's Ltd.: Two Hundred Years 1769–1969; Pevsner, Lond. ii. 238.
[42] Islington Gaz. 21 Sept. 1956.
[43] Hist. of W. H. Hayden Commercial Stationery Svce.; 150th anniv. (1979; booklet in Islington libr.).
[44] Ibid.
[45] Action Resource Centre, Survey of Cos. (TS. 1977, in Islington libr.); NE. Lond. Employment Group, 1st Ann. Rep. (1978).

Stepney,[46] which in 1349 included Barnsbury and Canonbury: 5s. was paid to him as the common fine from Islington, and 4s. from the Islington tenants of St. John of Jerusalem.[47] In 1510 the aletaster for Islington made presentments at the Stepney view and headboroughs for Barnsbury and Canonbury paid the fine and presented ditches in disrepair.[48] Islington had at least two constables in 1494.[49]

The prebendal manor held a court leet annually on Ascension day in 1649, at which the tenants of Canonbury owed service.[50] Rolls for view of frankpledge and court baron survive for 1654 to 1709; a keeper for the common pound was chosen in 1667, and ditches and infractions of the assize of bread were presented.[51] Courts at the Half Moon in 1823 were probably courts baron only.[52]

Court leet rolls for Newington Barrow survive for 1491 to 1519. Headboroughs were elected for Tollington and Stroud, Islington, and Newington Barrow, and a taster was chosen for the whole manor. Six women were among those presented for breaking the assize; others acted as collectors of rents for the manor. Damage to roads and houses was also presented.[53] The profits of the view of frankpledge and court leet were leased out by the Crown in 1563 and 1572.[54] In 1598 the leet was held at the George.[55] Rolls for the view and court baron exist for 1612 to 1622, but record only court baron business from 1618. Presentments concerned bridges, ditches, streams, and encroachments on the waste. In 1615 the stocks had decayed and the bailiff was to take timber to repair them.[56] In 1823 only the court baron was held, at the Blue Coat Boy, City Road.[57] In 1831 the steward of the manor was asked by the vestry to move the pound from High Street, because of the cholera scare.[58]

Court books for the manor of St. John of Jerusalem survive from 1776 to 1805, when a view of frankpledge was still held, and a constable and two headboroughs were elected for the liberty of St. Mary's, Islington. Several publicans and shopkeepers, at Battle Bridge and in Pentonville, were presented for giving light weight.[59] The courts leet and baron met annually on Holy Thursday in 1823, having recently moved to the White Conduit House from the Angel,[60] but no court leet was held for an Islington manor by 1857.[61]

PARISH GOVERNMENT TO 1856. The bishop complained to the vicar and churchwardens in 1662 that vestries were attended by people of 'adverse dispositions', who were to be replaced with 24 parishioners of good standing who conformed to the ecclesiastical laws.[62] Vestry minutes survive from 1663,[63] meetings then being held every two weeks but becoming more erratic until in 1666 affairs were in such disorder that a practice of meeting on the first Thursday of each month was revived.[64] The vestry was open in 1708,[65] and at least 13 parishioners were needed to make rates, according to the custom of the parish as stated in 1802.[66] Under a succession of Local Acts, however, most business, especially financial, passed to commissioners or trustees chosen from among the wealthiest parishioners: for lighting and watching in 1772, for a workhouse and poor relief in 1777, and for repair of roads and footpaths in 1795, together with an Act of 1751 for rebuilding the parish church, under which repairs were managed. The trustees appointed under the Act of 1772 were the vicar, churchwardens, and 61 parishioners with property valued at £20 a year, or £500 in personal estate. When the number fell below 40, nine or more trustees could elect new members, and they also fixed the rate.[67] An amending Act of 1806 allowed nine or more trustees to extend lighting and watching, levy additional rates for that purpose, and arrange for cleansing the streets. The trustees could also appoint officials.[68]

By the 1820s, a time of local controversy, John Nelson pointed out the dangers of a self-perpetuating 'junto', which contradicted the spirit of an open vestry.[69] The decision to seek the 1772 Act had been repealed by a meeting of male and female householders, and the Act had been obtained by a private group with the advice of the vestry.[70] Additional Acts apparently did not raise opposition in vestry until the second decade of the 19th century. In 1813 the vestry clerk was ordered to advertise each meeting on the church door and in 1814 printed bills were introduced.[71] Efforts to have meetings moved from the morning to the evening, because many parishioners were excluded, were defeated.[72] In 1816 the vestry considered seeking a general Act to cover all parish affairs, but in 1817 it decided that the existing Acts were adequate.[73] A proposal from Highbury residents in 1820 for their own lighting and watching Act, which would reduce their rating contribution to an eighth of its original level, was also defeated.[74] Another private Bill was introduced in 1823, however, to pave streets on the land of William and Thomas Rhodes,[75] which again threatened the power of the vestry and the trustees.

Further controversy was aroused in 1821 when plural voting was allowed in a ballot for churchwardens to some inhabitants under the Vestries

[46] Plac. de Quo Warr. (Rec. Com.), 475–6.
[47] P.R.O., SC 2/191/60, m. 16.
[48] Ibid. SC 2/191/63, m. 3.
[49] Cal. Pat. 1494–1509, 7.
[50] Guildhall MS. 11816B, p. 113.
[51] Ibid. 14225/1.
[52] Nelson, Islington (1823), 356.
[53] G.L.R.O., M83/NB/1.
[54] P.R.O., E 309/box 4/15 Eliz. I/14, no. 44.
[55] Ibid. E 134/40 Eliz. I/East. 30.
[56] Guildhall MSS. 3460/1, 2.
[57] Nelson, Islington (1829), 138.
[58] Vestry min. bk. 1824–38, 324.
[59] Islington libr., ct. bks., St. John of Jerusalem, 1776–92, 1793–1805.

[60] Nelson, Islington (1829), 62.
[61] Tomlins, Islington (1857), 7–8.
[62] Guildhall MS. 9182/2, file v.
[63] In Islington libr.
[64] Vestry min. bk. 1662/3–1708, 20.
[65] E. Hatton, New View of Lond. (1708), 380.
[66] 42 Geo. III, c. 28 (Local and Personal).
[67] 12 Geo. III, c. 17 (Priv. Act).
[68] 46 Geo. III, c. 1 (Local and Personal).
[69] Nelson, Islington (1829), 7 n.
[70] Vestry min. bk. 1735–77, 170v., 171v., 173–4.
[71] Ibid. 1812–24, 21, 46.
[72] Ibid. 69, 72, 80.
[73] Ibid. 113, 154.
[74] Ibid. 228, 236, 247–8.
[75] Ibid. 373–4.

Act, 1818, after dissatisfaction with a show of hands.[76] Legal advice that the Act did not over-rule ancient parish usage, so that plural voting was illegal, as were votes by women householders even by proxy,[77] may have stimulated attempts to obtain a general parish Act. Passed in 1824, the Act ensured that the trustees were elected by the vestry, but fixed a property qualification for trustees at £30 a year and vestrymen at £20, created a select vestry, and introduced plural voting. Besides allowing rates for the poor, roads, lighting, and church and chapel expenses, the Act empowered the trustees to pave and light streets, make roads and drains, and deal with nuisances, dangerous buildings, house numbering, drovers, and cleansing.[78] Vestry meetings, however, continued to be troubled with filibustering and motions for adjournment, concerned in particular with attempts to amend the Local Act and abolish plural voting.[79] In 1827 there were complaints about the retiring trustees and demands for a ballot for their successors, reflected in one of a series of satirical pamphlets on events in the 'Town of Hillhausen'. After a decision in King's Bench in 1831 in favour of a ballot, trustees who had been appointed when a ballot was refused were dismissed. The victorious party, hoping that rates which had been spent on entertainments would be better used henceforth,[80] also pressed for adoption of the Vestries Act in 1831.[81] A proposal in 1832 to give parishioners rated at £10–20 a year the same right to elect trustees as they now had to elect their M.P. was discussed in detail but finally defeated.[82]

A cholera committee was set up in 1831, superseded by the Islington board of health in 1832, concentrating on clothing for the poor and a hospital for cholera victims.[83] After the Poor Law Amendment Act, 1834, relief continued to be administered by the parish trustees until 1867.[84]

Wrangling over rates and accounts, and attempts to obtain a meeting place other than the parish church, recurred. By 1852 a committee had been appointed to consider a new local Act to extend the franchise to all ratepayers, and to allow the provision of another meeting place. The spread of population led to a scheme to divide the parish into equal voting districts, whose ratepayers would elect equal numbers of vestrymen and trustees. A motion against seeking a new Act was carried,[85] but the Metropolis Management Act, 1855, gave effect to many of the committee's aims.[86]

There were three churchwardens in 1561 and four sidesmen;[87] only two churchwardens were listed in the 1580s but there were three again by 1612,[88] and they served upper, middle, and lower divisions of Islington by 1663.[89] One churchwarden was said to have been sworn in by the dean and chapter for their precinct in the parish, but by 1708 he was sworn by the archdeacon of London.[90] In 1663 the fine for non-performance of parish office was raised from £3 or £4 to £10 or more because the choice of men to serve was so small,[91] and in 1676 residents were listed in order that none should serve a second time while others had not served once.[92] There were four overseers of the poor in 1577, and in 1663 two of them served the town of Islington and two the 'outsiders and landholders'.[93] A parish clerk was mentioned in 1636[94] and chosen by the vicar in 1668.[95] In 1708 the parish officers were three churchwardens, who chose the three sidesmen to assist them, four overseers and collectors, and four surveyors of the highways, besides six constables and six headboroughs nominated by the manorial courts.[96] Salaried officers included a sexton by 1663, to whose post a woman was appointed in 1671 and 1741,[97] and a beadle by 1671, who received a livery from the overseers in 1755;[98] watchmen assisted the beadle in 1706.[99] Other posts were those of engine-keeper (1717), who was also greenkeeper from 1789, clerk to the workhouse committee (1729), master and mistress of the workhouse (1731), apothecary (1732), five pew-openers for the new church (1754), lamp-lighter (1760), and assistant beadle (1805).[1] The number of surveyors was reduced to two in 1718 after the establishment of the Islington turnpike trust.[2] By 1762 the vestry nominated constables for four of the six liberties, when the justices complained that 'mean persons' were serving, and in 1767 the justices requested a list of all those qualified to serve as constables and headboroughs in the liberties where no court leet was held.[3] Other employees were appointed by the trustees under the Local Acts. In 1811 the vestry appointed the three churchwardens, assisted by sidesmen, two overseers, and an assistant overseer who was also the beadle. The surveyor of highways and footpaths came under the trustees for roads; there were two supervisors of the watch. The parish was divided into six districts derived from the manors: St. John of Jerusalem, Upper Barnsbury, Lower Barnsbury, Canonbury, the Prebend, and Highbury or Newington Barrow. One constable and one headborough was appointed for each district except St. John of Jerusalem, where the lord appointed one constable and two headboroughs. General business was conducted by the vestry clerk, who

[76] Vestry min. bk. 1812–24, 284; 58 Geo. III, c. 69.
[77] Vestry min. bk. 1812–24, 321–3.
[78] 5 Geo. IV, c. 125 (Local and Personal).
[79] Vestry min. bk. 1824–38, *passim*.
[80] Ibid. 76, 210, 215, 273; B.L., Broadsides, vol. I, ff. 131–4; Islington libr., pamphlet printed by C. Pritchard, poem by 'Paul Pry at Hillhausen'.
[81] Vestry min. bk. 1824–38, 303.
[82] Ibid. 373, 382–6.
[83] Ibid. 360, 365, 396–7.
[84] Below, bd. of guardians.
[85] Vestry min. bk. 1852–6, 72–3, 88.
[86] 18 & 19 Vic. c. 120.
[87] Guildhall MS. 9537/2, f. 24v.
[88] Ibid. 5, f. 115v.; 6, f. 112v.; 7, f. 111; 8, f. 80v.; 11, f. 84.

[89] Vestry min. bk. 1662–1708, 6.
[90] Newcourt, *Rep.* 676.
[91] Vestry min. bk. 1662–1708, 5.
[92] Ibid. 95.
[93] Guildhall MS. 9537/4, f. 85v.; vestry min. bk. 1662–1708, 3.
[94] Guildhall MS. 9537/14, f. 37v.
[95] Vestry min. bk. 1662–1708, 29.
[96] Hatton, *New View of Lond.* 380.
[97] Vestry min. bk. 1662–1708, 8, 53; 1735–77, 34.
[98] Ibid. 1662–1708, 53; 1735–77, 94.
[99] Ibid. 1662–1708, 367, 371; below, pub. svces.
[1] Vestry min. bks. *passim*.
[2] Vestry min. bk. 1708–34, 82.
[3] Ibid. 1735–77, 120, 142v.

was also clerk to the trustees of the poor and probably to the other trustees.[4] By 1822 the assistant overseer acted as relieving officer.[5] By 1831 the parish paid the following officers, whose salaries it could find no grounds for reducing: beadle, organist, organ-blower, engine- and greenkeeper, pew openers, sexton, master of the workhouse, apothecary, relieving officer, chaplain at the workhouse, matron and apothecary of the infants' poorhouse, surveyor and assistants for the highways, and inspector of lamps.[6] Under the Act of 1824 the watchmen were sworn as constables, 12 vestrymen were to act as assessors, three overseers were chosen by the justices from a list of eight, and the trustees could appoint a salaried relieving officer.[7]

Income in 1663 came from collections at the church door for the poor and for church repairs, rates for repairs, and for poor relief, fines for refusing office, rent from Stonefields, and sums from annuities and charities for the poor.[8] A new terrier was drawn up in 1663 for assessments, with a separate book for each of the six liberties or districts, towards the church rate.[9] Churchwardens' and overseers' accounts do not survive until 1730.[10] The parish assessment was called the poor's book in 1667, when a relief was granted to a former churchwarden for expenses during the plague of 1665, and another assessment was raised on it in 1668 towards the new workhouse at Clerkenwell.[11] A dispute arose in 1677 between resident and non-resident landholders, the latter claiming an ancient rating custom of 4d. per 20 a. instead of the rate on the value which had been ordered. The vestry abandoned both methods and from 1678 20 a. was to equal a house rent of £40 a year, and householders were to be rated on their goods in the parish, goods worth £1,000 to equal 20 a.[12] A flat rate of 5s. a house was instituted in 1706 for the watch, if the householder did not want to watch in person, and in 1761 householders paid a rate of 4d. in the £ for lighting, to be superseded by the Act of 1772, which made possible a lighting and watching rate, not to exceed 1s. 2d.[13] Rates for the poor and for the highways were also made under the Local Acts of 1777 and 1795 respectively. The Act of 1824 provided for five rates: for the poor, for lighting and watching (not to exceed 3s. in the £), for the highways (not to exceed 3s.), to repay the annuities and for expenses of the chapel of ease (not to exceed 2s. 6d.), and for repairing the parish church and churchwardens' expenses.[14] It was amended in 1832, when rates for repairs to

the chapel and the parish church were to be levied only on the district of St. Mary's.[15]

Separate overseers' accounts start in 1759, when a poor rate of 16d. yielded £728 4s. and a net amount of £92 12s. was received from charities and gifts.[16] The rate fluctuated widely: 13d. in 1760, 22d. in 1767, 18d. in 1768, and 20d. in 1775. It was levied according to the Land Tax under the Local Act of 1777, until many redeemed their tax under the Act of 1798 and could no longer be rated for the poor. Accordingly a Local Act of 1802 extended the rating to anyone who owned or occupied property in the parish, assessed either on annual rent or improved value.[17] By 1813 the rate had risen to 2s. 10d.; in 1814 it was 3s. 6d., assessed on rack-rents which were about four fifths of the real rent and realized £11,794. The increased rental value of the parish allowed the rate to fall to 2s. 6d. in 1823, and to 1s. 8d. in 1824.[18]

The vestry petitioned the justices in 1663 for amendment of their poor rate and additional relief for Islington's numerous poor.[19] Poor children were apprenticed.[20] Increased poverty led the vestry in 1664 to enforce the Statute against building cottages without 4 a., requiring the builders to give security against charges on the parish.[21] There followed in 1674 an order to the beadle to report all new or divided houses and newcomers at each monthly vestry.[22] In 1693 the churchwardens lodged ten paupers with Thomas Benitt, who was to teach them spinning and thereafter keep them in work; Benitt received 50s. towards the reels and wheels.[23] In April 1708 £5 was paid to 19 pensioners and 6s. each to 12 children. In March 1719 the monthly totals were £17 17s. to pensioners, £21 3s. to 11 children.[24] In 1759–60 payments ranging from 2s. a week to 3d. a month were made to 14 pensioners, with others for casual relief, workhouse charges, apprentices, carriage to hospital, and burials.[25]

There were two parish almshouses with two hearths each in 1663.[26] The churchwardens were responsible for repairing two almshouses in 1668, which may have been attached to the church,[27] and they repaired others by the Nine Elms in 1670.[28] In 1710 the vestry had six small almshouses built,[29] perhaps those on the east side of Islington Green in 1735.[30]

The vestry took a house at Stroud Green as a workhouse in 1726.[31] A more convenient site was planned in 1728 and a workhouse was built or hired in Holloway Road, near Ring Cross, probably by 1731; both buildings were shared with

[4] Nelson, *Islington* (1829), 7–8; *Rep. Sel. Cttee. on Poor Laws*, H.C. 462, p. 49 (1817), vi.
[5] Nelson, *Islington* (1829), 8.
[6] Vestry min. bk. 1824–38, 230.
[7] 5 Geo. IV, c. 125 (Local and Personal).
[8] Vestry min. bk. 1662–1708, *passim*; below, charities.
[9] Vestry min. bk. 1662–1708, 1–2.
[10] In Islington libr.
[11] Vestry min. bk. 1662–1708, 24, 34.
[12] Ibid. 104, 112.
[13] Ibid. 371; 1735–77, 117v.
[14] 5 Geo. IV, c. 125 (Local and Personal).
[15] 2 Wm. IV, c. 26 (Local and Personal).
[16] Islington libr., Chwdns.' and Overseers' Accts. 1759–1832, 1, 14.
[17] Vestry min. bk. 1777–1811, 141v.; 42 Geo. III, c. 28

(Local and Personal).
[18] Vestry min. bk. 1812–24, *passim*.
[19] Ibid. 1662–1708, 4.
[20] Ibid. 6.
[21] Ibid. 10.
[22] Ibid. 74.
[23] Ibid. 303.
[24] Islington libr., Accts. of Payments to Poor, 1708–19.
[25] Islington libr., Chwdns.' and Overseers' Accts. 1759–1832, pp. 5–10.
[26] P.R.O., E 179/252/32, p. 28.
[27] Vestry min. bk. 1662–1708, 35, 43.
[28] Ibid. 48.
[29] Ibid. 1708–34, 18, 22.
[30] Nelson, *Islington*, plan (1735).
[31] Vestry min. bk. 1708–34, 159–60.

Hornsey.[32] An apothecary treated the poor there, and a malt mill was installed in 1740.[33] In 1741 the workhouse was again found inconvenient, and hired houses were sought. The house used in 1757 was decayed, and one in Lower Street near the chapel was rented in 1758, possibly the old soap house or Ward's Place which was said to have been used for the poor. The master and mistress were to employ the poor in spinning, picking oakum, and other tasks, and received £20 a year and board.[34] The workhouse was too small in 1767, and two rooms were added on the east side of the yard with another two rooms over them in 1772.[35] A Local Act was sought in 1776 to provide a new workhouse for 120 inmates on the Hundred Acre in the Back Road, given to the parish by Mrs. Amy Hill.[36] Built in 1777, partly with money raised through annuities, the brick building consisted of a centre with two wings, and had a vegetable garden.[37] The centre was extended in front in 1802, and included an infirmary.[38] In 1814 there were 407 inmates: 95 men, 186 women, 67 boys, 48 girls, 11 lunatics; with room for about 50 more. The men picked oakum and mended footpaths, the women did slop-work and nursing.[39]

Following an Act for poor children of 1767,[40] between three and five parish guardians met about once a month to send children under 7 years to nurse in outer Middlesex.[41] By 1814 an infants' poor house had been established at Ford's Green, in Southgate, which had 48 children under 7 in 1814[42] and 32 in 1822.[43] Disease was reduced in 1834 by allowing only two children to a bed instead of four or five, and by a better diet. By 1837 girls were kept until 10 years, doing housework and needlework, instead of going to the adult workhouse at 7 years with the boys.[44] The parish also kept an infants' poor establishment at Park House, in Hackney, from 1849 to 1855, when the children were transferred to no. 5 Colebrooke Row.[45]

ISLINGTON BOARD OF GUARDIANS. The parish formed Islington poor law union under the Poor Law Amendment Act, 1834, but was one of several large London parishes where the Act's full application was precluded by a Local Act.[46] Although the Poor Law Board ordered relief to be administered by a board of guardians from 1837, the parish trustees apparently continued as before. When the medical officer told the Poor Law Board of bad conditions for the sick in the workhouse, he was dismissed by the parish trustees.[47] In 1867, however, an order established a body of 18 guardians to be elected by the ratepayers and 2 ex-officio members.[48]

The workhouse in Liverpool Road, with the same accommodation as in 1814, rapidly became overcrowded. In addition to housing the parish poor, it had to give overnight shelter to vagrants, whose average number was 48 each night during the summer of 1867.[49] A new workhouse with an infirmary was built between 1865 and 1872 in St. John's Road, Upper Holloway, to accommodate 1,142 adults, and was first used in 1870. From 1872 the old workhouse became the board of guardians' district relieving office and smallpox vaccination centre.[50] The new workhouse had 634 inmates in 1871 and 1,260 in 1881; during the winter numbers greatly exceeded the total officially allowed, even though some men were sent to the old workhouse and to Poplar. Since the Local Government Board would not allow an extension to be built in the workhouse grounds, the guardians in 1882 bought the City of London union workhouse on 5 a. in Cornwallis Road, Holloway,[51] which was adapted to hold 611 inmates. In 1882 c. 100 local inmates were housed, at first together with 200 inmates from St. Saviour's union and 100 from Shoreditch. In 1886 there were 623 inmates,[52] although, as at the other workhouse, numbers fluctuated by c. 100 during the year. In particular the sick poor at St. John's Road often exceeded their allowed accommodation of 540 during the 1880s.[53]

In 1893 the guardians leased Bowes Park in Edmonton, where they housed c. 20 old men until 1897.[54] In 1895 the Local Government Board insisted that the guardians find better accommodation for the infirmary, as the current one had 168 patients over the allowed number and the overcrowded workhouse also contained 160 sick; medical staff was inadequate and facilities were meagre.[55] In 1896 the guardians bought the smallpox hospital at Highgate Hill, with 9 a., for an infirmary,[56] which opened in 1901.[57] By 1913 St. John's Road had become a secondary infirmary and there were proposals to provide sick wards at Cornwallis Road.[58] St. John's Road Institution, as it was called in the 1920s, kept some old men and women for observation before sending them on to mental hospitals.[59] The workhouse was taken over by the G.L.C. as

[32] Ibid. 183, 185, 192, 220; Nelson, *Islington* (1829), 90, plan (1735).
[33] Below, pub. svces.; vestry min. bk. 1735–77, 2v., 29v.
[34] Ibid. 33v., 101v., 104v., 107; Nelson, *Islington* (1811), 85.
[35] Vestry min. bk. 1735–77, 144, 176v.
[36] Ibid. 198–199v.; below, charities.
[37] Vestry min. bk. 1777–1811, 9 and v., 153; Islington libr., Trustees of Poor min. bk. 1777–86; Nelson, *Islington* (1829), 89–90.
[38] R. H. Semple, *On Treatment of Sick Poor in Workho. in St. Mary's, Islington* (2nd edn. [1854], copy in Islington libr.), p. 4.
[39] *Rep. Sel. Cttee. on Poor Laws*, H.C. 462, pp. 49–53 (1817), vi.
[40] 7 Geo. III, c. 39.
[41] Islington libr., min. bk., guardians of poor chldn. 1767–99.
[42] *Rep. Sel. Cttee. on Poor Laws*, 49–53.
[43] Nelson, *Islington* (1829), 90.

[44] Vestry min. bks. 1824–38, 425, 476.
[45] G.L.R.O., P83/MRY1/827.
[46] Owen, *Govt. of Victorian Lond.* 276, 296.
[47] Islington libr., vestry min. bk. 1824–38, 470; Semple, *On Treatment of Sick Poor*, 1.
[48] G.L.R.O., Is.B.G. 1.   [49] Ibid. P83/MRY1/1162.
[50] *Return of Expenditure on Bldgs. for Paupers*, H.C. 86, p. 113 (1876), lxiii; E. A. Willats, 'People's Jnl. 1872–1972', *Holloway & Islington Jnl.* 15 Dec. 1972; G.L.R.O., Is.B.G. 6, p. 306.
[51] G.L.R.O., Is.B.G. 17, pp. 14, 74–5, 562.
[52] Ibid. Is.B.G. 79.
[53] *Return of Accn. in Met. Wkhos. etc.* H.C. 93, p. 745 (1888), lxxxvii.
[54] G.L.R.O., Is.B.G. 72/1; *V.C.H. Mdx.* v. 151.
[55] *The Times*, 4 Feb. 1893, 9f; 19 Apr. 1895, 4g.
[56] Ibid. 9 May 1896, 9e.
[57] Islington libr. *Local Govt. Bd. Orders, S.M.I. Infirmary*, 1901.
[58] G.L.R.O., Is.B.G. 78.   [59] Ibid. 168.

Hillside, closed in 1972, and demolished for housing and a public park.[60] Cornwallis Road workhouse was taken over by the G.P.O. during the Second World War.[61]

In 1853 a new infants' poor establishment was built on Porter's Acre, Hornsey Road,[62] for 90 boys, 60 girls, and 30 infants, with room for enlargement. Boys and girls were in separate departments, with a common dining hall, and there were infirmaries and accommodation for a master, schoolmaster, and schoolmistress.[63] There were 111 boys and 75 girls in 1864[64] and 219 in all in 1866.[65] The adjoining no. 86 Reform Street was rented in 1867-8.[66] In 1871, when it was enlarged for an extra 12 with accommodation for industrial teachers, the school formed a 'sort of juvenile workhouse', where 95 boys, 86 girls, and 72 infants were clothed and taught. They were found to be inferior in intelligence to children enjoying the freedom of the streets; instruction suffered because the master had too many duties, the infants had no regular teacher, and the girls had been doing nothing for seven weeks except preparing clothes for older girls who were about to emigrate.[67] In 1877 some children kept in the old workhouse were transferred to Hornsey Road.[68] Extensions were built in 1879 and 1885,[69] and the average number in the school in the 1880s was 363.[70]

LOCAL GOVERNMENT AFTER 1856. Under the Metropolis Management Act, in force from 1856, parishes with more than 2,000 ratepayers were divided into wards.[71] Islington was divided into eight: Upper Holloway (with 9 vestrymen), Lower Holloway (12), Highbury (15), Thornhill (18), Barnsbury (18), St. Mary's (15), Canonbury (15), St. Peter's (18).[72] The parish was one of six

BOROUGH OF ISLINGTON. *Per fess gules and argent, a cross counter-changed; in the first quarter a cross potent or, in the second a lion rampant argent, in the third an eagle displayed sable, and in the fourth a water-bouget sable*

[Granted 1901]

electing two members to the Metropolitan Board of Works (M.B.W.) and was among those which took over some sewers of the Metropolitan Commissioners, while main sewers passed to the M.B.W.[73] The vicar ceased to chair the vestry except at Easter, for ecclesiastical matters, and

until 1887 a chairman was elected at each meeting. Thereafter the new vicar, W. H. Barlow, regularly presided at metropolitan vestry meetings, being chosen annually even after the incumbent's right to preside had been abolished under the Local Government Act, 1894.[74] The parish had an additional member on the M.B.W. from 1885.[75] In 1896-7 the wards were increased to eleven and the 120 vestrymen were redistributed.[76] By the time vestry government ended, committees existed for most functions: baths and washhouses; cemetery; electric lighting; excise; finance; parliamentary and general purposes; public health; valuation; works.[77]

LONDON BOROUGH OF ISLINGTON. *Barry wavy argent and azure, a maltese cross argent surmounted by an open book proper edged and on a chief gules a crescent between two annulets or*

[Granted 1966]

In 1864 the parish paid 31 officers: vestry clerk, chief clerk, accountant, medical officer, surveyor of sewers, surveyor of highways, 2 sanitary inspectors, inspector of lamps and dust, office-keeper, housekeeper, streetkeeper, greenkeeper and constable, 8 rate-collectors, and 10 clerks. In addition, 4 foremen and c. 70 labourers were employed on the roads, and a foreman and 5 labourers for the sewers.[78]

Islington Metropolitan Borough was established under the Local Government Act, 1899, and the number of wards and councillors was fixed in 1900, when aldermen were to be one sixth of the number of councillors. The eleven wards were retained with two slight changes of name, but representation was halved to 60 councillors.[79] In 1965 Islington and Finsbury M.B.s were merged to form the London Borough of Islington, with 10 aldermen and 60 councillors for the enlarged area. In 1977 there were seven standing committees, and councillors represented one of the 19 wards for four years. Aldermen, elected by the councillors for six years, were abolished in 1978.[80] In 1982 there were 20 wards, 18 of them covering the former parish of Islington, and 2 or 3 of the 52 councillors served each ward for four years. There were 17 committees.[81]

In 1894 the Progressive (Liberal) vestrymen included a Labour group of eleven, but by 1899

[60] *Holloway & Islington Jnl.* 15 Dec. 1972.
[61] *Bavaria Rd. Estate Tenants' Handbk.* [1979], p. 4 (copy in Islington libr.).
[62] Below, charities.
[63] G.L.R.O., P83/MRY1/821.
[64] Ibid. MRY1/824.
[65] *V.C.H. Mdx.* i. 229.
[66] G.L.R.O., Is.B.G. 1, p. 21.
[67] P.R.O., ED 3/4.
[68] G.L.R.O., Is.B.G. 13, pp. 211, 213, 414.
[69] *Rep. of M.B.W. 1879*, H.C. 212, p. 483 (1880 Sess. 2), lxii; *Rep. of M.B.W. 1885*, H.C. 170, p. 425 (1886), lvii.
[70] J. H. Bridges, *Health of Met. Pauper Schs.* (1890), 4.

[71] 18 & 19 Vic. c. 120.
[72] Islington libr., min. bk. of Ward 6, par. of St. Mary, Islington; Plan [c. 1853].
[73] 18 & 19 Vic. c. 120.
[74] *Life of W. H. Barlow*, ed. M. Barlow, 90, 93.
[75] *Rep. of M.B.W. 1885*, H.C. 170, p. 387 (1886), lvii.
[76] Vestry mins. Apr. 1896–Mar. 1897, 41–3.
[77] Ibid. Apr.–Nov. 1900, 104–6.
[78] *Return of Property, Pop. and Officers in each Par.* H.C. 379, p. 54 (1864), l.
[79] Vestry mins. Apr.–Nov. 1900, 104–6; 62 & 63 Vic. c. 14.
[80] Islington L.B. *Official Guide 1977–8*, 13.
[81] Islington L.B. *Islington Svces.* (Sept. 1983).

Progressives and Labour had split.[82] Moderates controlled the council in 1900 but in 1903 there were 26 Moderates to 34 Progressives. The Municipal Reform party (Moderates or Conservatives) captured 58 seats in 1906, when Progressives won only two, and kept control in 1909 and 1912, when Labour won one seat.[83] Labour's share later reached 22, although in 1931 Municipal Reformers took all the seats, and in 1934 Labour won 34 to take control,[84] which except for a brief period they retained thereafter until 1981. In that year the emergence of a left-wing group in the local Labour party, the result of gentrification, caused many Labour councillors to join the Social Democratic party, giving it the largest group on the council, but in 1982 Labour won all but one seat.[85] The S.D.P. regained two seats in 1983.[86]

In 1826 the vestry, which still met in the church, authorized the parish trustees to hire more convenient premises, perhaps the two rooms of the Mansion House or Sandy's House, Essex Road at the corner of Windsor Street, that were being rented in 1833 for meetings of committees and the board of health.[87] The vestry clerk later had an office in Milner Square. A vestry hall and offices were built, at the corner of Florence and Upper streets in 1859 and additions were made as local government expanded.[88] The building was sold in 1925,[89] after a new town hall, of which the first part was completed in 1923, had been built at Tyndale Place, Upper Street. The council chamber and extension were opened in 1925, and the public hall was completed in 1929.[90] From 1965 it housed the chief executive and borough secretary, besides council meetings.

Islington became a parliamentary borough under the Reform Act, 1832.[91] The Liberals held Islington West and Conservatives the other three seats in 1900, but in 1906 all the seats were won by Liberals.[92] In 1910 the Unionists won Islington North and in 1918 the Coalition Unionists won all four seats. The Conservatives held all four in 1923 but Labour won Islington West and South in 1924 and the others in 1929. Conservatives took all four in 1931 but Labour regained West and South in 1935, and the other two in 1945. The constituencies were altered for the 1950 election to East, North, and South-West, all three won and thereafter held by Labour. Reorganization in 1974 revised Islington North and set up Islington Central, and Islington South and Finsbury, all won by Labour.[93] In 1981 ideological differences led all three M.P.s to leave the

Labour party and two of them to join the Social Democratic party.[94] In the 1983 election, however, when the three seats had been reorganized as two, North, and South and Finsbury, they lost to Labour candidates.[95]

PUBLIC SERVICES. Islington was well provided with springs, which supplied water for London and Clerkenwell in the 15th century. A conduit in Cowlese, called conduit field in 1650,[96] north-east of Canonbury House, had supplied St. Bartholomew's hospital for some time by 1433 and in 1538 and 1544.[97] A conduit nearby in Highbury, probably the one in conduit field opposite no. 14 Highbury Place, fed a reservoir in St. Giles, Cripplegate, built in the early 15th century, and in 1546 springs between Islington and Hoxton supplied a conduit at St. Mary Lothbury.[98] From 1430 the London Charterhouse had a piped supply from the place in Barnsbury[99] where the White Conduit House became a popular resort,[1] and its aqueduct was mentioned in 1545 and 1553.[2] Similar springs presumably served much of the parish until the 19th century: one near Upper Street supplied a cold bath used by Mr. Flower's school in 1810.[3]

The New River, passing through the most populous parts, was of great benefit to Islington's inhabitants, who were probably among those accused of cutting the banks to let out the water, contaminating it, and carrying it away.[4] Nude bathing was a continual problem in the 18th century and in 1804 police officers were called on to stop it, because of indecency rather than pollution.[5] In the mid 18th century only householders in the very southern end of the parish, around the Angel, had water piped by the New River Co., others having to buy water taken from the stream at $\frac{1}{2}d.$ a pail. Piped supplies seem to have been extended in the town by 1809, but Holloway, Canonbury, and beyond relied on a pump in the river at Hopping Lane, for which the owner paid 20s. a year to the company.[6] The company refused to pipe a supply to Holloway, and George Pocock, who had built several houses there, dug a 172-ft. well near George Place. An Act of 1810 formed a company for Pocock's Holloway waterworks and a steam engine was used to pump supplies. The New River Co. immediately laid pipes to Holloway and closed the Hopping Lane pump, but householders preferred Pocock's water. Eventually his under-capitalized waterworks was forced out of busi-

[82] P. Thompson, *Socialists, Liberals and Labour: Struggle for Lond. 1885–1914* (1967), 309.
[83] Ibid. 315–16; *The Times*, 3 Nov. 1906, 5a; 3 Nov. 1909, 10a, b; 4 Nov. 1912, 11a.
[84] *The Times*, 31 Oct. 1934, 14e; 3 Nov. 1934, 7c.
[85] Ibid. 8 Sept. 1981, 1; 9 Sept. 1981, 2; *Observer*, 21 Feb. 1982, 9.
[86] *The Times*, 28 Oct. 1983, 2f.
[87] Vestry min. bk. 1824–38, 67, 385; Cromwell, *Islington*, 232.
[88] Islington libr. *4th Ann. Rep. of Vestry* (1860), 3; Islington M.B. *Illus. Guide to Housing and Local Govt. Exhib.* (1946), 7.
[89] Islington libr., Sale Cat. of Islington town hall, 1925.
[90] Islington M.B. *Souvenir of Opening*, 1925; *Illus. Guide to Housing and Local Govt. Exhib.* 8.

[91] P. Glanville, *Lond. in Maps* (1972), 46.
[92] *The Times*, 16 Jan. 1906, 10b.
[93] *Whitaker's Almanack* (1915 and later edns.).
[94] *The Observer*, 21 Feb. 1982, 9.
[95] *The Times*, 11 June 1983, suppl. vi.
[96] Islington libr., deed box I/23.
[97] E. A. Webb, *Rec. of St. Bartholomew's, Smithfield* (1921), ii. 191, 193; P.R.O., E 211/166.
[98] Nelson, *Islington* (1829), 147.
[99] *Cal. Pat.* 1429–36, 105; P.R.O., E 326/6645; *V.C.H. Mdx.* i. 163.   [1] Above, social.
[2] *L. & P. Hen. VIII*, xx(1), p. 303; *Cal. Pat.* 1553–4, 208.
[3] Nelson, *Islington* (1811), 115.
[4] *Acts of P.C.* 1615–16, 212.
[5] Islington libr., vestry min. bk. 1777–1811, 157v., 166.
[6] Nelson, *Islington* (1811), 106.

ness and by 1823 houses in Holloway were connected to the New River Co.'s pipes.[7]

In 1846 a committee was appointed to look into ways of obtaining a constant water supply to improve sanitation in the poorer districts.[8] Several courts and alleys in the town were supplied for only a short period three times a week by standpipes shared by as many as 21 houses.[9] Since wells were expensive and uncertain, the New River Co. was approached to service tanks for pumps, in order that 53 of the worst streets and courts could receive additional cleansing.[10] By the 1880s a pumping station had been built in Hornsey Lane, with two engines and a covered reservoir, and another on the east side of Dartmouth Park Hill, with two covered reservoirs.[11] Water was turned on for only a few hours each day until 1889, when some parts of Islington received a continuous supply.[12]

Cholera in the 1840s led to organized attempts to improve sanitation in accord with the Metropolitan Commission of 1848–9, which was attempting to abolish cesspools.[13] Five district sanitary committees were set up in 1848, each with its own inspector who reported weekly on health hazards, nuisances, and roads.[14] In 1853 there were still areas with filthy privies, cesspool drainage, and no water supply.[15] The Metropolitan Commissioners of Sewers were undertaking a scheme which included Islington when they were superseded by the M.B.W. in 1856,[16] and the Caledonian Road sewer was completed that year.[17] Drainage in the northern part of the parish was improved by the Northern High Level sewer, completed in 1861, from Hampstead to the river Lea, replacing Hackney brook which the medical officer saw as a major nuisance.[18] Between 1855 and 1870 the M.B.W. constructed 9 miles of sewers in Islington as part of the general scheme for the metropolis, and a further 32 miles of sewers and 208 miles of pipe-drains were constructed privately under the vestry's supervision. Several open sewers were covered and outlet sewers constructed by the vestry; 20 urinals were also built. From 1856 parish drainage was the responsibility of three inspectors and a superintendent under the sanitary committee and medical officer of health.[19]

Under the Act of 1824 the parish trustees could contract out the cleansing of roads and sale of dust,[20] and tenders were sought, to let the dust for a year.[21] The contractor was criticized in 1865, when in many poor localities the dust was left for several weeks.[22] By the 1930s the borough had its own disposal works in Ashburton Grove, Hornsey Road, whence the refuse was taken away by rail. In 1937 the works was modernized; refuse from Stoke Newington was also handled there.[23]

Sixty street lamps were to be supplied and maintained at 3s. 4d. each a month in 1761 and were lit from Michaelmas to Lady Day in 1763.[24] The Local Act of 1772 empowered trustees to raise a lighting and watching rate and supervise the lamps and watchmen.[25] By the winter of 1811–12 there were 455 lamps maintained by a contractor.[26] In 1823 the lamp and watch committee arranged for part of the parish to be lit by the Imperial Gas Co., which had laid some pipes in Upper Street and Essex Road, c. 80 lamps being required to replace c. 170 oil lamps. In 1824 the Imperial Gas Co. agreed to light the rest of the parish, laying a main from the Back Road to the Crown at Holloway. The part of City Road that lay in the parish was lit by the Gas Light Co. of Brick Lane.[27] By 1870 there were 2,939 lamps, all lit by Imperial except for 12 in City Road lit by Chartered Gas Co.[28]

Islington vestry started its own electricity undertaking in 1894 with a generating station at Eden Grove,[29] which began the supply in 1896,[30] and new streets were to be lit with electricity instead of gas in 1906.[31] In 1936 offices and showrooms were built at the corner of Holloway and Camden roads,[32] which become London Electricity Board showrooms after nationalization.

The fire engine shed on the north side of the church porch was rebuilt in 1716.[33] In 1747 the two decayed fire engines were to be replaced by a large and a small one, with 40 feet of leather pipe.[34] The engineer received 40s. a year in 1717[35] and John Ashley succeeded his father at the same salary in 1753.[36] The engine house was moved near the watch house, probably on Islington green in 1751 when the old church was demolished, and was rebuilt there in 1767.[37] In 1770 the vestry decided to sell the engines and buy a large new one.[38] There were two engines by 1821, when one was to be kept at Holloway.[39] In 1861 the parish paid £304 for fire engines, £400 to the Royal Society for the Protection of Life for fire-escape ladders, and £152 in rewards; payments were made out of the churchwardens' rate.[40]

[7] Ibid. (1829), 103–4; 50 Geo. III, c. 150 (Local Act).
[8] G.L.R.O., P83/MRY1/736/1.
[9] Ibid. 11.
[10] Ibid. 1.
[11] P. A. Scratchley, *Bolton's Lond. Water Supply* (1888), 45, 71.
[12] Met. Water Bd. *Lond.'s Water Supply* (1953), 5; *Rep. of M.B.W. 1888*, H.C. 326, p. 753 (1889), lxvi.
[13] D. Owen, *Govt. of Victorian Lond. 1855–89* (1982), 48.
[14] G.L.R.O., P83/MRY1/721, 727, 730, 731.
[15] Ibid. 747.
[16] *Rep. of M.B.W. 1857*, H.C. 234, p. 16 (1857 Sess. 2), xli.
[17] Ibid. *1859*, H.C. 178, p. 290 (1859 Sess. 2), xxvi.
[18] Ibid. *1861*, H.C. 11, p. 403 (1862), xlvii; M.O.H. *1st Ann. Rep.* (1856), 10.
[19] *Return of Sanitary and Street Improvements since 1855*, H.C. 298, p. 14 (1872), xlix.
[20] 5 Geo. IV, c. 125 (Local).
[21] Islington libr., Lamp and Watch min. bk. 1806–24.
[22] *Rep. of M.O.H. 1865*, p. 17.
[23] Islington M.B. *Official Opening of Reconstructed Refuse Disposal Works* (brochure 1937); Islington M.B. *Illus. Guide to Housing and Local Govt. Exhib.* (1946), p. 16. (both in Islington libr.).
[24] Vestry min. bk. 1735–77, 117v., 125.
[25] 12 Geo. III, c. 17 (Priv. Act).
[26] G.L.R.O., P83/MRY1/655.
[27] Islington libr., Lamp and Watch min. bk. 1806–24.
[28] *Return of San. and Street Improvements*, p. 14.
[29] *Illus. Guide to Housing and Local Govt. Exhib.* p. 22.
[30] Islington M.B. *Official Guide* (1917), p. 43.
[31] *The Times*, 27 June 1906, 8a.
[32] Islington M.B. *Illus. Guide*, 20.
[33] Vestry min. bk. 1708–34, 58.
[34] Ibid. 1735–77, 59v.–60.
[35] Ibid. 1708–34, 66.
[36] Ibid. 1735–77, 87.
[37] Ibid. 139.
[38] Ibid. 167.
[39] Ibid. 1812–24, 268.
[40] *Return of Amounts paid by Pars. for Fire Engines in 1861*, H.C. 197, p. 334 (1862), xlvii.

Under the Metropolis Fire Brigade Act, 1865, the M.B.W. asked the parishes to maintain stations for four districts until the brigade could make permanent arrangements. Islington was the only parish that refused,[41] but may have agreed later.[42] The parish had temporary stations in 1866 at Florence Street, off Upper Street, and at Holloway Road. The first was replaced by a permanent station at Astey's Row, Essex Road, completed in 1868.[43] A station at Seven Sisters Road, Holloway, was opened in 1872[44] and enlarged in 1882.[45] Behind it no. 84 Mayton Street was bought in 1899 to take more firemen[46] and nos. 80 and 82 were bought in 1900.[47] The station was extended on the Mayton Street site in 1908.[48] In 1935 the Holloway station had 26 men. A new station was built next to Hornsey Road baths c. 1970.[49] A central station was opened in Upper Street in 1900, with accommodation for 19 firemen, two coachmen, and four horses,[50] and had 25 men in 1935.[51] It was extended on part of the site of the former Unity church after the Second World War.[52]

In 1887 the New River Co. provided 59 fire hydrants for Islington.[53] A substation in Blackstock Road opened in 1902.[54] In 1903 the L.C.C. purchased nos. 158–64 (even) Copenhagen Street for a substation, which had closed by 1927, and in 1905 nos. 45–51 (odd) Calverley Grove, Upper Holloway, for a similar purpose.[55]

A watch house, cage, and whipping post were to be set up in 1675, and permission was received from the justices in 1680. The beadle was allowed one watchman to assist him from July to September 1706, and after that the constables were to ask each inhabitant whether he would pay the rate for a watch, or to watch himself; the following month six men were appointed to watch each night until Lady Day.[56] A reward was instituted in 1739 for apprehending any of the footpads and highwaymen infesting the parish.[57] The justices ordered the rebuilding of the watch house, whipping post, stocks, and cage in 1763, and in 1767 a new watch house and cage were built on the site of the old.[58] The Local Act of 1772 enabled the trustees to use the rate for a watch and to appoint personnel. Two supervisors from sunset to midnight and two from midnight till 7 a.m. were to oversee the watchmen, inspect the lamps, and prevent civil nuisances.[59] Despite a regular watch, the Islington Reward Society was formed in

1781, meeting at the King's Head tavern, to encourage the apprehending of thieves. In 1830 the fund was in arrears and a further subscription was called for to wind up the society.[60]

The watch house which stood in the middle of Islington green was decayed again in 1797 and a new one was to be built at the corner of the green in 1798.[61] In 1828 the parish employed 14 officers to prevent nuisances and for other duties by day, including the salaried streetkeeper and his deputy, and the 6 constables and 6 head-boroughs. At night there were a paid constable, 4 supervisors, and 160 watchmen operating in two shifts, besides 10 watchmen employed privately. Foot patrols covered c. 20 miles of the parish roads at night, leaving c. 16 miles not covered; the cost of the parish's policing was c. £4,000 on average.[62] Islington came within the new metropolitan police area from 1829.[63] The police took over the old watch house in 1831, and leased premises in Bird's Buildings in 1853. A freehold site was bought in Upper Street in 1857 and the station there opened in 1864.[64] In 1863 the parish was divided between Finsbury, Islington, and Hampstead divisions.[65] In 1982 Islington had stations at nos. 277 Upper Street, 284 Hornsey Road, and 211 Blackstock Road,[66] the latter opened in 1910. Clerkenwell County Court stood in Duncan Street by c. 1853.[67]

There were leper hospitals at Kingsland Green, founded in 1280, and at the foot of Highgate Hill, founded in 1473.[68]

In 1732 four apothecaries, one a woman, were to treat the poor for one year each, and from 1735 an agreement was made annually with an apothecary to treat the poor and attend the workhouse.[69] A house in the possession of Dr. Robert Poole from 1740 served as a smallpox hospital, which the parish tried to get removed in 1748, although it was still there in 1749.[70] The vestry arranged in 1772 that the smallpox hospital in Clerkenwell should admit their cases for 5 gn. a year.[71] The hospital moved to Battle Bridge in St. Pancras in 1793 and to a site between Dartmouth Park Hill and Highgate Hill in 1850.[72] In 1867 the hospital had about 100 beds and was supported mainly by voluntary contributions, being intended for paying patients but taking paupers if beds were available. Until the Metropolitan Asylums Board made provision from c. 1869 it was one of only two isolation hospitals in London, the other

[41] Owen, *Govt. of Victorian Lond.* 129–30, 385 n. 15.
[42] *Rep. of M.B.W. 1865–6*, H.C. 34, pp. 627–8 (1867), lviii.
[43] Ibid. *1867–8*, H.C. 23, p. 702 (1868–9), li.
[44] Ibid. *1871*, H.C. 294, p. 497 (1872), xlix; *1872*, H.C. 146, p. 474 (1873), lvi.
[45] Ibid. *1882*, H.C. 169, p. 582 (1883), lix.
[46] L.C.C. *Ann. Rep. 1898–9*, p. 43.
[47] L.C.C. *Lond. Statutes*, ii. 418.
[48] Foundation stone.
[49] G.L.R.O., FB/GEN/1/51.
[50] *The Times*, 27 July 1900, 10d.
[51] G.L.R.O., FB/GEN/1/51.
[52] Below, prot. nonconf.
[53] *Rep. of M.B.W. 1887*, H.C. 159, p. 602 (1888), lxxxvii.
[54] L.C.C. *Ann. Rep. 1898–9*, p. 40; datestone.
[55] *Lond. Statutes*, ii. 526, 636; *P.O. Dir. Lond.* (1927).
[56] Vestry min. bk. 1662–1708, 85, 367, 369, 371; photocopy of sessions rec. in Islington libr.
[57] Vestry min. bk. 1735–77, 27.
[58] Ibid. 124v., 139, 144v.

[59] 12 Geo. III, c. 17 (Priv. Act), printed 1823, with copy of watchmen regulations in front.
[60] Islington libr., min. bks. Islington Reward Soc., 1781–1831.
[61] Vestry min. bk. 1777–1811, 119; inf. from Mr. J. C. Connell.
[62] *Rep. of Sel. Cttee. on Police of Metropolis*, H.C. 533, App. M, pp. 344, 374 (1828), vi.
[63] 10 Geo. IV, c. 44.
[64] Inf. from Mr. J. C. Connell.
[65] *Return of Police in Islington and Finsbury*, H.C. 398, p. 342 (1863), l.
[66] *Police and Constabulary Almanac 1982*; date on rainwater heads.
[67] Plan [c. 1853].
[68] *V.C.H. Mdx.* i. 210–11, 205–6.
[69] Vestry min. bk. 1708–34, 230; ibid. 1735–77, 2v., *passim.*
[70] Ibid. 1735–77, 63, 66v.
[71] Ibid. 175v.
[72] *V.C.H. Mdx.* v. 297.

being the London Fever hospital in Liverpool Road.[73] Although the smallpox hospital was apparently not taken over directly by the board,[74] it was the board which sold it with its 9-a. site to the Islington guardians in 1896 as a new work-house infirmary.[75] By 1920 five linked blocks had been added south of the original hospital.[76] By 1944 it had been taken over by the L.C.C. and formed the St. Mary, Islington, hospital in the Archway group, with 836 beds and more modern premises than the other two hospitals in the group. Those were Highgate, on the St. Pancras side of Dartmouth Park Hill, formerly St. Pancras infirmary, with 545 beds, and Archway, facing Archway Road, formerly Holborn workhouse infirmary, with 564 beds.[77] In 1977 the three formed the three wings of Whittington hospital under the North London Group Hospital Management Committee.[78] By 1980 new buildings on the St. Mary's site included a six-storeyed psychiatric wing. Whittington was principally an acute-case hospital with 804 beds, within the Camden and Islington Area Health Authority.[79]

The London Fever hospital, founded in 1802 beside the smallpox hospital at Battle Bridge, moved to Liverpool Road in 1850, despite much local opposition.[80] During 1850 it admitted 562 patients and had 49 at the end of the year.[81] It too depended on voluntary contributions and took mainly paying patients, having 182 beds in 1867.[82] The hospital was still a voluntary one in 1944 when it had 209 beds including 52 for pulmonary tuberculosis, mainly in old buildings with a new cubicle block. Its use as a fever hospital had declined with the increase in municipal facilities and from 1948 it was amalgamated with the Royal Free hospital, Holborn, as a general hospital. In 1973 it housed women's wards and a private wing.[83] In 1980 it was managed by the Camden and Islington Area Health Authority, and was the temporary headquarters of the area's Community Health Council.[84]

The old workhouse in Liverpool Road was taken over by the Metropolitan Asylums Board in 1871 as a temporary smallpox convalescent annexe to Hampstead isolation hospital, with 300 beds. A division was made in the building to seal it off from the part used for employment of outdoor poor.[85]

Islington dispensary was founded in 1821, and financed by subscriptions, dividends, and collections. In the 1850s the staff consisted of 3 physicians, 3 surgeons, a surgeon-dentist, and a paid resident medical officer.[86] Over 6,000 patients were treated in 1850–1.[87] The dispensary was in Upper Street near the parish church by 1886, when it was sold for road-widening, and it was rebuilt further back.[88] It was closed in 1946, and Islington Medical Centre (formerly Medical Mission) took over the building in 1949.[89]

A dispensary was opened in 1840 to serve Highbury and Upper and Lower Holloway. The staff in the 1850s were 2 consulting physicians, a consulting surgeon, 6 honorary local medical officers, and a paid resident medical officer and a dispenser. Besides the principal dispensary house in Francis Place, Lower Holloway, there were branches at Upper Holloway and Highbury Vale. In 1852–3 the dispensary treated 5,104 patients and was financed by subscriptions, collections, and dividends. A new dispensary house was about to be built c. 1854.[90] In 1886 it was in Palmer Place.[91]

The Royal Northern hospital was founded in 1856 as the Great Northern hospital at no. 11 York Road (later Way), facing the side of King's Cross station.[92] Sherard Freeman Statham established it at his own expense to provide medical attendance for the poor of north London for two hours each day and to receive as many as it could treat, regardless of preference or recommendations. Urgent cases would be taken at all hours. A maternal charity was established for married women at home. In the first six months 11,718 patients were treated, including 262 dental cases and 46 in-patients; there were 16,337 repeated attendances. Sometimes 300 people attended in one day, and patients included 1,800 children under two. The staff was expanded to 20 doctors, surgeons, and dentists in 1857, when the acquisition of nos. 9 and 10 York Road with adjoining yards and workshops increased the number of beds from 16 to 50. Financial difficulties at first often prevented full use of the beds; the medical staff gave support when donations were not adequate. In 1859–60 there were 19,000 new out-patients and 240 in-patients.

In 1862 the premises were bought by the Metropolitan Railway Co. and the hospital amalgamated with the Spinal hospital, no. 84 Portland Road, which became the orthopaedic department of the Great Northern, temporarily housing in-patients. Out-patients moved to no. 286 Penton-ville Road, provided by the railway company, and in 1863 to no. 294. The lease of Pembroke Villa, Caledonian Road, at the corner of Twyford Street, was acquired and the in-patients moved there in 1864. Nos. 229, 231, and 233 Caledonian Road were bought in 1866, and by 1868 the hospital occupied the whole block between

---

[73] G. M. Ayers, *Eng.'s First State Hosps. and Metropolitan Asylums Bd. 1867–1930* (1971), 12.
[74] Ibid.; M.A.B. *Work of Met. Asylums Bd. 1867–1930* (1930).
[75] *The Times*, 9 May 1896, 9e.
[76] O.S. Map 6″, Mdx. XII. SW. (1920 edn.).
[77] Min. of Health, *Hosp. Survey* (1945), 65–6.
[78] Islington L.B. *Official Guide 1977–8*, 70.
[79] *Hosps. and Health Svces. Year Bk. 1982*, 151.
[80] Ayers, *Eng.'s First State Hosps.* 12; Cruchley's *New Plan* (1829); S. Lewis, *Islington As It Was*, 59; *Rep. of Cttee. to oppose erection of Lond. Fever Hosp.* (1848, copy in Islington libr.).
[81] *49th Ann. Rep. of Lond. Fever Hosp.* (1851, copy in Islington libr.).

[82] Ayers, *Eng.'s First State Hosps.* 12–13.
[83] Min. of Health, *Hosp. Survey* (1945), 60; P. Zwart, *Islington: Hist. and Guide* (1973), 121.
[84] *Hosps. and Health Svces. Year Bk. 1982*, 151.
[85] Ayers, *Eng.'s First State Hosps.* 52–3; G.L.R.O., Is.B.G. 6, p. 521.
[86] Lewis, *Islington As It Was*, 77–8.
[87] *Rep. of Islington Dispensary* (1851, copy in Islington libr.).
[88] *Rep. of M.B.W. 1886*, H.C. 157, p. 563 (1887), lxxi.
[89] Inf. from Mr. J. C. Connell.
[90] Lewis, *Islington As It Was*, 78–9.
[91] Bacon, *Atlas of Lond.* (1886).
[92] Following 4 paras. based on E.C.O. Jewesbury, *Royal Northern Hosp. 1856–1956* (1956).

Stanmore and Twyford Streets, later the site of the public baths. Assistance came with some large legacies from 1865 and more donations, including regular contributions from the Midland, Great Northern, and Metropolitan Railway Cos., whose employees often received treatment. In 1883, having failed to buy the freehold to permit rebuilding, the hospital amalgamated with a committee whose projected central hospital for Highbury, Holloway, and Stoke Newington, on a different system combining free treatment with graduated payments, would duplicate the Great Northern's work.

The combined hospital was called the Great Northern Central and was a general and free hospital with pay wards. The committee bought the 1¼-a. Grove House site, Holloway Road, in 1884, and the first block, designed by Keith Young and Henry Hall, was opened in 1888 with 68 beds out of the 150 planned and out-patients' and administration units. Islington parish partially endowed one ward to commemorate the Golden Jubilee and thereafter the vicar, senior churchwarden, and vestry clerk sat on the management committee. In 1895 the hospital was officially recognized as a place of instruction for medical students. The Prince Albert Victor wing was opened, with 19 pay-beds fronting Holloway Road and a circular block of three wards for 65 patients; further wards in the block were opened 1898. In 1902 funds from the Stonefield charity estate were given to the hospital and a ward named Richard Cloudesley was set aside for the sick poor of Islington; the charity was also used to found a convalescent home at Clacton-on-Sea (Essex), opened in 1909. An electrical department was opened in 1908, and a separate X-ray department in 1918. The freehold of nos. 4 and 5 Manor Gardens was bought in 1917 for a new nurses' home, and adjacent property was acquired at about that time. A casualty department, funded by the Islington War Memorial Fund, and a nurses' home, designed by H. Percy Adams, were started in 1922. From 1921 the hospital was amalgamated with the Royal Chest hospital, City Road, whose in-patients had a special wing at Holloway until the chest hospital closed in 1954. A home of recovery in Hornsey Lane in 1918 was continued in Fortis Green Road from 1919 to 1921 when a permanent home was opened at Grovelands, Southgate.[93]

From 1921 the hospital was called the Royal Northern hospital. The Royal Northern Group consisted of 200 beds at Holloway, the Royal Chest hospital, Grovelands (60 beds), and Reckitt Convalescent Home (30 beds). The three-storeyed St. David's wing, designed by L. G. Pearson, was started in 1929, for patients of moderate means, especially residents of north London. The wing, on the Manor Gardens side, had 55 single and 5 double rooms; it was built with £57,000 from Sir Howell J. Williams, representative for South Islington on the L.C.C.

and the hospital's greatest benefactor with gifts totalling over £158,000, and was to be self-supporting. In 1944 there were 307 beds at Holloway, including 22 maternity, and 60 beds at Grovelands; 85 beds at the Royal Chest had been destroyed by bombing.[94] In 1948 the hospital ceased to be voluntary and became a state hospital in the North-West Metropolitan Region. On the closure of the Royal Chest hospital the South Islington chest clinic moved from there, together with the North Islington chest clinic from Holloway Road, to the Whittington hospital. Nos. 11 and 12 Highbury Crescent housed the nurses' preliminary training school from 1952. The Ingleby Arms, Tollington Way, became the occupational therapy department in 1955. More than 20 houses in Ingleby Road had been bought in the 1930s for nurses and most of the block between Tollington Way and Manor Gardens was bought for future development. In 1980 the hospital had 262 beds, including 23 private, and took mainly acute cases.[95]

Mildmay Memorial hospital originated as a small cottage hospital near Mildmay Road run by the nursing branch of the Mildmay Deaconess Institution, started 1866. It was replaced by the Tudor-style Memorial Cottage hospital, opened in 1883 in the centre of the Mildmay compound and provided by Lady Hay in memory of the Revd. William Pennefather and her son Duncan Hay.[96] In 1944 it treated mainly private patients, with 26 children's and general beds and 21 pay beds, 12 of them added since 1938 for special cases.[97] It had closed by 1980.

North Islington Infant Welfare Centre and School for Mothers, nos. 6–9 Manor Gardens, was founded in 1913 by some local women concerned at the very high infant mortality rate.[98] It started in a Presbyterian mission hall, Elthorne Road, one afternoon a week with a voluntary doctor treating 12–15 mothers and babies, aiming to educate mothers in the correct care of their children. It leased no. 9 Manor Gardens in 1915 and started a scheme of home helps, taking over the adjoining house in 1916 and nos. 6 and 7 in 1918. It had 18 hospital beds for children and an out-patients' department in 1944, when amalgamation with the Royal Northern was suggested,[99] but maintained its voluntary status in 1973 while also carrying out social work for the council. The centre was still active in 1981.

The City of London Maternity hospital moved its in-patients to no. 65 Hanley Road, Tollington Park, c. 1956, having agreed in 1947 to amalgamate with the gynaecological and obstetric departments of the Royal Northern.[1] In 1980 it was a maternity hospital under the Camden and Islington Area Health Authority, with 86 beds.[2]

Islington Medical mission met in Britannia Row in 1932, one of two missions run by Highbury Quadrant Congregational church, and provided basic medical attention for the poor. Its premises were destroyed in the Second World

[93] V.C.H. Mdx. v. 180.
[94] Min. of Health, Hosp. Survey (1945), 66.
[95] Hosps. and Health Svces. Year Bk. 1982, 151.
[96] H. J. Cooke, Mildmay; Story of First Deaconess Institution (1892), 130–1, 138–9; below prot. nonconf., missions.
[97] Min. of Health, Hosp. Survey (1945), 59, 86.

[98] Para. based on mem. plaque; Story of North Islington Infant Welfare Centre and Sch. for Mothers, 1913–1973 (booklet in Islington libr.).
[99] Min. of Health, Hosp. Survey, 66, 90.
[1] Jewesbury, Royal Northern, 126.
[2] Hosps. and Health Svces. Year Bk. 1982, 150.

War and it moved to Islington chapel, Upper Street, for a few years. The committee decided to move to Clerkenwell, but the superintendent and some staff remained as Islington Medical Centre, moving in 1949 to the former Islington dispensary at no. 303 Upper Street next to the parish church. Both medical treatment under the National Health scheme and missionary work were carried out. In 1969 the centre moved to no. 28 Cross Street, returning to the renovated no. 303 Upper Street in 1971.[3] In 1981 there were health centres, at Goodinge Road, Highbury Grange, and River Place, Essex Road.[4]

Islington burial board, appointed under the Burial Act of 1852,[5] in 1853 bought 30 a. of the land in East Finchley sold to St. Pancras burial board, sharing the cost of chapels and roads with St. Pancras.[6] By 1867 there were 3,000 burials a year and in 1876 the cemetery was enlarged.[7] A crematorium was added and in 1970 modernized.[8] Trent Park cemetery at Cockfosters in Southgate, a lawn-type cemetery of 1.3 a., was consecrated in 1960.[9]

Several lending libraries were provided by churches in the 19th century, besides those attached to the parochial schools and the Union chapel and Wesleyan Sunday schools.[10] The library connected with St. Peter's district had 390 titles in 1849, comprising religious, natural history, travel, and children's books, and the subscription was 2d. a month.[11] The Unitarian chapel, Highgate Hill, provided a free reading room and lending library open five nights a week, with some 7,000 volumes lent to 1,500 families of all classes, of whom only 11 were Unitarian; it also provided religious, ladies', and literary periodicals, in addition to the daily papers.[12] The reading room was used as a temporary public library in 1904.[13] Efforts were made from 1855 to adopt the Act to levy a rate for a library, but it was not until 1904 that the Public Library Acts were adopted. Andrew Carnegie offered to provide a central library and four branches, of which the North branch was the first to be opened, in 1906, on the site of nos. 14–19 Manor Gardens, Holloway. It was designed by Henry T. Hare who also won the competition for the Central library, part of which opened in 1907. The West branch, Lofting Road, Thornhill Square, designed by A. Beresford Pite, also opened in 1907. The reference section of the Central library opened in 1908. The South-East branch was built during the First World War, but was used as a recreation hall by the unemployed, who had to be evicted

in 1920, and it was opened as a library only in 1921. In 1946 the first sub-branch was opened in two converted shops at Archway next to the Methodist central hall; it became a full branch library in 1947 and moved to the new shopping precinct near Archway station c. 1980. Lewis Carroll children's library, Copenhagen Street, was opened in 1952; Mildmay, nos. 19–23 Mildmay Park, in 1954; Arthur Simpson library, Hanley Road, Crouch Hill, in 1960; and the Dick Whittington junior library, Giesbach Road, Upper Holloway, in 1962, closing in 1982 when its services were transferred to the enlarged Archway library. The latest new library was the John Barnes, no. 275 Camden Road, Holloway, in 1974.[14]

Public baths were started in 1892 in Caledonian Road, on the site of the old Great Northern hospital. Baths in Hornsey Road on the site of Devonshire House[15] were completed in 1895 with four swimming and 125 slipper baths, a laundry, and a washhouse. Part of the building was bombed in 1941 and part of the original main building was rebuilt, the whole being reopened in 1964.[16] Caledonian Road had three swimming baths, one of which was used as a hall seating 800 in winter, besides slipper baths and washhouses. It was rebuilt on the same site after the Second World War. Tibberton Square, later Essex Road, baths, Greenman's Lane, were opened c. 1897.[17] All three buildings were in use in 1982.

Copyhold known as Islington green was held of the manor of Canonbury by trustees for the parish from 1777 at 2s. 6d. a year.[18] Rails around it were to be rebuilt and repainted in 1781.[19] The green covered ½ a. in 1865, when it had been recently planted and furnished with seats.[20] Islington's need for open spaces was recognized early: its inhabitants were among those who initiated the scheme to create Finsbury park, which the M.B.W. pursued from 1856,[21] and Islington's medical officer in 1861 urged that the park was much needed for the health of the poor.[22] The park, a small part of which lay in Islington, was opened in 1869.[23] Islington also contributed towards the cost of Clissold park, in Stoke Newington, opened in 1889.[24] Newington green, which lay in Islington, was fenced and laid out as a garden by the M.B.W. and transferred to Islington vestry to maintain in perpetuity.[25] The M.B.W. bought the 25-a. Highbury Fields in 1885 for £60,000, of which Islington paid half, drained and levelled the ground, planted trees, and provided seats.[26]

[3] Islington Medical Centre, *Ann. Rep. 1957–8, 1970–1* (copies in Islington libr.).

[4] *Hosps. and Health Svces. Year Bk. 1982*, 151.

[5] 15 & 16 Vic. c. 85.

[6] Guildhall MS. 19224/436, file 2.

[7] *Return of Met. Burial Grounds*, H.C. 447, p. 727 (1867), lviii; *V.C.H. Mdx.* vi. 53.

[8] Islington L.B. *Official Guide 1977–8*, 47.

[9] Ibid.; Guildhall MS. 19224/436, file 4.

[10] Lewis, *Islington*, 380–1.

[11] *Cat. of Bks. in Lending Libr. in St. Peter's dist.* (1849), in Islington libr.

[12] Booth, *Life and Labour*, 3rd ser. (1), 125–6.

[13] Rest of para. based on E. A. Willats, 'Hist. of Islington Pub. Librs.' (T.S. c. 1965 in Islington libr.); inf. from Mr. J. C. Connell.

[14] Brochure on opening, in Islington libr.

[15] Vestry min. bk. 1891–2, 83, 238.

[16] *Opening of Hornsey Rd. Baths 1964* (bklet. in Islington libr.).

[17] Vestry min. bk. 1896–7, 166.

[18] G.L.R.O., P83/MRY1/406, no. 22.

[19] Vestry min. bk. 1777–1811, 23v.

[20] *Return of Commons and Open Spaces*, H.C. 461, p. 476 (1865), xlvii.

[21] *Rep. of M.B.W. 1857*, H.C. 234, p. 10 (1857 Sess. 2), xli.

[22] M.O.H. *Ann. Rep.* 1861, p. 14.

[23] *V.C.H. Mdx.* vi. 111, 145.

[24] Ibid. 111; *Rep. of M.B.W. 1888*, H.C. 326, p. 725 (1889), lxvi.

[25] *Rep. of M.B.W. 1876*, H.C. 225, p. 577 (1877), lxxi.

[26] L.C.C. *Lond. Statutes*, i. 665–6; *Rep. of M.B.W. 1885*, H.C. 170, p. 383 (1886), lvii; *1886*, H.C. 157, p. 479 (1887), lxxi.

In 1906 Newington and Islington greens were among several open areas to be preserved under the London Squares and Enclosures Act. Other areas included Canonbury, Thornhill, and Edward's squares, and Thornhill Gardens and Crescent.[27] Despite those and other pieces of land which gradually passed into municipal ownership, Islington's open space was still relatively meagre and the council incorporated more in its redevelopment schemes after the Second World War. The New River Walk was opened from St. Paul's Road to Astey's Row in 1954[28] and extended in the 1970s. By 1977 the council was responsible for 130 a. of open spaces and, as part of a 20-year plan, proposed to provide another 119 a. during rebuilding, particularly as play areas for children.[29] Among the areas thus created are the large park on the north side of Copenhagen Street, Bingfield park with the Crumbles play castle, small areas beside the Regent's canal, Paradise park between Sheringham and Mackenzie roads which in 1981 included the Freightliner farm moved from the west side of York Way, Wray Crescent off Tollington Park, and parks formed between Cressida Road and St. John's Way on part of the former workhouse site and at Archway roundabout.

CHURCHES. Islington church served the whole parish until 1814. It was recorded in the settlement, enrolled between 1163 and 1180, of a dispute about the rectory and advowson between the dean and chapter of St. Paul's and the nuns of St. Leonard's priory, Stratford-at-Bow. The dean and chapter received the church from the bishop and thereupon presented the nuns, who were to pay them 1 mark a year and find a chaplain to serve the church.[30] Thereafter the nuns held the rectory and advowson until the priory was dissolved in 1536. In 1539 the rectory and advowson were granted by the Crown in fee to Sir Ralph Sadler, reserving the rent of 1 mark to the dean and chapter.[31] In 1548 Sadler was licensed to grant the rectory and advowson to Thomas Perse or Percy of Islington,[32] who in turn was licensed in 1565 to sell the rectory to Roger Martin, alderman of London, and Humphrey his son.[33] Humphrey Martin sold it in 1582 to John Cheke,[34] but Percy had retained some interest because he was involved in a dispute with Humphrey Martin over a tenement called the Grange belonging to the vicarage of Islington, as was his son Jerome in 1586.[35] In

1587 Percy, Martin, and Cheke surrendered to Humphrey Smith of the Inner Temple a house, 2 gardens, an orchard, and 45 a. of the rectory, with all tithes and offerings and the advowson.[36] By 1618 the rectory had passed to Sir Walter Smith, M.P., of Great Bedwyn (Wilts.),[37] who presented to the living in 1639.[38] Early in 1646 he settled the rectory on his cousin Duke Stonehouse and his heirs,[39] but as a royalist Smith secured a reduction of his fine when in 1647 he settled the rectory in trust for the parishioners of Islington, who also presented to the living.[40]

The advowson and rectory reverted to private ownership at the Restoration, and Duke Stonehouse presented in 1662, followed by George Stonehouse in 1691 and 1720 and Francis Stonehouse in 1733 and 1738.[41] George Stonehouse, vicar 1738–40, resigned the living and conveyed the advowson in 1740 to Robert Holden in trust for Sir Gilbert Williams, Bt., vicar 1740–68, but retained some interest in the building known as the parsonage house at least, of which he granted a lease in 1755. In 1768 Holden presented Richard Smith (d. 1772), and in 1771 the advowson was sold to Richard Smith (d. 1776), a West India merchant of London and probably father of the vicar.[42] Under Smith's will the advowson was to go to whichever son of his son Benjamin became an Anglican clergyman; by 1811 it had passed to the Revd. Richard Smith who sold it to William Wilson, a London merchant.[43] Wilson (d. 1821) left the living to his kinsman and son-in-law Daniel Wilson, who presented himself in 1824 and his son Daniel in 1832, conveying the advowson thereafter to Evangelical trustees, possibly the Simeon Trust.[44]

The rectory estate was in the possession of the vicar in 1792[45] and seems to have passed to the Wilson family with the advowson, but there is no indication of how it was conveyed. In 1832 the land was held by trustees for the benefit of the vicar.[46]

The benefice was valued at 15 marks in 1254,[47] and the vicar was taxed on £5 in 1379.[48] In 1535 the value of the rectory and tithes was £5 13s. 4d. on average,[49] but in 1539 the farm of the rectory had been let to Richard Wheteley for £8 a year,[50] while the vicar received £30 a year in 1548.[51] In 1645 the rectory was valued at £40 a year,[52] and c. 1650 the rectory, vicarage, and all tithes were worth £111 together.[53] In 1708 the benefice was rated at £30 a year; the tithes were then valued at c. £100,[54] but in 1732[55] and in the late 18th century at c. £200.[56] In 1841 the vicar

[27] Lond. Statutes, ii. 732–3.
[28] Official Opening of New River Walk 1954 (brochure in Islington libr.).
[29] Islington L.B. Official Guide 1977–8, 34, 50.
[30] Letters and Charters of Gilb. Foliot, ed. A. Morey and C. N. L. Brooke, p. 440.
[31] L. & P. Hen. VIII, xiv (1), p. 161, no. 403(44); P.R.O., E 318/Box 19/969.   [32] Cal. Pat. 1547–8, 279.
[33] Ibid. 1563–6, 300.   [34] Lysons, Environs, iii. 147.
[35] Acts of P.C. 1586–7, 264.
[36] P.R.O., CP 25(2)/172/29–30 Eliz. I Mich.
[37] Guildhall MS. 15747, deed 1618.
[38] Hennessy, Novum Rep. 230.
[39] Guildhall MS. 15747, deed 1645/6.
[40] Cal. Cttee. for Compounding, ii. 949; Home Counties Mag. i. 56–7.   [41] Hennessy, Novum Rep. 230.
[42] Ibid. 230–1; M.L.R. 1740/3/21; Lewis, Islington, 104–5;

M.I. in par. ch. recorded in ibid. 215.
[43] Lewis, Islington, 105; P.R.O., CP 25(2)/1367/51 Geo. III. Trin.
[44] J. G. Bateman, Life of Rt. Rev. Dan. Wilson (1860), i. 231; Hennessy, Novum Rep. 230; P.R.O., C 54/13314, no. 15.
[45] Ch. Com. file 71145, Glebe.
[46] Ch. Com. deed 250,661.
[47] Val. of Norw. ed. Lunt, 326.
[48] Church in Lond. 1375–92 (Lond. Rec. Soc. xiii), 11.
[49] Valor Eccl. (Rec. Com.), i. 409.
[50] P.R.O., E 318/Box 19/969.
[51] Lond. and Mdx. Chantry Certs. 1548 (Lond. Rec. Soc. xvi), 62.   [52] Cal. Cttee. for Compounding, ii. 949.
[53] Home Counties Mag. i. 57.
[54] E. Hatton, New View of Lond. (1708), 379.
[55] Co. of Par. Clks. New Remarks on Lond. (1732), 234.
[56] Guildhall MS. 9550.

received a modus of 4*d*. an acre, 2*d*. a cow, and 2*d*. a calf, and no tithes were payable to anyone else.[57] In southern Islington, which was largely built over, most of the tithes had already been commuted by 1849, when the remaining tithes were commuted.[58] By 1851 the value of the benefice had greatly increased: although tithe composition amounted to only £60, the benefice was endowed with land worth £373 a year, glebe worth £57, and other permanent income of £40, beside pew rents, fees, and offerings, in all worth £1,073.[59]

The estate in the possession of the vicar in 1792 consisted of 9½ a. of freehold lying in two blocks, 4 a. bounded later by Liverpool Road, Sermon Lane (later Mantell Street), White Conduit Street, and Cloudesley Place, and 5½ a. bounded later by Ball's Pond Road, Wall Street, Wakeham Street, and Essex Road.[60] The origin of the estate is unknown: in 1890 the Ecclesiastical Commissioners could find no terriers and noted that the Local Act of 1792 was the earliest known title.[61] It is uncertain whether the land belonged to the vicarage, or, more likely, was part of the rectory and settled on the vicar. The parcel at Ball's Pond Road lay on the north side of Iveney, given to St. Paul's in 1239,[62] and may therefore once have been part of that estate and bestowed on the vicar by the dean and chapter; it was called the Parsonage field in 1554.[63] Another possibility is that land was settled on the vicar in the 17th century when there seems to have been a reduction in the land belonging to the rectory. In 1587, 15 a. of land, 10 a. of meadow, and 20 a. of pasture belonging to the rectory were conveyed,[64] but only 15 a. of pasture were mentioned in 1694.[65] The rectory's glebe and tithes were held by lessees or their subtenants from 1539 to 1561, in 1583, and in 1636.[66] Building leases were granted on the Liverpool Road block from 1807 and the Ball's Pond block from 1822. In 1891 the vicar sold the glebe to the Ecclesiastical Commissioners, who thereby acquired 133 houses at Liverpool Road and 155 at Ball's Pond. The Liverpool Road estate was sold to the L.C.C. in the 1950s.[67]

The vicarage house stood in Upper Street near the later site of Theberton Street, and a new house was built in its grounds, probably in the late 17th century; the two were known as the vicarage house and the parsonage house in 1755, when the latter was let on a long lease.[68] The vicarage house was a boarding school in 1754.[69] The vicar did not live there in 1810,[70] and Daniel Wilson and his son lived at no. 8 Barnsbury Park.

In 1888 the M.B.W. sold a site adjoining the churchyard for a vicarage,[71] which was built in 1897, designed by W. H. Barlow, and was still in use in 1970.[72]

A guild or fraternity of the Holy Trinity existed by 1427 and had its own priest in 1428 and 1432; it was mentioned in wills until 1467.[73] The fraternity of St. Thomas Martyr was founded in the 1440s, apparently for both men and women, and was mentioned until 1473.[74] The brotherhood of Jesus was founded by 1479 and maintained a priest to keep a continuous mass, being mentioned until 1541.[75]

Two obits were recorded in 1548. In 1517 Richard Cloudesley left £1 a year from the Stonefields estate for an obit, 6*s*. 8*d*. for the prayers of the poor, and 26*s*. 8*d*. to the brotherhood of Jesus for singing masses. At an unknown date John England gave a copyhold close valued at £4 6*s*. 8*d*. a year to the parish for an obit for himself and to support an honest priest to say mass.[76]

Pluralist vicars, often holding London rectories, were common, especially in the 16th to 18th centuries, and many held important ecclesiastical posts.[77] John Wardale, vicar 1455–72, was also prebendary of Twyford. Edward Vaughan, ?1499–1509, later bishop of St. David's, held the vicarage while prebendary of Brondesbury and of Harlesden and treasurer of St. Paul's. Dr. John Cocks, 1522–45, was Dean of the Arches. William Jennings, 1550–66, was also the first dean of Gloucester. Meredith Hanmer, 1583–90, also vicar of Shoreditch, was noted as a historian and his writing came under official notice in the 1580s.[78] William Cave, 1662–91, also rector of All Hallows the Great, chaplain to Charles II, and canon of Windsor, was known chiefly for writing on church history; described in 1690 as a learned and eloquent preacher, it was thought that his small congregation in Islington did not understand his sublime doctrine.[79] Cornelius Yeates, 1707–20, was also archdeacon of Wiltshire. George Stonehouse, 1738–40, supported the Methodists[80] and on his resignation joined the Moravian Brethren.[81] George Strahan, 1772–1824, also held three rectories and a prebendal stall at Rochester, and was non-resident for half the year. He attended the deathbed of Samuel Johnson, a close friend who frequently stayed with him at Islington towards the end of his life.[82]

John Bancks, mercer of London, in 1630 left property worth £178 to endow sermons at the Mercers' chapel and at Islington.[83] Daniel Parke

[57] Lewis, *Islington*, 105.
[58] P.R.O. IR 30/21/33.
[59] P.R.O., HO 129/10/2/1/5.
[60] Act to enable Vicar of Islington to grant bldg. leases of glebe lands (copy in Islington libr.).
[61] Ch. Com. file 71145.
[62] Above, other est.
[63] Guildhall MS. (formerly St. Paul's MS. C (Deans Reg.) Sampson, ff. 304v–5).
[64] P.R.O., CP 25(2)/172/29–30 Eliz. I Mich.
[65] Ibid. CP 25(2)/853/6 Wm. & Mary Trin.
[66] Ibid. E 318/Box 19/969; ibid. C 1/1362/6; Guildhall MSS. 9537/5, 14.
[67] Ch. Com., deed 250,661 and file 71145.
[68] Lewis, *Islington*, 105.
[69] Vestry min. bk. 1735–77, 91.
[70] Guildhall MS. 9558, f. 460.

[71] *Rep. of M.B.W. 1888*, H.C. 326, p. 823 (1889), lxvi.
[72] T. Hornsby, *Of People, Bldgs. and a Faith* (1970), 16; M. Barlow, *Life of Wm. Hagger Barlow* (1910), 81.
[73] Guildhall MSS. 9171/3, ff. 190v., 199, 312; 6, f. 30v.
[74] Ibid. 4, f. 240v.; 5, f. 371; 6, f. 123.
[75] Guildhall MSS. 9171/8, f. 143; P.R.O., PROB 11/28 (P.C.C. 36 Alenger, will of Rog. Gere).
[76] B.L. Harl. MS. 601, f. 44; *Lond. and Mdx. Chantry Certs. 1548* (Lond. Rec. Soc. xvi), 62.
[77] Para. based on Hennessy, *Novum Rep.* 230–1.
[78] *D.N.B.*; Hist. MSS. Com. 9, *Hatfield Ho.* xiii, p. 394.
[79] *D.N.B.*; *T.L.M.A.S.* xiii. 141–2, 155.
[80] Below, prot. nonconf.
[81] D. Benham, *Memoirs of Jas. Hutton* (1856), 267–8.
[82] Guildhall MS. 9557, p. 32; *D.N.B.*
[83] W. K. Jordan, *Chars. of Lond.* 283.

bequeathed a rent charge of 10s. in 1649 for a sermon on Christmas day, and Mrs. Amy Hill left 13s. 4d. a year for a sermon c. 1659.[84] In 1678 Ephraim Skinner bequeathed 5s. each Sunday to the minister for catechizing the poor.[85] In the 19th century Margareta Browne left £1,400 stock to provide £20 a year for the minister for catechizing children, the surplus to be used to buy prayer books as prizes.[86]

A lectureship[87] originated in the provision of a reader to assist William Cave in 1667, who was too weak to read the service and preach twice each Sunday. The vestry ordered £12 a year to be paid out of the parish lands.[88] In 1673 a lecturer was appointed from year to year; in 1675 the stipend was £30 to preach a sermon each Sunday afternoon, and in 1676 the money came from the Stonefields estate.[89] In 1679 the vestry again decided to obtain a reader, at £10 a year,[90] and a lecturer and reader was elected, to be paid by subscription.[91] Thereafter the lecturer was chosen by the vestry from several candidates, and the stipend was apparently met by an annual collection. By the 1820s it averaged £100 and, as only the Sunday afternoon duty was required,[92] the lectureship was often held with other preferments. Thomas Brett, the nonjuring divine, was lecturer 1691–6 at the beginning of his career.[93] William Hendley, lecturer 1718–24, was also lecturer at St. James's, Clerkenwell.[94] George Gaskin, later prebendary of Ely, held the lectureship from 1776 to 1822, while successively curate and rector of Stoke Newington.[95] On the resignation of John Denham in 1826, the vicar Daniel Wilson undertook to provide for the afternoon service and the lectureship lapsed, after some inhabitants had vainly sought legal advice.[96]

There was a chaplain in addition to the vicar in 1379,[97] and there were curates in 1517, 1531, and the 1540s.[98] Thereafter there was always an assistant curate, who in 1592 taught the Sunday school.[99] Two curates served in 1859, 3 by 1907, 1 in 1926, 3 in 1947, and 7 in 1965.[1] Among those of distinction were Hugh R. Gough, later archbishop of Sydney, curate 1928–31, vicar 1946–8, F. Donald Coggan, later archbishop of Canterbury, curate 1934–7, and David S. Sheppard, later bishop of Liverpool, who played cricket for England while an assistant curate at Islington, 1955–7.[2]

Two services were held each Sunday in 1667,[3] and until the 1820s; during the 18th century communion was held monthly and prayers were read on Wednesdays, Fridays, Saturday evenings, and holy days. Only 80–100 attended communion

in 1810 out of a population of 15,000.[4] Despite the opening of a chapel of ease in 1814, church sittings were still inadequate, especially for the poor, so Daniel Wilson started Sunday evening services c. 1824, at which all the seats were free. He also introduced an early communion, later changed to the evening when attendance trebled, use of the litany on Wednesdays and Fridays, and a service every saint's day.[5]

The vicars who succeeded Dr. Strahan in 1824 ministered to an expanding population, which led to the foundation of c. 40 district churches, and presided over a rural deanery which became as large as some dioceses.

The investiture of Daniel Wilson, 1824–32, seen as the chief Evangelical event of early 19th-century London,[6] changed the religious outlook and activity of the parish, establishing a notable tradition[7] which embraced many daughter churches in the vicar's gift. Under Dr. Strahan, a fine, old-fashioned clergyman and scholar, 'Islington slept; under his successor it awoke and has never slept since.'[8] Wilson immediately set in train the building of three churches: St. John's, Upper Holloway (1828), St. Paul's, Ball's Pond (1828), and Holy Trinity (1829). He started extra services;[9] districts were mapped out and house-to-house visitors enrolled; nine Sunday schools were opened straightaway and soon increased to fifteen. When he left to become bishop of Calcutta, the parish was renowned for the efficiency of a regime which had been established without losing all the original congregation, despite the dislike for Evangelicals felt by seatholders who thought that their vicar should minister only to those who paid.[10]

Wilson's activities extended beyond purely parochial matters. The Islington Clerical Meeting began when he invited 12 clerical friends to discuss prayer in the context of current church and international problems, a practice which became annual and was continued by Wilson's son Daniel, vicar 1832–86 and prebendary of Chiswick. Under the younger Wilson, a leader among London Evangelicals, the meetings grew to become a major Evangelical conference. In 1855 they were transferred to the hall of the Church Missionary College in Upper Street and in 1860 to the first Bishop Wilson Memorial hall. By the 1880s there were always more than 300 clergy present and the meetings, dealing primarily with spiritual matters, often in relation to topical issues, were preferred by Evangelicals to the church congresses, which dealt more with ecclesiastical matters.[11] The meetings later

[84] G.L.R.O., P83/MRY1/406, nos. 9, 23.
[85] Ibid. no. 24.
[86] Ibid. no. 26.
[87] There is no evidence for the assumption by Lewis and others that Rob. Browne, the separatist, was a lecturer in Islington ch. in the 1570s: below, prot. nonconf.
[88] Lewis, Islington, 108 n; Bateman, Life of Wilson, i. 248.
[89] Lewis, Islington, 114–15; below, charities.
[90] Lewis, Islington, 108 n.
[91] Ibid. 115.
[92] Bateman, Life of Wilson, 248.
[93] D.N.B.
[94] Lewis, Islington, 115.
[95] Ibid. 116; D.N.B.; Guildhall MS. 9557, p. 32.
[96] Lewis, Islington, 118; Bateman, Life of Wilson, i. 248.
[97] Ch. in Lond. 1375–92 (Lond. Rec. Soc. xiii), 11.

[98] Guildhall MS. 9171/9, f. 49; P.R.O., PROB 11/24 (P.C.C. 11 Thower, will of Rog. Flower); PROB 11/30 (P.C.C. 27 Pynning, will of Wm. Hobson); Lond. Consistory Court Wills 1492–1547 (Lond. Rec. Soc. iii), pp. 77, 84, 121.
[99] Guildhall MS. 9537/8, f. 80v.
[1] Clergy List (1859); Crockford (1907 and later edns.).
[2] Who's Who, 1980.   [3] Lewis, Islington, 108 n.
[4] Hatton, New View of Lond. 308; Guildhall MSS. 9550; 9557, p. 32; 9558, f. 460.
[5] G. R. Balleine, Hist. of Evangelical Party in Ch. of Eng. (1951), 156–7; O. Chadwick, Victorian Church (1972), ii. 316.
[6] Balleine, Hist. of Evangelical Party, 156.
[7] Chadwick, Victorian Ch. ii. 316.
[8] Bateman, Life of Wilson, i. 232.   [9] Above.
[10] Balleine, Hist. of Evangelical Party, 156–7.
[11] Ibid. 216–17.

moved to Mildmay conference hall, but outgrew it and were transferred to Church House, Westminster, from 1920, where they continued annually as the Islington Clerical Conference.[12]

Sermons by the elder Wilson were published and led to the formation of the Lord's Day Observance Society in 1831 by his cousin Joseph Wilson.[13] A local association had already been formed in 1830 with 340 residents and clergy, who agreed to try to persuade tradesmen to close on Sundays and to check sales by street traders.[14]

Wilson also inaugurated an association to assist the Church Missionary Society (C.M.S.) in 1827; thereafter Islington became a missionary parish, with mission sermons in St. Mary's and the district churches, and meetings addressed by notable men such as William Wilberforce.[15] The C.M.S., whose college was the first Anglican institution for training missionaries, had taken a house in Barnsbury Park in 1820, replacing it in 1822 with a copyhold house and land in Upper Street[16] for the principal and 12 students. A college with hall, library, and lecture room for 50 students was built in 1824 in the grounds[17] and remained in use until 1917. Its students held Sunday services and schools in three areas of South Islington, St. Matthew's, St. Peter's, and the 'Irish Courts' near the Angel, one of the roughest parts of the parish. The C.M.S. home for the children of missionaries overseas was in Milner Square from 1849, then from 1853 in a purpose-built home for 50 children at the corner of Highbury New Park and Highbury Grove.[18]

Another big Anglican institution, the London School of Divinity, was involved in local church life.[19] Founded in 1863 by the Revd. Alfred Peache and his sister Kezia as a strictly Evangelical theological college, it opened in temporary premises in St. John's Wood, and moved in 1866 to the former Highbury College, Aubert Park,[20] which was renamed St. John's Hall. There were 22 students in training in 1866 and 44 in 1870; 142 students from the college had been ordained by 1876. It aimed to provide a degree-level course, but few of the students reached the standard required. In 1909 the college opened St. John's Hall (later College) at Durham to enable its students to take a B.A. degree there, but in 1934 the college became the Associate London College of Divinity in London University. The college's first tutor was Charles Henry Waller, formerly a curate at St. Jude's, Mildmay Park, and local clergymen, including W. H. Barlow, then principal of C.M.S. college, gave lectures and examined admissions, while the students undertook voluntary work with local Sunday schools and open-air and mission services. The college left Highbury in 1939 and did not return, moving eventually to Northwood.[21]

Evangelicalism influenced many Islington lay-men. In 1835 a group led by Frederick Sandoz publicized the need for a home missionary society to serve the new industrial urban centres and combined with a group from the City to form the Church Pastoral-Aid Society in 1836.[22] During the Tractarian disputes, when in 1842 Bishop Blomfield ordered his clergy to preach in surplices rather than the customary black gown, many congregations walked out, and when confirmations in Islington were due to take place, the local incumbents and their congregations forced the bishop to give way.[23]

Despite the nine new churches opened between 1828 and 1850, the rapid growth in house building meant that by 1851 there were 16,548 Anglican sittings for a population of 95,329. Only about a third of the seats were free and none of the churches was in a style likely to attract the poor.[24] Soon afterwards the Islington Churches Extension Society was formed to provide more buildings and clergy. It appealed for 10 new churches within 10 years, each with accommodation for 1,000, and founded St. Luke's, West Holloway, in 1855.[25] Churches opened regularly thereafter, between five and ten in each decade, until the last, St. Andrew's, Whitehall Park, opened in 1895. They still catered mainly for middle-class inhabitants, however, leaving the missions to attract the working class. By the end of the century the Evangelical impetus had worn itself out and the Church of England had lost ground to nonconformity, particularly because of Islington's changing social composition. In 1851 Anglican services had three-fifths of all church attendances, double those at nonconformist churches; in 1903 fewer than two-fifths of worshippers were Anglicans, whereas more than half were nonconformists.[26] Anglican churches c. 1900 were active where they had middle-class congregations, mainly in the northern half of the parish, but were largely empty in the southern half, their successful work being in the day and Sunday schools. The decline had also troubled nonconformist churches in the south part and was attributed less to the type of services than to the replacement of middle-class residents, especially shopkeepers, by workers who did not go to church. The successful churches farther north attracted congregations with bright, varied services and a range of social activities which irritated purist Evangelical clergymen by their ritualism, secularism, and pleasure-seeking.[27] Decline in attendance continued in the 20th century as population changes continued. The Second World War removed several churches and others were amalgamated after the war and in the 1970s. In 1982 only 20 remained in full use for Anglican worship.

A bishop suffragan of Islington was appointed in 1898 and continued until 1923.[28]

[12] Hornsby, *People, Bldgs. and a Faith*, 18.
[13] Ibid. 14; Bateman, *Life of Wilson*, i. 20.
[14] *Procs. of Cttee. of Assoc. for Promoting Due Observance of Lord's Day in Islington* (1832) (in Islington libr.).
[15] Para. based on J. Rooker, *Islington's Centenary Missionary Story 1828–1928*.   [16] P.R.O., C 54/10110, nos. 4, 7.
[17] Lewis, *Islington As It Was*, 56.
[18] In 1983 site of Highbury Grove sch.
[19] Para. based on G. C. B. Davies, *Men for the Ministry* (1963), 16, 18, 21, 24, 28–9, 32, 35, 57, 59, 86, 93.

[20] Below, prot. nonconf.
[21] For details of bldg. see above, growth.
[22] Balleine, *Hist. of Evangelical Party*, 139–42.
[23] Ibid. 174.   [24] Lewis, *Islington As It Was*, 52–3.
[25] Clarke, *Lond. Chs.* 8; *Consecration of St. Geo.'s, Tufnell Pk.* (booklet, 1975, supplied by vicar).
[26] P.R.O., HO 129/10/1–2; Mudie-Smith, *Rel. Life*, 169–70.
[27] Booth, *Life and Labour*, 3rd ser. i, 127–34.
[28] *Crockford* (1926 edn.).

The church of *ST. MARY*, so called by 1392,[29] has been rebuilt at least three times on the same site. A stone from a building of the earlier 12th century was found in the walls of the crypt in 1938,[30] but the church demolished in 1751 was apparently of the mid 15th century:[31] it contained a monument of 1454, and the date 1483 was found at the south-east corner of the steeple when the west gallery was removed. A chapel of St. Thomas, Martyr, existed on the south side of the church by 1454, and a chapel of the Holy Trinity existed by 1467, both connected with parish fraternities.[32] Built of brick and boulders, the church had a tiled roof in 1708, Gothic columns and windows, and a square tower with steeple. A gallery was built in 1663 and an altarpiece in 1671. The roof inside was panelled and painted over the chancel. The walls were wainscotted. Among many monuments was the large marble tomb of Dame Alice Owen, parts of which were incorporated in the new church of 1751–4. The tower contained a peal of six bells: the treble was recast in 1683, and two others were recast in 1706;[33] a clock and sundial were added in 1708. At the west end was a two storeyed porch, which housed the charity school from 1710.[34]

The fabric was decaying in 1708 and repairs were frequently needed.[35] Accommodation was said to be inadequate in 1718, when the parishioners unsuccessfully sought rebuilding under the London Churches Act of 1711.[36] An Act was obtained in 1750 to allow rebuilding and the old church was demolished in 1751 by Samuel Steemson, who blew up the tower. Steemson also built the new church, which opened in 1754. Designed by Launcelot Dowbiggin, joiner of London, it did not strictly accord with any architectural style, but consisted of a plain rectangle of brick with stone quoins and dressings, containing an aisled nave, a short chancel, and galleries supported by oak Tuscan columns. At the west entrance was a semicircular portico of four Tuscan columns. The west tower had an octagonal balustrade, open circular stage, and an obelisk spire, in diminishing stages; it was flanked by vestries. The organ was built in 1771 by John Byfield the younger.[37]

The new church, which seated 1,500 in 1851,[38] had above the altar a painting by Nathaniel Clarkson, who lived in Church Street.[39] The picture made way for a stained glass window

when a chancel was added in 1902–4; a colonnade at the west porch was also added and the interior extensively altered by Sir A. W. Blomfield. The church was bombed in 1940. Everything except the tower was rebuilt in 1954–6 on the 18th-century plan in an adapted Georgian style by Seely & Paget, with the addition of transepts at the east end, within which the sanctuary is marked with slender pillars, the choir and organ being placed behind the congregation. The font, two brasses of the Fowler family, the lectern eagle, and the coat of arms of George II are from the previous church and the organ is from the demolished church of St. Mary, Bourdon Street, Berkeley Square.

The peal of eight bells survived from the previous church; they were cast in 1775 by Pack and Chapman at the Whitechapel Bell Foundry,[40] and the old bells were ordered to be sold, but may have been recast.[41] The plate in 1685 consisted of two silver flagons, two gilt bowls and covers, a silver paten and a silver plate,[42] which were in use in 1666.[43] After the Second World War there were 2 patens dated 1636 and *c.* 1636, 2 flagons of 1637, and 2 dishes of 1783.[44] The registers date from 1557 and are virtually complete except for 1648–61.[45]

Although the opening of district churches had reduced its congregation, at the end of the 19th century the parish church remained fairly successful in its work, in contrast with more moribund Anglican churches around it, and the example of its simple services was recommended to others.[46] Attendance in 1851 was 1,500 a.m.; 1,250 p.m.; and in 1903 was 283 a.m.; 326 p.m.[47]

The churchyard, which was enlarged in 1793, was closed for burials in 1853, and several graves were removed in 1885 when Upper Street was widened. It was laid out as a public garden of 1½ a. in 1885.[48]

Other C. of E. chs. were:[49]

ALL SAINTS, Caledonian Road. Dist. formed 1839 from Holy Trinity.[50] Parts assigned to St. And., Thornhill Sq., 1854, and St. Silas, Penton Street (Clerkenwell), 1868. Patron V. of Holy Trinity. Three asst. curates 1892, 2 in 1907, none in 1926; included a Lond. City missioner in 19th cent. Served St. Matthias, Caledonian Rd., 1859.[51] Joined to St. Silas under 1972 Pastoral Scheme,[52] but svces. held in ch. hall under V. of St. And.[53] Attendance 1851: 752 a.m.; 160 aft.;

[29] Guildhall MS. 9171/1, f. 306v.
[30] Hornsby, *People, Bldgs. and a Faith*, 4.
[31] Description based on Hatton, *New View of Lond.* 377; Lewis, *Islington*, 195–7; below, plates 30, 31.
[32] Guildhall MSS. 9171/5, f. 133v.; 6, f. 19v.; 7, f. 10.
[33] Vestry min. bk. 1662/3–1708, 160, 364.
[34] Ibid. 1708–34, 15.
[35] Hatton, *New View of Lond.* 377; vestry min. bks. *passim*.
[36] Rest. of para. based on Clarke, *Lond. Chs.* 86–7; Lysons, *Environs*, iii. 140; below, plate 32.
[37] *V.C.H. Mdx.* ii. 190; Hornsby, *People, Bldgs. and a Faith*, 22.
[38] P.R.O., HO 129/10/2/1/5.
[39] Para. based on Clarke, *Lond. Chs.* 86–7; *D.N.B.* s.v. Clarkson; Hornsby, *People, Bldgs. and a Faith*, 20–2; G.L.R.O., P83/MRY1/92.
[40] G.L.R.O., P83/MRY1/86.
[41] Vestry min. bk. 1735–77, 186; Guildhall MS. 474, p. 5.
[42] Guildhall MS. 9537/20, p. 85.
[43] Vestry min. bk. 1662–1708, 17.
[44] Pevsner, *Lond.* ii. 226.

[45] In G.L.R.O.
[46] Booth, *Life and Labour*, 3rd ser. (i), 133; Hornsby, *People, Bldgs. and a Faith*, 16.
[47] P.R.O., HO 129/10/2/1/5; Mudie-Smith, *Rel. Life*, 169.
[48] L.C.C. *Return of Burial Grounds* (1895), 7; *Lond. Gaz.* 15 Apr. 1853, p. 1098; G.L.R.O., P83/MRY1/1163.
[49] Inf. about patrons and asst. curates is from *Clergy List, Crockford*, and *Lond. Dioc. Bk.* (various edns.); architectural descriptions based on Clarke, *Lond. Chs.*; seating and attendance figs. 1851 from P.R.O., HO 129/10/1–2; attendance figs. 1903 from Mudie-Smith, *Rel. Life*, 169–70. Liturgical directions are used in all architectural descriptions. The following abbreviations are used, in addition to those in the index: aft., afternoon; asst., assistant; Dec., Decorated; demol., demolished; Eng., England or English; evg., evening; mtg., meeting; Perp., Perpendicular; temp., temporary; V., vicar.
[50] *Lond. Gaz.* 8 Oct. 1839, p. 1881.
[51] *Clergy List* (1859).
[52] Islington Soc. *Six Redundant Chs.* [1973], 3.
[53] *Lond. Dioc. Bk.* (1981).

564 evg.; 1903: 87 a.m.; 162 p.m. Plain brick bldg. in mixed Gothic style by Wm. Tress 1837–8: rectangular nave with galleries; turret and pinnacles. Seated 1,116 in 1851; 1,150 in 1896.[54] Baptistry and NW. porch added 1914. Svces. ceased c. 1969 and held in hall by 1975. Ch. gutted by fire 1975 and demol.[55] Missions at All Saints' mission ch., behind nos. 90–2 White Lion Street (Clerkenwell), from c. 1838 until c. 1953;[56] St. John the Evangelist, Copenhagen Street (Church Hosp. mission) by 1879, closed between 1956 and 1961,[57] attendance 1903: 121 a.m.; 140 p.m.; All Saints' Mission, Thornhill Bridge Pl., attendance 1903: 103 a.m.; 187 p.m.; Crinan Street, York Way, attendance 1903: 66 p.m. All Saints' hall, Caledonian Rd., used as chapel of ease to St. And., Thornhill Sq., 1981.[58]

ALL SAINTS, Dalmeny Rd., Tufnell Park. Originated in mission ch. opened by St. Mat. 1881.[59] Dist. formed 1886 from St. John, Upper Holloway, and St. Geo., Tufnell Pk.[60] Patron trustees, Ch. Pastoral Aid Soc. by 1961. Three asst. curates 1892, 1 in 1896, none in 1926. Attendance 1903: 299 a.m.; 390 p.m. Bldg. of red brick with stone dressings in Perp. style by J. E. K. Cutts 1884–5: apsidal chancel with side chapels and E. vestry, aisled and clerestoried nave, W. vestibule, bellcot. Chapel of Resurrection by N. F. Cachemaille-Day 1935, given in memory of Mrs. Tufnell by her son.[61] Ch. severely damaged 1941 and 1944; restored by A. Llewellyn Smith and rededicated 1953.[62]

CHRIST CHURCH, Highbury Grove. Built following discussions by residents 1846.[63] Dist. formed 1849 from Islington par.[64] Parts assigned to St. Augustine, Highbury, 1871, and St. John, Highbury, 1882. Patron trustees. Usually 1 or 2 asst. curates between 1859 and 1966. Attendance 1851: 653 a.m.; 222 aft.; 387 evg.; 1903: 270 a.m.; 257 p.m. Served St. Padarn's Welsh mission ch. 1907.[65] United with St. John, Highbury, 1979,[66] and St. Saviour, Aberdeen Pk., 1981.[67] Bldg. of Kentish rag with ashlar dressings in Dec. style by Thos. Allom, on site given by Hen. Dawes, 1847–8: unusual plan, with large central octagon and nave, transepts, chancel, all aisled and clerestoried; apsidal sanctuary; NW. tower and spire. Not oriented. Nave extended 1872 by Williams & Crouch. Windows in apse 1954 and transepts 1955. Seated 750 in 1851, 825 in 1896,[68] 500 in 1982.[69] Church hall, Leigh Rd., opened 1881. Mission hall in Whistler Rd. opened 1899.[70]

EMMANUEL, Hornsey Road. Originated in small mission ch. from 1881 to 1884. Dist. formed 1886 from St. Mark, Tollington Pk., St. Paul, Upper Holloway, and St. Luke, W. Holloway.[71] Patron trustees, Ch. Pastoral Aid Soc. by 1961. One asst. curate 1892, 2 in 1896, none in 1926. Served St. Padarn's Welsh mission ch. 1922–30.[72] United with St. Barnabas, Hornsey Rd., 1945.[73] Attendance 1903: 93 a.m.; 153 p.m. Red-brick bldg. in Early Eng. style by F. R. Farrow & E. S. Harris 1884: aisled and clerestoried nave and chancel under one long roof, transepts, curious turret at junction, tower at W. of S. aisle. Not oriented. Seated 800 in 1982.[74]

HOLY TRINITY, Cloudesley Square. Dist. formed from Islington par. 1830.[75] Parts assigned to All Saints, Caledonian Rd., 1839, St. And., Thornhill Sq., 1854, and St. Thos., Barnsbury, 1862. Patron V. of Islington until 1851, then trustees.[76] Two asst. curates in 1859, 3 in 1896, none in 1926. Attendance 1851: 1,830 a.m.; 951 evg.; 1903: 360 a.m.; 476 p.m. Joined to St. And., Thornhill Sq., 1980 and ch. declared redundant.[77] Buff brick bldg. with stone dressings in Perp. style by Sir Chas. Barry, on site given by Stonefields char. estate, 1826–9: small sanctuary, aisled and clerestoried nave, N. vestry, W. front with octagonal corner turrets. E. bay of nave furnished as chancel by E. Christian. Reseated and N. and S. galleries removed 1900.[78] Seated 1,750 in 1851, 1,400 in 1896.[79] Registers closed 1978.[80] Bldg. taken over by Celestial Ch. of Christ 1980.

ST. ANDREW, Thornhill Square. Dist. formed 1854 from Holy Trinity and All Saints.[81] Parts assigned to St. Thos., Barnsbury, 1862, and St. Mic. 1864; latter restored 1881.[82] Patron V. of Trinity and Islington trustees. One asst. curate in 1866, 3 in 1896, 1 in 1907. Served St. Mic. until 1864.[83] United with St. Thos., Barnsbury, 1953, with St. Matthias 1956,[84] and with Holy Trinity 1980.[85] Evangelical: open-air mtgs. in Clayton (later Tilloch) Street a regular feature before 1914.[86] Attendance 1903: 219 a.m.; 348 p.m. Bldg. of Kentish rag with Bath stone dressings in Dec. style by Fras. B. Newman & John Johnson, on site given by Geo. Thornhill, 1852–4: chancel with N. and S. chapels, wide galleried transepts, aisled nave, SW. tower and broach spire. Seated 1,650; carved pulpit of Caen stone.[87] Mission hall in East (later Gifford) Street opened 1882, closed after 1952;[88] attendance 1903: 75 p.m. Helped

[54] Crockford (1896).
[55] C.C.C., survey files; G.L.R.O., P83/ALL1, ch. svces. reg.
[56] Crockford (1947, 1955–6).
[57] P.O. Dir. Lond. (1879); Crockford (1955–6, 1961–2).
[58] Lond. Dioc. Bk. (1981).
[59] Clarke, Lond. Chs. 98.
[60] Lond. Gaz. 15 Dec. 1885, p. 6051.
[61] All Saints Tufnell Pk. Year Bk. 1952–3 (copy in Islington libr.).
[62] Ibid.; Clarke, Lond. Chs. 99.
[63] Centenary Year Bk. 1848–1948: Christ Ch. Highbury (booklet in Islington libr.).
[64] Lond. Gaz. 10 July 1849, p. 2200.
[65] Crockford (1907).
[66] Inf. from V.
[67] C.C.C., survey files.
[68] Crockford (1896).
[69] Inf. from V.   [70] Cent. Year Bk.
[71] Inf. from area dean; Lond. Gaz. 12 Mar. 1886, p. 1200.

[72] G.L.R.O., P83/EMM 4.
[73] Inf. from area dean.
[74] Inf. from area dean.
[75] Lond. Gaz. 14 Sept. 1830, p. 1950.
[76] Hennessy, Novum Rep. 241.
[77] C.C.C., survey files.
[78] Ibid.; G.L.R.O., P83/MRY1/1138/40; Clarke, Lond. Chs. 89; below, plate 33.
[79] Crockford (1896).
[80] G.L.R.O., P83/TRI, registers.
[81] Lond. Gaz. 24 Mar. 1854, p. 936.
[82] Ibid. 10 May 1881, p. 2417.
[83] Clergy List (1859, 1866).
[84] Ch. Com., file NB 23/233, 1953 Scheme; G.L.R.O., P83/MTS, cal. note.
[85] C.C.C., survey files.
[86] Souvenir of Centenary of St. And., Thornhill Sq. (booklet in Islington libr.), 23.
[87] Souv. of Cent. of St. And. 3.
[88] Ibid. 14.

found Paget Memorial mission hall, Randall Street.[89]

St. Andrew, Whitehall Park. Originated in mission ch. built by St. John, Upper Holloway, 1887 to serve area between Highgate Hill and Holloway Rd.[90] Dist. formed 1897.[91] Patron trustees. No asst. curate 1907, 1 in 1947 and 1965. Attendance 1903: 351 a.m.; 363 p.m. Red-brick bldg. with stone dressings in an early Gothic style by Frederic Hammond, on triangular sloping site, 1894–5: apsidal chancel with vestries, transepts, aisled and clerestoried nave with transepts and bell flèche, W. porch. Seated 700 in 1907.[92] Two 16th-cent. figures of St. Jas. and St. Sim. from Ram's chapel, Homerton, in transept windows, with pulpit also from chapel.[93] Interior altered 1972 to accommodate par. hall at W. end of ch., retaining E. end for worship with seating for 250–300. Mission ch., Archway Rd., served as par. hall 1895–1972.[94] Mission svces. attendance 1903: 46 a.m.; 58 p.m.

St. Anne, Poole's Park. Dist. formed from St. Mark, Tollington Pk., 1871.[95] Patron V. of St. Mark,[96] trustees by 1881, Ch. Patronage Soc. 1961. One asst. curate 1892, 1926, 1947, 2 in 1907. Joined to St. Mark between 1966 and 1970.[97] Attendance 1903: 180 a.m.; 251 p.m. Iron ch. in Durham Rd. from c. 1866 until 1870, when it housed Nat. sch.[98] Bldg. of multicoloured brick in Romanesque style by A. D. Gough 1870: narrow chancel, large aisled nave, N. vestries; SW. tower and spire by H. R. Gough 1877.[99] Seated 1,050 in 1896.[1] By 1957 mostly derelict for some years and used as hall; demol. 1965.[2] Adjoining smaller ch. by Romilly Craze consecrated 1960; demol. by 1970. Mission in Palmerston Rd.; attendance 1903: 100 a.m.; 107 p.m.

St. Augustine, Highbury New Park. Temp. ch. built 1864 for new area.[3] Dist. formed 1871 from Christ Ch. and St. Paul.[4] Patron Hen. Rydon, H. J. Rydon, then trustees. Two asst. curates 1881 and 1907, none in 1926. Attendance 1903: 778 a.m.; 722 p.m. First V., Gordon Calthrop, a well known preacher.[5] Iron ch. in Highbury New Pk. built by Hen. Rydon on his estate in 1864, seating c. 850. Insufficient by 1868. Bldg. of stock brick in Dec. style with coloured bandings and stone dressings, seating 1,150, by Habershon & Brock paid for by Rydon, 1869–70:[6] chancel flanked by organ chambers with vestries underneath, aisled and clerestoried nave, SW. tower. Additional seating necessary by 1873; W. gallery seating c. 200 added 1878, later

removed. Choir vestry enlarged 1889. Ch. hall opened 1881.[7] All svces. in larger hall built inside W. end of ch. c. 1970, interior of ch. being allowed to deteriorate, but hall too small by 1981. Restored ch., seating c. 800, used for svces. from 1982.[8]

St. Barnabas, Harvist Rd., Hornsey Road. Dist. formed 1866 from parts of St. Mary, St. Jas., Lower Holloway, St. John, Upper Holloway, and St. Mark.[9] Patron trustees. One asst. curate 1866, 3 in 1896, none in 1926. Attendance 1903: 174 a.m.; 231 p.m. Joined to Emmanuel 1945.[10] Iron ch., possibly in Benwell Rd.,[11] used 1856–66.[12] Bldg. in early Dec. style by T. K. Green 1864–6. Closed for worship 1945 and stood empty in 1966;[13] demol. soon after, when area rebuilt as Harvist estate. Mission in former Wes. Meth. mission hall, Queensland Rd., from c. 1882. Attendance 1903: 57 a.m.; 156 p.m. Still in use 1924.[14]

St. Bartholomew, Shepperton Road. Dist. formed 1865 from St. Steph., Canonbury Rd.[15] Patron trustees. One asst. curate 1881, none in 1907. Attendance 1903: 96 a.m.; 83 p.m. Held svces. for St. Steph. 1927–38 and after St. Steph. was bombed 1940. Joined to St. Steph. unofficially in 1949 and officially from 1953.[16] Bldg. in Early Eng. style, on part of site of nos. 9 and 10 New Norfolk Street Terr. (later Popham Rd.) and no. 1 Shepperton Street (later Rd.), by E. Clare 1861–2.[17] Seated 1,000 in 1896.[18] Demol. c. 1970.

St. Clement, St. Clement's Street, Westbourne Road. Dist. formed 1862 from St. Jas., Lower Holloway.[19] Patron Cubitt fam., bp. of Lond. by 1955. One asst. curate 1881, 2 in 1896, 3 in 1907, none in 1947. Ch. founded by Geo. Cubitt, M.P., to be less Evangelical than other local chs. Attendance 1903: 134 a.m.; 232 p.m. From c. 1966 used as St. John the Baptist Greek ch. and by Anglicans on certain major festivals. Adjoining hall, bombed in Second World War, rebuilt with Anglican chapel seating c. 40 by 1973. Claimed to be only Anglo-Cath. ch. in area in 1973.[20] Par. joined to St. David 1976. Iron ch. in Westbourne Rd. by 1857.[21] Bldg. of stock brick with dressings of ashlar and coloured brick in Early Eng. style by Sir Gilb. Scott 1863–5: chancel with cradle roof, aisled and clerestoried nave with steeply pitched roof, W. end with large buttresses, 3 porches, and bellcot.[22] Derelict 1983.

St. David, Westbourne Rd., Barnsbury (West Holloway). Dist. formed 1869 from St. Luke, W. Holloway.[23] Patron trustees, Ch. Patronage Soc.

[89] *Souv. of Cent. of St. And.* 22; below, missions.
[90] Inf. from V.
[91] *Lond. Dioc. Bk.* (1981).
[92] *Crockford* (1907).
[93] C.C.C., Basil Clarke's MSS.
[94] Inf. from V.
[95] *Lond. Gaz.* 17 Jan. 1871, p. 159.
[96] Hennessy, *Novum Rep.* 232.
[97] *Crockford* (1965–6); *Lond. Dioc. Bk.* (1970).
[98] *Clergy List* (1881); P.R.O., ED 7/82.
[99] Pevsner, *Lond.* ii. 226; below, plate 39.
[1] *Crockford* (1896).
[2] Clarke, *Lond. Chs.* 100.
[3] *St. Augustine's Ch. Centenary Booklet* (1970, copy in Islington libr.).
[4] *Lond. Gaz.* 28 Mar. 1871, p. 1609.
[5] J. E. Ritchie, *Rel. Life of Lond.* (1870), 122–3, 127.

[6] *St. Augustine's Ch.*; below, plate 40.
[7] *St. Augustine's Ch.*
[8] Inf. from V.
[9] *Lond. Gaz.* 27 July 1866, p. 4228.
[10] Inf. from area dean.
[11] *Clergy List* (1866).
[12] G.L.R.O., P83/BAN/1.
[13] *Mackeson's Guide* (1889); Clarke, *Lond. Chs.* 95.
[14] Inf. from Mr. J. S. Ellis.
[15] *Lond. Gaz.* 12 Sept. 1865, p. 4367.
[16] G.L.R.O., P83/STE1, regs. and cal.
[17] P.R.O., C 54/15653, no. 3; *Mackeson's Guide* (1889).
[18] *Crockford* (1896).
[19] *Lond. Gaz.* 5 Sept. 1862, p. 4368.
[20] Islington Soc. *Six Redundant Chs.* 7.
[21] G.L.R.O., P83/CLE, bapt. reg.; *P.O. Dir. Lond.* (1863).
[22] Pevsner, *Lond.* ii. 226; *Mackeson's Guide* (1889).
[23] *Lond. Gaz.* 13 July 1869, p. 3945.

1961, 1973, bp. of Lond. 1981. One asst. curate 1892, 2 in 1896, 1 in 1907, none in 1947. Attendance 1903: 119 a.m.; 131 p.m. United with St. Clement 1976.[24] Bldg. in transitional Gothic style by E. L. Blackburne 1866–9, burned 1935, rebuilt in brick with stone dressings by T. F. Ford and rededicated 1936: arcades and pieces of walls from former ch.; rest very plain with shallow E. apse,[25] aisled and clerestoried nave with low-pitched roof. Seated 750 in 1896,[26] 250 in 1982.[27]

St. Francis of Assisi, see St. Luke.

St. George, Carleton Rd., Tufnell Park. Founded 1858 after Hen. Hampton, min. at St. Luke's temp. ch. resigned and with other influential seceders built new temp. ch. V. of dist., St. John's, Upper Holloway, objected to new ch. as unnecessary; Hampton not licensed by bp. and ch. not recognized for Anglican worship, whereupon its c. 900 members formed Free Ch. of Eng.[28] Despite ostracism, wealthy congregation flourished. Hampton left through an exchange in 1862 and first officially recognized V. took charge 1863.[29] Dist. formed from St. John, Upper Holloway, and St. Luke.[30] Patron trustees. One asst. curate 1881, 2 in 1896, none in 1926. Attendance 1903: 428 a.m.; 335 p.m. Temp. circular wooden ch. 1858, seating 900, in fields near present Chambers Rd., designed by Geo. Truefitt, surveyor to Tufnell Pk. estate: 84 ft. in diameter, 5 entrances, vestry and bell turret. Moved to Carleton Rd., Tufnell Pk. Rd., 1863. Permanent ch. of Kentish ragstone with ashlar dressings and banding of dark bricks in Dec. style, seating 1,022, built beside it, on land given by Tufnell Pk. estate trustees, by Truefitt 1866–7:[31] unusual design, following temp. ch. and possibly based on ch. of St. Geo. at Salonika (Greece).[32] Central octagon with circular ambulatory; apsidal-ended NW. and SW. arms; long apsidal chancel and long W. lobby; E. of aisles, chancel is surrounded by ambulatory leading to E. vestry. SW. porch added 1868. Detached tower with octagonal top and spire, later partly demol., 1875.[33] Closed for roof repairs 1963 but vandalized and not reopened; sold 1970 and used as Shakespeare theatre 1982.[34] Svces. in par. hall until new ch. to seat 500, at junction of Crayford and Carleton rds., by Clive Alexander, consecrated 1975: solid red-brown brick walls at ground level, with clerestory windows all round, flat roof; bell-frame outside front entrance, with tall free-standing cross. Mission ho. at no. 21 Ward Rd. 1895. No. 23 Hercules Rd. used as mission ho. from c. 1879 until Grafton hall, Eburne Rd., was built; survived 1975.[35] Attendance at 2 missions 1903: 69 a.m.; 67 p.m.; 27 a.m.; 45 p.m.

St. James, Chillingworth (formerly Victoria) Rd., Lower Holloway. Dist. formed 1839 as St. Jas. the Apostle, Islington, from Islington par.[36] Boundaries altered and name changed to St. Jas., Lower Holloway, 1846.[37] Parts assigned to St. Clement 1862, St. Luke 1861, St. Barnabas 1861. Patron V. of Islington. Two asst. curates 1859, 1 in 1881, 3 in 1896, none in 1907. Wm. Bell Mackenzie, divine, first V. 1838–70, when par. very poor.[38] Attendance 1851: 1,591 a.m.; 1,700 evg.; 1903: 477 a.m.; 866 p.m. Some svces. held at St. Luke after ch. badly bombed 1944. Joined to St. Mary Magdalene 1954.[39] Large neo-classical bldg. of stock brick with stone dressings, financed by private subscriptions, by H. W. Inwood & E. N. Clifton 1837–8 and enlarged at E. by Hambley of Holloway 1839: asymmetrical S. front with pedimented Ionic hexastyle centre-piece and short bell-tower; extended 1850.[40] Seated 1,800 in 1851; 1,858 in 1896.[41] Badly bombed 1944 and restored as par. hall constructed inside ch. 1952: derelict galleries and roof remain above. In 1982 used as hall for St. Mary Magdalene with St. Jas. Missions held at St. Jas.'s lecture hall, Eden Grove (built by 1879),[42] 1903: attendance 106 a.m.; 143 p.m.

St. James the Apostle, Prebend Street. Founded by Clothworkers' Company of Lond. under Act of 1872 to replace Lambe's chapel in Wood Street Sq. (Lond.).[43] Dist. formed 1875 from St. Peter and St. Phil.[44] Patron Clothworkers' Co. One asst. curate 1892, 2 in 1907, none in 1947. Attendance 1903: 117 a.m.; 173 p.m. Bldg. of Kentish rag in Early Eng. style by F. W. Porter, 1873–5: apsidal sanctuary, aisled and clerestoried nave with tower and spire on S. side. Figure of Lambe, 1612, from old chapel, in niche over door; 4 Flemish roundels, in old chapel 1577, placed here 1895.[45] Mission in Britannia Row; attendance 1903: 51 p.m. Mission hall in converted wareho. at nos. 37 and 39, Britannia Row, conveyed to ch. 1908; sold by 1974.[46]

St. John, Holloway Rd., Upper Holloway. Dist. formed 1830 from Islington par.;[47] ch. served extensive area until creation of 14 daughter chs. Parts assigned to St. Mark 1854, St. Luke 1861, St. Barnabas 1866, St. Geo. 1868 and 1883, St. Paul, Upper Holloway, 1870, St. Mary, Brookfield (in St. Pancras), 1877, St. Peter, Upper Holloway, 1880, St. Steph., Upper Holloway, 1881. Patron V. of Islington, trustees by 1859. One asst. curate 1859, 3 in 1881, 2 in 1892, none in 1926. Hen. Venn, V. 1834–46, sec. of Ch. Missionary Soc.[48] Attendance 1851: 1,300 a.m.; 200 aft.; 800 evg.; 1903: 632 a.m.; 752 p.m. Grey-brick bldg. with stone dressings in Perp. style, on site given by Corporation for Orphans

[24] Inf. from V.
[25] *Mackeson's Guide* (1889).
[26] *Crockford* (1896).
[27] Inf. from V.
[28] *Diamond Jubilee Souvenir of St. Geo.'s, 1867–1927* (booklet in Islington libr.); *Consecration of St. Geo.'s* (booklet, 1975, supplied by V.); G.R.O. Worship Reg. no. 8756.
[29] *Diamond Jubilee Souvenir.*
[30] *Lond. Gaz.* 15 May 1868, p. 2750.
[31] *Diamond Jubilee Souvenir; Consecration of St. Geo.'s.*
[32] *Consecration of St. Geo.'s.*
[33] Pevsner, *Lond.* ii. 226–7; below, plate 37.
[34] *Consecration of St. Geo.'s*; above, social.
[35] *Consecration of St. Geo.'s.*
[36] *Lond. Gaz.* 8 Oct. 1839, p. 1881.
[37] Ibid. 7 Nov. 1846, p. 3915.
[38] *D.N.B.*; Hennessy, *Novum Rep.* 235.
[39] G.L.R.O., P83/JAS1, note in cal.
[40] Pevsner, *Lond.* ii. 227; below, plate 35.
[41] *Crockford* (1896).
[42] *P.O. Dir. Lond.* (1879).
[43] 35 & 36 Vic. c. 154 (Local); inf. from V.; below, charities.
[44] *Lond. Gaz.* 10 Mar. 1875, p. 3985.
[45] C.C.C., survey files.
[46] Char. Com. files, St. Jas. Mission Hall fund.
[47] *Lond. Gaz.* 14 Sept. 1830, p. 1950.
[48] *D.N.B.*

of Clergymen, by Chas. Barry 1826–8: shallow sanctuary, aisled and clerestoried nave, slim pinnacled W. tower flanked with vestibules. Not oriented, Central pulpit removed 1900 and choir stalls inserted.[49] Seated 1,600 in 1851, 1,750 in 1896.[50] Mission, attendance 1903: 44 p.m.

ST. JOHN, Highbury Pk. (formerly Highbury Vale). Originated in iron ch. seating 400 in Park Pl. (later Conewood St.) opened 1875.[51] Dist. formed 1882 from Christ Ch.[52] Patron trustees. Asst. curates from 1887: one in 1892, none in 1896, 1907, one in 1926, none 1944–8; last one left 1970.[53] Attendance 1903: 240 a.m.; 310 p.m. Staunchly Evangelical except during incumbency of Hen. Martin Sanders, 1900–11. Par. joined to Christ Ch. 1978. Bldg. of stock brick in Dec. style, on part of Cream Hall estate, by Wm. Bassett Smith 1881: apsidal chancel with N. chapel divided off to form vestry, transepts, aisled nave. Closed from 1979 and stood disused 1981. Mission hall at no. 164 Blackstock Rd. from c. 1891 to 1934. Attendance 1903: 22 p.m. Par. hall 1936 on site in Conewood Street given by Misses Quick.[54]

ST. JOHN THE BAPTIST, Cleveland Road. Dist. formed 1873 from St. Paul, Ball's Pond.[55] Site for ch. conveyed 1860,[56] and chapelry served from St. Paul by 1866.[57] Patron V. of St. Paul. One asst. curate 1896 and 1947. Attendance 1903: 119 a.m.; 220 p.m. Registers closed 1967; benefice joined to St. Steph. 1971.[58] Simple bldg. of stock brick in Dec. style, by Wm. Wigginton on triangular corner site 1871–2: apsidal chancel, nave, N. and S. aisles. Damaged 1940, 1944; svces. held in ch. hall. Declared redundant 1971,[59] and demol. by 1981. Mission in James Street; attendance 1903: 71 p.m.

ST. JOHN THE EVANGELIST, Copenhagen Street, see ALL SAINTS, missions.

ST. JUDE, Mildmay Grove. Dist. formed 1856 from St. Paul.[60] Patron V. of St. Paul, trustees from 1907. Three asst. curates 1866, 1 in 1892 and 1981. Gave much support for missionary work: par. collected for 22 socs. and missions, home and abroad, 1899.[61] Wm. Pennefather, V. 1864–73, hymn-writer and leading churchman, founded Mildmay Conference which led to many permanent organizations for home and foreign mission work; few clergymen exercised a wider personal influence; known throughout England as mission preacher. His wid. Cath. (d. 1893), hymn-writer, continued religious work at Mildmay Pk.[62] Attendance 1903: 436 a.m.; 385 p.m. Joined with St. Paul 1982.[63] Bldg. of Kentish rag with Bath stone dressings in mixed Dec. and

Perp. styles by A. D. Gough 1855: originally chancel, transepts with galleries, nave with galleries at W., thin tower with spire centrally on S.; seated 1,072 in 1855.[64] Enlarged in similar style 1871 by Edwin Clare, with addition of long chancel, aisles, and clerestory. Choir vestry added on S. of chancel 1906. Seated 1,200 in 1896;[65] 350 in 1982.[66] Church forms part of group with Vicarage to W. and schs. and adjoining hos. to N. Missions in St. Jude's lecture hall, King Henry Street, attendance 1903: 36 p.m.; at St. Jude's schs., King Henry's Walk, attendance 1903: 88 a.m.; 73 p.m.

ST. LUKE, Penn and Hillmarton roads. One of chs. founded by Islington Ch. Extension Soc. 1855. Svces. in sch. room in York Rd., accommodating 200, until temp. ch. built.[67] Dist. formed 1861 from St. John, Upper Holloway, and St. Jas., Lower Holloway.[68] Parts assigned to St. Geo., Tufnell Pk., 1868, and St. David, W. Holloway, 1869. Patron trustees. One asst. curate 1866, none in 1926. Attendance 1903: 267 a.m.; 268 p.m. Circular wooden ch. 1855–6 at rear of Holloway Castle hotel, S. side Camden Rd.[69] Bldg. of Kentish rag and Bath stone in Middle Pointed style by Chas. Lee consecrated 1860: chancel, transepts, nave, NW. tower and spire; seated 967 in 1896.[70] Choir vestry and ch. room built 1903. N. transept destroyed 1941. Rededicated after repair 1956. New bldg. by A. Llewellyn Smith 1961 on site of N. transept. Seated 600 in 1982.[71] Mission hall in Goodinge Rd., North Rd., attendance 1903: 34 a.m.; 63 p.m. Demol. when area rebuilt, and replaced by a chapel of ease, St. Fras. of Assisi Ch. Centre, North Rd., 1976; seated 100 in 1982.[72]

ST. MARK, Tollington Park. Dist. formed 1854 from St. John, Upper Holloway.[73] Parts assigned to St. Mary, Hornsey Rise, 1865, St. Barnabas 1866, St. Paul, Upper Holloway, 1870, St. Anne 1871. Patron V. of St. John, Upper Holloway, until after 1972, Ch. Pastoral Aid Soc. 1981. One asst. curate 1859, 3 in 1881, 2 in 1926, 1 in 1981. Joined to St. Anne between 1966 and 1970.[74] Attendance 1903: 301 a.m.; 327 p.m. Bldg. of Kentish rag with Bath stone dressings in Early Eng. style by A. D. Gough 1853–4: chancel flanked by vestries, wide transepts into aisled and clerestoried nave, thin SW. tower and spire. Not oriented. Walls of nave and galleries in transepts removed 1884 and new aisles, by F. R. Farrow, built. New vestry and E. window 1904. Seated 950 in 1896, 700 in 1907.[75] Mission hall on W. side Hornsey Rd., near Tollington Way; attendance 1903: 83 a.m.; 77 p.m.

[49] Hist. of St. John's, Upper Holloway, 1826–1968 (booklet in Islington libr.).
[50] Crockford (1896).
[51] Thank You St. John's: St. John's Highbury Vale, 1881–1978 (TS. booklet in Islington libr.).
[52] Lond. Gaz. 8 Feb. 1882, p. 539.
[53] Thank You St. John's.
[54] Ibid.
[55] Lond. Gaz. 6 May 1873, p. 2268.
[56] P.R.O., C 54/15579, no. 15.
[57] Clergy List (1866).
[58] G.L.R.O., P83/JNB; C.C.C., survey files.
[59] C.C.C., survey files; Mackeson's Guide (1889).
[60] Lond. Gaz. 5 Feb. 1856, p. 417.
[61] St. Jude's, 34th Parochial Rep. 1899 (copy in Islington libr.).

[62] D.N.B.; inf. from V.; below, prot. nonconf., undenom. missions.
[63] Inf. from V.
[64] Islington Indicator, no. 1, July 1855 (copy in Islington libr.).
[65] Crockford (1896).
[66] Inf. from V.
[67] Diamond Jubilee Souvenir of St. Geo.'s Ch., Tufnell Pk. (booklet in Islington libr.).
[68] Lond. Gaz. 14 May 1861, p. 2048.
[69] Diamond Jubilee Souv.
[70] Crockford (1896); below, plate 38.
[71] Inf. from V.
[72] Ibid.
[73] Lond. Gaz. 15 Aug. 1854, p. 2514.
[74] Above, St. Anne's.
[75] Crockford (1896, 1907).

St. Mary, Ashley Rd., Hornsey Rise. Benefice formed 1861;[76] dist. 1865 from St. Mark.[77] Parts assigned to St. Paul, Upper Holloway, 1870, and St. Steph., Upper Holloway, 1881 (qq.v.). Patron Islington trustees. One asst. curate 1881, none in 1896, 2 in 1961. Attendance 1903: 305 a.m.; 252 p.m. Bldg. of Kentish rag in Dec. style by A. D. Gough 1860-1, on site presented by Mr. Warlters: small sanctuary, wide transepts, aisled and clerestoried nave; thin SW. tower and spire added 1868. New E. aisles built to transepts, N., S., and W. porches added, chancel roof altered, and W. gallery built 1883-4.[78] New W. porch after 1895. Fittings include screening formerly in St. Paul's, Hampstead.[79] Seated 650 in 1982.[80] Mission in Hornsey Rd., attendance 1903: 114 a.m.; 106 p.m. Mission hall in Marlborough Rd. 1961.

St. Mary Magdalene (formerly the chapel of ease), Holloway Road. First new ch. in Islington, built under Act of 1811 to relieve par. ch.[81] Renamed and dist. formed 1894.[82] Patron V. of Islington. One asst. curate 1859, 2 in 1896, 1 in 1947 and 1981. Strongly Evangelical under T. C. Ralph, V. 1931-44, and A. W. Goodwin Hudson, V. 1948-55, later dean of Sydney.[83] Attendance 1851: 1,336 a.m.; 1,100 p.m.; 1903: 495 a.m.; 748 p.m. United with St. Jas., Chillingworth Rd., 1954. Plain neo-classical bldg. of stock brick with Bath stone dressings, seating 1,324, by Wm. Wickings, Mdx. county surveyor, 1812-14. Paid for by par. rate and annuities, later found to be illegal; cost greatly exceeded estimate and led to much controversy.[84] Part of Stonefields char. income also used for maintenance, which became a fixed annual sum of £350 in 1902.[85] E. tower with Ionic pilasters and urns, flanked by vestibules with Tuscan porches; body of ch. a large galleried hall over crypts; Tuscan W. porch. Ceiling with coves and 3 roses. Upper galleries in NW. and SW. corners demol., windows inserted at ends of N. and S. galleries and W. ends of aisles, and reseated 1895. Restoration 1910 by J. R. Manning & W. Gilbee Scott. Seating increased to 1,371 in 1851; 1,500 in 1907. Changes to interior in 1983 greatly reduced nave to make way for offices and meeting rooms.[86] Site included 4 a. for burial ground, closed 1856 except for private vaults; taken over by vestry and L.C.C. 1894 as public pk.[87]

St. Matthew, Essex Road. Originated as temp. St. Paul's Episcopal chapel, New Norfolk Street (later Ecclesbourne Rd.), 1836-51, in bldg. formerly Wes. chapel, seating 300.[88] Attendance 1851: 282 a.m.; 237 evg. Dist. formed 1851 from

St. Paul, Ball's Pond.[89] Patron V. of St. Paul. One asst. curate 1866, 2 in 1892, 1 in 1907, none in 1947. Attendance 1903: 197 a.m.; 275 p.m. Joined to St. Steph., Canonbury, 1953.[90] Bldg. of Kentish rag with stone dressings in Perp. style by A. D. Gough 1850.[91] Chancel, transepts, aisled nave, SW. tower with spire. In damaged condition 1944.[92] Demol. by 1966. Rosemary Branch mission, Shepperton Street, extant 1872-9, 1895-1949;[93] attendance 1903: 111 a.m.; 219 p.m. Mission at ch. room next to no. 19 Ecclesbourne Rd. until c. 1946; attendance 1903: 138 p.m. Mission hall, Raynor Pl., until c. 1946.[94]

St. Matthias, Caledonian Road. Opened 1868 as chapel of ease to St. Luke in former Caledonian Rd. Presb. ch. Dist. formed 1888 from St. Luke, W. Holloway, and St. And.[95] Patron trustees. One asst. curate 1896, none in 1926. Joined to St. And., Thornhill Sq., 1956.[96] Ragstone bldg. in Gothic style with twin W. porches by John Barnett & Birch c. 1853; chancel and S. chapel by Wm. Smith 1883; consecrated 1886.[97] Used as chapel of ease to St. And. 1956-72;[98] nave used as sports hall 1970s. Declared redundant 1978.[99] Demol. by 1981.

St. Michael, Bingfield Street, York Way. Originated in temp. ch. in boys' sch., Bingfield Street, by 1853.[1] Perpetual curacy under St. And., Thornhill Sq., by 1859.[2] Dist. formed 1864 from St. And. and endowed with ground rents of £198.[3] Patron trustees 1866, Mrs. Shaw for life 1881 and 1892, G. Evans and Revd. W. A. Croft-Atkins 1907, bp. of Lond. by 1961. One asst. curate 1866, 2 in 1892, 1 in 1907. Attendance 1903: 370 a.m.; 189 p.m. Church 'very Oxford Movement' following incumbency of Clarence Simes, 1924-69.[4] Joined to St. And. 1977. Stock brick bldg. with red and black decoration by R. L. Roumieu 1863-4: apsidal chancel, with N. chapel and small S. sacrament chapel, aisled and clerestoried nave, large SW. porch. Reopened 1954 after repairs.[5] Closed 1973 and partly derelict 1981.

St. Padarn's Welsh Church (extraparochial), Salterton Rd., Seven Sisters Road. Temp. iron ch. opened by 1903 by Lond. community belonging to Ch. in Wales, in connexion with N. Lond. Welsh Ch. mission. Served from Christ Ch., Highbury, 1907, but own min. licensed 1909; served from Emmanuel 1922-30. Patron bp. of Lond. Attendance 1903: 13 a.m.; 50 p.m. Permanent ch. after 1909, possibly by 1912. Yellow-brick bldg. with red-brick dressings in Early Eng. style: sanctuary, nave, W.

[76] Lond. Dioc. Bk. (1981).
[77] Lond. Gaz. 9 May 1865, p. 2632.
[78] St. Mary's, Hornsey Rise, Centenary Souvenir 1861-1961 (booklet supplied by V.).
[79] St. Mary's, Cent. Souvenir; below, charities.
[80] Inf. from V.
[81] P.R.O., HO 129/10/1/1/1; 51 Geo. III, c. 134.
[82] Lond. Gaz. 20 July 1894, p. 4148.
[83] Fifty Years On: St. Mary Magdalen Holloway (1964) (booklet in Islington libr.), 16.
[84] Clarke, Lond. Chs. 87.
[85] P.R.O., HO 129/10/1/1/1; below, charities.
[86] Inf. from Mr. J. C. Connell.
[87] Fifty Years On, 7; Ret. of Met. Burial Grounds, H.C. 41, p. 40 (1857-8), xlviii.
[88] P.R.O., HO 129/10/2/1/2.

[89] Lond. Gaz. 12 Aug. 1851, p. 2070.
[90] Ch. Com., file NB 23/233, 1953 Scheme.
[91] Pevsner, Lond. ii. 228; Mackeson's Guide (1889).
[92] C.C.C., survey files (photos.).
[93] G.L.R.O., P83/MTW, regs.
[94] G.L.R.O., P83/MTW/31.
[95] Clarke, Lond. Chs. 93; P.R.O., C 54/16887, no. 9; G.L.R.O., P83/MTS; Lond. Gaz. 14 Aug. 1888, p. 4347.
[96] G.L.R.O., P83/MTS, cal. note.
[97] Mackeson's Guide (1889); C.C.C., survey files.
[98] Lond. Dioc. Bk. (1972).
[99] C.C.C., survey files.
[1] P.R.O., ED 7/82.   [2] Clergy List (1859).
[3] Lond. Gaz. 12 Apr. 1864, p. 2038.
[4] Islington Soc. Six Redundant Chs. 9.
[5] C.C.C., survey files.

vestibule. Closed 1970s, sold 1982 to British followers of Archbp. Lefebvre as Rom. Cath. ch.[6]

ST. PAUL, Essex Road. Dist. formed 1830 from Islington par.[7] Parts assigned to St. Mat. 1851, St. Jude 1856, St. Augustine 1871, and St. John the Baptist, Cleveland Rd., 1873. Patron trustees. One asst. curate 1859, 2 in 1866, none in 1926. Attendance 1851: 1,600 a.m.; 200 aft.; 900 evg.; 1903: 505 a.m.; 551 p.m. Most svces. held at St. Jude by 1981; par. to be joined to St. Jude 1982.[8] Bldg. of grey brick with stone dressings in Perp. style by Chas. Barry, 1826-8, on site given by marquess of Northampton: similar to St. John, Upper Holloway, with sanctuary, aisled and clerestoried nave and galleries, but with pin-nacled E. tower over altar, flanked by later apsidal vestries. Choir 1880, new choir vestry 1900. Tower contains entrances to galleries only.[9] Seated 1,800 in 1851; 1,000 in 1981.[10]

ST. PAUL, Kingsdown (formerly Brougham) Road. Dist. formed 1870 from St. John, Upper Holloway, St. Mary, Hornsey Rise, and St. Mark, Tollington Pk.[11] Patron trustees. Three asst. curates 1881, none in 1892, 1 in 1907. Attendance 1903: 254 a.m.; 291 p.m. Joined to St. Saviour, Tollington Pk., 1953.[12] Site for ch. conveyed to Bp. of Lond.'s Fund 1867 and ch. by Jarvis built but not consecrated by 1870.[13] Closed 1953 and demol.

ST. PETER, Devonia Rd., Islington Green. Dist. formed 1839 from St. Mary, Islington, and enlarged 1858.[14] Part assigned to St. Jas., Pre-bend Street, 1875. Patron V. of Islington. One asst. curate 1859, 2 in 1881, 4 in 1892, 1 in 1907. Attendance 1851: 1,220 a.m.; 970 evg.; 1903: 345 a.m.; 354 p.m. Joined to St. Jas., Prebend Street, 1982.[15] Stock brick bldg. in Early Eng. style by Chas. Barry 1834-5: plain and box-like, with corner pinnacles. Enlarged and embellished 1842-3[16] with NW. spire with flying buttresses, new W. front; transepts, short sanctuary, and vestry added later. Seated 1,500 in 1851. Re-seated 1884, when NE. porch replaced by vestry and upper galleries on each side removed.[17] Seated 1,060 in 1896.[18] By 1966 it housed the Angel's throne from Cath. Apostolic ch., Duncan Street.[19] Ch. declared redundant 1982, and alter-native use sought to preserve tower and W. front.[20]

ST. PETER, Dartmouth Park Hill. Opened as St. Peter, Highgate Hill, 1874.[21] Dist. formed 1880 from St. John, Upper Holloway.[22] Patron trustees. One asst. curate 1892, 2 in 1907, 1 in 1926, 1965. Attendance 1903: 272 a.m.; 461 p.m.

United with St. John, Upper Holloway, 1978.[23] Red-brick bldg. with stone dressings in Early Gothic style by C. L. Luck 1879-80: short sanctuary, aisled and clerestoried nave, W. front with octagonal turrets and large central bellcot; S. vestry added 1955. Seated 730 in 1896.[24] Mission at St. Peter's schs., Highgate; attendance 1903: 219 a.m.

ST. PHILIP, Arlington Square. Dist. formed 1858 from St. Steph., Canonbury, and St. Mary, Islington.[25] Part assigned to St. Jas., Prebend Street, 1875. Patron trustees. One asst. curate 1866, 2 in 1892, 1 in 1896, none in 1926. Attendance 1903: 183 a.m.; 271 p.m. Joined to St. Jas. under 1953 Scheme.[26] Bldg. of Kentish rag with stone dressings in ornate Norman style by A. D. Gough 1855: NW. tower square with short spire and Rhenish roof.[27] Closed 1953 and demol.

ST. SAVIOUR, Aberdeen Park. Ch. built by Revd. W. D. Morrice who owned land around it.[28] Patron W. D. Morrice and sons, followed by bp. of Lond. One asst. curate in 1881 and 1926. Attendance 1903: 205 a.m.; 140 p.m. Benefice joined to Christ Ch. 1981. Red-brick bldg. in Early Eng. style by Wm. White consec. 1866: chancel with N. organ chamber and S. chapel, transepts, aisled and clerestoried nave with short additional bay at W. end, central octagonal lantern tower with short spire. Square brick piers in nave.[29] Seated 450 in 1896.[30] Subject of poem by Sir John Betjeman, whose parents worshipped there. Attendance in single figures 1970s; svces. held in Vicarage 1980 and ch. closed. Declared redundant 1981. Highly thought of architectur-ally and efforts being made for its preservation 1982.[31]

ST. SAVIOUR, Hanley Rd., Tollington Park. Dist. formed 1888 from St. Mark, Tollington Pk., and St. Mary, Hornsey Rise.[32] Patron trustees, Ch. Pastoral Aid Soc. by 1961. One asst. curate 1892, none in 1907. Attendance 1903: 428 a.m.; 423 p.m. United with St. Paul, Kingsdown Rd., 1953. Red-brick bldg. with stone dressings in Dec. style by J. P. Cutts: aisled and clerestoried nave built 1887-8; chancel and vestries 1890; small bellcot over chancel arch; W. porches 1900. Proposed tower never built. Ch. repaired 1961. Seated 200 in 1982.[33]

ST. STEPHEN, Canonbury (formerly New North) Road. Dist. formed 1839 from St. Mary, Islington.[34] Parts assigned to St. Phil. 1858 and St. Bart. 1865. Patron V. of Islington. One asst.

---

[6] Para. based on *Sun. Telegraph*, 21 March 1982, 3; *Crockford* (1907); Guildhall MS. 19224/536; *P.O. Dir. Lond.* (1912).
[7] *Lond. Gaz.* 14 Sept. 1830, p. 1950.
[8] Inf. from V. of St. Jude.
[9] C.C.C., survey files.
[10] Inf. from V. of St. Jude.
[11] *Lond. Gaz.* 29 Nov. 1870, p. 5402.
[12] Ch. Com., file NB 23/233, 1953 Scheme.
[13] P.R.O., C 54/16873, no. 8; *Mackeson's Guide* (1889); Islington libr., deed no. 2765.
[14] *Lond. Gaz.* 8 Oct. 1839, p. 1881; 13 Apr. 1858, p. 1863.
[15] C.C.C., survey files.
[16] Ibid.; below, plate 34. Gough & Roumieu exhibited drawings for alterations, but Pevsner attributes them to E. B. Lamb: *Lond.* ii. 229. Lamb may have been the executive architect.
[17] Pevsner, *Lond.* ii. 229.

[18] *Crockford* (1896).
[19] Clarke, *Lond. Chs.* 89.
[20] C.C.C., survey files.
[21] G.L.R.O., P83/PET1.
[22] *Lond. Gaz.* 17 Dec. 1880, p. 6915.
[23] G.L.R.O., P83/PET1, note in cal.
[24] *Crockford* (1896).
[25] *Lond. Gaz.* 2 July 1858, p. 3133.
[26] Ch. Com., file NB 23/233, 1953 Scheme.
[27] Pevsner, *Lond.* ii. 229.
[28] Annotation to copy of Clarke, *Lond. Chs.* 95, in I.H.R.
[29] Pevsner, *Lond.* ii. 229; *Mackeson's Guide* (1889); below, plate 41.
[30] *Crockford* (1896).
[31] C.C.C., survey files.
[32] *Lond. Gaz.* 14 Aug. 1888, p. 4359.
[33] Inf. from V.
[34] *Lond. Gaz.* 8 Oct. 1839, p. 1881.

curate 1859, 2 in 1892, none in 1907. Attendance 1851: 874 a.m.; 406 aft.; 511 evg.; 1903: 152 a.m.; 281 p.m. United with St. Bart. 1939, and with St. Mat. 1953.[35] Pale brick bldg. in Gothic style by W. and H. W. Inwood & E. N. Clifton 1837–9: E. front with octagonal turret and spire and small turrets at sides, flying buttresses. Two E. porches added 1850, later removed, and ch. lengthened by A. D. Gough.[36] Seated 1,341 in 1851; 1,100 in 1896.[37] Bombed and burnt out 1940; reconstructed by A. Llewellyn Smith & A. W. Waters 1957. Shortened to make room for vestries and chapel, and interior reoriented. Organ incorporates organ from St. Mat.[38]

St. Stephen, Elthorne Road. Originated as mission ch. in Elthorne Rd. founded by St. John, Upper Holloway, c. 1877 to serve artisans in dist. and servants of those living near St. John's.[39] Dist. formed 1881 from St. John and St. Mary, Hornsey Rise.[40] Patron bp. of Lond. One asst. curate 1892, none in 1896, 1 in 1926, 1961. Attendance 1903: 76 a.m.; 161 p.m. Rebldg. of 30 a. around ch. from 1966 slowly destroyed congregation. Decision to join with St. Mary, Hornsey Rise, 1980.[41] Red-brick bldg. with stone dressings in an Early Eng. style by E. Christian 1879–80: small chancel without arch, nave with aisles, triple gabled W. front with vestibule, flèche. Not oriented. Seated 700–800. Unusual sloping floor to nave. Ch. closed 1980 and demol. 1983.[42] Mission ch. became ch. hall 1880.[43] Missions held there; attendance 1903: 47 a.m. Demol. 1970s.

St. Thomas, Hemingford Rd., Barnsbury. Dist. formed 1862 from St. And., Thornhill Sq., and Holy Trinity.[44] Patron trustees. One asst. curate 1892, none in 1896, 1907, 1 in 1926. Attendance 1903: 100 a.m.; 174 p.m. Joined to St. And. 1953.[45] Bldg. of Kentish rag with stone dressings in Dec. style by A. Billing consecrated 1860: nave, aisles. Seated 1,026 in 1896, 950 in 1907.[46] Registers closed 1946, and ch. demol. after 1953. St. Thos.'s mission room, Twyford Street, opened by 1902.[47] Attendance 1903 (as St. John, Twyford Street): 89 p.m.

St. Thomas, St. Thomas's Rd., Finsbury Park. Originated as mission dist. c. 1880; svces. in new but unlicensed public ho., then in brick mission room. Former iron nonconf. chapel erected on site for permanent ch. Par. formed 1888, consisting of 6–7,000 people nearly all of 'lower middle class', from St. Anne, Tollington Pk.[48] Patron abp. of Canterbury. Three asst. curates 1896, 2 in 1907, 1 in 1926. Attendance

1903: 495 a.m.; 443 p.m. Red-brick bldg. with stone dressings in Early Eng. style, built as successor to St. Mat., Friday Street (Lond.) by E. Christian 1889: chancel, nave with wide aisles, S. porch, triple gabled W. front with vestibule, flèche. Wagon roofs; dormer windows in chancel. Parsonage, vestry, and hall, 1901, built on S. Seated 900 in 1896, 800 in 1907.[49] Mission ho. at no. 100 St. Thomas's Rd. by 1894.[50]

ROMAN CATHOLICISM. Three recusants were reported in 1577 and two were named in 1588.[51] Many lodged in Islington[52] because it was near London yet separated by open country. Thomas Worthington, a priest from Douai, was arrested there in 1584,[53] a priest called Williams went to Mr. Talbot's house there in 1592, and a seminary priest, Thomas Clarke, spent several months in 1592 at the Crown at Islington.[54] Three priests sent to England c. 1600 were to lodge at Islington.[55] In 1626 it was feared that children were being brought up as Roman Catholics in a house where mass was evidently held.[56]

There were two suspected recusants in 1680, and one professed and one reputed Catholic in 1708.[57] Christopher Piggot, a seminary priest, passed some years in Islington, where he died in 1735, and by 1733 was said to have formed a community of converted gentlewomen in a village in north London, who gave large sums for Roman Catholics in London and colleges abroad.[58]

In the late 18th century there were three or four Roman Catholics,[59] but it was not until 1837 that two priests from Moorfields moved to the parish and built the school in Duncan Street which was used for worship until the church of St. John the Evangelist was built.[60] By 1840 there were 600 Roman Catholics living between Ball's Pond and City Road; a 'poor man' was very active in securing attendances at mass in Duncan Street. About a third of the families around City Road and the Angel were poor Irish Roman Catholics.[61]

In 1841 it seemed likely that the Roman Catholic congregation would become one of the most important in the suburbs.[62] Its rapid growth, in an Evangelical parish, led in 1846 to the establishment of the Islington Protestant Institute, whose defence of Protestantism included the conversion of Romanists; publications, meetings, sermons, petitions to parliament and the

[35] G.L.R.O., P83/STE1, cal. note; Ch. Com., file NB 23/233, 1953 Scheme.
[36] Pevsner, *Lond.* ii. 229.
[37] *Crockford* (1896).
[38] Clarke, *Lond. Chs.* 90–1.
[39] Inf. from V. of St. Mary, Hornsey Rise.
[40] *Lond. Gaz.* 15 Apr. 1881, p. 1859.
[41] Inf. from V. of St. Mary.
[42] Ibid.
[43] Ibid.
[44] *Lond. Gaz.* 7 Jan. 1862, p. 67.
[45] Ch. Com., file NB 23/233, 1953 Scheme.
[46] *Mackeson's Guide* (1889); *Crockford* (1896, 1907).
[47] *P.O. Dir. Lond.* (1902).
[48] *Handbk. of Grand Bazaar in aid of St. Thos., Finsbury Pk. 1894* (booklet in Islington libr.), 9; *Lond. Gaz.* 23 Nov. 1888, p. 6420.

[49] *Crockford* (1896, 1907).
[50] *Handbk. of Grand Bazaar*, 10.
[51] *Cath. Rec. Soc.* xxii. 46, 123; *Cal. S.P. Dom. Add.* 1566–79, 551.
[52] e.g. *Cal. S.P. Dom.* 1581–90, 277; 1591–4, 19.
[53] *D.N.B.*
[54] *Cal. S.P. Dom.* 1591–4, 176, 305.
[55] Hist. MSS. Com. 9, *Hatfield Ho.*, xi, p. 115.
[56] *Acts of P.C.* 1626, 178, 212.
[57] G.L.R.O., MR/RR 4, nos. 60, 61; MR/RR 11, m. 2; cf. Guildhall MS. 9800.
[58] G. Anstruther, *Seminary Priests*, iii. 170; J. Kirk, *Biogs. of English Caths.* (1909), p. 184.
[59] Guildhall MS. 9557, p. 32.
[60] Below.
[61] *Lond. City Miss. Mag.* v (1840), 103–4; vi (1841), 7.
[62] *Cath. Dir.* (1841), p. 19.

queen, and missionary work were all employed.[63] Re-establishment of the Roman Catholic hierarchy in England in 1850 provoked agitation and the parading of effigies of the pope and Cardinal Wiseman at St. John's church on Guy Fawkes day.[64] In the 1920s worshippers were still abused as they walked to mass in Eden Grove.[65]

A second centre of worship was started in 1854, to serve Lower Holloway, and in 1858 the Passionist Fathers founded St. Joseph's church and Retreat on Highgate Hill, where their congregation grew rapidly with the influx of Irish into Upper Holloway. The Ball's Pond area was served from 1854 by Our Lady and St. Joseph, Kingsland, just outside the boundary, which moved to a new church in Islington in 1964. No further churches were built until the church of the Blessed Sacrament was opened in Barnsbury in 1916 and services began in Highbury in 1918. A chapel was opened in Upper Holloway in 1928, for those unable to reach St. Joseph's, and one in Tollington Park c. 1925. An increased Roman Catholic population in north Islington from 1950 led to extra masses at both chapels, which eventually were replaced by parish churches.

Two separatist groups also appeared in Islington after the Second World War. The Old Roman Catholic Church, founded in England in 1908, established their British headquarters at no. 16 Aberdeen Road, where they opened a chapel in 1952.[66] They moved to no. 23 Drayton Park c. 1974 and opened a chapel there.[67] In 1982 followers of Archbishop Lefebvre, who held to the Latin Tridentine mass, bought St. Padarn's C.E. church, Salterton Rd., changing its dedication to St. Joseph and St. Padarn.[68] Individual churches and convents are described below.[69]

St. John the Evangelist, Duncan Terr., originated in svces. in sch. in Duncan Street, founded from St. Mary, Moorfields, Lond. 1837. Worshippers from wide area: Islington, Highbury, Stoke Newington, Kingsland.[70] Chapel on ground floor of sch. opened 1839. Large red-brick ch. in Anglo-Norman style by J. J. Scoles, started 1841 on site shared by schs., opened 1843; two towers and side chapels finished later; consec. 1873.[71] Seated 850 in 1851, when attendance 1,500 at three masses a.m., 201 aft., 1,179 evg.[72] Attendance 1903: 1,220 a.m.; 210 p.m. Major alterations to interior 1964 and 1973; seated 270 in 1982.[73]

Church of the Sacred Heart of Jesus originated in mission chapel at no. 5 Albany Pl., Ring Cross, founded 1854 by Canon Oakeley of St. John the Evangelist. Larger chapel of the Guardian Angels opened 1855 at no. 19 Cornwall Pl. (later Eden Grove), later site of Willow Ct.,[74] and reg. 1857 as chapel of St. Mary of the Angels:[75] two ground-floor rooms made into one. Site at top of Eden Grove bought 1867. Church opened 1870, renamed Sacred Heart of Jesus:[76] Early Eng. style with stone and brick façade, two side chapels.[77] Consec. 1928 after debt repaid.[78] Attendance 1903: 861 a.m.; 148 p.m. Seated c. 400 in 1982.[79]

Passionist Fathers from Hendon bought former Black Dog tavern, Highgate Hill, 1858, converting ground floor into chapel of St. Joseph, with accn. upstairs for community of 18.[80] Chapel behind opened 1860. New retreat begun 1875, as community had increased. Iron chapel built and old ch. demolished 1888; new ch. of St. Jos. on site opened 1889 to serve over 2,000:[81] white-brick with Doulton dressings in Romanesque style, with some Renaissance details; wide aisled nave; five side chapels inc. one with relics of St. Valeriana; dome 107 ft. high a landmark. Seated 800 in 1929.[82] Attendance 1903: 1,233 a.m.; 329 p.m.

Church of the Blessed Sacrament, Copenhagen St., started 1913 and opened 1916. Small, almost square, with organ gallery with hall underneath. New sacristy added c. 1929. Ch. doubled in length 1957; seated c. 300 in 1982.[83]

St. Joan of Arc, Highbury Pk., originated in svces. in Carmelite chapel, Highbury Pk., 1918. Temporary ch. seating 140 in Kelross Rd. opened 1920, possibly first to be dedicated to St. Joan of Arc (canonized 1920). Extended 1925 to seat extra 100. Sperati fam. gave ho., used as presbytery. Permanent ch. of brick with stone dressings, seating 760, on site of Carmelite chapel, by S. C. Kerr Bate 1961-2: bell by Whitechapel foundry; perspex statue of St. Joan by Arthur J. Fleischmann. Sunday mass centre opened in Portland hotel on parish boundary 1960. Attendance 1961: 3,000 at 10 masses at par. ch.; 300 at 3 masses at Portland hotel.[84] Temporary ch. became hall 1962.[85]

Iron chapel of ease, dedicated to St. Gabriel, built 1928 in Hatchard Rd., Upper Holloway, by Passionists from St. Jos. Seated 200, enlarged c. 1931.[86] Transferred to diocese and formed combined par. of St. Mellitus, Tollington Pk., and St. Gabriel 1939.[87] Three additional masses each Sunday 1955 to 1964. St. Gabriel became

[63] S. Lewis, *Islington As It Was* (1854), 65; Islington Prot. Inst. *Ann. Rep.* and published sermons (in Islington libr.).
[64] *St. John the Evangelist, Islington, 1843-1943* (booklet supplied by par. priest), 6-7.
[65] *Golden Jubilee of Consec. of Sacred Heart Ch. Eden Grove* (booklet supplied by par. priest).
[66] *Old Roman Cath. Ch.: Hist. and Purpose* (n.d., copy in Islington libr.); G.R.O. Worship Reg. no. 63460.
[67] G.R.O. Worship Reg. no. 73749.
[68] *Sunday Telegraph*, 21 Mar. 1983, p. 3.
[69] The following abbreviations are used, in addition to those in the index: accn., accommodation; consec., consecrated; reg., registered.
[70] *Cath. Dir.* (1837); *St. John the Evang.* 1.
[71] *St. John the Evang.* 2-3; Lewis, *Islington*, 365; P.R.O., C 54/15673, no. 12; *Cath. Dir.* (1981).
[72] P.R.O., HO 129/10/2/1/19.

[73] Inf. from par. priest.   [74] *Jubilee of Sacred Heart Ch.*
[75] G.R.O. Worship Reg. no. 8047.
[76] Ibid. no. 19836; *Jubilee of Sacred Heart Ch.*
[77] A. Rottmann, *Lond. Cath. Chs.* 214.
[78] *Jubilee of Sacred Heart Ch.*
[79] Inf. from par. priest.
[80] *V.C.H. Mdx.* v. 38; *Souvenir of Consec. of St. Jos. 1932*, 20; G.R.O. Worship Reg. no. 8554.
[81] *Souvenir of Consec.* 21-4; *V.C.H. Mdx.* vi. 183.
[82] Rottmann, *Lond. Cath. Chs.* 216-18; *Souvenir of Consec.* 28.
[83] Rottmann, *Lond. Cath. Chs.* 213; inf. from par. priest.
[84] *St. Joan of Arc, Highbury, 1920-62* (booklet in Islington libr.).
[85] G.R.O. Worship Reg. no. 47921.
[86] *Souvenir of Consec. of St. Jos.* 27.
[87] *Westm. Year Bk.* (1969), 201.

separate par. 1964.[88] Permanent ch. in Holloway Rd. seating 500–600, of dark grey brick with concrete and aluminium roof, by Gerard Goalen 1966–7: windowless walls to shut out traffic noise. Seats 500–600. Temporary ch. became hall.[89]

St. Mellitus's chapel, no. 140 Tollington Pk., reg. 1925,[90] replaced 1927 by asbestos ch. in Everleigh St.[91] Under care of canons regular at Stroud Green until par. formed 1939.[92] Moved to New Ct. Cong. ch., Tollington Pk., and Everleigh St. bldg. temporarily used by Congs. 1959. Ch. seated c. 900 in 1982 and former Sunday sch. converted into presbytery.[93]

Church of Our Lady and St. Joseph, Kingsland, moved from corner of Culford Rd. and Tottenham Street, Hackney, to no. 100A Ball's Pond Rd. 1964. Seated 600 in 1982.[94]

Polish Catholic Mission, set up 1894 to serve immigrants, moved from Shadwell St., Stepney, 1930 to former New Jerusalem ch. in Devonshire St. (Devonia Rd. from 1943). Ch. of Our Lady of Czestochowa and St. Casimir, seating c. 120–50, serves N. and E. Lond. and is residence of vicar delegate for Poles in Eng. and Wales.[95]

Sisters of the Sacred Heart of Jesus and Mary founded St. Pelagia's Home, nos. 25 and 27 Bickerton Road, Upper Holloway, in 1889 for mothers with illegitimate children. Chapel reg. for worship 1905. Closed c. 1924, and moved to no. 34 West Hill, Highgate.[96]

Convent of Discalced Carmelites, at no. 64 Highbury Pk. from St. John the Evangelist 1918, survived 1953. New ch. of St. Joan of Arc built on site 1962.[97]

Augustinian Sisters of Meaux formed convent and nursing home at Bethanie, no. 12 Hornsey Lane, 1922, for chronic invalids and convalescents.[98]

Franciscan Missionaries of the Divine Motherhood opened maternity home at no. 31 Highbury Hill, connected with the Crusade of Rescue in 1940s. Closed by 1966.[99]

Fathers of the Order of St. Camillus opened Ho. of Our Lady of Consolation, no. 100 Hornsey Lane, by 1953; closed between 1966 and 1979.[1]

Sisters of the Catholic Apostolate (Pallottine Sisters) reg. chapel at no. 7 Milner Pl., Barnsbury, 1969.[2]

Several congregations opened hos. in 1970s: Little Brothers of Jesus, no. 27 Bracey Street,

Tollington Pk.; Sisters of Providence, no. 17 St. John's Villas, Upper Holloway; Sisters of Loreto, no. 149 Hemingford Road, Barnsbury; Sisters of St. Paul of Chartres, no. 30 Aberdeen Pk., Highbury; Ursulines of Jesus, no. 8 King Henry's Walk, Ball's Pond Road.[3]

PROTESTANT NONCONFORMITY. Fields near Islington town were frequently used for secret gatherings. In 1558 c. 40 men and women at a prayer meeting in a back close were arrested and 13 of them were burnt.[4] Robert Browne, founder of the Brownist sect, was said to have preached at Islington, possibly in a gravel pit, in the 1570s.[5] Since it is unlikely that he came to London during that period, the tradition may refer to 1586–9, when Browne preached in and around London while a schoolmaster in Southwark.[6] A separatist church led by Francis Johnson and John Penry used woods near Islington as one of its meeting places. On one occasion c. 50 were arrested there, possibly in 1593 when Johnson and his father and his brother George were arrested.[7]

After the Restoration several deprived ministers settled in Islington, some running dissenting academies.[8] In 1672 Samuel Lee, ejected from St. Botolph's, Bishopsgate, was licensed to teach at his house at Newington Green, and the houses there of Daniel Bull and Mrs. Stock were licensed as Presbyterian meeting places. George Fowler, ejected vicar of Bridewell, was also licensed to teach at his house in Islington, and the houses of William Barker and George Thwing at Islington and of David King at Kingsland green were licensed as meeting places.[9] Presbyterianism declined thereafter, until revived in connexion with the Church of Scotland in the early 19th century.

George Whitefield and John Wesley preached in Islington from 1738, usually in private houses, and often stayed there. George Stonehouse, vicar 1738–40, invited Whitefield and John and Charles Wesley to preach in the parish church in 1738 and 1739.[10] In April 1739 Whitefield assisted the vicar in administering communion and afterwards addressed a large crowd in a room. The next day he was prevented by the churchwardens from entering the pulpit and preached in the churchyard. The vestry blamed Stonehouse for the frequent disturbances, by allowing unlicensed

[88] Ibid.; *Par. of St. Gabriel, Opening Souvenir* (booklet [1967] in Islington libr.).
[89] *Westm. Year Bk.* (1969), 201.
[90] G.R.O. Worship Reg. no. 49682.
[91] Ibid. no. 50716; inf. from par. priest.
[92] *Par. of St. Gabriel, Opening Souvenir*; and see St. Gabriel's above.
[93] Inf. from par. priest; below, prot. nonconf., Congs.
[94] Inf. from par. priest; G.R.O. Worship Reg. no. 69416.
[95] Inf. from sec. of Polish mission; R. Glass and others, *Lond. Aspects of Change* (1964), 326; G.R.O. Worship Reg. no. 52462; below, prot. nonconf., New Jerusalem ch.
[96] G.R.O. Worship Reg. no. 41269; Reformatory and Refuge Union, *Classified List of Child-Saving Institutions* (1912 and later edns.).
[97] *St. John the Evang.* 12; P. F. Anson, *Rel. Orders and Congs. of G.B. and Irel.* (1949), 203; *Westm. Year Bk.* (1953); *St. Joan of Arc, Highbury*, 1–2.
[98] Anson, *Rel. Orders*, 162; *Cath. Dir.* (1981).
[99] Anson, *Rel. Orders*, 274; *Westm. Year Bk.* (1966).

[1] *Westm. Year Bk.* (1953 and later edns.).
[2] G.R.O. Worship Reg. no. 71656.
[3] *Cath. Dir.* (1979, 1981).
[4] *Acts and Monuments of John Foxe*, viii. 468–9.
[5] E. Pagitt, *Heresiography* (1661), 66; R. Baillie, *A Dissuasive from the Errors of the Time* (1646), 13; *D.N.B.* There is no evidence to support the claim in Lewis, *Islington*, 113–14, that Browne was a lecturer in the par. ch.: H. M. Dexter, *Congregationalism of Last Three Hundred Years* (1970), 65 n.
[6] C. Burrage, *True Story of Rob. Browne* (1906), 62; F. J. Powicke, *Rob. Browne: Pioneer of Modern Congregationalism* [1910], 46; *Church Hist.* vi (1937), 292.
[7] M. R. Watts, *Dissenters*, i (1978), 36–9; *D.N.B.* s.v. Fras. Johnson.
[8] Below, educ.
[9] *Cal. S.P. Dom.* 1672, 11; G. E. Turner, *Orig. Rec. of Early Nonconf.* (1911), ii. 958; F. Bate, *Declaration of Indulgence*, App. xl.
[10] *John Wesley's Jnl.* ed. N. Curnock (1938), i. 460; ii. 94, 135, 219, 276, 350.

persons to preach, and made a presentment to the bishop. Representatives of both vicar and parish drew up a statement that the Wesleys and Whitefield would not be allowed to use the pulpit, which Stonehouse signed, but four months later he allowed John Westley Hall to preach and wanted to appoint him as curate. The vestry asked the bishop to prevent Hall or any other preacher in fields or private houses from being licensed, Hall was not appointed, and in 1740 Stonehouse resigned.[11] In 1778 there were said to be no Methodists in the parish,[12] although John Wesley frequently stayed at no. 25 Highbury Place towards the end of his life, at the home of John Horton who became one of his executors.[13]

The first dissenting chapel was built in 1744 in Essex Road by Independents,[14] followed by Islington chapel in Church Street which was begun in 1788, inspired by the preaching of Jeremiah Learnoult Garrett on Islington Green and at the old Rectifying House and old Soap House. There was some connexion with Calvinistic Methodists, which Garrett later joined, but the chapel was mainly used by Independent preachers.[15] It was described as Methodist by the vicar in 1810, together with Union chapel and Holloway chapel, probably because the denominations were not clear.[16]

From the 1790s dissenters certified many private houses for worship; in addition to those listed below under specific sects, unspecified groups registered a house in Lower Street, 1800, no. 17 Britannia Row, 1817, no. 4 Windsor Street, 1823, no. 13 Wells Row, 1823, no. 26 Popham Street, 1824, a house in Union Row, Kingsland, 1824, and a former schoolroom in Adelaide Square, opposite no. 24 Shepperton Street, 1840.[17] Besides the two chapels mentioned above, small groups of Independents were meeting by 1793, as were Wesleyans at King's Cross by 1807 and Holloway by 1811. Although Particular Baptists met at King's Cross c. 1800, Baptists did not appear by name in Islington town until 1830.[18]

Some of the meetings eventually founded chapels. Independents founded the first nonconformist chapel at Holloway in 1805, and Wesleyans followed there in 1821. Union chapel, 1799, promoted co-operation between free churchmen and Evangelical Anglicans before the established church in Islington had come to be influenced by the Evangelical movement. Nonconformity was reinforced when the Hoxton Academy moved to the new Highbury College in 1826, training young men for the Congregationalist ministry there until 1850.[19]

New sects appeared with the spread of housing from the 1820s. The Methodist New Connexion, English Presbyterians, the United Secession Church of Scotland, and the Catholic Apostolic Church all opened chapels in 1834, followed by Lady Huntingdon's Connexion in 1838, the Wesleyan Methodist Association in 1841, Brethren in 1843, the Established Church of Scotland in 1846, Latter-day Saints in 1850, and the New Church (Swedenborgians) in 1852. In 1851 Islington was one of 10 parishes with the highest numbers of nonconformist worshippers in Middlesex.[20] There were 15 sects by 1860 and 20 by 1870. Several of the churches came from the City, as their members moved to the suburbs. In 1903 out of 29 sects that had held services in Islington 20 survived. A few more arrived in the 20th century: Seventh-day Baptists before the First World War, the Elim Four-Square Gospel Alliance, Christian Scientists, Liberal Catholics, the Apostolic Faith Church, and Paracletians in the period between the World Wars, and Pentecostalists and Jehovah's Witnesses after 1945.

The large working- and lower middle-class areas probably accounted for the smaller and less rigidly organized denominations; Islington's social structure demanded an evangelistic approach, and in all periods missions were more successful than regular services, except in middle-class areas such as Highbury.[21] Some nonconformist churches, like Anglican ones, retained social distinctions in their seating in the early 20th century as in the 19th. The division in Islington chapel was one of the reasons why W. H. Dorman left and joined the Brethren in 1838: a brass trellis screen marked off the pews for the middle class, who also sat several inches higher than the poor, and gates at each end of the aisles shut out those who could not pay.[22] Most chapels and churches of the leading sects still used seat-holding.

As the Evangelical drive in the Anglican church died down, nonconformists increased their proportion of church attendances. In 1851 there were 13,451 attendances at nonconformist services on census Sunday, 32 per cent of the total attendances, while the Anglican churches had 60 per cent.[23] In 1903 nonconformist attendances accounted for 54 per cent of the total and Anglicans had declined to 38 per cent,[24] although, as elsewhere, only a minority of the population worshipped at all: $11\frac{1}{2}$ per cent attended nonconformist services, $8\frac{1}{2}$ per cent Anglican, and $1\frac{1}{2}$ per cent other services.[25] Both in 1851 and 1903 the Congregationalists had the most nonconformist attendances, with 60 per cent (8,086) in 1851 and 30 per cent (11,771) in 1903. All Methodist churches had 18 per cent in 1851 and 17 per cent in 1903; Presbyterians 8 per cent and 9 per cent. Baptists showed the greatest percentage increase, from 6 per cent (790) in 1851 to 15 per cent (5,900) in 1903. The Brethren, with

[11] *Proc. Wesley Hist. Soc.* v. 238–9; *Geo. Whitefield's Jnls.* (1960 edn.), 193, 196, 204, 224, 259–61.
[12] Guildhall MS. 9558, f. 460.
[13] *Wesley's Jnl.* vii. 229 and n.; viii. 343; J. Vickers and B. Young, *Meth. Guide to Lond. and SE.* (1980), 25.
[14] Below. Vicar called them Presbs. in 1778: Guildhall MS. 9558, f. 460. [15] *D.N.B.*; below, Congs.
[16] Guildhall MS. 9558, f. 459v.
[17] Guildhall MSS. 9580/2, p. 56; 4; 5; 8, p. 70.
[18] Para. and rest of section based mainly on lists of individual chs. below.

[19] P.R.O., C 54/10711, no. 9; C 54/13998, no. 4.
[20] *V.C.H. Mdx.* i. 147.
[21] Booth, *Life and Labour*, 3rd ser. (1), 120–32.
[22] W. H. Dorman, *Reasons for Retiring from Independent or Congregational Body* (1862).
[23] 1851 figs. based on P.R.O., HO 129/10/1, 2; 1903 figs. on Mudie-Smith, *Rel. Life*, 170–4.
[24] Above, churches, for discussion.
[25] Figs. based on Mudie-Smith, *Rel. Life*, 169–74; *Census*, 1901.

1,174 attendances, and the Salvation Army, with 1,997, were the only other denominations with over 1,000 in 1903, and all except one of the remainder were below 500.

All existing churches declined sharply from c. 1900, as members moved to the outer suburbs and the newly arrived poor had yet to be won over. The new sects' mainly evangelistic approach resulted, as in the 19th century, in a growing membership, while older denominations were closing and amalgamating their churches. In 1914, excluding missions, there were 13 Congregational churches, 10 Methodist (Primitive and Wesleyan), 13 Baptist, 13 Brethren's, and 5 Presbyterian, besides 22 others representing a further 13 sects.[26] By 1983 the largest sects, Congregationalists and United Reformed Church, Methodists, and Baptists, had respectively only four, four, and six churches remaining out of the many founded in the 19th century.

The following abbreviations are used in the accounts of protestant nonconformist churches, in addition to those used in the index: Bapt., Baptist; Cong., Congregationalist; demol., demolished; Ind., Independent; Met., Metropolitan; Meth., Methodist; mtg., meeting; Presb., Presbyterian; reg., registered; temp., temporary; Utd. Ref., United Reformed; Wes., Wesleyan. Attendance figures for 1886 are from *British Weekly*, 'Rel. Census of Lond.' 24 Oct. 1886, 41; attendance figures for 1903 are from Mudie-Smith, *Rel. Life*, 170-4. Information dated 1914 is from Harris and Bryant, *Chs. and Lond.* 399-401.

CONGREGATIONALISTS. Lower Street (Essex Rd.) chapel built 1744 with donations from Wm. Pearcy and Mr. Pike, S. corner Greenman's Lane, as first dissenting chapel in Islington. No regular min. until 1761. During ministry of John Gawsell, 1761-8, seceders met in Ward's Pl., old ho. just S. of chapel, but reunited when their min. left. Nos. rose after 1768 and galleries built. Known as Islington Mtg. c. 1800. Chapel much enlarged 1820, when front brought forward. Schoolroom for 200 later added.[27] Seated 800 in 1838,[28] 700 in 1851. Attendance 1851: 476 a.m.; 560 evg.[29] Lease expired 1865 and new chapel in River Street (later Pl.)[30] reg. 1864. Lecture room added by 1872.[31] Attendance 1903: 19 a.m.; 86 p.m. Closed 1909.[32]

Islington chapel[33] originated in privately owned chapel built 1788 in Church (later Gaskin) Street by John Ives, blacksmith, of Upper Street, assisted by Jeremiah Garrett, but not completed owing to lack of funds. Preachers included Revd. Mr. Clayton, Mr. Crole of Founders' Hall, Revd. Jos. Phillips, and Revd. John Marrant, American negro known as the Black Preacher. Chapel completed 1793 when Thos. Wills, formerly preacher to Ctss. of Huntingdon's Connexion and husband of Lady Huntingdon's niece,[34] took lease for life. Wills conveyed interest 1800 to Evan John Jones, min. 1800-27. Nos. increased and girls' sch. of ind. added. Sun. sch. of 300 was first of kind in Islington. Moved to new chapel in Upper Street, near corner Gaskin Street, built 1814: two-storeyed brick bldg. with cement facing in Grecian style, seating 1,389 including gallery.[35] Jones was criticized for material gains and large congregation;[36] also for profiting from New Bunhill Fields, burial ground created 1817 from garden of no. 5 Church Row, Upper Street, which he purchased and which adjoined grounds of old Church Street chapel. Jones conveyed chapel to trustees for Calvinists 1823,[37] having formerly had sole control of admissions. Anglican liturgy for Sun. svces. abandoned 1830. Chas. Gilbert, min. 1828-34, failed to regain sole control and with seceders founded Barnsbury chapel (q.v.). W. H. Dorman, min. c. 1835-8, joined Plymouth Brethren. Lecture hall built under chapel c. 1850. Attendance 1851: 869 a.m.; 719 evg.[38] Feuds reduced nos. to 49 by 1867. Revival attempted by John Spurgeon, min. 1873-6, whose s. Chas. Haddon Spurgeon preached anniversary sermons to large nos. Spurgeon resigned to allow amalgamation with Colebrooke Row Presb. chapel but public outcry defeated scheme. In 1877 chapel's 31 members sought financial aid of Lond. Cong. Union. In 1886 membership of 370 bought land to rebuild chapel after M.B.W. had taken premises for street improvements. New bldg. 1887-8 by Bonella & Paull: front in Norman Shaw style with large flat upper oriel window and cupola; two side entrances with four small arched windows between; galleried interior.[39] Attendance 1903: 322 a.m.; 720 p.m. Became Islington Chapel Utd. Ref. ch. 1972. Closed 1979.[40]

From late 18th cent. several premises were used by Inds.: room in ho. at corner of Union Row, Kingsland Rd., just inside par., 1793, whence worshippers moved to bldg. in Robinson's Row (near Kingsland Common or Crossway) just in Hackney, built 1794, reg. 1808;[41] room in ho. of Ric. Lawson, Elder Walk, Lower Rd., 1794;[42] Wm. Hodgson's ho., Hedge Row, Upper Street, Islington Green, 1800,[43] some members moving to Ann Morris's ho., no. 30 Cross Street, 1803;[44] Wm. Mackenzie's ho., Lower Street, 1802;[45] Geo. Thompson's ho., no. 7 Wells Row, 1806;[46] Rob. Martin's ho. at Holloway, 1803, replaced by Wm. Perfect's ho. there, 1804;[47] room of John Ankins, Hornsey Rd., 1816, worshippers using room at no. 13 Brand Street 1829;[48] Hornsey Rd. new schoolroom, 1820;[49] room on premises of John Hayes at Belle Isle, 1821;[50] Thos. Clark's ho. no. 16

[26] H. W. Harris and M. Bryant, *Chs. and Lond.* [1914], 399-401.
[27] Lewis, *Islington*, 412-13; G.L.R.O., N/C/10.
[28] *Lond. City Mission Mag.* iii (1838), 104.
[29] P.R.O., HO 129/10/2/1/9.
[30] A. Mearns, *Guide to Cong. Chs. of Lond.* (1882-4).
[31] G.R.O. Worship Reg. nos. 16275, 21070.
[32] Ibid. no. 16275.
[33] Para. based on L. D. Dixon, *Seven Score Years and Ten* [1938].
[34] *D.N.B.*   [35] Lewis, *Islington*, 263.
[36] B.L., Broadsides, f. 132.
[37] P.R.O., C 54/10109, no. 6.
[38] P.R.O., HO 129/10/2/1/12.
[39] Pevsner, *Lond.* ii. 230.
[40] G.R.O. Worship Reg. no. 31379.
[41] Guildhall MSS. 9580/1, p. 55; 3; Mearns, *Cong. Chs.*
[42] Guildhall MS. 9580/1, p. 66.
[43] Ibid. 2, p. 69.   [44] Ibid. 2, p. 107.
[45] Ibid. 2, p. 99.   [46] Ibid. 2, p. 171.
[47] Ibid. 2, pp. 106, 136.   [48] Ibid. 4; 6, pp. 256-7.
[49] Ibid. 5.   [50] Ibid.

Orchard Grove, 1829 and no. 14 Orchard Grove, 1829;[51] no. 8 Duddy's Rents, Lower Street, 1830.[52]

Union chapel originated in ch. formed 1799 which met in chapel (later private ho. no. 18) in Highbury Grove, after Hugh Worthington, min. at Salters' Hall chapel and former Unitarian, had preached at Highbury Grove 1793-6.[53] Established tradition of Anglican liturgy a.m. and free church worship p.m., providing union of Evangelical chs. of Eng. and Scotland and non-conf. chs. Thos. Lewis, Meth. lay preacher, first permanent min. 1802-52; became Cong. min. 1804.[54] New chapel in Compton Terr. built 1806,[55] seating 1,000 in 1838,[56] 1,100 in 1851.[57] Dan. Wilson at par. ch. drew away some attenders; Anglican liturgy dropped 1845, Cong. Union joined 1847. David Nasmith, member of Union chapel, founded Lond. City Mission, and out-stations from chapel. Hen. Allon, co-pastor from 1844, pastor 1852-92, twice president of Cong. Union, developed music in svces.[58] Attendance 1851: 882 a.m.; 664 aft. (for servants; attendance doubled owing to schs. collection); 770 evg.[59] Membership rose from 318 in 1844 to 692 in 1860. Chapel enlarged 1861. Rebuilt on same site 1876-7, when svces. held at Myddelton hall, Upper Street, and iron chapel in Highbury New Pk.:[60] red-brick bldg. in the style of Santa Fosca Torcello by Jas. Cubitt with big tower, completed 1889, dominating terr.; octagonal interior on plan of Greek Cross.[61] Lecture hall, Compton Terr., and Sun. sch., Compton Ave., added by 1901.[62] Attendance 1903: 786 a.m.; 608 p.m. Membership fell rapidly early 20th cent. with migration to outer suburbs.[63] Did not join Utd. Ref. Ch. but remained in Cong. Federation, with 18 members 1980.[64] Missions: Nichol Street, Bethnal Green; Morton Rd. mission and sch., 1855, seating 800; attendance 1903: 386 p.m.; became builder's office after Second World War; Union hall, Station Rd., seating 250, by 1884.[65]

Holloway chapel, at junction of Camden and Caledonian rds., originated in one built by Inds. 1804 in Holloway Pl. (S. side of Holloway Rd., just NW. of G.N.R. line).[66] Destroyed by fire, possibly deliberately, 1807 and rebuilt on same site 1808;[67] fittings from chapel in Highbury Grove.[68] No regular min., but served from Hoxton and other dissenting academies; Ingram Cobbin, sec. of British and Foreign Schs. Soc. and sec. of Home Mission Soc., officiated there.[69] Enlarged 1821 and 1834,[70] seated 550 in 1838.[71] Sold to Ch. of Scotland 1842. Chapel built on new site 1842.[72] Seated 650 in 1851,[73] 470 in 1884.[74] Attendance 1851: 540 a.m.; 109 aft. (Sun. sch. svce. only); 343 evg.[75] Attendance 1903: 104 a.m.; 179 p.m. Ch. destroyed 1940; Sun. p.m. svces. held in St. Luke's C.E. ch. 1940-8. Hall built 1948 and replaced 1960 with permanent ch. on same site, seating c. 80 and with facilities for playgroup and youth activities. Became Hollo-way Utd. Ref. ch. 1972.[76]

Maberly chapel, no. 49 Ball's Pond Rd., built 1824, opened 1826, by Hen. Ashley for Inds.[77] Seated 700 in 1851. Attendance 1851: 520 a.m.; 60 aft.; 300 evg.[78] Closed c. 1888.[79]

No. 31 Highbury Vale (later Blackstock Rd.) certified by Wm. Parker Bourne, student in theology, for Ind. worship 1826.[80] Mtg. ho. built in Highbury Vale 1850, seating 50. Attendance 1851: 22 aft.; 20 evg.[81] Nothing further known.

Inds. under Chas. Gilbert from Islington chapel (q.v.), worshipped in ho. of Mat. Jas. Starling at SW. corner of Experimental Gdns. (off York Way) 1833; Starling certified his sch. ho. on E. side of Little William Street (near York Way) for Inds. 1837.[82] Inds. from sch. ho. met in cottage seating 20 in same street 1851. Attendance: 17 evg.[83] Svce. for adults also in Little William Street chapel and Sun. sch. 1851, seating 160.[84] Nothing further known; mtgs. may have ceased on opening of Caledonian Rd. chapel later in 1851.[85]

Barnsbury chapel and sch. room, corner of Barnsbury and Milner streets, built 1835, under Chas. Gilbert after resigning Islington chapel.[86] Seated 500 in 1838.[87] Reopened 1841 after altera-tions, seating 550: stuccoed two-storeyed neo-classical bldg. with twin porticoes on Doric columns and tall round-arched windows.[88] In 1851 seated 708; attendance: 556 a.m.; 347 evg.; average attendance: 720 a.m.[89] Attendance 1903: 113 a.m.; 497 p.m. Restored 1876, seated 750.[90] Nos. declined from c. 1900 and chapel closed 1909.[91]

[51] Guildhall MS. 9580/6, pp. 223-4, 263.
[52] Ibid. 7, p. 6.
[53] R. Taylor, *150 Years Not Out* [booklet in Islington libr., ?1949], p. 9; Guildhall MS. 9580/2, p. 27; *D.N.B.*, s.v. Worthington; Nelson, *Islington*, 185.
[54] Taylor, *150 Years*, 9-11.
[55] Ibid. 9; P.R.O., C 54/11061, no. 5; above, plate 36.
[56] *Lond. City Mission Mag.* iii. 104.
[57] P.R.O., HO 129/10/2/1/11.
[58] Taylor, *150 Years*, 14; *D.N.B.*
[59] P.R.O., HO 129/10/2/1/11.
[60] Taylor, *150 Years*, 15-16; G.R.O. Worship Reg. no. 22459.
[61] Taylor, *150 Years*, 15-16; Pevsner, *Lond.* ii. 230.
[62] G.R.O. Worship Reg. nos. 38407-8; R. T. Jones, *Congregationalism in Eng. 1662-1962*, 327.
[63] Taylor, *150 Years*, 16.
[64] *Cong. Year Bk.* (1980-1), 102.
[65] Taylor, *150 Years*, 14, 19-20; Mearns, *Cong. Chs.* (1884).
[66] Guildhall MS. 9580/2, p. 137; Lewis, *Islington*, 300.
[67] P.R.O., C 54/8535, no. 4.
[68] Lewis, *Islington*, 301; above, Union chapel.
[69] Nelson, *Islington*, 104-5; *D.N.B.*

[70] Lewis, *Islington*, 301.
[71] *Lond. City Mission Mag.* iii. 104.
[72] Guildhall MS. 9580/8, p. 267; inf. from ch. sec.; below.
[73] P.R.O., HO 129/10/1/1/11.
[74] Mearns, *Cong. Chs.* (1884).
[75] P.R.O., HO 129/10/1/1/11.
[76] Inf. from ch. sec.
[77] Guildhall MS. 9580/6, p. 68; P.R.O., C 54/10719, no. 5; Lewis, *Islington*, 333.
[78] P.R.O., HO 129/10/2/1/10.
[79] *P.O. Dir. Lond.* (1888, 1889).
[80] Guildhall MS. 9580/6, p. 110.
[81] P.R.O., HO 129/10/2/1/13.
[82] Guildhall MS. 9580/7, pp. 123, 269.
[83] P.R.O., HO 129/10/1/1/15.
[84] Ibid. 10/1/1/12.
[85] Below.
[86] Guildhall MS. 9580/7, p. 174; P.R.O., C 54/11437, no. 3; above, Starling's ho. and Islington chapel.
[87] *Lond. City Mission Mag.* iii. 104.
[88] Lewis, *Islington*, 265.
[89] P.R.O., HO 129/10/1/1/13.
[90] Mearns, *Cong. Chs.*
[91] 'Lond. Cong. Chs. since 1850', *Trans. Cong. Hist. Soc.* xx, no. 1, 31.

Caledonian Rd. chapel, near Bingfield St., seating 1,000, built 1850-1[92] through efforts of Ebenezer Davies, min. Seated 800 in 1884.[93] Attendance 1903: 109 a.m.; 229 p.m. Closed 1948.[94]

Offord Rd. chapel founded by group from neighbouring chapel who worshipped in Twyford hall, Twyford Street, 1855.[95] Built 1856.[96] Evan Lewis min. 1868-9.[97] Seated 800 in 1884.[98] Attendance 1903: 130 a.m.; 138 p.m. Closed 1918.[99] Bldg. used as wareho. 1981.

Harecourt chapel, St. Paul's Rd., built 1855 with proceeds from sale of Hare Court chapel, Aldersgate.[1] Bldg. of Kentish rag by E. & W. G. Habershon: octagonal central plan with three short arms in main axes.[2] Seated 1,300 in 1884.[3] Attendance 1903: 247 a.m.; 183 p.m. Church Ho., no. 1 Alma (later Harecourt) Rd. reg. for worship 1930.[4] Renamed Utd. Ref. ch., Harecourt Rd., 1972.[5] Destroyed by fire c. 1982 and svces. held in adjoining ho. Mission work and schs. in Elder Walk, Essex Rd., 1861.[6] In 1884 missions at Hammond Sq., Hoxton, seating 150; Macclesfield Street, City Rd., seating 100. Harecourt also founded chapels in Milton Rd., Stoke Newington, and Rectory Rd., Hackney.[7]

Britannia Row cong. ch. originated in mission work in Elder Walk, Essex Rd., started by Harecourt chapel and continued under Lond. City Missionary. Branch formed 1865 with 16 members, mtg. in sch. room which seated 150. Membership rose to 152 in 1871, when ch. built 1871-2 in Britannia Row with aid from Harecourt.[8] Seated 500 in 1884.[9] Attendance 1903: 103 a.m.; 139 p.m. Bombed 1940 and not rebuilt.

Temp. Cong. chapel in York Pl. (later St. Clement Street), Barnsbury, 1861,[10] may have been forerunner of Arundel Sq. Cong. chapel and sch. room, opened nearby 1863 at corner Westbourne Rd. and Bride Street.[11] Galleries built 1865; seated 1,000 in 1884.[12] Attendance 1903: 170 a.m.; 232 p.m. Closed 1931.[13] Bldg. used by free Bapts. 1931-5, before sale to St. Giles Christian mission.[14] Chapel ran preaching station at G.N.R. station on Sundays 1884.[15]

Baxter Rd. Cong. ch. built 1862-3 by Congs. Sold to Bapts. 1864.[16]

Junction Rd. Cong. ch. reg. temp. ch. 1865 on N. side of Junction Rd., Upper Holloway. New ch. built nearby 1866-7 on island site at corner of Tremlett Grove:[17] Kentish rag in Decorated style. Seated 700 in 1884.[18] Attendance 1903: 416 a.m.; 506 p.m. Renamed Junction Rd. Utd. Ref. ch. 1972. Closed 1978.[19]

Seven Sisters Rd. Cong. ch., reg. 1865, replaced 1885 by Finsbury Pk. Cong. ch., corner of Seven Sisters and Palmerston (later Playford) rds.[20] Large membership under T. Eynon Davies 1880s. Attendance 1886: 1,021 a.m.; 1,170 p.m.[21] Attendance 1903: 489 a.m.; 943 p.m. Closed 1939 and moved out of Islington.[22]

New Court Cong. chapel, Tollington Pk., built 1871 by worshippers from New Ct., Lincoln's Inn Fields, whose chapel had been demol. for Law Courts.[23] Neo-classical bldg. by C. G. Searle, with giant Corinthian portico, seating 1,340 in 1884.[24] During ministries of Campbell Morgan and J. Ossian Davies often full, but attendances declined c. 1900 with migration to outer suburbs. Attendance 1886: 1,053 a.m.; 1,326 p.m.[25] Attendance 1903: 734 a.m.; 633 p.m. Chapel sold to St. Mellitus Rom. Cath. ch. 1959;[26] members moved to temp. chapel in Everleigh Street until 1961.[27] New Court Cong. ch., Regina Rd., opened 1961; closed 1976.[28] Mission at nos. 88 and 89, Campbell Rd., 1884, seating 300; svces. Sun. and Wed.[29]

Blenheim Rd. chapel, Upper Holloway, opened as mission by Park chapel, Crouch End,[30] and reg. 1871. Seated 450 in 1884.[31] Attendance 1903: 96 a.m.; 156 p.m. Replaced 1916 by Blenheim Cong. mission hall, Blenheim (later Bavaria) Rd. Closed by 1954.[32]

Crayford Rd. Cong. ch., Tufnell Pk., formed 1874 in Athenaeum, Camden Rd. In Crayford Rd. by 1880 seating 400 in 1884.[33]

Cong. ch. (possibly temp.), Highbury Quadrant, reg. 1880.[34] Permanent ch. in Highbury Quadrant built 1881; seated 1,370 in 1884.[35] Designed by John Sulman; galleries added. Attendance 1903: 580 a.m.; 683 p.m. Because of subsidence, replaced 1957 with new single-storeyed red-brick bldg. with small tower, seating 250.[36]

Gifford hall mission, Gifford Street, Caledonian Rd., reg. 1901.[37] Attendance 1903: 50 a.m.; 399 p.m. Closed 1918; bldg. used by undesignated Christians.[38]

[92] P.R.O., C 54/14344, no. 4; ibid. HO 129/10/1/1/[12A].
[93] Mearns, Cong. Chs.
[94] G.R.O. Worship Reg. no. 317.
[95] Coull, Islington, 123; Mearns, Cong. Chs.
[96] P.R.O., C 54/15168, no. 19; datestone.
[97] D.N.B.   [98] Mearns, Cong. Chs.
[99] G.R.O. Worship Reg. no. 7942.
[1] P.R.O., C 54/15130, no. 12.
[2] Pevsner, Lond. ii. 229-30.
[3] Mearns, Cong. Chs.
[4] G.R.O. Worship Reg. no. 52607.   [5] Ibid. no. 8750.
[6] Below, Britannia Row ch.
[7] Mearns, Cong. Chs.
[8] Islington libr., docs. found under foundation stone of chapel; G.R.O. Worship Reg. no. 21007.
[9] Mearns, Cong. Chs.
[10] Coull, Islington, 124.
[11] P.R.O., C 54/16852, no. 1.   [12] Mearns, Cong. Chs.
[13] G.R.O. Worship Reg. no. 15420.
[14] Below, Bapts.; undenom. missions.
[15] Mearns, Cong. Chs.
[16] P.R.O., C 54/16103, no. 4; G.R.O. Worship Reg. no. 15837; below, Bapts., Salters' Hall.

[17] G.R.O. Worship Reg. nos. 16565, 18037, 18353; datestone; P.R.O., C 54/16695, no. 8.
[18] Mearns, Cong. Chs.
[19] G.R.O. Worship Reg. no. 18353.
[20] Ibid. nos. 16693, 29033.
[21] Trans. Cong. Hist. Soc. xx, no. 1, 32.
[22] G.R.O. Worship Reg. no. 58931.
[23] Mearns, Cong. Chs.
[24] Pevsner, Lond. ii. 230.
[25] Trans. Cong. Hist. Soc. xx, no. 1, 32.
[26] Above, Rom. Cathm.
[27] Inf. from par. priest, St. Mellitus; G.R.O. Worship Reg. no. 67389.
[28] G.R.O. Worship Reg. no. 68387.
[29] Mearns, Cong. Chs.
[30] V.C.H. Mdx. vi. 186.
[31] Mearns, Cong. Chs.; G.R.O. Worship Reg. no. 19999.
[32] G.R.O. Worship Reg. no. 46931.
[33] Mearns, Cong. Chs.
[34] G.R.O. Worship Reg. nos. 24898, 26330.
[35] Mearns, Cong. Chs.
[36] Inf. from ch. sec.
[37] G.R.O. Worship Reg. no. 38387.   [38] Ibid.; below.

Regent Street chapel, Thane Villas, Seven Sisters Rd., reg. 1903 by Congs. meeting in Providence chapel, Regent Street, City Rd. 1879.[39] Attendance 1903 (as Calvinistic Inds.): 111 a.m.; 184 p.m. Closed 1947–52.[40]

Inds. who reg. new sch. room in Shepperton Street, New North Rd., adapted as chapel 1833,[41] may have been those from Pavement chapel, Moorfields, who moved to New North Rd. 1833. They moved to Southgate Rd., De Beauvoir Town, 1851.[42]

Sermon Lane Ragged sch., built 1849, used by Inds. 1851, seating 40. Attendance: 15 p.m.[43]

Lower part of Brand Street Ragged sch. used by Congs. 1851, seating 100. Attendance: 20 p.m.[44]

Islington Literary and Scientific Institution, Wellington Street, used by Congs. 1861–76.[45]

Rosslyn hall, no. 1 Church Street, used by Congs. 1882–96.[46]

Almshos. in Ball's Pond Rd. had mission svces. for 100 held by Kingsland Cong. ch., Hackney, 1884.[47]

Cong. mission, Lennox Rd., Upper Holloway; attendance 1903: 66 a.m.; 253 p.m.

Cong. mission, Myrtle (later Hurlock) Street, attendance 1903: 125 a.m.; 142 p.m. Highbury Vale mission, Hurlock Street, Blackstock Rd., reg. 1937. Used by undesignated Christians from 1948.[48]

BAPTISTS. Battle Bridge mtg. ho., near S. end of Maiden Lane (York Way), built c. 1775, and called Trinity chapel c. 1793. Belonged to Particular Bapts. before 1810.[49] Used by Wes. Meths. by 1807 and until 1825,[50] then became private ho.[51]

Room at no. 2 Brays Ct., Essex Rd., reg. 1830, formerly reg. 1823 by Chas. Thompson for protestants.[52] Same group reg. room at no. 60 Britannia Row, Essex Rd., 1830, and workshop in South (later Basire) Street, New North Rd., fitted up as Zion chapel 1831.[53]

Cross Street Bapt. ch. originated at Providence hall, Providence Pl., Islington Green (called Islington Green chapel 1851), built c. 1833 and purchased by Bapts. 1840. Joined Bapt. Union c. 1845.[54] Seated 320 in 1851, attendance: 240 a.m.; 170 evg.[55] Cross St. chapel built 1852, of Kentish rag with Bath stone dressings and two arched entrances, seating 600;[56] reg. by Particular Bapts.[57] Land added at rear and schs. built 1857; additional land c. 1882.[58] Attendance 1903: 152 a.m.; 182 p.m. Seated 650 in 1928.[59] Bombed 1940; rebuilt and reopened 1957, seating 250–300, flanked by manse and fellowship room.[60]

Bapt. mtg. in Denmark Terr., Copenhagen Street, formed 1848. Temp. accn. in British sch. room, Denmark Terr., 1851; attendance: 87 a.m.; 106 evg. Gone by 1862.[61]

Providence chapel, Highbury Pl., founded through work of Wm. Flack who reg. Jarman's sch., Church (later Gaskin) Street, for Bapts. 1849.[62] Eight members formed Particular Bapt. ch. 1850 at Birkbeck schs., Windsor Street.[63] Seated 150 in 1851, attendance: 60 a.m.; 41 aft.; 86 evg.[64] Five mtg. places by 1857, including Parkfield Street 1852. Moved to Tabernacle, Providence Pl., Islington Green, 1853, formerly used by Ctss. of Huntingdon's Connexion, and may have taken over Providence chapel next to it. Membership increased to 70: Myddelton hall, Upper St., sometimes hired for large nos. 1860s. Joined Met. Strict Bapt. Assoc. probably 1869[65] and left 1888. Declined to low point c. 1870, but increased again 1880s. Providence Bapt. chapel built 1888 in Highbury Pl., corner of Baalbec Rd. Side galleries added. Seated 450 in 1928. Attendance 1903: 160 a.m.; 147 p.m. Nos. declined after 1900 as members moved away. Open-air mtgs. 1890s in Highbury Fields and at Highbury Corner.

Zoar chapel, John (later Wedmore) Street, Upper Holloway, built 1852, and may have originated in mtgs. at no. 2 John Street in 1848.[66] Reorganized 1880, still at Wedmore Street 1884,[67] but moved to Zoar Bapt. chapel, Tollington Pk., by 1888.[68] Joined Met. Strict Bapt. Assoc. Attendance 1903: 19 a.m.; 26 p.m. Seated 200 in 1928, renamed Strict Bapt. by 1954, closed 1959; Zoar Bapt. ch., Tollington Pk., reg. on same date; closed by 1971.[69]

Park Ho. sch. room, St. George's Terr., Barnsbury Pk., reg. by Gen. Bapts. 1852; disused by 1876.[70]

Eliatha chapel, William Street North (later Pembroke Street), Caledonian Rd., reg. by Bapts. 1853; became a Brethren chapel by 1855.[71]

Salem chapel, centre of Wilton Sq., leased 1853 to Bapts. under Rob. Dunning, who had met in Dorchester Pl., Hoxton, 1845.[72] Wm. Flack min. from 1857. Reorganized 1866. Joined

[39] G.R.O. Worship Reg. no. 39577.
[40] P.O. Dir. Lond. (1947, 1952).
[41] Guildhall MS. 9580/7, p. 120.
[42] Mearns, Cong. Chs.; P.R.O., HO 129/10/1/1/14.
[43] Ibid. 129/10/1/1/19.
[44] Ibid. 129/10/2/1/14.
[45] G.R.O. Worship Reg. no. 14535.
[46] Ibid. no. 26228.
[47] Mearns, Cong. Chs.
[48] Mudie-Smith, Rel. Life, 172; G.R.O. Worship Reg. nos. 57631, 61941.
[49] Nelson, Islington, 73.
[50] J. J. Graham, Cent. of Methodism at King's Cross Wes. Ch. (1923), 20, 28.
[51] Lewis, Islington, 394.
[52] Guildhall MS. 9580/5; 6, p. 266.
[53] Ibid. 9580/6, p. 312; 7, p. 34.
[54] W. T. Whitley, Bapts. of Lond. (1928), 164.
[55] P.R.O., HO 129/10/1/1/16.
[56] Inf. from ch. sec.; Coull, Islington, 123.
[57] G.R.O. Worship Reg. no. 1; P.R.O., C 54/14550, no. 15.
[58] Whitley, Bapts. of Lond. 164; P.R.O., C 54/15744, no. 1; G.R.O. Worship Reg. no. 26156.
[59] Whitley, op. cit. 284.
[60] Inf. from ch. sec.; Cross Street Bapt. Ch. Year Bk. 1957–8 (copy in Islington libr.).
[61] Whitley, op. cit. 172; P.R.O., HO 129/10/1/1/17.
[62] Guildhall MS. 9580/9, p. 33. Para. based on Whitley, op. cit. 175; Remembering All the Way (centenary booklet 1950, in Islington libr.).
[63] Guildhall MS. 9580/9, p. 42.
[64] P.R.O., HO 129/10/2/1/16.
[65] G.R.O. Worship Reg. no. 19401.
[66] Ibid. no. 369; Whitley, Bapts. of Lond. 178; Guildhall MS. 9580/9, p. 2. [67] N. Suburbs Dir. (1884).
[68] Whitley, Bapts. of Lond. 178; G.R.O. Worship Reg. no. 31118.
[69] G.R.O. Worship Reg. nos. 31118, 67228.
[70] Ibid. no. 395. [71] Ibid. no. 877; below, Brethren.
[72] Para. based on Whitley, Bapts. of Lond. 169; G.L.R.O., P83/MRY1/119/1. Chapel reg. by Inds. 1852, but prob. an error: G.R.O. Worship Reg. no. 38.

Lond. Bapt. Assoc. for a while, then Met. Strict Bapt. Assoc. Attendance 1903: 37 a.m.; 62 p.m. Disbanded 1913. Lease of chapel assigned to vicar of Islington 1925. Demolished by 1981.

Camden Rd. chapel, corner of Ramsbury (later Camden) and Hilldrop roads, built 1853–4 by Bapt. Met. Chap. Bldg. Soc. for Particular Bapts.[73] Bldg. of Kentish rag by C. G. Searle in Perpendicular style, entrance flanked by octagonal towers; seated 700. Galleries added 1859, besides hall, vestries, classrooms.[74] Seated 1,050 in 1928. Joined Lond. Bapt. Assoc. by 1884.[75] Attendance 1903: 319 a.m.; 275 p.m.[76] Migration to outer suburbs from c. 1900 seriously reduced nos. Some increase 1926–32. Missions at Belle Isle (q.v.) 1870; Fakenham Street 1884, moved to Goodinge Street near Met. market same year and hall built; served by Lond. City Mission. Attendance 1903: 26 p.m. Closed 1919 and hall let to Salvation Army. Preaching in George's Rd. and no. 134 Holloway Rd. 1884.[77]

Highbury Hill Bapt. ch. originated in mtg. 1862 to form ch. on Highbury Hill. Chapel at corner of Highbury Hill and Aubert Pk. reg. 1862, disused by 1866; ch. met 1864 at Barnsbury hall, Upper Street, but extinct 1867.[78] New ch. formed 1871 under auspices of Lond. Bapt. Assoc. and met at Thornhill hall, Lower Holloway. Chapel built 1870–1 on Highbury Hill site and reg. by Particular Bapts.[79] Vestries and classrooms added by 1901.[80] Seated 1,060 in 1928.[81] Attendance 1903: 416 a.m.; 302 p.m. Chapel, severely damaged by 1952,[82] demol. 1959. Missions at Gillespie Rd. (q.v.) 1880s, Riversdale Rd. 1892.[83]

Salters' Hall chapel, formed in Cong. chapel, Baxter Rd., Essex Rd., bought 1864 by Particular Bapts. who had worshipped in bldg. in Oxford Ct. (Cannon Street, Lond.), formerly used by Presbs. from Salters' Hall. Seated 850 in 1928. Later joined Bapt. Union.[84] Attendance 1903: 285 a.m.; 472 p.m. Joined by Dalston Bapt. ch. from Ashwin Street, Hackney, 1967 to form Dalston and Salters' Hall Bapt. ch. Closed 1980 owing to dilapidation. Thereafter svces. in hall of St. Paul's C.E. ch. Maintained Sun. sch. and Girls' Brigade in German Lutheran ch., Ritson Rd., Hackney, until 1982.[85]

Ebenezer chapel, Birkbeck (later Elthorne) Rd., Upper Holloway, reg. 1864 by Particular Bapts.,[86] who may have reg. Newbury Ho., Hornsey Rise, 1864–8.[87] Member of Met. Strict Bapt. Assoc. until c. 1916. Seated 350 in 1928.[88]

Attendance 1903: 67 a.m.; 45 p.m. Closed by 1954.

Bethel chapel, Lavina Grove, King's Cross, opened 1865 by Joseph Thrift to replace that in Chapel Street, St. Pancras. Affiliated to Ampton Street chapel in St. Pancras c. 1885. Seated 80.[89] Attendance 1903: 53 p.m. Closed between 1927 and 1934.

Upper Holloway Bapt. ch., Holloway Rd., corner of Tollington Way, first ch. built with aid of new Lond. Bapt. Assoc. c. 1866–8; supported by Camden Rd. Bapt. ch. until self supporting.[90] Attendance 1903: 714 a.m.; 1,143 p.m. Entrance vestibule enlarged c. 1911, giving extra seating in gallery. Hall and rooms at rear provided when former brewer's yard roofed over c. 1926.[91] Seated 1,300 in 1928.[92] Ceiling of ch. collapsed c. 1977, and hall at rear seating c. 100 used for most svces. 1982; hall seating 250 used for larger mtgs.[93] Mission at Rupert Rd., Upper Holloway, from 1878;[94] attendance 1903: 55 a.m.; 145 p.m.

Hampden hall, Hampden Rd., Upper Holloway, reg. 1866, disused by 1896,[95] was probably the Free Bapt. mtg. ho. built 1866 at expense of a working man.[96]

Bapt. mtg. in Holloway Rd. under W. Durban 1866, gone 1873.[97]

Bapt. mtg. in Richmond Street, Caledonian Rd., 1867, moved to Thornhill hall, Barnsbury, 1872. Declined 1878, reconstructed 1881, but disappeared by 1888.[98]

Bapt. mtg. in Royal Agricultural Hall reg. 1867 for unknown period.[99]

Belle Isle ch. originated in mission from Camden Rd. Bapt. ch. to serve populous area S. of Metropolitan market; Sun. sch. in loft over cowshed. Hall built 1870 under deacon from Camden Rd. Separate ch. 1877 at Co-operative hall, Copenhagen Street. Moved to Brewery Rd. 1878 as Belle Isle mission chapel, seating 550 in 1928. Attendance 1903: 219 a.m.; 329 p.m. Bombed 1941; members returned to Camden Rd. ch. Opened branch in Blundell Street 1879, and may have run mission at Drovers' hall, North Rd.; attendance 1903: 119 p.m.[1]

Hornsey Rise Bapt. ch., Hazelville Rd., Upper Holloway, founded 1870 by Revd. F. M. Smith when site bought and iron chapel and Sun. sch. built. Permanent ch. built 1881, seating 500. Attendance 1903: 166 a.m.; 202 p.m. Owing to war damage and reduced membership inner ch. seating 70 built 1948 by boxing in centre pews;

[73] P.R.O., C 54/15880, no. 6; Whitley, *Bapts. of Lond.* 180.
[74] Pevsner, *Lond.* ii. 229; *Souvenir of Cent. of Camden Rd. Bapt. Ch. 1854–1954* (copy in Islington libr.), p. 4; P.R.O., C 54/15880, no. 5.
[75] Whitley, *Bapts. of Lond.* 180, 291.
[76] Mudie-Smith, *Rel. Life*, 176 (St. Pancras).
[77] *Souvenir of Cent.* 5–11; Whitley, *Bapts. of Lond.* 231.
[78] Whitley, op. cit. 196; G.R.O. Worship Reg. no. 15229.
[79] Whitley, op. cit. 211; G.R.O. Worship Reg. no. 20461; Islington libr., Highbury Hill chapel, docs. found under foundation stone; Pevsner, *Lond.* ii. 230.
[80] G.R.O. Worship Reg. no. 38436.
[81] Whitley, *Bapts. of Lond.* 284.
[82] Pevsner, *Lond.* ii. 230.
[83] Whitley, op. cit. 211.
[84] P.R.O., C 54/16747, no. 11; G.R.O. Worship Reg. no. 16428; Whitley, op. cit. 158, 284.
[85] Inf. from min.
[86] Not Birkbeck Rd., Hackney, as in Whitley, *Bapts. of Lond.* 197; G.R.O. Worship Reg. no. 18491.
[87] G.R.O. Worship Reg. no. 16595.
[88] Whitley, op. cit. 197.
[89] Ibid. 140, 284; G.R.O. Worship Reg. no. 16888.
[90] P.R.O., C 54/16978, no. 7; Whitley, op. cit. 206; inf. from ch. sec.
[91] Inf. from ch. sec.
[92] Whitley, op. cit. 284.
[93] Inf. from ch. sec.
[94] Whitley, op. cit. 223.
[95] G.R.O. Worship Reg. no. 17487.
[96] *Islington Gaz.* 15 May 1866.
[97] Whitley, op. cit. 200.
[98] Ibid. 202.
[99] G.R.O. Worship Reg. no. 17832.
[1] Whitley, *Bapts. of Lond.* 221, 284; *Souvenir of Cent. of Camden Rd. Ch.* (copy in Islington libr.), pp. 5, 17.

main ch. still used in summer. Forty-six members in 1895; 200 in 1931; 36 in 1982.[2]

Ebenezer Bapt. chapel, Britannia Row, Essex Rd., opened 1872 under Jabez Whitteridge. Closed 1877 when he left and went with members first to Philip Street, then built chapel in Gillespie Rd., Highbury Vale, 1878. Closed when Whitteridge left, 1886.[3]

Bapt. mtg. in Fonthill Rd., Seven Sisters Rd., 1875, gone by 1888.[4]

Ebenezer chapel, Caledonian Rd., organized 1876; closed c. 1887.[5]

Bapt. mission room, no. 8 Cornelia Street, Barnsbury, reg. 1886, closed by 1896.[6]

Providence hall, Providence Pl., a Bapt. chapel until 1888, reg. by Ind. Bapts. 1900, closed 1912.[7] Attendance 1903: 63 a.m.; 78 p.m.

Tollington Pk. Bapt. ch. originated in ch. formed 1893 in Hornsey Rd. under Edwin Smart.[8] Attendance 1903: 70 a.m.; 146 p.m. Replaced by Spurgeon Memorial Bapt. chapel, Pine Grove, Tollington Pk., reg. 1909.[9] Seated 450 in 1928.[10] Replaced by concrete bldg. built in front, possibly 1969 when name amended to ch. Renamed Tollington Park Bapt. ch. in 1970s. Affiliated to Fellowship of Ind. Evangelical Chs. 1971.[11]

Free Bapts. reg. the former Arundel Sq. Cong. ch., Westbourne Rd., 1931; closed 1935.[12]

SEVENTH DAY BAPTISTS. Ch. formerly mtg. at Mill Yard, Leman Street, Whitechapel, 1691 to 1885, used Mornington hall, Canonbury Lane, by 1911, sharing it with Christadelphians. Only surviving group in Lond., with 20–30 members 1914. Possibly same as group using no. 105 Seven Sisters Rd. by 1935.[13]

METHODISTS.[14] Wes. Trinity chapel, S. end of Maiden Lane (later York Way), by 1807 had 57 members; moved to new Battle Bridge chapel, Birkenhead Street, St. Pancras, 1825.[15]

Hornsey Rd. chapel founded by Wes. from City Rd., creating first soc. in N. Lond.[16] Svces. first in ho. of Chas. Broad, Duval's Lane (later Hornsey Rd.), 1811,[17] and Broad gave adjacent site for chapel E. side of Hornsey Rd. (N. of Seven Sisters Rd.).[18] Small nearly square bldg. of old Meth. type opened 1821. Part of 1st Lond.-City Rd. circuit until 1843, when part of new 8th

Lond.-Islington circuit. Seated 180 in 1851; attendance: 170 a.m.; 80 evg.[19] Chapel rebuilt, seating 700, on enlarged site 1858. Grey Kent stone bldg. with Bath stone dressings, by Mr. Trimen in 16th-cent. style; twin towers and two entrances at front.[20] Head of new Highgate circuit 1873.[21] By 1880s local poverty led to soc. receiving grants instead of giving to other areas as formerly. New chapels reduced nos., but mission work carried on in Andover Rd. from c. 1876, replaced by Alsen Rd. from c. 1881, and Hampden Rd. Became circuit mission 1898. Attendance 1886: 425 a.m.; 450 evg.; 1903: 201 a.m.; 407 p.m. Closed 1940; demol. 1960 for new police stn.[22]

Eliz. Emmins's sch., Norfolk Pl., adjoining no. 6 New Norfolk Street (later Ecclesbourne Rd.), used for Wes. worship 1822.[23] Chapel built in New Norfolk Street reg. 1829 and sold to Anglicans c. 1837.[24]

No. 5 Medlands Rents, Islington, reg. for Wes. worship 1823.[25]

Liverpool Rd. chapel, corner of Barford Street, built 1825 on site bought by Ric. Barford, member of City Rd. chapel, and opened 1826 by Wes. who had met in his wareho. nearby,[26] and before that at preaching station and Sun. sch. in butcher's shop, White Lion Street, in Clerkenwell.[27] Bldg. in neo-classical style, seating c. 950;[28] adjoining sch. in Barford Street added 1834.[29] Enlarged 1844, mainly with aid of Geo. Chubb, inventor of patent lock.[30] Rebuilt 1849 after fire,[31] in Decorated style by Jas. Wilson.[32] Seated 1,506 in 1851; attendance: 786 a.m.; 200 aft.; 674 evg., but said to average 1,100 a.m.; 1,200 evg.[33] Formed part of Wes. Lond. Central Mission from 1880s. Attendance 1903: 267 a.m.; 364 p.m. Chapel closed 1929, and work transferred to Highbury (q.v.). Bldg. bought by Royal Agricultural Hall Co. and demol. as site for New hall.[34]

Meth. New Connexion first met in Islington 1834 at ho. of Henry Webber, Sidney Street, off City Rd.[35] Soc. continued to meet in Shoreditch until dissolved 1852 for lack of suitable place; members met in private hos. Min. of Lond. circuit organized bldg. of Britannia Fields chapel 1854, at junction of Packington and Arlington streets, with aid from Josiah Bates and Ric. Barford, who had left Wes. Meths.[36] Brick bldg.

[2] Inf. from ch. sec.; Whitley, *Bapts. of Lond.* 209, 284.
[3] Whitley, op. cit. 213, 223; G.R.O. Worship Reg. no. 20772.
[4] Whitley, op.cit. 217.   [5] Ibid. 219.
[6] G.R.O. Worship Reg. no. 29349.
[7] Ibid. no. 37800.
[8] Whitley, *Bapts. of Lond.* 242.
[9] G.R.O. Worship Reg. no. 44024.
[10] Whitley, op. cit. 284.
[11] G.R.O. Worship Reg. no. 44024; Fellowship of Ind. Evang. Chs. *Handbk.* (1977), 9.
[12] G.R.O. Worship Reg. no. 53364; above, Congs.
[13] Harris and Bryant, *Chs. and Lond.* 290–1; *P.O. Dir. Lond.* (1911, 1935).
[14] The help of Mr. John S. Ellis in providing many refs. for this subsection is gratefully acknowledged.
[15] Graham, *Cent. of Methodism at King's Cross Wes. Ch.* 20, 28.
[16] Para. based on *One Hundred Years in Hornsey Rd. 1821–1921* (centenary souvenir in Islington libr.).
[17] Guildhall MS. 9580/3: reg. as 'Independent'.
[18] P.R.O., C 54/10443, no. 3.

[19] Ibid. HO 129/10/2/1/8.
[20] Ibid. C 54/15349, no. 2; *Illus. News of the World*, 9 Oct. 1858.   [21] Inf. from Mr. Ellis.
[22] Ibid.   [23] Guildhall MS. 9580/5.
[24] Ibid. 6, p. 228; P.R.O., C 54/11851, no. 7; ibid. HO 129/10/2/1/2; above, chs. (St. Mat.).
[25] Guildhall MS. 9580/5.
[26] Ibid. 6, p. 20; P.R.O., C 54/10340, no. 10.
[27] *This Is Mildmay* (centenary souvenir 1962, in Islington libr.), 3; E. C. Rayner, *Story of the Christian Community* (1909), 33.
[28] *Wes. Meth. Mag.* May 1826, p. 340.
[29] Guildhall MS. 9580/7, p. 231.
[30] Coull, *Islington*, 120.
[31] P.R.O., C 54/13791, no. 2.
[32] Inf. from Mr. Ellis.   [33] P.R.O., HO 129/10/1/1/8.
[34] E. H. Smith, *Short Story of Albany Mission* (1961), 7; 'Royal Agric. Hall' (hist. compiled by Eliz. Ledster c. 1976, in Islington libr.).
[35] Para. based on *Great the Heritage: 1854–1954* (Meth. ch., Packington Street, booklet in Islington libr.).
[36] P.R.O., C 54/14673, no. 8; inf. from Mr. Ellis.

with stone dressings in early Gothic style by J. McLansborough, with pinnacles at front corners, sch. room underneath. William Booth min. 1854–61 while young probationer; drew large nos. and gave firm foundation to evangelism. Allowed to use chapel for svces. of Salvation Army formed after he had left Connexion. Attendance 1903: 92 a.m.; 146 p.m. Nos. declined in early 20th cent. due to migration out of area, and chapel kept going by Connexion's Home Missions dept. Became part of Utd. Meth. Ch. 1907; in 1909, as Packington Street ch., belonged to Hackney circuit. New hall at rear 1932. Membership declined after Second World War, when neighbourhood rebuilt. Closed 1964 and demol.[37] Mission in Penton Street, in Clerkenwell, closed 1917.

Wes. chapel in gdn. of no. 2 George's Pl. (later Rd.), Lower Holloway, built 1837.[38] Seated 134 in 1851; attendance: 65 a.m.; 28 aft.; 50 evg.[39] Closed 1857, and leased to Soc. of Friends;[40] 31 members transferred to new Highbury chapel (q.v.).

Rob. Stodhart's sch. in Providence Pl. reg. 1838, for Calvinistic Meths. of Ctss. of Huntingdon's Connexion.[41] Known as Islington tabernacle by 1845.[42] Connexion still there 1850,[43] but in 1851 said to be Ind. chapel, part converted, part built c. 1846, seating c. 150. Attendance 1851: c. 50 a.m.; c. 30 evg.[44] Taken over by Strict Bapts. 1853.[45] Chapel and sch. N. side of Charlotte (later Carnegie) Street, Caledonian Rd., built by Wes. Meth. Assoc. 1841.[46] Seated 325 in 1851; attendance: 272 a.m.; 132 evg.[47] Joined Utd. Meth. Free Ch. 1857; Utd. Meth. Ch. 1907.[48] Attendance 1903: 186 a.m.; 431 p.m. Also known as King's Cross mission by 1927.[49] Destroyed by land mine 1941. Members met in temp. premises, including Caledonian Rd. Liberal club, but joined King's Cross Meth. ch., Birkenhead Street, in St. Pancras, 1960.[50]

No. 4 Wilson Street, Barnsbury Pk., and no. 3 York Pl., Belle Isle, Maiden Lane (later York Way), used for Wes. mtgs. 1843.[51]

Bethel chapel at corner of Wilton Sq. and Wilton Pl. built by Welsh Calvinistic Meths. 1853; rebuilt 1884.[52] Seated 400 c. 1894.[53] Attendance 1903: 95 a.m.; 232 p.m. Sect became Presb. Ch. of Wales 1933. Chapel closed between 1947 and 1953; restored as hostel 1955 by St. Vincent's Housing Assoc.[54]

Providence chapel, Hornsey Rd. (no. 1 Hooper Street), reg. by Primitive Meths. 1854;[55] closed by 1857.[56]

Frog Lane (later Popham Rd.) chapel, S. side at corner of south (later Basire) Street, built by Primitive Meths. 1854–5 who had met in rented room for several years. Built with aid from Jas. Staley; first chapel built by Primitive Meths. in Lond.; 52 new members in first year. Attendance 1886: 92 a.m.; 162 evg. Closed 1897.[57]

Chapel in Clayton (later Tilloch) Street, Caledonian Rd., said to be part of Meth. New Connexion 2nd Lond. circuit 1856. Nothing further known.[58]

Highbury Wes. chapel, Drayton Pk., founded by members of Liverpool Rd. chapel, because George's Pl. chapel insufficient.[59] Thirty-one members transferred from George's Pl., 31 from Liverpool Rd. Bldg., with aid from Fras. (later Sir Fras.) Lycett, in Gothic style by Chas. Law 1857: Kentish rag with Bath stone dressings, seating 1,023. Day schs. built 1864. Part of Wes. Lond. Central Mission from 1880s. Attendance 1903: 139 a.m.; 195 p.m. Closed 1930.[60]

Islington Central hall, built 1929 on site of schs. at corner of Drayton Pk. and Horsell Rd. to replace Highbury Wes. chapel.[61] United with Liverpool Rd. soc. Large two-tier auditorium seating 1,300.[62] First min. Donald (later Lord) Soper, 1929–36, drew large congs. and provided social functions for unemployed.[63] Closed 1953 owing to heavy maintenance costs; let for ind. use, stood empty 1982. Work transferred to Albany mission, Albany Pl., Hornsey Rd., reg. 1954,[64] given by Smith fam. Closed 1961 for slum clearance, and svces. held in German Meth. mission until Islington Central Meth. ch. (q.v.), Palmers Pl., opened 1963.

Coffee ho. and dining rooms, no. 3 Whittington Terr., Upper Holloway, reg. for Wes. worship 1859;[65] closed by 1863.[66] Probably forerunner of Archway Rd. Wes. Meth. chapel (q.v.).

Primitive Meths. rented Market Street hall, Market Street, Caledonian Rd., 1860, St. George's hall, Richmond Rd., 1863, then hall in Hemingford Street, before Caledonian Rd. Primitive Meth. chapel built 1870 by S. gate of Met. market.[67] Part of 2nd Lond. circuit 1879.[68] Attendance 1903: 95 a.m.; 251 p.m. Became Caledonian Rd. Meth. ch. 1932.[69] Restored and reopened 1953; seated 375 in 1955, 250 in 1972. Funds raised 1980 to clean exterior, revealing fine Italianate bldg. of buff and red brick.[70]

---

[37] *Meth. Recorder*, 19 Nov. 1964.
[38] Guildhall MS. 9580/7, p. 264; P.R.O., C 54/12081, no. 2.
[39] P.R.O., HO 129/10/1/1/10.
[40] Inf. from Mr. Ellis; W. Beck and T. F. Ball, *Lond. Friends Mtgs.* (1869), 264; below.
[41] Guildhall MS. 9580/8, p. 5.
[42] *P.O. Dir. Lond.* (1845).   [43] Ibid. (1850).
[44] P.R.O., HO 129/10/1/1/14.
[45] Above, Bapts., Providence chapel.
[46] P.R.O., C 54/13395, no. 17.
[47] Ibid. HO 129/10/1/1/9.
[48] G.R.O. Worship Reg. nos. 3559, 17911; *Churches and Churchgoers*, ed. R. Currie, A. Gilbert, L. Horsley (1977), 146.
[49] *P.O. Dir. Lond.* (1927).
[50] Inf. from Mr. Ellis.
[51] Guildhall MS. 9580/8, pp. 177, 184.
[52] P.R.O., C 54/14833, no. 4; datestones.
[53] Inf. from Mr. Ellis.

[54] Ibid.; G.R.O. Worship Reg. no. 28933; *P.O. Dir. Lond.* (1947).   [55] G.R.O. Worship Reg. no. 5375.
[56] *P.O. Dir. Lond.* (1857).
[57] G.R.O. Worship Reg. no. 12774; P.R.O., C 54/15278, no. 9; *Prim. Meth. Mag.* Jan. 1855, p. 48; inf. from Mr. Ellis.
[58] *Great the Heritage*, 8.
[59] Para. based on P.R.O., C 54/15174, no. 2; C 54/16830, no. 1; L. Hale, *Highbury Methodism* (1924); inf. from Mr. Ellis.   [60] G.R.O. Worship Reg. no. 8103.
[61] Ibid. no. 52251. Rest of para. based on inf. from Mr. Ellis.
[62] E. H. Smith, *Albany Mission*, 7.
[63] W. Purcell, *Portrait of Soper* (1972), 65.
[64] G.R.O. Worship Reg. no. 64287.
[65] Ibid. no. 9015; inf. from Mr. Ellis.
[66] *P.O. Dir. Lond.* (1863).
[67] J. Vickers and B. Young, *Meth. Guide to Lond. and SE.* (1980), 25; inf. from Mr. Ellis.
[68] *P.O. Dir. Lond.* (1879).
[69] *Meth. Guide to Lond.* 25.   [70] Inf. from Mr. Ellis.

Elwood Street chapel, Highbury Vale, originated in Park Pl. chapel, no. 2 Park Pl. (later Conewood Street), reg. by Primitive Meths. 1861, but possibly in use 1859. Closed by 1863.[71] Perhaps used Workman's hall E. side of Highbury Vale by 1869 and mission hall at corner of Blackstock Rd. and Myrtle (later Hurlock) Street, from c. 1870,[72] before opening Elwood Street chapel, 1889, whose members had previously met in rented halls.[73] Attendance 1903: 45 a.m.; 42 p.m. New sch. built 1927; young people's ch. and sch. reg. 1929. Chapel and sch. closed 1951,[74] and sold to L.C.C. as site for flats.

Elder Walk Ragged sch. reg. for Wes. worship 1861; ceased by 1876.[75]

Mildmay Pk. Wes. chapel, next to no. 4 Mildmay Pk., founded by Fras. Lycett, Wm. Lamplough, and S. D. (later Judge) Waddy, built 1862, first to be aided by new Met. Wes. Chapel Bldg. Fund.[76] Seated 1,150; choir in front gallery over clock; pulpit against E. wall until organ installed 1866; communion space enlarged 1893. Apse at E. end and vestibule added 1912. Income largest of any Meth. chapel in Lond. 1875. Helped maintain mission chapel in Matthias Rd., in Stoke Newington. Attendance 1886: 329 a.m.; 492 evg.; 1903: 401 a.m.; 331 p.m. Migration to suburbs brought growing deficit 1930s and membership dwindled after Second World War. Closed 1964;[77] area later cleared for housing. Lecture hall and sch. built 1878 at rear, given up 1938. Ran Mildmay Wes. mission room, no. 44 Newington Green Rd., reg. 1891, closed 1912.[78]

Caledonian Rd. Wes. ch., at junction of Caledonian and Hillmarton rds., originated in svces. held by 1863 in sch. room, York Pl. (later St. Clement's Street), under a home missionary.[79] Ch. in Gothic style with lofty spire, seating 1,000, with sch. room below, built 1866 on site obtained with aid from Fras. Lycett.[80] Attendance 1903: 151 a.m.; 213 p.m. Closed 1916; used as furniture wareho. until taken over by Liberal Catholic Ch. 1926.[81]

Archway Central Hall, corner of Archway Rd. and St. John's Way, originated in iron Archway Rd. Wes. chapel, built 1864 in St. John's Rd., seating 200.[82] Outlying part of Islington (Liverpool Rd.) circuit. Founded by local Meths. formerly mtg. at no. 3 Whittington Terrace (q.v.) and recent migrants from inner suburbs. Permanent chapel and sch. built on adjoining site 1872–3: cruciform Romanesque bldg. of light brick with terracotta dressings, by

J. Johnson. Head of Highgate circuit 1873. Library started 1868. Attendance 1903: 442 a.m.; 373 p.m. Iron hall built 1933 in grounds of St. Mary's hosp. used until old ch. replaced[83] by last Central Hall to be built in Lond. 1934.[84] Main hall seating 1,300, lesser hall 300–400, with chapel, classrooms. Mission at no. 51 Vorley Rd. started 1884, ceased by 1896.[85]

Welsh Calvinistic Meth. chapel, Sussex Way, Holloway, built 1865, seating 500.[86] Attendance 1903: 74 a.m.; 220 p.m. Sect became Presb. Ch. of Wales 1933 and chapel renamed Holloway Welsh Presb. ch.[87]

No. 4 Bowmans Pl., Seven Sisters Rd., reg. as Wes. mtg. 1867; closed by 1876.[88]

Queensland Rd. Wes. mission started 1867 in room lent for purpose; 10 full members and 32 on trial 1868.[89] Hall leased in Queensland Rd., reg. 1873,[90] and lay missioner engaged. Part of Highbury circuit. Svces. transferred to Highbury Wes. day schs. 1882, and hall let to St. Barnabas's C.E. ch. Mission work transferred to Highbury chapel (q.v.).

Twyford hall Wes. mission, Twyford Street, Caledonian Rd., seating 200, opened 1872 as continuation of Penton Street mission, in Clerkenwell 1866–71. Attendance 1886: 45 a.m.; 160 evg. Closed 1890.[91]

Holly Pk. Meth. ch., Crouch Hill, opened by Wes. 1875 in iron chapel provided by Sir Fras. Lycett, who made large grant for permanent ch. built 1881–2 by Elijah Hoole, seating 650; clock tower and spire added 1910. Schs. and vestries built at rear 1886–7. Attendance 1903: 287 a.m.; 252 p.m. Ch. replaced by one of buff brick, by Mic. Pipe, seating 192, opened 1961. Rest of site used for block of flats. Mission at Weston Pk., Hornsey Vale, in Hornsey, c. 1882–1912.[92]

Primitive Meth. chapel, Anatola Rd., Dartmouth Pk. Hill, reg. 1877.[93] Larger chapel and sch. built 1883.[94] Attendance 1886: 140 a.m.; 167 evg.; 1903: 142 a.m.; 165 p.m. Closed 1936 after Archway Central Hall opened.[95]

Primitive Meth. chapel, Durham Rd., Seven Sisters Rd., reg. 1877. Attendance 1903: 67 a.m.; 58 p.m. Closed 1917.[96]

Gillespie Rd. Wes. chapel, Highbury Vale, founded 1878 by members of Finsbury Pk. or Wilberforce Rd. chapel in Hornsey.[97] May have held svces. in former Primitive Meth. chapel, E. side of Highbury Vale, 1876–8.[98] Attendance 1903: 119 a.m.; 91 p.m. Closed c. 1933 and soc. joined Elwood Street chapel.[99]

Ind. Meth. chapel in Windsor Street, Essex

[71] Inf. from Mr. Ellis; G.R.O. Worship Reg. no. 12772; *P.O. Dir. Lond.* (1863).
[72] *Islington Dir.* (1870 and later edns.).
[73] Inf. from Mr. Ellis.
[74] G.R.O. Worship Reg. nos. 38426, 50805.
[75] Ibid. no. 12078.
[76] Para. based on *This Is Mildmay*.
[77] G.R.O. Worship Reg. no. 15349.   [78] Ibid. no. 32590.
[79] L. Hale, *Highbury Methodism*, cap. 3.
[80] P.R.O., C 54/16844, no. 6; *2nd Rep. Met. Wes. Chapel Bldg. Fund* (1869).
[81] G.R.O. Worship Reg. no. 17324; *Westm. Gaz.* 28 Oct. 1926; Hale, *Highbury Methodism*, cap. 4; below, Lib. Cath. Ch.
[82] Para. based on 'Archway Meth. Centenary 1864–1964' (TS. booklet in Islington libr.); G.R.O. Worship Reg. no. 16462.

[83] G.R.O. Worship Reg. nos. 22170, 54730.
[84] Ibid. no. 55587; *Meth. Guide to Lond.* 26.
[85] G.R.O. Worship Reg. no. 28101.
[86] Inf. from min.
[87] *Chs. and Churchgoers*, 152; G.R.O. Worship Reg. no. 27105.
[88] G.R.O. Worship Reg. no. 18200.
[89] Para. based on Hale, *Highbury Methodism*, cap. 4.
[90] G.R.O. Worship Reg. no. 21222.
[91] Inf. from Mr. Ellis.
[92] *Meth. Recorder*, 7 Dec. 1905, 9 Feb. 1911; inf. from Mr. Ellis.   [93] G.R.O. Worship Reg. no. 23234.
[94] *Prim. Meth. Mag.* Mar. 1883, p. 188.
[95] *Islington Gaz.* 21 Aug. 1936.
[96] G.R.O. Worship Reg. no. 23660.
[97] *V.C.H. Mdx.* vi. 186.
[98] Above, Park Pl.   [99] Inf. from Mr. Ellis.

Rd., reg. 1879.[1] May have become Windsor hall Wes. mission, founded c. 1866 and attached to Liverpool Rd. chapel by 1887.[2] Hall between nos. 12 and 14 Windsor Street. Attendance 1903: 53 a.m.; 57 p.m. Windsor hall reg. at no. 6, 1906; closed by 1935.[3]

Primitive Meth. mission hall, Story Street, Caledonian Rd., reg. 1882; closed by 1896.[4]

Primitive Meth. mtg. at Jubilee Ho., ho. 473 Hornsey Rd., 1887,[5] reg. Hornsey Rise mission at no. 21 Station Parade, Hornsey Rise, 1901. Attendance 1903: 44 a.m.; 103 p.m. Replaced 1908 with chapel built at no. 425 Hornsey Rd. Closed 1930,[6] and taken over by Spiritualists.

German Wes. Meth. mission, no. 10A (later 30) Drayton Pk., founded at Spitalfields 1864, moved from Bateman Street in Westm. 1929, with membership of c. 100. Premises included mtg. rooms, flat for min., and rooms for mission home. Svces. held without min. during Second World War, until new min. sent from Germany 1948. Small hostel for young German speakers opened c. 1951. Moved to King's Cross Meth. mission, Birkenhead Street, in St. Pancras, 1971.[7]

Meth. chapel in Nat. Children's Home and Orphanage, no. 85 Highbury Pk., reg. 1935. Became interdenominational 1954.[8]

Islington Central Meth. ch., Palmer Pl., Holloway, built 1962-3 with aid from Joseph Rank Benevolent Trust and Lond. Mission and Dept. for Chapel Affairs, to continue work of Albany mission and Liverpool Rd. and Drayton Pk. chs. Seats 170. Part of premises used by Islington Bus Co. (community char.), 1982.[9]

PRESBYTERIANS. Islington Presb. ch., River Terr. (later Colebrooke Row), also known as Scotch ch., built 1834 to replace chapel in Chadwell Street, Clerkenwell, in Presb. Synod of Eng. in connexion with Ch. of Scotland. Became identified with Free Ch. of Scotland, formed 1843; later part of Presb. Ch. of Eng., formed 1876. Bldg. in Early Eng. style, with three pinnacles on front, seating 630 including gallery. Enlarged after members increased from 70 to 340, seatholders from 121 to 1,063, 1844-7, and sch. room added.[10] Seated 1,000 in 1851; attendance: 640 a.m.; 498 evg.; 433 communicants on roll.[11] Nos. fell then rose again 1862-91 under Revd. J. Thain Davidson, who held svces. in Berner's hall, 1868, Royal Agric. Hall, and St. Mary's hall, sometimes for 3,000; organized many interdenominational mission svces. in

Evangelical revival of 1860s and 1870s. Svces. also in Wilmington mission. Attendance 1903: 254 a.m.; 429 p.m. Svces. in St. Peter's schs. owing to condition of ch.; members disbanded 1923 and bldgs. sold.[12]

Colebrooke Row chapel, no. 1 Colebrooke Row, reg. by Rob. Simpson, min. of Utd. Secession Ch. of Scotland, 1834. Nothing further known.[13]

South Street chapel, seating 150, said to be Presb. in 1838,[14] possibly former Bapt. chapel.

Caledonian ch., Holloway Rd., see below, Est. Ch. of Scotland.

Caledonian Rd. Presb. ch., just N. of Brewery Rd., built by 1855 in terrace, designed by John Barnett & Birch. Closed by 1868, when transferred to trustees of Bp. of Lond.'s Fund and opened as St. Matthias's C.E. ch.[15]

Trinity Presb. ch., Church (later North Church) Rd., Southgate Rd., originated as old Scots ch. mtg. at Founders' Hall from 1672 and London Wall from 1764. Moved to Islington 1857 on expiry of lease. Ch. and manse opened 1858; lecture hall added 1880s. Nos. declined in 1890s to almost nothing; served by missioner 1897-9. John Kerr Craig's ministry 1899-1910 increased membership again. Attendance 1903: 77 a.m.; 149 p.m. Closed between 1934 and 1942.[16]

Park ch., Grosvenor Ave., Highbury, built after Scotch cong. at Myddelton Hall, Upper Street, increased under Revd. John Edmond.[17] One of three Utd. Presb. chs. in Lond. founded with aid of John Henderson of Renfrewshire.[18] Later part of Presb. Ch. of Eng., formed 1876.[19] White brick bldg. 1861-3, by E. Habershon, seating 1,200. Only façade remained 1952: neo-Hawksmoor type with low portico, SW. tower Italianate but with spire.[20] Lecture hall added by 1901.[21] Attendance 1903: 204 a.m.; 159 p.m. Membership over 400 c. 1870,[22] 169 in 1927, 94 in 1937.[23] As dist. had no poor, ch. supported City missioner in Hoxton by 1870, with Sun. and day schs. in Harvey Street and Albert Sq., Hoxton, in Shoreditch.[24] Ch. closed c. 1950.[25]

Crouch Hill Presb. ch., Holly Pk., originated in iron ch. built by cttee. in Finsbury Pk. area, formed 1873.[26] Site bought with help of Mr., later Sir Geo., Bunce. Lecture hall and vestries built 1876; svces. in hall, seating 320, until permanent ch. opened 1878. Brick bldg. with stone dressings in Gothic style, seating 620; three-stage corner tower with short spire. Enlarged, seating 830 by 1885. New hall for over 500 and other rooms behind ch. begun 1889.

[1] G.R.O. Worship Reg. no. 24808.
[2] Islington Gaz. 27 Apr. 1887.
[3] G.R.O. Worship Reg. no. 41929.
[4] Ibid. no. 26275.   [5] Inf. from Mr. Ellis.
[6] Ibid.; G.R.O. Worship Reg. nos. 38463, 43198.
[7] Hundred Years of Meth. German Mission in Lond. 1864-1964 (per Mr. Ellis); G.R.O. Worship Reg. no. 52244.
[8] G.R.O. Worship Reg. no. 56229; above, growth, Highbury.
[9] G.R.O. Worship Reg. no. 69164; inf. from Mr. Ellis; above, social.
[10] Islington Presb. Ch. Souvenir Programme (1908, copy in Islington libr.); Lewis, Islington, 364-5; Guildhall MS. 9580/7, p. 275; Rep. of Bldg. Cttee., Scotch Ch., 1833-4 (in Islington libr.).
[11] P.R.O., HO 129/10/2/1/17.
[12] Islington Presb. Ch. Souv.; Jnl. Presb. Hist. Soc. of Eng. ii, no. 4 (1923), 207-8, 211; below, missions.
[13] Guildhall MS. 9580/7, p. 135.

[14] Lond. City Mission Mag. iii. 104.
[15] G.R.O. Worship Reg. no. 6676; P.R.O., C 54/15734, no. 14; C 54/16887, no. 9; Clarke, Lond. Chs. 93; above, churches.
[16] Jnl. Presb. Hist. Soc. of Eng. i (1914-19), 88-9, 115, 185-6; G.R.O. Worship Reg. no. 8605; P.O. Dir. Lond. (1934, 1942).
[17] J. E. Ritchie, Rel. Life of Lond. (1870), 139.
[18] P.R.O., C 54/16352, no. 4.
[19] G.R.O. Worship Reg. no. 23369.
[20] Pevsner, Lond. ii. 230; Ritchie, Rel. Life of Lond. 139-40.   [21] G.R.O. Worship Reg. no. 38459.
[22] Ritchie, Rel. Life of Lond. 140.
[23] Presb. Ch. of Eng., Park Ch. Ann. Rep. (1927-37, copy in Islington libr.).
[24] Ibid.; Ritchie, Rel. Life of Lond. 141.
[25] P.O. Dir. Lond. (1947, 1952).
[26] Para. based on J. Menzies, Story of Crouch Hill Presb. Ch. 1876-1926 (jubilee pamphlet, 1926), 3-6, 8-9, 12.

Attendance 1903: 780 a.m.; 774 p.m. Closed 1975[27] and bldg. demol. Mission at Andover Rd. established 1884; hall, no. 61, reg. 1898.[28] Attendance 1903: 135 a.m.; 315 p.m. Closed by 1954.

Thrift hall, Grovedale Rd., Upper Holloway, reg. 1901. Attendance 1903: 97 a.m.; 40 p.m. Closed 1913 and bldg. used by Spiritualists.[29]

Mission hall, Elthorne Rd., Upper Holloway, reg. 1929; closed by 1954.[30]

CATHOLIC APOSTOLIC (IRVINGITES). Revd. Edw. Irving, after expulsion from National Scotch Ch. 1832, preached in the open in Britannia Fields and other parts of Islington. Ch. in Duncan Street built 1834 by Duncan Mackenzie of Barnsbury Pk., former elder at Irving's Regent Sq. Scotch ch. and one of 12 Apostles of Catholic Apostolic Ch. from 1835 to 1840. Designed and built by Messrs. Stevenson & Ramage of Theobalds Rd. in Holborn, seating 350 in 1835,[31] 300 in 1851.[32] Single-storeyed neo-classical bldg. of brick with stone dressings, with recessed portico on two Ionic columns; N. end with coved semicircular recess with chairs for elders.[33] Attendance 1851: 234 a.m.; 171 aft.; 227 evg.[34] Attendance 1903: 200 a.m.; 124 p.m. Closed between 1964 and 1975.

Catholic Apostolic ch., Gloucester (later Salterton) Rd., Holloway, in use by 1880.[35] Attendance 1903: 169 a.m.; 109 p.m. Moved to Tottenham 1906.[36]

BRETHREN. Room in yard of no. 24 Coles Terr., Barnsbury Rd., home of John Parnell, Baron Congleton, reg. 1843 for protestant dissenters, probably Brethren, as about that time Congleton furnished a fellowship room for Brethren who came from distant areas to Camden Town mtg. Congleton moved 1846.[37]

Pembroke Street (formerly William Street North) hall, Caledonian Rd., used by Brethren from 1853–5.[38] Attendance 1903: 23 a.m.; 43 p.m. Known as Eliatha chapel 1914. Closed c. 1948.[39]

The Priory, no. 198 Upper Street, in 1870s said to be one of three principal Brethren mtgs. in London.[40] Possibly moved to no. 57 Park Street (q.v.).

Park Street hall, no. 57 Islington Park Street, opened 1875.[41] Attendance 1903: 161 a.m.; 159 p.m. Endowment by Art. Jas. Chitty administered under Scheme of 1934.[42] Known as Brethren ch. 1982.

Archway assembly, no. 6A Junction Rd., founded c. 1880 when dancing academy hired on Sun. evgs. First communion svce. 1883. Premises later taken over completely,[43] reg. as Christian Assembly Hall, 1901.[44] Attendance 1903: 41 a.m.; 104 p.m. Premises taken for Archway Underground sta. c. 1907; cong. moved to Archway assembly hall, Hargrave Rd., reg. 1911, renamed Hargrave hall 1943.[45] Closed between 1975 and 1981.[46] Premises used by community centre 1981.

Finsbury Pk. room, behind no. 48 Blackstock Rd., reg. by Brethren 1885, cancelled 1901. Park hall, no. 48 Blackstock Rd., reg. 1901. Attendance 1903: 47 a.m.; 52 p.m. Still in use 1914. Used by Christadelphians from 1932.[47]

Canonbury hall, no. 96 Canonbury Rd., reg. 1902. Attendance 1903: 7 a.m.; 35 p.m. In use 1914. Closed by 1954.[48]

Barnsbury Rd. meeting, possibly at no. 70,[49] attendance 1903: 26 a.m.; 42 p.m. In use 1914. Barnsbury gospel hall, no. 10 Barnsbury Rd., reg. 1931, closed 1934.[50] Bethany hall, nos. 70–2 Barnsbury Rd., reg. 1934, closed 1976.[51]

Mtgs. also held 1903 at Terret's Pl. room, Upper Street, attendance: 39 a.m.; 33 p.m.; at Eversleigh Street hall, Tollington Pk., attendance: 27 a.m.; 35 p.m.; at Hazelville room, St. John's Rd., Upper Holloway, attendance: 123 a.m.; 114 p.m.; at Wedmore Street mtg. room, Upper Holloway, attendance: 11 a.m.; 25 p.m.; at Duncombe Rd., Upper Holloway, attendance: 12 a.m.; 25 p.m. All in use 1914 except Wedmore Street. Also used in 1914: Argyle hall, no. 105 Seven Sisters Rd.; no. 145 Holloway Rd.; Central hall, no. 102 Ball's Pond Rd.

Brethren meeting room, no. 93 Mildmay Pk., reg. 1930, closed by 1954.[52]

Mtg. room, no. 5A Drayton Pk., reg. 1932, closed by 1964.[53]

LATTER-DAY SAINTS. Latter-day Saints worshipped in basement of no. 3 Halton Pl., 1850, and schoolroom, no. 1 Cornwall Pl., Eden Grove, Holloway, 1851.[54]

Lecture hall, West Pl., Islington Green, reg. 1852; closed by 1876.[55]

Latter-day Saints chapel, Church Lane, behind no. 20 Church (later Gaskin) Street, reg. 1855; closed by 1876.[56]

Church of Jesus Christ of Latter-day Saints, no. 88A Archway Rd., reg. 1951, in former Highgate synagogue.[57]

[27] G.R.O. Worship Reg. no. 23361.
[28] Ibid. no. 36869.
[29] Ibid. no. 38479; below.
[30] G.R.O. Worship Reg. no. 51777.
[31] Lewis, *Islington*, 362–3; P.R.O., C 54/14229, no. 27; R. A. Davenport, *Albury Apostles* (1970), 76, 117, 146, 371.
[32] P.R.O., HO 129/10/2/1/18.
[33] Lewis, *Islington*, 362–3.
[34] P.R.O., HO 129/10/2/1/18.
[35] *N. Suburbs Dir.* (1880).
[36] G.R.O. Worship Reg. no. 32291; *V.C.H. Mdx.* v. 363.
[37] Guildhall MS. 9580/8, p. 183; H. H. Rowdon, *Origins of Brethren: 1825–50* (1967), 162; H. Groves, *Memoir of Ld. Congleton* (1884), 69–71.
[38] *P.O. Dir. Lond.* (1853, 1855).
[39] Ibid. (1948, 1949).
[40] C. M. Davies, *Unorthodox Lond.* (1876), 105.

[41] Inf. from trustee.
[42] Char. Com. files.
[43] D. J. Beattie, *Brethren: Story of a Great Recovery* [1939], 102.
[44] G.R.O. Worship Reg. no. 38493.
[45] Beattie, *Brethren*, 77; G.R.O. Worship Reg. nos. 44748, 60527.   [46] *P.O. Dir. Lond.* (1975).
[47] G.R.O. Worship Reg. no. 28923; below.
[48] G.R.O. Worship Reg. no. 39244.
[49] *P.O. Dir. Lond.* (1902).
[50] G.R.O. Worship Reg. no. 53225.
[51] Ibid. no. 55520.
[52] Ibid. no. 52626.   [53] Ibid. no. 53942.
[54] Guildhall MS. 9580/9, pp. 38, 91.
[55] G.R.O. Worship Reg. no. 583.
[56] Ibid. no. 6226.
[57] Ibid. no. 63187; below, Judaism.

CHURCH OF THE NEW JERUSALEM (SWEDEN-BORGIANS). Hen. Bateman of Islington and his children founded Emanuel Coll. 1845 to promote doctrines and prepare students for ministry. Coll. at first in care of New ch., Argyle Sq., St. Pancras, but Bateman purchased from Thos. Cubitt site in Devonshire Street (later Devonia Rd.), where chapel opened 1852, with residence above and schoolroom below in wing completed by 1854.[58] By 1867 completion of large central chapel and sch. left original wing for coll.[59] Attendance 1903: 32 a.m.; 57 p.m. Closed 1930 and bldgs. sold to Polish R.C. mission.[60]

New Jerusalem ch., Camden Rd., built 1873–4 to replace ch. in Cross Street, Hatton Gdn.[61] Svces. in adjacent Athenaeum, Camden Rd., while ch. being built. Gothic style with SW. tower and spire, lecture hall, sch. room. New entrance from Parkhurst Street and hall opened 1908, when ch. held largest colln. of New Ch. literature in Eng. Attendance 1903: 156 a.m.; 94 p.m. In 1924 had 206 members, 60 of them not resident in area. Lease expired 1952 and ch. closed 1954, later used by Islington Boys' club. Most members joined N. Finchley ch., offshoot of study circle started by Camden Rd.

SOCIETY OF FRIENDS. Holloway Preparative mtg., with c. 30 members, first met 1858 in former Wes. chapel, George's Pl. (later Rd.), Lower Holloway. Mtg. ho. in Mercer's Rd., Upper Holloway, built 1864: two-storeyed brick bldg. with stone dressings and central pediment. Large hall seating over 100. Libr. opened 1866; classroom, cloakrooms, with schoolroom over for large Sun. sch., added 1888. Bldg. accn. over 600. Membership, with movement out of City, rose from 1860s to c. 150 in 1880s and became one of largest in Westm. Monthly Mtg. 1880–95. Mission work at Quaker centre, Bunhill Fields. From 1900 membership declined with movement farther out. Attendance 1903: 36 a.m.; 27 p.m. Falling nos. and dilapidation led to sale 1938 and purchase of no. 404 Camden Rd., altered for mtgs., seating 70. In 1958 became an Allowed Mtg., too small to manage business functions, and attached to Muswell Hill Mtg.; bldg. sold to N. Lond. Soc. for Mentally Handicapped Children 1963, with reservation of room for Sun. mtgs. for 5 yrs., but mtgs. ceased by 1966.[62]

Worshipping group formed 1979 by wife of V. of St. David's C.E. ch., meeting at vicarage, no. 43 Eden Grove, Lower Holloway. Average attendance 12 in 1982.[63]

UNITARIANS. Unity ch., Upper Street, founded from Carter Lane, St. Paul's, since several members lived in Islington. Schs. and vestry built 1860 on former nursery ground; svces. in sch. until ch. opened 1862. Bldg. in Gothic style with spire, by T. Chatfeild Clarke, seating c. 500. Window to Jos. Chamberlain (d. 1837) and tablet to s. Jos. (d. 1874), grandfather and father of politician Jos., who was worshipper there. Attendance 1903: 64 a.m.; 75 p.m. Preston memorial rooms added 1906–7 next to sch. Ch. and sch. destroyed 1941 and plain bldg., by Kenneth Tayler, seating c. 100 and also used as hall, provided 1958 by War Damage Com. on site of sch., facing Florence Street. Site of ch. on Upper Street sold to adjoining fire station.[64]

Highgate Unitarian ch., Despard Rd., High-gate Hill, built 1885; sch. ho. opened 1885, ch. 1890.[65] Attendance 1903: 146 a.m.; 104 p.m. Closed 1962[66] and demol.

SANDEMANIANS (GLASITES). Mtg. ho. at corner of Barnsbury Grove and Bride Street used from 1862 when London ch., founded 1762 by Rob. Sandeman, moved from Paul's Alley, Barbican.[67] Simple bldg. of white brick seating c. 300; two rows of raised seats at far end for elders. Mic. Faraday (1791–1867), discoverer of electricity, an elder until 1864. Membership 118 in 1785, c. 100 in 1870s; mostly poor. Membership 34 in 1901, when mtg. moved to no. 3 Highbury Crescent.[68] Attendance 1903: 45 a.m.; 25 p.m. Possibly last remaining Sandemanian ch. in Eng., with 13 members and only 1 elder in 1982; thought unlikely to survive.

Seceders from Barnsbury Grove reg. Christian mtg. ho., no. 18 Albion (later Furlong) Rd., Holloway, 1886. Attendance 1903: 36 a.m.; 37 p.m. Ch. closed 1935.[69]

CHRISTADELPHIANS. Ecclesia of c. 50 members meeting in dancing academy, top of Gower Street, St. Pancras, moved early 1870s to Wellington hall, Wellington (later Almeida) Street.[70] Attendance 1903: 48 a.m.; 57 p.m.

Other mtgs. 1903 at Barnsbury Street hall, attendance: 54 a.m.; 44 p.m.; in use 1911;[71] Mornington hall, Canonbury Lane, attendance: 67 a.m.; 69 p.m.; in use 1914; Wortley hall, no. 242 Seven Sisters Rd., attendance: 55 a.m.; 73 p.m.; in use 1914.

Christadelphian hall, no. 48 Blackstock Rd., Finsbury Pk., formerly used by Brethren, reg. 1932.[72] In use 1982.

[58] P.R.O., C 54/14812, no. 2; G.R.O. Worship Reg. no. 192.

[59] G.R.O. Worship Reg. no. 18047.

[60] Above, Rom. Cathm.

[61] Para. based on Camden Rd. Soc. of New Ch. 1924–54; Jubilee of Camden Rd. Soc. 1924; Short Hist. Camden Rd. Soc. of New Jerusalem Ch. 1908 (booklets in B.L.); V.C.H. Mdx. vi. 91.

[62] C. A. Humpage Pryer, 'Quakers in Holloway: Hist. of Holloway Mtg. 1858–1966' (TS. 1975, copy in Friends' Libr., Euston Rd.); Beck and Ball, Lond. Friends' Mtgs. 264; G.R.O. Worship Reg. nos. 8623, 16444; P.R.O., C 54/16523, no. 19.

[63] Inf. from Mrs. Beth Allen.

[64] P.R.O., C 54/15749, no. 15; A. V. Fox, Christian Faith and Christian Freedom [1966] (tercentenary vol., in Islington

libr.); C. Titford, Hist. of Unity Ch. (1912); inf. from hon. treasurer.

[65] V.C.H. Mdx. vi. 188; G. E. Evans, Vestiges of Prot. Dissent (1897), 148. [66] G.R.O. Worship Reg. no. 32194.

[67] Para. based on inf. from Mr. E. S. Williams; S. P. Thompson, Mic. Faraday: Life and Work (1898), 286, 289, 294–5, 297; Davies, Unorthodox Lond. 171, 173; J. H. Gladstone, Mic. Faraday (1873), 36; W. Wilson, Hist. and Antiquities of Dissenting Chs. and Mtg. Hos. in Lond. iii (1810), 220, 233, 261, 365; Ritchie, Rel. Life of Lond. 314–16; Guildhall MS. 16938, f. 115.

[68] G.R.O. Worship Reg. no. 38592.

[69] Ibid. no. 29551; inf. from Mr. E. S. Williams.

[70] Davies, Unorthodox Lond. 142.

[71] P.O. Dir. Lond. (1911).

[72] G.R.O. Worship Reg. no. 53985.

BLUE RIBBON GOSPEL ARMY. Hall at no. 5A Northampton Pl., Holloway, reg. 1882, closed by 1896.[73] Duncombe Road chapel, Upper Holloway, reg. 1883, closed 1884.[74] No. 148 Holloway Rd. reg. 1886, closed 1912.[75]

SALVATION ARMY. Temperance hall, no. 134 Holloway Rd., reg. 1884, closed 1886.[76] Highbury hall, no. 65 Holloway Rd., reg. 1886, re-reg. 1888 as Salvation Army hall, no. 324 Holloway Rd.; closed by 1896.[77]

St. Mark's mission hall, no. 300 Hornsey Rd., reg. 1885. Renamed barracks 1892.[78] Attendance 1903: 18 a.m.; 64 p.m. Closed 1904.[79]

Barracks, no. 2 Salisbury Rd., Highgate Hill, reg. 1888, closed by 1896.[80]

Wellington Castle barracks, Almeida St., Upper St., reg. 1890; renamed citadel 1902.[81] Attendance 1903: 104 a.m.; 209 p.m. Closed 1959.[82]

Citadel, Ronald's Rd., Lower Holloway, reg. 1891.[83] Attendance 1903: 112 a.m.; 284 p.m. Replaced 1968 by citadel, no. 30 Junction Rd., Upper Holloway (q.v.).[84]

Barracks, no. 11 Elthorne Rd., Upper Holloway, reg. 1896, closed 1900.[85]

Barracks, no. 83 Ball's Pond Rd., reg. 1898. Attendance 1903 (at no. 81): 55 a.m.; 115 p.m.[86] Closed by 1911.[87]

Citadel, between nos. 30 and 32 Junction Rd., reg. 1899. Attendance 1903: 257 a.m.; 635 p.m. Closed 1965,[88] but reopened 1968 to replace citadel in Ronald's Rd. (q.v.).

Temperance hall, Church Passage, Upper St., used 1903; attendance: 39 a.m.; 56 p.m.

Finsbury Pk. hall, no. 6 Station Rd. and no. 225 Seven Sisters Rd., formerly used for svces. by Y.M.C.A., reg. 1903.[89] Attendance 1903: 55 a.m.; 164 p.m. Moved to barracks, no. 382 Hornsey Rd., Upper Holloway, 1904. Closed 1916.[90]

Hall, Cornelia St., Lower Holloway, reg. 1904; closed 1912.[91]

Hall, Durham Rd., Finsbury Pk., reg. 1917, closed 1920.[92]

Hall, Corporation Street, York Way, formerly Goodinge Rd. Bapt. mission, reg. 1920; probably closed 1952 when hall was sold.[93]

Mildmay Conference Hall, Mildmay Pk., reg. 1922 to 1952.[94]

Hall, Turle Rd., Tollington Pk., reg. 1926,[95] closed by 1934.[96]

Hall, ground floor of bldg. at corner of Paddington St. and Campbell Rd., Finsbury Pk., reg. 1932, closed by 1954.[97]

Hall, no. 112 Fonthill Rd., Finsbury Pk., reg. 1936, closed by 1954.[98]

SEVENTH-DAY ADVENTISTS.[99] Conversion work in Lond. began 1887 at the Chaloners, Anson Rd., Tufnell Pk., with 20–30 baptisms 1888. Mtgs. also at the Athenaeum, Camden Rd., and Duncombe hall, from which several chs. emerged. First training sch. also at Duncombe hall, then Manor Gdns., Holloway, until move to Watford 1907. Publishing works opened at no. 451 Holloway Rd. 1887.

Svces. at Duncombe hall, Duncombe Rd., Hornsey Rise, Sat., Sun. evg., some weekday evgs. Attendance 1903: 50 p.m. (Sun.; main svces. Sat.).

Stroud Green hall, no. 15 Jacksons Bldgs. (the Parade), Stroud Green Rd., reg. 1910.[1] Members organized lecture programme and svces. in several N. Lond. halls. In use 1914, but by 1919 replaced by Scala cinema.[2]

Seventh-day Adventist ch., no. 395 (later 381) Holloway Rd. Built 1927–8 as New Holloway hall, seating 650–700, with aid of national Conference as representative ch. and conference H.Q., also as permanent ch. for earliest N. Lond. congregation, which previously met in hos. and hired halls. Membership 242 in 1927.

SPIRITUALISTS. Svces. held 1903 at no. 19 Stroud Green Rd., attendance: 15 p.m.; and at no. 51 Monsell Rd., Finsbury Pk., attendance: 12 p.m.

Grovedale hall, no. 40B Grovedale Rd., Upper Holloway, taken over from Presbs. 1913. Moved to N. Lond. Spiritualist Assoc. New ch., no. 425 Hornsey Rd., 1931. Renamed N. Lond. Spiritualist ch. 1964.[3] Sanctuary of Hope, no. 23 Duncan Terr., reg. by Christian Spiritualists 1938. Moved to no. 42 Canonbury Rd. 1941; closed by 1954.[4]

Spiritualist Ch. and Healing Sanctuary, no. 806A Holloway Rd., reg. 1943; closed by 1954.[5]

St. John's Healing Sanctuary, no. 9 Hillmarton Rd., reg. 1956.[6]

ELIM FOUR-SQUARE GOSPEL ALLIANCE. Zion Tabernacle, Duncombe Rd., Hornsey Rise, reg. 1929; closed by 1971.[7]

ELIM PENTECOSTALS. Mission work began 1928 with mtgs. at Caledonian Rd. baths, Rink

[73] G.R.O. Worship Reg. no. 26533.
[74] Ibid. no. 26816.
[75] Ibid. no. 29105.
[76] Ibid. no. 28076.
[77] Ibid. nos. 29814, 31152.
[78] Ibid. nos. 29004, 33466.
[79] Ibid. no. 33466.
[80] Ibid. no. 30619.
[81] Ibid. nos. 32480, 39032.
[82] Ibid. no. 39032.
[83] Ibid. no. 32882.
[84] Ibid. no. 71529.
[85] Ibid. no. 35298.
[86] Mudie-Smith, *Rel. Life*, 66 (under Hackney).
[87] G.R.O. Worship Reg. no. 36923.
[88] Ibid. no. 37273.
[89] Ibid. nos. 39546, 28597.
[90] Ibid. no. 40278.

[91] Ibid. no. 40776.
[92] Ibid. no. 47000.
[93] Ibid. no. 47832; above, Camden Rd. Bapt. ch.
[94] G.R.O. Worship Reg. no. 48691; see below for Mildmay hall.
[95] G.R.O. Worship Reg. no. 50239.
[96] *P.O. Dir. Lond.* (1927, 1934).
[97] G.R.O. Worship Reg. no. 53686.
[98] Ibid. no. 57005.
[99] Section based on G. D. Hagstotz, *Seventh-day Adventists in Brit. Isles 1878–1933* (1935), 95–9, 113; Seventh-day Adventists, *Missionary Worker*, vol. 29, no. 15, 8–9, 15; vol. 32, no. 5, 1–2; vol. 33, no. 5, 1, 3.
[1] G.R.O. Worship Reg. no. 44080.
[2] *County Suburbs Dir.* (1919).
[3] G.R.O. Worship Reg. nos. 45578, 53276.
[4] Ibid. nos. 58045, 59738.   [5] Ibid. no. 60394.
[6] Ibid. no. 65319.   [7] Ibid. no. 52098.

cinema, Finsbury Pk., and central libr. Vacant ch. in Fowler Rd. rented 1929 and opened for regular svces. as Elim tabernacle. Bombed 1944 and replaced by rented shop, no. 111 Essex Rd. Moved to disused Meth. ch. in Highbury 1947-51. Joined Hornsey ch. temporarily 1951 then moved to Newcourt ch. hall, Lennox Rd., Finsbury Pk., reg. 1951. Attendance *c.* 30 in 1970s. Bought Newcourt Cong. ch., Regina Rd., and opened Newcourt Elim Pentecostal ch. there 1977, seating 300. Membership increased steadily to 100 in 1979.[8]

PENTECOSTALS. Pentecostal Fellowship Mission, Station hall, Hornsey Rd. sta., reg. 1951; closed 1959. Anglo-West Indian Assembly reg. by Pentecostals at same address 1959; closed by 1964.[9]

Stroud Green Christian Assembly, Everleigh hall, Everleigh Street, Finsbury Pk., reg. 1957 by Assemblies of God. Renamed Stroud Green Pentecostal ch. 1971.[10]

OTHER DENOMINATIONS. German Evangelical (Utd.) Ch. reg. chapel in new rd. (later Fowler Rd.), off Halton Street, 1862. Attendance 1903: 119 a.m.; 58 p.m. Mtg. room in Fowler Rd. reg. 1905. Both chapel and room closed by 1925.[11]

St. Luke's Free Eng. ch., Duncombe Rd., Hornsey Rise, reg. 1866; closed by 1876.[12]

Followers of Joanna Southcott met at no. 9 Elder Walk, Essex Rd., *c.* 1870, under John Whatmore, 'muddle-headed, well meaning mystic' and open-air preacher.[13]

Aged Pilgrims Asylum (later Home) chapel, Hornsey Rise, reg. 1872 by sect refusing to be designated. Known as Calvinistic Ind. ch. 1903; attendance: 56 p.m. Closed 1974.[14]

Church Mission hall, Blackstock Rd., Finsbury Pk., reg. by Reformed Episcopalians 1880, closed by 1896. St. George's ch., George's Rd., Holloway, reg. by same 1881, closed by 1896.[15]

Christian Soldier hall, Church (later Gaskin) Street, reg. 1882; closed by 1896.[16]

All Saints' schoolroom, Hemingford Rd., and mission hall, Thornhill Bridge Pl., Caledonian Rd., reg. by Church Army 1883. Both closed by 1896.[17]

Fifth Ch. of Christ Scientist at no. 137 Stroud Green Rd. by 1914.

Fifth Ch. of Christ Scientist, no. 58 Crouch Hill, reg. 1925, consisting of nine rooms including Sun. sch. in 1935. Moved 1964 to Blythwood Rd.,[18] where ch. closed by 1982 and used as community centre.

Tower hall, no. 12 Warltersville Rd., Crouch

Hill, reg. by Apostolic Faith Ch. 1926. Renamed Utd. Apostolic Faith ch. 1933. Closed 1970 and moved to Hornsey.[19]

St. Mary's ch., in former Meth. ch. at junction of Caledonian and Hillmarton rds., reg. by Liberal Catholics 1926 to replace ch. in St. Pancras. Closed 1976 and moved to Kensington.[20]

First-floor room, no. 129 Seven Sisters Rd., reg. by Paracletians 1934, closed 1937. Neo-Paracletians reg. same room, then part of Co-op. Social hall, 1954; closed by 1971.[21]

Kingdom hall, no. 16A Highbury Pl., reg. by Jehovah's Witnesses 1961. Closed 1973.[22]

ESTABLISHED CHURCH OF SCOTLAND. The Caledonian church was opened *c.* 1846 in the former Holloway Independent chapel, Holloway Rd. It seated 600 in 1851, and was attended by 250 in the morning, including the children of the Royal Caledonian asylum, and 100 in the evening of census Sunday.[23] It closed *c.* 1956, when the building was used by Islington Boy Scouts,[24] and was demolished *c.* 1960 to make way for a new Scout H.Q.[25]

UNDENOMINATIONAL   MISSIONS.[26] Nineteenth-century Islington attracted a great deal of missionary work, some connected with churches and chapels, but much, although evangelistic, attached to no particular denomination. Besides their religious importance, the missions played a significant role in social welfare.

LONDON CITY MISSION.[27] Founded 1835 by David Nasmith, then member of Union chapel. Assoc. for Islington founded soon after, supporting missionary in Lower Rd. for area between Britannia Row and Greenman's Lane by 1840; of 900 people visited, only dozen showed sign of religion. Three more missionaries 1841, covering areas around City Rd. and Angel, Lower Holloway and Liverpool Rd.; eight by 1846. Working men in one dist. formed own assoc. to support separate missionary for White Conduit Fields. Missionaries, generally working-class under superintendent, visited hos., formed ragged schs., and worked at request of local Anglican and nonconf. chs. Continued work in Islington in 1983, holding mission svces. and assisting vicars.

MILDMAY.[28] One of most influential home and overseas missionary organizations in Eng., which led to founding of many other bodies. Founded

[8] Inf. from min.; G.R.O. Worship Reg. nos. 51810, 60960, 63135.
[9] G.R.O. Worship Reg. nos. 62922, 67530.
[10] Ibid. no. 66229.
[11] P.R.O., C 54/16228, no. 10; G.R.O. Worship Reg. nos. 15259, 31633, 41027.
[12] G.R.O. Worship Reg. no. 17196; above, churches (St. Geo.).
[13] Ritchie, *Rel. Life of Lond.* 320, 326.
[14] G.R.O. Worship Reg. no. 20833.
[15] Ibid. nos. 25260, 25575.   [16] Ibid. no. 26604.
[17] Ibid. nos. 27009, 27016.
[18] Ibid. nos. 49687, 56112, 69766.
[19] Ibid. nos. 50467, 54734; *V.C.H. Mdx.* vi. 188.
[20] G.R.O. Worship Reg. no. 50379.

[21] Ibid. nos. 55451, 64638.   [22] Ibid. no. 68408.
[23] P.R.O., HO 129/10/1/1/18.
[24] *P.O. Dir. Lond.* (1952); E. & W. Young, *Old Lond. Chs.* (1956), 228.   [25] Inf. from Mr. J. C. Connell.
[26] The same abbreviations are used as in the accounts of protestant nonconformist chs. above.
[27] Para. based on *Lond. City Mission Mag.* v (1840), 11-12, 103-4; xi (1846), 207-20; K. Heasman, *Evangelicals in Action* (1962), 35.
[28] Para. based on Heasman, op. cit. 37-40, 42, 109, 113-14; H. J. Cooke, *Mildmay; Story of First Deaconess Institution* (1892), *passim*; *Svce. for King: Rec. of Mildmay missions and Assoc. of Women Workers* (March 1899, copy in Islington libr.); G. Balleine, *Hist. of Evangelical Party*, 194; C. Hanbury, *Life of Mrs. Albert Head* [1905], 86, 113-15.

at Barnet by Revd. Wm. Pennefather, who held first conference for interdenominational missionary work in 1856 and started Deaconess Institution 1860. Both transferred to Mildmay Pk. 1864, when Pennefather became vicar of St. Jude's, and were greatly expanded. Mildmay conference hall built 1869 on land south of Newington Green bought from Mildmay est., to replace iron room from Barnet: three-storeyed brick bldg., seating 2,500–3,000, with gallery on three sides and platform. Used for conferences, Evangelical svces., missionary and prayer mtgs.; Sun. sermons by different denoms.; 20 socs. met there on weekdays 1892. Rooms below hall for night sch., attended by up to 600 men, mtgs., annual teas, needlework classes, cookery for sick. Attendance at mission svce. 1903: 588 a.m.; 2,725 p.m. Hall closed after Second World War, but hosp. (below) remained.

Deaconess Institution, first of kind in English-speaking world, offered full-time careers for young women of good educ., with two years at Mildmay before going to outlying missions in Lond. and elsewhere. Careful theoretical and practical training copied by other institutions and influenced 19th-cent. soc. work and later soc. science courses in universities. About 200 deaconesses at any one time; distinctive uniform allowed them to work in roughest areas unmolested. Served 20 missions, 12 in Lond., started at invitation of vicars, 1892. H.Q. at Deaconess Ho. built 1871 next to conference hall. Nursing branch started 1866; served Mildmay cottage hosp.,[29] nursing home for deaconesses, medical mission at Bethnal Green started from Mildmay 1874, and other hosps. and homes in Eng. and abroad. From 1885 nurses lived in nos. 9 and 10 Newington Green, possibly Alderman Halliday's old ho.[30] Training home opened at the Willows, near Clissold Pk., Stoke Newington, given by Mr. Alexander.

Other organizations started at Mildmay or receiving impetus from it were: Dorcas scheme for training in needlework, which had 400 women in 1892; Bible Flower mission, which distributed 2,000 bunches of flowers each week in summer to Lond. hosps. and workho. infirmaries, started under Caroline Hanbury (later Mrs. Albert Head) of Stoke Newington; orphanage opened 1872 at no. 3 Newington Green, which trained 30–40 girls as servants; Mildmay Lads' Institute, started 1867 to provide recreation for working boys; Metropolitan Free Dormitory Assoc., organized by Ld. Shaftesbury and Wm. Pennefather in 1857 to provide meals and accn. for respectable but homeless people in seven areas including Holloway. Working Girls' Institute (founded 1855) and body to link those engaged in soc. work for girls were brought together 1877 by Mrs. Pennefather as Y.W.C.A., which had central office at Mildmay until 1884. Railway Mission was formed 1881 following annual teas for N.L.R. employees from 1874 and bible

classes in waiting rooms, organized by Caroline Hanbury, and also had H.Q. at Mildmay. Children's Special Svce. Mission originated in mission by American, Payson Hammond, 1867 at invitation of Wm. Pennefather; success led to Sun. evg. children's svces. at St. Jude's sch., after which svce. mission, interdenominational like most Mildmay institutions, was set up, spreading throughout Lond. and Eng.[31]

ALBANY MISSION, Albany Pl., Hornsey Rd. Date founded unknown; by 1874 was Sun. sch. and branch mission attached to Holloway chapel. Chapel member L. J. Smith became superintendent, and when chapel gave up the mission, probably for financial reasons, took over mortgage. In 1891 became undenominational Christian ch. with monthly communion and Sun. sch. for up to 400 children from rough area. Attendance 1903: 77 a.m.; 56 p.m. Smith's fam. taught at sch. In 1924 two rooms built at back of hall. By 1950 c. 70 attended sch.[32] Closed by 1980.

MOODY AND SANKEY MISSION.[33] D. L. Moody, preacher, and I. D. Sankey, singer, American evangelists invited to Eng. by Wm. Pennefather 1873, drew thousands to mtgs. and converted hundreds, continuing Evangelical revival of 1860s to which local mins., such as Davidson of Scotch ch., had contributed.[34] Royal Agricultural Hall, Upper Street, was Lond. venue 1875, where several prominent philanthropists and evangelists were inspired. Wilson Carlile, young layman who played organ at the Agricultural Hall, spoke at mtgs. held to take overflow from Hall, and went on to form Church Army 1875; it became part of C.E. 1885.

PAGET MEMORIAL MISSION HALL, Randells Rd., York Way. Built 1911 by Revd. Sholto Doug. Campbell-Douglas, Ld. Blythswood, in memory of w. Violet Mary Paget (d. 1908), who before marriage had held bible classes at the site 1887–9, while a Mildmay deaconess. Additions made 1915. Interior, unusually decorated with richly carved figures, contains breakfast set given to the couple by Queen Victoria. Svces. held 1983 under auspices of Lond. City Mission.[35]

ST. GILES'S CHRISTIAN MISSION, Westbourne Rd. Founded 1860 at Seven Dials, Westm., and pioneered prison gate mission work from 1877. Moved from Lt. Wild Street to former Arundel Sq. Cong. chapel at corner of Bride Street and Westbourne Rd. 1935. Chapel adapted and partly rebuilt. Religious and soc. activities for all ages. Despite rebldg. of area 1970s and decline in prison work, mission continued as soc. focus for Lower Holloway and Barnsbury.[36]

OTHERS. Mission halls and other premises reg. for worship by unsectarian groups in: Blackstock Rd., Highbury Vale, 1884, closed by 1896;[37]

[29] Above, pub. svces. (hosps.).
[30] Above, other est. (Mildmay).
[31] Balleine, *Hist. Evangelical Party*, 196–7.
[32] E. H. Smith, *Fifty Years and More at Albany* [1950].
[33] Para. based on Balleine, *Hist. Evangelical Party*, 198–200.
[34] Above, prot. nonconf., Presbs.
[35] P. Zwart, *Islington: Hist. and Guide*, 135; *Souvenir of Cent. of St. And.* 22; Burke, *Peerage* (1931); G.R.O. Worship Reg. no. 52547; datestones.
[36] St. Giles' Christian Mission, *Ann. Rep.* (1960, 1970–2).
[37] G.R.O. Worship Reg. no. 27846.

Finsbury Pk. mission to poor children, no. 33 Stroud Green Rd., 1910, closed by 1954;[38] Gifford Rd., Caledonian Rd., 1918, in former Cong. mission hall, closed by 1971;[39] Tollington Pk. People's mission hall, no. 91 Tollington Pk., 1935, closed by 1954;[40] Chorley Memorial hall, no. 9 King Henry's Walk, Ball's Pond, 1937, became NE. Lond. Gospel Mission in 1954,[41] in use 1983; Trent hall, no. 61 Hanley Rd., Stroud Green, 1938, closed by 1954;[42] N. Lond. Evangelical mission, no. 93 Tollington Way, Holloway, 1946;[43] Hazelville room, St. John's Way, Upper Holloway, 1954, closed by 1964;[44] St. Bernard Ch. of Divine Healing, no. 169 Upper Street, 1955, closed 1956;[45] Fishers of Men mission hall, no. 86 Caledonian Rd., 1956, closed by 1964;[46] Kingsdown Christian mission, nos. 209–11 Sussex Way, Upper Holloway, 1958, closed 1960 and moved to Hackney.[47]

JUDAISM.[48] A few Jews had settled in Canonbury by the early 19th century, and the widespread building in Barnsbury brought a large number of middle-class Jews from the City from c. 1840. Regular religious services were not started until the 1860s, however, by which time there were nearly 1,000 Jews in the area.

Sephardim were the first to propose a synagogue, in 1860, although Solomon Haim Andrade's private synagogue at Spencer House, Lower Road, was opened only c. 1865. In 1886 Andrade's congregation opened a synagogue at no. 39 Mildmay Park. Attendance on the first day of Passover, 1903, was 96.[49] Mildmay Park synagogue closed in 1937.[50]

Ashkenazim had organized services at Barnsbury hall by 1864, and in 1868 opened the North London synagogue, John Street (later Lofting Road), Barnsbury, a two-storeyed rectangular building with a long ornate front,[51] built with aid from the Great Synagogue. It was admitted to the United Synagogue in 1878.[52] In 1872 it had 126 seatholders, but migration northward, especially to Highbury, and the opening of Dalston synagogue, caused its membership to decline before rising again to 271 in 1883. It fell again to 163 in 1890, and rose to 267 in 1913. Attendance on the first day of Passover 1903 was 275.[53] The synagogue was amalgamated with Dalston (see below) in 1958, and the building in Lofting Road was closed.[54]

From the late 1860s many Jews moved into Highbury and Mildmay Park, and by 1878 most members of the North London synagogue lived in Highbury or Canonbury. In 1874 there were said to be 700 Jewish families living within half an hour's walk of Dalston Junction but farther from the synagogue, whereupon a synagogue was established for Dalston and Ball's Pond Road. Services were held in Ridley Road, Hackney, and a synagogue opened in Birkbeck Road, Hackney; in 1876 it moved to a leased building in Mildmay Road, and in 1885 to Poet's Road off Newington Green, retaining the name Dalston synagogue, and was admitted to the United Synagogue.[55] Membership rose from 268 in 1886 to 365 in 1913. Attendance on the first day of Passover 1903 was 774.[56] The congregation from the North London synagogue joined it in 1958, but in 1967 Dalston synagogue was amalgamated with Stoke Newington synagogue, Shacklewell Lane, Hackney, and the building closed.[57]

South Hackney synagogue moved to Mildmay Road in 1885, and to Devonshire Road, in Hackney, in 1892. A Beth Hamedrash was established in Newington Green Road in 1886, moving to Ferntower Road in 1892. Another Beth Hamedrash was registered at no. 24A Highbury New Park in 1915, closing by 1954.[58] An orthodox synagogue was opened at no. 13A Highbury New Park in 1926, closing by 1971.[59] Highgate synagogue was registered 1930 at no. 88 Archway Road, bought by an orthodox Jewish community in 1929, was replaced in 1937 by a new building adjoining it, seating c. 400, and in 1950 moved to no. 200 Archway Road, Hornsey.[60]

The West London Synagogue had opened a 1¼-a. burial ground and hall by 1851 in Kingsbury Road near the N.L.R. It was still in use in 1895, and was the West London Cemetery of British Jews in 1975.[61]

MOSLEMS. The Moslem Welfare Centre at no. 15 St. Thomas's Road, Finsbury Park, was registered for worship in 1976.[62]

HINDUS. The Shree Swaminarayan Hindu temple was opened a few years before 1974 in Elmore Street, Essex Road, in the former mission hall of St. John's, Cleveland Road.[63] It was still there in 1983.

EDUCATION. The parish had a schoolmaster from c. 1588,[64] and from 1613 Owen's school in Clerkenwell provided free education for 24 Islington children.[65] A boy from a school at

[38] Ibid. no. 44306.
[39] Ibid. no. 47254.
[40] Ibid. no. 55992.
[41] Ibid. no. 57548.
[42] Ibid. no. 58168.
[43] Ibid. no. 61508.
[44] Ibid. no. 64482.
[45] Ibid. no. 65034.
[46] Ibid. no. 65627.
[47] Ibid. no. 66662.
[48] Section based on *Trans. Jewish Hist. Soc.* xxi. 85–8, 100.
[49] Mudie-Smith, *Rel. Life*, 265.
[50] *Jewish Year bk.* (1937).
[51] *Illus. Lond. News*, 3 Oct. 1868.
[52] A. Newman, *United Synagogue 1870–1970* (1976), 5, 216.

[53] Mudie-Smith, *Rel. Life*, 265.
[54] Newman, *United Synagogue*, 216–17; G.R.O. Worship Reg. no. 18455.
[55] Newman, *United Synagogue*, 216–17.
[56] Mudie-Smith, *Rel. Life*, 265.
[57] Newman, *United Synagogue*, 216–17; G.R.O. Worship Reg. no. 23059.
[58] G.R.O. Worship Reg. no. 46399.
[59] Ibid. no. 50458.
[60] Ibid. nos. 52413, 57262; *V.C.H. Mdx.* vi. 189.
[61] P.R.O., HO 107/10/2/33; L.C.C. *Return of Burial Grounds* (1895), 7; *P.O. Dir. Lond.* (1959, 1975).
[62] G.R.O. Worship Reg. no. 74494.
[63] Inf. from Mr. J. C. Connell.
[64] Guildhall MS. 9537/7, f. 111.
[65] Below, private schs.

Islington was admitted to Magdalene College, Cambridge, in 1644.[66] Peter Vowell; schoolmaster at Islington, appeared before the House of Commons in 1643, and was hanged in 1654 for plotting against Cromwell.[67] In 1679 children maintained by the parish were to be sent out for schooling and a master and mistress were to receive 2d. a week for each child.[68] Dame Sarah Temple, by will proved in 1699, left £500 for a rent charge to be paid to the minister and churchwardens for maintaining and educating poor children. The money was obtained from her executor, Sir Thomas Draper, Bt., in 1702 after a Chancery case, and c. 22 a. at Potters Bar (Herts.) were purchased. Two boys were maintained at a boarding school at Chertsey (Surr.), where they received elementary instruction in 1843.[69] Two girls were maintained and educated by the charity in 1895.[70] In 1710 the minister and parishioners subscribed to form charity schools to educate and clothe 24 boys and 20 girls, in a room over the church porch.[71] A bequest of £300 in annuities by John Westbrook (d. 1768) for young children to be taught to read the catechism paid for three boys and four girls at the charity schools in 1769. The charity's stock was increased by a gift of £100 from Isaac Needham in 1809. Six 'Westbrook children' were taught at a private school at no. 10 Smith's Buildings in 1827 and ten in 1828. In 1836 the trustees decided to extend the charity by leasing a room in Smith's Buildings and employing a regular mistress.[72]

In 1819 the charity schools and the two charities provided the only free primary schooling,[73] although a school of industry for girls had been founded by Islington chapel in 1801, and Union chapel had a girls' school founded in 1807 and a boys' founded in 1814.[74] By 1833 provision had greatly increased, with the opening of several infants' and National schools, and the charity schools had also established a connexion with the National Society. There were 4 infants' schools, supported by subscriptions and private gifts, and 11 day schools, similarly supported and in some cases charging school pence. In addition there were 51 private day schools, including one attended by eight 'Westbrook children', a proprietary school, and 38 boarding schools. More advanced education for the poor was available only for boys at Owen's school. In all 578 infants, 642 boys, and 447 girls received free or almost free education; 578 boys and 536 girls attended private day schools, and 798 boys and 421 girls attended private boarding schools. Sunday schools also provided free basic education, and 719 boys and 769 girls attended the four Anglican and five nonconformist ones.[75]

The growth in population brought more places for the poor, mainly linked with the provision of new churches or with the ragged school movement. By 1847 there were 27 infants' and National schools attached to 11 Anglican churches.[76] Although as many as nine in ten of Islington's schools in 1851 were private, they taught less than half of the district's schoolchildren.[77]

The London school board was formed in 1870 with Islington as part of Finsbury Division.[78] Under the Elementary Education Act of 1871 the board inspected all elementary schools offering education for 9d. a week or less: Islington had 35 public schools held under trusts, including National, British, and other church schools, 20 schools run by private committees, mainly the ragged and mission schools, and 139 adventure schools, being mainly small dame schools. All but three of the public schools and over half the privately managed schools were found efficient. Many of the adventure schools refused inspection and others had closed when the inspectors called; of the rest only two were efficient, two others were efficient in instruction but not premises, and another might be made efficient. Most of those not recognized appalled the inspectors. In all, 47 schools for working-class children could be recognized, giving places for 7,675 boys and 6,165 girls of all ages. Night schools were of value for children who worked during the day and had not received basic instruction when younger. In 1871 sixteen schools, including three adventure schools, provided evening classes for 922 boys and 467 girls, aged 9 and up. The schools were usually held for six or seven months in the winter, although two were open all year, and their hours varied from three to ten a week.[79]

By early 1875 the board had completed four new schools in Islington, with three more under way.[80] When the L.C.C. took over responsibility for elementary education in 1904, the board had 38 local schools with c. 43,000 places, including schools transferred to the board.[81] In 1906 many voluntary schools had to reduce their intake or make other improvements, and some, having survived competition from board schools, were obliged to close or transfer to the L.C.C. for financial reasons.[82]

Three schools, Montem Street, Upper Hornsey Road, and Duncombe Road, had about a third of their pupils in higher grade classes by 1900, and Montem Street's upper boys formed a science school.[83] In 1903 Islington had nine secondary and higher educational establishments administered by the Board of Education, including evening classes at two board schools.[84] In 1904 the first higher grade school was opened by the L.C.C. at Barnsbury Park, followed by Camden

[66] Hist. MSS. Com. 4, 5th Rep. p. 482.
[67] Cal. S.P. Dom. 1641-3, 476; Walker Revised, 262.
[68] Islington libr., vestry mins. 1663-1708, 125.
[69] Digest of Schs. and Chars. for Educ. H.C. 435, pp. 614-15 (1843), xviii.
[70] G.L.R.O., P83/MRY1/406, no. 2; P83/MRY1/133, f. 18; P.R.O., C 5/309/6; vestry mins. 1663-1708, 335.
[71] Vestry mins. 1708-34, 14-15; below, St. Mary C.E. sch.
[72] G.L.R.O., P83/MRY1/140; below, Westbrook char. sch.
[73] Digest of Returns on Educ. of Poor, H.C. 224, p. 550 (1819), ix (I).

[74] For individual schs., see below.
[75] Educ. Enq. Abstract, 565-6.
[76] Nat. Soc. Inquiry, 1846-7, Mdx. 8.
[77] V.C.H. Mdx. i. 237.
[78] T. A. Spalding, Work of Lond. Sch. Bd. (1900), 27.
[79] P.R.O., ED 3/4-6.
[80] J. F. B. Firth, Municipal Lond. (1876), 459, 461.
[81] S.B.L. Final Rep. of Sch. Bd. for Lond. 1870-1904 (1904), maps.   [82] P.R.O., ED 16/201; Nat. Soc. files.
[83] Spalding, Lond. Sch. Bd. 195.
[84] Sec. Schs. under Admin. of Bd. 1902-3 [Cd. 1752], p. 405, H.C. (1903), lii.

secondary school in 1907.[85] In 1908 four private secondary schools were recognized as efficient,[86] of which Highbury Hill High school was taken over by the L.C.C. in 1912. Higher grade classes in elementary schools were gradually replaced by separate central schools. From 1927 most Islington council schools were reorganized into senior and junior schools, though a few all-age schools, many of them denominational, remained to be adapted after the Second World War. The London school plan, drawn up between 1944 and 1947, laid down a complete scheme of primary and comprehensive secondary education but included several aided grammar schools which remained outside the reorganization.[87] By 1955 Islington had 36 council primary schools, some divided into separate junior and infants' sections, 12 voluntary aided primaries, 16 county secondary schools, and 5 voluntary aided secondaries.[88] Some single-sex secondary schools were amalgamated into mixed schools in 1957–9; former grammar or high schools remained single-sex but had become comprehensive by 1982, again taking pupils from other secondary schools. In 1980 there were 26 county and 13 voluntary aided primaries (6 of them Roman Catholic and 7 Anglican), 8 county secondary schools (5 single-sex), and 3 voluntary aided Roman Catholic secondary schools (all single-sex).[89]

Special centres were opened, at Laycock school to teach English to pupils with other mother tongues and at the Islington Centre, Delhi Street, to give basic education to immigrants of secondary school age. A centre for persistent truants from Archway and Tollington schools was set up in 1971 at no. 6 Cromartie Road, Upper Holloway; it had 16 attenders in 1976.[90]

Public schools.[91] Basic historical information and numbers in existing schools have been supplied by head teachers and Mr. A. R. Neate of the G.L.R.O. Except where otherwise stated, the remaining historical information and figures of accommodation and average attendance have been taken from: files on Church of England schools at the National Society; P.R.O., ED 3/4–6; ED 7/76, 80, 82; ED 14/5, 35; *Return of Sums expended for Educ.* H.C. 444 (1843), xl; *Mins. of Educ. Cttee. of Council, 1846* [787], H.C. (1847), xlv; *1849* [1215], H.C. (1850), xliii; *1852–3* [1623], H.C. (1853), lxxix; *Rep. of Educ. Cttee. of Council, 1865–6* [3666], H.C. (1866), xxvii; *1878* [C. 2342-I], H.C. (1878–9), xxiii; *Return of Schs. 1893* [C. 7529], H.C. (1894), lxv; *Return of Non-Provided Schs.* H.C. 178-XXIII (1906), lxxxviii; *List of Sec. Schs. Recognised as Efficient* [Cd. 4374], H.C. (1908), lxxxiii; *Bd. of Educ., List 21, 1908–38* (H.M.S.O.); L.C.C. *Educ. Svce. Particulars* (1937 and later edns.); L.C.C. (I.L.E.A. from 1965) *Educ. Svce. Inf.* (1951 and later edns.).

The following abbreviations are used in addition to those in the index: a.a., average attendance; accn., accommodation; amalg., amalgamated, amalgamation; B, boy, boys; Bapt., Baptist; C.E., Church of England; Cong., Congregationalist; demol., demolished; dept., department; G, girl, girls; J, JB, JG, JM, junior, junior boys, girls, mixed; I, infant, infants; M, mixed; mod., modern; Meth., Methodist; Nat., National; parl., parliamentary; perm., permanent; R.C., Roman Catholic; reorg., reorganized; roll, numbers on roll; S, SB, SG, SM, senior, senior boys, girls, mixed; S.B.L., School Board for London; sch., school; sec., secondary; sep., separate; tech., technical; temp., temporary; vol., voluntary; V., vicar; Wes., Wesleyan. The word 'school' is to be understood after each named entry. Separate departments are indicated by commas: B, G, I; JM, I.

ALBANY DAY AND SUNDAY, 14 Albany Pl., Hornsey Rd. Opened by 1848 by Independents. Roll 1871: 52 B, 44 G, all ages; accn. 87 M, 90 I. Financed by sch. pence, subscriptions. Instruction not adequate but good moral training 1871. Not recognized by Bd. of Educ. and day sch. probably closed soon after 1871.

ALFRED PRICHARD PRIMARY, see Wellington Rd.

ALL SAINTS' NAT. AND I, Muriel Street. I sch. for 140 with teacher's ho. built 1842 W. of Muriel Street.[92] Praised by inspector 1846. 1849 accn. 161, a.a. 130; 1852 accn. 200. Nat. sch. for 272 B, 272 G built 1852 E. of Muriel Street,[93] with grants from parl., Nat. Soc. Roll 1853: 206 B, 96 G, 130 I; a.a. 176 B, 96 G, 130 I. Financed by sch. pence, vol. contributions, parl. grants. Small evg. sch. in winter, 6 hrs. a week. Roll 1871: 238 B, 191 G, 171 I; 1878 accn. 584 M, I, a.a. 292; 1908 accn. 134 M, 190 I, a.a. 238 M, 123 I. Reorg. 1927–32 for 289 JM & I. 1935 a.a. 207. Closed 1947–51.

AMBLER PRIMARY, Blackstock Rd., Finsbury Pk. Opened 1898 as Ambler Rd. bd. sch. for B, G, I. 1908 accn. 300 B, 300 G, 333 I, a.a. 242 B, 212 G, 123 I; 1911 a.a. 723. Reorg. 1932–6 to form Finsbury Pk. Junior B, Junior G, with 348 JB, 351 JG (see also Finsbury Pk. primary). Reorg. for JM c. 1949, and renamed Ambler primary. Amalg. 1971 with Finsbury Pk. primary to form Ambler primary for JM & I. Nursery block added c. 1971. Adjoining ho. demol. for playground c. 1975. Roll 1982: c. 250 JM & I.

ANGEL CT. RAGGED, 41 Rufford's Bldgs., Islington High Street. Possibly Rufford's Bldgs. ragged sch. opened 1854 for G & I, supported by Turnpike Cts. Dist. Visiting Soc. Took pupils from Protestant Institute's Parsley Ct. sch. leaving latter mainly for B.[94] By 1871 a free sch. run by Ch. Missionary Coll., Upper Street. Roll 1871: 60 B & 38 G, 127 I; evg. sch. 3 hrs. a week 21 B, 22 G. Irregular attendance but sch. capable of meeting Bd. of Educ.'s standards 1871. Nothing further known.

ANGLERS GDNS., see Charles Lamb.

<hr>

[85] Below.
[86] *Sec. Schs. Recognized as Efficient* [Cd. 4374], p. 306, H.C. (1908), lxxxiii.
[87] S. Maclure, *One Hundred Years of Lond. Educ. 1870–1970* (1970), 146–7, 170.
[88] L.C.C. *Educ. Svce. Inf.* (1955).

[89] I.L.E.A. *Green Bk.* (1980).
[90] R. Grunsell, *Born to be Invisible* (1978), *passim.*
[91] Private schs. are treated separately below.
[92] P.R.O., C 54/12848, no. 2.
[93] Ibid. C 54/14349, no. 3.
[94] Lewis, *Islington As It Was*, 84.

ARCHWAY SEC., Duncombe Rd., Upper Holloway. Formed 1959 for SM from Archway sec. B, Duncombe Rd., and Archway sec. G, which moved to Duncombe Rd. 1957 (see Duncombe; Cottenham Rd.). Took over whole of Duncombe Rd. site, with annexe at Whittington sch. Additions to bldg. after 1959. Roll 1981: 750 SM. Amalg. 1981 with Tollington Pk. sch. to form George Orwell (q.v.).

ARLINGTON SQ., see St. Philip.

ASHMOUNT, Ashmount Rd., Hornsey Lane. Opened 1957 as Ashmount primary for JM, I. Rolls 1982: 172 JM, 146 I.

BALL'S POND RD. MISSION (St. Jude's), 37 Ball's Pond Rd. Opened 1866 in iron bldg. for 225 M. Roll 1871: 61 B & 68 G, all ages, under 1 mistress; a.a. 60–70. Financed by sch. pence (2d.), vol. contributions, parl. grants. 1878 accn. 159, a.a. 109. Closed by 1893.

BARFORD STREET WES., Liverpool Rd. Day and Sun. sch. built c. 1834 adjoining chapel. Existed 1849, but no longer a day sch. 1871.[95]

BARNSBURY B CENTRAL, see Barnsbury sec. for B.

BARNSBURY CENTRAL, see Barnsbury sch. for G.

BARNSBURY PK., Liverpool Rd. Opened 1910 by L.C.C., taking pupils from Harvist Rd. temp. 1911 accn. 320 M, 180 I. Reorg. 1927–32 for 320 JM, 156 I; 1932–6 for 196 I. In 1947 was day special sch. for M, age 5–14. Closed by 1951.

BARNSBURY SCH. FOR G, Barnsbury Pk.[96] Opened 1904 as Offord Rd. Higher Grade county sch. for 400 SM; renamed Barnsbury Pk. c. 1905. 1908 a.a. 355. Commercial subjects introduced. Renamed Barnsbury Central 1911. 1919 a.a. 404; 1922 accn. 444 SM; 1927 a.a. 471. Reorg. 1931 as Barnsbury Girls' Central for 400 SG; B went to Barnsbury Boys' Central (see Barnsbury sec.). Renamed Barnsbury sec. for G 1947–51, Barnsbury Sch. for G c. 1966. Roll 1982: 780 SG.

BARNSBURY SEC. FOR B, Geary Street, Eden Grove, Holloway. Opened 1931 as Barnsbury B Central for 400 SB from former Barnsbury Central (above). Renamed Barnsbury sec. for B 1947–51. Closed 1967 and pupils moved to Highbury Grove (q.v.).

BARNSBURY STREET. Bd. sch. opened 1878 for BG as feeder for new permanent sch. in Thornhill Rd. (q.v.).

BELLE ISLE BRITISH, Brewery Rd., York Way. Opened by Camden Rd. Bapt. chapel; moved to Brewery Rd. 1871. Roll 1871: 99 B & 85 G, all ages; accn. 200, a.a. 140. Financed by sch. pence. Efficient 1871 but probably closed by 1878.

BISHOP GIFFARD R.C. SEC., Gifford Street. Vol. aided R.C. sec. sch. opened 1961 in former Gifford Street sch. Closed 1967; bldg. later used by St. William of York (q.v.).

BLACKSTOCK RD., see Finsbury Pk.

BLENHEIM RD., Hornsey Rd. Opened 1872 by S.B.L., B in iron room belonging to Park chapel, Hornsey, G & I in Blenheim hall. Sch. pence (2d.). 1872 a.a. 50 B, 115 G & I, 66 I. Closed by 1878; probably replaced by Hornsey Rd. bd. (q.v.).

BLESSED SACRAMENT R.C. PRIMARY, Boadicea Street, Copenhagen Street. Opened 1965–7 as vol. aided sch. for JM & I. Roll 1982: 217 JM & I.

BLUNDELL STREET, see Robert Blair.

BOWMAN'S PL., see Grafton.

BREWERY RD. (temp.), York Way. Opened 1877 by S.B.L. in rented premises for BGI. Sch. pence (2d.). 1878 accn. 232 M, a.a. 191. Closed by 1893.

BRITANNIA ROW, Essex Rd. Opened 1872 by S.B.L. in rented premises for 130 G, 100 I. Sch. pence (1d.). Closed by 1878.

BRITANNIA ROW (ISLINGTON) RAGGED, 36 Britannia Row. Opened by 1868.[97] Efficient but overcrowded 1871: accn. 150 M, 105 G and I. Roll 1871: 78 B, 89 G under master; 145 I under mistress; evg. sch. 40 B, 47 G, from age 10. Nothing further known.

BRUNSWICK RD. TEMP., Upper Holloway. Opened 1895 by S.B.L. for BGI in former St. Peter's Nat. sch., until Hargrave Pk. enlarged (q.v.).

BUCKINGHAM STREET, see Copenhagen primary.

CALEDONIAN RD., Bingfield Street. Opened 1872 by S.B.L. for B in premises belonging to Caledonian Rd. chapel. Caledonian Rd. G and I mission bd. sch. opened by 1878, accn. 187, a.a. 154. Both schs. replaced by new sch. for BGI 1878. Sch. pence (3d.). 1893 accn. 1,104, a.a. 1,027; 1927 accn. 797 BGI, a.a. 708. Closed 1931.

CAMDEN SEC. FOR B, see Holloway.

CANONBURY, Canonbury Rd.[98] Originated as Union Chapel British schs. for 50 G, opened 1807, and 50 B, opened 1814. New sch. built in Compton Mews 1836, for B, G. Roll 1838: 161 B, 95 G. Financed by subscriptions, collections, sch. pence (2d., 3d.). Roll 1850: 132 B, 120 G. I sch. opened 1853; used room under vestry behind chapel from 1868. Sch. pence (2d.). Roll 1871: 103 B, 92 G, 153 I. Sch. and bldg. in Compton Mews transferred to S.B.L. 1873, accn. 239 BG. I sch. taken over 1875 and moved to iron bldg. in Canonbury Rd. 1876. Perm. bd. sch. opened 1877 at Canonbury Rd. for B, G, I. 1878 accn. 572, a.a. 296. Additions to bldgs. 1893, 1910, 1972. 1908 accn. 929, a.a. 850; 1912 accn. 1,252. a.a. rose to 1,146 in 1914, fell to 904 by 1927. Reorg. 1932–6 for 358 SB, 360 JM, 390 I. SB left 1947–51; reorg. for JM, I. Rolls 1982: 172 JM; 120 I & 73 nursery.

CHAPEL OF EASE PAROCHIAL, see St. Mary Magdalene C.E.

CHARLES LAMB PRIMARY, Popham Rd. Opened 1875 as Anglers Gdns. bd. sch. for 1,090 B, G, I. Sch. pence (1d.). 1878 accn. 1,147, a.a. 948; 1893 accn. 1,213, a.a. 921. Renamed Popham Rd. and remodelled 1903. JM, I depts. opened 1914 in new bldg. 1919 accn. 339 B, 304 G, 240 JM, 288 I, a.a. 317 B, 275 G, 223 JM, 292 I. Reorg. 1932–6 for 359 JB, 318 JG, 369 I. Renamed Chas. Lamb primary for JM, I, c. 1949. JM & I

---

[95] P.R.O., C 54/11458, no. 17; C 54/12523, no. 20; C 54/13791, no. 1.
[96] Additional inf. from *Barnsbury Central Sch.* (jubilee hist. 1954, in Islington libr.); Barnsbury Central sch. log. bk., in Islington libr.

[97] *Ragged Sch. Union Mag.* xx (1868), p. 181.
[98] Additional inf. from Lewis, *Islington*, 260; P.R.O., C 54/11627, no. 9; Brit. and Foreign Sch. Soc. *Rep.* (1838), 35; (1850), 32.

amalg. 1972; old J bldg. replaced 1972 by one-storeyed bldg. and extended playground. Roll 1982: 232 JM & I, 35 nursery.

CHARLOTTE STREET, Barnsbury. Opened 1872 by S.B.L. in bldg. at corner of Bryan Street rented from Free Meth. chapel. GI only. Sch. pence (3d., 2d.). Closed by 1878; may have been feeder for Caledonian Rd. (q.v.).

CHRIST CHURCH NAT., see St. John's, Highbury Vale.

CHRIST THE KING R.C. PRIMARY, Tollington Pk. Originated as independent mixed prep. sch. run by Sisters of St. John of God. Became vol. aided R.C. primary for JM & I 1961. Roll 1982: 501 JM & I.

CLOUDESLEY STREET TEMP., see Holy Trinity.

COPENHAGEN STREET RAGGED, 119 Copenhagen Street. Opened as part of N. Lond. Industrial Home for destitute boys, Bryan Street, c. 1852 with c. 80 B.[99] New bldg. 1862 with sch. over industrial sch., built by Islington Reformatory Cttee., B, G, I. Financed by contribution to reformatory and grant from Ragged Sch. Union, which ceased 1872 when sch. pence (1d.) charged. Efficient 1872. Roll 1872: 90 B, 81 G, 32 I; accn. 332. Sch. closed by 1878, but home for destitute boys remained there 1912.[1]

COPENHAGEN PRIMARY, Treaty Street, Copenhagen Street. Opened 1887 as Buckingham Street bd. sch. for 1,033 B, G, I. Sch. pence (2d.). 1893 a.a. 970; 1908 a.a. 1,072. Reorg. 1927 for 280 JB, 320 JG, 334 I. Renamed Copenhagen council sch. 1938. Reorg. 1964 for JM, I. Reorg. 1979 for JM & I with 2 nursery classes. Admin. block and nursery wing added 1970. Roll 1982: 230 JM & I.

COTTENHAM RD., Cottenham Rd. (later Sussex Way), Upper Holloway. Opened 1873 by S.B.L. for 966 B, G, I. Sch. pence (2d.). 1893 accn. 1,108, a.a. 981; 1908 accn. 446 B, 446 G, 570 I, a.a. 395 B, 356 G, 415 I. Reorg. 1931 for 320 SB, 320 SG, 389 I. Renamed Hanley sch. 1938. Reopened c. 1945 as Hanley sec. G (renamed Archway sec. G 1951), and Hanley I (renamed Hanleigh I 1951); SB moved to Duncombe Rd. (see Archway sec.). Hanleigh I closed 1957; Archway sec. G exchanged sites with Duncombe primary 1957 (see Archway sec.).

CROSS STREET CHAPEL BRITISH, Grove Rd. Opened 1857 by Cross Street Bapts., with 73 BI, 23 G. Financed by sch. pence (4d. to 1s.), vol. contributions. Roll 1871: 76 B, 27 G, all ages. Nothing further known.

DENMARK TERR. (temp.), see South Islington and Pentonville British.

DRAYTON PK. PRIMARY, Drayton Pk., Holloway. Opened 1860 as Highbury Wes. sch. for BG in room under ch. Financed by sch. pence (4d.), vol. contributions, parl. grants from 1866. Roll 1860: 58 B & 27 G. New bldg. 1866 for B, G, I; a.a. 125 B, 45 G, 60 I. Roll 1871: 161 B, 135 G, 132 I; 1878 accn. 578, a.a. 433. Vol. sch. in 1906 but taken over by L.C.C. and renamed Drayton Pk. council sch. by 1908 with same accn. Reorg. 1927 for 240 JM, 260 I in sep. depts. in new bldg.

JM, I amalg. 1966. Nursery opened 1980 in part of I accn. Roll 1982: 200 JM & I.

DUDDY'S RENTS, see Protestant Institute.

DUNCOMBE, Sussex Way, Upper Holloway. Temp. bd. sch. for c. 74 B opened 1878 in Duncombe Rd. Perm. sch. opened 1881 for B, G, I. 1893 accn. 1,591, a.a. 1,437. Higher grade classes 1905–10; one-storeyed bldg. added 1905. 1908 accn. 382 SM, 480 JB, 480 JG, 607 I, a.a. 404 SM, 654 JM, 507 I. Reorg. 1911 for 382 B, 308 G, 508 JM, 510 I. 1913 a.a. 1,666; 1927 a.a. 1,498. Reorg. 1931 for SB, JB, JG, I. Reopened c. 1945 as Duncombe Rd. primary (Rd. omitted from 1951) with JB, JG, I, and Duncombe Rd. sec. B (renamed Archway sec. B 1951) with SB from Cottenham Rd. (see Archway sec.). Primary sch. exchanged sites with Archway sec. G and moved to Sussex Way 1957 (see Cottenham Rd.). Reorg. for JM, I 1965. Roll fell from 350 in 1970 to lowest point c. 1979. Rolls 1982: 188 JM; 150 I.

ECCLESBOURNE PRIMARY, Ecclesbourne Rd., New North Rd. Opened 1886 as Ecclesbourne Rd. bd. sch. for 1,209 B, G, I. Sch. pence (2d.). 1893 accn. 1,209, a.a. 1,035; 1908 accn. 472 B, 472 G, 562 I. Reorg. 1932–6 for 396 SB, 356 SG, 400 I. Reorg. 1947–51 for JM, I. Roll 1982: 251 JM & I.

ELDER WALK RAGGED, Elder Walk, Essex Rd. Opened 1848 by Congs. with funds raised by local missioner for one of poorest and most populous areas; a.a. 60–80, reached 105 in winter. Bldg. enlarged 1850 for 120. 1851 a.a. 90 I at day sch. with 8 vol. teachers and 1 paid.[2] Roll 1871: 90 M, 68 I; evg. sch. 3 hrs. a week 39 B & 51 G. Attendance irregular and 1 accn. cramped 1871. New premises being built in Britannia Row 1871, but nothing further known.

FINSBURY PK., Blackstock Rd. Opened 1888 as Blackstock Rd. bd. sch. for B, G, I. Sch. pence (3d.). 1893 accn. 1,002, a.a. 1,050; 1908 accn. 416 B, 416 G, 552 I, a.a. 320 B, 309 G, 286 I. Accn. reduced 1927 to 280 B, 280 G, 336 I. Reorg. 1932–6 as Finsbury Pk. SB, SG and I council sch. for 400 SM, 324 I (for JB, JG, see Ambler). Reorg. 1947–51 as Finsbury Pk. sec. for SM, and Finsbury Pk. primary for I. Primary sch. closed 1960 and I joined Ambler primary. Sec. sch. closed c. 1964.

FORSTER, see William Forster.

FROG LANE, Popham Rd. Opened 1872 by S.B.L. in rented premises. Roll: 120 B. Sch. pence (1d.). Probably replaced by Anglers Gdns. (see Charles Lamb).

GEORGE ORWELL, Turle Rd., Tollington Pk. Comprehensive sec. sch. opened 1981 with SM pupils from Tollington Pk. and Archway schs. (qq.v.). Annexes at Duncombe Rd. and Highgate Hill. Roll 1981: 1,390 SM.

GIFFORD SEC., Gifford Street, Caledonian Rd. Opened 1872 as Gifford Street bd. sch. in mission hall with 80 M, 152 I. Sch. pence (3d., 2d.). New sch. opened 1877 for 1,104 B, G, I. 1878 a.a. 938. Gifford Hall, Gifford Street, and Blundell Street temp. schs. reopened 1879 as

[99] Additional inf. from Lewis, *Islington As It Was*, 83–4.
[1] Reformatory and Refuge Union, *Class. List of Child-Saving Institutions* (1912), 26.
[2] *Ragged Sch. Union Mag.* ii (1850), 56, 305; iii (1851), 207.

feeders for enlargement of Gifford Street. 1893 accn. 1,988, a.a. 1,520. Bldg. remodelled 1915–16. Reorg. 1927–32 for 480 SB, 480 SG, 516 I. Reorg. 1947–51 as Gifford sec. for SM. Closed 1960. Site used for Bishop Giffard (q.v.).

GILLESPIE PRIMARY, Gillespie Rd., Highbury. Opened 1878 as Gillespie Rd. bd. sch. for B, G, I. 1893 accn. 1,200, a.a. 1,175. Reorg. 1932–6 for 256 I. Reorg. 1947–51 as primary for JM, I. Reorg. as JM & I 1957. Roll 1982: 150 JM & I.

GORDON CT. RAGGED, see St. John, Upper Holloway, ragged.

GRAFTON, Eburne Rd., Holloway. Opened 1879 as Bowman's Pl. bd. sch. for B, G, I. Sch. pence (3d., 2d.). Renamed Grafton Rd. by 1893; accn. 1,300, a.a. 1,088. Reorg. 1927–32 for 280 JB, 382 JG, 304 I. Reorg. 1936 for 360 JM, 304 I. Primary sch. for JM, I from 1947. Rolls 1982: 138 JM, 158 I.

GREENMAN'S LANE BRITISH, see Lower Road British.

HANLEIGH (HANLEY), see Cottenham Rd.

HANOVER PRIMARY, Noel Rd., Islington Green. Opened 1877 as Hanover Street bd. sch. for B, G, I. Sch. pence (2d., 1d.). 1878 accn. 828, a.a. 788; 1893 accn. 1,229, a.a. 1,026. Reorg. 1932–6 for 280 JB, 280 JG, 336 I. New bldg. 1936, after subsidence caused by canal. Renamed Hanover sch. 1938: accn. 200 JB, 200 JG, 280 I. Reorg. 1947–51 for JM, I. Became JM & I c. 1966. In 1983 top floor occupied by Children's Theatre Group, performing at Islington primary schs. Roll fell to 150 JM & I c. 1980. Roll 1983: 205 JM & I.

HARGRAVE PK. PRIMARY, Junction Rd., Upper Holloway. Opened 1877 as Hargrave Pk. Rd. bd. sch. for B, G, I; I dept. used initially as covered playground. 1878 accn. 528, a.a. 341; 1893 accn. 1,328, a.a. 909. Reorg. 1927–32 for 358 JB, 359 JG, 391 I. Reorg. 1936–8 for 400 JM, 391 I. Primary sch. from 1947. Included unit for partially hearing by 1977.

HARVIST RD. TEMP., Hornsey Rd. Opened possibly in former St. Barnabas sch. c. 1901. 1908 accn. 207 G, 201 I. Closed 1910 and replaced by Shelburne (q.v.).

HIGHBURY, see Highbury Grove.

HIGHBURY FIELDS, Highbury Hill.[3] Founded as Home and Colonial Sch. Soc.'s Mayo, or Middle-Class, sch. in Gray's Inn Rd. 1844 and moved to Highbury Hill Ho. 1894, with non-government part of training coll. and nucleus of 17 pupils. Alterations 1899 to provide great hall. Students housed in Highbury New Pk., and then no. 5 (later 15) Highbury Hill, which was used for Kindergarten Training Coll. and sch., leaving Ho. for high sch. only. No. 27 Highbury Hill leased from 1903 for junior sch. L.C.C. grants for laboratories and maintenance from 1902. As Highbury Hill, with 130 G, the sch. was recognized as efficient sec. sch. 1903. Sch. transferred to L.C.C. 1912 and training coll. and kindergarten

closed; roll 280 including 70 under 10 years. 1914 roll 350, later reduced as new bldgs. postponed. Four-storeyed bldg. for 450 SG opened in garden 1928. Ho. demol. Additional land 1936. Roll 1939: 400 SG; 1946: 465; 1954: 480. Reorg. 1981 as Highbury Fields comprehensive for G, with SG from Shelburne; annexes in Annette and Benwell rds. Roll 1982: 1,118 SG.

HIGHBURY GROVE, Highbury New Pk.[4] Sec. sch. founded 1901 by governors of Northern Polytechnic, Holloway Rd.; SM from 1902, with 140 B, 98 G in 1908; fees £7 16s. Reorg. for SB 1912. Transferred to L.C.C. and moved to Highbury Grove as Highbury county sch. 1922. As part of 1947 plan, amalg. with Laycock SB and Barnsbury SB to form Highbury Grove comprehensive 1967, in new bldgs. on Highbury site. Roll 1982: 1,280 SB.

HIGHBURY HILL HIGH, see Highbury Fields.

HIGHBURY QUADRANT PRIMARY, Highbury New Pk. Opened 1956 for JM, I. Classrooms added. Reorg. for JM & I c. 1973. Roll 1982: 378 JM & I.

HIGHBURY VALE C.E., see St. John, Highbury Vale, C.E.

HIGHBURY WESLEYAN, see Drayton Pk.

HIGHGATE HILL R.C., see St. Joseph's R.C. primary.

HOLLOWAY, Hilldrop Rd., Camden Rd.[5] Opened 1907 by L.C.C. as Camden sec. sch. for B, including top form of commercial section of University Coll. sch. Fees 10 gns. 1908. Three-storeyed bldg. with four-storeyed wings. Renamed Holloway sch. by 1927. Acquired premises of Camden Sch. of Art, Dalmeny Ave., 1923 as annexe; new wing 1927 and further additions 1930s. Bldgs. on 3½-a. site in Carleton Rd. opened 1956; sch. reorg. as comprehensive for SB. Roll 1955: 1,250 SB. Teaching included tech. subjects, accounting. Roll 1982: 1,156 SB.

HOLLOWAY FREE AND RAGGED, Brand Street, Hornsey Rd.[6] Opened 1846 and moved to purpose built sch. in Brand Street by 1854, accn. 300. In 1851, 60 B, 30 G, 80 I at day sch.; 20 B, 10 adults at evg. sch.; 17 vol. teachers and 2 paid. Included penny bank and working-class lectures. New sch. 1866 in Ingram Pl., opposite side of Hornsey Rd. 1867 a.a. 86 B, 90 G, 125 JM, 93 I; evg. sch. 38 B, 40 G. Roll 1871: 166 G at Ingram Pl.; 164 B and 172 I at Hornsey Rd.; 53 B at evg. sch. Schs. transferred to S.B.L. 1872; closed by 1878.

HOLY TRINITY NAT. AND I, Cloudesley Street.[7] I sch. opened 1830; in rooms adjoining Oldfield's dairy until sch. and master's ho. built 1830. Roll 1835: 240 I, with 60 older children in evg. sch. Nat. sch. built 1839–40 behind I. Roll 1840: 133 B, 224 I. Roll 1858: 116 B, 74 G, 171 I. Financed by vol. subscriptions, sch. pence (2d., 1d.), endowment of £5 a year by 1893. Roll 1871: 189 B, 119 G, 193 I; 1875 a.a. 551. Premises found unsuitable for perm. sch. 1905; accn. reduced

[3] Para. based on *Highbury Hill High Sch.: Short Hist.* (booklet c. 1958, in Islington libr.).
[4] Additional inf. from G.L.R.O., EO/HFE/5/107, *Rep. of Northern Polytechnic 1930–31; Sec. Schs. Recognised as Efficient*, 306; I.L.E.A. *Highbury Grove Sch.* (TS. prospectus in Islington libr.).
[5] Para. based on R. J. King and T. H. Price, *Holloway*

Sch. Jubilee Retrospective 1907–57 (1957, copy in Islington libr.); inf. from sch. librarian.
[6] Para. based on *Ragged Sch. Union Mag.* xix (1867), 125; iii. 207; xx. 239; Lewis, *Islington As It Was*, 82; P.R.O., C 54/15557, no. 16.
[7] Additional inf. from Lewis, *Islington*, 343–4; P.R.O., C 54/12082, no. 16.

to 394, a.a. 447. Transferred to L.C.C. and renamed Cloudesley Street temp. 1908. Closed 1915 and replaced by Laycock.

HOPE STREET, see Ring Cross.

HORNSEY RD. WES. DAY. Opened 1871 adjoining chapel, with 91 B & 29 G under 1 master; a.a. 90–100. Financed by vol. subscriptions, sch. pence (4d., 6d.), parl. grants. 1878 accn. 219 M, a.a. 218; 1893 accn. 403 M, a.a. 128. Bldg. transferred to S.B.L. 1893 for 3 years for temp. bd. sch., and later demol. (see Hornsey Rd., Upper).

HORNSEY RD. BD. Opened 1875 for 486 B, G, I.[8] 1878 accn. 860, a.a. 645. Demol. 1887 and pupils temporarily transferred to Pakeman Street (see Hornsey Rd., Upper).

HORNSEY RD., UPPER, near Seven Sisters Rd. Temp. bldgs. at Pakeman Street sch. used for Hornsey Rd. pupils 1888–93. Hornsey Rd. Wes. sch. opened 1893 as temp. sch. for B, G, I, by S.B.L., and site later used for perm. sch. In 1894 two iron rooms opened for I. Upper Hornsey Rd. perm. bd. sch. opened 1897 for B, G, I. 1908 accn. 552 B, 552 G, 543 I, a.a. 447 B, 461 G, 430 I. Reorg. 1927–32 for 462 SB, 455 SG, 447 I. Reorg. 1947–51 as Isledon primary for I, and Isledon sec. for SM. Reorg. 1957 when Isledon sec. joined Tollington Pk. (q.v.), Isledon primary closed; Montem (q.v.) took over bldg.

HUNGERFORD I, North Rd.; HUNGERFORD J, Hungerford Rd., York Way. Opened 1896 as Hungerford Rd. bd. sch. for B, G, I. 1908 accn. 480 B, 485 G, 528 I, a.a. 346 B, 331 G, 365 I. Reorg. 1927–32 for 379 JB, 387 JG, 440 I. Renamed Hungerford primary c. 1947. Reorg. 1967 for JM, I; class taught in Welsh for pupils from all over Lond. 1960s. I moved to new open-plan bldg. in North Rd. 1971; further bldg. 1981. Included 3 nursery classes (1 off-site) from 1975. Rolls 1982: 266 JM; 200 I & 100 nursery.

ISLEDON PRIMARY, SEC., see Hornsey Rd., Upper.

ISLINGTON CHAPEL, Church (later Gaskin) Street.[9] Sch. of industry opened 1801 to clothe and educate 30 G aged 8 to 13 years, in room adjoining chapel. N. Lond. and Islington Royal British Free Sch. Soc. formed 1817, fitted up chapel as sch. for 200 G; many still clothed. Financed by subscriptions. Roll 1820: 247 G; needlework taught. Sch. pence charged by 1838 (1d., 2d.). Roll 1838: 140 G. Sch. closed c. 1841 and former chapel sold to St. Mary's parochial sch. 1842. Probably replaced by Lower Rd. British (q.v.). By 1850 G sch. reopened in Church Street, probably adjoining new Islington chapel at corner of Upper Street. Roll: 125 G. Closed by 1871.

ISLINGTON GREEN, Prebend Street. Opened 1886 as Queen's Head Street bd. sch. for B, GI. Sep. I opened 1887 with additional accn. for 320.[10] Sch. pence (3d.). 1893 accn. 1,460, a.a. 1,176; 1908 accn. 446 B, 460 G, 474 I, a.a. 447 B, 426 G, 420 I. Reorg. 1911 for 494 B, 460 G, 319 JM, 404 I,

taking pupils from Arlington Sq. and St. Bartholomew's. 1911 a.a. 1,311; 1922 a.a. 1,540. Reorg. 1932–6 for 560 SB, 556 SG, 424 I. Reorg. 1947–51 as Tudor sec. for G and Tudor sec. for B. Reorg. for SM 1954. Reorg. as Islington Green comprehensive for SM 1965 on same site. Tudor G block demol. 1963–4; six-storeyed teaching block and two-storeyed houseroom block built. Roll 1982: 860 SM.

ISLINGTON GUARDIANS' RECEIVING HOME TEMP., 'Sandal Magna' and 1–2 Cromartie Rd., Hornsey Rise. Opened 1913 by L.C.C. in bd. of guardians' premises, for M & I. 1914 accn. 116 M & I; a.a. 81. Closed 1915.

ISLINGTON WORKHOUSE SCH., see above, local govt.

ISLINGTON AND N. LOND. SHOE-BLACK BRIGADE, 15 York Rd. (later Way), King's Cross.[11] Formed 1857 in Church Street as refuge for c. 20 B, employed c. 25 more as shoe-blacks, and provided evg. sch. Self supporting by 1867: 307,925 pairs of boots cleaned @ 1d. a pair in 1866. Moved to York Rd. 1867. 107 B passed through refuge in 1866. Roll 1871: 47 B from age 13. Received parl. grants. 1878 accn. 100, a.a. 36. Moved to no. 146B King's Cross Road by 1912 when accn. 29. Nothing further known.

ISLINGTON RAGGED, see Britannia Row (Islington).

LAYCOCK, Laycock Street, Upper Street. Opened 1915 as Laycock Street council sch. for B, G, I, replacing Cloudesley Street temp. 1919 accn. 395 B, 395 G, 462 I, a.a. 315 B, 310 G, 291 I. Reorg. 1927–32 for 395 SB, 355 SG, 395 JB, 395 JG, 462 I. In 1939 JM, I in Laycock Street, SB, SG in former Station Road sch. Reorg. 1947–51 as Laycock primary, Laycock Street, for JM, I, and Laycock sec., Highbury Station Rd., for SB. Laycock sec. amalg. 1967 with other SB schs. to form Highbury Grove (q.v.), and bldg. used for Isledon Teachers' Centre and media resources bldg. for local schs. 1982. Primary reorg. for JM & I c. 1971, and included unit for partially hearing from c. 1974. Roll 1982: c. 250 JM & I.

LITTLE WILLIAM STREET BRITISH. Opened c. 1851 with 130 B & G. Sch. pence (3d., 4d.).[12] Closed by 1852.

LOWER RD. BRITISH, Greenman's Lane. Opened 1844 for B; success soon led to opening of G sch. to replace Islington chapel sch. Roll 1844: 142 B, 100 G.[13] Financed by sch. pence (2d.), parl. grants, vol. contributions. Roll 1845: 286; a.a. 120 B, 100 G, geography and history taught. By 1850 for B only; G sch. reopened in Church Street (see Islington chapel sch.). 1850 roll 190 B.

MARRIOTT RD. CENTRAL, see Tollington Pk.

MATTHIAS RD., see Newington Green.

MILTON YARD RAGGED, Elizabeth Terr., Liverpool Rd.[14] Opened 1856 as evg. sch. only, a.a. 15–20. Moved to larger premises, a.a. 30. Enlarged 1862, a.a. 62 during winter. Roll 1866:

---

[8] Firth, *Municipal Lond.*, 459.
[9] Para. based on *Rep. of Cttee. of Islington chapel sch. of industry for G* (1845, in Islington libr.); Lewis, *Islington*, 263; British and Foreign Sch. Soc. *Rep.* (1817), 26, 131; (1820), 113–14; (1821), 128; (1838), 35; L. D. Dixon, *Seven Score Years and Ten*, 17.   [10] S.B.L. *Rep. 1886–7* (1887), 18.

[11] Para. based on *Ragged Sch. Union Mag.* xx. 11–12; Reformatory and Refuge Union, *Class. List* (1912), 30.
[12] British and Foreign Sch. Soc. *Rep.* (1851), 39.
[13] Ibid. (1844), 55.
[14] Para. based on *Ragged Sch. Union Mag.* xix. 192; xx. 263.

350 B; a.a. 73 summer, 95 winter. G included later. Penny bank and lending libr. In 1868 sch. 'crammed' each evg.; B sch. 4 evgs. a week, a.a. 120 winter, 90–100 summer, aged 10–20. Roll 1871: 164 B, 120 G. Nothing further known.

MONTEM, Hornsey Rd. Opened 1886 as Montem Street bd. sch., Montem Street, Tollington Pk., with 1,000 B, G, I. Sch. pence (4*d.*, 3*d.*). 1893 accn. 1,400, a.a. 1,389; 1908 accn. 452 B, 420 G, 276 SG, 520 I. SB organized into Montem Street higher elementary sch. until 1910 when it became Montem Street central; SG joined central 1911 (see Tollington Pk.). Reorg. 1927–32 for 400 JB, 360 JG, 419 I. Reorg. 1947–51 as Montem primary for JM, I. Moved to former Upper Hornsey Rd. sch. bldg. 1957. Reorg. as sep. JM, I schs. 1962. Noteworthy conversion of buildings by John Harvey 1969–72. Roll *c.* 1970: 400 JM, 250 I. Rolls 1982: 214 JM; 130 I & 30 nursery.

MONTEM STREET CENTRAL, see Tollington Pk.

MORTON RD., 30 Morton Rd., Essex Rd. Opened 1850 by Congs. as ragged sch.; moved to new bldg. 1865. Roll 1871: 43 B & 34 G, 126 I; 340 B at evg. sch. run by vol. teachers; a.a. 66 M, 72 I. Apparently transferred to S.B.L. as Morton Rd. bd. sch. 1878 accn. 168, a.a. 125; later closed. Reopened 1885 as Morton Rd. temp. for M, I, as feeder for Ecclesbourne Rd. (q.v.).

MOUNT CARMEL R.C. G, Eden Grove, Holloway. Opened 1967 as vol. aided sec. sch. for SG, replacing Our Lady of Sion sch. on same site. By 1970 upper sch. in Eden Grove, lower sch. in former Wellington Rd. bldg., Westbourne Rd. Roll 1982: 588 SG.

NEW NORTH RD., see St. Bartholomew's C.E.

NEWINGTON GREEN, Matthias Rd. Opened 1884 as Matthias Road bd. sch. for 360 B, 360 G, 460 I. Sch. pence (2*d.*, 3*d.*). Enlarged by 1893 for 476 B, 476 G, 605 I, a.a. 1,063. Reorg. 1927–32 for 353 JB, 360 JG, 435 I. Rebuilt 1930s but largely destroyed in Second World War. Existing temp. bldg. opened 1951 with Newington Green JM and Newington Green I in sep. schs. Roll 1982: 240 JM; 131 I & 65 nursery.

OFFORD RD. HIGHER GRADE, see Barnsbury sch. for G.

OUR LADY OF SION SEC., Eden Grove, Holloway. Opened as private day and boarding sch. (below). Became vol. aided R.C. sec. sch. for SG 1947–51. Closed 1967; replaced by Mount Carmel (q.v.).

OUR LADY OF THE SACRED HEART R.C., Eden Grove, Holloway. Opened 1868 with 35 B, 30 G in Eden Grove. Financed by vol. contributions, sch. pence (2*d.*, 1*d.*), parl. grants. Moved to new ho. 1869 with *c.* 90 M and to bldg. adjoining presbytery 1869. Roll 1871: 81 B, 135 G. Over half pupils admitted free. 1878 accn. 274 BGI, a.a. 152; 1908 accn. 120 B, 180 G, 195 I, a.a. 101 B, 121 G, 91 I. Wing on S. side of ch. 1904 for G and I; B remained in old bldg. Hut on playground opposite ch. used for meals; replaced by community centre 1973. 1912 a.a. 409; 1922 a.a. 444. Reorg. 1949 as JM and I primary. Annexe at St. Joan, Highbury Pk. (q.v.), became sep. sch. 1956.

Annexe at Westbourne Rd. opened 1965; 2 floors of former Alfred Prichard bldg. used 1982. Roll 1982: 302 JM & I.

PAKEMAN, Hornsey Rd., Holloway. Opened 1888 as Pakeman Street bd. sch. with G, I from Hornsey Rd.; B in iron bldg. nearby until new Upper Hornsey Rd. sch. opened. Reorg. 1889 for JM, I. Sch. pence (2*d.*, 1*d.*). 1893 accn. 1,051, a.a. 575 M, I; 1908 accn. 360 SM, 300 JM, 391 I, a.a. 284 SM, 273 JM, 299 I. Reorg. 1915 for 286 B, 283 G, 293 I. 1919 a.a. 721. Reorg. 1927–32 for 235 JB, 234 JG, 261 I. Reorg. 1947–51 as primary for JM only. Reorg. for JM & I *c.* 1971. Roll 1982: 277 JM & I.

PAROCHIAL CHAR. SCHS., see St. Mary, Islington, C.E.

PARSLEY CT., see Protestant Institute.

PENTON PRIMARY, Ritchie Street, Liverpool Rd. Opened as Richard Street bd. sch. 1891 for B, G, I. Sch. pence (2*d.*). 1893 accn. 1,193, a.a. 957; 1908 accn. 360 B, 356 G, 473 I, a.a. 338 B, 332 G, 380 I. Renamed Ritchie council sch. 1938; accn. 266 B, 306 G, 328 I. Reorg. as Ritchie sec. for SG 1947–51. Closed 1969. Penton J & I sch. moved to site 1969 from White Lion Street (Clerkenwell). Renamed Penton primary for JM & I 1971. Roll 1982: 183 JM & I.

POOLE'S PK., Lennox Rd., Finsbury Pk.[15] Opened 1876 as Poole's Pk. bd. sch. for 716 B, G, I. Sch. pence (2*d.*). Too small within 6 months. 1878 accn. 1,016, a.a. 706; 1893 accn. 1,058, a.a. 1,058. Accn. for B, G increased over covered playground 1906. Bldg. demol. 1938; new three-storeyed bldg. on same site unfinished 1939. Reopened 1946 as primary sch. for JB, JG, I. Additions to bldg. 1949, 1970. Reorg. for JM, I 1959. In 1960s half pupils of Cypriot origin. Rolls 1982: 210 JM; 161 I.

POPHAM RD., see Charles Lamb.

PROTESTANT INSTITUTE RAGGED SCHS. Institute opened two schs. in 1851 mainly for children of R.C.s. One in Duddy's Rents, Lower Rd.: 1853 a.a. 93 BGI. One in Parsley Ct., Islington High Street: a.a. 38, also evg. sch.[16]

QUEEN'S HEAD STREET, see Islington Green.

RICHARD STREET, see Penton.

RING CROSS PRIMARY, Eden Grove, Holloway. Opened 1931 as Hope Street council sch. for 392 JM & I. Renamed Ring Cross 1936 for 353 JM & I. 1939 accn. 132 JM & 178 I. Reorg. 1947–51 for I only. Moved to Chillingworth Rd. by 1955. Ring Cross J opened *c.* 1969 at Eden Grove. Reorg. 1977–80 as JM & I at Eden Grove site. Roll 1982: 215 JM & I.

RITCHIE COUNCIL and SEC., see Penton.

ROBERT BLAIR PRIMARY, Blundell Street, Caledonian Rd. Temp. schs. opened 1872 by S.B.L. with 161 B in Blundell Street mission rooms, 139 G in room under Primitive Meth. chapel. Perm. Blundell Street bd. sch. opened 1873 for B, G, I. 1878 accn. 830, a.a. 825; 1893 accn. 1,433, a.a. 1,357; 1908 accn. 439 B, 428 G, 566 I, a.a. 402 B, 396 G, 418 I. 1913 a.a. 1,108; 1927 a.a. 969. Sch. rebuilt 1923–4. Reorg. 1927–32 for 440 SB, 400 SG, 320 JM, 298 I. Renamed Rob. Blair 1936. Reorg. 1947–51 for

[15] Additional inf. from *Poole's Pk. Schs. Islington 1876–1976* (centenary booklet supplied by junior sch. head).
[16] Lewis, *Islington As It Was*, 83.

1. Regent's Canal Opening behind Duncan Terrace

2. Islington Green from the south in 1808

ISLINGTON

3. Canonbury House from the south in 1731

4. Ward's or King John's Place, Lower Street, in 1860

5. Fisher's house in Lower Street, demolished in 1845, from the garden

ISLINGTON

6. Highbury Barn c. 1800

7. Archway tavern with horse trams c. 1900

8. Queen's Head, Essex Road, in 1827

ISLINGTON

10. Scholefield Road, nos. 38 to 46. Demolished c. 1970.

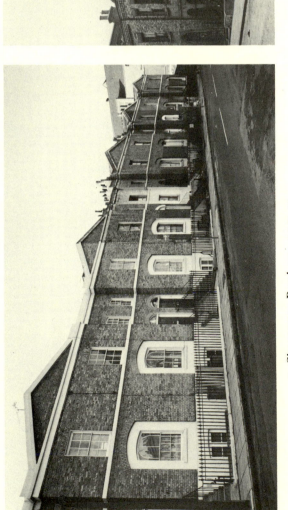

9. Shepperton Road, nos. 35 to 53

12. Arundel Grove, nos. 21 to 33. Demolished early 1960s.

11. Balfe Street, nos. 17 to 35

ISLINGTON

15. Highbury New Park, no. 31

14. Myddleton Cottage, Canonbury Park South

17. Thornhill Square, nos. 23 to 30

13. Houses on site of Highbury Quadrant school,
Highbury New Park

16. Whitehall Park, nos. 29 to 35

ISLINGTON

18. Ridley's Floor-Cloth Manufactory, Lower Road, *c.* 1830. The Rosemary Branch white lead mills are in the background.

19. Brickmaking on the Stonefields estate. Liverpool Road and the workhouse are in the background.

ISLINGTON

20. Beaconsfield Buildings, Rufford Street　　　21. Clarence Terrace, Rufford Street

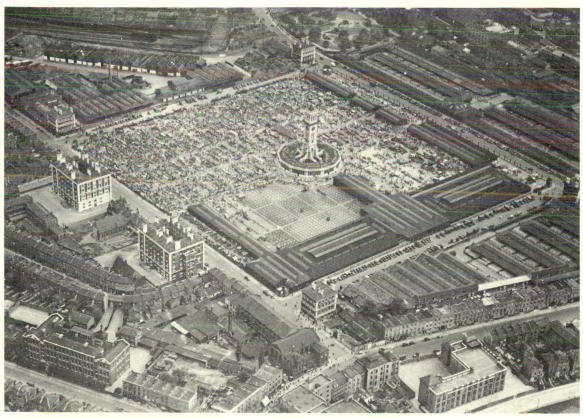

22. Metropolitan Market from the air, looking east, *c.* 1930

ISLINGTON

23. Highbury College, Highbury Park, in 1826

24. Church Missionary College, formerly Harvey's house, Upper Street, in 1824

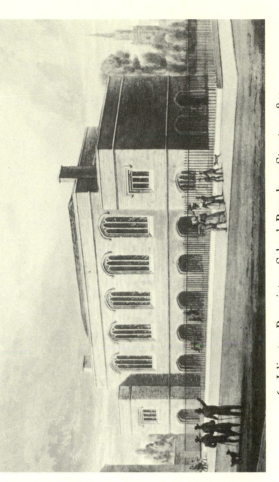

26. Islington Proprietary School, Barnsbury Street, c. 1850

25. St. James's, Holloway, district schools, George's Road, in 1854

ISLINGTON

29. Holloway prison: reception block

27. Church Missionary Society's Children's Home, Highbury Grove, c. 1855

28. Pentonville prison in 1842

ISLINGTON

32. St. Mary's new church in 1793

30. St. Mary's old church from the north-west in 1750

31. St. Mary's old church from the north-east in 1750

ISLINGTON

34. St. Peter's Chapel, River Lane, c. 1840

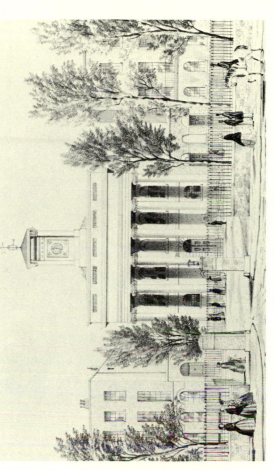

36. Union Chapel, Compton Terrace, c. 1850

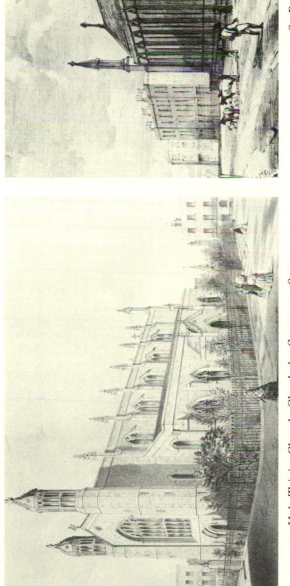

33. Holy Trinity Church, Cloudesley Square, c. 1850

35. St. James's Church, Chillingworth Road, between the World Wars

ISLINGTON

37. St. George's Church, Tufnell Park

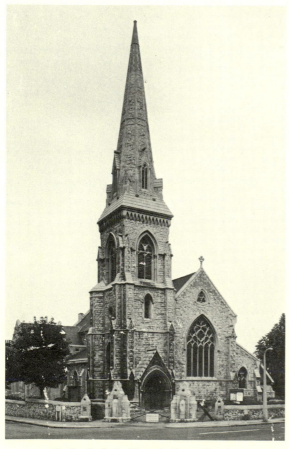

38. St. Luke's Church, Penn Road

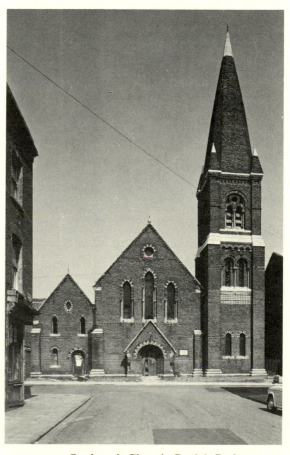

39. St. Anne's Church, Poole's Park

ISLINGTON

40. St. Augustine's Church, Highbury New Park

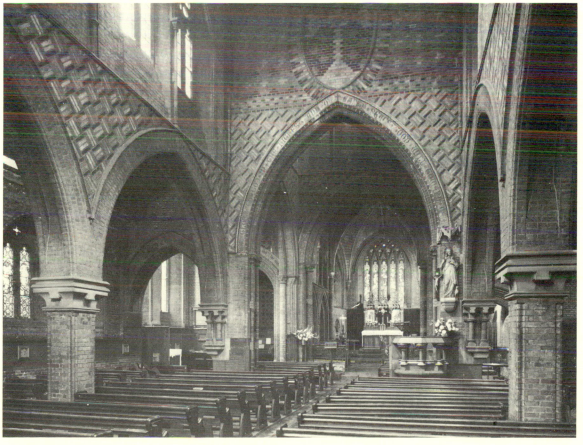

41. St. Saviour's Church, Aberdeen Park

ISLINGTON

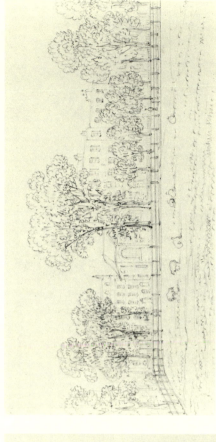

43. Newington Green in 1843. The chapel is in the centre.

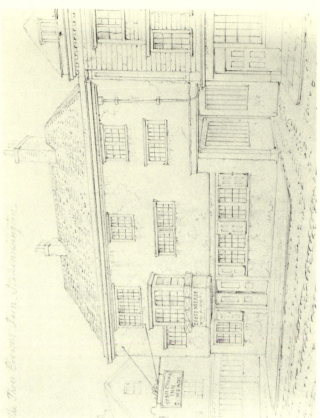

44. Three Crowns, High Street, *c.* 1843

42. Old manor gateway, behind Edward's Lane

STOKE NEWINGTON

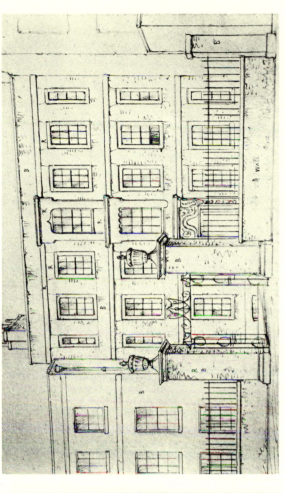

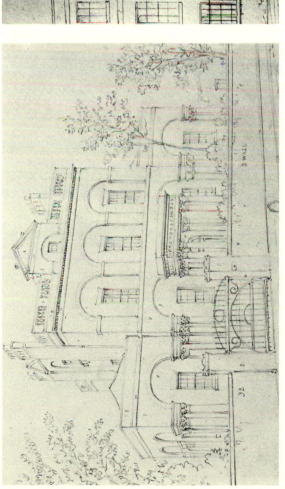

45. Newington Hall c. 1844

46. Mr. Foster's, formerly Thos. Day's, House in 1843

47. Fleetwood House, garden front, c. 1843

48. Abney House, garden front, c. 1843

STOKE NEWINGTON: CHURCH STREET

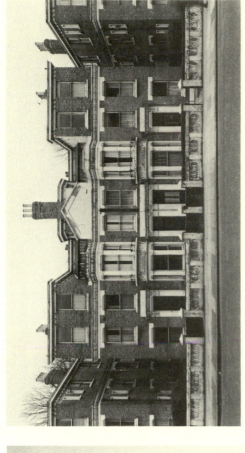

50. Manor Road, nos. 40 to 46, flats

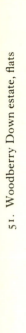

51. Woodberry Down estate, flats

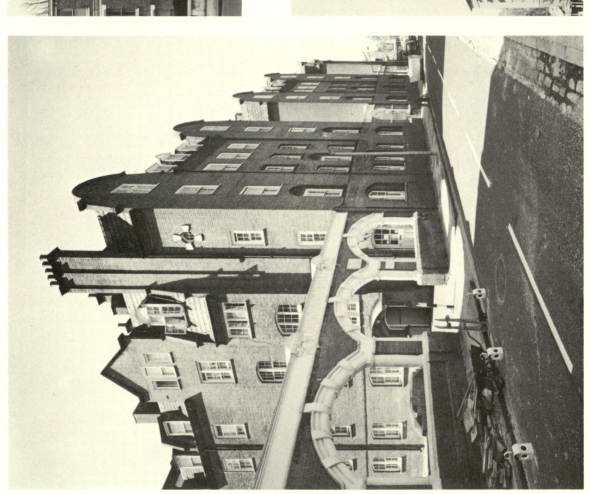

49. Coronation Avenue, Victorian Grove, flats

STOKE NEWINGTON

53. Green Lanes pumping station

STOKE NEWINGTON

52. Town Hall

56. St. Mary's new church

54. St. Mary's old church *c.* 1850

55. Newington Green chapel *c.* 1843

STOKE NEWINGTON

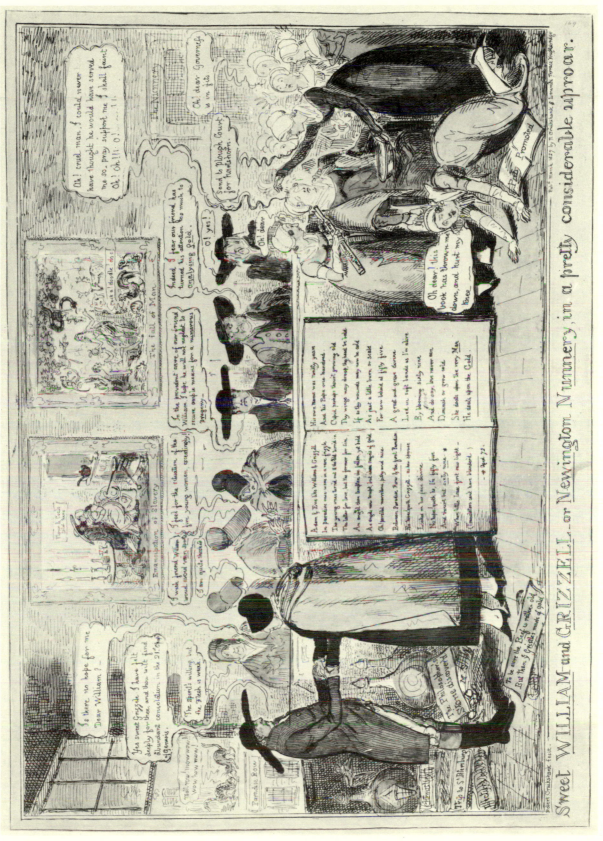

57. Cartoon on the marriage of William Allen to his third wife Grizell, *née* Hoare, 1827, satirizing his girls' boarding school and circle of Quakers

STOKE NEWINGTON

58. Olney Cottage, Cowper Road. St. Matthias's Church, built in 1849, is on the right.

59. Stoke Newington from the north-west *c.* 1750. Beyond the New River are the church and, on the right, Paradise Row.

STOKE NEWINGTON

JM, I. Later amalg. as JM & I. Roll 1982: 169 JM & I.

ROMILLY LODGE PRIMARY, 59 Hornsey Rise. Opened *c.* 1947 as temp. primary for 200 JM & I in former Romilly Lodge special sch. Closed 1957.

ROTHERFIELD, Rotherfield Street, Essex Rd. Opened 1898 as Rotherfield Street bd. sch. for B, G, I. 1908 accn. 360 B, 360 G, 435 I, a.a. 309 B, 325 G, 308 I. Reorg. 1932–6 for 548 JG, 360 I. Rotherfield primary from 1947. JB from Shepperton Rd. amalg. 1957 with JG to form JM. Additions to bldg. 1967. Rolls 1982: 167 I & 30 nursery; 212 JM.

RUFFORD'S BLDGS., see Angel.

ST. ALOYSIUS COLLEGE, Hornsey Lane, High-gate. Founded 1879 by Brothers of Mercy as private R.C. sec. sch. for B. Became vol. aided grammar 1950.[17] Largely rebuilt 1969–71 on same site, as comprehensive for *c.* 1,000 SB. Roll 1982: 1,020 SB.

ST. ANDREW CH., 22A Storey Street, Cale-donian Rd. Possibly opened by 1861. Roll 1871: 146 B, 170 G, all ages; accn. 4 rooms for 50, a.a. 50 M, 80 I. Financed by sch. pence, vol. contri-butions. Not recognized as efficient and probably soon closed.

ST. ANNE, TOLLINGTON PK., C.E., Poole's Pk. Opened 1870 with Nat. Soc. grant in former St. Anne's iron ch., Durham Rd. Roll 1871: 111 B, 248 G, all ages; evg. sch. 6 hrs. a week, 27 B, 19 G. New schs. for B, G, I completed 1877 next to ch. Financed by sch. pence (3*d.*, 4*d.*), vol. contri-butions, parl. grants. Roll 1877: 148 B, 139 G, 120 I. 1893 accn. 353, a.a. 328; 1898 a.a. 117 B, 124 G. Closed 1898.

ST. BARNABUS NAT., Harvist Rd., Hornsey Rd. Opened 1872 for 200 B, 200 G, 230 I. Also evg. sch. Financed by sch. pence (2*d.*–4*d.*), vol. contributions, parl. grants. 1878 accn. 724, a.a. 590; 1893 accn. 744, a.a. 587. Bd. schs. drew away pupils, until B closed *c.* 1899, G and I 1900. Premises may have been let to S.B.L. 1901 for Harvist Rd. temp. (q.v.).

ST. BARTHOLOMEW C.E., Shepperton Rd., New North Rd. Opened 1856 in Newhall Street, off Popham Rd., moving to ho. in Shepperton Rd. 1857, for B, G, I. Financed by sch. pence (2*d.*, 1*d.*), vol. contributions, and grants from parl., Islington Ch. Home mission, C.E. Educ. Soc. Roll 1858: 60 B, 40 G, all ages. 1865 a.a. 84. New schs. in Shepperton Rd.[18] opened 1871 for 450 BG. Roll 1871: 101 B, 70 G. I sch. for 140 by 1874 when enlarged for 220 I. 1893 accn. 469 B, M, a.a. 305. Sch. amalg. with St. Matthew C.E. 1894; Shepperton Rd. bldg. used for B. Trans-ferred to S.B.L. 1901 and renamed New North Rd. bd. for B. 1908 accn. 294 B. Closed 1911 and replaced by Queen's Head Street.

ST. CLEMENT NAT., Cumberland (later Ponder) Street, Roman Way. Opened 1861. New sch. in Cumberland Street 1866, for 260 B, G, I, in one dept. until bldg. finished.[19] Sep. depts. by 1871. Roll 1871: 236 B, 170 G, 220 I. Financed by sch.

pence, parl. grants. 1878 accn. 722, a.a. 605; 1893 a.a. 492; 1908 accn. 192 B, 192 G, 165 I, a.a. 177 B, 152 G, 132 I. 1932 a.a. 166 B, 142 G, 95 I. Reorg. 1947–51 as vol. aided primary for B, JG & I; and for JM & I by 1955. Closed 1972–4.

ST. DAVID C.E. NAT., Wellington Rd., St. James's Rd., Holloway. Iron room for 120 M opened 1869. Roll 1871: 95 B, 128 G, all ages; accn. 90, a.a. 120 M and I under 1 mistress. New sch. for 450 B, G, I on same site completed 1874; a.a. 80 B, 61 G, 140 I. Financed by sch. pence (2*d.*–8*d.*), parl. grants. 1878 accn. 594, a.a. 377. Transferred to S.B.L. 1879, and probably became Wellington Rd. (q.v.).

ST. GEORGE, TUFNELL PK., C.E., Grafton Rd., Holloway. Opened by 1871 with 63 B, 40 G, 120 I; a.a. 52 B, 28 G, 96 I. Evg. sch. 70 B, G. Closed 1874 as new site unobtainable.

ST. JAMES NAT. and I, George's Rd., Holloway. Built 1838 with Nat. Soc. grant on part of ch. grounds, for M & I until new schs. built. Roll 1840: 210 I.[20] Roll 1846 215; accn. 250; 1852 a.a. 160 M. New schs. built 1854[21] for 142 B, 142 G, 142 I. B enlarged by 100 in 1861. 1865 a.a. 432. Financed by parl. grants, sch. pence, vol. contri-butions. Roll 1871: 253 B, 163 G, 227 I; a.a. 208 B, 131 G, 178 I. 1878 accn. 716, a.a. 572. By 1908 recognized accn. reduced to 422 B, G, I, a.a. 448. Reorg. 1925 for 200 SM, 192 JM & I. Closed 1947–51.

ST. JAMES MISSION ROOM, Rosemary Street, Islington. Opened by 1871 for 350 I; a.a. 130 I to age 11. Not recognized by Bd. of Educ. and probably soon closed.

ST. JOAN OF ARC R.C. PRIMARY, Northolme Rd., Highbury Pk. Opened at 66–70 Highbury Pk. as war emergency sch. and became annexe to Our Lady of the Sacred Heart primary 1947–51. Became sep. vol. aided R.C. primary for JM & I, 1956. Annexe in Aberdeen Pk. opened 1963. New bldg. on adjoining site in Northolme Rd. 1964. Old bldg. demol. for playground. Roll 1982: 324 JM & I.

ST. JOHN, UPPER HOLLOWAY, C.E. PRIMARY, Pemberton Gdns., Upper Holloway.[22] Sch. for G and I in Hornsey Lane by 1828; temp. sch. for B in two rented cottages at 11 Gordon Pl. opened 1829 with 41 B. Both schs. in union with Nat. Soc. 1829, roll 63 B, 56 G. Site adjoining St. John's ch. intended for parsonage presented by Corporation of Sons of Clergy 1830. Sch. designed by Sir Chas. Barry[23] opened 1831. Roll 1831: 74 B, 52 G. Extended 1858, 1867. I by 1867. Roll 1871: 193 B, 174 G, 282 I; a.a. 168 B, 130 G, 219 I. Financed by vol. contributions, parl. grants, sch. pence (2*d.*). Improvements to accn. required by L.C.C. 1904. Reorg. 1945 as vol. aided C.E. primary for JM & I. New sch. built on site of 14–30 Pemberton Gdns. and 51–9 St. John's Grove; part moved 1967, remainder 1972. Nursery unit added 1977. Roll 1982: *c.* 220 JM & I.

ST. JOHN, UPPER HOLLOWAY, RAGGED, Gordon Ct., Highgate Hill. Opened *c.* 1864 in converted

[17] *V.C.H. Mdx.* i. 262; below, private schs.
[18] P.R.O., C 54/16900, no. 12.
[19] Ibid. C 54/16450, no. 8.
[20] Lewis, *Islington*, 377; P.R.O., C 54/14573, no. 14.
[21] Above, plate 25.
[22] See St. Mark C.E. for I sch. in Grove Lane.
[23] Colvin, *Dict. Brit. Architects*, 91.

ho. as Gordon Ct. I sch. by V. of St. John's and cttee., as free sch. Roll 1870: 60 I. Sch. pence (1d.) charged from 1870. 1871 accn. 35, a.a. 50 B, 30 G, all ages, under 1 teacher. New sch. built 1872 in Vorley Rd. for 200 I and known as St. John's mission I sch. Financed by vol. contributions, parl. grants, sch. pence. Roll 1875: 146 G and 476 I. 1878 accn. 182, a.a. 129. Not receiving grants by 1893.

St. John, Highbury Vale, C.E. primary, Conewood Street, Blackstock Rd.[24] Opened 1836 as Highbury Vale sch. with 102 M, with aid of parl. grant, by ladies who founded chapel; accn. 186, a.a. 68 in 1849. Site enlarged and sch. rebuilt 1864; B, G, I and known as Christ Ch. Nat. schs. Financed by vol. contributions, parl. grants, sch. pence (2d.–4d.). Praised by inspector 1852. Roll 1871: 58 B, 76 G, 109 I; a.a. 53 B, 68 G, 84 I. 1878 accn. 279, a.a. 270. Handed over to new ch. of St. John's 1883. New I room built 1884 and B, G enlarged 1885, with aid from Nat. Soc. 1893 accn. 541, a.a. 380. Roll fell by over half after Free Educ. Act. L.C.C. required thorough repairs 1908; accn. 108 B, 108 G, 145 I, a.a. 140 B, 140 G, 112 I. Playgrounds added 1934, 1937. Reorg. 1947–51 as vol. aided C.E. primary for JM & I. New I block 1982. Roll 1982: c. 210 JM & I.

St. John the Evangelist R.C. primary, Duncan Street, Islington Green. Built 1839 behind ch. site, B on ground floor, G on first, with teacher's ho. Roll 1857: 55 B, 50 G & I. Connected with R.C. Poor Sch. Cttee. Financed by vol. contributions, parl. grants, sch. pence when possible. 1865 a.a. 283. Roll 1871: 190 B, 200 G & I; evg. sch. 8 hrs. a week for 48 B. Third of pupils free. 1878 accn. 569, a.a. 250; 1908 accn. 236 B, 176 G, 192 I, a.a. 213 B, 173 G, 138 I. Reorg. 1947–51 as vol. aided R.C. primary for JM & I. Roll 1982: 293 JM & I.

St. John the Evangelist R.C. sec., Duncan Street. Opened 1947–51 with pupils from St. John the Evangelist primary R.C. and on same site, as vol. aided sch. for SM. Closed 1957.

St. John's Rd. (temp.), Upper Holloway. Opened 1879 by S.B.L. in rented premises as feeder for perm. sch. on Highgate Hill. B, GI. Sch. pence (3d.).

St. Joseph R.C. primary, Highgate Hill. Opened 1860 in temp. room fronting Dartmouth Pk. Hill for BGI. Financed by vol. contributions, parl. grants, sch. pence (1d.). 1863 a.a. 33 M. New bldg. opened 1867 for B, G. Sch. pence (1d.–3d.). Roll 1871: 125 B all ages in 1 dept., 76 G & 75 I in 1 dept.; majority did not pay. 1878 accn. 424, a.a. 147; 1893 accn. 379, a.a. 264. 1908 accn. 204 B, 225 G, 98 I, a.a. 113 B, 114 G, 75 I. G & I still in 1 dept. 1932. Reorg. 1947–51 as vol. aided R.C. primary for M & I. Reorg. 1961 for JM & I. Roll 1982: 405 JM & I.

St. Jude, Mildmay Pk., C.E. primary, King Henry's Walk. Opened 1857 in Mildmay Grove beside ch. with 37 B, 40 G, 40 I.[25] Replaced by St. Jude elementary C.E. sch. 1865. Financed by vol. contributions, parl. grants, sch. pence (1d.). Roll 1866: 88 B, 54 G, 118 I; a.a. 233. B moved to St. Jude Dist. B sch. 1870 in iron room in Woodville Grove, Mildmay Rd. Roll 1870: 116 B. New sch. for B, I opened 1885 in King Henry's Walk; G remained in Mildmay Grove. 1893 accn. 840, a.a. 586. B, I sch. burned down 1924; new bldg. on same site opened 1926. Reorg. 1953 as vol. aided C.E. primary for JM in King Henry's Walk, I in Mildmay Grove. Roll 1982: 180 JM & I.

St. Jude mission, see Ball's Pond Rd. mission.

St. Luke, Cattle Market, Holloway. Opened 1868 by V. of St. Luke in three rooms at Queen's Arms bldg., Cattle Market, for c. 110 I who could not reach bd. sch. New bldg. opened 1878 belonging to par. Financed by vol. contributions, sch. pence (2d.). Not recognized.

St. Mark C.E. primary, Sussex Way, Upper Holloway. I sch. of two rooms with teacher's ho. above in Grove Lane or Rd. (later Tollington Way), built 1836 and maintained by Hen. Venn, V. of St. John, Upper Holloway. Roll 1842: 71 I.[26] Enlarged 1846. Premises given to St. Mark's dist., which it served after 1851. Financed by vol. contributions, sch. pence (1d., 2d.). Site at corner of Tollington Way and Mitford Rd. conveyed by Venn 1863 for Nat. and I schs. for St. Mark and St. Mary, Hornsey Rise, jointly. Opened 1863, 1 bldg. for I, 1 for B, G; playground acquired 1865.[27] 1863 a.a. 63 B, 72 G, 130 I. Roll 1871: 141 B, 115 G, 338 I. 1908 accn. 148 B, 143 G, 150 I, a.a. 146 B, 132 G, 178 I. Reorg. 1927–32 for 359 JM & I. New bldgs. after Second World War, also iron huts. Roll 1982: 207 JM & I.

St. Mary, Islington, C.E. primary, Halton Rd. Char. schs. founded by subscription 1710 to clothe, board, educate, and apprentice 24 B, 20 G in sep. schs.; subscriptions c. £100 in 1712.[28] Schs. in room over ch. porch.[29] Lease of ho. and gdn. near corner of Cross and Upper streets devised by Geo. Sayer for benefit of schs. 1725 and renewed 1741.[30] Schs. moved 1751 from ch. to new ho. on S. side of Cross Street; adjoining Corner Ho. bought by sch. trustees 1779 and freehold of adjoining property in Cross Street 1788, with 1½ a. of waste of Canonbury manor (later site of 27 Cross Street). Schs. enlarged 1788 and rest of property leased.[31] In 1810 schs., in Rufford's Row, corner of Cross and Upper streets, had 46 B, 34 G supported by char. and clothed, in grey for B, blue for G; clothing continued until c. 1860.[32] New schs. for 400 B, G and teacher's ho. designed by John Wm. Griffith, surveyor to Jas. Rhodes's est., built 1815 on c. ½ a. in Liverpool Rd. near chapel of ease, given by Sam Rhodes. Bldg. financed by subscriptions, donations, and Nat. Soc. grant.[33] Old bldg. then

[24] Para. based on J. Hall, *Hist. Highbury Vale Schs. 1834–1936* (TS. booklet c. 1977 supplied by head); P.R.O., C 54/16186, no. 4; C 54/16288, no. 6.

[25] P.R.O., C 54/15039, no. 11.

[26] Lewis, *Islington*, 299.

[27] P.R.O., C 54/16031, no. 6; C 54/16442, no. 15.

[28] *Acct. of Char. Schs. in G.B. & Irel.* (1712), 13.

[29] G.L.R.O., P83/MRY1/156, p. 8.

[30] Ibid. MRY1/157/9, 12.

[31] Ibid. MRY1/156, p. 9; 158/1, 13, 15; 159/1, 2; P.R.O., C 54/6532, no. 8; C 54/5846, no. 4.

[32] G.L.R.O., P83/MRY1/276/8; MRY1/156, p. 9.

[33] Ibid. MRY1/232; P.R.O., C 54/9473, no. 13; Lewis, *Islington*, 380; Colvin, *Dict. Brit. Architects*, 366.

let.[34] Roll 1816: 250 B, G (only 80 clothed, etc., under char.);[35] 1818: 225 B, 125 G, and steadily increased.[36] I admitted until sep. sch. set up by 1822, when roll 100 I. New sch. for I in Greenman's Lane, Essex Rd., opened 1825.[37] Roll 1828: 368 B, 174 G, 244 I. G spent half of sch. time making char. clothing. G sch. included c. 50 I living too far from I sch. until St. Jas. opened 1838.[38] Roll 1841: 205 B, 113 G, 215 I.[39] Par. bought lease of former Islington chapel, Church Street, 1841 and in 1842 schs. were split into par. ch. branch at Church Street, and chapel of ease branch at Liverpool Rd. bldg.[40] (see St. Mary Magdalene). Roll 1846: 125 B, 69 G, accn. in both Nat. schs. 300 B, 200 G; results found insufficient for amount spent. Par. ch. branch obtained leases of 6 Little Cross Street 1851[41] and adjoining land where new sch. built 1859.[42] 1865 a.a. 482. Roll 1871: 215 B, 126 G; evg. sch. 27 B, 95 G. I sch., established 1847, moved to new bldg. 1850 in Church Passage, off Cross Street. Roll 1864: 228; new bldg. required by inspector. Land bought in Little Cross Street adjoining Nat. schs. and I sch. built 1867–8 fronting Grove Street.[43] Roll 1871: 201 I; a.a. 155. 1878 accn. 667 B, G, I, a.a. 470. Financed by parl. grants, sch. pence (1d.–6d.); 7 B, 5 G free under Westbrook's char. Roll 1888: 200 B, 186 G, 247 I, accn. 240 B, 240 G, 250 I, a.a. 164 B, 150 G, 179 I. Under Scheme 1888, Grace Jackson's char. assisted G to remain after legal requirement.[44] Steady decrease in BG, increase in I; free scholarships needed to put sch. in range of poor.[45] 1908 accn. 194 B, 194 G, 198 I, a.a. 172 B, 197 G, 173 I. Reorg. 1909 for 150 SM, 150 JM, 180 I, a.a. 155 SM, 197 JM, 173 I. Reorg. 1925 for 270 M, 168 I. Reorg. 1947–51 as vol. aided C.E. primary for JM & I. Bombed 1944 and housed at William Tyndale 1944–62, 1964–7, Canonbury 1962–4. Bldg. on old site opened 1967 for c. 160, and enlarged for 280 1969–70. Roll 1982: 150 JM & I.

St. Mary Magdalene C.E. primary, Liverpool Rd., Lower Holloway. Originated as chapel of ease branch of St. Mary, Islington (q.v.), 1842, remaining in Liverpool Rd. bldg. with B, G, I. Financed by vol. contributions, sch. pence, small endowment. Roll 1875: 260 B, 258 G, 271 I; a.a. 227 B, 220 G, 220 I. 1878 accn. 898. Hambleton memorial sch. rooms for I built 1874 in memory of previous V. Old bldg. remodelled 1908 through aid of C. E. Perceval. 1908 accn. 216 B, 174 G, 220 I, a.a. 230 B, 239 G, 227 I. Bombed 1940; sch. used Wellington Rd. until pupils dispersed 1945. Bldg. for 320 JM & I on old site opened 1954, as vol. aided C.E. primary. Roll 1982: 166 JM & I.

St. Matthew M and I C.E., New Norfolk (later Rotherfield) Street, Essex Rd. I sch. opened 1837 adjoining St. Paul's Episcopal chapel, New Norfolk Street, as branch of St. Paul, Canonbury, I sch.[46] Enlarged 1838 for 140 I. Chapel became M sch. for St. Mat.'s dist. 1851, in addition to I sch. Roll 1858: 253 BGI; a.a. 160. Financed by vol. contributions, sch. pence (2d., 1d.). Land in Queen's Pl. adjoining sch. bought 1862 for new sch. and teacher's ho. Nat. Soc. grant for bldg. 1865; new bldg. used for G & I, old bldg. converted for 234 B. Roll 1871: 110 B in Rotherfield Street, 82 G, 191 I in Queen's Pl. 1878 accn. 450 BGI, a.a. 344. Amalg. with St. Bartholomew (q.v.) 1894; G and I moved to Rotherfield Street. Closed 1901.

St. Matthew, City Rd., Nat., Nelson Pl.[47] Built 1851–3 for 150 B, 150 G; additional bldg. 1858 for B, allowed accn. for 90 I. 1878 accn. 408, a.a. 346; evg. sch. 55. Financed by parl. grants, vol. contributions, sch. pence. 1906 accn. 403. 1908 accn. 91 B, 88 G, 135 I, a.a. 111 B, 115 G, 119 I. Reorg. 1932–6 for JM & I. Damaged by bombs 1940. Closed by 1955.

St. Matthias mission, Blundell Street, Caledonian Rd. C.E. sch. in two rooms opened by 1871 for G, I. Roll in G sch. 38 B, 35 G; 43 I. G sch. recognized as efficient 1871, but not receiving parl. grant 1878.

St. Michael C.E., 74, 76, 78 Bingfield Street, Caledonian Rd. Opened 1853 in new bldgs. owned and managed by John Randell, who met expenses not covered by sch. pence. 1865 a.a. 382. Sep. rooms for B, G, I and accn. for I and B teachers by 1871. Roll 1871: 236 B, 138 G, 157 I; a.a. 177 B, 99 G, 116 I. Not receiving grant 1878.

St. Paul Nat. and I, Dorset Street (later Dove Rd.), Ball's Pond.[48] Sch. for 150 I and teacher's ho. fronting Dorset Street built 1829. One-storeyed Nat. schs. for 140 B and 140 G with master's ho. built on adjacent land fronting Henshall Street 1833 with parl. grant. Roll 1840: 100 B, 46 G, 128 I. Financed by subscriptions, vol. contributions, sch. pence, and grant from Betton's char. c. 1851. Additional I sch. in New Norfolk Street 1838 (see St. Matthew C.E.). B, G schs. and ho. rebuilt 1862 as two-storeyed bldg. for B, G. 1862 accn. 542 B, G, I. Roll 1871: 110 B, 93 G, 188 I; a.a. 80 B, 66 G, 146 I. 1878 a.a. 310. Accn. reduced by L.C.C. to 164 B, 110 G, 134 I in 1908; a.a. 172 B, 156 G, 151 I. I bldg. demol. 1908 and replaced by two-storeyed bldg. for G and I; B took over former G dept. 1909 accn. 248 B, 186 G, 126 I; 1939 accn. 259 B, 204 G, 126 I. Reorg. 1947–51 as vol. aided C.E. sch. for M, I. Reorg. 1954 into primary and sec. schs. with 93 SM and 107 I. Primary closed 1955. Roll 1969: 220 SM. Closed 1971.

St. Paul Nat., Blenheim Rd., Upper Holloway. Opened 1875 in mission hall with accn. for 308 M to replace sch. in mission ho. Financed by vol. contributions, sch. pence (3d., 4d.), C.E.

[34] G.L.R.O., P83/MRY1/159, no. 3; Digest of Returns on Educ. of Poor, 550.
[35] Rep. of Sel. Cttee. on Educ. of Lower Orders of Metropolis, H.C. 497, p. 314 (1816), iv.
[36] Par. Schs., List of Subs. and Accts. (1818, in Islington libr.).
[37] G.L.R.O., P83/MRY1/187/1, 2, 4.
[38] Ibid. MRY1/187, Ann. Reps.
[39] Lewis, Islington, 380.
[40] P.R.O., C 54/12864, no. 14; G.L.R.O., P83/MRY1/160/1; MRY1/156, p. 11.
[41] G.L.R.O., P83/MRY1/162.
[42] Ibid. MRY1/156, p. 11; P.R.O., C 54/15443, no. 5.
[43] P.R.O., C 54/16824, no. 6.
[44] G.L.R.O., P83/MRY1/137/6.
[45] Ibid. MRY1/285/4.
[46] Lewis, Islington, 330.
[47] Para. based on O. C. Taylor, Our Parish Story: St. Mat.'s Ch., City Rd. [1932], 15–16 (booklet in Islington libr.).
[48] Additional inf. from Hist. St. Paul's Sch., Canonbury, 1829–1969 (booklet in Islington libr.); Char. Com. files.

Educ. Soc. grant. 1878 accn. 322, a.a. 228; 1893 accn. 340 M, a.a. 256. Closed 1901.

St. Peter Nat., Devonia Rd., Islington Green. I sch. and master's ho. built in Devonia Rd. adjoining ch. 1840 with grants from Nat. Soc. and Thos. Cubitt.[49] Financed by subscriptions, sch. pence (2d.). Roll 1846: 122 B, 74 G. New G and I sch. built 1850 for 166 G, 166 I; old G room added to sch. for 300 B, using additional land fronting Grantbridge Street. Roll 1871: 190 B, 112 G; evg. sch. 42 B, 35 G. Closed c. 1878; bldgs. later used as German sch. (below, private schs.).

St. Peter, Highgate Hill, Nat. G, Brunswick Rd., Upper Holloway. Opened c. 1871 as I sch. Reopened 1879 as G sch. with Nat. Soc. grant. Closed c. 1893; premises later used for Brunswick Rd. sch. (q.v.).

St. Philip the Evangelist Nat., Hale (later Rees) Street, New North Rd. Sch. for G and I opened 1856. New bldg. 1861. Roll 1870: 197 G and I; a.a. 125. Bldg. enlarged for I and sep. schs. for BG built 1871 with Nat. Soc. grant. 1871 accn. 150 B, 120 G, 180 I. Financed by vol. contributions, sch. pence. Evg. sch. for BG from 1873. 1878 accn. 492, a.a. 391. Transferred to S.B.L. 1901 and opened as Arlington Sq. (St. Phil.) temp. bd. 1908 accn. 138 B, 120 G, 132 I, a.a. 125 B, 115 G, 129 I. Closed 1911 and bldg. returned to St. Phil. par.

St. Silas, Penton Street, Nat., Vittoria Pl., Half Moon Crescent. B sch. opened c. 1862 in temp. room. Schs. for B, G, I built on site of 1–3 Vittoria Pl. 1869–70,[50] with Nat. Soc. grant. Roll 1871: 198 B, 127 G, 162 I; a.a. 155 B, 95 G, 105 I. Financed by vol. contributions, parl. grants, sch. pence. Probably closed soon after transfer to S.B.L. c. 1875.

St. Stephen Nat. and I, River Street, Essex Rd.[51] Built 1842 for 293 B, G, I with Nat. Soc. grant. 1849 accn. 266, a.a. 195. Financed by subscriptions, sch. pence. I sch. built 1860 in Hayes Pl. behind ch. Roll 1871: 130 B, 99 G, 145 I; a.a. 105 B, 76 G, 123 I. Closed 1880s; I sch. sold 1882.

St. Thomas, Barnsbury, C.E. primary, Everilda Street.[52] Opened 1856 as M sch. Reopened 1857 for B. G and I sch. opened in temp. rented bldg. in Alma Grove (later Pulteney Terr.). 1857 a.a. 73 B; 1860 a.a. 96 G and I; 1865 a.a. 320 BGI. Financed by vol. contributions, C.E. grants including Islington Ch. Home Mission, sch. pence (2d., 1½d.). New schs. for B, G, I 1866–7 replaced 13 hos. in Everilda Street near ch. Roll 1871: 340 B, 259 G, 384 I; a.a. 272 B, 196 G, 223 I; evg. sch. all year, 29 B, 29 G. 1906 accn. 672 B, G, I reduced to 440 in 1908, 340 in 1909. Reorg. for M, I 1941; closed 1945 due to bomb damage, but reopened by 1955 as vol. aided primary for M, I. Management passed to St. And.; reorg. as M & I

1957. Reorg. for JM & I 1959. Roll 1982: 163 JM & I.

St. William of York R.C. sec., Brewery Rd., Caledonian Rd. Opened 1957 as vol. aided sec. for SM in Blundell Street. From 1968 upper sch. used former Bishop Giffard bldg., Gifford Street, lower sch. shared Robert Blair, Brewery Rd. Reorg. 1978–80 for SB, with lower sch. at Gifford Street and upper at Brewery Rd. Roll 1982: 390 SB.

Sebbon Street, see William Tyndale.

Sermon Lane ragged, Liverpool Rd.[53] Opened 1849 on Clerkenwell side, but almost entirely supported by Islington inhabitants. Housed in loft over blacksmith's shop; accn. 100, a.a. 40 B, 30 G, 30 I. Industrial classes each afternoon for 50 G; evg. sch. for 23 B, 7 adults; 3 paid teachers, 10 vol. New bldg. 1851 with aid of subscriptions. 1867 a.a. 90 B, 50 G, 40 I, with other occasional pupils; evg. sch. a.a. 50–60 in summer, 140 in winter. 1869 a.a. 182. Nothing further known.

Shelburne, Annette Rd., Holloway. Opened 1910 as Shelburne Rd. council sch. taking pupils from Harvist Rd. 1910 accn. 320 M, 175 I. Enlarged 1922 for 360 M, 223 I. Reorg. 1924 for 232 B, 232 G, 309 I. Reorg. 1927–32 for 520 SM, 309 I. Reorg. 1947–51 as Shelburne primary for I, and Shelburne sec. for SM on same site. Primary moved to Pakeman Street 1958 and closed c. 1960. Sec. reorg. 1958 for SG. Annexe at York Way opened 1961. Moved to former William Forster bldg., Benwell Rd., c. 1963. By 1967 upper sch. at Benwell Rd., lower sch. at Annette Rd. Amalg. as part of Highbury Fields c. 1981; bldgs. in Benwell and Annette rds. used as annexes.

Shepperton Road bd., New North Rd. Opened 1879 by S.B.L. for B, G, I. Sch. pence (2d.). 1893 accn. 998, a.a. 962. Accn. reduced 1922–7 to 264 B, 248 G, 272 I. Reorg. 1932–6 for 472 JB. Primary for JB from 1947. Closed 1957 and replaced by Rotherfield primary (q.v.).

South Islington and Pentonville British, Denmark Terr., Cloudesley Rd.[54] Opened 1842 in purpose built sch. with covered playground with aid of parl. grant; accn. 250 I on ground floor, 600 B on 1st, sch. of industry for 200 G on 2nd. Roll 1845: 60 I, 189 JB & 131 SB, 95 G. 1852 a.a. 245 B, 245 G & I; 1865 a.a. 380. Roll 1871: 216 B, 121 G, 82 I; a.a. 178 B, 81 G, 72 I. Recognized but by 1883 transferred to S.B.L. as Denmark Terr. bd. sch. Temp. sch. reopened 1885 for B, G, I to test demand. Closed by 1893.

Station Rd., Upper Street. Opened 1885 by S.B.L. in new bldg. for B, G, I. Sch. pence (3d., 2d.). 1908 accn. 355 B, 355 G, 397 I, a.a. 301 B, 292 G, 241 I. Accn. reduced 1922–7 to 275 B, 315 G, 311 I. Closed 1927; bldg. used by Laycock (q.v.).

[49] Additional inf. from P.R.O., C 54/12307, no. 18; C 54/14143, no. 3; Lewis, *Islington*, 361.

[50] P.R.O., C 54/17010, no. 1.

[51] Additional inf. from *Nat. Soc. Inquiry, 1846–7*, Mdx.; P.R.O., C 54/15250, no. 1; C 54/15310, nos. 18, 19; G.L.R.O., P83/STE1/27/1.

[52] Additional inf. from *Souvenir of Centenary of St. Thomas's C.E. Sch.* (booklet supplied by head); P.R.O., C 54/16579, no. 1.

[53] Para. based on Lewis, *Islington As It Was*, 84; *Ragged Sch. Union Mag.* iii. 207; xix. 103; xx. 24.

[54] Additional inf. from Lewis, *Islington*, 344; P.R.O., C 54/12513, no. 2; ibid. ED 14/5; *Ann. Rep. of Cttee. of S. Islington & Pentonville British Schs. 1843, 1845* (in Islington libr.).

THORNHILL, Thornhill Rd., Barnsbury. Opened as Thornhill Rd. bd. sch. 1881 for B, G, I. Sch. pence (4*d.*, 2*d.*). 1893 accn. 1,204, a.a. 1,146; 1908 accn. 480 B, 480 G, 577 I, a.a. 442 B, 438 G, 474 I. Reorg. 1927–32 for 410 JB, 410 JG, 432 I. Reorg. 1947–51 as primary for JM, I. Reorg. for JM & I 1972–4. Roll 1982: 279 JM & I.

TOLLINGTON PK., Turle Rd., Upper Holloway. Originated as Montem Street central 1910 with B from Montem Street higher elementary; SG from Montem Street 1911. 1911 accn. 300 B, 240 G. Renamed Marriott Rd. central 1914. Reorg. 1925 into sep. Tollington Pk. B central and G central, Turle Rd. (same site); accn. 320 B, 320 G. Amalg. again 1957, and with Isledon sec. formed Tollington Pk. sec. for SM at Turle Rd. Finsbury Pk. sec. joined sch. 1964. Technical block built 1960s, drama hall early 1970s. Roll 1981: 710 SM. Amalg. 1981 with Archway sch. to form George Orwell (q.v.).

TUDOR SEC., see Islington Green.

TUFNELL PK. PRIMARY, Dalmeny Rd. Opened 1955 for JM & I. Roll 1982: 240 JM.

UNION CHAPEL BRITISH, see Canonbury.

UNITY CHURCH DAILY, Florence Street, Upper Street. Opened 1864 in rooms behind ch. Financed by vol. contributions, sch. pence (3*d.*, 2*d.*). Roll 1871: 24 B, 39 G, all ages; evg. sch. 10 B, 37 G. 1878 accn. 169, a.a. 71. Closed by 1893.

UPPER HORNSEY RD. BD., see Hornsey Rd., Upper.

VITTORIA PRIMARY, Half Moon Crescent, Barnsbury. Opened 1879 as Vittoria Pl. bd. sch. for G, I. New bldg. for G, I opened 1881; B and cookery centre in old bldg. Sch. pence (2*d.*, 1*d.*). 1893 accn. 1,398, a.a. 791; 1908 accn. 318 B, 318 G, 392 I, a.a. 302 B, 292 G, 310 I. Reorg. 1947–51 for JM, I. New bldg. one of two experimental primary schs. built by Architectural Development Group of D.E.S., with split-level classrooms.[55] Reorg. for JM & I 1952. Roll 1982: 125 JM & I.

WARD'S PL. RAGGED, Lower Rd. Opened *c.* 1856 in old bldg.; connected with Union chapel. Rebuilt and enlarged *c.* 1858. Included evg. sch.[56] Nothing further known.

WELLINGTON RD., Wellington (later Westbourne) Rd., Lower Holloway. Temp. bd. sch. for BGI opened 1879 in leased bldg., probably former St. David Nat. Nearby bldg. opened 1892; temp. bldg. continued in use until enlargement of new sch. complete. 1893 accn. 1,163, a.a. 884; 1908 accn. 352 B, 345 G, 428 I, a.a. 321 B, 318 G, 393 I. Reorg. 1927–32 for 256 JB, 263 JG, 304 I. 1939 accn. 396 JM, 299 I. Renamed Alfred Prichard primary for JB, JG, I 1947–51. Closed by 1965; bldg. partly used as Our Lady of Sacred Heart annexe.

WESTBROOK CHAR. SCH. Opened 1836 in Smith's Bldgs. by trustees of Westbrook's char. Subscriptions and donations augmented income from £400 stock. Roll 1836: 77. 1838 a.a. 60–70; 1841–51 a.a. 50. In 1855 premises taken over by Turnpike Cts. Dist. Visiting Soc. to expand Angel Ct. sch. and ragged schs. of Protestant Institute, which had reduced need for Westbrook. Endowment used by soc. to support 20 poor children at its schs. until 1859, when income paid to St. Mary's I sch. for 12 Westbrook children placed there by char.'s trustees. Payments still made 1904.

WHITTINGTON, Highgate Hill. Opened 1882 by S.B.L. for B, G, I. 1893 accn. 1,000, a.a. 772. Reorg. 1927–32 for 536 SG, 313 I. Reorg. 1932–6 for 477 SG. Reorg. 1947–51 as Whittington primary for I. Closed 1957; bldg. used as annexe for Archway sec. and later George Orwell.

WILLIAM FORSTER PRIMARY, Benwell Rd., Holloway. Opened 1889 by S.B.L. as Forster bd. sch. for BGI. Sch. pence (1*d.*). Staff transferred from Pakeman Street. 1893 accn. 988, a.a. 908; 1908 accn. 360 B, 300 G, 378 I. Reorg. 1932–6 for 360 JM, 237 I. Primary sch. for JM & I 1951; renamed Wm. Forster *c.* 1955. Closed 1961; bldg. used by Shelburne (q.v.).

WILLIAM TYNDALE PRIMARY, Sable Street, Canonbury Rd. Iron bldg. opened by L.C.C. in 1914 as Sebbon Street sch. for 144 JM & I, a.a. 76. Replaced 1916 by perm. sch. for 272 B, 272 G, 324 I, a.a. 178 B, 203 G, 220 I. Reorg. 1932–6 for 280 SG, 280 JM, 294 I. Renamed Wm. Tyndale 1949 for JM, I. By 1970s had many poor children, including recent immigrants, but was popular with middle-class parents. Changed teaching methods in mid-1970s led to divisions among staff that involved parents and managers; teachers' strike and long legal inquiry followed, giving rise to many studies of sch. system.[57] Roll 1974: 217 JM & I. Roll 1982: 246 JM & I.

WINDSOR STREET BD., Essex Rd. Opened by 1872 when it moved to leased bldg. on Packington estate used as a Sun. sch. B only; G, I in sep. bldgs. nearby. Roll 1872: 150 B. 1878 accn. 102. Closed by 1893.

YERBURY PRIMARY, Foxham Rd., Upper Holloway. Opened 1884 by S.B.L. as Yerbury Rd. bd. sch. for 360 B, 360 G, 473 I. Sch. pence (3*d.*, 2*d.*). Extension built 1895; accn. 478 B, 478 G, 633 I. Reorg. 1927–32 for 348 JB, 348 JG, 394 I. Reorg. 1947–51 for JM, I. JM & I amalg. by 1977. Roll 1982: 110 JM, 67 I, 50 nursery.

YORK RD. (later WAY) BD., Delhi Street, King's Cross. Opened 1874 for B, G, I. Sch. pence (1*d.*–3*d.*). 1878 accn. 1,388, a.a. 1,288; 1893 accn. 1,451, a.a. 1,153. Bldg. remodelled 1910. Reorg. 1927–32 for 384 JB, 382 JG, 358 I. Reorg. 1947–51 as primary for I. Closed *c.* 1969; bldg. used as annexe for Risinghill sch., Clerkenwell, in 1977.

Special schools. AMBLER RD., Blackstock Rd. Centre for 60 physically and mentally handicapped children opened 1900 in Ambler Rd. bd. sch.

BARNSBURY PK., Liverpool Rd. Opened 1932 for 100 partially sighted children of all ages in part of council sch. Closed 1947–51.

CLOUDESLEY, Dowrey Street, Richmond Ave. Opened 1909. 1937 accn. for 123 mentally handicapped B all ages, and 90 physically handicapped SB. Reorg. by 1951 as sec. sch. for

---

[55] Maclure, *One Hundred Years of Lond. Educ.* 163.
[56] *Ragged Sch. Union Mag.* xi. 9.

[57] J. Gretton and M. Jackson, *Wm. Tyndale: Collapse of a Sch. – or a System?* (1976).

physically handicapped SB; for SM by 1964. Closed 1972; site used for Samuel Rhodes (q.v.).

COLEBROOKE, Colebrooke Row, Islington Green. Opened 1914 for mentally handicapped children. 1937 accn. 168 SG and JM. Reorg. by 1951 for educationally subnormal SG until move to Chequers sch., E.C.1 1960. Reopened as all-age sch. for maladjusted children. Roll 1982: 50 M.

DEAF AND DUMB CENTRE, opened in Winchester Street, and temp. centre at Barnsbury Street sch. in 1887.[58]

EDWARD SEGUIN, Prah Rd., Finsbury Pk. Opened as sec. sch. for educationally subnormal SB c. 1963 in part of Finsbury Pk. sch. Closed c. 1975; bldg. used for Jack Ashley (q.v.).

FORSTER, Hornsey Rd. Opened 1904. 1937 accn. for 84 physically handicapped SG and JM in William Forster bldg. Closed by 1947.

HARBOROUGH, Elthorne Rd., Upper Holloway. Opened 1913 as Elthorne Rd. for delicate children. Reorg. by 1937 for 102 physically handicapped B. Closed by 1951. Harborough M primary and sec. schs. for partially sighted opened by 1951, sharing Laycock primary. Moved to Elthorne Rd. by 1955. Reorg. 1967 as M sch. for autistic children. Roll 1982: 25 M.

JACK ASHLEY, Prah Rd., Finsbury Pk. Sch. for deaf SM opened in former Edw. Seguin bldg. c. 1975, named Jack Ashley 1976.

OFFORD. Opened 1905 in Offord Rd., sharing site with Barnsbury G. 1937 accn. for 100 mentally handicapped JM. Sharing Ring Cross sch. as M primary for educationally subnormal 1951, but returned to Offord Rd. by 1955. Moved to former Wellington Rd. sch. 1957. Closed c. 1967.

ROMILLY LODGE, 59 Hornsey Rise. Opened 1902. 1937 accn. for 99 mentally handicapped B. Used as a temp. primary by 1947.

ROSEMARY, 75 Prebend Street. Opened 1970-2 for educationally subnormal children and including special care unit. Annexe at Camden Rd. United Reformed ch., 577 Caledonian Rd.

SAMUEL RHODES, Dowrey Street, Richmond Ave. Opened 1972 as all-age sch. for educationally subnormal children. New bldg. on site of former Cloudesley sch. Roll 1982: c. 150 M.

Technical education. The Polytechnic of North London was founded as the Northern Polytechnic Institute with aid from London Parochial Charities funds, under a Scheme of 1892, and substantial donations from the Clothworkers' Company of London.[59] The first building, designed by Charles Bell, was opened in 1896 fronting Holloway Road, with blocks added on 1½ a. behind. The great hall (later the theatre) was opened in 1897 and large additions were made in 1902, designed by A. W. Cooksey. In 1923 the polytechnic acquired ¾ a. between the existing buildings and Hornsey Road, which had been cleared of slums, and the women's department

rooms were built in 1927. Nevertheless, in 1929 overcrowding had led to the use of Forster board school nearby, and a grant was received to extend the building department. Further extensions were needed in 1937 but prevented by war.[60] New premises for the National College of Rubber Technology (below) were opened in Benwell Road in 1952 and additional catering facilities in 1954 and 1955. Shortage of space persisted, despite a tower block opened in 1966[61] and the use of Marlborough House office block from 1974,[62] and in 1980 the polytechnic had annexes in Prince of Wales Road in St. Pancras, Ladbroke House, Highbury Grove, nos. 207-225 Essex Road, and nos. 2-16 Eden Grove.[63]

Early courses were varied, mainly in evening classes, providing technical instruction for mechanics and artisans, besides general education for 14-year olds.[64] There was also a training school for teachers and a day school, which in 1902 became a mixed secondary school and later Highbury Grove school.[65] Among the first courses were natural sciences, engineering, architectural and building studies, and domestic subjects for women, and the polytechnic was soon approved by the University of London for teaching internal degrees in sciences. A domestic economy school, started in 1899 to train girls for domestic service, from 1916 evolved into a secondary school with a domestic bias and in 1930 made way for more advanced work in the women's department. From 1913 rationalization amongst polytechnics caused the Northern to give up engineering and the arts, and concentrate on sciences, building, and women's classes. From 1915 a music trades' school trained apprentices in local industries, especially the making of pianos, organs, and brass instruments. It gave rise to radio courses in 1929 and eventually to the department of Electronic and Communications Engineering. In 1920 courses in rubber technology were started, forming in 1948 the foundation for the polytechnic's College of Rubber Technology, which had its own building from 1952. The School of Architecture also emerged as a major training centre, with courses recognized by the R.I.B.A. from 1925.[66]

After the Second World War full-time day courses became more important than evening and part-time. The three secondary schools associated with building, rubber, and music trades, which had 236 boys, had been reduced by 1939 and in 1951 were moved out, but facilities for post-graduate research remained restricted until the polytechnic became one of the 24 regional colleges set up in 1956 to cater for advanced study, and more premises were built. In the 1960s the major departments were rubber; electronic engineering; architecture, surveying and building; chemistry; physics; mathematics. In 1967 the polytechnic covered 4½ a. with 200 full-time and 250 part-time staff, and 1,100 full-time and 4,000 part-time students, including 360

[58] S.B.L. *Rep. 1886-7* (1887), 20.
[59] *Times Higher Educ. Supplement*, 24 Apr. 1981, 10; *Northern Polytechnic 1892-1967* (75th anniv. booklet).
[60] G.L.R.O., EO/HFE/5/107.
[61] *N. Polytechnic 1892-1967*.
[62] Islington L.B. *Official Guide 1977-8*, 67.

[63] I.L.E.A. *Green Book* (1980).
[64] *N. Polytechnic 1892-1967*.
[65] G.L.R.O., EO/HFE/5/170; above.
[66] *N. Polytechnic 1892-1967*; G.L.R.O., EO/HFE/5/170; Islington L.B. *Official Guide 1977-8*, 67.

taking postgraduate courses or research and 800 taking postgraduate short courses. In 1971 the Northern polytechnic was amalgamated with the North-western to form the large Polytechnic of North London, with 4,000 full-time and 3,000 part-time students in addition to those taking specialized short courses.

North London Day College run by the L.C.C. was housed in the Working Men's College in Crowndale Road, St. Pancras, in 1955, with evening departments in Islington at Offord, Finsbury Park, and Shelburne schools.[67] The college moved to Camden Road c. 1967,[68] and was the North London College for Further Education in 1977.[69]

Private schools. Dame Alice Owen's free school, founded c. 1613 on the Hermitage fields in St. John Street, Clerkenwell, took 24 children from Islington and 6 from Clerkenwell. Further grammar education for Islington was provided when a girls' school was added in 1886. Having become voluntary aided under the Education Act, 1944,[70] the schools, as a co-educational comprehensive, moved to South Mimms in 1976.[71]

Israel Tonge (1621-80), divine, taught a successful grammar class in the gallery of Sir Thomas Fisher's house, 1659-60. He is also said to have held an academy teaching Latin and Greek to girls.[72]

John Mitchell, a nonconformist ejected from a Dorset living, kept boarders who may have been pupils at his house in Islington in 1669.[73] Other nonconformist ministers kept academies, many at Newington Green.[74] Theophilus Gale (1628-78) formed an academy there in 1665, which was continued after his death by his pupil Thomas Rowe (1657-1705).[75] Rowe moved away but had returned to Islington when Isaac Watts was a pupil there, and remained until c. 1705. Other pupils included John Evans, D.D., Daniel Neal, Henry Grove, John Hughes (d. 1720), poet and dramatist, Jeremiah Hunt, D.D., and Josiah Hort, archbishop of Tuam. Rowe was the first to desert the traditional text books, introducing 'free philosophy', and one of the earliest exponents of John Locke.[76] Ralph Button (d. 1680) moved his academy to Newington Green in the early 1670s, where his pupils, some of them for the dissenting ministry,[77] included Sir Joseph Jekyll (1663-1738), Master of the Rolls. Charles Morton (1627-98),[78] who received most of Button's students at his death, formed an academy at Newington Green, possibly in 1667 and certainly by 1673, which became the principal Independent academy in London. In 1682 he had

two houses with at least 60 boarders. A range of traditional and newer subjects was taught, to university standard, including modern languages and politics as a science, and Morton was a pioneer in the use of English as a medium of instruction.[79] His pupils included Timothy Cruso, whose family lived at Newington Green, Daniel Defoe, and Samuel Wesley, father of John and Charles. The vicar of Islington reported on the school in 1685 and Morton left England that year; his school continued until c. 1696 under Stephen Lobb, William Wickens, and Francis Glasscock. Thomas Doolittle (1632?-1707) in 1672 moved his academy to Islington,[80] where in 1680 he had 28 students and where the historian Edmund Calamy (1671-1732)[81] attended. It closed temporarily in 1685, when Doolittle was compelled to move. Robert Woodcock, clothworker of London, ran a girls' boarding school 1679-87 in the house formerly belonging to the Draper family behind the church;[82] his school and Morrett's, both reported on by the vicar along with Morton's in 1685,[83] may have been nonconformist.

Mrs. Smith had a pew in the parish church for herself and her scholars in 1664. In 1668 too many seats had been given to schools and none was to be so allotted, although galleries might be built. In 1673 Capt. Stacy applied to take over a gallery for his school.[84] Hannah, wife of the musician and publisher John Playford, kept a boarding school for girls in Upper Street, opposite the parish church, at her death in 1679.[85]

Islington had several day and boarding schools in the 18th and early 19th centuries, few of which outlived their founders. In 1787 nine boarding schools had pews in the church: Messrs. Young and Co., Rosomans Buildings, Mr. Charron, Lower Street, Mr. Duff, Hornsey Row (Upper Street), Mrs. Weaver, Mrs. Gibbs, Mrs. Blackstone, all Upper Street, Miss Reynolds, Canonbury, Mrs. Cockburn, Newington Green, and Mrs. Dubois.[86] In the 1790s 14 schools were listed: Charron's French boarding school for young ladies, boarding schools under Childs, Mrs. Clark, Ann Harris, Kirkman, and Miss Weaver, girls' boarding schools under Cotton, Samuel Morley, and Samuel Reynolds, academies under William Frances, John Price, A. Rae, and the Revd. A. Croles, and a ladies' school under Frances Longbottom.[87]

Mrs. Science, wife of a watchmaker, kept a boarding school for young ladies in a house in Upper Street (later no. 107) c. 1740, where her son-in-law John Shield (d. 1786) opened a boys' school which acquired a high reputation. Pupils

[67] L.C.C. *Educ. Svce. Inf.* (1955), 84.
[68] G.L.R.O., EO/HFE/5/278.
[69] Islington L.B. *Official Guide 1977-8,* 67.
[70] For details see *V.C.H. Mdx.* i. 310-11. Treatment of sch. bldgs. reserved for article on Clerkenwell.
[71] M. Ball, *Worshipful Co. of Brewers* (1977), 67-8, 99, 117-18; *V.C.H. Mdx.* v. 305.
[72] *D.N.B.*   [73] *Calamy Revised,* 351.
[74] Rest of para. based on I. Parker, *Dissenting Academies in Eng.* (1914), 138; 'Early Nonconf. Academies', *Trans. Cong. Hist. Soc.* iii (1907-8), 274-88, 395; 'Islington', *Jnl. of Presb. Hist. Soc. of Eng.* ii, no. 4 (1923), 207.
[75] *D.N.B.*

[76] Ibid.
[77] Ibid.; *Calamy Revised,* 95; R. T. Jones, *Congregationalism in Eng. 1662-1962* (1962), 88.
[78] *D.N.B.*
[79] Jones, op. cit. 88; *Cal. S.P. Dom. 1682,* 551; Parker, *Dissenting Academies,* 59-60.
[80] *D.N.B.*   [81] Ibid.
[82] P.R.O., C 6/259/11.
[83] Guildhall MS. 9537/20, p. 85.
[84] Islington libr., vestry min. bk. 1663-1708, 7, 32, 67.
[85] Nelson, *Islington,* 361; *D.N.B.*
[86] Guildhall MS. 474, par. ch. seating plan.
[87] *Univ. Brit. Dir.* (1791-7).

included William Hawes, M.D. (1736–1808), founder of the Royal Humane Society, William Tooke (1744–1820), historian, and John Nichols (1745–1826), printer and author. E. Flower ran a highly regarded boarding school in the same house, adding a large schoolroom, in 1810,[88] and still did so in 1828.[89] By 1844 the school, belonging to T. E. Edgeworth, had closed and the building of 20 rooms with its 35 school beds was sold.[90]

Mrs. Paul ran a boarding school for young ladies in the vicarage in 1754, as she had before the old church was demolished in 1751.[91]

The Revd. John Rule kept a well reputed academy for young gentlemen in the house at the north end of Colebrooke Row in the 1760s and 1770s.[92]

Mary Wollstonecraft transferred her school from Islington to Newington Green in 1783. It closed in 1785 but provided the experience for her books on the education of girls.[93]

Mr. Crole kept a school in Queen's Head Lane, where Thomas Uwins (1782–1857), painter, was a day boy for 6 years c. 1790.[94]

John Evans (1767–1827), a Baptist minister, opened a school at Hoxton Square, Shoreditch, in the 1790s, moving to no. 7 Pullins Row, Islington, by c. 1800, and continuing until his death. Charles Whittingham (1795–1876), printer, was among his pupils.[95]

A girls' boarding school was housed for many years in the original no. 1 Colebrooke Row, at the north corner with Gerrard Road. It was followed by a boys' boarding school known as Colebrooke House academy, where in 1828 the Revd. R. Simpson, with two assistants, offered classics, mathematics, and English literature.[96] In 1835 Simpson's academy exemplified an advanced system of infants' education.[97] It had closed by 1851.[98]

In 1828 there were advertised 26 girls' boarding schools and 14 boys' including Flower's and Colebrooke House. Almost all were in or near the town, with one or two at Highbury, Ball's Pond Road, Highgate Hill, and along Holloway Road.[99] In 1833 the parish had 38 boarding schools, of which several took day pupils and all but one had started since 1818: 15 had 773 boys, 21 had 396 girls, and two had 50 boys and girls. In addition there were 51 day schools for fee payers: 34 were single-sex schools, although two boys' schools provided evening classes for a few girls. The 506 girls and 425 boys educated in those schools, besides another 61 children of unspecified sex, excluded the proprietary school (below) with 160 boys.[1] Islington's many adventure schools were generally short lived. Other private

schools soon included some, mainly day schools, held under trusts, providing professional and commercial education for a growing number of middle-class boys. In 1851 there were 28 boarding schools for girls and 16 for boys, only four of them traceable from schools existing in 1828. In 1879 there were 17 schools of note for older boys, mainly boarding, and 9 similar schools for girls in 1884.[2] Some of the longer lived schools are noticed below.[3]

South Islington Commercial and Mathematical school was established in 1818, offering mathematics, commercial accounts, elementary classics, and modern languages. In 1851 it was at Parkfield House, Parkfield Street, owned by Frederick J. Minasi, who was still there in 1879.

Islington Proprietary school, Barnsbury Street, was founded in 1830 in union with King's College for day boys, in a building designed for it by John Newman.[4] Proprietors could nominate one free pupil for each share held, paying fees for additional admissions; consent of the directors was required if a boy was not the proprietor's son. The roll of 99 in 1831 increased to 150 in 1832, 160 in 1833, 170 in 1835. Boys were offered classics, mathematics, modern languages, and Hebrew, and preparation for university, commerce, and government examinations. Scholarships to Oxford or Cambridge were available. The proprietors were professional men or had businesses outside the parish, local traders being excluded, and the headmaster was to be an Anglican clergyman. In 1865 there were 137 boys; in 1879 c. 140, aged 7 to 18.[5]

South Islington Proprietary school, in union with King's College, London, stood on the north-east corner of Duncan Street by 1839 and was still there in 1842;[6] it had been replaced by the county court by 1851.[7]

The College, nos. 3–4 Turle Road, Tollington Park, was established in 1833 as a day and boarding school for boys, in union with the College of Preceptors. Classics, mathematics, and languages were offered, with preparation for university and professional examinations. In 1851 it had 32 boarders, aged 6 to 16, under William Griggs and three assistant masters. G. Moxon was the master in 1879.

Roxburgh House Collegiate school for boys, no. 328 Liverpool Road, was established in 1820, and took a few boarders in 1879. Subjects included English, classics, and languages, and preparation was given for Oxford Local examinations.

Histon House College, Barnsbury Park, was established in 1830 in a purpose built house with garden and croquet-lawn. Day girls and

[88] Nelson, *Islington*, 113–15; *D.N.B.* s.v. Hawes, Nichols.
[89] *Boarding Sch. and Lond. Masters' Dir.* (1828), 34.
[90] Sale cat. in Islington libr.
[91] Vestry min. bk. 1735–77, 91.
[92] *N. & Q.* 2nd ser. iv. 9; *V.C.H. Mdx.* i. 247; Nelson, *Islington* (1829), 195.
[93] *Oxford Literary Guide to Brit. Isles* (1977), 220.
[94] *D.N.B.*
[95] *D.N.B.* s.v. Evans, Whittingham; A.D. Morris, *Hoxton Sq. and Hoxton Academies* (priv. print. 1957, copy in Islington libr.), 5.
[96] *Boarding Sch. Dir.* (1828), 41; Nelson, *Islington* (1829), 195.

[97] *Rep. Sel. Cttee. into State of Educ. of People*, H.C. 465, p. 941 (1835), vii.   [98] P.R.O., HO 107/10/2/5.
[99] *Boarding Sch. Dir.* (1828).
[1] *Educ. Enq. Abstract*, 565–6.
[2] Figs. from P.R.O., HO 107/10/1–2; F. S. de Carteret-Bisson, *Our Schs. and Colls.* (1879), 707–13, 930; (1884), 428, 530–2.
[3] Inf. on schs. taken from 1851 census: P.R.O., HO 107/10/1, 2; Bisson, op. cit. (1879, 1884).   [4] Above, plate 26.
[5] Cromwell, *Islington*, 349–54; *Schs. Inquiry Com. 1865* [3966-IX], pp. 242–6, H.C. (1867–8), xxviii (9).
[6] P.R.O., C 54/15673, no. 12, plan; Lewis, *Islington*, 367.
[7] P.R.O., HO 107/10/2/2.

boarders were offered an English education with music and French, and preparation for Oxford and Cambridge Local and university entrance examinations. There were 12 boarders, aged 13 to 17, in 1851 under Elizabeth Matthews; Miss S. A. Fitt was headmistress in 1884.

East Islington Commercial school, Lower Road, opened next to the new market in 1841. Designed for fee payers who could not afford the proprietary schools, it catered only for day boys in 1851.[8]

The School of Commerce, no. 32 New North Road, was established in 1840, to prepare day boys and boarders for commerce and the professions, and for professional examinations in 1879.

Alexander Stewart, a Congregationalist minister, had a school at Palmer House, no. 1 Palmer Terrace, Lower Holloway, from 1847, assisted by his two sons. In 1851 he had 26 boys boarding aged 9 to 15 years. The school may have continued until his death in 1874; his sons entered the ministry, one of them, Halley (later knighted), working at Caledonian Road before going into business.[9]

George Darnell (1798-1857) for many years conducted a large day school at Islington. He composed very popular handbooks designed to make beginning schoolwork more inviting to both pupil and teacher, and his famous copybooks started c. 1840. He died at Gibson Square.[10]

Barnsbury Park Collegiate school, no. 1 Barnsbury Park, was established by 1849 for the sons of gentlemen, both day and boarding, with particular advantages for the sons of clergymen. The curriculum included modern languages, physical science, mercantile subjects, and preparation for public school, university, and other examinations. A junior school took boys from 4 years of age. The school had 23 boarders aged 8 to 15 in 1851. It closed between 1879 and 1897.[11]

Manor House school, Holloway, was a boys' boarding school under Mr. Softley in 1828 and 1831. In 1851 it was kept by E. Dukes, with 26 boarders aged 7 to 15 years. In 1879 subjects included English, classics, modern languages, mathematics, and land surveying, with preparation for the Indian Civil Service, Sandhurst, and other professional examinations.[12]

Miss Oates in 1828 ran a finishing school for girls at no. 7 Canonbury Place,[13] where by 1851 Emma Springett's girls' school had 17 boarders aged 6 to 19. Caroline Bifield ran a similar school at no. 6, with 26 boarders in 1851 and a staff including teachers for English, music, and drawing.

In 1878 the Girls' Public Day School Trust, in connexion with the National Union for Improving the Education of Women, opened

Highbury and Islington High school at nos. 6 and 7 Canonbury Place, part of the east range of Canonbury House. It offered a broad education with preparation for Oxford and Cambridge Schools Board examinations. There were 215 pupils in 1884, with a kindergarten, and priority was given to nominees of shareholders. It was a recognized secondary school in 1908 with 144 girls. The first head was Miss M. C. Whyte; Miss M. A. Minasi was head in 1884 and 1908. The school closed in 1911.[14]

Mr. Sprange ran a boarding school for 20 boys at no. 21 Arundel Place, White Conduit Fields in 1828.[15] He was probably the Daniel Sprange who had eight boarders aged 8 to 14 at no. 5 Lonsdale Square in 1851, when he was assisted by his wife, son, and two other teachers.

William Baker ran a finishing seminary for boys at no. 1 Francis Place, Holloway, in 1828.[16] In 1851 he had 47 boarders aged 8 to 16, and subjects offered included English, classics, French, and mathematics.

William Barker's finishing seminary for boys, in Lower Street in 1828,[17] had 15 boarders aged 8 to 15 at no. 37 Lower Street in 1851.

Charlotte Brady and her sister advertised their school for young ladies at nos. 22-3 Portland Place (Canonbury Road) in 1837.[18] In 1851 they had 8 boarders, aged 5 to 16.

The Church of England Metropolitan Training Institution, which opened at Highbury College in 1849 to train men and women for Anglican schools, included a model school which had 175 boys in 1854. It closed c. 1865.[19]

The School of Science and Art, Windsor Street, Essex Road, was a secondary or middle-class school connected with the Science and Art Department, South Kensington. It was established in 1852 to teach sons of tradesmen and artisans all the sciences, including human physiology, besides English, book-keeping, and mathematics, as required by the Civil Service.[20] Boys were admitted from 7 years into the junior division and in 1879 there were 220.

Highbury New Park Collegiate school was established in 1855, and offered classics, mathematics, and modern languages, including Hindustani and Persian for careers in India.[21] Preparation was given for all major examinations. In 1879 there were c. 50 boys aged 10 to 18. Possibly the school continued as the Highbury Park New College listed in 1903.[22]

Thornhill College for Ladies, no. 1A Thornhill Crescent, from 1854 offered a broad education, including French, drawing, and music, and preparation for university and public examinations. In 1884 there were 40 boarders and day pupils.

Queen's College Institution for Ladies, Brecknock Road, was founded c. 1847 with Mrs. Anna Maria Morel as principal, and stood

[8] Lewis, *Islington*, 330.
[9] *Trans. Cong. Hist. Soc.* xv (1945-8), 75.
[10] *D.N.B.*
[11] *Hist. of 353 (Lond.) Medium Regt. R.A. (T.A.), 1861-1961* (in Islington libr.).
[12] *Boarding Sch. Dir.* (1828), 41; *V.C.H. Mdx.* i. 275; Cromwell, *Islington*, 327.
[13] *Boarding Sch. Dir.* 20.
[14] Girls' Public Day Sch. Trust, *1872-1972, Cent. Review*,

26, 29; *List of Sec. Schs. recognised as Efficient* [Cd. 4374], p. 306, H.C. (1908), lxxxiii.
[15] *Boarding Sch. Dir.* 41.
[16] Ibid. 28.   [17] Ibid.
[18] *Cath. Dir.* (1837).
[19] Lewis, *Islington As It Was*, 57-8; *1st Ann. Rep. of Cttee.* (1850, in Islington libr.).
[20] *V.C.H. Mdx.* i. 273.
[21] Ibid. i. 276.   [22] Paton, *List of Schs.* 381.

in c. 2 a. on the edge of Tufnell Park. It offered preparation for all examinations open to women, and had finishing, senior, middle, and junior schools in 1884. In 1851 there were 64 boarders aged 5 to 19 and 14 governesses, including an Italian for singing and teachers of French, German, and music. In 1879 Miss Button was principal, succeeded by Mr. and Mrs. James Baker Pyne by 1881. The school closed c. 1888.[23]

Alfred House Collegiate Institute for Young Ladies was run by Trevillian Spicer, who in 1849 aimed to prove that women's intellectual capacity was equal to men's. Subjects included higher mathematics, classics, geography, German literature, and English history.[24]

The Church Missionary Children's Home kept a boarding school for the children of overseas missionaries in Milner Square from 1850 and in a purpose built school in Highbury Grove from 1853. In 1865 there were 39 boys and 38 girls. The boys received a classical education and left at 15, many for public schools; the girls were taught languages, English, and music, and left at 16. The home had closed by 1891, when the S.B.L. opened a truant school in its building.[25]

Holloway College, nos. 2, 4, 6 Spencer Road, Hornsey Road, was established in 1864 and provided a commercial education, including French, English, science, and music, for 250 boys in 1879. A girls' department existed.

A boys' day school at no. 45 Ellington Street, Arundel Square, was established in 1856 and offered classical, mathematical, and commercial subjects. A girls' school was connected with it in 1879.

A Ladies' College, no. 3 Marquess Grove, Canonbury, was established in 1865, giving a broad education to c. 35 day girls, with preparation for public examinations in 1884.

Tollington Park College was bought in 1879 by W. Brown, who had increased it from 80 to 400 boys by 1893. In the absence of endowed schools it filled a need for languages and science. A branch opened in Muswell Hill in 1902.[26]

Other boys' schools in 1879 included a day preparatory school at no. 18 Alwyne Place, Canonbury Park North, which had 25 boys in 1919; a school at no. 23 Devonshire Street (later Devonia Road) preparing boys for City of London school; Englefield College, no. 127 Englefield Road, Islington, established in 1877 with 130 day boys from 6 years, offering a commercial education with Latin, French, and natural sciences; Higher Middle Class school, no. 18 Mildmay Grove, established in 1870 for boarders and day pupils; Castle House Collegiate school, nos. 44 and 46 Mildmay Grove, established in 1869 for boarding and day boys, preparing for university and Civil Service examinations.

Girls' schools in 1884 included Kinnoull House, Highbury New Park, a boarding school; Owthorne, Highbury Crescent, a boarding school established in 1873; Manston House, Junction Road, Upper Holloway, boarding and day; Clyde House, no. 65 Tufnell Park Road, a boarding school established in 1873. Most prepared girls for public examinations.

A Roman Catholic grammar school for boys was at Cornwall Villa, Eden Grove, Holloway, by 1879, connected with the church of the Sacred Heart.[27] Brothers of Mercy opened St. Aloysius' College in 1879 as a secondary school, with 405 boys in 1919. It was voluntary aided from 1950.[28]

Sisters of Our Lady of Sion at Aberdeen Park, Highbury, ran a day and boarding school for girls in 1949; in 1960 they ran a mixed pre-preparatory boarding and day school, which apparently had closed by 1966.[29]

The convent of Our Lady of Sion at Eden Grove, Holloway, was established in 1870, when the nuns assisted with the parish school. A private boarding and day school had opened at the convent by 1919. It became voluntary aided c. 1950, but continued to take fee paying boarders and closed 1967.[30]

The Company of the Daughters of Mary Notre Dame ran a convent boarding school at no. 55 Tollington Park by 1908, when it had 85 girls. In 1919 there were 60 girls. It was still a boarding school in 1934, but took only day girls in 1952 and 1960 and had closed by 1975.[31]

Sisters of the Cross and Passion ran a school at their convent, no. 41 Duncan Terrace, Islington Green, in 1919 when it had 77 boys and girls including senior pupils. In 1934 it was a girls' day school and in 1952 a preparatory school. Called St. Gabriel's Preparatory school in 1969, when recognized as an efficient independent school, it had closed by 1975.[32]

Sisters of St. John of God ran a mixed preparatory school which became voluntary aided in 1961 as Christ the King R.C. primary school.[33] In 1975 the convent had an independent mixed preparatory school at no. 81 Wray Crescent, Tollington Park.[34]

The Home and Colonial Society moved its boarding school for girls from Gray's Inn Road to Highbury Hill House in 1894. It prepared for London matriculation examinations and for the Society's teacher training college. The school was transferred to the L.C.C. in 1912.[35]

Arundell House school, no. 137 Highbury New Park, was established by 1903 and offered a broad education for day girls and a few boarders, with boys taken up to 7 years. In 1919 it had 114 pupils. It had closed by 1934.[36]

In 1908 only five secondary schools in Islington were recognized as efficient by the Board of Education: Camden Secondary, run by the

[23] A. S. J. [Jones], 'College Gdns. Story' (TS. 1967 in Islington libr.).
[24] V.C.H. Mdx. i. 263; Islington libr., local colln. cutting 1849.
[25] Schs. Inquiry Com. 1865 [3966–IX], pp. 247–9, H.C. (1867–8), xxviii (9); S.B.L. Final Rep. 256.
[26] V.C.H. Mdx. i. 274; vi. 195.
[27] Ibid. i. 262.
[28] Above (pub. schs.).
[29] Cath. Dir. (1949 and later edns.).
[30] Above (pub. schs.); P.R.O., ED 15/23.
[31] List of Sec. Schs. recognised as Efficient [Cd. 4374], p. 306, H.C. (1908), lxxxiii; P.R.O., ED 15/23; P.O. Dir. Lond. (1934 and later edns.).
[32] P.R.O., ED 15/23; P.O. Dir. Lond. (1934 and later edns.); Cath. Dir. (1969).
[33] Above (pub. schs.).
[34] P.O. Dir. Lond. (1975).
[35] Above (pub. schs., Highbury Fields).
[36] P.R.O., ED 15/23; P.O. Dir. Lond. (1934).

L.C.C., Notre Dame High, Highbury and Islington High, Highbury Hill High, and the Northern Polytechnic Secondary.[37] In 1919 there were 31 private schools offering some secondary education but not recognized as efficient, though a few were recognized later. Those not already mentioned included Colebrooke School at no. 29 Duncan Terrace, with c. 90 boys and girls in 1919, a mixed preparatory school under Caroline Mariben in 1934; Marquess Garden school, no. 8 Marquess Road, with 16 boys in 1919, a mixed school under Clara Tappe in 1934; Clarke's High School, Bridge House, Anson Road, with 179 girls in 1919, which had become a branch of Clark's College by 1934, providing business training for boys and girls.[38]

In 1934 there were 14 private schools listed in Islington, including Clark's and Pitman's business colleges. The other schools were 2 boys' and 2 girls' boarding, a boys' and a girls' day, 3 mixed or unspecified, 2 mixed preparatory, and a kindergarten.[39] By 1952 only three private schools, all convent schools, were listed. There was one, at the convent of St. John of God, in 1975.[40]

CHARITIES FOR THE POOR. Between 1730 and 1810 the income from the Stonefields estate and other legacies was distributed by the churchwardens from a single account without regard for the donors' intentions.[41] Most of the distributive charities, separately mentioned below and benefiting the whole parish, were brought together in a United Charities Scheme in 1901, slightly modified in 1960: the charities of Burge, Cooper, Ferris, Geary, Haines, Hobson, Hull, Loane, Marshall, May, Morton, Owen, Parke, Parsons, Wilson, and the poor's stock. The annual income, £1,089 in 1963 and £740 in 1973, was used as follows: £1 to the verger of the parish church, 10s. for a sermon on Christmas day, 10s. each to 10 poor parishioners, and the residue for the poor.[42]

Cloudesley (Stonefields estate) charity. Richard Young *alias* Cloudesley, by will dated 1517/18, left land called Stonefields or the Fourteen acres, let for £4 a year, the income to be distributed by six men chosen each year by the parishioners: 20s. was for an obit, with 6s. 8d. for the prayers of the poor there, 26s. 8d. was for the brotherhood of Jesus to sing masses, and 10s. was for the six men for their trouble. No instructions were given about the residue.[43] Following the 1548 Act concerning superstitious uses, the Crown seized the whole income, then £7, until 1551, when the court of Exchequer allotted 53s. 4d. a year to the Crown and the rest to parish feoffees. In 1561 new feoffees declared trusts to pay the residue to

the churchwardens to be distributed as six or eight parishioners decided.[44] In the 18th century the churchwardens distributed the rent from their charity account as they saw fit;[45] in 1748 it amounted to £42 p.a.[46] In 1811, after the rents had been used for repairs to the parish church, an Act allowed the trustees to grant building leases of the property, consisting of 16¾ a. on the west side of the Back Road, and to use the rents for repairs to the new chapel of ease.[47] Under a further Act of 1832, the income up to £1,000 a year was to be divided equally between the chapel of ease and Trinity, St. John's, and St. Paul's district churches for expenses of worship, any residue to go towards the churchwardens' rate.[48] In 1850–1 it was unsuccessfully proposed that the charities should be applied to almshouses and other charitable purposes.[49] By 1895 the income consisted of ground rents from c. 240 houses in Cloudesley Square, Liverpool Road, Cloudesley Street, Stonefield Street, Richmond Road, and Cloudesley Road, on leases which would fall in between 1899 and 1916, and the Charity Commissioners ordered the income surplus to the four churches' £1,000 to be banked.[50] Under a Scheme of 1902 the existing funds were to be divided between rebuilding or restoring the parish church and enabling the Great Northern Central hospital to place poor Islington patients in convalescent homes. From the future annual income of the estate, £100 each was to be paid to St. Mary Magdalene's, Holy Trinity, St. John's, Upper Holloway, and St. Paul's, Ball's Pond, and £500 to the parish church and £250 to St. Mary Magdalene's for maintenance. Half of the remaining income was to go to other churches and half to hospitals or medical and nursing charities, including the Great Northern hospital as long as it should be open to the poor of Islington and one ward should be named after Richard Cloudesley.[51] The ground rents of 71 houses and 2 shops were sold in 1937,[52] but in 1980 the charity still owned property in Cloudesley Square, Cloudesley Road, and Cloudesley Street, including two blocks of mansion flats, besides the capital from sales invested in stocks. A Scheme of 1980 simplified the application, only specifying £500 a year for the upkeep of the parish church and £250 for St. Mary Magdalene's. In 1981 the remainder of the income, c. £21,000 net, was used to create a welfare fund for quick response to personal need, and for grants to medical charities benefiting Islington and for repairs to local churches.[53]

Almshouse charities. Dame Alice Owen's almshouses for 10 elderly widows, built in 1609 just inside Clerkenwell parish, were intended for widows of Islington and Clerkenwell.[54]

Davis's almshouses were founded by John

[37] *List of Sec. Schs.* [Cd. 4374], p. 306; above (tech. educ.) for Northern Polytechnic sch.
[38] P.R.O., ED 15/23; *P.O. Dir. Lond.* (1934).
[39] *P.O. Dir. Lond.* (1934).
[40] Ibid. (1952, 1975).
[41] MS. copy of rep. to vestry on Cloudesley est. 1851 (in Islington libr.), p. 14.
[42] Char. Com. files.
[43] Guildhall MS. 9171/9, ff. 75–7.
[44] Rep. to vestry, p. 1.   [45] Ibid. p. 14.

[46] G.L.R.O., P83/MRY1/133, f. 3.
[47] Rep. to vestry, p. 15; 51 Geo. III, c. 216 (Local and Personal).
[48] 2 & 3 Wm. IV, c. 26 (Local and Personal).
[49] Rep. to vestry, p. 15; pamphlets in Islington libr.
[50] G.L.R.O., P83/MRY1/406, no. 1.
[51] Copy of 1902 Scheme in Islington libr.
[52] Sale cat. in Islington libr.
[53] Char. Com. files.
[54] *D.N.B.* Reserved for treatment under Clerkenwell.

Davis (d. 1793) of Islington, carpenter, who left £2,000 to build and endow them. Eight small houses were built in 1794 on the south side of Queen's Row (later Queen's Head Lane) and were endowed with £670. They housed married couples or widows aged 50 or more, Anglicans, but not necessarily from Islington. To prevent the almshouses becoming a 'nursery for nurses', no doctor or apothecary was to be a trustee.[55] By 1895 the charity possessed £3,500 in stock, part bequeathed by John's widow Jane Davis, who had directed that the almshouses should not be under the control of the parish officers. The interest was to be used first for maintenance of the eight houses and the residue distributed amongst the inmates.[56] Under an order of 1964 the site of the houses, nos. 65–79 (odd) Queen's Head Street, was sold for rebuilding and the proceeds were invested. The income, £605 in 1969, was thereafter used for the poor in Islington M.B.[57]

Distributive charities. Richard Martin, by will proved 1602, requested that the 20s. a year given to the poor by his father be paid by his wife and son, and left a further 20s. a year to the church-wardens for the poor.[58] Nothing more is known of the charity.

Dame Alice Owen left £60 to Christ's Hospital on condition that the governors paid 1s. a week to buy bread for Islington's poor. In 1895 £2 12s. was paid annually to the churchwardens and distributed with similar charities.[59]

Thomas Hobson in 1614 surrendered his copyhold known as the Cock, subject to a rent charge of £5 4s. to the churchwardens for gifts of 2d. each to 12 poor people every Sunday.[60] In 1895 the sum was charged on no. 61 Upper Street.[61]

Nathaniel Loane of St. Sepulchre-without-Newgate, by will dated 1625, left £5 4s. from property in Little Old Bailey, to the vicar and churchwardens of Islington to be distributed each Sunday as 12d. in bread and 12d. in money to 12 of the poorest parishioners of good conversation.[62] From 1768 Islington received ⅙ of the rent of the property, which was let at £40 a year until 1830 and thereafter £180.[63] In 1895 the property was let at £500 p.a., of which Islington received £81 5s. 4d.[64]

Daniel Parke, by will dated 1649, gave a rent charge of 40s., 10s. for a sermon on Christmas day and the remainder for bread on Sundays. The rent charge was replaced c. 1881 by £75 invested in stock, producing £2 1s. 4d. a year.[65]

Mrs. Amy Hill at an unknown date left £50 to purchase land producing 50s. a year; 30s. was for 30 poor on St. Thomas's day, 13s. 4d. for a

sermon, and 3s. 4d. each for the clerk and sexton. In 1659 c. ¾ a. near the Back Road was bought and in 1777 a workhouse was built there, whereupon the payments ceased. The building became the property of the guardians following the Metropolitan Poor Act, 1867, and in 1895 was used for their offices and as a vestry depot.[66]

Ephraim Skinner gave £700 to Christ's Hospital in 1678, the governors to pay 5s. each Sunday to the minister of Islington for catechizing the poor and £5 a year for distribution, but the gift to become void if no catechizing took place for two consecutive Sundays. In 1895 the sums were paid direct to the vicar.[67]

Dr. William Crowne of London, physician, left £50 for the Islington poor, received by the vestry in 1685, the interest to buy bread every Sunday.[68] Dame Mary Sadlier, Crowne's widow, by will proved c. 1707, augmented his gift by £50, to buy bread to the value of 12d. every Sunday.[69] The sum was received in 1707, but nothing further was recorded of either gift.

Robert Hull of Islington, bricklayer, by will dated 1694, gave £3 a year to the vicar and churchwardens after the death of his wife Jane, for the use of the poor, and another £3 a year to Islington or to the Bricklayers' Company as his wife decided.[70] By deed of 1701 Jane Hull gave both sums to Islington to be paid out of property in Great and Little Bardfield (Essex).[71] The rent charge of £6 was received in the 18th and 19th centuries,[72] but in 1893 the sum was £5 16s. 6d., spent on coal, bread, blankets, and gifts of money.[73] Maj. Haines gave £2 of a rent charge on nos. 11–20 Paradise Row, Essex Road, which was paid to the churchwardens in 1895 and distributed with Hull's charity.[74]

John Parsons, by will dated 1700, left the rent of a close called Porter's acre in the manor of Newington Barrow to the vicar for the poor of Islington, the income to buy coals in summer at the cheapest rate. The rent was £4 in 1700,[75] £32 in 1820–7, and £15 in 1827–34.[76] In 1853 the land, 2⅛ a., was let to the guardians for 99 years at £50 a year and was the site of the infants' poor house and schools, Hornsey Road. The churchwardens bought coal tickets with the rent in 1895.[77]

John Smith was said in the early 18th century to have bequeathed a rent charge of 52s. from a house in Hedge Row for distribution in bread to the poor at 12d. a week.[78] Nothing further is known of the charity.

Mrs. Ann May, of Wotton (Surr.), by will of unknown date, left half the residue of her estate to the poor of Islington and half to the parish school for Christian instruction. In 1807 the gift consisted of £156 6s. 10d. stock.[79] In 1895 the

[55] P.R.O., C 54/7237, no. 14.
[56] G.L.R.O., P83/MRY1/406, no. 29.
[57] Char. Com. files.
[58] P.R.O., PROB 11/100 (P.C.C. 51 Montague).
[59] G.L.R.O., P83/MRY1/406, no. 8.
[60] Ibid. 133, ff. 4–6.
[61] Ibid. 1095, f. 6; 406, no. 7.
[62] Ibid. 133, ff. 7–8.
[63] Ibid. 1095, f. 7v.
[64] Ibid. 406, no. 4.
[65] Ibid. no. 9.
[66] Ibid. no. 23; above, pub. svces.

[67] G.L.R.O., P83/MRY1/406, no. 24.
[68] Vestry min. bk. 1662/3–1708, 169.
[69] G.L.R.O., P83/MRY1/133, ff. 16–17.
[70] Ibid. ff. 10–11.
[71] Ibid. ff. 12–14; 406, no. 5.
[72] Ibid. 1095, f. 13.
[73] Ibid. 406, no. 5.
[74] Ibid. no. 6.
[75] Ibid. 133, f. 9.   [76] Ibid. 1095, f. 9.
[77] Ibid. 406, no. 3; above, pub. svces.
[78] G.L.R.O., P83/MRY1/133, f. 15.
[79] Ibid. 1095, f. 28.

income for the poor was spent on bread, coal, and other gifts.[80]

Rosamond Marshall of Islington before 1807 left £100 stock, the interest to be distributed amongst poor not receiving relief. Her husband added a further £100 stock.[81] In 1895 the church-wardens bought bread, coal, and other gifts.[82]

Property thought to have come to the parish on the death of a 'pauper' named Cooper and consisting of ½ a. at Ball's Pond, also known as the Kingsland Common estate, was let in 1812 at £16 a year, used for the poor. It was sold in 1865 for £1,112, which was invested; the income of £30 11s. 8d. in 1895 was spent by the churchwardens on bread, coal, and other gifts.[83]

Mrs. Mary Morton of Colebrooke Row, by will dated 1813, left £500 stock for repair of her tomb, any residue to be distributed as charity.[84] In 1895 the proceeds were used for bread, coal, and other gifts.[85]

Mrs. Susan Acburn (d. 1820) left £200 to the churchwardens for 20 poor Anglicans and £100 stock for repair of her tomb.[86]

Mrs. Sarah Blasson left £4,000 stock by will proved 1844, to provide £10 each for 10 female Anglican parishioners over 60 years of age on midsummer's day.[87] Under a Scheme of 1975, the sums were paid as directed.[88]

Joseph Hankins Burge, of New (later Cole-brooke) Terrace, by will dated 1846, left the dividends on £300 stock; £5 a year was to provide bread for the poor on the last Sunday of every month, and £3 was for repair of his tomb.[89]

Following an Act of 1872, the charity estab-lished by William Lambe and the Clothworkers' Company by deed of 1568 and Lambe's will of 1574, attached to Lambe's chapel in Wood Street Square (Lond.), was transferred to St. James's, Prebend Street. Clothing or blankets and shoes to the value of £14 14s. were provided each year for 12 men and 12 women living in the district, who had to attend a sermon.[90] The charity was carried out as directed in 1982.[91]

William Henry Schroder, by will proved 1873, left £1,000 in annuities, the interest to be divided annually between 15 women and 15 men, all aged 50 or more and living in the parish of St. Philip the Evangelist, Islington. The income was £22 10s. in 1966 and was distributed as directed.[92]

Alderman Col. Samuel Wilson placed a sum with the Weavers' Company of London, from whom the Islington churchwardens received £5 p.a. from 1885, distributed in gifts of 10s. to 10 parishioners not receiving parish relief.[93]

A fund called the poor's stock was formed when each recipient of some waste of Highbury manor contributed a sum for the Islington poor; the fund totalled £212 10s. stock in 1895. Dividends were paid to the churchwardens and used to buy bread, coals, and other gifts.[94]

Mrs. Ann Geary, before 1895, left £50 invested in stock, to provide £1 10s. a year to buy bread for the poor.[95]

Mrs. Isabella Ferris, before 1895, left £300 for the repair of Elizabeth Sebbon's tomb, the surplus to be spent on fuel for the poor.[96]

Thomas Dickenson, before 1895, left £4,000 stock to the incumbent of St. John's, Upper Holloway, and trustees, the income to buy bread, potatoes, and coals for 20 families atten-ding St. John's. By 1895 the charity had been divided among churches formed from St. John's district.[97] Under a Scheme of 1975 the income, c. £150 in 1978, relieved members of St. John's and of St. Mark's with St. Anne's.[98]

Mary Ann Crease,[99] by will proved 1895, left a sum to provide coal annually for the poor of St. Stephen's, Canonbury. Mary Georgiana Allen, by will proved 1925, left a small sum for the same purpose. In 1982 the charities, together producing an income of between £10 and £25 p.a., were managed under a Scheme of 1963.

Mrs. Phebe Eliza Rowarth, by will proved 1895, left £1,000 stock to the churchwardens of St. Mary's, Hornsey Rise, for payments to elderly widows every Christmas. In 1966 the income of £34 was distributed to 27 widows.

The Heartwell charity, established by Mrs. Louisa and Miss Emily Heartwell under a will proved 1896, provided for bread, potatoes, and coal to be given in winter to 20 poor of St. John's, Upper Holloway, or of St. Peter's and All Saints', to the value of 4s. each per week. In 1968 groceries worth £50 were distributed.

Thomas Lyon, by will proved 1905, left shares which realized £215 9s. 8d., the income to be divided equally among 20 poor of St. John's, Upper Holloway. In 1972 the income was £7 8s. 2d., and in 1982 the charity was managed under a Scheme of 1975.

Henrietta Thresher Glenny, by will dated 1912, left £1,200 each to the parishes of Christ Church, Highbury, and St. John's, Highbury Vale, for their poor. The sums were invested, and under a Scheme of 1980, following the union of the parishes, the joint income of £30 was disbursed by the vicar of Christ Church.

Miss Penelope Flinders Baldwin, by will proved 1924, left £100 for the poor of St. Paul's, Canonbury. The income in 1961 was £5 2s. 10d.

Emma Elizabeth Jones left houses at Southend-on-Sea (Essex) to establish a fund named, after her father, the Charles William Jones Trust, which was set up in 1949. The property had been sold and £3,960 4s. 9d. invested by 1962, the income being spent on poor people striving to help themselves, preferably resident in Upper Holloway.

Mary Lowthion Naile, by will proved 1949, left the residue of her estate in reversion to

80 Ibid. 406, no. 15.
81 Ibid. 1095, f. 27.
82 Ibid. 406, no. 14.
83 Ibid. no. 12.
84 Ibid. 1095, f. 30.
85 Ibid. 406, no. 16.
86 Ibid. no. 10.
87 Ibid. no. 27.
88 Char. Com. files.
89 G.L.R.O., P83/MRY1/1095, f. 33.

90 35 & 36 Vic. c. 154 (Local); above, churches.
91 Char. Com. files.
92 Ibid.
93 G.L.R.O., P83/MRY1/406, no. 11.
94 Ibid. no. 13.
95 Ibid. no. 17.
96 Ibid. no. 20.
97 Ibid. no. 28.
98 Char. Com. files.
99 Rest of subsection based on Char. Com. files.

Islington M.B. to assist middle-class women, the charity being named after her father John Shepperd Naile. Under a Scheme of 1969, £3,600 8s. was invested; in 1971 the income was £114 15s. 9d., of which £50 was distributed.

Charlie Reid, by will dated 1968, left all his furniture, personal belongings, and £100 to form the Charlie Reid fund for the sick and elderly of Islington. Stock worth £1,595 was purchased, producing £100 to £136 in 1971–5.

William Heron Welfare Trust. William Heron, woodmonger of London, in his will dated 1580 left land to the Clothworkers' Company of London, who were to pay £8 a year to the upkeep of roads in Islington, Clerkenwell, and St. Pancras. After a considerable increase in the value of the estate a Chancery order reapportioned the income: most of it went to the poor of Islington, Clerkenwell, and St. Pancras, but in 1983 Islington received £158 for repairing parish highways. Under Schemes of 1972 and 1980 the income was to be used for the relief of aged poor in Islington L.B. and the provision of recreational and other facilities.[1]

---

[1] G.L.R.O., P83/MRY1/1095, f. 24; ibid. 406, no. 2; Char. Com. files.

STOKE NEWINGTON

STOKE NEWINGTON[1] parish, known for its connexions with Dissent and literature, lies some 5 km. north of Bishopsgate on Ermine Street. A small, narrow parish 3.2 km. long at its farthest point and under 1.6 km. wide, it did not include the district east of the London road, which was often called Stoke Newington and included a common of that name but lay within Hackney parish. Two ancient roads formed a large part of Stoke Newington's boundaries:[2] the London road divided it from Hackney and Green Lanes,[3] with its continuation Coach and Horses Lane, from Islington and Hornsey on the west and Islington on the south. Cock and Castle Lane (Crossway), which joined the two main roads, formed the short south-east boundary, with Hackney. Field boundaries divided Stoke Newington from Tottenham on the north and Hackney on the north-east. There was no apparent logic in the boundaries with the prebend of Brownswood in Hornsey, which left three blocks of South Hornsey embedded in the southern part of Stoke Newington and some 29 a. of Clissold Park jutting into the northern part. The effect was to isolate the south-eastern corner (later Palatine ward) from the rest of the parish. There was controversy over boundaries between Stoke Newington and Brownswood in the 16th century,[4] and disputes arose with Hackney over Cock and Castle Lane in the early 19th century[5] and with Hornsey over Green Lanes and the western boundary in the 1860s and 1870s.[6] When Stoke Newington M.B. was formed in 1900, boundaries were altered, not only by the inclusion of the detached portions of South Hornsey and the rest of Brownswood, the western boundary following Seven Sisters, Blackstock, and Mountgrove roads, but by minor adjustments to the south-western boundary with Islington[7] and to the north-eastern boundary with Hackney, which thereafter followed the Great Eastern railway line and Bethune Road.[8] Stoke Newington parish contained 639 a. and the M.B. 863 a.[9] From 1965 Stoke Newington has formed the north-western part of Hackney L.B. The present article includes both the ancient parish of Stoke Newington and the detached parts of South Hornsey.[10]

London Clay covers the whole area, itself overlain by river deposits of the Boyn Hill stage: brickearth extends south across the centre from just north of Church Street, and gravel covers the south and south-east.[11] The resulting soil was a heavy clay in the north, roughly coinciding with the manorial demesne, a strong loam on the brickearth, and a gravelly soil in the south.[12] The land, 'generally much on a level',[13] lies about 25 m. above sea level, rising slightly in the north and west to 30 m.[14] The openness on the east to winds made the parish cold in winter but was thought conducive to health.[15]

Hackney or Manor brook, a tributary of the Lea, crossed the parish from Islington to Hackney.[16] When building spread in the early 19th century it became an open sewer,[17] which was eventually replaced by the High Level sewer after the formation of the Metropolitan Board of Works in 1855.[18] Apart from tributaries in the north-east, the whole of Hackney brook disappeared into culverts.[19] The New River, completed in 1613, meandered through the north end of the parish, with another loop in the Hornsey part of Clissold Park.[20] The original course extended into Hackney but was shortened by a new cut c. 1724.[21]

In 1825 the New River Co. agreed to improve the flow of the New River through Stoke Newington after complaints about leakage and interference with drainage,[22] and in 1831 took a lease of 50 a. of demesne land for reservoirs.[23] In 1833 two reservoirs were constructed alongside the New River partly as a reserve and partly to purify the water. In accordance with the Metropolis Water Act of 1852,[24] the company constructed filter beds and built, to the designs of William Chadwell Mylne, a large pumping station in Green Lanes, in the style of a medieval Scottish castle with towers and turrets, in 1856, having acquired another 14 a. from the Eade estate in 1855. The Metropolitan Water Board, which in 1904 superseded the New River Co., made considerable additions to the pumping station in

---

[1] The article was written in 1982–3.
[2] W. Robinson, *Hist. and Antiquities of Stoke Newington* (1820), frontispiece map.
[3] Boundary ran W. of rd. at SW. corner, probably originally including roadside waste.
[4] Guildhall MS. 14233/1, s.v. 1570; *Mdx. County Rec.* i. 62, 64.
[5] Vestry mins. 1819–38, 4, 48, 50.
[6] Ibid. 1862–89, 46, 59, 229, 294; Hackney dist. bd. of wks. *Ann. Rep.* (1874), 1–2.
[7] From Green Lanes along Petherton and Leconfield rds. to Green Lanes.
[8] Stoke Newington vestry, *Ann. Rep.* (1899–1900), 12; *N. Lond. Guardian*, 30 Jan. 1900 (G.L.R.O., AR/BA/2/49).
[9] *Census*, 1861, 1901.
[10] Brownswood is treated in *V.C.H. Mdx.* vi.
[11] Geol. Surv. Map 6", Mdx. XII. SW., SE. (1934 edn.); *V.C.H. Mdx.* i. 7.
[12] Robinson, *Stoke Newington*, 5; Foot, *Agric. of Mdx.* 9.
[13] *Bibliotheca Topographica Britannica*, ii, no. 9 (1783), 2.
[14] O.S. Map 1/10,000, TQ 38 NW. (1975 edn.).
[15] Stoke Newington vestry, *M.O.H. Rep.* (1895), 75.
[16] Robinson, *Stoke Newington*, frontispiece map.
[17] Mins. of Cttee. of Health, 1831 (HA P/M/BH 1); P.R.O., MH 13/261, no. 307/48.
[18] *Metropolitan Drainage*, H.C. 233, p. 271 (1857 Sess. 2), xxxvi; below, pub. svces.
[19] O.S. Map 1/2,500, Lond. V, X (1870 edn.).
[20] *V.C.H. Mdx.* vi. 102.
[21] Memo. by official of New River Co. 1793 (transcript of docs. in possession of New River Co., S.N.L. cuttings 46.2, LC 901); Robinson, *Stoke Newington*, map facing p. 37; H. W. Dickinson, *Water Supply of Gtr. Lond.* (1954), 40.
[22] Guildhall MS. CC. 212290.
[23] Ibid. 33412. The co. had 55 a. by 1848: tithe (1848), nos. 43–7, 78–9.
[24] 15 & 16 Vic. c. 84.

1936 but ceased to use it and the filter beds in 1946.[25] From that date the New River terminated at the pumping station, leaving a stretch of ornamental water in Clissold Park.[26] The board purchased the freeholds of the reservoirs from the Church Commissioners in 1958.[27]

COMMUNICATIONS. Ermine Street, the Roman road to Lincoln,[28] was locally called in the 16th century London Way[29] or High Street[30] and later,[31] from north to south, Stamford Hill, High Street, and Stoke Newington Road. Responsibility for the road was assigned in 1713 to Stamford Hill turnpike trust[32] and in 1826 to its successor, the metropolitan turnpike roads commissioners.[33] By the Middlesex Roads Act of 1789 the parish paid a composition to the trust in lieu of statute labour[34] and in 1829 the commissioners were paid arrears unpaid since 1824.[35] Responsibility returned to the local authorities after the abolition of turnpike tolls in 1865, passing to Hackney district board of works.[36]

Green Lanes was probably ancient, although unlikely to have been the original Ermine Street.[37] Its course was certainly established by 1577.[38] In the 18th century it was still literally green lanes, a shifting track over common land which apparently left its mark on Stoke Newington's western boundary.[39] In 1786 Stoke Newington's surveyors applied to Islington and Hornsey parishes about repairing the portion of the road between Paradise Row and Newington Green[40] but in 1789 the Stamford Hill trustees were made responsible for the whole of Green Lanes from Newington Green to Bush Hill in Edmonton.[41] Stoke Newington's inhabitants were exempted from payments at the toll gate at Paradise Row.[42] The trustees widened Green Lanes at Newington Green in 1791.[43] After the abolition of turnpike tolls Hackney district board of works was in dispute with Islington and Hornsey over Green Lanes.[44] In 1892 Hackney board and Islington

vestry jointly asked the L.C.C. to widen the road at the junction with Albion Road at Newington Green because of the great increase in traffic.[45]

The road from Kingsland to Green Lanes at the corner of Newington Green, which Camden believed part of the Roman route,[46] certainly existed in 1577[47] and may be identifiable with Kellers (1569) or Kyllary (1576) Street.[48] By 1793, when an agreement was reached with Islington and Hornsey for its repair, it was called Coach and Horses Lane after an inn in Islington.[49] The southern section was called Prospect Place in 1829,[50] Back Road in 1832 and c. 1861,[51] and Boleyn Road after 1877.[52] The north-west section became Matthias Road after the opening of St. Matthias's church in 1853.[53] Stoke Newington's south-eastern boundary was formed by a road joining Stoke Newington Road at Kingsland to Coach and Horses Lane. It existed in 1577,[54] was called Cock Lane in 1735,[55] Cock and Castle Lane in the early 19th century, when responsibility for its repair was disputed between Stoke Newington and Hackney,[56] Castle Lane c. 1885,[57] and Crossway in 1913.[58]

Church Street, which divided the parish in two,[59] existed by 1329.[60] Possibly called Newington (Newton) Lane in 1403, 1449, and 1500,[61] it was Church Street in 1576[62] and Stoke Newington Church Street from 1937. It was widened in 1872,[63] in 1899, when the junction with High Street was enlarged,[64] and during the 1930s.[65]

The only other road mapped in 1577, known in the 19th century as Cut Throat Lane, ran northward from Coach and Horses Lane to a large house[66] and was probably ancient, since it bounded two of the detached parts of South Hornsey. By 1638 it was described as a little lane from Kingsland to the lands of Roger Corbett.[67] In the 18th century it formed a through route from Kingsland to High Street and Church Street, although the northern part was only a footpath.[68] By c. 1861 the southern portion was named Wordsworth Road[69] and its continuation

[25] Guildhall MS. CC. 20359; H. W. Dickinson, *Water Supply of Gtr. Lond.* (1954), 75; Metropol. Water Bd. *Water Supply of Lond.* (1953 edn.), 221; *Illus. Lond. News*, 22 Nov. 1856 (S.N.L. cuttings 46.2).

[26] M. Cosh, *New River* (Islington libr. 1982), 12.

[27] Ch. Com., Surveys S2, p. 911.

[28] Cf. *V.C.H. Mdx.* v. 133, 309.

[29] P.R.O., MPF 282 (map of Mdx. 1577).

[30] Guildhall MS. 14233/1 (s.v. 1570).

[31] *Cruchley's New Plan* (1829).

[32] 12 Anne, c. 19. Inf. on London rd. and Green Lanes based on D. O. Pam, *Stamford Hill, Green Lanes Turnpike Trust*, i, ii (Edmonton Hund. Hist. Soc. 1963, 1965).

[33] 7 Geo. IV, c. 142 (Local and Personal).

[34] 29 Geo. III, c. 96; vestry mins. 1784–1819, 474; 1819–38, 143–6.

[35] Vestry mins. 1819–38, 286; G.L.R.O., P94/MRY/300–5.

[36] Hackney dist. bd. of wks. *Ann. Rep.* (1865), 2–3.

[37] *V.C.H. Mdx.* v. 309.

[38] P.R.O., MPF 282.

[39] Robinson, *Stoke Newington*, map (1734) facing p. 37; Cuttings of Stoke Newington 1722–1895, p. 2 n. (S.N.L. 80, LC 2411).

[40] Vestry mins. 1784–1819, 62.

[41] 29 Geo. III, c. 96. Cf. *V.C.H. Mdx.* v. 133, 311.

[42] Vestry mins. 1784–1819, 464; Robinson, *Stoke Newington*, 14, 21; Act 55 Geo. III, c. 59 (Local and Personal).

[43] Pam, *Stamford Hill, Green Lanes Turnpike Trust*, ii. 24.

[44] Hackney dist. bd. of wks. *Ann. Rep.* (1865), 3.

[45] Ibid. (1892), 5.

[46] *V.C.H. Mdx.* v. 309.

[47] P.R.O., MPF 282.

[48] Identification suggested by abutments: Guildhall MS. 14233/1.

[49] Vestry mins. 1784–1819, 179; Robinson, *Stoke Newington*, frontispiece map.

[50] *Cruchley's New Plan* (1829).

[51] Mins. of Cttee. of Health, 1831 (HA P/M/BH1); *Cassell's Map of Lond.* (c. 1861–2).

[52] L.C.C. *Names of Streets* (1912), 53.

[53] *Cassell's Map of Lond.* (c. 1861–2); below, churches.

[54] P.R.O., MPF 282.

[55] Tomlins, *Islington*, map facing p. 12.

[56] Vestry mins. 1819–38, 4, 28, 50, 143–6.

[57] *Bacon's Map of Parl. Boro. & Sch. Bd. Dist. of Hackney* [c. 1885] (S.N.L. 85.2, LC 1360).

[58] L.C.C. *List of Streets* (1929).

[59] P.R.O., MPF 282.

[60] Guildhall MS. (formerly St. Paul's MS. B 103).

[61] Lond. Mus. MS. 57.17/1; Guildhall MSS. 9171/4, ff. 258v–259; 8, f. 225.

[62] Guildhall MS. 14233/1.

[63] Hackney dist. bd. of wks. *Ann. Rep.* (1872), 5.

[64] Stoke Newington vestry, *Ann. Rep.* (1899–1900), 8, 63.

[65] Below, Church Street.

[66] P.R.O., MPF 282.

[67] Ibid. C 93/16/18.

[68] Tomlins, *Islington*, map (1735) facing p. 12; Rocque, *Map of Lond.* (1741–5), who labels it Green Lane; Milne, *Land Use Map of Lond.* (1800); Robinson, *Stoke Newington*, frontispiece map.

[69] *Cassell's Map of Lond.* (c. 1861–2).

by 1870 Nevill Road. In 1870 part of the footpath was stopped up, breaking the connexion between the southern portion and Hussey's Lane, an alley and hedged footpath from Church Street.[70] Hussey's Lane was replaced by Oldfield Road in the 1880s and 1890s.[71] A branch to the east at High Street, perhaps more important than the access to Church Street in the mid 18th century,[72] and known as Pawnbroker's Lane by c. 1861,[73] was cut off from the rest in 1870 and had disappeared by c. 1885.[74]

Lordship Road existed by 1649[75] and was named Lordship Lane by 1694.[76] In the mid 18th century it continued as a footpath to Hangar's Lane in Tottenham.[77] Its course was altered by the Act of 1814 which opened up building on the demesne. A new road (Woodberry Down) was driven from Green Lanes to Lordship Lane, the northern part of which was stopped up.[78] In 1869 Lordship Road was one of the principal routes to Finsbury Park and Alexandra Park.[79]

A bridle way across the glebe to Newington Green was stopped up by the rector c. 1475 and in 1569 the manor court ordered its reopening.[80] It was a footpath by 1713,[81] which, as Church Path or Walk, it remained, despite attempts to close it in 1838 and 1858,[82] until rebuilding in the 1960s left truncated sections from Church Street and Newington Green respectively.[83]

North of Church Street, Queen Elizabeth's Walk and Edward's Lane probably dated from the early 18th century, although not mentioned by name until 1734[84] and 1756 respectively.[85] Queen Elizabeth's Walk was 'ground used as a public walk', associated with Church Row, in 1704.[86] Edward's [sic] Lane was named after Job Edwards the builder (fl. 1697–1717).[87] By 1800 they were linked by Lordship Terrace.[88] Meadow Street, its extension eastward to Lordship Lane, existed by 1814.[89] Red Lion Lane existed by 1781[90] and Barn Street by 1825.[91]

Two later roads were important for general access. Albion Road, which joined Church Street to Newington Green, was completed by 1829.[92] The metropolitan roads commissioners opened the remainder of Seven Sisters Road from Green Lanes to Tottenham High Street in 1833.[93] There were 7½ miles of road in Stoke Newington in 1854,[94] 17 miles in 1897,[95] and 25 miles in 1905.[96] In 1937 the names of 23 roads were changed to avoid confusion with others in London.[97]

Money was left in 1449 to repair the 'sordid ways' towards the church[98] and in 1581 and 1611 to mend the ways from Newington to Islington.[99] Ermine Street, from the 14th century onwards, was frequently in a very bad state. Hazards in 1713 included quicksands at Kingsland and Stamford Hill, requiring a great deal of gravel.[1] The Palatine estate, formerly called Gravelpit fields, may once have provided gravel for the adjacent highway.[2] There were sloughs in Green Lanes in 1767[3] and the disrepair of the road, in some parts impassable for carriages, was given as the reason for turnpiking it in 1789.[4] Stoke Newington vestry, which feared that traffic from west London would pass along Green Lanes and Church Street to Stamford Hill, protested that Green Lanes was 'in as good repair as it has been within memory'.[5]

Highway robbery was a worse problem than the poor state of the roads. Attacks at Stoke Newington, recorded from 1575,[6] became frequent on the London road in the mid 18th century,[7] and there were others in Green Lanes[8] and Queen Elizabeth's Walk.[9] In 1830, after the parish joined the metropolitan police district, there were complaints that Cut Throat Lane, Lordship Road, Woodberry Down, and the farther part of Green Lanes were insufficiently protected.[10]

After Green Lanes and Seven Sisters Road had been disturnpiked in 1870, the Local Government Board paid Hackney district board of works an annual contribution for their maintenance until 1888, when responsibility passed to the L.C.C. In 1899 there was a clash between the L.C.C. and Stoke Newington vestry, which thereafter had to pay three-eighths of the cost.[11]

Stamford, originally Sanford, the sandy ford,

[70] O.S. Map 1/2,500, Lond. X (1870 edn.); cutting 30 Apr. 1870 (S.N.L. cuttings 48.1, LC 173); Giltspur [J. R. Spratling], *Story of Church Street* (1893), 47.

[71] S. pt. blt. by c. 1885: *Bacon's Map of Hackney* [c. 1885]. Completed by 1894: O.S. Map 1/2,500, Lond. XXX (1894–6 edn.).

[72] Rocque, *Map of Lond.* (1741–5).

[73] *Cassell's Map of Lond.* (c. 1861–2). Possibly named after Thos. Parsons, pawnbroker, who leased adjacent property in 1824: Abstract of Ct. Rolls 1802–31, 286.

[74] *Bacon's Map of Hackney* [c. 1885].

[75] Guildhall MS. 11816B, p. 129.

[76] P.R.O., C 7/636/25; Robinson, *Stoke Newington*, map (1734) facing p. 37.

[77] Rocque, *Map of Lond.* (1741–5).

[78] Robinson, *Stoke Newington*, 47 and frontispiece map.

[79] Hackney dist. bd. of wks. *Ann. Rep.* (1869), 5–6.

[80] Guildhall MS. 14233/1, s.vv. 1569, 1570, 1576.

[81] Vestry mins. 1681–1743, 163; Rocque, *Map. of Lond.* (1741–5).

[82] G.L.R.O., P94/MRY/309; *Islington Times*, 20 Mar. 1858 (S.N.L. cuttings 48.1).

[83] O.S. Map 1/1,250, TQ 3286 SE. (1952, 1970 edns.).

[84] Robinson, *Stoke Newington*, map facing p. 37.

[85] P.R.O., C 54/5975, pt. 1, no. 21, mm. 7–9.

[86] M.L.R. 1760/2/164.

[87] Below, settlement and growth to 1870.

[88] Milne, *Land Use Map of Lond.* (1800).

[89] Robinson, *Stoke Newington*, frontispiece map.

[90] Guide for assessors of par. 1781–2.

[91] Vestry mins. 1819–38, 143–6.

[92] *Cruchley's New Plan* (1829).

[93] G.L.R.O., MRC 11, pp. 274, 303; *V.C.H. Mdx.* v. 311.

[94] *Returns relating to Paving, Cleansing and Lighting within Metropol. Dists.* H.C. 127, pp. 5–6 (1854–5), liii.

[95] Stoke Newington vestry, *Ann. Rep.* (1897–8), 3.

[96] L.C.C. *Lond. Statistics*, xvi (1905–6), 323.

[97] Stoke Newington, *Official Guide* [1955], 57.

[98] Guildhall MS. 9171/4, ff. 258v.–259.

[99] P.R.O., PROB 11/63 (P.C.C. 15 Darcy, will of John Dudley); PROB 11/118 (101 Wood, will of Thos. Sutton).

[1] Pam, *Stamford Hill, Green Lanes Turnpike Trust*, i. 1–3.

[2] Below, other est.

[3] Pam, op. cit. 16.

[4] 29 Geo. III, c. 96.

[5] Vestry mins. 1784–1819, 107–8.

[6] *Cal. Pat.* 1572–5, 466, 481–2; Cal. Mdx. Rec. ii. 14; *Mdx. Sess. Rec.* iii. 132.

[7] e.g. robbery of 2 stage coaches and 3 postchaises betw. Shoreditch and Newington on one occasion in 1760: Cuttings of Stoke Newington 1722–1895, p. 4b (S.N.L. cuttings 80, LC 2411); cf. ibid. pp. 4a, 7a.

[8] Ibid. p. 2e, n.

[9] Ibid. p. 4f.

[10] Vestry mins. 1819–38, 307.

[11] Hackney dist. bd. of wks. *Ann. Rep.* (1890), 13; L.C.C. *Ann. Rep.* (1899), 66–7.

was where the London road crossed Hackney brook.[12] There was a wooden bridge there in 1675[13] and a 'great bridge' by 1687.[14] In 1826, called Newington bridge, it was a two-arched brick bridge nearly 40 ft. wide, built and maintained by the turnpike trustees at the expense of the county.[15] In 1830 a landlord, who planned to build along Stamford Hill, petitioned for the widening of the bridge on the Stoke Newington side where the parapet wall extended dangerously into the road. There was, however, disagreement about paying for the widening and it seems unlikely that it was done.[16] The brook was culverted in the 1850s; the old bridge was uncovered by excavations in 1910.[17]

There were several bridges where Green Lanes crossed the New River, including Green Lanes bridge in the north and Newington Green bridge in the south. The New River Co. was responsible for their maintenance. By 1826 Hackney brook was culverted where it passed under Green Lanes.[18] In 1734 the parish surveyors were to mend Stoke Newington's part of the bridge over the New River in Church Street, at the boundary with Hornsey.[19] In 1882 Hackney district board of works negotiated with the New River Co. to widen Lordship Road bridge over the New River.[20] Park Lane (later Clissold Crescent) bridge over the New River was demolished when the road was widened in 1931.[21]

A stage coach plied along the London road to Stoke Newington in 1760[22] and Samuel Hoare (d. 1796) made daily journeys from Paradise Row to the City by coach.[23] There were hourly coach services from Stoke Newington to Gracechurch Street by 1820, hourly and half-hourly services to Bishopsgate, and daily services to Skinner Street and Covent Garden by 1822.[24] In 1838–9 four omnibuses ran to Bishopsgate Street, six omnibuses and one short-stage coach to the Bank, an omnibus to Oxford Street, and a short-stage coach to Fleet Street.[25] By 1845 omnibuses ran to the City every 15 minutes and to the west end of London every half hour.[26] In 1849 four omnibus proprietors ran frequent vehicles to Bishopsgate, Piccadilly, Charing Cross, and the Exchange.[27] Six owners from Stoke Newington handed 11 omnibuses over to the London General Omnibus Co. in 1856.[28] The company leased coach houses at the rear of no. 83 Church Street from 1867 to 1910.[29]

In 1885 the L.G.O.C. had 17 buses at Stoke Newington, each making five journeys a day from Stamford Hill to Victoria station via Church Street, Albion Road, and Essex Road; the number had doubled by 1889 and reached 280 journeys each way by 1893.[30] In 1881 Henry Marshall, jobmaster of Stoke Newington, started a private omnibus service from Brownswood Park to Stoke Newington station, in Hackney, via Manor Road.[31] He was making 48 journeys each way by 1889. By 1893 the omnibuses of Messrs. Rackshaws and Roberts were making 120 journeys and private buses 28 journeys on that route.[32] In 1895 vehicles of the L.G.O.C. made 160 journeys each way from Stamford Hill on the Church Street and Albion Road route to Victoria and 198 journeys each way from Stamford Hill to London Bridge along Ermine Street, while 56 private buses ran from Stoke Newington station to Brownswood tavern and another 56 from the station to Finsbury Park station, both along Manor Road.[33]

Proposals in the 1860s for railway lines across Stoke Newington came to nothing[34] but in 1872 the Great Eastern Co. opened a station called Stoke Newington just outside the parish, in Hackney, on its line to Bishopsgate (after 1874 Liverpool Street) station.[35]

In 1871 the district board of works welcomed the Tramways Act of 1870, hoping that tramways would save the roads.[36] A line from the City along the London road to Stamford Hill was completed in 1872[37] and another from Newington Green along Green Lanes to Clissold Park in 1874, extended to Manor House in 1883.[38] In 1885 there were 169 daily journeys each way on the North Metropolitan Tramways Co.'s service between Stamford Hill and Moorgate Street and another 53 journeys between Stamford Hill and Bishopsgate, both services operating along the London road.[39] The North London Tramways Co. opened a line along Seven Sisters Road from Tottenham to Manor House in 1885 and along Green Lanes from Manor House to Wood Green in 1887.[40] In 1889 the North Metropolitan Tramways Co. operated three services along the London road from Stamford Hill: red cars to Moorgate Street (137 journeys daily each way), yellow to Bishopsgate (12 journeys), and green to Holborn (142 journeys). It also operated green cars from Finsbury Park along Green Lanes to Moorgate Street (203 journeys). The North

---

[12] P.N. Mdx. (E.P.N.S.), 107.
[13] J. Ogilby, Britannia (1675), plate betw. pp. 8 and 9.
[14] Cal. Mdx. Sess. Bks. viii. 36.
[15] Rep. on Bridges in Mdx. 142.
[16] G.L.R.O., MJ/SPB 457–65. The hos. were not built until later: below, Lond. rd.
[17] N. Lond. Guardian, 17 June, 8 July 1910 (HA Bagust xiv. 8).
[18] Rep. on Bridges in Mdx. 142–3.
[19] Vestry mins. 1681–1743, 373.
[20] Hackney dist. bd. of wks. Ann. Rep. (1882), 9.
[21] Plaque on site.
[22] Cuttings of Stoke Newington 1722–1895, p. 4a, b (S.N.L. 80, LC 2411).
[23] Memoirs of Sam. Hoare (1911), ed. F. R. Pryor, 3.
[24] Robson's Lond. Dir. (1820), 106; Pigot's Lond. Dir. (1822–3), 36.
[25] Hist. Lond. Transport, i. 402.
[26] P.O. Dir. Six Home Counties (1845).
[27] Hackney and NE. Lond. Dir. (1849), 265–7.

[28] Hist. Lond. Transport, i. 404.
[29] Guildhall MS. CC. 212398; Kelly's Dir. Stoke Newington (1890–1911).
[30] Hackney dist. bd. of wks. Surveyor's Rep. (1885), 22; ibid. (1889), 32–3; ibid. (1893), 32.
[31] Appeal to inhabs. of Stoke Newington (S.N.L. cuttings 48).
[32] Hackney dist. bd. of wks. Surveyor's Rep. (1889), 33; ibid. (1893), 33.
[33] Stoke Newington vestry, Surveyor's Rep. (1895), 134.
[34] Hackney dist. bd. of wks. Ann. Rep. (1864), 8–9, 12; C. Klapper, Lond.'s Lost Rlys. (1876), 52.
[35] Hackney dist. bd. of wks. Ann. Rep. (1872), 4; C. J. Allen, Gt. Eastern Rly. (1955 edn.), 58.
[36] Hackney dist. bd. of wks. Ann. Rep. (1871), 7.
[37] Ibid. Surveyor's Rep. (1884), 13.
[38] Hist. Lond. Transport, i. 185; 'Rodinglea', Tramways of E. Lond. (1967), 222–3.
[39] Hackney dist. bd. of wks. Surveyor's Rep. (1885), 23.
[40] Ibid. (1886), 8; Hist. Lond. Transport, i. 259.

London Tramways Co. ran a service along the rest of Green Lanes and Seven Sisters Road.[41]

In 1892 the North Metropolitan Tramways Co. acquired the North London Tramways Co.'s services. It ran yellow cars and increased the journeys along Green Lanes from Finsbury Park to Wood Green to 78 by 1892 and 98 by 1895, while blue cars increased those along Seven Sisters Road to 71 by 1892 but reduced them to 64 by 1895. Services along the London road similarly increased.[42] The North Metropolitan Tramways Co. was allowed in 1898 to build stables at its depot on the north side of Seven Sisters Road.[43] In 1904 the Metropolitan Electric Tramways Co., which had acquired the lines of the North Metropolitan Tramways Co. in the area, electrified the lines along Seven Sisters Road and the northern part of Green Lanes from Manor House to Wood Green.[44]

The question of steam- or electric-powered trams was raised in 1890, since horse-droppings were greatly impeding road sweeping. There were steam trams on parts of Green Lanes and Seven Sisters Road and although they were considered unsightly, they were normally less noisy than the horse trams.[45] In 1895 the L.C.C. purchased the North Metropolitan Tramways' system within its boundary on a lease-back arrangement[46] and by the London County Tramways (Electrical Power) Act of 1900, it obtained powers to electrify.[47] Nevertheless it was not until 1907 that the L.C.C. electrified the line from London to Stamford Hill and in 1912 the southern part of Green Lanes as far as the Manor House.[48] A new service along Amhurst Park to link the Seven Sisters Road trams with those at Stamford Hill was opened in 1924.[49]

An inquiry in 1925 found that there were six tram and three motor bus services along the London road, trams along Green Lanes and Seven Sisters Road, and motor buses 'in all directions' in Stoke Newington, but that there was great overcrowding at Finsbury Park station and traffic congestion in Stoke Newington High Street. Stoke Newington was felt to be greatly in need of a tube railway.[50] There had been an abortive scheme to bring a railway along the London road in 1903 and in 1906 a line (later the Piccadilly) opened between Hammersmith and Finsbury Park, which remained Stoke Newington's

nearest tube station until the line was extended in 1932 with a station at Manor House.[51]

The London Passenger Transport Board, to which transport by bus, tram, and underground railway had passed in 1933,[52] under a series of Acts from 1934 to 1937[53] converted the trams into trolleybuses, starting with Seven Sisters Road (1936), then the northern parts of the Green Lanes and London road routes (1938), and ending with the southern part of the London road (1939).[54] By 1959 Stoke Newington was served by 16 trolleybus, 5 other London Transport motor bus services, and 3 Green Line coach routes.[55] In 1961 trolleybuses were replaced by motor buses, of which there were 18 services in 1980.[56]

GROWTH. SETTLEMENT AND BUILDING TO 1870. Abney Park cemetery forms part of an extensive palaeolithic working floor containing axes, hammer stones, and flakes.[57] Continuous occupation, however, probably dates only from the late Saxon period, and the 'ing' form of the name Newington is not recorded before the 13th century.[58] The first mention was as Neutone in 1086 when there were four villeins and 37 cottars with an amount of cultivated land which suggests that approximately half the area was still woodland.[59] The prefix Stoke, first recorded as a suffix in 1274[60] and used to distinguish the vill from Newington Barrow and Newington Berners in Islington, may refer either to tree-stumps, suggesting clearance of woodland, or to a timber structure.[61]

The medieval village was probably set in a landscape of open fields and woodland, with homesteads, closes, and gardens surrounding the cottages along Church Street, the London road and, by the later Middle Ages, Newington Green.[62] The woodland was gradually cleared: three loads of timber were taken from Newington to the Tower of London in 1528,[63] and in the 1560s and 1570s the manorial demesne, the glebe, and waste along Green Lanes all suffered from illegal felling, while there was still woodland on the copyhold in the north-east part of the parish.[64] Woodland covered 77 a. of the demesne in 1649,[65] some 27 a., mostly in the extreme north, in 1734[66] and had apparently disappeared

[41] Hackney dist. bd. of wks. *Surveyor's Rep.* (1889), 32–3.

[42] To 193, 79, 197, and 236 respectively: Stoke Newington vestry, *Ann. Rep.* (1894–5), 134; Hackney dist. bd. of wks. *Sanitary Inspector's Rep.* (1892), 31; G.L.R.O., CL/LOC/1/70. And see *V.C.H. Mdx.* v. 312.

[43] Stoke Newington vestry, *Ann. Rep.* (1897–8), 10.

[44] *Hist. Lond. Transport*, ii. 30–1, 100–1.

[45] Hackney dist. bd. of wks. *Ann. Rep.* (1890), 25–61. Cf. *V.C.H. Mdx.* v. 312.

[46] *Hist. Lond. Transport*, i. 270.

[47] 63 & 64 Vic. c. 271 (Local Act).

[48] *Hist. Lond. Transport*, ii. 100–1.

[49] 12 & 13 Geo. V, c. 80, pt. 2 (Local Act); *Hackney and Kingsland Gaz.* 12 May 1922 (S.N.L. cuttings 48); *Illus. Leader*, 21 Mar. 1924 (S.N.L. illus. 48, LC 2396).

[50] Min. of Transport, *Lond. Traffic Act, 1924, Publ. Inq.* 20 Oct. 1925 (S.N.L. 48.1, LC 2345).

[51] Klapper, *Lond.'s Lost Rlys.* 57; cutting Jan. 1927 (S.N.L. cuttings 48.5); Stoke Newington, *Official Guide* [1955], 55, 57.

[52] Lond. Passenger Transport Act, 23 & 24 Geo. V, c. 14.

[53] 24 & 25 Geo. V, c. 96 (Local and Personal); 25 & 26

Geo. V, c. 90 (Local and Personal); 1 Edw. VIII and 1 Geo. VI, c. 90 (Local and Personal).

[54] *Hist. Lond. Transport*, ii. 300.

[55] Stoke Newington, *Official Guide* (1959).

[56] Lond. Transport, *Map & List of Routes* (1980).

[57] *V.C.H. Mdx.* i. 11, 16, 20; Worthington G. Smith, *Man the Primeval Savage* (1894), 196–7, 204–5.

[58] *P.N. Mdx.* (E.P.N.S.), 159.

[59] *V.C.H. Mdx.* i. 122.

[60] P.R.O., JUST 1/538, m. 20d.

[61] *P.N. Mdx.* 159; *P.N. Elements* (E.P.N.S.), ii. 156.

[62] Guildhall MS. (formerly St. Paul's MS. B 103); B.L. Add. Ch. 44737; G.L.R.O., M83/NB/1; Tomlins, *Islington*, 209. The evolution of Church Street and Newington Green is separately treated above, Islington, and below.

[63] As with many early references, it is impossible to know whether Newington in Mdx. or Surrey is meant: *L. & P. Hen. VIII*, iv (2), p. 2236.

[64] Guildhall MS. 14233/1, unpag., s.v. 1569, 1570, 1572; ibid. MS. (formerly St. Paul's MS. A 37/1114).

[65] Ibid. MS. 11816B, p. 129.

[66] Robinson, *Stoke Newington*, map facing p. 37.

entirely from the parish by the mid 18th century.[67] Stoke Newington was sufficiently near London to attract residents from outside, like the earl of Oxford, in 1593 living in 'a very proper house there'.[68] From the burial of a servant of the countess of Essex, then wife of the earl of Leicester, in the church in 1582 it has been argued that Leicester was himself a resident. Leicester and his wife, however, were in the parish as guests of the widow of Leicester's kinsman John Dudley. It was probably the visits of Queen Elizabeth I to the Dudleys that were commemorated in Queen Elizabeth's Walk.[69] Houses were increasingly leased to outsiders, mostly London merchants but also foreigners. Two Flanders men were living in Newington in 1436[70] and two Italian merchants in 1572.[71] In 1616 a merchant, Cyprian Gabrie, himself possibly foreign, complained of the obstruction of a watercourse from his house in Stoke Newington by Sir Noell Caron, ambassador from the United Provinces, who was presumably his neighbour,[72] and in 1643 the same house was occupied by Reynatus Augier, apparently another foreigner.[73]

The parish was affected by religious and political movements. A clergyman was gaoled for repeating London gossip about the queen in 1562[74] and in 1623 a tailor from Newington near London was in trouble for remarks about James I.[75] The parish was strongly parliamentarian during the Civil War, and Col. Alexander Popham and, after 1664, Gen. Charles Fleetwood were among its inhabitants.[76] The Fleetwoods and Hartopps, and later the Abneys, were the protectors of nonconforming ministers and teachers who settled at Newington Green after the Restoration. In 1661 Henry Danvers (d. 1687), who had been a parliamentary colonel and who had a house at Stoke Newington, was described as one of a group of dangerous men in London who were preparing a rising.[77] In 1675 a shot was fired at the king from a house which was probably in High Street.[78] In 1681 Titus Oates was at Newington, presumably to see Danvers, whom he met there in 1682, and in 1685 Danvers was accused of 'treasonous practices', probably in connexion with Monmouth's rebellion.[79] Daniel Axtel (d. 1687), whose house at Stoke Newington was searched in 1678 for seditious libels, was the son of an executed regicide and fled to Carolina.[80]

There were 100 communicants in 1548,[81] and during the 16th and 17th centuries burials averaged between 4 and 10 a year. During plague years 13 were buried in 1563, 34 in 1593, 65 in 1603, 52 of whom 40 died of the plague in 1625, and 25 at least during the 'sad visitation' of 1665.[82] In 1649 the parish was said to be small and most of the inhabitants attended Islington church, while many from west Hackney came to Stoke Newington church.[83] Sixty houses were assessed for hearth tax in Stoke Newington village in 1674 and another 24 at Newington Green. Another 19 cottages not chargeable in 1664 should probably be added to the total. There were 13 houses in Stoke Newington village and one at Newington Green with 10 or more hearths.[84] By manorial custom houses could be replaced by buildings of equal value, as happened in the 1680s. Tenementing, like the division of the Three Pigeons into five tenements by 1692, also implies a demand for housing.[85] There was considerable building during the 18th century, especially in Church Street, and by 1782 there were 191 houses in the parish, of which two thirds were in Church Street and one fifth along the London road.[86] In 1795 there were c. 200 houses,[87] and 208 inhabited and 13 uninhabited houses in 1801.[88]

Protestant nonconformity and London commerce, exemplified in Daniel Defoe,[89] featured strongly in local society. In 1698 a London gentleman, wishing to find a place out of town for his mother, rented a house in Stoke Newington.[90] In 1708 a London mercer, whose sick wife needed to live in the country, leased a house in Church Street and found that he could make a living from wealthy lodgers.[91] In 1720 Stoke Newington was 'pleasantly situated and full of fine country houses for citizens, being about 3 or 4 miles from London'.[92] In 1798 merchants' country retreats, where the women could spend much of their time, especially in summer, included 'genteel villas and pleasure grounds' near the New River.[93]

Hitherto building had been limited to the frontage to existing roads, especially Church Street and the London road. Manorial custom prohibited subleasing on copyhold for more than three years without licence. In 1805 the lord of the manor allowed John Graham, owner of Stonefields, 30 a. of copyhold in the south-east of the parish, to sublease for 61 years without

[67] Rocque, *Map. of Lond.* (1741–5).
[68] Norden, *Spec. Brit.* 37. Hen., s. of Edw. Vere, earl of Oxford bapt. in ch. 1593: Sage and Spratling, *Extracts from par. regs.*
[69] Robinson, *Stoke Newington*, 50–3. There is no evidence for tradition that Eliz. hid in ho. belonging to Leicester during Mary's reign.
[70] *Cal. Pat.* 1429–36, 537.   [71] Guildhall MS. 14233/1.
[72] *Acts of P.C.* 1615–16, 492.
[73] B.L. Harl. Ch. 111, C44.
[74] *Cal. S.P. Dom.* 1601–3, *Addenda*, 525; below, church.
[75] *Cal. S.P. Dom.* 1619–23, 496.   [76] *D.N.B.*
[77] *Cal. S.P. Dom.* 1670, *Addenda*, 661. Danvers's ho. was assessed for 13 hearths in 1664: G.L.R.O., MR/TH 1, m. 37.
[78] *Cal. S.P. Dom.* 1675–6, 471. The evolution of High Street (the London road) is separately treated below.
[79] *Cal. S.P. Dom.* 1680–1, 307; 1682, 237; 1685, 5; *D.N.B.*
[80] *Cal. S.P. Dom.* 1678, *Addenda*, 290, 294; P.R.O., PROB 11/389 (P.C.C. 90 Foot). Axtel's ho. was assessed for 10 hearths in 1674: P.R.O., E 179/143/370, m. 38d.

[81] *Lond. and Mdx. Chantry Certificates* (Lond. Rec. Soc. xvi), 72.
[82] Lysons, *Environs*, iii. 294.
[83] *Home Counties Mag.* i. 60.
[84] P.R.O., E 179/143/370, mm. 38d.–39. Several entries for 1664 are illegible and it is not clear how much of Newington Green, listed after Islington, was in Stoke Newington: G.L.R.O., MR/TH 1, mm. 31d.–32, 37 and d.
[85] Guildhall MSS. 14233/2, 3.
[86] Guide for assessors of par. 1781–2. Cf. Rocque, *Map of Lond.* (1741–5); c. 195 hos. in 1783: *Bibliotheca Topographica Britannica*, ii, no. 9 (1783), 1.
[87] Lysons, *Environs*, iii. 294.
[88] *Census*, 1801.
[89] For Defoe, below, Church Street, Newington Green.
[90] P.R.O., C 10/526/45.
[91] Ibid. C 7/644/5.
[92] John Stow, *Survey of Lond. and Westm.* ed. J. Strype (1720 edn.), ii, bk. 6, p. 131.
[93] Middleton, *View*, 12, 403.

demanding a larger fine than two years' ground rent on any building erected by him. In 1810 a similar agreement was made with James Kibble-white, who had purchased 9½ a. from Graham.[94] As a result 92 new houses and cottages fronted Stoke Newington Road, Castle Lane, and Coach and Horses Lane by 1813.[95] They included Nelson Lodge,[96] set well back from Stoke Newington Road, and houses at the corner of 'Berrett Street',[97] which was presumably Barrett's Grove although mapped in 1814 only as a footpath.[98]

In 1814 Stoke Newington's vicinity to London was said to make it capable of great improvement. Persuaded by the Eades, lessees of the manor, the prebendary obtained an Act enabling him to lease the manor for 99 years and empowering the lessees to grant subleases for terms up to 99 years. The same Act permitted enfranchisements, so opening up both demesne and copyhold land to builders.[99] There were 379 houses in the parish on the eve of the Act.[1] The numbers increased[2] to 442 in 1821 and 670 in 1831, but by 1832 a general depression had brought building to a standstill.[3] Twelve houses were built in 1841, ten in 1842, and eight in 1843; in 1844, when there were 705, it was thought that few would be built in the next years.[4] Annual returns of buildings erected from 1856[5] show that within increases of 29 per cent between 1851 and 1861 and 68 per cent between 1861 and 1871 the number varied from 16 in 1861 to 113 in 1868. By 1871 there were 1,816 houses in Stoke Newington parish and another 1,087 in South Hornsey.

Construction was by scores, if not hundreds, of independent builders, mostly on a very small scale. Albert Town, for example, was built in the 1850s by 53 builders, the largest of whom, James Witcombe of Islington, built 35 houses. Many others put up a single house.[6] Best known was Thomas Cubitt and local ones included Meshard Izzard, a carpenter from High Street, and Thomas Widdows of Church Street, described in 1839 as 'a most lascivious old fellow'.[7] Architects who designed their own houses were John Young c. 1845 and James Brooks in 1862.[8] There was a contrast between the area north of Church Street, mainly demesne land over which the lords of the manor exercised some control, and that to the south, fragmented among numerous owners. In the north it was possible to lay out roads like Seven Sisters Road, Manor Road, and Lordship Park spanning the whole parish, while in the south small estates were developed piecemeal.

There were 31 houses and cottages on the demesne in 1813, mostly on the north side of Church Street from Church Row to Lordship Lane (later Road) but including four in Edward's Lane and two in Lordship Lane. Woodberry Down, from Green Lanes to Lordship Lane, had been formed although it was still called New Road and had no houses.[9] Building after the Act proceeded modestly on the existing roads close to Church Street, mostly with small terraced houses. There were six in Meadow Street by 1818[10] and Meshach Izzard built another 13 there in 1820–1.[11] A terrace of 10 brick cottages had been lately built in Edward's Lane in 1820.[12] From 1821 to 1828 10 houses, with gardens of 1 a. and ½ a., were built in Lordship Road.[13] Building started in Green Lanes in 1821 with a large house at the junction with Woodberry Down[14] and in 1824 with three detached houses at a crossing of the New River.[15] At the northern end of Green Lanes Northumberland House, a three-storeyed building with a pillared entrance, balustrade, and urns on its roof, had been built by 1824[16] and Thatched Cottage, with Gothic windows, on the Tottenham border by 1825.[17] Woodberry Down Cottages, four detached houses on the south side of Woodberry Down, had been built by 1829.[18] Thomas Widdows had built Manor House public house at the junction of Green Lanes and Seven Sisters Road by 1832.[19] By 1837 the large River House, at the bend of the New River on the south side of Seven Sisters Road, had been built by builders from Clerkenwell[20] and Homefield Place, six cottages in Lordship Road, by Thomas Widdows.[21] In the 1840s larger houses were built in the central portion of Lordship Road,[22] in Green Lanes north of those built in the 1820s,[23] and on the north side of Seven Sisters Road. There was an ambitious but abortive scheme in 1846 for roads and 34 detached houses on land bounded by Seven Sisters Road, the New River, and Manor House tavern.[24] One house was built in Queen Elizabeth's Walk by

[94] 54 Geo. III, c. 128 (Local and Personal).
[95] Robinson, *Stoke Newington*, frontispiece map; ref. bk. to Wadmore map (1813) s.v. Graham (nos. 420–58), Kibble-white (nos. 459–64), Hindle (nos. 465–531); below, other est. (Stonefields).
[96] Ref. bk. to Wadmore map (1813), nos. 465–8; Abstract of Ct. Rolls 1832–82, 343.
[97] Ref. bk. to Wadmore map (1813), nos. 447–8.
[98] Map on p. 146.
[99] 54 Geo. III, c. 128 (Local and Personal).
[1] Ref. bk. to Wadmore map (1813). Cf. 364 in 1811: *Census*, 1811.
[2] Based on *Census*, 1821–71. Figures include uninhabited hos. and those being built.
[3] Ch. Com. file (return by prebendary 1832).
[4] G.L.R.O., P94/MRY/207 (return under New Metropol. Bldgs. Act 1844).
[5] G.L.R.O., MBW 1772–8 (abstracts of monthly returns 1856–88); AR/BA 4/718–28 (abstracts 1901–20). Rest of section based on dist. surveyors' monthly returns, bound together annually under local authorities: G.L.R.O., MBO (1845–52); MBW (1871–88); AR/BA 4 (1889–1939).
[6] M. Hunter, *Victorian Villas of Hackney* (Hackney Soc. 1981), 16.

[7] Cuttings of Stoke Newington 1722–1895, p. 7k (S.N.L. 80, LC 2411). [8] Below, from 1940.
[9] Robinson, *Stoke Newington*, App. vi, pp. 289–94; ref. bk. to Wadmore map (1813); Guildhall MS. CC. 212290.
[10] Ch. Com. file 30341 pt. 1 (schedule of leases).
[11] Guildhall MSS. CC. 212317, 212320–2, 212326–7.
[12] Abstract of Ct. Rolls 1802–31, 272; photos. (S.N.L. illus. 80.5 EDW, LC 472, 475, 3028).
[13] Guildhall MSS. CC. 212306–8, 212321, 212323, 212331, 304979. [14] Ch. Com. file 30341 pt. 1 (schedule of leases).
[15] Guildhall MSS. CC. 212309, 212324.
[16] It became a private lunatic asylum in 1830: *Prospectus of Northumberland Ho. Asylum*, 1835 (S.N.L. 47.3, LC 1211); photo. (S.N.L. illus. 80.1 WOD, LC 47).
[17] Guildhall MS. CC. 212290; photos. c. 1865 (S.N.L. illus. 57.2 SPE, LC 49–50).
[18] *Cruchley's New Plan* (1829).
[19] Guildhall MS. CC. 282581. [20] Ibid. 212354.
[21] G.L.R.O., O/238/1.
[22] Guildhall MS. CC. 2418; tithe (1848), nos. 92–103.
[23] Guildhall MSS. CC. 2413–15; tithe (1848), nos. 60, 63–4.
[24] Guildhall MS. CC. 2417; ibid. Prints S4/La. Pr. I/SEV (wrongly labelled Islington); tithe (1848), nos. 22–4.

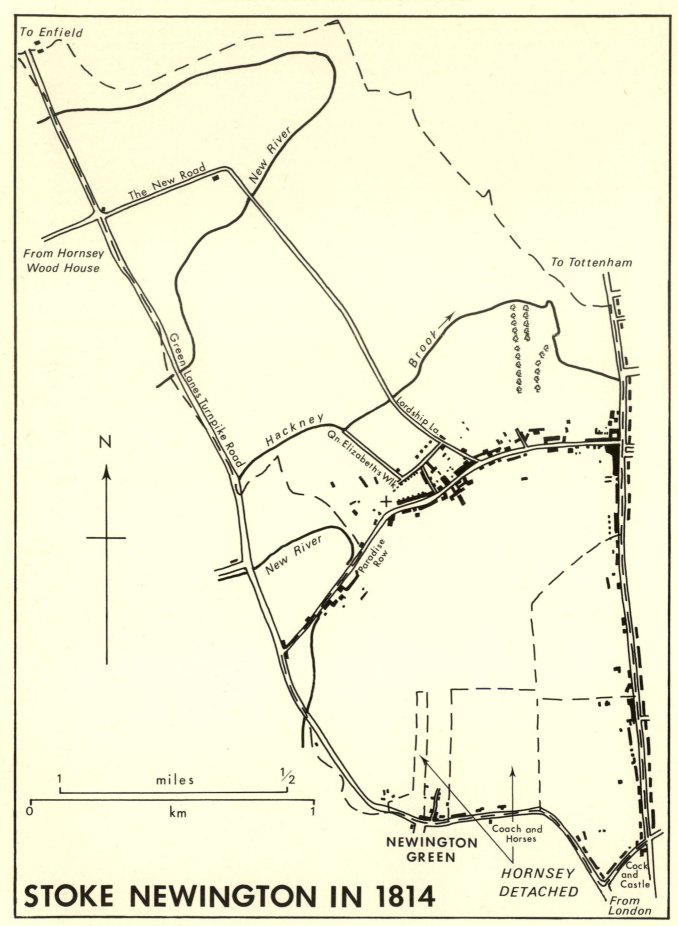

To Enfield

From Hornsey
Wood House

The New Road

New River

To Tottenham

Brook

Green Lanes Turnpike Road

Lordship La.

Hackney

Qn. Elizabeth's Wlk.

N

New River

Paradise Row

1   miles   ½

0   km   1

Coach and
Horses

NEWINGTON
GREEN

HORNSEY
DETACHED

Cock
and
Castle

From
London

STOKE NEWINGTON IN 1814

1846.[25] By 1848 there were 134 houses and cottages on the demesne.[26]

The south-eastern part of the area north of Church Street was not demesne. By 1829 Park Street (later Yoakley Road), with houses on either side, had been driven north from Church Street.[27] A Quaker meeting house and alms-houses opened in 1829 and 1834 respectively[28] and 12 houses were built between 1845 and 1851 by Thomas Widdows and others. Manor Road (called Park Grove in 1848) had been driven from Stamford Hill to Lordship Road by 1827 and during the 1840s housing spread westward on Thomas Maughan's estate. The builder was Richard Ashby, who occupied a large detached house on the south side of the road.[29] In 1840 most of the remaining land in the south-east corner north of Church Street became part of Abney Park cemetery, providing a permanent open space, as did the 50 a. of demesne land taken for reservoirs in 1831.[30]

Except for glebe, all the land south of Church Street was copyhold. In 1821 the largest estate, the Pulteney estate of 60 a. occupying most of the western side of the parish between Church Street and Newington Green, was for sale in lots of 1 a. or 2 a. fronting Green Lanes and two projected new roads, Albion Road and Clissold Crescent.[31] Thomas Cubitt[32] bought seven lots (12 a.) mostly on each side of the northern part of Albion Road. In 1822 he purchased two adjoining lots (3½ a.) from John Merrington, a local surveyor. Cubitt assumed responsibility for making and maintaining Albion Road until it was adopted by the vestry in 1837, and he constructed the sewers.[33] He started with houses at the north end in 1823, some being built by his own men and some, for example, Clarence Cottages (nos. 191–3), which were completed by John Payn in 1827, by small builders. Construction slowed in 1829 and some of the builders went bankrupt, but Cubitt in 1833 started building again, completing houses in South Place which he had left unfinished since 1829. Before 1834 he let land on the north-east to a nurseryman, but building continued during the 1830s on other sites to meet a new demand for larger detached or semi-detached houses[34] and by 1839 was virtually complete. Within 20 years Cubitt had added more than 70 houses, mostly of a quality to preserve Stoke Newington's character as a select residential area, al-

though a contemporary in 1841 complained that Albion Road 'has spoilt all the quiet of the fields and brought London nearer to Stoke Newington by 50 miles'.[35]

The building lots on the east side of the southern part of Albion Road were divided among several purchasers, including Thomas Cubitt's brother William.[36] A few houses were built before 1829[37] and more during the 1840s[38] until by 1848 they formed a continuous line from South Place southward for more than half the length of Albion Road.[39]

Benjamin Massey bought five lots (11 a.) of the western part of the Pulteney estate and was leased another 4 a.[40] He had built Newington Hall for himself at the junction of Church Street and Green Lanes and two houses adjoining it fronting Green Lanes, called Paradise Place, by 1829.[41] The rest of Paradise Place was built in 1846–8.[42] Cubitt's original purchase in 1821 had included 2 a. between the New River and Clissold Crescent, which he leased in 1822 and 1823 to Massey and to Joshua Ramsay. By 1836 Ramsay had built one house fronting Clissold Crescent and another three facing the New River, forming the northern part of what, after 1839, was named Aden Terrace.[43] Massey built at the southern end of the terrace and in Millfield Place on the west side of Green Lanes in 1846–8. By 1848 there were 27 houses and a tavern, the Pegasus, on his land.[44] South of Millfield Place some 20 houses and the Royal Oak tavern were built between 1829 and 1846 on 1½ a. sold in 1821 to George Brown.[45]

Although Samuel Rhodes of Islington, an important North London developer, bought nearly 15 a. in the centre of the Pulteney estate, he did not build there.[46] James Rhodes, his son, enfranchised most of it in 1824[47] and by 1848 it had passed to Massey and others.[48] Some 9 a. to the east, joining the small portion of South Hornsey detached, was bought in 1821 by James Browning and was still held by his descendants in 1848, as part of farmland stretching to Albion Road.[49]

Soon after Victoria's accession Victoria Grove was driven westward from the London road on James Cockburn's estate in the eastern part of South Hornsey. Eleven houses had been built there by 1841[50] and building was active during the 1840s. By 1848 Victoria Road had been built and Victoria Grove extended[51] until by 1849

[25] Guildhall MS. CC. 2416; below, from 1940.
[26] Tithe (1848), nos. 1–106, 118–244.
[27] *Cruchley's New Plan* (1829).
[28] Below, prot. nonconf.
[29] Tithe (1848), nos. 321–3, 384–9. For Manor Rd., see above.
[30] Below, pub. svces.
[31] Guildhall MS. 14233/18, 52 sqq.; below, other est. (Pulteney).
[32] Inf. on Cubitt from H. Hobhouse, *Thos. Cubitt: Master Builder* (1971), 19, 42–9.
[33] Vestry mins. 1819–38, 198.
[34] Though Hobhouse, *Thos. Cubitt*, 45, mentions larger hos. adjoining Church St., backing on glebe land, the earlier, northern hos. were mostly terraced and smaller: tithe (1848), nos. 631–56. For nursery, below, econ., nurseries and mkt. gdns.
[35] *Chamber's Edinburgh Jnl.* [1841], 310–11 (S.N.L. cuttings 80).
[36] Hobhouse, *Thos. Cubitt*, 43; Guildhall MS. 14233/18, 52 sqq.
[37] *Cruchley's New Plan* (1829).
[38] Abstract of Ct. Rolls 1832–82, 347.
[39] Tithe (1848), nos. 778–818.
[40] Guildhall MS. 14233/18, 52 sqq.
[41] *Cruchley's New Plan* (1829).
[42] Tithe (1848), nos. 699–705.
[43] Ibid. nos. 706–11; Hobhouse, *Thos. Cubitt*, 44; Pevsner, *Lond.* ii. 411. By 1848 part of Cornelius Hanbury's est.
[44] Tithe (1848), nos. 713–20, 728–43.
[45] Ibid. nos. 744–59, 762–6; *Cruchley's New Plan* (1829); Miller, *Plan of Stoke Newington* (1846); Abstract of Ct. Rolls 1832–82, 339.
[46] Guildhall MS. 14233/18, 52 sqq.; Hobhouse, *Thos. Cubitt*, 43.
[47] Abstract of Ct. Rolls 1832–82, 341; HA D/F/RHO.
[48] Tithe (1848), nos. 673, 724–5, 767–9.
[49] Ibid. nos. 770–6; Guildhall MS. 14233/18, 52 sqq.
[50] P.R.O., HO 107/663/4; photo. (S.N.L. illus. 80.8 VIC/b, LC 565); Haringey L.B., Rec. of St. Mary Hornsey (D/PH/2B/26, quoted in S.N.L. 92, LC 3275).
[51] J. Wyld, *Map of Lond. & Environs* (1848).

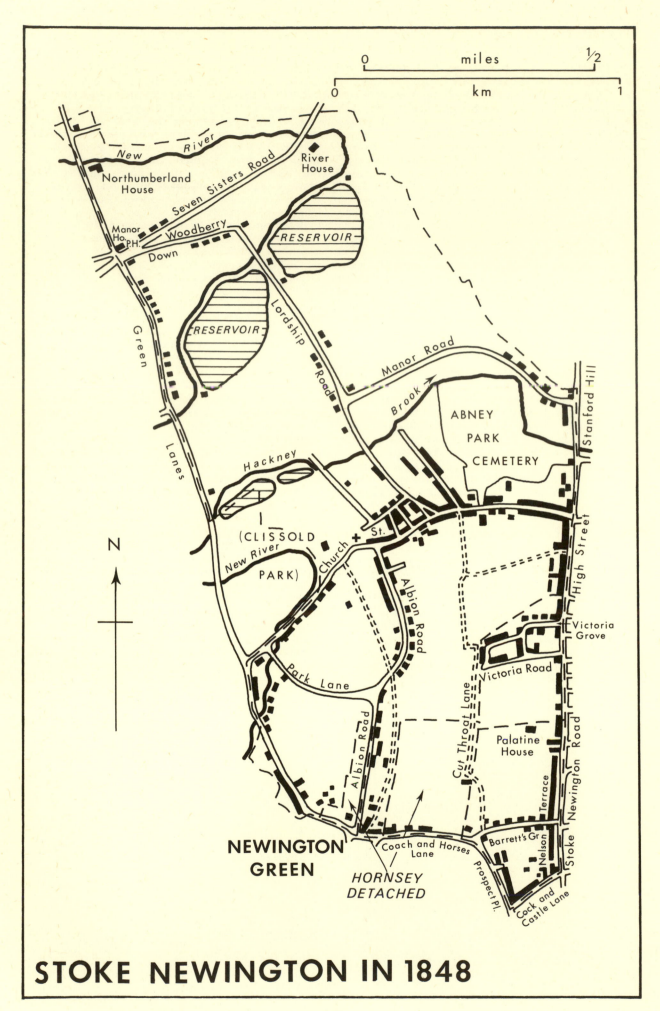

STOKE NEWINGTON IN 1848

there were 79 houses, mostly terraced,[52] and 107 in the Grove and 42 in the Road by 1851. Among the craftsmen, commercial travellers, and clerks who lived there in 1851 were two builders, one of whom, George Major of Albert Terrace in Victoria Road, employer of 30 men, may have built many of the houses nearby.[53]

In 1849 the Foy estate east of Albion Road, consisting of 28½ a. in the central part of South Hornsey[54] and, adjoining it on the north-west, 6 a. in Stoke Newington,[55] much of which had been leased as brickfields, was conveyed by the assignees of Offley Shore, a bankrupt, to the National Freehold Land Society.[56] By 1852 the society had laid out the roads, named after poets, of what by 1854 was known as Albert Town,[57] possibly to complement the name Victoria in the eastern section of South Hornsey. The society also laid down sewers, relieving fears of fever resulting from stagnant water in brickpits.[58] In 1851 the land was sold in lots[59] and building started in Albion Grove and Milton and Shakespeare roads. St. Matthias's school was built on the eastern borders of the estate, in Stoke Newington, in 1849 and the neighbouring church in 1853 to serve the built up area to the east and south but also in awareness of growth to the west. Houses were 'springing up' near the church in 1854[60] and building was probably complete by 1855.[61] Built to produce Liberal voters,[62] Albert Town was inhabited mainly by the middle class, especially clerks and craftsmen, but included brickmakers and labourers in the smaller terraced houses, besides such wealthy residents as Mary King who, supported by railway dividends, lived in Olney Cottage in Cowper Road and John Thomas, landowner, in Albion Grove in 1861.[63]

In 1850 the rector, who had relinquished glebe land for the building of Glebe Place in Church Street, granted a lease on 11¼ a. to Charles Birch and others with provision for 21 houses, 9 facing Church Street to contain at least 10 rooms each, and the rest on the west side of a new road, Park (later Clissold) Road.[64] Birch made the new road, which he asked the vestry to adopt in 1853.[65] Several builders worked on 39 houses in 1851–2 and by 1855 the Church Street site (Park Crescent) and the east side of Park Road were completed; on the west side there were eight houses at the southern and two detached at the

northern end.[66] The rest of the houses were completed by c. 1862.[67]

A plan to divide the central portion of the Pulteney estate for building existed in 1846,[68] and two houses were built in Grange (later Burma) Road in 1851, but there were still only four in 1855[69] and seven c. 1862.[70] Two others were built in Aden Grove South in 1846 but the rest of the project was to wait 25 years. At the northern end of the Pulteney estate Massey built a few houses at the western end of Clissold Crescent between 1848 and 1855.[71] York Villas in Albion Road were built in 1852 and Ebor Terrace stood on the eastern side at the southern end of the road by 1855.[72] On the Victoria estate in South Hornsey, Gordon Road[73] with its two side roads, Warwick and Gainsborough roads, had appeared by c. 1862, although the only building was the Edinburgh brewery.[74]

North of Church Street building continued at Woodberry Down during the 1850s,[75] and by 1855 large houses covered its south side.[76] The Ecclesiastical Commissioners had acquired land on the western borders of Abney Park cemetery by 1848[77] and in 1859 they agreed that John Rodda of Canonbury, who had already worked on the rectory estate, should construct a road, Bouverie Road, from Church Street to Manor Road, lay sewers and drains by 1861, and build eight houses a year on 11 a. The commissioners kept tight control, providing the plan and elevation of the houses, which were to be terraced, three-storeyed and three-bayed, with Ionic columns flanking substantial doorways.[78] Rodda was building houses and a chapel in the road in the 1860s and by 1870 had reached northward almost half-way up the new road on both sides.[79] The 11 a. included a tongue of land projecting westward at the north end and by 1868 Grayling Road joined Bouverie and Lordship roads and Rodda was building Claremont Terrace there.[80]

In 1855 an extension of Manor Road to Green Lanes was projected,[81] although it was not until 1864 that an application for it was made to the M.B.W. by the Hackney board.[82] Semi-detached houses, each with a bay window and stepped porch, called Lordship Park, were built on either side of the road, then called Manor Road, during the 1860s, mostly by Thomas John Angell, who was probably a speculator rather than a builder.[83]

[52] Hackney and NE. Lond. Dir. (1849).
[53] P.R.O., HO 107/1702/1/4.
[54] G.L.R.O., MR/DE/HOR, nos. 708–10; Guildhall MS. CC. 184832, f. 5v.   [55] Tithe (1848), no. 623.
[56] Conveyance to John Morland of Croydon and Conrad Wilkinson of Beckenham, presumably trustees for soc.: G.L.R.O., Acc. 1274/26–41.
[57] G.L.R.O., M.C.S. 498/703; min. bks. of Hornsey par. (HA P/HOR/L).
[58] Freeholders' Circular, 1 Apr. 1852 (S.N.L. cuttings 41.8 ALB, LC 3573).
[59] G.L.R.O., Acc. 1274/26–41.
[60] Mary E. Shipley, Barbara Pelham [1906], 92.
[61] Miller, Plan of Stoke Newington (1855).
[62] E. J. Cleary, Building Soc. Movement (1965), 51.
[63] P.R.O., RG 9/152/11/7; RG 9/792/5; Olney Cottage (HA ST 183); above, plate 58.
[64] G.L.R.O., P94/MRY/96 (deed, 1850).
[65] Vestry mins. 1838–62, 364.
[66] Miller, Plan of Stoke Newington (1855).
[67] Cassell's Map of Lond. (c. 1861–2); P.R.O., RG 9/152/11/3; photos. (S.N.L. illus. 80.6 CL1, LC 279, 492).

[68] Miller, Plan of Stoke Newington (1846).
[69] Ibid. (1855).
[70] Cassell's Map of Lond. (c. 1861–2).
[71] Tithe (1848), nos. 721, 723; Miller, Plan of Stoke Newington (1855).
[72] Miller, Plan of Stoke Newington (1855); Cassell's Map of Lond. (c. 1861–2).
[73] Presumably named after Gordon Ho. and est., not after the general: P.R.O., RG 9/791/4.
[74] Cassell's Map of Lond. (c. 1861–2).
[75] Guildhall MSS. CC. 267386–7 (Marlborough Ho.); 292944, 292953 (Silvermere).
[76] Miller, Plan of Stoke Newington (1855).
[77] Tithe (1848), nos. 305, 309, 311, 313, 315.
[78] Guildhall MS. CC. 41744.
[79] Ibid. MSS. CC. 53651, 95904, 109551, 351807; O.S. Map 1/2,500, Lond. X (1870 edn.).
[80] Guildhall MSS. CC. 121959, 125394–6, 125399.
[81] Miller, Plan of Stoke Newington (1855).
[82] Hackney dist. bd. of wks. Ann. Rep. (1864).
[83] Guildhall MSS. CC. 96857, 102801–5, 120760, 374448. Angell was described as 'gent. of Maida Hill West'.

At about the same time Angell was involved with Finsbury Park Villas, a terrace of at least 12 houses, which, starting with Finsbury Park tavern, ran northward along Green Lanes from its junction with the new Woodberry Grove.[84] Building also proceeded during the 1860s in Lordship Road[85] and was continuous on the west side up to Manor Road by *c.* 1870.[86] During the 1860s it spread westward along new roads like Brook (later Grazebrook) Road[87] and Lordship Grove[88] and continued eastward along the north side of Seven Sisters Road, built by Angell and a London builder Thomas Oldis.[89] An architect,

South of Church Street, Green Lanes was in 1861 a growing neighbourhood,[94] and between 1861 and 1870 terraced houses were built on the east side of the road opposite the Pegasus as far south as Aden Grove. Terraces were also built on the west side of Grange Road and on the south side of Park Lane, on land leased in 1848 as a brickfield from Benjamin Massey.[95] The most extensive building during the 1860s, however, was on the Walford estate between Albert Town and the Victoria estate, the southern part of which it included. Acquired by the Walford family from Martha Carr, most of the area by 1870 had been

1844   1877   1904

STOKE NEWINGTON: EVOLUTION OF SETTLEMENT 1844–1904

(1 inch to 1 mile)

William Reddall of Finsbury, was among those who leased the detached houses built from 1868 to 1870 at the east end of Seven Sisters Road with gardens running to the New River.[90] At the east end 3 a. on the south side were leased in 1867 for four detached or nine 'substantial' houses; three detached houses were built by 1871.[91] Woodberry Down was dedicated in 1868,[92] when it was extended eastward from Lordship Road, and villas were built on the south side in the late 1860s.[93]

covered with terraced houses, of which, in the Stoke Newington part, there were 332 in 1871.[96]

Stoke Newington had many handsome residences in 1826[97] and was 'eminently respectable' in 1834,[98] when the dwellings of the poor totalled 110, about a fifth of the whole.[99] In 1845 the neighbourhood was 'retired and picturesque'.[1] In 1864 Shirley Hibberd observed that nightingales were still there, although 'all around the builders are drawing a close cordon of bricks'.[2] Until 1870 Stoke Newington remained pre-

[84] Guildhall MSS. CC. 120758–9, 135621–2, 371256.
[85] Ibid. 97731.
[86] O.S. Map 1/2,500, Lond. X (1870 edn.).
[87] Guildhall MSS. CC. 102821–2, 120749, 120754–5, 212395.
[88] Miller, *Plan of Stoke Newington* (1855); O.S. Map 1/2,500, Lond. X (1870 edn.).
[89] Guildhall MSS. CC. 102793–4, 120761–5, 131743, 294282, 348976.
[90] Ibid. 135653–5, 146201, 149325, 340462.
[91] Ibid. 212302.
[92] Hackney dist. bd. of wks. *List of Rds.* (1877) (HA J/BW 28).

[93] Guildhall MSS. CC. 135620, 135657.
[94] Hackney dist. bd. of wks. *Ann. Rep.* (1861), 3.
[95] Tithe (1848), no. 724; *Cassell's Map of Lond.* (*c.* 1861–2); O.S. Map 1/2,500, Lond. X (1870 edn.).
[96] F. W. Baxter, 'Stoke Newington Street Names' (S.N.L. 80, LC 2330); O.S. Map 1/2,500, Lond. X (1870 edn.); P.R.O., RG 10/311/9/1c.
[97] *Pigot's Lond. Dir.* (1826–7), 492.
[98] Pigot, *Nat. Com. Dir.* (1834), 930.
[99] *Rep. Com. Poor Laws*, H.C. 44, p. 178i, no. 50 (1834), xxxvi.
[1] *P.O. Dir. Six Home Counties* (1845).
[2] Quoted in Pevsner, *Lond.* ii. 427.

dominantly middle-class, with a birth rate said to be very low because of the many unmarried servants.[3] Since the great majority of servants were female, wealth was reflected in the preponderance of women. Females formed 63 per cent of the population in 1801, 57 per cent in 1831, 59 per cent in 1841, over 60 per cent in 1851 and 1861, and 57 per cent in 1871, when in the wealthy district west of Albion Road they formed 69 per cent.[4]

The chief cause of growth was that Stoke Newington provided good houses in an attractive setting within easy reach of commercial London. Merchants, bankers, and stockbrokers spread from Church Street and the London road to the newer Aden Terrace, Albion Road, Paradise Place, Park Road, Manor Road, Lordship Road, Woodberry Down, and Seven Sisters Road. Clerks, commercial travellers, retailers, craftsmen, and small manufacturers, inhabited the medium-sized houses, especially in Albert Town. Brickmakers, labourers, and scavengers lived in crowded courtyards off High Street, the smaller streets off Church Street, and the south-east corner of the parish.[5]

George Grote (1794–1871), a banker who became a classical historian and founder of London University, lived in Paradise Place in the 1820s.[6] Thomas Hancock (1786–1865), who was involved in the discovery of waterproofing with rubber, lived in Marlborough Cottage, Green Lanes, in 1848.[7] Stoke Newington was the home of James Smetham (1821–89), painter and essayist, in 1855,[8] and John Burnet, painter and engraver, retired to Victoria Road in 1860 and died there in 1868.[9] William Monk, professor of music and organist at St. Matthias's, lived in a Gothic house, no. 59 Clissold Road, in 1861.[10]

FROM 1870 TO 1914. From 1,816 houses in 1871, there was an increase of 127 per cent to 1881. The rate slackened considerably thereafter, to 34 per cent in the next decade and 17 per cent from 1891 to 1901. Only 163 dwellings were built between 1901 and 1911, when there were 7,962 in Stoke Newington borough.[11]

The scale of building was much larger after 1870. In 1880 the agents of the Ecclesiastical Commissioners said that the buildings on the estate were very varied, ranging from inferior cottages and old residences at rack rents, other houses for various terms, and good residences granted on building leases.[12] From the late 1870s the Eade trustees, the Commissioners' lessees of the demesne, let blocks of up to 11 a. on 99-year leases to builders or speculators who subleased houses to the buyer, selling the lease back to the

Commissioners. The latter in 1881 bought out the interest of the Eade trustees.[13] Among the holders of building leases on the demesne were Jesse Chessum, a builder who lived in Paradise Place in 1871, Holly Bush Lodge, Green Lanes in 1877, and Amhurst Park Road in 1881, when he employed 60 men.[14] Francis Hobson, a City surveyor and land agent, who held a building lease on the demesne in 1877, was also involved in constructing the Wentworth House estate in 1883 and the Willows estate in 1892. Edward Paget Nunn, who lived in Lordship Park, took part in numerous building projects, mostly on the demesne in the 1870s and 1880s, and in local politics. The largest builder was probably William Osment of Palatine Road, who had developed the Browning estate (1871–2), Palatine estate (1874–8), and land in Hackney (1876) before working on several sites on the demesne (1879–86).[15]

In 1866 the part of the Pulteney estate which had been bought in 1821 by William Browning was enfranchised[16] and in 1870 the part of the Browning estate adjoining it in South Hornsey was put up for sale. In addition to the family mansion fronting Newington Green, the land included 1 a. divided into 26 lots fronting the western side of Albion Road.[17] The rest of the estate was presumably sold for building at the same time. Four houses were built in Albion Road by Thomas Catling in 1871 and another 11 by Henry Foot in 1875. In 1871–2 roads following the shape of the elongated Browning estate were constructed and houses put up by Osment, Foot, Thomas Thomas, and others: Lavell Road (3 houses), Lilford (later Winston) Road (89 houses), Lidfield Road (34 houses), and Reedholm Villas (11 houses). In the same period 14 houses were built in Green Lanes, 8 of them by Thomas, probably also on the Browning estate. At the northern end of the estate 8 houses were built in Park Lane in 1872–3. There was also building on the neighbouring Rhodes estate, where 53 houses were built in Aden Grove and 41 in Aden Grove North (later Springdale Road) in 1871–3.

During the early 1870s the Walford estate spread north from Broughton (later Barbauld) Road, to Sandbrook (4 houses in 1871), Harcombe (17 houses in 1871), Oldfield (64 houses in 1871–3), Nevill (51 houses in 1871–5), and Brighton roads.[18] The neighbouring Palatine estate, south of Brighton Road, was the subject of a building agreement in 1874 with William Osment, who was to build 40 houses fronting Wordsworth Road and the newly constructed Palatine Road. Other agreements were made in

[3] Hackney dist. bd. of wks. *M.O.H. Rep.* (1858), 4.
[4] *Census*, 1801–71; P.R.O., RG 10/310/9/1B.
[5] P.R.O., HO 107/1503/11/1–6; HO 107/1702/1/4; RG 9/152/11/1–6; 791/4–5; RG 10/309/9/1A–C.
[6] *D.N.B.*
[7] Ibid.; *Hornsey Jnl.* 19 May 1939 (S.N.L. cuttings 78 Hancock); tithe (1848), no. 60.
[8] [W. E. Baxter], 'Association of Stoke Newington with Eng. Literature' (MS. of talk 1914, printed in *N. Lond. Guardian*, 13 Mar. 1914, S.N.L. 51, LC 1135).
[9] *D.N.B.*
[10] P.R.O., RG 9/152/11/3; photo. (S.N.L. illus. 80.6 CL1, LC 492).

[11] *Census*, 1871–1911.
[12] Ch. Com. file 30341 pt. 1 (letter from Clutton's 1880).
[13] Guildhall MS. CC. 210856.
[14] Ibid. 212381; P.R.O., RG 10/310/9/1B; RG 11/281/10/3.
[15] Below. For Osment's work in Hackney, see Hunter, *Victorian Villas*, 49.
[16] Abstract of Ct. Rolls 1832–82, 397.
[17] Sales parts. 1870 (S.N.L. 60.5, LC 1637).
[18] Brighton Rd. was in S. Hornsey: Abstract of Ct. Rolls 1832–82, 425.

1875 and 1877 with Osment,[19] who built 93 houses on the estate in 1874–8. North-east of the Walford estate 18 a., mostly brickfields, were enfranchised in 1857 by Henry Lee,[20] and in 1874 building started in Kynaston Road, constructed on the route of Pawnbrokers Lane from the London road to link with Nevill and Oldfield roads on the Walford estate; 85 houses were built there between 1874 and 1877 by several builders, including Charles Hunt and Thomas Finney. In 1876–8 work proceeded on the surrounding new roads: Kersley (38 houses, mostly by Thomas Casey), Brodia (28 houses), Chesholm (45 houses, mostly by George Messenger and James Pullin), Dynevor (115 houses), Lavers (45 houses, all by Thomas Finney), and Dumont (39 houses, mostly by Charles Hunt) roads. In 1873–4 large houses with extensive grounds stretching south from Church Street to the Walford estate were for sale and 31 houses were built there in 1875–6 in Woodlea Road and 136 in Hawkesley Road by Alfred Capsey of Tottenham, Thomas G. Bricknell, Joseph Dawson, and others. In the extreme south part of the parish, on the Stonefields estate, there was considerable growth on the Hindle estate where 95 houses were built in 1874–5, many in new roads.[21]

North of Church Street, Matthew Allen of Finsbury, builder and member of the Stoke Newington Quaker family, in partnership with the Industrial Dwellings Co. built flats for the middle classes in 1873–5 on a corner site between Bethune Road and Manor Road. The flats, which used much artificial stone but little wood, and whose facilities included a croquet lawn, bowling green, gardener, and rooms for billiards and dancing, excited the admiration of contemporary architects.[22]

In 1872 the Ecclesiastical Commissioners entered into an agreement with George Blackmore for building in Bouverie Road, Grayling Terrace, and Lordship Road.[23] Between 1874 and 1878 some 102 houses were built in Bouverie Road, many by Thomas G. and Alfred Bricknell, to whom Blackmore subcontracted. Blackmore also appears to have subcontracted for the Grayling Terrace houses, of which 27 were built in 1874–6. Nine houses were built in Lordship Road in 1874.[24]

At the eastern end of the northern border Amhurst Park Road, begun in 1864,[25] had reached Stamford Hill station by 1873 when the owners and lessees of the demesne agreed to continue it westward to Seven Sisters Road.[26] In 1877 they reached agreement with the owners of the Hermitage estate in Tottenham to widen the private Hermitage Road.[27] Woodberry Grove had been constructed north of Seven Sisters Road by 1874.[28]

There was some building on the north side of Seven Sisters Road in the 1870s[29] and five houses were built on the south side in 1877. Two-bedroomed semi-detached houses in Green Lanes between Lordship Park and the nursery north of Clissold Park had been planned in 1858.[30] As Buckingham Gate and Bertram Villas they were built in 1877 and 1879 by Samuel Sabey of Finsbury.[31] Most of the demesne, however, retained a rural character in the early 1870s. In 1874 Manor Road was private, with a toll payable on animal traffic,[32] and farmland stretched from Lordship Road to Stamford Hill.[33]

Most building on the demesne took place in the late 1870s and the 1880s, following agreements[34] in 1877 with Francis Hobson, a City surveyor and land agent, for 10 a., with George Blackmore of Bouverie Road for 10 a., with James Smith, gentleman of Green Lanes, and Edward Wells, iron merchant of Shoreditch for 8½ a., with David Bowker Catling for 4 a., and with Jesse Chessum for 2½ a. There was one agreement in 1878, with Charles Gatliff, gentleman, of Finsbury Circus for 3 a. There were further agreements with Hobson in 1879 for 7 a., with Joseph Wilkinson, a Shoreditch timber merchant, for 11 a., and with William Williamson, a contractor from Lower Holloway, Edward Paget Nunn, and William Osment for smaller sites. In 1880 some 37 a. were available for building on the Commissioners' estates. There were further agreements for small sites with Nunn in 1880 and 1881. Other agreements were made in 1881 with William Osment for 8 a.,[35] in 1882 with William Hardy of Stroud Green for 5½ a.,[36] in 1883 with Stephen Goodall of Dynevor Road for an unknown acreage,[37] and in 1884 with Nunn for 4 a.[38] and with H. A. Wickes, timber merchant of Finsbury Park, for 7 a.[39]

Francis Hobson's 10 a. lay in a block south of Fairholt Road, between Heathland and Bethune roads.[40] In Bethune Road 94 houses were built between 1880 and 1884. Building on the west side between Fairholt and Grangecourt roads was complete by 1882.[41] Hobson used several builders, including Edward Tidman of Bethune Road on nos. 1, 7, and 9 in 1880[42] and William Kelland of Bouverie Road at nos. 63 and 65 in 1883.[43] In 1880 Tidman also built 10 houses in Heathland Road, which formed the western boundary of Hobson's estate; another 6 were built in

[19] Spratling, *Palatine Estate*, 35–7, 41; *Endowed Chars. (County of Lond.)*, H.C. 128, pp. 15, 18 (1897), lxvi, pt. 1; Hackney dist. bd. of wks. *Surveyor's Rep.* (1874), 5.
[20] Abstract of Ct. Rolls 1832–82, 379.
[21] i.e. Hayling, Millard, and Shellgrove rds.
[22] *Bldg. News*, 31 Dec. 1875; *Builder*, 24 June 1876; *Architects Jnl.* 18 Oct. 1972 (S.N.L. cuttings 41.8, LC 3164–6); *The Times*, 21 Feb. 1876, 4c; Guildhall MSS. CC. 212302, 212356, 212358, 212395; above, plate 50; below.
[23] Guildhall MS. CC. 176895.
[24] Ibid. 174926–9, 176313–16, 176893, 181119–20, 291576–7, 375842.
[25] Hackney dist. bd. of wks. *Ann. Rep.* (1864), 2.
[26] Guildhall MS. CC. 180813.
[27] Ibid. 197450.
[28] Hackney dist. bd. of wks. *List of Rds.* (1877).

[29] Guildhall MSS. CC. 164480, 172554, 172556, 172558.
[30] Ibid. Print S4/La. Pr. S4.
[31] Ibid. MSS. CC. 183638–9, 198560, 198563.
[32] S.N.L. illus. 80.2 LOR, LC 96–7.
[33] *Evening News*, 24 Apr. 1925 (S.N.L. cuttings 80, LC 113A).
[34] With builders unless otherwise stated.
[35] Guildhall MS. CC. 212302; Ch. Com. file 30341 pt. 1 (letter from Clutton's 1880).
[36] Guildhall MS. CC. 208840.
[37] Ibid. 209916–19, 329002, 347816, 348806.
[38] Ibid. 212246.
[39] Ibid. 248409.
[40] Ibid. 212380.
[41] Ibid. 209202–3.
[42] Ibid. 201143–5.
[43] Ibid. 359861, 372471.

1881. Another new road, called St. Kilda's Road by 1880, passed through the southern part of Hobson's estate and Tidman built 10 houses there in 1880.[44] It may have been an otherwise unknown road, St. Lawrence Road, Manor Park, where Tidman built 10 houses in 1879. Grange-court Road, wholly within Hobson's estate, was built up by others, among them William Prescott of Ball's Pond Road and Francis Paxley of Hornsey Rise, in the early 1880s.[45] Hobson's northern boundary was Fairholt Road where 5 houses were built in 1881 and where Prescott built another 12 in 1883.[46]

Blackmore's 10 a. lay in three blocks fronting the north side of Manor Road, west of Bethune Road, and the east side of Lordship Road, south of the reservoir.[47] He subcontracted to Thomas Bricknell, who built 10 houses, probably Manor Park Villas, large semi-detached houses in Manor Road, in 1877. Two more were built by 1879.[48] The site on the north side of Manor Road west of the villas was occupied from 1876 to 1884 by St. Andrew's temporary church,[49] and in 1879 Osment, to whom Blackmore assigned the lease, built 22 houses next to it, stretching almost as far as Lordship Road.[50] The Presbyterian church stood on the corner site from 1883.[51] Heathland Road provided a northern continuation of Bouverie Road by 1880, a small portion passing through Blackmore's and Osment's estate, and Osment had built on the eastern side by 1880.[52] The western boundary was a long frontage on Lordship Road, where most of the 37 houses erected between 1879 and 1881 were by Osment.[53]

The 8½ a. of Smith and Wells lay west of Lordship Road, south of the reservoir.[54] They were speculators who subleased to Thomas James of Hackney, who built on the west side of Lordship Road by 1879[55] and George Wilson, who built houses in Queen Elizabeth's Walk[56] (which had been extended northward beyond Lordship Park and eastward to Lordship Road, mostly through Smith and Wells's estate) and at the eastern end of Allerton Road in 1881.[57] David B. Catling, whose lease of 1877 was for Woodberry Grove, built a terrace of four houses in 1878.[58] In 1879 he assigned some work to Charles D. Lavington, possibly his partner,[59] who built 24 houses between 1879 and 1881. Jesse Chessum's 2½ a. lay at the bend of the New River where Amhurst Park

and Bethune Road met.[60] He put up large detached houses in 1878 in Amhurst Park Road[61] and by 1879 on the east side of Bethune Road[62] and semi-detached houses on the north side of Amhurst Park Road by 1883.[63]

Following the agreement of 1878 with Charles Gatliff for 3 a.,[64] 16 houses were built in Woodberry Down between 1879 and 1886 and 7 in Seven Sisters Road in 1889. The largest area leased for building in 1879 was the 11 a. at Bethune Road, between Hobson's and Chessum's estates, which was leased to Joseph Wilkinson.[65] His builder, Arthur Hancock of Lower Clapton, had built at least 18 houses in Bethune Road in 1882, including Hillcrest, no. 143,[66] and he was presumably also responsible for part of Fairholt Road, the eastern end of which formed the southern boundary of the estate.[67] William Williamson had built 8 houses at the northern end of Green Lanes, between the New River and Hermitage Road, by 1879[68] when he concluded a building agreement for land adjoining it on the east, fronting Hermitage and Eade roads.[69] Williamson was building houses there in 1884, when he was described as of the Potteries, Green Lanes.[70] Eleven houses were built in Eade Road in 1881 and 1882 and 16 in Hermitage Road between 1880 and 1884.[71]

Edward Paget Nunn, in 1876 of Lordship Park, was building houses there in the 1870s,[72] some 27 between 1878 and 1880. He built 9 on the west side of Queen Elizabeth's Walk and 6 in Brook (later Grazebrook) Road, a side road, in 1879, and 7 on the east side of Edward's Lane in 1880.[73] On 6½ a. leased in 1881 between Hobson's and Blackmore's estates, Nunn built 5 houses in Heathland Road in 1882 and most of the 28 erected there between 1882 and 1885.[74] He was responsible for most of the 28 houses built in St. Kilda's Road between 1882 and 1884.[75]

Osment's agreement in 1879 was for a small area on the south side of Manor Road, where 7 houses (four by William Wyeth) were built in 1879 and 1880[76] and another 3 in 1880. Six had already been built, probably those opposite Allen's flats, in 1877. The 8 a. leased by Osment in 1881 stretched southward from the eastern reservoir and included most of Fairholt Road, where he had built some semi-detached houses by 1883[77] and another 23 in 1885.[78] Altogether,

[44] Ibid. 206575, 364148.
[45] Ibid. 206572, 209202, 380111.
[46] Ibid. 209202.
[47] Ibid. 212302.
[48] Ibid. 349298.
[49] Ibid. 212315; below, churches.
[50] Guildhall MSS. CC. 201190, 212302, 341866, 344960, 355705.
[51] Ibid. 216104.
[52] Ibid. 203509.
[53] Ibid. 203516, 210843-4, 210847, 210849-51, 212302.
[54] Ibid. 212382.
[55] i.e. Brooklyn and Ufford Hos., S. of junction with Queen Eliz. Walk: Guildhall MSS. CC. 198518-19.
[56] e.g. Kenilworth Terrace: Guildhall MSS. CC. 206511, 206514, 206517.
[57] Guildhall MS. CC. 209198.
[58] Ibid. 375121.
[59] Both were described as of Finsbury Pk. Villas: ibid. 199897, 202867, 375121.
[60] Ibid. 212381.
[61] e.g. Leith Ho. at junction with Seven Sisters Rd. and

Aberglaslyn at junction with Bethune Rd.: ibid. 197432, 339148.
[62] Ibid. 20041.
[63] Ibid. 358425.
[64] Ibid. 212385.
[65] Ibid. 212302.
[66] Ibid. 369051; cf. ibid. 214208-9, 214212-13.
[67] Below.
[68] Guildhall MS. CC. 198557. Possibly in 1876: G.L.R.O., MBW 1659/135, no. 21.
[69] Guildhall MS. CC. 212302.
[70] Ibid. 214217.
[71] For Hermitage Rd. in 1880, see S.N.L. illus. 80.1 HER, LC 6.
[72] Guildhall MSS. CC. 179386-7, 183654, 183658, 197473, 197476-86, 345101, 353438, 366019.
[73] Ibid. 212390.
[74] Ibid. 209224-5, 351036.
[75] Ibid. 210995, 211694, 335920.
[76] Ibid. 212388.
[77] Ibid. 211035-6.
[78] Ibid. 350955.

STOKE NEWINGTON: BUILDING LEASES

Church Commissioners' estates: 1 Rodda (1859), 2 Allen (1874), 3 Hobson (1877), 4 Blackmore (1877), 5 Smith & Wells (1877), 6 Catling (1877), 7 Chessum (1877), 8 Wilkinson (1879), 9 Nunn (1881), 10 Osment (1881), 11 Hardy (1882), 12 Nunn (1884), 13 Wickes (1884). *Other building estates*: 14 Graham, 15 Kibblewhite, 16 Thos. Cubitt's purchases, 17 Massey, 18 Rhodes, 19 Victoria, 20 Maughan, 21 Albert Town, 22 Glebe (Birch), 23 Walford, 24 Browning, 25 Lee, 26 Wentworth Ho., 27 The Willows. The boundary is that of the metropolitan borough.

between 1881 and 1886 over 100 houses were built in Fairholt Road and the 'new road', probably St. Andrew's Road.[79] The latter was named by 1888 when 6 houses were built there.[80]

The estate leased by Hardy in 1882 consisted of 5½ a., west of the Smith and Wells estate, where he had to complete Allerton Road, including the drainage and sewerage, and built at least 10 houses a year.[81] Sixty-six houses were built in Allerton Road between 1882 and 1888, not all by Hardy himself.[82] In 1882 Goodall leased land on the east side of Queen Elizabeth's Walk, where 14 houses were built in 1886.[83]

Nunn's lease in 1884 was for 4 a. north of the 6½ a. which he had leased in 1881. Work began in Paget Road, which he constructed, together with drains and sewers,[84] in 1885, and by 1887 there were 34 houses in terraces of four.[85] He built 8 houses in St. Andrew's Road at the western end of the estate in 1889. The other building lease of 1884 was of 7 a. on the northern border, east of Williamson's estate, which was leased to H. A. Wickes.[86] In 1886 the Ecclesiastical Commissioners purchased the Clissold Park estate for housing but a year later they bowed to local pressure and it became a permanent open space.[87]

Of the remaining area north of Church Street, 11 houses were built in Grayling Road and Park Street in 1881, and the rest of the Maughan estate, at the eastern end of Manor Road, was built up in 1882–4. Sixteen houses were built in Martaban Street and 103, by George Earl, Henry Marston, and others, in Listria Park.[88]

During the 1880s building south of Church Street included 16 shops in Aden Grove in 1880, 11 houses, mostly by J. Edmundson & Son, in Albion Road in 1884–5 and 6 houses there in 1889, 3 in Hawkesley Road in 1887, and 3 (nos. 91A–C) in Dynevor Road in 1889.

In 1881 George Robert Green, who had inherited the estate of his great-uncle, James Kibblewhite in 1870, enfranchised it and began to develop it. The land was in two sections, part of Stonefields in the south-east and part of the Pulteney estate in the west.[89] On the Stonefields section 19 houses, shops, and stables were built in Boleyn (formerly Back) Road in 1881–4; 31 houses were built by Henry Dunkerly in 1883 and 25 by Stephen Goodall in 1887 in Barrett's Grove. Most of the remaining houses were by Goodall, 29 in 1884 in Truman's Place, 90 in 1884–6 in Pellerin Road, 48 in 1888 in Cressington Road, the last two being new roads. The Pulteney estate comprised 3½ a. south-east of Grange (later Burma) Road and west of Green Lanes: 32 houses were built in Grange Road in 1882–3 and 15 houses and shops in 1882 and 10

shops in 1884 in Green Lanes. Another 6 houses built in Park Lane in 1883 were probably also part of the estate.

In 1883 the rector made a building agreement with Francis Hobson for the Wentworth House estate.[90] Terraced houses had already been started in 1882, when 16 were built in the new Painsthorpe Road; 34 were built in Ayrsome Road in 1883–4 and 12 in Oldfield Road, which formed the eastern boundary of the estate, in 1883.

Building started on two of the remaining open spaces in the 1890s. After the death of G. W. Alexander, the Willows and some 10 a., originally the northern part of the Pulteney estate, were put up for auction in 1891.[91] In 1892 the sanitary inspector considered the plan by F. S. Hobson, presumably one of the purchasers, for new streets on the north side of Park Lane (later Clissold Crescent) 'highly objectionable'.[92] In 1893 H. C. Foulkes's application to form a new road, Carysfort Road, out of Park Lane was approved[93] and 76 houses were built in Park Lane, mostly by Foulkes and W. Whymark. Another 11 were built there by Foulkes in 1894 and 9 by Thomas Pryor in 1897; 88 houses were built, partly by Foulkes and Whymark, in Carysfort Road in 1894.[94]

In 1894 W. Hicklin obtained permission to construct three roads on the Graham portion of Stonefields, north of Barrett's Grove.[95] Work on terraced houses proceeded rapidly on the new roads: Prince George Road (135 houses in 1894–5, mostly by A. Adams, William Levitt, Herbert Hext, and C. W. Payne), Wiesbaden (later Belgrade) Road (48 houses and 2 shops in 1894 by Thomas Pryor), and Princess May (129 houses in 1894–6, mostly by Pryor and Harreson Bros.).[96]

Most building during the 1890s was small-scale, infilling or replacement. South of Church Street 9 houses were built in 1893–4 in Church Path, 9 by G. and E. Flaxman in 1891, 5 in 1893, 7 houses and 3 shops in 1894, 6 houses on the site of Ebor Lodge in 1895, a block of flats in 1899, all in Albion Road, and 6 blocks of flats in 1896 in Salcombe Road in the south-east. At the opposite end of the parish 5 houses were built in Hermitage Road in 1891. William Williamson built 3 fronting Hermitage Road in 1892 and 5 houses and shops in 1895.[97] Nearby 6 houses were built in 1889 and 4 in 1894 in Eade Road, 7 in Seven Sisters Road in 1889, and 6 in Woodberry Grove in 1895. Another 8 were built in Bouverie Road in 1889.

In 1894–6 a peak in building produced 400 houses; a report of 200 dwellings in course of erection on the Willows estate and 600 on Hicklin's estate was considerably exaggerated.[98]

[79] There were 88 hos. in Fairholt Rd.: O.S. Map 1/2,500, Lond. XXI (1894–6 edn.).
[80] Ch. of St. And. built 1884 but not in the rd.
[81] Guildhall MS. CC. 208840.
[82] Ibid. 223093, 239002–3, 353299, 375724.
[83] Ibid. 209916–19, 329002, 347816, 348806.
[84] Ibid. 212246.
[85] O.S. Map 1/2,500, Lond. XXI (1894–6 edn.).
[86] Guildhall MS. CC. 248409.
[87] Below, pub. svces.
[88] Map in Marcham, Digest, pt. 3.
[89] Abstract of Ct. Rolls 1832–82, 408–10, 431.

[90] Guildhall MSS. CC. 216721–3.
[91] Sales parts. 1891 (S.N.L. 60.5, LC 1637); cf. Guildhall MS. 14233/18, p. 64, lots 21, 25–9.
[92] Hackney dist. bd. of wks. Sanitary Inspectors' Rep. (1892), 39.   [93] Ibid. Surveyor's Rep. (1893), 38.
[94] Stoke Newington vestry, Ann. Rep. (1897–8), 67.
[95] Hackney dist. bd. of wks. Surveyor's Rep. (1894), 31.
[96] O.S. Map 1/2,500, Lond. XXX (1894–6 edn.); II.15 (1915 edn.).   [97] Guildhall MS. CC. 253077.
[98] Stoke Newington vestry, Ann. Rep. (1894–5), 129–30. Annual totals of new bldgs. were 128 (1894), 169 (1895), 102 (1896).

Thereafter numbers dropped to 30 new build-ings in 1897 and only 9 in 1899, when Stoke Newington was 'chock-full'.[99] Workshops and factories but virtually no new housing appeared between 1900 and 1914, although there was much rebuilding. In Albion Road no. 143 was converted to flats in 1908. In 1905 working-class housing included 114 three-roomed tenements erected by the Stoke Newington Dwellings Syndicate Ltd. and 184 tenements were provided in 1904. There were 326 tenements by 1906.[1]

Between 1870 and 1914 Stoke Newington was transformed. In increasing more than fourfold, building covered not only all available farmland but even gardens, leaving only one small space (behind Paradise Row) to be developed south of Church Street. North of Church Street the reservoirs, Abney Park cemetery, and Clissold Park provided some open space, and although there was little land left for building and many of the new houses were terraced, they all had larger gardens and streets were less cramped than in the south.[2] In 1870 land fronting Albion Road which had been bought at £100 an acre was being sold at £2,200 an acre.[3] Builders crammed as many houses as possible on a site. Following legislation in 1864, working men were attracted by cheap fares on the G.E.R. line just outside Stoke Newington's eastern boundary.[4] New houses, especially south of Church Street, were smaller and terraced. In 1872 Stoke Newington was said to be 'suffering from a fearful eruption of bricks and mortar of a very low type'.[5] In 1876 the death rate had risen as a consequence of jerry building: natural earth was replaced with refuse and damp was a constant problem.[6] In 1877 the surveyor commented on the remarkable increase of houses[7] and in 1879 on the poor condition of many roads, which were made up by the freeholder[8] but usually adopted by the local authority only when building was completed.[9]

The population in Stoke Newington was said in 1875 to be increasing faster than in other districts, partly because of building but also because its social character was changing. Many immigrants were of child-bearing age and the proportion of the elderly and unmarried diminished as the large houses began to be replaced by streets of smaller ones.[10] A gradual reduction in the ratio of females reflected a fall in the number of servants. From 57 per cent in 1871, it declined to 56 per cent in 1901, 55 per cent in 1911, and 54 per cent in 1921, which, considering the loss of men in the First World War, was a significant drop. There was considerable local variation, Lordship ward in the north having more than 61 per cent of women in 1901 and 1911, com-pared with Palatine ward, which had under 52 per cent.[11]

In 1902 a social decline was observed, follow-ing immigration from inner London.[12] It began in the south-east and spread northward. The once highly respectable area of Nelson Terrace was already in decline by 1871. Overcrowding and poor sanitation led to disease and squalor: there were 16 cases of cholera in Cock and Castle Lane in 1871[13] and 6 people in one room in the Palatine houses in 1874.[14]

The neighbourhood of St. Matthias was said in 1878 to be not too poor, but in 1882 the popula-tion was 'increasing at extraordinary speed'.[15] By 1888 most of the wealthy had left, and in 1892 the character of the population had 'much degener-ated', one street being described by a magistrate as the 'worst in north London'.[16] By 1894 South Hornsey had been fully built up with no new building erected for the last five years. The three parts of South Hornsey together comprised 65 a., with 1,333 houses and 9,353 people. The most densely populated area was Albert Town, 28 a. containing 687 houses and 4,831 people, a density of 24 houses and 172 people to the acre. The Victoria area, joining the London road, had 574 houses and 4,018 people on 32 a., 18 houses and 125 people to the acre, while the most recently developed portion, 5 a. west of Albion Road, had 72 houses and 504 people, 14 houses and 101 people to the acre.[17] Stoke Newington, with 4,973 houses, had 440 a. north of Church Street occupied by 12,189 people, only 28 to the acre, and 199 a. south of Church Street occupied by 20,719 people, 104 to the acre. In the south part the death rate was 10.2 per 1,000, compared with 8.3 per 1,000 in the north, and many died of tuberculosis, bronchitis, and similar diseases.[18] By 1897 there were 5,600 houses in Stoke New-ington and the death rate had risen to 16.7 per 1,000 in the south. The increased crowding and poverty was also occasioned by a higher birth rate.[19]

In 1894 there was said to be no extreme poverty although there was a 'considerable number' of tenemented dwellings, especially in the south, where houses built for one family were occupied by several or turned into lodging houses.[20] There was one common lodging house run by the L.C.C. for men at no. 81 Church Street from 1900 to 1914 with, in 1905, accom-modation for 37. A register of houses let in lodgings was begun in 1900 and recorded 180 houses in 1903, another 39 in 1904, and 259 by 1906. The number reached a peak of 273 in 1910, falling to 220 by 1913 but rising again to 259 in 1921. Those in South Hornsey in

[99] Cutting Oct. 1899 (S.N.L. cuttings 55.4).
[1] L.C.C. *Lond. Statistics*, xvi (1905–6), 132, 134; xvii (1906–7), 145.
[2] O.S. Maps 1/2,500, Lond. IV, IX, X, XVIII (1870 edn.); II. 11, 14, 15; V. 3 (1915 edn.); below, pub. svces.
[3] *The Times*, 5 May 1870, 11c.
[4] D. J. Olsen, *Growth of Victorian Lond.* (1976), 317.
[5] *N. & Q.* 4th ser. ix. 364–5.
[6] Hackney dist. bd. of wks. *M.O.H. Rep.* (1876), 16, 23, 26, 36.   [7] Ibid. *Surveyor's Rep.* (1877), 14.
[8] Ibid. (1879), 16.
[9] e.g. Grange, Lidfield, Lavell, Reedholm, and Londes-borough rds. in 1877: ibid. (1877), 14.

[10] Hackney dist. bd. of wks. *M.O.H. Rep.* (1875), 5–6.
[11] *Census*, 1871–1921.
[12] Booth, *Life and Labour*, 3rd ser. (1), 159–60.
[13] Hackney dist. bd. of wks. *M.O.H. Rep.* (1872), 34.
[14] Ibid. (1874), 24.
[15] Nat. Soc. files, St. Matthias.
[16] Ibid.; G.L.R.O., P94/MTS/35/1 (scrapbk. of St. Matthias, pp. 126, 144).
[17] G.L.R.O., Off. Acc. 1965/46 (*Rep. Local Inqs.* 1889–94, S. Hornsey 1894).
[18] Stoke Newington vestry, *M.O.H. Rep.* (1895), 77–81, 98.   [19] Ibid. *Ann. Rep.* (1897–8), 8, 11.
[20] Ibid. *M.O.H. Rep.* (1895), 77, 98.

1914 housed industrious tenants 'well above the pauper line'.[21]

In 1902 it was estimated that 13.5 per cent of Stoke Newington borough was subject to over-crowding and 18.5 per cent to poverty, and in a table of 50 London districts arranged in ascending order of social conditions it ranked no. 45.[22] It had a high proportion of upper classes (11.6 per cent) and of servants (7.5 per cent),[23] which was expressed in 1901 as nearly 28 servants for every 100 families.[24] The part of the borough north of Lordship Park and Manor Road consisted of well built houses with long gardens. In the part stretching south to Park Lane (later Clissold Crescent), Albion Grove, and the northern boundary of Hornsey detached, 17.9 per cent of the people lived in poverty. It included the wealthy in Paradise Row, Park Crescent, and Church Row. The poverty was concentrated in Barn Street and other small areas north of Church Street, in the courtyards off the London road, and to a lesser extent in the newer streets south of Church Street, between Defoe and Kynaston roads. Most of the area was characterized by houses rented at about £30 a year to clerks and skilled mechanics. In the area to the south, which included all the formerly detached parts of Hornsey, 27.5 per cent lived in poverty. Some of the houses at Newington Green were 'very comfortable' and Aden Terrace and Burma Road were well-to-do, but most of the rest contained a mixed population of 'artisans, policemen, shopmen, and labourers' and some houses were in a poor state and very crowded. Many of the newer houses had been built and rented for £30–35 a year.[25]

In 1903 a writer in St. Mary's parish magazine commented on changes since 1886: the rich had moved out and the poor flocked in and only 50 out of 200 families were the same.[26] In 1874 the congregation of Green Lanes Methodist chapel consisted of men of wealth and social influence. By 1906 they had all gone, Jews had moved in, and many houses had become boarding houses for young foreigners.[27] In 1907 there were very few above working class in St. Matthias's parish and many on the verge of destitution.[28] In 1913 the same district, originally a pleasant suburb for City merchants and businessmen, was 'becoming an East End parish', especially in Albert Town, its streets tenanted chiefly by Jews.[29]

In spite of the decline Stoke Newington was described in 1896 as a 'well-established and reputable suburb'.[30] In 1903 it was noted that except in the south and south-east parts Stoke Newington was largely upper middle-class, with a few of the 'very well-to-do' about Clissold Park.[31] In 1905 a survey among the Anglican incumbents pointed up the differences between north and south. St. Matthias's had 'none but poor', much drunkenness among women, and an above average of rough districts, with many 'living in sexual vice'; All Saints' had no wealthy, many thieves, much drinking, and a shifting population with a prevalence of Jews and non-conformists; the chief difficulty in St. Faith's was gross indifference. In the northern parishes by contrast the moral conduct of St. Mary's was 'exceptionally good', of St. Andrew's 'very respectable', and of St. Olave's 'above average'.[32]

In 1871 some of Rodda's houses in Lordship Road were advertised as 'suitable only for respectable families'.[33] Most of the new houses in northern Stoke Newington were for men involved in the commercial life of London, many of whom had moved from outside or from older houses in the parish. In 1877 a lead merchant from High Street moved to Manor Park Villas[34] and in 1880 a shipowner moved from Albion Road to Manor Road.[35] In the 1870s there was an insurance broker from the City, an architect, a flour factor, a chemical manufacturer from Clapton, and a shipping agent from the City in Bethune Road.[36] Similar professional or business men lived in Lordship Road,[37] Lordship Park, including Henry Sarson, vinegar merchant of New North Road,[38] St. Kilda's Road,[39] and Queen Elizabeth's Walk.[40] Most of those involved in Stoke Newington's local government lived in the area, including John Joseph Runtz at Hillcrest, no. 143 Bethune Road,[41] F. A. Dod at Stoke Lodge, no. 186 Lordship Road,[42] and Sir Herbert J. Ormond at no. 83 Lordship Road.[43] William Jamrach, a naturalist with a world-wide trade in wild animals, lived at no. 63 Lordship Road in 1896[44] and E. J. Sage (d. 1905), a local historian, lived at no. 64 Lordship Park.[45] Another local historian was John Robert Spratling (d. 1934), editor of the *North London Guardian*, for which he wrote under the name 'Giltspur'. He served on the borough council from 1916 to 1922 and lived for many years at no. 22 Lordship Terrace.[46]

A certain cosmopolitanism, present in the upper reaches of Stoke Newington society in the

[21] Ibid. *Ann. Rep.* (1899–1900), 46; Stoke Newington boro. *M.O.H. Rep.* (1914), 142, 160; L.C.C. *Lond. Statistics*, xvi (1905–6), 98–9; xvii (1906–7), 111; xxi (1910–11), 140–1; xxiv (1913–14), 176–7.

[22] Booth, *Life and Labour*, final vol. 14, 17; cf. Hampstead no. 48, Islington no. 19.

[23] Booth, op. cit. 22, 25.

[24] L.C.C. *Lond. Statistics*, xvi (1905–6), 56.

[25] Booth, *Life and Labour*, 1st ser. (2), App. p. 22; 3rd ser. (1), pp. 159–60, map facing p. 164.

[26] Quoted in I. G. Brooks, *Par. of St. Mary, Stoke Newington: a Short Hist.* (booklet 1973, copy in S.N.L. 14.01, LC 3286).

[27] *Story of Green Lanes Wes. Ch.* (S.N.L. 18.3, LC 1374).

[28] Nat. Soc. files, St. Matthias.

[29] T. F. Bumpus, *An historical Lond. ch.* (booklet 1913, S.N.L. 14.04, LC 2207).

[30] *Daily Telegraph*, 18 Sept. 1896, quoted in Stoke Newington vestry, *Ann. Rep.* (1896–7), 44.

[31] Mudie-Smith, *Rel. Life*, 129.

[32] Guildhall MS. 17885/6/27–34.

[33] *Hackney Gaz.* 31 May 1871, reproduced in Hunter, *Victorian Villas*, 22.

[34] Guildhall MS. CC. 349298.

[35] Ibid. 201193.

[36] Ibid. 214201, 214208–9, 214212–13.

[37] Ibid. 359877, 359879, 373659.

[38] Ibid. 343965, 343970, 343976, 345101.

[39] Ibid. 335920, 364148.

[40] Ibid. 209916, 329002, 347816.   [41] Ibid. 369051.

[42] S.N.L. illus. 57.2 DOD, LC 123.

[43] Ibid. 57.2 ORM, LC 120.

[44] *Gentleman's Jnl.* 1 May 1896 (S.N.L. cuttings 78 Jamrach, LC 91).

[45] *N. Lond. Guardian*, 8 Dec. 1905 (S.N.L. cuttings 78 SAGE).

[46] *Hackney & Kingsland Gaz.* 5 Dec. 1934 (S.N.L. cuttings 78 Spratling).

old settlements, spread to the newly built up areas in the north. German 'gentlemen' from the City came to live in Lordship Park in 1878, 1881, 1887, and 1896.[47] In the southern area immigrants included many East End Jews who greatly stimulated the growth of the clothing and furniture industries.

BETWEEN THE WORLD WARS. In 1919, when no working-class houses had been built for 10 years, about half of the 8,028 houses were working-class and threequarters were tenemented. Overcrowding was particularly acute in South Hornsey where there were on average more than two occupants to a room.[48] In 1921 Stoke Newington was 'not one of the worst boroughs', with an average of 1.67 families to a dwelling. There were then 103 blocks of flats (housing 2,390) and the population was densest in Palatine and Church wards, with 147 and 122 people to the acre, and lowest in Lordship and Manor wards, with 19 and 35 to the acre.[49]

Eleven houses were built in the northern part of Green Lanes in the 1920s and J. Pryor put up three in Queen Elizabeth's Walk in 1923.[50] The southern side of Woodberry Grove was built up during the 1920s, partly by Rock Estates, which also built at the north-east end of Seven Sisters Road and at Woodberry Down in the late 1920s and early 1930s, accounting for most of the 89 houses and flats built between 1918 and 1930.[51] By 1931 there were 8,196 occupied and 172 vacant dwellings.[52]

There was a little private building during the 1930s, mostly north of Church Street: 9 houses on the north side of Eade Road and 7 shops in Trumans Road and Stoke Newington Road in 1932;[53] 4 houses in Bethune Road behind no. 93 Amhurst Park and 3 by Bernstein Properties behind no. 289 Seven Sisters Road in 1933; 6 by Bernstein behind no. 287 and 9 by other builders on the site of nos. 307 and 331 Seven Sisters Road, 6 in Woodberry Down and 6 by Foux in St. Andrew's Road in 1934. In 1928 nos. 203-5 Albion Road were converted into flats (Alexandra Villas), as was no. 241 Green Lanes in 1933. Flats were built at no. 182 Green Lanes in 1935, at no. 100 Amhurst Park in 1936, and by Lydford Estates in Green Lanes in 1937. The last were probably part of the redevelopment, necessitated by the opening of Manor House tube station in 1932, in which the hotel was rebuilt, the street

widened, and new flats and shops were erected.[54] During the 1920s and 1930s large factories took most of the few remaining vacant spaces, often within a triangle or rectangle formed by the backs of houses. The largest space, on the Willows estate, was covered with the factory buildings of Carysfort Road and Shelford Place.[55]

In 1921 Stoke Newington borough council built its first flats on land purchased from the Church Commissioners in Lordship Grove, at the southern end of Lordship Road.[56] The 18 flats, however, were already said to be in danger of collapse in 1928.[57] In an attempt to relieve overcrowding, 111 families from Stoke Newington were rehoused in L.C.C. estates outside the borough in 1927-30.[58] In 1933 the borough council declared seven clearance areas under the 1930 Housing Act: Masons Court and Place, Rochester Place, and White Hart Court, all off the London road, Selsea Place, off Crossway, Hewling Street, once part of the Grove House estate, and Leonard Place in Albert Town. Barn Street was added in 1934.[59] The Church Commissioners sold a site at the corner of Queen Elizabeth's Walk and Lordship Terrace to the council, which in 1934 opened three blocks (Ormond, Clissold, and Lordship houses), 100 flats in all, for those displaced by clearance. At the same time land south of the council flats of 1921 and stretching to Lordship Terrace was sold by the commissioners to the L.C.C., which agreed to an exchange,[60] and in 1937 the borough council opened four more blocks, named after trees and containing 96 flats, east of the existing 100 flats.[61] The site acquired in the exchange was Glebe Place, which had been purchased in 1927 by the borough for swimming baths, built in 1928, and public housing.[62] In 1937 the L.C.C. opened blocks, named after rectors of Stoke Newington, of 74 flats in all on the Glebe Place site and Clissold Court in Greenway Close, north of Clissold Park.[63]

In 1937 the Church Commissioners erected Denman House, the first of five blocks for 89 families on land adjoining the borough council's flats, south of Lordship Terrace, between Lordship Road and Edward's Lane, replacing 50 early 19th-century cottages.[64] By 1937 Stoke Newington contained 6,764 undivided houses and 1,257 flats.[65] Another three blocks containing 90 flats were built on the Hewling Street site between Howard and Matthias roads in 1939.[66]

[47] Guildhall MSS. CC. 343965, 343970, 345103-4.
[48] Stoke Newington boro. M.O.H. Rep. (1919), 324.
[49] Census, 1921.
[50] Cutting 23 Mar. 1923 (S.N.L. cuttings 55.4).
[51] Stoke Newington boro. M.O.H. Rep. (1930).
[52] Census, 1931.
[53] G.L.R.O., CL/LOC/1/64 (L.C.C. Local Govt. Cttee.).
[54] Stoke Newington, Official Guide (1938), 47.
[55] O.S. Maps 1/2,500, Lond. II. 10, 11, 14, 15; V. 3 (1915, 1936 edns.); below, econ., industry.
[56] Stoke Newington boro. M.O.H. Rep. (1921); cutting 29 June 1921 (S.N.L. cuttings 41.8 LOR); Ch. Com., Estate maps, Stoke Newington Estate 3.
[57] Stoke Newington Recorder, 8 June 1928 (S.N.L. illus. 41.8 LOR, LC 2709).
[58] Stoke Newington boro. M.O.H. Rep. (1930); The Times, 14 Nov. 1933, 11c.
[59] Official Opening of Lordship Rd.-Lordship Terr. Housing Est. 1934 (S.N.L. cuttings 41.8 LOR, LC 471).

[60] The Times, 2 Aug. 1933, 7c; 29 Sept. 1934, 14c; Builder, 21 Sept. 1934 (S.N.L. illus. 41.8 LOR, LC 1913); Ch. Com. file 6439 pt. 2.
[61] The Times, 25 Jan. 1937, 14d; Official Opening of Lordship Terr.-Queen Eliz.'s Walk, 1937 (S.N.L. 41.8, LC 1590).
[62] Opening of Pub. Swimming Bath, 1930 (S.N.L. cuttings 46.26).
[63] Stoke Newington, Official Guide (1938), 46, 57-9; (1950), 58; L.C.C. Lond. Statistics, xli (1936-8), 150.
[64] The Times, 3 May 1937, 11a; Architect and Bldg. News, 6 Aug. 1937 (S.N.L. illus. 41.8 DEN, LC 2389); Stoke Newington, Official Guide (1938), 59.
[65] Stoke Newington boro. Ann. Rep. 1936-7 (S.N.L. 34.3).
[66] Stoke Newington B.C. Mins. 1937-8, 30; Builder, 25 Aug. 1939 (S.N.L. illus. 41.8 HEW, LC 2178, 2369-71); N. Lond. Recorder, 8 July 1938 (S.N.L. cuttings 41.8 HEW, LC 3101); Stoke Newington, Official Guide [1955], 58.

The most ambitious housing scheme was for a vast L.C.C. estate on 64 a. at Woodberry Down. Herbert Morrison proposed in 1936 to replace the 185 houses occupied by 1,200 people, only 200 of whom were working-class, by flats for 12,000 slum-dwellers from the East End. His supporters argued that many old houses were in multiple occupation and others were 'rotten property'. Opponents, who included the borough council and most local organizations, objected that the scheme would demolish well built houses and completely change the character of Stoke Newington;[67] instead of replacing dingy streets in the south part of the borough it involved planting thousands of Labour voters in the heart of a Conservative area.[68] A compulsory purchase order was confirmed in 1937. The L.C.C. produced a scheme for 1,667 flats in 1938.[69] In 1939 it bought the freehold of the triangular area bounded by the New River from the Church Commissioners,[70] whereupon progress was halted by the war.

The ratio of females in the population, 54 per cent, remained the same in 1921 and 1931 and was cited in 1921 as an indication that, although changed, Stoke Newington was not yet an industrial borough.[71] In 1921 there were 16,307 employed men, of whom the largest proportion, 146 per 1,000, worked in commerce, finance, and insurance, and 107 per 1,000 were clerks and draftsmen. Stoke Newington ranked first among London boroughs in the number of commercial travellers (21 per 1,000) and second in that of clerks.[72] The City clerk portrayed in Priestley's *Angel Pavement*, published in 1930, lived in a six-roomed house 'between the High Street and Clissold Park'.[73] The largest category of industrial workers in 1921 was those in metal, with 61 per 1,000. There were 9,428 women in paid employment. Domestic service was still the largest category, with 276 per 1,000, but the clothing industry, which employed 203 per 1,000, was catching up and there were 178 per 1,000 female clerks and typists and another 81 per 1,000 women in commerce and finance. Forty-three per cent of the working population were employed outside the borough, 4,445 of them in the City. In 1932 it was observed that Stoke Newington had, since the 18th century, been mainly a residential district for people working in the City but that there was no longer so high a proportion of the well-to-do. Most inhabitants, 73.4 per cent in 1921, had been born in London and probably included part of the 'considerable influx' of Jews within the last 30 years.[74] First-generation Jewish

immigrants were represented in 1921 by some 1,270 born in Russia, Poland, or Germany.[75]

Slums, caused by an increasing population and shortage of land, were a dominant problem in the period between the World Wars. In 1930 it was said that most houses had been built between 1870 and 1890 and were leasehold. Widespread subletting had 'a lowering effect on the general status of the district', added to which was the tendency, especially in the south, for private houses to be used by small businesses. Landlords failed to enforce repair clauses, causing a general dilapidation. The resulting damp and the inhabiting of basements, which were sometimes rat-infested, led to an increase in rheumatism and respiratory disease. Stoke Newington, long noted for its health, had a death rate by 1930 (12.2) that was higher than London's average, with tuberculosis the fourth largest cause of death.[76] The clearance areas of 1933 were in 1929-30 'below Booth's poverty line' and the whole of Albert Town, a 'mass of unskilled labourers etc. above the poverty line', was also overcrowded and included decayed 19th-century property and ill kept blocks of tenements. The rest of the area south of Church Street, and also stretching north of Church Street to Grayling Road and including land in the north-west, north of Woodberry Grove, housed 'skilled workers and similar'.[77] Migration alleviated some of the overcrowding in the south and by 1931 the density in Palatine and Church wards had improved to 133.5 and 113.6 people to the acre. During the 1930s the worst of the slums were replaced by council housing.

The contrast between north and south continued throughout the 1920s and 1930s. The Jews who settled during the 1930s in St. Olave's parish in the north[78] were unlike the poor Jews who had previously flooded in farther south. They followed Jewish purchases of Church Commission property in the north between 1916 and 1929, who included a furrier from Commercial Street, a Hatton Garden jeweller, a mantle manufacturer from Howard Road, and a merchant and a clothier from Bow.[79] Jacob Gestetner, brother and partner of the founder of the duplicating-machine firm, moved to no. 21 Lordship Park in 1920.[80] In 1928 the Woodberry Down site coveted by the L.C.C. contained large houses with gardens backing on the New River and reservoirs, inhabited by, among others, Sir John Baddeley (d. 1926), lord mayor of London 1921-2,[81] Albert Chevalier (d. 1923), the music hall singer and comedian,[82] H. J. Beavis, prominent in local government,[83] and Sir G. W. H.

[67] *The Times*, 24 Feb. 1936, 9g; *Hackney Gaz.* 28 Feb. 1936 (S.N.L. cuttings 41.8); L.C.C. Woodberry Down Housing Scheme (S.N.L. illus. 41.8 WOO, LC 1493); G.L.R.O., CL/HSL/2/55 (L.C.C., Housing and Pub. Health Cttee. rep. on Woodberry Down site).
[68] *N. Lond. Recorder*, 28 Feb. 1936 (S.N.L. cuttings 41.8).
[69] G.L.R.O., CL/HSL/2/55.
[70] Ch. Com., Estate maps, Stoke Newington Estate 3.
[71] In industrial areas there were more men and the pop. was younger: *Census*, 1921.   [72] *Census*, 1921.
[73] The name of the rd., Chaucer Rd., is fictitious: J. B. Priestley, *Angel Pavement* (Everyman edn. 1953), 52.
[74] *New Lond. Life and Labour*, iii, Social Survey, I. 369-71.
[75] *Census*, 1921.
[76] Stoke Newington boro. *M.O.H. Rep.* (1930); *The Times*, 14 Nov. 1933, 11c.

[77] *New Lond. Life and Labour*, iii, Social Survey, I. 369-71; (1929-30), IV, Map of Eastern Area, sheets 1, 3; (1931), Map of overcrowding.
[78] B. Murray, 'Short hist. of St. Olave's' (TS. pamphlet 1969, S.N.L. 14.02, LC 3220).
[79] Guildhall MSS. CC. 345106, 359861, 369055, 369059, 372471.
[80] Ibid. 366028; inf. from Gestetner International Ltd. 1983.
[81] *Who Was Who, 1916-28*, 40.
[82] *Who was Who in the Theatre* (1912-76), i. 436.
[83] Stoke Newington, *Official Guide* (1928); photo. (S.N.L. illus. 80.1, LC 32); *Stoke Newington Recorder*, 8 Apr. 1927 (S.N.L. cuttings 35); MS. note by J. Dailey 1973 (S.N.L. cuttings 78 BAD); cutting 15 Nov. 1912 (S.N.L. cuttings 78 BEA).

Jones, Stoke Newington's M.P.[84] In 1929–30 the whole area between Seven Sisters Road and Manor Road was classified as wealthy,[85] although pressure on housing eventually led to a change even there. In 1934 the Church Commissioners wanted to use the Lordship Terrace site for good-class houses and flats, but under threat of compulsory purchase put up working-class housing.[86] In the late 1930s, before building started on the Woodberry Down estate, the area began to run down as people left or neglected property in anticipation of purchase by the L.C.C.

FROM 1940. During the Second World War 474 buildings were destroyed and many more damaged.[87] The County of London Plan of 1943 discussed an expansion of open space, a reduction of population to an overall density of 100 to the acre, and a separation of industry from residential areas.[88] The need to give priority to housing, however, together with vigorous objections by firms to residential zoning, ensured that the plan was never put into effect.[89] By 1951 there were 10,446 dwellings in the borough, an increase of almost a quarter over 1931.[90] Numbers of dwellings built since the war were 3,244 by 1957, 3,834 by 1960, and 4,507 by 1964.[91] In 1961 there were 15,037 dwellings in the borough.[92]

The shift in the balance between private and public housing, which had begun during the 1930s, was completed after the Second World War. The Church Commissioners, having relinquished the freehold of Woodberry Down, sold numerous other sites. The borough council acquired nos. 206–16 (even) Green Lanes in 1950, nos. 23–33 (odd) Lordship Road in 1951, nos. 58–78 (even) Bethune Road and nos. 96–122 (even) Manor Road in 1955, nos. 1–11 (odd) Queen Elizabeth's Walk and the rear of Lordship Park in 1955, and nos. 87–121 (odd) Lordship Road in 1957. The L.C.C. acquired nos. 63–93 (odd) Bethune Road and nos. 2–16 (even) Fairholt Road in 1951, Northumberland House, nos. 338–52 (even) Green Lanes and nos. 1–25 (odd) Woodberry Grove in 1954, and no. 54 Bouverie Road in 1958.[93]

The borough council set up a housing department in 1948 and, largely using its direct labour force,[94] undertook an extensive replacement of

Victorian houses with blocks of flats, mainly in the south. They included Hawkesley Court (128 flats and 23 houses) finished in 1948, Milton Gardens (76 flats) in Albert Town in 1949,[95] Amwell Court (116 flats) in Green Lanes next to the reservoir in 1950,[96] Gordon Lodge at the northern end of Queen Elizabeth's Walk in 1951,[97] Londesborough Road (80 flats)[98] and Manor Road (54 flats, probably Rosedale House) in 1953,[99] and Defoe Road (36 flats) by 1955.[1] Lordship South estate (121 flats) on the western side of Lordship Road was begun in 1956 but not finished until 1959, by which time other recently completed estates were Hillcourt (146 flats) on the north side of Manor Road, and Burma Court (129 flats) south of Aden Terrace.[2] The borough had built 1,336 dwellings between 1945 and 1957 and at the end of 1960 owned 2,335, including pre-war estates. By the end of 1964 the numbers had risen to 2,889.[3]

The L.C.C. in 1946 started work on the first eight blocks containing 1,765 dwellings as part of an amended scheme for Woodberry Down.[4] One eight-storeyed block, the largest yet built for the L.C.C., was opened in 1949.[5] Building continued until by 1961 there were 1,797 dwellings on the original site, mostly in five-storeyed blocks, while another 219 dwellings, mostly in ten-storeyed blocks, were being built on the site of Northumberland House.[6] The L.C.C. built 1,845 dwellings in Stoke Newington between 1945 and 1957, owning 2,041 dwellings there by the end of 1960 and 2,324 by the end of 1964.[7]

Other flats built during the 1950s were Medway and Crawshay houses in Clissold Crescent between 1954 and 1959,[8] Queen Elizabeth's Close on the site of nos. 1–11 (odd) Queen Elizabeth's Walk between 1952 and 1960,[9] and Shannon Court off Dynevor Road between 1952 and 1962.[10] During the next decade Listria Lodge replaced two large houses at the Stamford Hill end of Manor Road between 1953 and 1966,[11] Sandor Court, four- and six-storeyed blocks, replaced Bethune Close between 1954 and 1963,[12] Meadowcroft replaced nos. 83–93 (odd) Bethune Road between 1954 and 1970,[13] Arbor Court (48 flats) was built on a site bounded by Queen Elizabeth's Walk, Lordship Park, and Lordship Road, Queen's and Palm's courts were built in Queen Elizabeth's Walk north of Lord-

[84] 'Stoke Newington', vol. 2 (scrapbk. of cuttings S.N.L. 80, LC 1661).
[85] New Lond. Life and Labour (1929–30), iv, Map of Eastern Area, sheet 3.
[86] Ch. Com. file 6439 pt. 2.
[87] Stoke Newington, Official Guide (1950), 77.
[88] G.L.R.O., AR/TP2/157 (L.C.C. Town Planning Scheme 19).
[89] Ibid. TP4/33.
[90] Census, 1951.
[91] Thereafter the figures for Stoke Newington were included in those for Hackney: L.C.C. Lond. Statistics, N.S. iii (1947–50), 110; v (1951–60), 98; vii (1955–64), 101.
[92] Census, 1961.
[93] Ch. Com., Surveys S2, pp. 910 sqq.; Estate maps, Stoke Newington Estate 1.
[94] Below, local govt.
[95] Stoke Newington, Official Guide (1950), 77, 83–4.
[96] The Times, 13 Nov. 1950, 2e; Official Opening of Amwell Ct. Housing Est. 1950 (S.N.L. cuttings 41.8, LC 2166).
[97] Official Opening of Gordon Lodge, 1951 (S.N.L. cuttings 41.8 GOR, LC 2387).

[98] Londesborough Rd. Housing Scheme, 1953 (S.N.L. cuttings 41.8 LON).
[99] O.S. Map 1/1,250 TQ 3287 SE. (1953, 1954 edns.).
[1] Stoke Newington, Official Guide [1955], 22.
[2] Ibid. (1959); Lond. Boro. of Hackney, Street Plan [n.d.]; The Times, 25 Apr. 1961, 8a; 21 Nov. 1961, 6d.
[3] L.C.C. Lond. Statistics, N.S. iii (1947–56), 110; v (1951–60), 94–5, 98; vii (1955–64), 98, 101.
[4] Hackney Gaz. 21 Feb. 1944 (S.N.L. cuttings 41.8); Stoke Newington, Official Guide [1947], 36; above, plate 51.
[5] The Times, 18 Feb. 1949, 2d.
[6] Stoke Newington, Official Guide [1961], 10–13; O.S. Map 1/1,250, TQ 3287 NE., NW., SW. (1953, 1954, 1962 edns.).
[7] L.C.C. Lond. Statistics, N.S. iii (1947–56), 110; v (1951–60), 94–5, 98; vii (1955–64), 98, 101.
[8] O.S. Map 1/1,250, TQ 3285 NE. (1954, 1959 edns.).
[9] Ibid. TQ 3286 NE. (1952, 1960 edns.).
[10] Ibid. TQ 3386 SE. (1952, 1962 edns.).
[11] Ibid. TQ 3386 NE. (1953, 1966 edns.).
[12] Ibid. TQ 3387 SW. (1954, 1963 edns.).
[13] Ibid. TQ 3387 NW. (1954, 1970 edns.).

ship Park between 1960 and 1970,[14] and flats replaced Victorian houses on a site bounded by Lordship, St. Kilda's, and St. Andrew's roads between 1960 and 1975.[15] Flats continued to be built south of Church Street. The Milton Gardens estate in Albert Town was extended, more than 200 flats in blocks named after poets being built between 1954 and 1970,[16] and to the west flats replaced houses in Howard Road and the old town hall in Milton Grove between 1959 and 1970.[17] The other area of development was in the south-west where flats were built between Green Lanes and Statham Grove and on the site of All Saints' church in Aden Grove between 1959 and 1970.[18] All the houses on the east side of Clissold Road were demolished after 1952, and Clissold Park school opened there in 1969 and Glebelands old people's home about the same time. In 1972 Crusoe House opened on the site of nos. 41–51 (odd) Clissold Road.[19] Chestnut Close replaced nos. 15–35 (odd) Lordship Road, Juniper Court was built in Grazebrook Road, and Sandale Close was built on the site of no. 97B Carysfort Road between 1970 and 1980.[20] Two large estates by Hackney L.B. in the 1980s were Shellgrove in the south-east, bounded by Boleyn Road, Crossway, Pellerin Road, and Selsea Place, and Yorkshire Grove in the old Victoria area of South Hornsey, bounded by Victoria Grove, Yorkshire Close (formerly Victoria Grove West), Nevill, Walford, and Beatty (formerly Gordon) roads.

The immediate post-war policy of replacing Victorian houses with blocks of flats gradually moderated. By 1964 the borough council had converted 346 houses to flats and the L.C.C. 42.[21] Under the Civic Amenities Act, 1967, Hackney L.B. designated the Clissold Park area, including nos. 169–223 (odd) Church Street, a conservation area.[22] In 1972 it prevented rebuilding on the site of Allen's flats in Bethune Road.[23] In 1974 a list of protected buildings included large numbers of Victorian houses throughout Stoke Newington.[24] In 1975 Hackney L.B. was opposed by the inhabitants of some 40 houses in the Barbauld (formerly Broughton) Road area, which it wanted to replace by flats, and in 1976 the G.L.C. expressed concern about displacing small firms from the large gardens at the back of Albion Road.[25] In 1983, although there were modern flats at the western end of Barbauld Road, most of the street retained its Victorian terraces. In 1976 Hackney designated for rehabilitation an 'action area' named Shakspeare Walk, north of the new flats in Albert Town and west of Nevill Road. Houses in Cowper Road were accordingly demolished to provide an open space, while shops and houses in

Milton Grove and Allen Road were restored. In 1981 the council designated an 'action area' called Palatine Road, east of Albert Town between Beatty and Prince George roads, and a general improvement area called Martaban (Listria Park, near Stamford Hill). In 1982 the council proposed two new conservation areas, one extending the Clissold Park area to include the whole of Church Street and the second comprising Milton Grove and parts of Albion Road and Shakspeare Walk.[26]

Density in 1951 varied from 100 people to the acre in Palatine and 83 in Church ward to 36 in Manor ward; 65 per cent of households shared a dwelling.[27] In the decade to 1961 the number of dwellings increased by more than a half and the wards were reorganized. Manor ward, reduced in size, was still the most spacious, with 33 people to the acre, and Palatine the most crowded, with 97. Woodberry ward had been created for the Woodberry Down estate, which had 71 to the acre. In 1961 nearly 40 per cent of accommodation was rented, private, and unfurnished, nearly 27 per cent was rented from the local authority, and only 25 per cent was owner occupied.[28]

In spite of additional housing, overcrowding was greater than before.[29] The most prosperous moved farther from London and slum clearance transferred many of the original inhabitants to new towns. The old who were left sublet to immigrants, whose proportion to the total population rose from 105 per 1,000 in 1951 to 192 in 1961[30] and 240 in 1966. Many were West Indians, of whom 68 per cent shared dwellings in 1973, compared with 25 per cent of the English, while only 8 per cent of West Indian households had all facilities, compared with 40 per cent of the English. There was higher unemployment among the West Indians, who often lived in furnished, rented accommodation. By 1971 Clissold and Defoe wards, comprising the whole area south of Lordship Park and Manor Road, respectively had 26 per cent and 23 per cent of their residents with both parents born in the New Commonwealth. Overcrowding (10 per cent) and lack of amenities (64 per cent) were then highest in Brownswood ward,[31] where in 1971 there were 0.79 people to a room and 136 people to the hectare. While there were fewer people per room (0.74 or 0.75) in the other wards, the density was usually greater, 195 to the hectare in Clissold and 174 in Defoe, but only 107 in New River. The population in all wards had gone down since 1961.[32]

In the 1960s and 1970s the Jews who had settled between the late 19th century and 1940 were replaced by more recent immigrants. In

[14] Ibid. TQ 3286 NE. (1960, 1970 edns.).
[15] Ibid. TQ 3287 NE. (1960, 1975 edns.).
[16] Ibid. TQ 3385 SW. (1954, 1970 edns.).
[17] Ibid. TQ 3285 NE. (1959, 1970 edns.).
[18] Ibid. TQ 3285 NE. (1959, 1970 edns.).
[19] Ibid. TQ 3286 SE. (1952, 1970, 1980 edns.); below, educ.
[20] Ibid. TQ 3286 NE., SE. (1970, 1980 edns.).
[21] L.C.C. *Lond. Statistics*, n.s. vii (1955–64), 98.
[22] *Lond. Gaz.* 31 Jan. 1969, p. 1176.
[23] *Architect's Jnl.* 18 Oct. 1972 (S.N.L. cuttings 41.8).
[24] Listed Bldgs. under 1971 Act, 1974 (S.N.L. cuttings 55).

[25] *Hackney Gaz.* 7 Oct., 25 Nov. 1975 (S.N.L. cuttings 41.8 BAR, LC 3320–1); *Evening Standard*, 10 June 1976 (S.N.L. cuttings 41.8, LC 3206).
[26] *Hackney Gaz.* 30 Nov. 1979 (S.N.L. cuttings 55.4, LC 3666); *Hackney Boro. Plan, Stoke Newington Area* (1982), SN 3–4, 9–11, maps 3.11, 8.1, 9.6.
[27] *Census*, 1951.   [28] Ibid. 1961.
[29] Passage based on P. J. Mason, 'Immigration and Housing in Stoke Newington' (TS. 1973, S.N.L. 41.6, LC 3305).
[30] Cf. average for L.C.C. area: 93 in 1951, 141 in 1961.
[31] START, *Interim Rep. on Social Trends in L.B. of Hackney* (S.N.L. 40.4).   [32] *Census*, 1971.

addition to West Indians, there were Hassidim from Europe who settled in large numbers north of Church Street,[33] Greek Cypriots in Finsbury Park,[34] and Turks in the south-west part of Stoke Newington.[35] In 1981 Green Lanes from Newington Green to Harringay and Wood Green was described as the spinal cord of Cypriot London.[36] By the 1980s gentrification was spreading from Islington. In addition to the renovation of Victorian houses by the borough council and housing associations, there was a growth of owner occupation and a new appreciation of Victorian architecture.[37]

In 1983 Stoke Newington was sharply divided between Victorian housing and modern, predominantly post-war, blocks of flats. The old centres of settlement are treated separately below. Among buildings[38] north of Church Street is the mid 19th-century engine house of the Metropolitan Water Board, a large castle-like structure or 'amazing folly',[39] and Fairview, no. 14 Queen Elizabeth's Walk, a detached two-storeyed stock-brick house with original ironwork, built for the nurseryman Alfred Kendall by 1846.[40] At the east end of Manor Road no. 4, stock-brick and of three storeys and basement, with a segmental bay, survives from the early 19th century.[41] The Allen flats, nos. 24-54 (even) Manor Road and nos. 2-56 (even) Bethune Road, resemble three-storeyed semi-detached houses of grey brick and painted stucco.[42] Modernization of some blocks was in progress in 1983. On the southern side of Manor Road the older houses are mostly three-storeyed semi-detached buildings of the late 1870s. In Lordship Road, where many houses have disappeared since 1974, there remain two pre-Victorian cottages, nos. 10 and 12, at the Church Street end and St. Mary's Lodge, no. 73, a two-storeyed stock- and red-brick detached house built by John Young, an architect, for himself c. 1845.[43] Farther north survive a derelict villa of the mid 19th century and, in its own grounds opposite St. Kilda's Road, one of slightly earlier date. The east side of Yoakley Road is lined with yellow-brick houses, mostly two-storeyed and in pairs or short terraces, all mid 19th-century.

South of Church Street are houses dating from the 1820s and 1830s, notably those by Cubitt and others in Albion Road, which contains a mixture of 19th-century villas and terraces in varying states, some recently restored, mostly as flats, and some in industrial use. Nos. 143-9 (odd) on the west side are detached and semi-detached symmetrical stuccoed houses with pedimented

entrances.[44] The more noteworthy buildings are on the east side: no. 76, a two-storeyed, three-bayed detached house with a massive porch, nos. 108-18 (even), formerly South Place, a terrace built after 1839 by John Adams,[45] nos. 154-62 (even), detached and semi-detached houses mostly in poor condition, and nos. 166-78 (even), an impressive three-storeyed terrace undergoing restoration. Other noteworthy houses include no. 68, two-storeyed with a basement, and nos. 78-86 (even) and 92-104 (even), two three-storeyed terraces of stock-brick and stucco, in poor condition although some houses are being renovated, and nos. 180-4 (even), a semi-detached pair and a single house that might have been the end of a terrace, all three-storeyed and plain. A small yellow-brick terrace at the Church Street end (nos. 238-46 even) is notable as having been built by Cubitt's own labourers.[46]

Early 19th-century houses survive in Victorian (formerly Victoria) Grove, including Albion Villas, nos. 9 and 11, a semi-detached two-storeyed pair with basement and attics and semi-circular bays. The flanking semi-detached pairs, nos. 5 and 7 and 13 and 15, are of similar date. In spite of the demolition in Albert Town, many of the original houses, dating from the early 1850s, remain. In Milton Grove no. 66, of two storeys with an Ionic porch, is being rehabilitated, and nos. 64 and 68 are of similar date. Eden Villa, no. 104, is two-storeyed, with iron balconies, railings, and pilasters, and nos. 2-16 (even) Albion Grove, are three-storeyed houses in groups of four, with Italianate features of the 1850s. Other houses in the same roads and in Shakspeare Walk display similar details.[47] Also of the 1850s are the Albion public house in Clissold Road and, opposite, nos. 1-39 (odd), Italianate houses of three storeys and basements, in groups of four; most are in a poor state, awaiting rehabilitation.[48] No. 3 Aden Grove, a narrow three-storeyed house with basement, survives from a pair that existed in 1848,[49] and no. 42 Clissold Crescent, formerly the Grange, Park Lane, a red-brick Gothic detached house built by the architect, James Brooks, for himself in 1862, where he died in 1901,[50] is being refurbished. Nos. 93 and 95 and 99-103 (odd) Green Lanes are the remains of Millfield Place, a three-storeyed terrace built in 1846-8.[51]

Whole streets of houses of the 1870s and 1880s remain. Features include the twin pillars at the entrance to Lordship Park from Green Lanes, surmounted by a lion and griffin, sculpted motifs on the terraced houses of Hermitage and Eade roads, the ecclesiastical appearance of Bethany,

[33] Below, Judaism.
[34] *Time Out*, 20-6 June 1980 (S.N.L. cuttings 80.3, LC 3760).
[35] Ibid. 1 Aug. 1980 (S.N.L. cuttings 23.1, LC 3761).
[36] *New Society*, 26 Mar. 1981 (S.N.L. cuttings 41.6, LC 3794).
[37] Hunter, *Victorian Villas*, 62.
[38] Listed Bldgs. under 1971 Act, 1974 (S.N.L. cuttings 55).
[39] Pevsner, *Lond.* ii. 429-30; D. Batchelder and others, *From Tower to Tower Block: Bldgs. of Hackney* (Hackney Soc. 1979), unpag., plate 39; above, plate 53.
[40] *From Tower to Tower Block*, plate 24; Guildhall MS. CC. 2416; tithe (1848), no. 121. For Kendal, below, econ., nurseries.
[41] Tithe (1848), no. 389.

[42] *From Tower to Tower Block*, plate 26; above, plate 50.
[43] Guildhall MSS. CC. 2410, 359874, 359877; tithe (1848), no. 99.
[44] *From Tower to Tower Block*, plate 14.
[45] Hobhouse, *Thos. Cubitt*, 48.
[46] Ibid. 46.
[47] *From Tower to Tower Block*, plate 25; Hunter, *Victorian Villas*, 17, 43, 45.
[48] *Hackney Boro. Plan, Stoke Newington Planning Area* (1982), SN 3-7.
[49] Tithe (1848), nos. 767-8.
[50] *From Tower to Tower Block*, plate 32; Victorian Soc. 'The Grange, 42 Clissold Cres.' (R. Dixon, TS. 1972, S.N.L. cuttings 57.2); S.N.L. cuttings 78 Brooks.
[51] Tithe (1848).

no. 53 Bethune Road, in 1983 housing a religious community, and tiled paths in Lordship Park and Queen Elizabeth's Walk.[52] Of the 20th-century buildings, Nicholl House by Sir Leslie Martin (1948), one of the first blocks on the L.C.C.'s Woodberry Down estate, is starkly functional in style. On a later extension of the estate, Lincoln Court at Bethune Road (1969) was built by Howes, Jackman and Partners as high-rise rectangular blocks on pedestals overlooking the reservoirs.[53] Much of the Woodberry Down estate, however, in contrast to the low-rise brick flats of the borough council, is in grey concrete and reminiscent of Soviet architecture of the early 1950s.[54]

The population, 1,462 in 1801, more than doubled to 3,480 in 1831, reached 6,608 in 1861, and rose to 9,841 in 1871, and, during the decade of most building, to 22,781 in 1881. Overcrowding, rather than building, was reflected in the rise from 30,936 in 1901 to 50,659 in 1911 and 52,172 in 1921. The population then declined, falling to 31,370 in 1941, rose steadily to a new peak of 52,301 in 1961, but fell to 45,684 in 1971.[55]

CHURCH STREET.[56] The main medieval settlement grew up in Church Street around the church and stone manor house on the north side and parsonage and parish pond on the south, stretching eastward to the London road. There was some building in brick at the church and manor house in the 1560s by William Patten, but the parsonage, which he also repaired, was of timber, as were most of the houses. Fleetwood House, a large brick house, was built at the eastern end of the street probably in the 1630s.[57] Thomas Stock built five houses on the north side of Church Street at its junction with High Street before 1664,[58] and John Pride had recently built a house at the west end of Church Street by 1677.[59] In 1686 Andrew Yardley, a London lawyer, was permitted to pull down a house provided that he rebuilt it.[60] The replacement may have been the brick house, stable, and coach house on the south side of Church Street 'lately erected' in 1701 and later called Wentworth House,[61] of five bays and two storeys with attics and a steep roof.[62] In

1700 Abney House was built west of Fleetwood House.[63]

In the 1670s settlement was concentrated at the eastern end of Church Street.[64] The western end was built up mostly in the early 18th century, when the scattered timber cottages were replaced by brick houses singly and in terraces. In 1695, after the demolition of the old manor house, its site was leased for 99 years to John Knight, a London scrivener, who divided the ground and leased it, mostly to Timothy Mathews, a grocer, William Gardiner, tiler and bricklayer, Job Edwards, carpenter, and Christopher Bostock, glazier, all Londoners. Mathews leased his section, mostly to Edwards, who built the greater part of Church Row, nine houses in a terrace east of the churchyard. Although the eighth and ninth houses had datestones of 1706 and 1709 respectively they were referred to in 1696 and 1697 and probably all were completed by 1700.[65] Edwards, who had died by 1717, also built five houses between Church Row and Edward's Lane by 1710.[66] By 1717 Edward Newens, bricklayer of Stoke Newington, had built four brick houses on the site of one old house on the south side of Church Street, probably the terrace called Sisters Place after it was inherited by four sisters in 1813.[67]

The land upon which Newens built had formed part of the Pulteney estate which Henry Guy sold to John Drury (d. 1716) in 1700.[68] Drury's son Robert, who was shipwrecked off Madagascar in 1703 and not rescued until 1717, was probably the inspiration for Robinson Crusoe.[69] Daniel Defoe was living in a rented house on the north side of Church Street by 1709.[70] He moved, possibly by 1714, to the later no. 95 on the south side, which he rebuilt as a handsome three-storeyed house with a central block of three bays, pediment, and porch, flanked by single-bayed wings. There was a stable block and a large garden bounded on two sides by Hussey's and Pawnbroker's lanes.[71]

In 1721 Newens and Silvanus Horton, a London carpenter, took a lease of 3 a. of the Lloyd estate on the south side of Church Street, west of the glebe,[72] upon which they had built several houses by 1723.[73] Six had been built by 1734,[74] c. 12 by 1744,[75] and c. 15 by 1764[76] in what

[52] The black and white chequered pattern may have been a feature used by Wm. Osment: Hunter, *Victorian Villas*, 49.
[53] *From Tower to Tower Block*, plates 49, 50.
[54] Above, plate 51.
[55] *Census*, 1801–1971; L.C.C. *Statistical Abstract for Lond.* xxxi (1939–48), 5. Figures to 1891 inclusive for parish, 1901–61 for borough, 1971 for wards comprising area of former borough.
[56] After 1937 called Stoke Newington Church Street. House nos. are wherever possible those of 1983. The nos. were changed in 1880 and 1937.
[57] Below, manor, other est., churches.
[58] One was occupied by Dan. Bull; the others conveyed for Stock's char.: below, charities.
[59] Guildhall MS. 14233/2, s.v. 1679.
[60] Ibid. 3; P.R.O., C 5/584/6.
[61] 'Formerly dwelling ho. of And. Yardley': G.L.R.O., P94/MRY/83–4 (lease and schedule 1701); tithe (1848), nos. 549–50.
[62] S.N.L. illus. 57.2 WEN, LC 645.
[63] For Abney and Fleetwood hos., below, manor; other est.
[64] J. Ogilby, *Britannia* (1675), plate betw. pp. 8 and 9; Ogilby, *Map of Mdx.* [1677].

[65] Robinson, *Stoke Newington*, 54–7; P.R.O., C 8/357/197; G.L.R.O., P94/MRY/108 (deed 1740). For 1st ho., mentioned in 1695, see M.L.R. 1730/2/3.
[66] M.L.R. 1710/3/381; 1715/3/39.
[67] Ibid. 1717/5/95–6; 1718/4/158, 241; Guildhall MSS. 14233/5, m. 2; 8, m. 4d.; 'Sisters Place' (TS. by Ref. Libr. 1959, S.N.L. cuttings 57.2). No. 171 bears date 1714: *From Tower to Tower Block*, plate 8.
[68] Guildhall MS. 14233/5, m. 2; M.L.R. 1717/5/96.
[69] A. J. Shirren, *Dan. Defoe in Stoke Newington* (1960), 12–15.
[70] Will of Nic. Clarke, quoted in Shirren, *Defoe*, 18–19.
[71] Whether Defoe repaired and beautified or 'newly built' is disputed: Shirren, *Defoe*, 22. Views suggest at least complete refronting: ibid. facing p. 14; S.N.L. illus. 57.2 DEF, LC 3688, 3690; tithe (1848), nos. 541–3.
[72] M.L.R. 1722/2/233; below, other est.
[73] M.L.R. 1723/4/193. Cf. plan in B.L. Maps, King's Topog. XXX. 10. g.
[74] Marcham, 'Digest', pt. 3.
[75] Abstract of Ct. Rolls 1740–63, 91.
[76] Ibid. 1763–1801, 123, 129.

by 1738 was named Paradise Row.[77] The houses were mostly three-storeyed and five-bayed[78] but Paradise House consisted of a three-bayed central portion with a pedimented porch, Corinthian pillars, and projecting wings.[79] One, formerly the home of John Zachary, a merchant, was advertised in 1755 as 'new and well built', paved with marble, with a large garden.[80]

Other 18th-century houses included Halstead House and the adjoining houses (nos. 199–203 odd in 1925), a five-bayed central block with two-bayed side wings,[81] and two large houses at the eastern end of Church Street, a three-storeyed square one lying back from the street west of Abney House[82] and Compton House opposite Abney House by 1814.[83] Thomas Rigby built four cottages on the south side of Church Street, at the eastern end, between 1788 and 1816 and eight were built at Falcon Court behind the inn between 1798 and 1816.[84] In 1822 Meshach Izzard, a local carpenter, was licensed to replace the five old houses next to the dilapidated Three Crowns with four larger ones.[85] Thomas Widdows, the Church Street builder, was accumulating property in the 1820s.[86] Newington Hall, a large, classical house, stood by 1829 at the western end of the street, beyond Paradise Row, with grounds backing on the New River.[87] Four houses built by Widdows fronting Church Street on the glebe soon after 1835 may be identified with the semi-detached pairs with Ionic porches known as Glebe Place.[88]

Widdows built four brick houses on the site of four old, probably timber ones, on the north side and another two on the south side of Church Street by 1840.[89] One house in Paradise Row had been 'lately built' as two houses by 1845[90] and between 1827 and 1854 the old Falcon made way for a new inn and a house.[91] In 1856 nos. 5–7 Church Street were demolished as dangerous and their site was sold to an auctioneer.[92] At the western end of the street Park Crescent was built east of Glebe Place in the early 1850s[93] and in 1855–8 the timber rectory house was replaced by the handsome new church and parsonage.[94]

In 1841 Church Street was famed for its 'mansion-like residences' with their large gardens, many of which stretched into pleasure grounds and paddocks where the owners made their own hay and kept cows.[95] The residents were merchants and, attracted by the dissenting tradition, writers who in turn attracted others.[96] The inhabitants of Fleetwood House included two Turkey merchants, Sir Nathaniel Gould (d. 1728) and Thomas Cooke (d. 1752), a stockbroker, Henry Guinard, in 1766–9, and an exchange broker, Charles Rebotier, c. 1770.[97] Thomas Day (d. 1789), author of Sandford and Merton, spent his early childhood at nos. 109 and 111, then set behind wrought-iron gates and pillars topped with urns.[98] John Aikin (d. 1822), the writer, obliged to quit 'the close atmosphere of London', had settled by 1799 at the three-storeyed, three-bayed house on the north side of Church Street (no. 106, later called Abney House) which his daughter Lucy (d. 1864), herself a writer, called in 1806 'the white house at Newington'.[99] It had previously housed Adam Anderson (1679–1765), a trustee for establishing the colony of Georgia and historian of commerce, and Solomon de Medina, the Jewish merchant.[1] Opposite, at no. 113 from 1802 until her death in 1825, lived Aikin's sister Anna Letitia, a leading literary figure, and her husband the Revd. Rochemont Barbauld (d. 1808). Many writers visited the two houses in Church Street,[2] where Mrs. Barbauld's circle included the Eades at Abney House and the Rivaz family,[3] descendants of Huguenots who in 1848 occupied Hugonin House near the Falcon inn and another house opposite Fleetwood House. They were businessmen, Henry Rivaz being described in 1851 as a dealer in stocks and the railway, and prominent in local politics.[4] Pishey Thompson (d. 1862), author of a history of Boston, lived at no. 122, a two-storeyed ten-bayed house on the north side of Church Street.[5]

Most of the houses in Church Row had two storeys and attics, five bays, pedimented doorways, and decorative gate pillars.[6] No. 8 (later no.

[77] M.L.R. 1738/4/150. Of 15 hos. mentioned in 1744 and 18 in 1764 some were on the N. side of street, at the W. end, where there were 3 in 1781–2: Guide for assessors of par. 1781–2.
[78] e.g. photos. of the Grange: S.N.L. illus. 57.2 GRA, LC 280–2, 295–6; Stoke Ho.: S.N.L. illus. 57.2 STO, LC 290.
[79] S.N.L. illus. 57.6, LC 1267–8; W. Shepherd, 'Paradise Row c.1914' (TS. 1976, S.N.L. cuttings 49.2, LC 3348).
[80] Cuttings of Stoke Newington 1722–1895, p. 3c (S.N.L. 80, LC 2411).
[81] Hist. Mon. Com. W. Lond. 92; Sunday Times, 26 Oct. 1930 (S.N.L. illus. 57.2 HAL, LC 2069); photo. (S.N.L. illus. 57.2 HAL, LC 727).
[82] W. Beck, Church Street, 11; tithe (1848), no. 312.
[83] Robinson, Stoke Newington, frontispiece map; tithe (1848), no. 523.
[84] Abstract of Ct. Rolls 1802–31, 266–7.
[85] Vestry mins. 1819–38, 12.
[86] Abstract of Ct. Rolls 1802–31, 289.
[87] T. H. Shepherd, drawing 1844 (HA S 248 (164)): above, plate 45. Cruchley's New Plan (1829).
[88] Ch. Com. file 47064 (letter 1872); S.N.L. illus. 57.2 GLE, LC 277).
[89] G.L.R.O., o/238/2/1.
[90] Abstract of Ct. Rolls 1832–82, 357, i.e. ref. bk. to Wadmore map (1813), no. 125.
[91] Abstract of Ct. Rolls 1832–82, 373, 400.
[92] Ibid. 376.
[93] Above, settlement and growth to 1870.

[94] Below, churches.
[95] Chamber's Edinburgh Jnl. [1841], 310–11 (S.N.L. cuttings 80).
[96] e.g. Three Score Years and Ten: Reminiscences of Sophia Eliz. De Morgan, ed. Mary A. De Morgan (S.N.L. cuttings 78 De Morgan, LC 1974).
[97] Robinson, Stoke Newington, 80–1, 99, 178–9; below, other est. (Fleetwood Ho.).
[98] D.N.B.; Shepherd's drawings: Portrait of Lond. Suburb, item 17; HA 5702 DAY 771; tithe (1848), no. 545.
[99] Aikin letters (HA M 3712, 3723); Portrait of Lond. Suburb, item 19; HA WP 8574; ref. bk. to Wadmore map (1813), no. 211.
[1] Tithe (1848), no. 248; Abstract of Ct. Rolls 1802–32, 271; 1832–82, 416; 'List of Bldgs. in Stoke Newington having historical interest' (TS. 1912, S.N.L. cuttings 57.2, LC 2231); D.N.B.
[2] Ref. bk. to Wadmore map (1813), no. 190; D.N.B.; Oxford Literary Guide to Brit. Isles, ed. D. Eagle and H. Carnell (1977), 219–20.
[3] Barbauld letters (HA M 3728).
[4] Tithe (1848), nos. 525, 558; P.R.O., HO 107/1505/11/3; ibid. RG 10/310/9/1B. Hugonin Ho. was possibly no. 137: J. Dailey, 'Stoke Newington in brief' (TS. 1972, S.N.L. cuttings 80, LC 3160).
[5] S.N.L. illus. 57.2 THO, LC 649–83; 'List of Bldgs. in Stoke Newington having historical interest'.
[6] S.N.L. illus. 57.2 CHU, LC 702, 713, 716–18, 723, 862–3.

168 Church Street)[7] was owned by Mrs. Lardeau, a widow whose young lodger John Howard (?1726–90), later the prison reformer, married her and in 1755 inherited her property.[8] In 1781–2 Church Row housed James Brown,[9] either the father (1709–88) or son (1750–1839). The elder James, merchant and author of a Persian dictionary, settled in Stoke Newington in 1734 and was buried in the church. The younger James, who wrote the account of the parish for the *Bibliotheca Topographica Britannica* in 1783, lived in Stoke Newington until 1799.[10] Benjamin D'Israeli (d. 1816), a London stockbroker and grandfather of the earl of Beaconsfield, lived at no. 7 (no. 170), where he was visited by literary men, including the publisher John Murray.[11] The same house was visited in the 1840s by Dickens and Thackeray when it housed Frederick Mullet Evans (d. 1870), proprietor of *Punch*.[12] At the same time nos. 6 and 9 (respectively nos. 172 and 166 Church Street) were occupied by members of the Quaker Moline family, Sparks and Edward, who had helped to found the meeting house in 1829. Sparks's daughter Isabella (d. 1923) was active in running the invalid asylum in High Street.[13] Wynne Baxter (d. 1920) lived at no. 170 at least since 1883, followed by his son Francis William (d. 1932), the local historian, upon whose death the whole row, which was owned or held in trust by the Baxter family, was surrendered for demolition.[14]

Stoke Newington's main claim to notice during the 18th and 19th centuries was its Quaker community, made up of a few families, inter-connected by marriage, deeply concerned in philosophical and political issues, mostly deriving their wealth from the City and resident in Church Street, especially in Paradise Row.[15] Samuel Hoare the elder (d. 1796), a merchant of 'ample fortune', occupied Paradise House, the largest in the row, from 1775.[16] His son Samuel the younger (1751–1825), the banker, lived in the row from 1785 until the damp of the New River induced him to leave Stoke Newington in 1790. The elder Samuel's second son Jonathan, a merchant and the black sheep of the family, occupied a 'late erected' house belonging to his father before

1792 and owned Grafton House, another house in the row, after 1819.[17] His sister Margaret married Joseph Woods, a London woollen merchant who by 1781–2 was living in another house in the row, probably Vincent House; their son Joseph (1776–1864) was the architect and botanist.[18] Woods and Samuel Hoare the younger campaigned to abolish slavery[19] and Paradise Row was often visited by fellow campaigners like William Wilberforce and his brother-in-law James Stephen (d. 1832), master in Chancery, whose father James (d. 1779) had come to Stoke Newington in 1774 to live in the Summerhouse on the north side of Church Street, described by the younger James c. 1820 as 'the first respectable-looking house on the right' from the London road.[20] Also present at the meetings against slavery was William Allen (1770–1843), founder of the chemical firm, promoter of the Lancasterian school movement and friend of princes, who retired to Stoke Newington in 1795 and lived at no. 135 Church Street, the home of his second wife Charlotte Hanbury (d. 1816) from their marriage in 1806 until 1827. After his marriage, the subject of a cartoon by Cruikshank, in that year to Grizell (d. 1835), the widowed daughter of Samuel Hoare, he moved to her home, Paradise House.[21] Allen's nephew and partner Cornelius Hanbury (d. 1869) lived at Warwick House in 1848[22] and later at Stoneleigh House, both in Paradise Row, before leaving the parish 1857. Hanbury's son Cornelius married Sarah, daughter of Frederick Janson (d. 1832) of Lloyds, member of another prominent Quaker family, who followed Allen at no. 135 Church Street.[23] The younger Cornelius lived successively in three houses in Paradise Row; about 1863 he and his wife began attending Anglican services and their son was a supporter of St. Matthias's.[24] The Harrises, who lived east of the Red Lion in 1823 and moved to Stoke House in Paradise Row in 1837 were also Quakers,[25] as were the Listers, John, a wine merchant and his son Joseph Jackson (1786–1869), the microscopist, and sister Mary, who founded the invalid asylum in 1825 and owned Vincent House in Paradise Row by 1810.[26]

---

[7] Church Row was numbered 1–9 from W. to E. No. 1 was pulled down in 1841 and in 1882 the hos. were renumbered, from E. to W., 166–80 (even): J. Dailey, 'Church Row' (note 1969, S.N.L. cuttings 57.2).
[8] *D.N.B.*; cutting 22 Jan. 1935 (S.N.L. cuttings 57.2).
[9] Guide for assessors of par. 1781–2.
[10] *D.N.B.*; *Gent. Mag.* lviii (2), 1128; Jas. Brown, 'Autograph letters & notes 1782–1836' (MS., S.N.L. 78, LC 1640).
[11] *D.N.B.* s.v. Isaac D'Israeli; [W. E. Baxter], 'Assoc. of Stoke Newington with Eng. lit.' (MS. talk 1914, printed in *N. Lond. Guardian*, 13 Mar. 1914, S.N.L. 51, LC 1135).
[12] 'Assoc. of Stoke Newington with Eng. lit.'; S.N.L. cuttings 57.2, LC 1455; tithe (1848), no. 156; M. H. Spielmann, *History of 'Punch'* (1895), 33.
[13] Tithe (1848), nos. 154, 157; F. W. Baxter, letter and *The Friend*, 16 Nov. 1923 (both S.N.L. cuttings 78 MOL, LC 1757).
[14] Cutting 1 Oct. 1920 (S.N.L. cuttings 78 BAX, LC 60); J. Dailey, MS. note (S.N.L. cuttings 78 BAX).
[15] For the hos. in the row see W. Shepherd, 'Paradise Row c. 1914' (TS. 1976, S.N.L. cuttings 49.2, LC 3348).
[16] Guide for assessors of par. 1781–2; print (S.N.L. cuttings 78 Hoare, LC 1012); tithe (1848), no. 689. For the Hoares, see *Gent. Mag.* lxvi(2), 793; *Memoirs of Sam. Hoare*, ed. F. R. Pryor (1911), pp. x, 2, 22, 25, 47; Marcham, Digest, pt. 2.

[17] Tithe (1848), no. 681; below, other est. (Clissold Park).
[18] Guide for assessors of par. 1781–2; tithe (1848), no. 692; *D.N.B.*
[19] Passage based on *Life of Wm. Allen* (1846), i. 80; ii. 394, 441, 446, 452; A. J. Shirren, 'Wm. Wilberforce and the Anti-slavery campaign in Stoke Newington' (TS. of articles publ. in *St. Mary Stoke Newington Par. Mag.* 1959–60, S.N.L. 41.6, LC 3391); 'Stoke Newington', vol. 1 (scrapbk. of cuttings from *Hackney & Kingsland Gaz.* 1924, S.N.L. 80, LC 1660).
[20] Cutting (S.N.L. cuttings 78 Wilberforce, LC 1978); *D.N.B.* s.v. Stephens.
[21] *D.N.B.*; J. Dailey, 'Bilney Lodge, 135 Church Street' (MS. 1969, S.N.L. cuttings 57.2 BIL); above, plate 57.
[22] Tithe (1848), no. 693.
[23] Dailey, 'Bilney Lodge, 135 Church Street'; Isabella Harris, *Family Memorials* (1869), 164.
[24] *Charlotte Hanbury, an Autobiography*, ed. Mrs. Albert Head (1901), 3, 11, 17, 71; Charlotte Hanbury, *Life of Mrs. Albert Head* (1905), 1–5, 16; 'Stoke Newington', vol. 1 (S.N.L. 80, LC 1660).
[25] Harris, *Family Memorials*, 237, 290; *Friends of a half century 1840–90*, ed. W. Robinson (1891), 186–202.
[26] *D.N.B.*; 'Stoke Newington', vol. 1 (S.N.L. 80, LC 1660); tithe (1848), no. 692.

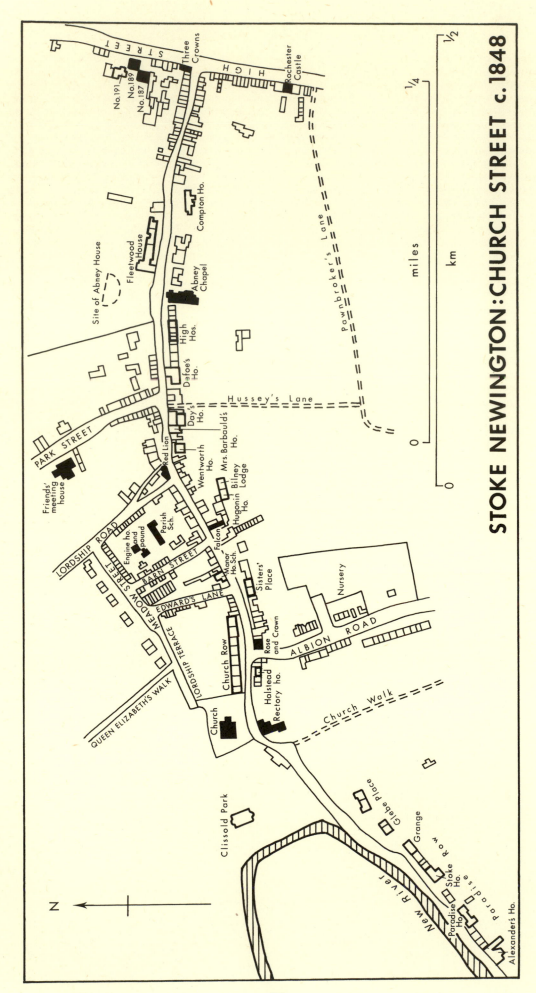

STOKE NEWINGTON : CHURCH STREET c.1848

166

George William Alexander, a banker, lived in the westernmost house in Paradise Row, which was set in 3 a. bordered by the New River, facing Clissold Park. There in 1850 he was visited by Alphonse de Lamartine and in 1853 by Harriet Beecher Stowe, who wrote that his 'place is called Paradise' and looked on a beautiful park.[27] By 1870 Alexander had pulled down the old house, itself large, and replaced it with an even larger one, the Willows, later called Kennaway Hall.[28] Another inhabitant of Paradise Row was the poet Samuel Rogers's nephew Samuel Sharpe (1799–1881), the Egyptologist, who spent much of his childhood at the Grange.[29] William Beck (d. 1907), a London surveyor and Quaker architect and historian, lived at no. 3 Glebe Place, east of Paradise Row.[30]

Boarding schools were kept in Church Street from the 18th century and by the 1830s and 1840s were a prominent feature.[31] During the same period shop fronts were fitted to the 18th-century houses, especially at the eastern end of the street.[32] One house in Paradise Row was used as a weaver's factory in 1813[33] but the growth of industry in Church Street came later.

Church Street began to be transformed during the late 19th century, with terraces and shops replacing the large houses and with small-scale industry taking over the back rooms and gardens. Between 1872 and 1880 36 houses and shops replaced larger houses, besides old timber buildings like that taken down for Carter, Paterson & Co. in 1878[34] and the forge and adjoining cottages and shops cleared for Church Street board school in 1892.[35] Where houses with extensive gardens were sold for building, side streets, usually of small terraced houses, replaced them. A Hackney builder bought no. 42 (later no. 43), on the south side of the street, in 1870.[36] Defoe's house and estate were sold in the 1860s, and by 1870 the house had been demolished and Defoe Road started, although only the assembly rooms had been built;[37] 53 terraced houses were built there in 1875–6. The Rose and Crown and its adjoining house were advertised in 1868 as having a frontage to Church Street for five or six houses.[38] When Fleetwood House was demolished in 1872, a contemporary complained that most of the old houses were disappearing.[39] Fleetwood Street, 16 small houses, replaced it in the same year.

The Laurels, square built and standing back from the road, residence in 1861 of a High Church banker, was sold in 1873 with 2 a. stretching southward from Church Street. It was thought that shops could front Church Street and some 35 houses similar to those on the adjacent Walford estate then being 'rapidly developed' could be built behind.[40] In 1874 the 2-a. estate adjoining it on the east, stretching south from no. 48, was put up for sale on similar terms.[41] The house, one of the so-called Manor Houses, an 18th-century five-bayed building behind fine iron gates, was demolished in 1875 and replaced by nos. 163–7 (odd) Church Street.[42] At the east end of Church Street three houses were built in 1874 and another seven in 1876 in Lancell Street on the site of Compton House.[43] On the north side, almost opposite, 16 houses were built in 1877, mostly by Alfred Capsey, in Summerhouse Road on the site of the house of that name. At the other end of Church Street 32 houses were built in 1876–7 in Statham Grove on the site of Newington Hall.[44] Wentworth House, dilapidated in 1849 but later repaired[45] and occupied by Joseph Janson, a banker who cultivated rare plants, had a narrow frontage to Church Street and 3 a. stretching southward; in 1882 the rector enfranchised the estate and in 1883 he made a building agreement with F. S. Hobson, the land agent, whereupon the house made way for Marton Road.[46] An 18th-century house called Manor House, standing back from the north side of Church Street, square and three-storeyed with a portico, whose owner c. 1860 had relinquished land for building Bouverie Road, was in 1886[47] replaced by seven houses and shops. In 1891 the public library was built on the site of Job Edwards's early 18th-century houses.[48]

In 1881 Paradise Row still housed bankers, brokers, merchants, and manufacturers, although Paradise House had become a school. Elsewhere there was much division into tenements[49] and industry was growing. By 1914 there were 22 firms engaged in manufacture.[50] From the 1880s some of the houses became the homes of institutions like St. Mary's mission house and club at nos. 106 and 110 or political clubs at nos. 83, 91, and 179.[51] Rignold Mansions replaced nos. 120–4 (even) in 1925[52] but there was little new building until the 1930s. Three of the group of four old houses east of Red Lion Lane, including John Aikin's house, were pulled down in 1931

[27] Tithe (1848), nos. 696–7; 'Stoke Newington', vol. 1 (S.N.L. 80, LC 1660); Harriet Beecher Stowe, *Sunny Memories of Foreign Lands* (1854), 252–3.
[28] Cf. tithe (1848), no. 696 and O.S. Map 1/2,500, Lond. X (1870 edn.).
[29] A. J. Shirren, *Sam. Rogers* (priv. print., Stoke Newington pub. libr. 1963, unpag.); *Islington Gaz.* 21 June 1940 (S.N.L. cuttings 50.3).
[30] 'Stoke Newington', vol. 1 (S.N.L. 80, LC 1660); inf. from Friends' Ho., Euston Rd.
[31] Below, educ., private.
[32] Below, econ., trade and industry.
[33] Ref. bk. to Wadmore map (1813), no. 125.
[34] Ink sketch (S.N.L. illus. 57.2 DAY).
[35] Ink sketch and photo. (S.N.L. illus. 80.5 CHU, LC 376); below, educ.
[36] Abstract of Ct. Rolls 1832–82, 412–13.
[37] Tithe (1848), nos. 542–3; O.S. Map 1/2,500, Lond. X (1870 edn.); below, social.
[38] Sales parts. 1868 (HA M 3895).

[39] *N. & Q.* 4th ser. ix. 296, 364.
[40] Beck, *Church Street*, 18; sales parts. 1873 (HA M 3895); P.R.O., RG 9/152/11/4.
[41] Sales parts. 1874 (HA M 3895).
[42] Sketch of ho. 1875 (S.N.L. illus. 57.6, LC 1464); P.R.O., RG 9/152/11/4; RG 10/309/9/1A; letter 1924 by dau. of Thos. Jackson (HA M 3784).
[43] O.S. Map 1/2,500, Lond. X (1870 edn.).
[44] 'Stoke Newington', vol. 1 (S.N.L. 80, LC 1660).
[45] Guildhall MS. CC. 216716.
[46] Tithe (1848), nos. 549–50; Guildhall MSS. CC. 216721–3; Beck, *Church Street*, 15.
[47] Sales parts. 1886 (HA M 3895); tithe (1848), no. 312; O.S. Map 1/2,500, Lond. X (1870 edn.); Beck, *Church Street*, 11.
[48] Guildhall MS. CC. 252182.
[49] P.R.O., RG 11/281/10/1.
[50] Below, econ., industry.   [51] Below, social.
[52] *Kelly's Dir. Stoke Newington* (1924–5); photos. (S.N.L. illus. 57.2 THO, LC 649–50, 683).

after some years as shops and the site became part of Whitbread's bottling yard.[53]

Street widening caused a truncation of nos. 57, 73, and 93 and of Abney chapel in 1927.[54] The narrowness of the street at its junction with Albion Road prompted the authorities to acquire the freehold of nos. 197–205 (odd) in 1923[55] although it was not until 1930 that the houses, decayed and including Halstead House (no. 201), were demolished. The Rose and Crown, as part of the same operation, was rebuilt on the west side of Albion Road. The frontage of Church Row was pushed back but the 'magnificent and varied' gates, piers, and railings were re-erected on the new line.[56] Church Row did not survive long, however, being bought in 1932 by the borough council which built the new town hall on the site in 1937.[57] In 1930 a new building was erected at nos. 10–11 Paradise Row and Stoke House was converted into flats. In 1934 the stretch of Church Street between the church and Green Lanes was 'one of the most charming sites in London' but leases were falling in, one old house became a stonemason's yard, and another was about to make way for a factory.[58] Factories and flats were being built on the south side in Shelford Place, and Warwick House had become a toy factory.[59] In 1936 the L.C.C. built flats on the sites of Glebe Place, Paradise House, and other houses in Paradise Row.[60] The westernmost houses in the row, Vincent and Warwick houses and Kennaway Hall, were replaced by L.C.C. flats (Garland and Taverner houses) c. 1953.[61] In 1976 a council estate, Brett Close, transformed the frontage on Church Street between Red Lion Lane and Yoakley Road.[62] Other new buildings included a rebuilt Abney chapel in 1957 and a fire station replacing a Victorian terrace on the site of Fleetwood House in 1977.[63]

Church Street declined as a shopping centre until by the 1980s it was distinctly seedy, containing small-scale industry, dilapidated buildings, and sites cleared by demolition. In 1982, however, the entire street was declared a conservation area and several of the old houses, of which in 1983[64] a large number remains, were being restored, usually as flats. Only the gates and piers of Abney House survive from the 18th century on the north side of Church Street. On the south side nos. 9 and 11, three-storeyed buildings with 19th-century shop fronts, are of the 18th or early 19th century and the early 18th

century respectively. To the west, nos. 75–9 (odd), an early 19th-century group of three storeys, with basements and dormers in yellow brick, are west of Abney chapel. The next four houses, nos. 81–7 (odd) were built in 1734 and known as the High Houses and later as Park Terrace; of buff brick with red-brick dressings and subsequently altered, they have four storeys, basements, and a carriage entrance in the centre. No. 83 was converted to flats in 1972 by Actel Housing Association.[65] On either side of nos. 81–7 are early 19th-century terraces of yellow brick, of which no. 89 is very dilapidated. Buildings of the 1870s flank Defoe Road but nos. 105–17 (odd) are earlier, including the three-storeyed building, nos. 109 and 111, of buff brick with red-brick dressings, associated with Thomas Day, and no. 113, much altered since the 18th century, where Mrs. Barbauld lived. Bilney Lodge, no. 135, a three-storeyed yellow-brick building of five bays with pedimented doorcase, set back from the road, was rebuilt in 1769 by Henry Sanford and associated with the Hanburys, William Allen, and the Jansons and converted into flats in 1949.[66] The adjoining no. 137, in the process of rehabilitation, is also 18th-century. Opposite Edward's Lane and the library nos. 169–85 (odd), once Sisters Place, mostly behind later shop fronts, date from 1715 and include nos. 171 and 173, a red-brick building still used as a residence, with iron gates and piers with urns.[67] Behind shop fronts, nos. 179 and 181 form a similar pair. Park Crescent (nos. 207–23 odd) between Church Walk and Clissold Road, was owned by the G.L.C. and converted into flats, its façade restored in 1968 by Hubert Bennett. The remnants of Paradise Row, nos. 235–43 (odd), survive and, although refronted, retain some 18th-century features.[68] Terraces of Victorian houses and shops remain, especially at the eastern end of the street, the western end being dominated by blocks of flats. At the west end, however, is an ornate terrace (nos. 273–81 odd) dating from the 1870s, which, with similar houses behind, replaced Newington Hall.

THE LONDON ROAD (STOKE NEWINGTON ROAD, HIGH STREET, and STAMFORD HILL). Settlement was probably early along the London road, the Roman Ermine Street, especially at its junction with Church Street. There were roadside inns[69] and by 1570 at least three houses on the Stoke

[53] i.e. nos. 36–9, changed in 1880 to nos. 106–12 (even). The remaining ho., no. 112, became no. 130 in 1937: J. Dailey, 'Site of Whitbread's brewery, Stoke Newington Church Street' (MS. 1976, S.N.L. cuttings 14.016, LC 3283); S.N.L. illus. 57.2 HAR, LC 639.
[54] Stoke Newington Recorder, 18 Oct. 1926; 11 Mar. 1927 (S.N.L. cuttings 55.4).
[55] Cutting 21 Mar. 1923 (S.N.L. cuttings 55.4).
[56] Architect and Bldg. News, 7 Nov. 1930, suppl. (S.N.L. illus. 57.2 HAL, LC 725); Stoke Newington, Official Guide (1931), 28.
[57] J. Dailey, Notes on Town Hall site (S.N.L. cuttings 31.3).
[58] The Times, 6 Jan. 1934, 6d.
[59] Below, econ., industry.
[60] Stoke Newington, Official Guide (1938), 46–9; L.C.C. Lond. Statistics, xli (1936–8), 150; O.S. Map 1/2,500, Lond. II. 11 (1936 edn.).
[61] O.S. Maps 1/1,250, TQ 3286 SE. (1952, 1970 edns.);

Stoke Newington, Official Guide (1959); Reg. of Electors (1945, 1953, 1954).
[62] Hackney Herald, summer 1976 (S.N.L. cuttings 14.016).
[63] Below, pub. svces.; prot. nonconf.
[64] Rest of section based on 'Listed Bldgs. 1952' and 'Listed Bldgs. under 1971 Act, 1974' (S.N.L. cuttings 55); E. M. Thomas, 'Study of Church Street' (N.W. Polytechnic Lond. teachers' certificate thesis, 1972, copy in S.N.L. 80); O.S. Map 1/1,250 TQ 3286 SE. (1980 edn.); 3386 SW. (1962 edn.); NE. (1966 edn.); NW. (1971 edn.); J. Summerson, Georgian Lond. (1945), 294.
[65] 'Official Opening 1972' (S.N.L. cuttings 57.2, LC 3161); J. Dailey, 'No. 83 Stoke Newington Church Street' (TS. 1972, S.N.L. cuttings 57.2).
[66] J. Dailey, 'Bilney Lodge, 135 Church Street' (MS. 1969, S.N.L. cuttings 57.2 BIL).
[67] From Tower to Tower Block, plate 8.
[68] Pevsner, Lond. ii. 431.
[69] Below, social.

Newington side of High Street, of which two were occupied by a tailor and a shoemaker respectively. A house (*domus*) was built in High Street in 1571.[70] Settlement was concentrated at the junction with Church Street in the 17th century.[71] A fine group of town houses was built north of the junction with Church Street in the early 18th century, one of which (no. 187), dated 1712, may have been built by the merchant Edward Lascelles,[72] whose daughters sold it in 1755 to John Wilmer (d. 1764). Wilmer, a wealthy Quaker, was buried in a brick vault in the garden with a bell attached to his wrist, for fear of being buried alive.[73]

In the 1740s buildings stretched from Church Street northward half-way to Hackney brook and southward to Cut Throat Lane. There were scattered buildings a little to the south, one of them the White Hart at the northern tip of South Hornsey detached, which had existed since 1723 and possibly since 1625. Farther south again there was a gap before the isolated Palatine houses.[74]

The Palatine houses were built following a decision by the parish in 1709 to house four families of Protestant refugees from the Rhine Palatinate.[75] In 1710 the parish estate was leased to Thomas Thompson, gentleman of Stoke Newington, on condition that he spent £100 on building.[76] One house subleased by Thompson in 1720 had been rebuilt as a substantial brick house by Thomas Slennet, a gardener, by 1736.[77] The White Lion existed by 1723 and in 1736 a piece of the parish field was leased to a Shoreditch bricklayer,[78] who had built one house by 1738[79] and three by 1740. At that date the Palatine houses consisted of the large house built by Slennet, the White Lion, three other houses, and the three recently built.[80] There were nine houses by 1752[81] and ten (two of them described as new) by 1782.[82] There were two taverns on the estate in the mid 18th century, one probably the ancestor of the Hare and Hounds, which by the end of the century was in the middle of a terrace fronting the London road. One large house, Palatine House, lay well back from the main road on the north of the estate and four cottages ran back from the road at the southern border.[83] In 1781–2 Palatine House was occupied by Charles Greenwood, a London upholsterer, and used as a retreat by his friend John Wesley.[84] The largest and most northerly of the terraced houses may

formerly have been the White Lion but by 1781–2 was occupied by Thomas Ellis (d. 1802), a stockbroker.[85] In the 1820s the Quaker Anna Sewell (1820–78), author of *Black Beauty*, lived with her mother Mary (1797–1884), herself an author, in the converted coach house west of Palatine House. The Sewells remembered it as 'very pretty', with 4 a. of garden and meadow.[86] In 1830 a 'proper public house' was built on the site of the Hare and Hounds.[87]

Two cottages were built by 1774 abutting southward on South Hornsey.[88] There were 43 houses fronting the London road in 1781–2, of which 13, including the Three Crowns, lay north of the junction with Church Street; 30, including the Green Dragon, stretched southward, of which 10 were on the Palatine estate.[89] By 1796 there were 17 houses, including 10 in Diapason Row, on the Hornsey estate, where there had been one or two in the 1740s.[90]

In 1801 the Green Dragon and two houses were acquired by Richard Payne (d. 1809) of Rochester, who built the 'Rochester Castle' and Rochester Terrace on their site.[91] In 1813 his daughters owned some 50 houses and cottages in courts, alleys, and terraces on High Street between Church Street and the White Hart.[92] In 1804 the Stonefields estate in the southern corner of the parish was acquired by the auctioneer John Graham, whose agreement with the lords of the manor in 1805 enabled him to begin large-scale building.[93] He had built Nelson Terrace fronting Stoke Newington Road by 1810,[94] and by 1814 building was continuous from Kingsland to the Hornsey border.[95]

Between 1801 and 1813 two cottages were built in Chapel Court and by 1833 there were five, described as newly erected.[96] Manor Road had been driven westward from Stamford Hill by 1827[97] and Thomas Maughan had built semi-detached houses fronting Stamford Hill by 1829, although his plan for a terrace between them and Hackney brook was frustrated by the dangerously projecting bridge. Freshfield had built houses south of the brook by 1830[98] and they apparently made way in the 1840s for Abney Park cemetery with its lodges.[99] Between 1829 and 1841 houses were built bordering the London road in South Hornsey, Victoria Grove and Road being constructed, presumably in or after 1837, as side roads, together with the Victoria tavern and cottages in terraces, places, and courts off the

[70] Guildhall MS. 14233/1.
[71] Ogilby, *Map of Mdx.* [1677].
[72] Date on rainwater head; M.L.R. 1720/4/84.
[73] J. Dailey, 'No. 187 Stoke Newington High St.' (TS. 1969, S.N.L. cuttings 57.2); S.N.L. cuttings 78 Wilmer, LC 1882, 2036).
[74] Rocque, *Map of Lond.* (1741–5); below, social.
[75] Vestry mins. 1681–1743, 129, 131; below, other est.
[76] Vestry mins. 1681–1743, 141.
[77] M.L.R. 1721/1/325; 1736/3/448.
[78] Ibid. 1736/4/239.
[79] Ibid. 1738/1/333.
[80] Vestry mins. 1681–1743, 466.
[81] J. R. Spratling, *Hist. of Palatine Estate* (Stoke Newington Recs.), 21–2.
[82] Guide for assessors of par. 1781–2.
[83] Spratling, *Palatine Estate*, plan (1797) facing p. 24.
[84] Guide for assessors of par. 1781–2; J. Vickers and B. Young, *Methodist Guide to Lond. and SE.* 27.
[85] Guide for assessors of par. 1781–2; Spratling, *Palatine*

Estate, plan (1797) facing p. 24; Robinson, *Stoke Newington*, 180; M.L.R. 1782/3/95.
[86] *D.N.B.*; Mrs. Bayly, *Life and Letters of Mrs. Sewell* (1889), 61–3.
[87] Spratling, *Palatine Estate*, 27; Shepherd watercolour (HA WP 8628). [88] Marcham, Digest, pt. 1.
[89] Guide for assessors of par. 1781–2.
[90] Guildhall MS. CC. 184832; G.L.R.O., MR/DE/HOR (map and award). [91] Marcham, Digest, pt. 1.
[92] Ibid.; ref. bk. to Wadmore map (1813), nos. 320–72.
[93] Above.
[94] Plan of turnpike roads from Shoreditch to Enfield, 1810 (copy in S.N.L.).
[95] Robinson, *Stoke Newington*, frontispiece map.
[96] Abstract of Ct. Rolls 1832–82, 321; ref. bk. to Wadmore map (1813), nos. 316–17.
[97] Guildhall MS. CC. 212291.
[98] *Cruchley's New Plan* (1829); Abstract of Ct. Rolls 1802–31, 307; G.L.R.O., MJ/SPB 457–65.
[99] Cf. tithe map.

main road.[1] On the Rochester estate seven houses, called Duke's Buildings, had been 'lately erected' in 1840.[2] Five houses were built in High Street in 1846 and another 13 in 1848-9, the latter probably including the terrace south of Abney Park cemetery.[3]

By 1851 there were 132 houses on the west side of the London road between Kingsland and Church Street, with another 65 in courts, yards, and alleys. North of Church Street there were 8 old and 11 new buildings, some still unoccupied, before the entrance to Abney Park. In Stamford Hill there were 10 on Maughan's estate.[4] Three more houses were built on Stamford Hill in 1852 and Maughan's terrace, south of his semi-detached houses, was probably built in the late 1850s, after the culverting of Hackney brook removed the dangerous bridge.[5]

On the South Hornsey part of the London road, Gordon Road was constructed between 1855 and 1861 and Walford Road between 1861 and 1870. Terraces on the London road were constructed during the same period,[6] as was the police station (1868) at no. 33 High Street and the Devonshire Square Baptist chapel (1870) at the junction with Walford Road.[7] Nelson Terrace was rebuilt in 1868-9,[8] and in 1873, when there were still only 15 houses and cottages on the Palatine estate, the trustees were authorized to enfranchise it, construct roads and sewers, and make building agreements. Palatine Road was constructed through the centre of the property and in the 1870s William Osment replaced the 18th-century houses (except Palatine House) and the Hare and Hounds with houses, shops, and a new public house.[9] Brighton Road was built through the site of Sisters Cottage at the southern end of the Hornsey portion by 1878.[10] Shops and houses (nos. 83-93 odd) were built in High Street in 1887. In 1894 three side roads were constructed on the remaining part of the Stonefields estate between Barrett's Grove and Palatine Road and 24 houses and shops were built fronting Stoke Newington Road, some on the site of earlier houses.[11] In 1899 the London school board's Princess May school replaced houses at the corner of Stoke Newington Road and Barrett's Grove.[12] In 1900 a 2-a. building site fronting the London road between Gordon and Victoria roads in South Hornsey was for sale.[13] In 1902 its

purchaser, the Four Per Cent. Industrial Dwellings Co., commissioned Dove Bros. of Islington to build a block of artisans' dwellings, completed in 1903.[14] Adjacent blocks were built by the company in 1915-18 in Coronation Avenue, which had been constructed in 1910, and Imperial Avenue.[15]

Throughout the 19th century the London road remained the principal shopping centre of Stoke Newington, full of crowds and traffic, its 'lively and bustling appearance' noted in 1826.[16] Merchants and brokers still lived there: at Palatine House in 1841,[17] in other Palatine houses, Nelson Terrace, no. 189 High Street, and Stamford Hill in 1851,[18] in Nelson Terrace in 1861.[19] A newspaper proprietor lived in Stamford House (? no. 191 High Street), a silk manufacturer and several retired people with servants in Stamford Hill in 1871.[20] Many buildings, particularly the larger houses, were taken over by institutions. In 1794 no. 187 High Street was occupied by a schoolmaster[21] and from 1832 until the Second World War by the invalid asylum for respectable women. No. 189 was in private occupation until 1864 when it became a dispensary, which it remained until after the Second World War.[22] No. 191 housed an infant orphan asylum in 1848,[23] reverted to residential use during the 1850s when it was occupied by the rector,[24] had become a girls' school by 1860[25] and a private house by 1871,[26] and from 1884 until the Second World War housed the London Female Penitentiary.[27] Many private schools opened in the London road.[28] Most of the smaller houses in High Street and Stoke Newington Road were occupied by retailers living above their shops, by clerks, dressmakers, craftsmen, and, especially in the cottages in the courts off the main road, labourers in the brickfields or nurseries. Small-scale industry occupied the upper floors and back yards.[29] At the end of the century the Alexandra theatre was built in Stoke Newington Road.[30]

At the beginning of the 20th century Stamford Hill, High Street, and Stoke Newington Road north of Gordon Road were classified as well-to-do, while the portion to the south was fairly comfortable. Several of the courts off High Street were moderately or very poor.[31] By 1915 the private schools had gone from the London road but several cinemas had been built.[32] Most of the courts were declared clearance areas in

[1] *Cruchley's New Plan* (1829); P.R.O., HO 107/663/4.
[2] Abstract of Ct. Rolls 1832-82, 333.
[3] Tithe (1848), no. 348.
[4] P.R.O., HO 107/1503/11/1, 3, 6; HO 107/1702/1/4.
[5] Above, communications.
[6] Miller, *Plan of Stoke Newington* (1855); *Cassell's Map of Lond.* (c. 1861-2); O.S. Map 1/2,500, Lond. X (1870 edn.); P.R.O., RG 9/791/4.
[7] Below, pub. svces.; prot. nonconf.
[8] Above.
[9] Spratling, *Palatine Estate*, 35-7, 41; *Endowed Charities (County of Lond.)*, H.C. 128, pp. 15, 18 (1897), lxvi, pt. 1.
[10] E. Stanford, *Map of Lond. & Environs* (1878).
[11] Hackney bd. of wks. *Surveyor's Rep.* (1894), 3; O.S. Map 1/2,500, Lond. XXX (1894-6 edn.); II. 15 (1915 edn.).
[12] Cutting Feb. 1899 (S.N.L. cuttings 55.4).
[13] Sales parts. 1900 (S.N.L. 60.5, LC 1638).
[14] D. Braithwaite, *Building in the Blood* (1981), 42, 129.
[15] *Reg. of Electors* (1914-15, 1918); *Kelly's Dir. Stoke Newington* (1900-23).
[16] *Pigot's Lond. Dir.* (1826-7), 492.

[17] P.R.O., HO 107/663/4.
[18] Ibid. HO 107/1503/11/1, 5.
[19] Ibid. RG 9/152/11/5.
[20] Ibid. RG 10/309/9/1A.
[21] Marcham, Digest, pt. 3.
[22] Tithe (1848), nos. 344-5. For asylum and dispensary, below, pub. svces.
[23] Tithe (1848), no. 346.
[24] Letters 1924, 1927 by dau. of Thos. Jackson (HA M 3784).
[25] Below, educ., private.
[26] P.R.O., RG 10/309/9/1A.
[27] J. Dailey, 'Stoke Newington in brief' (TS. 1972, S.N.L. cuttings 80, LC 3160).
[28] Below, educ., private.
[29] P.R.O., HO 107/663/4; HO 107/1503/11/1, 3; HO 107/1702/1/4; ibid. RG 9/152/11/4-5; RG 9/791/4; RG 10/310/9/1B.
[30] Below, social.
[31] Booth, *Life and Labour*, 3rd ser. (1), map facing p. 164.
[32] O.S. Map 1/2,500, Lond. II. 15, V. 3 (1915 edn.); below, social.

1933[33] and, together with part of High Street, demolished in 1936.[34]

There was some redevelopment after the Second World war. The Alexandra theatre was replaced by a probation office and flats (Alexandra Court) between 1954 and 1964 and most of the cinemas closed.[35] A block of flats, Hugh Gaitskill House, replaced nos. 35–9 (odd) Stamford Hill in 1964 and another, Ockway House replaced no. 41 about the same time.[36]

By the 1980s the run-down state of High Street which, with Church Street, constituted the town centre of Stoke Newington, provoked the borough council to declare nos. 183–91 (odd) High Street a development site.[37] Nos. 187–91 (odd), early 18th-century houses each of three storeys and five bays, formed an 'uncommonly impressive trio'.[38] In 1961 a preservation order was put on no. 187 but it suffered further damage in 1968[39] and during the 1970s,[40] despite efforts by the G.L.C. to save all three houses.[41] In 1976 shopkeepers complained that Stoke Newington had declined markedly in the last ten years, partly because the one-way traffic system diverted business to Dalston and partly because of the growth of Wood Green as a shopping centre.[42] In the same year a fire at Whincop & Son's timber yard at the junction of Church Street and High Street prompted the decision to pull down houses and shops in Aldam Place (behind the Three Crowns) and nos. 183 and 185 High Street and replace them by offices. No. 187 was refurbished and extended in 1983. No. 189, nearer the road and with a massive Victorian porch, was restored in 1982 as Newington House, 'unusually elegant offices'.[43] No. 191, also being refurbished and with additions made at the rear in 1901,[44] appears to have been built with a wide central passage dividing the ground floor. The only other surviving 18th-century building is no. 107 Stoke Newington Road, Palatine House, three-storeyed and with a large semicircular bay,[45] in a poor condition behind a housebreakers' yard.

Most of the buildings on Maughan's estate at Stamford Hill survive, including the terrace of nos. 1–19 (odd) which, standing well back from the road, is of three storeys with attics and basements and has paired Ionic porches. Some of the houses are used as industrial premises or are dilapidated but others are being renovated as flats. Other Victorian survivals include the

Egyptian-style entrance to Abney Park cemetery, dating to the 1840s, many terraces behind projecting shop fronts in High Street and Stoke Newington Road, and Oak Lodge, no. 127 Stoke Newington Road. Oak Lodge was built in the 1850s, a detached house on the South Hornsey estate.[46]

NEWINGTON GREEN.[47] Newington Green, first mentioned by name in 1480,[48] was fringed in the 1490s by cottages, homesteads, and crofts, at least on the three sides in Newington Barrow manor in Islington.[49] The northern side, all copyhold, was divided between the prebendal manors of Stoke Newington and of Brownswood in South Hornsey. By 1541 there was a common well on the green and there were houses on the northern side within Stoke Newington parish.[50] In the 1570s most if not all the area north of the green belonged to the London butcher Richard Heard. His estate included at least two houses and a cottage among the copyhold of Stoke Newington prebend[51] and a house among that of Brownswood. Heard himself probably lived in the Brownswood house, which was sited in 24½ a. of meadow and woodland on the east side of the green.[52]

No. 42 Newington Green, the large house belonging to the Brownswood estate, on the west side of Albion Road, possibly dated from c. 1680, had timber framing, and in 1870 contained oak panelling attributed to Grinling Gibbons[53] but probably some 60 years later. A Presbyterian (later Unitarian) meeting house replaced one or more houses in the centre of the north side of the green in 1708.[54] By the 1730s houses on the north side included the Golden Lion inn and a house which was leased to a carpenter by Edward Newens, the builder of much of Church Street.[55]

In 1742 the green, previously 'a most rude wilderness with large old trees' was railed in.[56] At that time building on the north side was continuous, except for Church Walk west of the chapel. Building had begun along the walk and there were isolated farmhouses to the west (on the Pulteney estate) and east (probably on the site of Heard's house).[57] In 1761 Newington Green was a 'pleasant village' consisting of a 'handsome square' surrounded by generally well built houses, with a row of trees on each side and an extensive grass plat in the centre.[58] There were

[33] Above.
[34] Stoke Newington B.C. *Ann. Rep.* 1936–7.
[35] O.S. Map 1/1,250 TQ 3385 NE. (1954, 1964 edns.); below, social.
[36] O.S. Map 1/1,250 TQ 3386 NE. (1953, 1966 edns.); MS. note by J. Dailey on Dod, 1979 (S.N.L. cuttings 32 DOD, LC 3717).
[37] *Hackney Boro. Plan, Stoke Newington Planning Area* (1982), SN 4-2.
[38] Summerson, *Georgian Lond.* 294; Pevsner, *Lond.* ii. 430.
[39] Pevsner, *Lond.* ii. 430; *The Times*, 9 Jan. 1968, 6g; S.N.L. cuttings 78 Wilmer, LC 1882; photos. (S.N.L. illus. 57.2 HIGH, LC 3011–20).
[40] List sent to Scotland Yd. of items stolen (S.N.L. cuttings 57.2, LC 3640).
[41] *The Times*, 12 Feb. 1971, 3c.
[42] *Hackney Gaz.* 25 June, 17 Aug. 1976 (S.N.L. cuttings 80, LC 3346–7).
[43] Pevsner, *Lond.* ii. 430; *Hackney Gaz.* 8 Oct. 1979 (S.N.L. illus. 57.2 HIG, LC 3644); *Daily Telegraph*, 5 Apr. 1982, 14 Nov. 1983.

[44] S.N.L. illus. 57.2 HIG, LC 3183; J. Dailey, 'Lond. Female Penitentiary & Guardian Soc.' (TS. 1977, S.N.L. cuttings 41.32, LC 3351); *Hackney Boro. Plan, Stoke Newington Planning Area* (1982), SN 4-2.
[45] Photos. (S.N.L. illus. 57.2 GRE, LC 628).
[46] P.R.O., RG 9/791/4; O.S. Map 1/2,500, Lond. X (1870 edn.).   [47] For the part in Islington, see above.
[48] *P.N. Mdx.* (E.P.N.S.), 159.
[49] G.L.R.O., M83/NB/1.
[50] Consistory of Lond. Rec., Bks. of Depositions and Answers, vi (1541), f. 22 (copy in S.N.L. letters 78 Arnold, LC 2123).   [51] Guildhall MS. 14233/1.
[52] P.R.O., SP 12/113/17; cf. ibid. STAC 8/182/21.
[53] S.N.L. illus. 57.6, LC 602; sales parts. 1870 (HA M 3895).
[54] Marcham, Digest, pt. 1; below, prot. nonconf.
[55] M.L.R. 1735/4/28; 1738/4/548.
[56] Lewis, *Islington*, 311; Stoke Newington, *Official Guide* (1950).   [57] Rocque, *Map of Lond.* (1741–5).
[58] R. & J. Dodsley, *Lond. and its Environs described* (1761), v.

some 11 dwellings and the chapel in the Stoke Newington part in 1781–2[59] and 5 houses in the Brownswood parts in 1796.[60] Among the inhabitants was Daniel Defoe (c. 1660–1731), who was educated at Morton's academy and in 1684 married a girl from Newington Green, where in 1692 he tried to raise civet cats.[61] Others included Abraham Price (d. 1756), the first manufacturer of wallpaper in England, and Rawson Aislabie (d. 1806), a former soapboiler from East Smithfield.[62] Thomas Holloway (d. 1827), the line engraver and painter, lived at no. 37 in 1797[63] and James Mill (1773–1836), the philosopher, lived from 1810 to 1813 at Newington Green, which his son John Stuart, then a small boy, described as an almost rustic neighbourhood.[64]

Three cottages were 'lately erected' in 1804 behind the meeting house, at the southern end of Church Walk, to be replaced in turn by two houses, Howard and Warwick houses, by 1854.[65] By 1809 there were four houses on the Pulteney estate, some at least of which had been built since 1784.[66] In 1821 the estate was sold for building but, apart from the construction of Albion Road to link Newington Green with Church Street, there was little immediate change at the green because the adjoining land was bought by James Browning, whose estate in South Hornsey centred on his house in the western angle of the green and Albion Road.[67] The north side of Newington Green retained an essentially 18th-century façade until the 1890s, although building in the 1870s on the Browning estate on the west side and on the Grove House site on the east made Newington Green part of one continuous line of building.[68] When Albion Road was widened at its junction with Newington Green in 1892, the two three-storeyed 18th-century houses between Albion Road and Church Walk were demolished and a bank in Italianate style was built on the narrowed site.[69] In 1893 an application was made to build the Mildmay club on the site of old houses at no. 34,[70] although the foundation stone of the present building is dated 1900.

In 1820 Newington Green was said to be principally inhabited by merchants and gentlemen,[71] of whom at least three owned land and houses on the Stoke Newington part of the green in the 1820s.[72] William Browning, who in 1841 and 1851 lived in the large house on the westernmost Brownswood portion, was an oil merchant.[73] In 1851 the inhabitants included capitalists and merchants, Dr. Robert Brett, the High Church general practitioner, and 13 servants.[74] By 1851 Grove House had been built on Brownswood land as a private lunatic asylum,[75] and in 1871 one of the houses on the green was a boarding school.[76] In 1888 one house was occupied by the East Highbury Liberal club.[77]

The green was still a middle-class, comfortable area in 1900 and 1930, but it was close to slums in the north-east[78] and in 1909 a factory was built adjoining no. 42 on the west side of Albion Road.[79] By 1929 all the buildings on the north side of the square, except for the bank, chapel, and Mildmay club, had become shops.[80] No. 42, at different times called Holland (probably after Edward Hollands who bought it in 1870)[81] and Olympic House, a three-storeyed, five-bayed, red-brick house with quoins, probably dating from the early 18th century with a later porch,[82] made way c. 1965 for factory buildings[83] which in 1983 stood empty behind the 18th-century iron gates and railings of the house. The chapel survives in 1983, together with the remaining 18th-century houses, nos. 35–9,[84] three- and four-bayed terraced buildings of three storeys with a plain façade, mostly hidden behind projecting shop fronts.

SOCIAL AND CULTURAL ACTIVITIES.

Stoke Newington probably had inns at an early date because of its position on a major road to London. There were 8 licensed victuallers in 1553[85] and the line 'To Hogsden or to Newington where ale and cakes are plenty' dates from 1613.[86] In 1679 respectable inhabitants complained that alehouses had lately 'very much increased'[87] and in 1716 there were only 5 licensed victuallers. The numbers increased to 9 in 1723 and 12 in 1751, but declined again to 10 in 1765, 8 in 1779, and 6 in 1800 and 1823.[88] By 1848 there were 8 taverns and two beershops.[89]

Le Bell on the Hoop or Hope existed in Newington Lane, possibly Church Street, in 1403.[90] There were at least two inns, the Rose and the Hind, on the west side of High Street in 1570

[59] Guide for assessors of par. 1781–2; *Bibliotheca Topographica Britannica*, ii, no. 9 (1783), 19.
[60] Guildhall MS. CC. 184832 (nos. 72–8).
[61] *D.N.B.*; B.L. Add. MS. 28094, ff. 165–6; above, Church Street; below, econ., industry; educ.
[62] Cuttings of Stoke Newington 1722–1895, pp. 3i, 5p (S.N.L. 80, LC 2411); *Mdx. & Herts. N. & Q.* i. 23; above, plate 44.
[63] Holloway letters (HA M 3781–2); List of Bldgs. in Stoke Newington having historical interest (TS. 1912, S.N.L. cuttings 57.2, LC 2231).
[64] *D.N.B.*; John Stuart Mill, *Autobiography* (1873), 6.
[65] Marcham, Digest, pt. 1.
[66] Abstract of title, Albion Rd. 1837 (HA M 3894); below, other est.   [67] *Cruchley's New Plan* (1829); above.
[68] O.S. Maps 1/2,500, Lond. X (1870 edn.); XXX (1894–6 edn.); above, plate 43.
[69] Photos. (S.N.L. illus. 80.9 NEW, LC 579–80).
[70] G.L.R.O., AR/BA 4/40, vol. 287, no. 22.
[71] *Ambulator* (12th edn. 1820), 234–5.
[72] Abstract of Ct. Rolls 1802–32, 278, 282, 290.
[73] P.R.O., HO 107/663/4; HO 107/1702/1/4.
[74] Ibid. HO 107/1503/11/2. For Brett, see below, churches.

[75] P.R.O., HO 107/1702/1/4.
[76] P.R.O., RG 10/311/9/1C.
[77] *Highbury, Stoke Newington Dir.* (1888–9).
[78] Booth, *Life and Labour*, 3rd. ser. (1), map facing p. 164; *New Lond. Life and Labour*, iv, Map of Eastern Area, sheets 1, 3.
[79] *Kelly's Dir. Stoke Newington* (1929); sales parts. 1923 (S.N.L. cuttings 60.5, LC 1718).
[80] *Kelly's Dir. Stoke Newington* (1929).
[81] Sales parts. 1923 (S.N.L. cuttings 60.5, LC 1718).
[82] Listed Bldgs. 1952 (S.N.L. cuttings 55); 1953 (S.N.L. 55). It is wrongly numbered 35 in Summerson, *Georgian Lond.* 294, and Pevsner, *Lond.* ii. 432.
[83] K. Janzon and A. Johnson, *Changing Face of Newington Green* (1977), 10.
[84] Listed Bldgs. under 1971 Act, 1974 (S.N.L. cuttings 55).
[85] Named: G.L.R.O., MR/LV1 [f. 15].
[86] *The Knight of the Burning Pestle*, 4. Interlude, line 54 in *Dramatic Works in Beaumont and Fletcher Canon*, ed. F. Bowers (C.U.P. 1966), i. 76.
[87] G.L.R.O., Cal. Mdx. Sess. Bks. vi. 22–3.
[88] Following three paras. based on G.L.R.O., MR/LV3/3, 103; LV7/8, 10; LV8/40; LV9/86; LV10/87; LV23/326–31.
[89] Tithe (1848).   [90] Lond. Mus. MS. 57.17/1.

and a wine tavern at Stamford Hill in 1600.[91] Other early inns were the Bull (1576–1624),[92] the Flower de Luce (1603–85),[93] the Cock (1608–25),[94] the Black Bull (1624),[95] the Sun (1624–1713),[96] the Spread Eagle (1658),[97] and the Three Pigeons (1678–92).[98]

A Green Dragon was mentioned in 1668[99] as at Newington Green but the main inn of that name, recorded from 1721, was in High Street.[1] It survived in 1801 but a new house, probably the Rochester Castle, had been built there by 1809.[2] The Three Crowns was mentioned in 1683 as 'formerly the Flower de Luce' but in 1687 as 'formerly the Cock and Harp' (fl. 1663).[3] It occupied the key position at the junction of the London road with Church Street and the name is said to allude to James I, who, on his way to take the English throne in 1603, first glimpsed London from Stamford Hill. The inn, a meeting place of the vestry in the late 18th and the early 19th century, was rebuilt c. 1871 and in 1898,[4] and survived in 1983. The White Hind (1625–87)[5] can probably be identified with the White Hart (1723), which was in High Street, within the detached portion of South Hornsey,[6] and survived as a Victorian public house in 1983. One of the Palatine houses was the White Lion in 1723[7] and was apparently one of the three taverns at the Palatine houses in 1765 called the Hare, the George (both licensed in 1751), and the Greyhound and Hare. About 1781 there were the Hare and the Hare and Hounds; the Greyhound was also mentioned but empty and had not been licensed in 1779, and neither it nor the Hare were licensed in 1800.[8] The Hare and Hounds was rebuilt in 1830 and in the 1870s[9] and in 1983 it existed as one of the Victorian public houses in High Street.

There were several inns in Church Street. The Rose and Crown existed by 1612.[10] The timber framed and gabled inn was replaced in 1815 and again in 1932 when it was moved to the west side of Albion Road where it survives in 1983.[11] The Red Lion stood on the north side of Church Street by 1697 and was in 1839 a meeting place for respectable tradesmen;[12] a public house called the Red Lion was still on the site in 1983. The Falcon, named in 1723 and almost certainly in existence by 1716 and rebuilt in 1854, stood on the south side until the 1930s.[13] The White Horse, in Paradise Row by 1734[14] and called the White Horse and Half Moon in 1765, had closed by 1779. Another, apparently short lived, White Horse was in Church Street in 1751.

There was an inn at Newington Green in 1614, possibly identifiable with the Green Man of 1668.[15] The Golden Lion existed on the north side of the green from c. 1735 to c. 1779.[16]

Public houses multiplied during the 19th century. The Rochester Castle had opened in High Street by 1813 and the Victoria in the South Hornsey part of High Street by 1839.[17] Manor House, which replaced the Three Crowns as the vestry's meeting place, was built at the junction of Green Lanes and Seven Sisters Road in 1832.[18] By 1848 there were two other taverns, the Pegasus and the Royal Oak, in Green Lanes,[19] the Horse and Groom on the south side of Church Street,[20] and two beershops on the southern border.[21] The Peacock in Park Street and a beershop, probably the Free Trader, in Edward's Lane, had opened by 1849.[22] By c. 1870 there were some 25 taverns and beershops in Stoke Newington and the detached portions of South Hornsey, many at the corners of new roads.[23] In spite of opposition, mainly from nonconformist Sunday schools and abstinence associations,[24] the numbers had reached 28 by 1905 and 37 by 1918.[25] Most still existed in 1980, when Victorian taverns with names drawn from England's royal and aristocratic families incongruously housed North London 'pop' groups and Rastafarians.[26]

In 1649 the manor house had a room for hawks.[27] For the gentler recreation of the City businessmen and dissenting ladies who were later lords of the manor, there was a bowling green at Abney House in 1783.[28] There were others at

[91] Guildhall MS. 14233/1; Lysons, *Environs*, iii. 296.
[92] *Acts of P.C.* 1575–7, 105; F. W. Baxter, note on inns named in burial regs. (MS. 1909, S.N.L. cuttings 23.1, LC 2283).
[93] Guildhall MS. 14233/2; Baxter, op. cit.
[94] P.R.O., C 2/Jas. I/W 5/46; Baxter, op. cit.
[95] E. J. Sage and J. R. Spratling, *St. Mary Stoke Newington. Extracts from Par. Reg.* (publ. in *N. Lond. Guardian*, 1888–9, S.N.L. 31, LC 2244). A Black Bull of 1707 was probably in Hackney: P.R.O., C 6/353/38.
[96] Baxter, op. cit.; Guildhall MS. 14233/2 (1683). Converted into 3 tenements by 1713: Guildhall MS. 14233/7.
[97] Baxter, op. cit.
[98] Guildhall MS. 14233/2. Converted into 5 tenements by 1692: ibid. 3.
[99] Baxter, op. cit.
[1] Vestry mins. 1681–1743, 230. In 1723 on road from Lond. to Ware (Guildhall MS. 14233/9); ho. of Wm. Chaddock, licensee 1779, was in 1781 at S. end of High Street: Guide for assessors of par. 1781–2.
[2] Abstract of Ct. Rolls 1763–1801, 222, 225; 1802–31, 246–7.
[3] Guildhall MS. 14233/2; ibid. 3; Baxter, op. cit.
[4] Guildhall MS. 14233/16, *passim*; 19, p. 1; *Portrait of Lond. Suburb, 1844*, item 16; *Kelly's Dir. Mdx.* (1871).
[5] Baxter, op. cit.; 'formerly the White Hind' in 1687: Guildhall MS. 14233/3.
[6] Listed s.v. Stoke Newington in licensed victuallers' returns for 1723, but not subsequently.

[7] Vestry mins. 1681–1743, 466.
[8] M.L.R. 1765/3/7; Guide for assessors of par. 1781–2.
[9] Above, the Lond. rd.
[10] Baxter, op. cit.
[11] *Portrait of Lond. Suburb, 1844*, item 13; Stoke Newington, *Official Guide* [1934], 27.
[12] Guildhall MS. 14233/4; cuttings of Stoke Newington 1722–1895, p. 7k (S.N.L. 80, LC 2411).
[13] *Kelly's Dir. Stoke Newington* (1929); *Kelly's Dir. Lond.* (1936); Abstract of Ct. Rolls 1832–82, 373.
[14] Vestry mins. 1681–1743, 373; M.L.R. 1738/4/150.
[15] *Mdx. Sess. Rec.* ii. 31.
[16] M.L.R. 1735/4/28.
[17] Cuttings of Stoke Newington 1722–1895, p. 8f; ref. bk. to Wadmore map (1813).
[18] Guildhall MS. CC. 282581; below, local govt.
[19] Tithe (1848), nos. 728, 744.
[20] Ibid. 544.
[21] Ibid. 932, 940.
[22] *Hackney and NE. Lond. Dir.* (1849); Guildhall MS. CC. 135628.
[23] O.S. Map 1/2,500, Lond. IV, V, IX, X, XVIII (1870 edn.); G.L.R.O., MA/C/L 1879/13.
[24] G.L.R.O., MA/C/L 1879/4–12.
[25] L.C.C. *Lond. Statistics*, xvi (1905–6), 212; xxvi (1915–20), 205.
[26] *Daily Telegraph*, 23 June 1975.
[27] Guildhall MS. 11816B, p. 128.
[28] Robinson, *Stoke Newington*, 38.

Morton's academy in the 1680s[29] and in Newington in 1737, where rules included 'no swearing on the green'.[30] There was a fight at Stoke Newington in 1759 between 'four noted bruisers', in which two women beat two men.[31] In 1798, in fear of a French invasion, Stoke Newington raised subscriptions and formed an armed association, which still met in 1803.[32] A cricket match took place in 1811 on Newington Green between teams of women from Hampshire and Surrey.[33] There was wrestling in the 1820s at the sluice house of the New River in Green Lanes, and on one occasion, when a participant failed to appear, the audience adjourned to a public house for dog-fights and rat-killing.[34]

Public houses were used for many social activities. The Golden Lion at Newington Green had skittle grounds in 1736.[35] Four houses, the Clarence, the Londesborough, the White Hart, and the Three Crowns, had billiard licences in 1879;[36] the Manor House converted its assembly room into a billiard saloon in 1883[37] and the Three Crowns built a bigger billiard room in 1898.[38] The Manor House had a concert room seating 300 from 1852 to 1903 and the Pegasus was licensed for music from 1852 to 1874.[39] A social club met at the Rochester Castle in 1839[40] and almost all the friendly societies met at taverns for, apart from a coffee house in the mid 18th century[41] and the assembly rooms of the 19th century, there were no other secular meeting places.

A box club existed in 1752.[42] The Rochester Castle was the meeting place of the True Brothers of Stoke Newington and Hackney Improved Birmingham benefit society from 1840 to 1866,[43] of the Ancient Order of Foresters from 1852 to 1868,[44] and of the Combined Friends of Stoke Newington Improved Working Man's Friend benefit society in 1861.[45] A provident and friendly society also met in High Street, next to the dispensary, in 1842[46] and the Pride of Stoke Newington met at the Londesborough tavern in Londesborough Road from 1860 to 1864.[47] Another Ancient Order of Foresters group met at the Falcon from 1863 to 1869[48] and the Hand and Heart United friendly society started meeting at the Freemasons tavern in Howard Road in 1863, moving in the same year to Allen Road where it remained until 1868.[49] Other so called Stoke Newington friendly societies met between 1802 and 1858 at public houses in Hackney.[50]

Much social life centred on the churches and chapels. In the 18th century the Unitarian chapel made Newington Green 'one of the cultural spots in London', as did the Quaker residents of Paradise Row in the early 19th century. In 1842 a conversation society, which was still flourishing in 1898, was founded at the Unitarian chapel, which formed a library about the same time.[51] Abney chapel had lending libraries for girls and boys from 1829 and 1834 respectively and a literary society from 1866.[52] The Quakers had founded Stoke Newington Mutual Instruction society by 1850 and it still flourished in 1863.[53] Libraries were formed at St. Matthias's by the 1860s, at Raleigh Memorial Congregational church in 1880, and at St. Mary's by the 1880s.[54] Lecture halls were attached to Raleigh in 1880 and to Devonshire Square Baptist chapel in 1890, and St. Mary's sponsored lectures on church history in 1900.[55] There was a society for theological study at the Unitarian chapel by the 1880s,[56] a literary society at the Presbyterian chapel from 1887,[57] another at All Saints' by 1913, and a dramatic society at St. Olave's in the 1920s.[58] Parish magazines were started by St. Mary's in 1882, St. Andrew's in 1884, St. Faith's c. 1885, the Presbyterian chapel in 1889, St. Matthias's in 1893, Abney chapel in 1896, and All Saints' by 1913. St. Mary's had a drum and fife band by 1882, St. Andrew's held subscription concerts in 1884,[59] and several chapels supported bands of hope, usually as adjuncts to their temperance societies.[60] There were sports clubs: cricket and cycling at the Unitarian chapel, football at Abney from c. 1886 and at St. Olave's by the 1930s, lawn tennis at St. Andrew's by 1889, and athletics at St. Faith's by 1901.[61]

The churches provided some support for the

[29] [S. Wesley], *Letter from a Country Divine concerning Educ. of Dissenters* (1703), 7; *Cal. S.P. Dom.* 1680–1, 307.

[30] Newspaper cutting, 1737 (S.N.L. cuttings 26.17).

[31] Cuttings of Stoke Newington 1722–1895, p. 3d.

[32] Ibid. p. 5n; vestry mins. 1784–1819, 239; Stoke Newington, *Official Guide* [1921], 36.

[33] *Illus. News*, Aug. 1885 (S.N.L. cuttings 26.17); S.N.L. illus. 80.27, LC 1254, 1477.

[34] *Morning Chron.* 15 Oct. 1824 (S.N.L. cuttings 26.1, LC 75). [35] M.L.R. 1736/4/351.

[36] G.L.R.O., MA/C/L 1879/9.

[37] Guildhall MS. CC. 282598.

[38] G.L.R.O., AR/BA 4/87, no. 57.

[39] D. Howard, *Lond. Theatres and Music Halls 1850–1950* (1970), 148, 174.

[40] Cuttings of Stoke Newington 1722–1895, p. 8a.

[41] G.L.R.O., MR/LV7/10 (1751); LV8/40 (1765).

[42] Robinson, *Stoke Newington*, 102.

[43] P.R.O., FS 2/7/2032, 3424.

[44] Ibid. FS 2/7/3054, 4349. [45] Ibid. FS 1/490/4074.

[46] Ibid. FS 2/7/2364. [47] Ibid. FS 2/7/3911.

[48] Ibid. FS 2/7/4249. [49] Ibid. FS 2/7/4253.

[50] Ibid. FS 2/7/924, 1052, 1057, 1436, 1654, 1679, 3527.

[51] H. G. Pritchard, *Stoke Newington and its Associations* (paper read to soc. 1898) (S.N.L. 80, LC 1260); J. L. Tayler, *A Little Corner of Lond.: Newington Green* (1925), 41, 44.

[52] A. C. Upstill, 'Hist. of Abney Cong. Ch.' (TS. 1962, S.N.L. 18.1, LC 3107); *Abney Quarterly* (1896) (S.N.L. 18.1, LC 1446).

[53] *Stoke Newington Mutual Instruction Soc., session 1850–1* (S.N.L. cuttings 50.2); *Ann. mtg. 1863* (S.N.L. cuttings 19.1, LC 2461).

[54] G.L.R.O., P94/MTS/35/1 (scrapbk. of St. Matthias, p. 53); *Bldg. News*, 11 June 1880 (S.N.L. illus. 18.1, LC 552, 3378); [*St. Mary's*] *Par. Mag.* (1882) (S.N.L. 14.01, LC 1485).

[55] *Bldg. News*, 11 June 1880; *St. Mary Ch. Monthly* (1900) (S.N.L. 14.01, LC 1503); below, prot. nonconf.

[56] M. Thorncroft, *Trust in Freedom: Story of Newington Green Unitarian Ch. 1708–1958* (pamphlet, S.N.L. 18.4, LC 2889).

[57] *Stoke Newington Presb. Ch. 'Our Work'* (par. mag. 1889–1901) (S.N.L. 18.5, LC 1552).

[58] *All Saints' Par. Mag.* (1913) (S.N.L. 14.07, LC 1587); B. Murray, 'Short Hist. of St. Olave's' (TS. 1969, S.N.L. 14.02, LC 3220).

[59] [*St. Mary's*] *Par. Mag.* (1882); *St. And.'s Monthly Paper*, Feb. 1884 (S.N.L. 14.03, LC 1563); *St. Faith's Par. Mag.* Nov. 1901, no. 187 (S.N.L. cuttings 14.05, LC 2227); *Stoke Newington Presb. Ch. 'Our Work'* (par. mag. 1889); *St. Matthias Par. Mag.* June 1983 (S.N.L. illus. 14.04, LC 617); *Abney Quarterly* (1896); *All Saints' Par. Mag.* (1913).

[60] e.g. Unitarian chapel: Thorncroft, *Newington Green Unitarian Ch.*; Presb. chapel: *Stoke Newington Presb. Ch. 'Our Work'*. St. Mary's also had a temperance soc. in 1881: [*St. Mary's*] *Par. Mag.* (1882).

[61] Thorncroft, *Newington Green Unitarian Ch.*; *Abney Quarterly* (1896); Murray, 'St. Olave's'; G.L.R.O., AR/BA 4/4, no. 24; *St. Faith's Par. Mag.* 1901.

poor, rivalling the friendly societies. St. Mary's formed a district visiting society in 1843 to promote self-help and encourage saving during summer employment, and in 1882 the society formed a sick club.[62] The Unitarian chapel ran a domestic mission society in the mid 19th century.[63] St. Matthias's had a work society to assist the poor in winter in the 1860s, a £20 provident society which met at the Freemasons tavern in 1865, and a home in Walford Road by 1871.[64] In 1880 St. Faith's formed the guild of St. Mary, a social club to advance 'all womanly virtues' and later the guild of the Holy Child, which collected toys for poor children.[65] St. Mary's working men's club started in 1881 in a room in Edward's Lane and moved to no. 106 Church Street, which opened in 1882 as the Amethyst club and coffee room. It soon had 80 members and in 1885 moved to larger premises at no. 110, where it remained until 1917. Also associated with St. Mary's were a girls' friendly society (1882), a day nursery at no. 99 Church Street (1884-1906) and then at no. 106 (1906-18), a working men's club at the Good Shepherd mission (1889), the order of St. Barnabas (1891) for 'work amongst rough lads', a perseverance guild, a guild of St. Ambrose to instruct confirmed boys in carpentry and similar skills (1892), and a guild of St. Agnes (1893) for girls.[66] There were young men's and women's provident societies at the Unitarian chapel and a young men's guild at the Presbyterian chapel in the 1880s;[67] the Abney brotherhood was founded in 1907.[68]

When Abney chapel was built in 1838 the old Congregational chapel on the north side of Church Street, between nos. 46 and 48, became Manor rooms,[69] the parish assembly rooms until new ones were built in Defoe Road in 1868. In 1872 additions were made to the Defoe Road rooms, which in 1905 were sold to St. Mary's for use as a mission room.[70] By that date a public hall at the public library in Church Street seated 550 and another hall at the Manor House public house in Green Lanes seated 300.[71] An assembly hall seating 616 besides 146 in the balcony formed part of the town hall buildings opened in 1937.[72]

There was a workmen's hall at no. 46 Back (later Boleyn) Road from c. 1871 to c. 1880[73] and an Eden hall at no. 127 Stoke Newington Road from c. 1876 to c. 1897.[74] By 1936 two halls had been built in Albion Road and Woodberry hall at no. 218 Green Lanes;[75] no. 59 Clissold Road, a former Mormon chapel, was opened as a hall of remembrance in 1945.[76] Manor Park club existed by 1884 at Grayling Terrace (later no. 49 Grayling Road);[77] it had a skittle club by 1904.[78] Stoke Newington social club met at no. 119 Stoke Newington Road from 1913 to 1915.[79] In 1914 a trust company was to acquire no. 7 Albion Grove as headquarters for the Stoke Newington Reserve. In 1934 the premises were leased to Stoke Newington club, primarily for ex-servicemen. The club had moved to nos. 25-6 by 1966 and had closed by 1968.[80]

Concerts and illustrated lectures on music were held at the Manor rooms in 1844.[81] There was a Stoke Newington book society in 1844, which met at members' houses.[82] Stoke Newington Literary and Scientific Institution, mentioned in 1847, was on the Hackney side of High Street and probably housed the society of that name which met in 1855.[83] In 1888 the rector proposed a society for the middle classes, since the lower classes were catered for but the young should be shielded from 'the temptations abounding everywhere'. As a result the Literary and Scientific association was founded, which met once a month, sometimes at the 'Mansion House' possibly Clissold House, until 1938.[84] A literary reading society, which included the local historian Francis William Baxter (d. 1932), met at no. 170 Church Street to read plays, lapsed in 1897 but revived again in 1902 and lasted until 1920.[85] The Amethyst literary and debating society was meeting at the Amethyst club by 1896.[86] In 1921 there was an attempt to found another debating society, Stoke Newington parliament.[87]

Stoke Newington and South Hornsey Conservative association had been founded at no. 179 Church Street by 1885.[88] By 1890 the premises had become the Primrose League institute and there were two other political clubs in Church Street, North Hackney Radical club at no. 83 and a Conservative club at no. 91. East Highbury Liberal club had opened at Newington Green, at the junction with Albion Road.[89] The Conservatives moved again, to no. 20 Church Street by

[62] [St. Mary's] Par. Mag. (1882).
[63] Thorncroft, Newington Green Unitarian Ch.
[64] Scrapbk. of St. Matthias, p. 53; P.R.O., FS 2/7/4419; Kelly's Dir. Mdx. (1871).
[65] St. Faith's Par. Mag. Nov. 1901.
[66] [St. Mary's] Par. Mag. (1882); MS. notebk. by Sister Annie Jefferson, in charge of Mission Ho. (HA M 3898); 'Amethyst Club' (TS., S.N.L. cuttings 14.016); J. Dailey, 'Site of Whitbread's brewery, Stoke Newington Church Street' (MS. 1976, S.N.L. cuttings 14.016, LC 3283).
[67] Thorncroft, Newington Green Unitarian Ch.; Stoke Newington Presb. Ch. 'Our Work' (par. mag. 1889).
[68] Notes on Abney chapel (S.N.L. cuttings 18.16 ABN, LC 2488).
[69] Beck, Church Street, 10; Kelly's Dir. Lond. Suburbs (1860).
[70] J. Dailey, 'St. Mary's Ch. Rooms, Defoe Rd.' (MS. 1968, S.N.L. cuttings 14.016); G.L.R.O., MBW/1628/104, no. 21.
[71] L.C.C. Lond. Statistics, xvi (1905-6), 198, 203.
[72] G.L.R.O., AR/BA 4/644, no. 36; Stoke Newington, Official Guide [1938], 26.
[73] Kelly's Dir. Mdx. (1871): Ellis's Dir. Stoke Newington (1880).
[74] Ellis's Dir. Stoke Newington (1876-7); Kelly's Dir. Stoke

Newington (1896-8). A mechanics' hall listed among institutions at no. 16 Church Street in Highbury, Stoke Newington Dir. (1885) probably refers to the Amethyst club (above) at no. 106.
[75] O.S. Map 1/2,500, Lond. II. 14, 15 (1936 edn.).
[76] Below, prot. nonconf., other denominations.
[77] Norris's Dir. Stoke Newington (1884); Kelly's Dir. Stoke Newington (1890).
[78] MS. programme 1904 (S.N.L. cuttings 24).
[79] Kelly's Dir. Stoke Newington (1912-16).
[80] Rep. of town clerk, gen. purposes cttee. 21 Oct. 1947 (HA SN/G 12).
[81] Programme (S.N.L. cuttings 54.3); poster (S.N.L. illus. 54).   [82] Notice of mtg. (S.N.L. cuttings 50.3).
[83] T. Kelly, Geo. Birkbeck, 314; corresp. with T. Kelly in S.N.L.; T. Jackson, Stoke Newington (lecture to soc. 1855) (S.N.L. 80, LC 1202).
[84] Min. bks. (HA D/S/31); The Times, 18 May 1922, 7g.
[85] Min. bk. and sec.'s record bks. (HA D/S/32).
[86] Programme (S.N.L. cuttings 50.3).
[87] Hackney Gaz. 29 June 1921 (S.N.L. cuttings 50.3).
[88] Highbury, Stoke Newington Dir. (1885).
[89] Kelly's Dir. Stoke Newington (1890); photo. of Newington Green chapel (S.N.L. illus. 18.4, LC 1485).

1920 and to no. 99 by 1925. In 1920 the Liberals were at no. 132 and by 1925 there was a Labour party at no. 99 Belgrade Road.[90] Mildmay Radical club opened in 1888 at no. 36 Newington Green Road (Islington) and moved to a newly built clubhouse at no. 34 Newington Green, near the Unitarian chapel, in 1893, when the vicar of St. Matthias castigated its 'pernicious influence among the young'. In 1930 it changed its name to Mildmay club and institute, and became non-political; in the 1950s it staged weekly variety shows.[91]

Stoke Newington borough had its own military band by 1910 and open-air concerts were held in Clissold Park by 1916.[92] A Stoke Newington choral society, existing by 1925, met in Upper Clapton, Hackney.[93] Stoke Newington schools' music association was founded in 1937 and survived in 1953.[94] Alexander Henry Chalmers (d. 1927), a local inhabitant, bequeathed paintings and other *objets d'art* to the borough council, with an endowment to add to the collection, which was exhibited in a gallery converted from the library hall in 1964.[95]

Stoke Newington was noted in the 1850s and 1860s for its garden flowers and still had many fruit trees.[96] The first English chrysanthemum society, later the National Chrysanthemum Society, was founded in Stoke Newington in 1846.[97] Flower shows were held in the large gardens of Stamford Hill in the 1870s and a horticultural society held its first show in 1911. Hackney, Stoke Newington and District fanciers' association, founded in 1914 for those who wished to breed rabbits and birds, met at the Amethyst club.[98]

Stoke Newington was playing cricket against Edmonton in 1866 and in 1869 there was a cricket club with its own grounds in Albion Road.[99] In 1900 Brownswood bowling club, established in 1871 in King's Road, Brownswood, in Hornsey, purchased Marlborough Cottage, no. 256 Green Lanes, with extensive grounds where it opened new greens in 1913. By 1936 it had tennis courts and a putting green but it had gone by 1940 when the site was purchased for Woodberry Down estate.[1] Another bowling club, called Clissold, existed by 1911 and was one of the first to play in

a public park.[2] Bethune lawn tennis and bowling club existed in Bethune Road by 1929.[3] Stoke Newington harriers, founded in 1881, had their headquarters at Clapton Common, in Hackney.[4] Pavilions were built by the lawn tennis association behind Fairholt Road in 1883 and by Queens lawn tennis club, which existed by 1890, in Princess Road, Brownswood, in 1922.[5] In 1929 Finsbury Park tennis club, founded before 1885, had courts in Queen Elizabeth's Walk, Mildmay Park Wesleyan guild had a tennis club in Church Walk, and there were also grounds in Clissold Road and Woodberry Down.[6] Stoke Newington rifle club, founded in 1907, opened a new range and headquarters in a converted factory at no. 49 Grayling Road in 1912.[7] Rifle ranges were added to the facilities of Mildmay club in 1907 and 1921 and to the premises at no. 7 Albion Road by 1920.[8] Stoke Newington schools' athletic association was formed in 1921 and held annual contests.[9]

After disruption caused by the Second World War, the borough council in 1946 joined with the L.C.C. to sponsor weekly lectures on the arts, with the intention of stimulating societies.[10] Clubs founded under the sponsorship of the council included the Mozart social club (which became the A. D. Saray club in 1972) at no. 66 Albion Road, a photographic society, a poultry and rabbit club, and a swimming club, all dating from 1946, a gardeners' guild (1947), a gramophone society 'soon after the war', the Progress Players (1951), and a library club for the blind.[11] There was an aquaria society by 1955[12] and societies for art, boxing, and cage birds, a Caribbean social club, and a variety club by 1959.[13] The Stoke Newington Society was founded after 1965 with the aim of rehabilitating Church Street.[14] An annual field day was held in Clissold Park from 1953, and from 1959 the borough held annual gala weeks, which were continued after 1965 as Hackney festival.[15]

The Alexandra theatre was built to the designs of Frank Matcham at nos. 65 and 67 Stoke Newington Road in 1897. It accommodated 1,710 and among those who played there in its early years were Henry Irving, Ellen Terry, Lily Langtry, and Dan Leno. Called the Palace Theatre of Varieties from 1906 to 1909, it was run by the

[90] *Kelly's Dir. Stoke Newington* (1920, 1925).
[91] Ibid. (1890–5); *Stoke Newington: Coronation of Eliz. II* (brochure, 1953 in S.N.L.); Nat. Soc. files, St. Matthias; G.L.R.O., AR/BA 4/40, no. 22.
[92] *Kelly's Dir. Stoke Newington* (1910–11); cutting 15 Sept. 1916 (S.N.L. cuttings 54.3).
[93] *Kelly's Dir. Stoke Newington* (1925).
[94] *Stoke Newington: Coronation of Eliz. II.*
[95] Stoke Newington pub. librs. cttee. *Chalmers Bequest* (pamphlet in S.N.L.); inf. from Hackney L.B. Directorate of Leisure Svces. (1982).
[96] J. L. Tayler, *Little Corner of Lond.: Newington Green*; sales parts. of ho. at S. end of Albion Rd. 1870 (HA M 3895).
[97] *Gardening from Which?* June 1983, 180.
[98] *Hackney and Stoke Newington Recorder*, 30 June 1911, 5 Dec. 1913; rules of assoc.; cutting 9 Nov. 1928 (all in S.N.L. cuttings 53).   [99] Cuttings (S.N.L. cuttings 26.17).
[1] G.L.R.O., CL/HSL/2/55; *Kelly's Dir. Stoke Newington* (1890); *Brownswood Ltd. Brochure* (S.N.L. 26); *Daily Sketch*, 28 Apr. 1913 (S.N.L. illus. 26.173, LC 2595); *Kelly's Dir. Lond.* (1939–40); O.S. Map 1/2,500, Lond. II. 14 (1936 edn.).
[2] *N. Lond. Guardian*, 28 Sept. 1911; *Stoke Newington Recorder*, 30 Mar. 1928 (both in S.N.L. cuttings 24).
[3] *Kelly's Dir. Stoke Newington* (1929).

[4] Cutting 1888 (S.N.L. cuttings 26.1; illus. 26.12, LC 1436).
[5] G.L.R.O., MBW 1721/197, no. 24; AR/BA 4/388, no. 33; *Kelly's Dir. Stoke Newington* (1890).
[6] *Highbury, Stoke Newington Dir.* (1885); *Kelly's Dir. Stoke Newington* (1929).
[7] *N. Lond. Guardian*, 1 Feb. 1907; cutting 29 Nov. 1912 (both in S.N.L. cuttings 24); *Daily Graphic*, 25 Nov. 1912 (S.N.L. illus. 26.25, LC 2594); G.L.R.O., AR/BA 4/249, no. 46.
[8] Official opening card 1907 (S.N.L. cuttings 24); G.L.R.O., AR/BA 4/373, no. 33; *Kelly's Dir. Stoke Newington* (1920).
[9] *Hackney and Kingsland Gaz.* 20 June 1921 (S.N.L. cuttings 26.1).
[10] *Evening News*, 30 July 1946 (S.N.L. cuttings 50).
[11] *Stoke Newington: Coronation of Eliz. II*; *Kelly's Dir. Lond.* (1945–6, 1971–2).
[12] Stoke Newington, *Official Guide* [1955], 20.
[13] Ibid. [1959]; Royal Commission on Local Govt. in Greater Lond. *Mins. of Evidence* (1959), 8, pp. 309–26.
[14] Ch. Com. file 6440, pt. 2 (letter from soc. 1972).
[15] Stoke Newington, *Gala Official Guide* (1959) (S.N.L. 22.4, LC 2655).

Alexandra Theatre Stock Co. from 1910 until 1912, when it housed variety and cinema shows. It became a cinema in 1917 but reverted to being a theatre in 1920, when it provided films, circus, and pantomime besides plays. It closed in 1935, reopened in 1939, and from 1947 to 1949 was the home of the New Yiddish Theatre Co. It closed again in 1950 and made way for Alexandra Court.[16]

Two cinemas[17] were built in 1911:[18] the Albion at no. 4 Albion Parade, Albion Road, which closed in 1952, and the Coliseum at nos. 31–3 Stoke Newington Road, which seated 600 and closed in 1972. Biograph Theatre Ltd., at no. 181 High Street just north of the Three Crowns, from 1911 to 1919, had opened a cinema there by 1915 but it had become billiard rooms by 1924.[19] The Apollo cinema opened with 1,080 seats in 1915 at no. 117 Stoke Newington Road, next to the Baptist chapel. Renamed the Ambassador in 1936, it closed in 1963, and housed bingo until 1974 when it reopened as the Astra. The Savoy cinema was built with 1,800 seats at nos. 11–15 Stoke Newington Road, south of the junction with Truman's Road, in 1935.[20] It was an ABC cinema from 1962 until 1977 when it became the independent Konak cinema.

The *Stoke Newington and Hackney Recorder* originated as the *Ball's Pond Advertiser* (1871–88), and was called the *Stoke Newington and Islington Recorder* (1897–1907), the *Hackney and Stoke Newington Recorder* (1908–26), and the *North London Recorder* (1926–39).[21] A weekly published in Church Street, it was in its early years 'fiercely blue' but by 1939 considered itself to have no political bias.[22] It was suspended in 1939 and later incorporated in *The Recorder* (1943–61). *The Hackney Monthly and Stoke Newington Review* (1920), founded in 1919 as the *Churchman's Hackney Monthly and Review*, was incorporated into the *Hackney Review and Stoke Newington Chronicle*, a twice monthly paper, in 1921 but closed in 1922. In 1924 the *Hackney and Stoke Newington Illustrated Leader* printed 28 issues. The *Stoke Newington and Hackney Observer* (1940–71) was founded in 1939 as the *North London Observer*, an independent paper printed in Manor Road and later in Allen Road and in Hornsey. The *Stoke Newington Citizen* was published monthly by the London Co-

operative Society political committee from 1930 to 1939. In 1983 the only local newspaper serving Stoke Newington was the *Hackney Gazette*, founded in 1869 as the *Hackney and Kingsland Gazette* and called the *Hackney Gazette and North London Recorder* since 1926.

MANOR. Although not mentioned by name in any extant Anglo-Saxon charter, *STOKE NEWINGTON* (Neutone) formed part of the demesne of St. Paul's cathedral in 1086, when the canons had 2 hides there,[23] and may have formed part of the 24 hides 'next the wall of London' which King Athelbert gave St. Paul's.[24] A prebendary of Stoke Newington was recorded from *c.* 1104,[25] and the manor, co-extensive with the parish, remained the property of the prebendary until vested in the Ecclesiastical Commissioners in 1843 under the Act of 1840,[26] except during the Interregnum when parliamentary commissioners sold it to the lessee.[27] In 1972 the Church Commissioners refused a request by the Stoke Newington Society to buy the lordship of the manor.[28]

The lordship, with all its profits, was leased to Thomas Gibbes, mercer, in the 1460s.[29] John Young, prebendary 1512–16, leased the demesne, the rents of freeholders, and the right to sell wood to Richard Lee.[30] In 1541 the prebend, without perquisites of court or woods, was leased to George Bysmore, a Londoner, to whom in 1545 a further lease was made, including the perquisites.[31] Bysmore was still lessee in 1549[32] but *c.* 1552 a lease was made to William Patten, teller of the Exchequer and humanist scholar. Writing in 1572 Patten referred to Newington where he had lived for almost 20 years.[33] He received a new lease in 1560[34] and another in 1565, for 99 years from 1576, of the manor, profits of courts, and woods.[35] Patten assigned the lease to Sir William Cordell, Master of the Rolls, from whom it had passed by 1569 to John Dudley, a rich brewer (d. 1580).[36] It passed to trustees for Dudley's young widow Elizabeth (d. 1602), who *c.* 1582 married the very wealthy Thomas Sutton (d. 1611), original of Ben Jonson's Volpone, and Dudley's daughter Anne.[37]

Anne's husband Sir Francis Popham (d. 1644)[38]

[16] R. W. Heasman, 'Alexandra Theatre' (TS. in S.N.L. 28, LC 3216); *Hackney Gaz.* 19 Sept. 1978 (S.N.L. cuttings 28, LC 3562); photocopy (ibid. LC 3561); G.L.R.O., AR/BA 4/78, no. 57; L.C.C. *Lond. Statistics*, xvi (1905–6), 187.

[17] Para. on cinemas based on *Kelly's Dir. Stoke Newington* (1911–29); *Kelly's Dir. Lond.* (1934 and later edns.); M. A. F. Webb, *Lond. Suburban Cinemas 1946–80* (priv. print., S.N.L. 28); inf. from A. C. Ward (1982).

[18] G.L.R.O., AR/BA 4/233, no. 46.

[19] O.S. Map 1/2,500, Lond. X (1915 edn.).

[20] G.L.R.O., AR/BA 4/622; L.C.C. *Lond. Statistics*, xl (1935–7), 196.

[21] Para. based on B.L. Newspaper cat. and *Willing's Press Guide* (1922 and later edns.).

[22] *N. Lond. Recorder*, 21 Apr. 1939 (S.N.L. cuttings O. 18.16).

[23] *V.C.H. Mdx.* i. 122, no. 29.

[24] *Early Charters of St. Paul's* (Camd. 3rd ser. lviii), pp. xxiv, 13–14.

[25] Le Neve, *Fasti, 1066–1300, St. Paul's, Lond.* 65.

[26] *Lond. Gaz.* 9 May 1854, p. 1439; 3 & 4 Vic. c. 113, vesting estates in Eccl. Com. on vacancy of prebend.

[27] Guildhall MS. (formerly St. Paul's MS. CA 9, pre-

bendal estates 1649–52, ff. 141–5); P.R.O., C 54/3472, no. 17; below.

[28] Ch. Com. file 6440, pt. 2.

[29] P.R.O., C 1/4/73.

[30] Ibid., C 1/449/9.

[31] Guildhall MS. 9531/12, ff. 119v.–120v.

[32] P.R.O., C 1/1251/14.

[33] B.L. Lansdowne MS. 739, f. 12v.; Guildhall MS. (formerly St. Paul's MS. C (Sampson), ff. 382v.–383). Robinson, *Stoke Newington*, 29, dates the lease 1550, which is not supported by his source. For Patten, see *Trans. Camb. Bibliograph. Soc.* iv (1964–8), 192–200.

[34] Guildhall MS. (formerly St. Paul's MS. A 40/1446).

[35] Ibid. (A 37/1114).

[36] Guildhall MS. 14233/1, s.vv. 1569–70, 29 Mar. 1581; P.R.O., REQ 2/222/41; which undermine the statement that Patten assigned the lease to Dudley in 1571, in Lysons, *Environs*, iii. 281, and Robinson, *Stoke Newington*, 29–30. For Cordell see P.R.O., PROB 11/63 (P.C.C. 15 Darcy, will of John Dudley); Robinson, *Stoke Newington*, 227 n.

[37] B.L. Harl. Ch. 79. G. 16; *D.N.B.* s.v. Sutton; *Aubrey's Brief Lives*, ed. O. L. Dick, 452–3.

[38] *D.N.B.*

was succeeded by his second son Alexander, a parliamentary colonel who purchased the manor in 1649[39] and obtained a new lease for three lives when the prebendal estates were restored in 1661.[40] The lease, renewed for lives in 1674, 1695, and 1700, passed in the direct line from Alexander (d. 1669) to Francis (d. 1674) and Alexander, who sold it in 1699 to Thomas Gunston, a merchant who had been buying copyhold in Stoke Newington since 1688.[41] Gunston (d. 1700) was succeeded by his sister Mary (d. 1750), wife of Sir Thomas Abney (d. 1722), lord mayor of London and a founder of the Bank of England, who obtained a new lease in 1701.[42] Leases for lives were renewed in 1730, 1732, and 1738.[43]

Mary Abney was succeeded by her only surviving child, Elizabeth (d. 1782), under whose will the lease of the manor was sold for the benefit of dissenting ministers. The buyer, Jonathan Eade, obtained a new lease in 1783[44] and died in 1811, leaving his interest to his two sons, William and Joseph, in common.[45] They obtained a new lease for lives in 1812,[46] and an Act in 1814 enabled the prebendary to grant a 99-year lease and the lessees to grant building subleases; the Act also allowed enfranchisement of the copyhold.[47] The prebendary leased the manor for 99 years to William and Joseph Eade in 1814.[48] William in 1815 assigned his moiety to Joseph (d. 1828),[49] who left the manor to trustees to sell on the death of his widow (d. 1862). Robert Henty, Joseph's son-in-law and the sole surviving trustee in 1862, postponed the sale and from 1864, after an action brought by the children of one of Joseph's daughters, the trustees continued to manage the estate under a Chancery Scheme.[50] Accordingly, a new 99-year lease to run from 1864 was made in 1868 to Henty and the Revd. Edward Eade.[51] In 1881 they sold the leasehold interest to the Ecclesiastical Commissioners,[52] who leased the manorial demesne piecemeal until the 1950s when they sold most of the freehold.[53]

The demesne occupied most of the land north of Church Street with the manor house at its southern end, next to the church.[54] In the 1930s the foundations were uncovered of a medieval building of chalk and Kentish ragstone and of a 16th-century brick house facing the church.[55] In 1558 the manor house was said to have been badly neglected and to have suffered from being 'utterly destitute of water'.[56] By 1565 Patten had carried out extensive repairs, especially to the outbuildings.[57] In 1590 when it was subleased to Sir Roger Townshend (d. 1590) and his wife, the house contained 20 chambers besides two dining chambers, a gallery, a kitchen, and outhouses.[58] The house in 1649 was of brick, containing a large hall, fair staircase, wainscotting, courtyards, gatehouse, and numerous farm and other outbuildings. Popham was resident in 1649 and possibly in 1664[59] but from 1672 to 1692 the house was occupied by John Upton; it was assessed for 25 hearths.[60] In 1695, alleging that it was too large, the lessees obtained permission from the prebendary to pull it down, and several houses, forming Church Row, were built on the site.[61] The eastern gate survived as a dilapidated Gothic structure until 1892.[62] The lessees moved to Abney House, built on their copyhold estate.[63]

OTHER ESTATES.[64] John Donnington (d. 1544), salter of London and member of a family which had connexions with London and Stoke Newington at least from the mid 15th century,[65] left his estates in Stoke Newington to his daughter, Margaret (d. 1561). Margaret's first husband Sir Thomas Kytson (d. 1540), mercer and sheriff of London, had a house and chapel in Stoke Newington, part of an estate held of the manor for 16s. 2d. a year. She afterwards married Sir Richard Long and, in 1548, John Bourchier, earl of Bath.[66] Kytson's estate was inherited by his son Thomas, and Margaret's jointly by Thomas and his half-brother Henry Long. In 1569 Thomas conveyed all his customary lands and tenements to Edward Tursett (or Turfett), longbow-stringmaker of London, to whom Richard Donnington quitclaimed all his rights in Stoke Newington in 1576.[67] By will proved 1590 Tursett divided his estates among his four sons John, George, Edward, and Stephen, who received land at Stamford Hill in Hackney;[68]

[39] P.R.O., C 54/3472, no. 17; Guildhall MS. (formerly St. Paul's MS. CA 9, prebendal estates 1649-52, ff. 141-5).
[40] Guildhall MS. (formerly St. Paul's MS. C (Barwick 1661-4), ff. 7v.-8).
[41] Ibid. (Sancroft 1670-7), ff. 235-7; (Tillotson and Sherlock 1689-1700), ff. 156v.-159; (Sherlock 1700-7), ff. 10v.-13; Guildhall MS. 14233/3. For the Gunstons see G.L.R.O., MR/TH/1, m. 31d.; Guildhall MS. 14233/2; Robinson, Stoke Newington, 36.
[42] Guildhall MS. (formerly St. Paul's MS. C (Sherlock 1700-7), ff. 49-52v.); D.N.B.
[43] Guildhall MSS. CC. 212277-9.
[44] Ibid. 212281, 212283.
[45] The eldest son, Jonathan Bowles Eade,, who lived in Church Street, was an imbecile: L.J. xlix. 740, 790, 795, 873.
[46] Guildhall MS. CC. 212285.
[47] 54 Geo. III, c. 128 (Local and Personal).
[48] Guildhall MS. CC. 2375.
[49] Ibid. 212288.
[50] Ibid. 212302; Ch. Com. file 30341, pt. 1.
[51] Guildhall MS. CC. 137921.
[52] Ibid. 212299; Ch. Com. file 30341, pt. 1.
[53] Ch. Com., Surveys S 2, pp. 911-14.
[54] Robinson, Stoke Newington, map facing p. 37.
[55] Stoke Newington M.B. Opening of New Municipal Bldgs. (1937) in S.N.L.; photos. (S.N.L. illus. 57.2 MAN, LC 850, 852, 857, 860-1).
[56] Guildhall MS. (formerly St. Paul's MS. C (Sampson), ff. 382v.-383).
[57] Ibid. (formerly St. Paul's MS. A 37/1114).
[58] Inventory of contents of residences of Sir Rog. Townshend (1590) (HA M 1528); D.N.B.
[59] Guildhall MS. 11816B, pp. 127-81; Robinson, Stoke Newington, 155.
[60] P.R.O., E 179/143/370, m. 38d.; Robinson, Stoke Newington, 48.
[61] Guildhall MS. (formerly St. Paul's MS. C (Tillotson and Sherlock 1689-1700), ff. 155-9; above, Church Street.
[62] Robinson, Stoke Newington, 56; [R. M. Panther], Old North Lond. (1928), 56; S.N.L. illus. 57.2 MAN, LC 637, 688, 1232, 3392-6; HA WP 8577; above, plate 42.
[63] Below.
[64] All the estates were copyhold of Stoke Newington manor.
[65] Guildhall MS. 9171/4, ff. 258v.-259; B.L. Add. Ch. 44737.
[66] P.R.O., PROB 11/30 (P.C.C. 3 Pynning, will of Donnington); Kytson Accts. 1566-7 (W. Suff. Rec. Off. E 3/15.51/1-2); D.N.B. s.v. Kytson; Complete Peerage, s.v. Bath.
[67] Guildhall MS. 14233/1.
[68] P.R.O., PROB 11/76 (P.C.C. 56 Drury).

George still had connexions with Stoke Newington in 1598 and his son was buried there in 1605.[69] In 1570, however, Kytson and Henry Long, as heirs of Margaret, herself described as heir of Thomas (*recte* John) Donnington, conveyed all their lands, which included some held from Stoke Newington manor for 2s. a year, to William Parker, draper of London, whose property in 1571 included a mansion house described as once Henry Long's.[70]

By will proved 1576 Parker, who was childless, left his capital messuage and other customary premises to his wife Agnes for life with remainder to William Parker of Coventry.[71] Within a year Agnes had remarried and in 1580 the younger Parker quitclaimed his rights in the property, identifiable from its borders as that held for most of the 17th century by the *CORBETT* family, to Agnes, her second husband, Humphrey Corbett (d. 1609) and his heir.[72] Agnes enjoyed the property, described in 1609 as a capital messuage and lands worth £100 a year, until her death at an unknown date, when it passed to Humphrey's nephew and heir, Rowland Corbett,[73] who was assessed for £5 on land in 1611-12.[74] In 1615 Humphrey Corbett, merchant of London, either Rowland's son or another nephew, was fined 20s. for the poor of Stoke Newington.[75] A Mr. Corbett had 20 a. in the parish in 1617 and 50 a. in 1639.[76] In 1638 Roger Corbett (d. 1639), another nephew, owned the estate,[77] which was held in 1657 by his son Edmund, merchant of London, when it totalled 21 a. Edmund (d. 1687)[78] mortgaged it to Mary Hobby, widow of London, who foreclosed in 1688, after Corbett's son Henry had been admitted.[79]

Mary Hobby (d. 1708) devised the estate to Humphrey Primatt (d. 1729), grocer of London, whence it descended to his sons Humphrey (d. 1740) and Nathaniel, a London chemist, who sold it in 1741 to Thomas Lingood, merchant of London. When Lingood became bankrupt in 1743 the estate was sold to James Ogilvie (d. 1757), whose widow Catherine married Rowland Johnson (d. 1773). It passed to Johnson's son William (d. 1790) and then to William's aunt Ann Nevill, who married William Carr (d. 1804)[80] as her second husband. Carr's daughter Martha had 23 a. of arable in 1813.[81] She enfranchised the estate in 1840 and by 1848 had leased it as brickfields to William Webb.[82]

There were several houses on John Donning-ton's estate[83] and Sir Thomas Kytson had a house and chapel in Stoke Newington.[84] In 1571 William Parker had two mansion houses: one he presumably lived in and the other 'once Henry Long',[85] one of them presumably the large house on the border of Hornsey detached in 1577.[86] Humphrey Corbett (d. 1609) had lived in a capital messuage,[87] which was owned by Edmund Corbett but empty when assessed for 7 hearths in 1664.[88] In 1693 Mary Hobby conveyed two houses to Edmund Corbett, who sold them in that year.[89] The conveyance included a footpath to the London road, which suggests that the houses probably joined the main estate, and one of the houses, once occupied by Ann Corbett and in 1693 apparently tenemented, could have been the mansion of 1577. Probably already dilapidated, it had gone by the 1740s.[90] There was no house on Martha Carr's estate in 1813 but cottages, probably for brickmakers, had been built by 1848.[91]

The *PULTENEY* estate, 60 a. in the southwest,[92] probably originated in the estate of John Stokker (d. 1502), who by will dated 1500 left two tenements in Newington Lane to William and Thomas Broughton and the rest of his copyhold in Stoke Newington to John Stokker Jekyll, his grandson in the care of his daughter Margaret and her husband William Jekyll.[93] John Stokker Jekyll (d. 1549) left his property, one great messuage, a cottage, and at least 32 a. in Stoke Newington, to his wife Anne for life with remainder to his brother Bartholomew, who disputed with Anne and her second husband Drew Barentyn.[94] Bartholomew, alive in 1559,[95] had been succeeded by 1569 by John Stokker Jekyll of London, perhaps his son, who in 1570 conveyed all his customary lands, three houses, and some 49 a. to Richard Heard. Heard, a London butcher (*lanius*), also acquired two houses, a cottage, and 10 a. at Newington Green from William Patten in the same year.[96] In 1577 Heard had a house and 28 a. of copyhold of Brownswood manor in Hornsey detached, the abutments of which show that he had land fronting the whole of the north side of Newington Green.[97] Heard (d. 1579) left his estate to his grandson Richard Heard, although his widow Alice, admitted to one third,[98] was apparently still in control in 1588-9 when she was assessed on £8 of goods.[99] Richard Heard had land in Brownswood manor in 1611[1] and by will proved 1628 left all his estates

[69] Ibid. REQ 2/222/41; G.L.R.O., P94/MRY/1, f. 48 (Burial Reg.).
[70] Guildhall MS. 14233/1; Kytson Accts. 1566-7 (W. Suff. Rec. Off. E 3/15.51/1-2).
[71] P.R.O., PROB 11/58 (P.C.C. 5 Carew).
[72] Guildhall MS. 14233/1; P.R.O., SP 12/113/17. Cf. ibid. C 142/314/129; *V.C.H. Herts.* iv. 8; G. Baker, *Hist. of Northants.* 335.
[73] P.R.O., PROB 11/114 (P.C.C. 114 Dorset). For Corbett's nephews and their descendants, see *Visit. Rutland, 1618-19* (Harl. Soc. iii), 3.
[74] P.R.O., E 179/142/284.
[75] *Mdx. Sess. Rec.* ii. 211.
[76] Robinson, *Stoke Newington*, 252-3.
[77] P.R.O., C 93/16/18; vestry mins. 1681-1743, loose leaves at front [1674].
[78] P.R.O., C 8/159/95.
[79] Guildhall MS. 14233/3; P.R.O., C 5/70/42; C 8/377/123.
[80] Marcham, Digest, pt. 2.

[81] Ref. bk. to Wadmore map (1813), nos. 395-7.
[82] Tithe (1848), nos. 504, 603, 622.
[83] Kytson Accts. 1566-7 (W. Suff. Rec. Off. E 3/15.51/1-2).
[84] *D.N.B.* s.v. Kytson.
[85] Guildhall MS. 14233/1.
[86] Depicted on map of 1577: P.R.O., MPF 282.
[87] P.R.O., PROB 11/114 (P.C.C. 114 Dorset).
[88] G.L.R.O., MR/TH 1, m. 37d.
[89] Guildhall MS. 14233/3.
[90] Rocque, *Map. of Lond.* (1741-5).
[91] Ref. bk. to Wadmore map (1813), nos. 395-7; tithe (1848), nos. 504.
[92] Guildhall MS. 14233/18, pp. 15, 52 sqq., 64.
[93] Ibid. 9171/8, f. 225; G.L.R.O., M 83/NB/1.
[94] P.R.O., C 1/1200/4; C 1/1237/47.
[95] *Cal. Pat.* 1558-60, 157.
[96] Guildhall MS. 14233/1; cf. P.R.O., C 3/100/15.
[97] P.R.O., SP 12/113/17.
[98] Guildhall MS. 14233/1.
[99] P.R.O., E 179/269/41.   [1] Ibid. STAC 8/182/21.

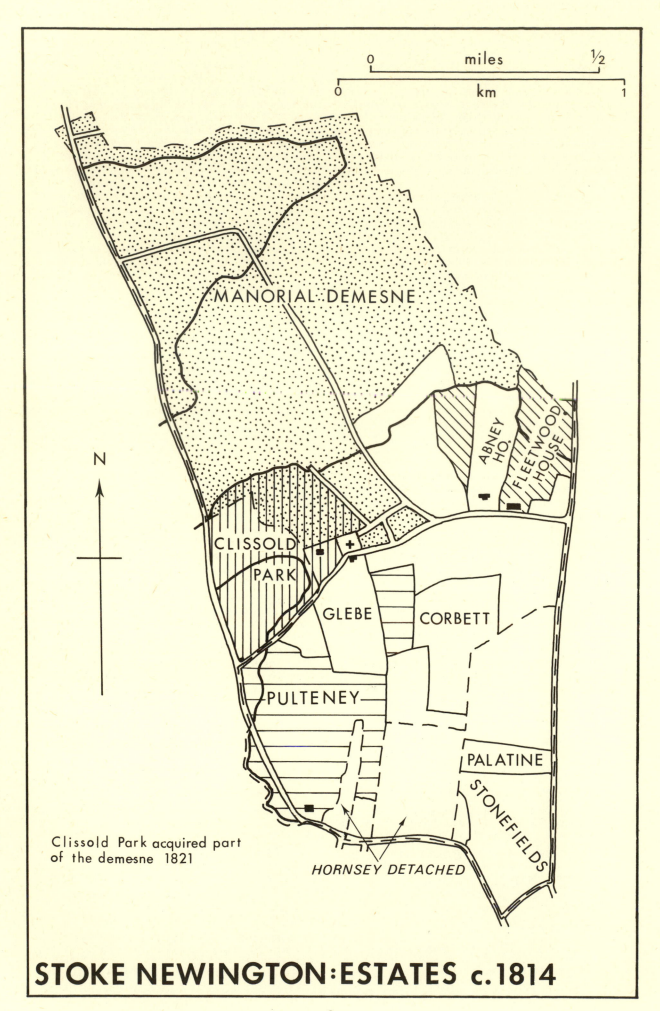

0   miles   ½

0   km   1

MANORIAL DEMESNE

N

ABNEY HO.

FLEETWOOD HOUSE

CLISSOLD PARK

GLEBE

CORBETT

PULTENEY

PALATINE

STONEFIELDS

Clissold Park acquired part of the demesne 1821

HORNSEY DETACHED

STOKE NEWINGTON: ESTATES c.1814

in Stoke Newington, Hornsey, and Brownswood to his wife Elizabeth towards payment of his debts.[2]

There is a gap in the evidence until 1677 when Henry Guy, M.P. and secretary of the Treasury, had property in Stoke Newington.[3] He died in 1711 seised of 60 a. which he left in trust for the heirs of Sir William Pulteney.[4] The beneficiaries were successively Sir William's grandson William Pulteney, created earl of Bath (d. 1764), presumably the earl's brother Harry (d. 1767), and Sir William's great-granddaughter Frances (d. 1782), wife of Sir William Pulteney (formerly Johnstone), whose daughter Henrietta Laura, created countess of Bath (d. 1808), was admitted to the estate in 1784. Henrietta's heirs were William Harry Vane, earl of Darlington, and John Paddy, descendants from Sir William Pulteney's daughter Anne. Paddy's share passed by will on his death in 1816 to John Brooks who in 1821, together with Darlington, sold the estate in lots for building and brickfields.[5]

There were at least two houses and a cottage at Newington Green on Richard Heard's Stoke Newington estate in the 1570s.[6] There was a farmhouse in Green Lanes by the mid 18th century[7] and there were three other houses on the estate at Newington Green by 1809.[8]

The *PALATINE* estate[9] was earlier called the parish lands or Gravelpit fields. The statement that it originated in a gift to the parish in John Stokker's will dated 1500[10] is evidently wrong.[11] The parish had 3 a. of land and 1 a. of wood in 1548,[12] which it probably owned long before 1500. John Stokker Jekyll in 1565 quitclaimed his right in a croft called Claydiches or Littlestones, which he held by lease from the churchwardens.[13] In 1638 the parish successfully claimed against the lord, Sir Francis Popham, 5 a. of pasture on the west side of the London road, which the parish had held time out of mind until Popham's seizure of the rent in 1623, using all the rent, subject to a quitrent to the chapter of St. Paul's, for the repair, ornament, and 'necessary occasions' of the church.[14]

The parish lands were leased at £6 a year during the 17th century, the right to dig gravel being reserved. In 1685 the vestry complained that the rent had been spent 'promiscuously' with other money by the churchwardens and ordered that it should be used only for the church.[15] The rent was raised to £7 in 1687.[16] In 1709 the parish agreed to settle four Protestant families from the Rhine Palatinate and built houses for them in the parish field.[17] The estate was leased for 99 years in 1710 and mortgaged in 1717 to raise money to enlarge the church.[18] Annuities charged on the estate in 1806[19] and 1816 were sold to raise money to repair the church and enlarge the churchyard. In 1809 a vestry committee rejected the surveyor's recommendation that the field should be leased for building.[20] The rent from existing houses,[21] however, under new leases from 1809, raised the income to some £312 a year.[22] In 1824 the income was being illegally applied to the repair of the highways, in 1827 the estate was again used as security for a loan to pay church expenses, and in 1828 new trustees were admitted at the manor court at a cost of £1,000, secured by a further loan.[23]

A Scheme of 1859 directed that property was to be let for terms of less than 21 years, that building leases might be granted, and that income was to be used for the repair and ornament of the parish church, with any surplus invested in stock.[24] Following enfranchisement in 1873 roads and sewers were laid out, houses built, and the income from the estate raised from £378 in 1873 to £839 by 1888.[25]

Resentment was expressed in 1854, 1879, and 1888 by the daughter churches that the income was used exclusively for the mother church.[26] Under a Scheme of 1888 the trustees were to include representatives of the daughter churches and to raise £6,000 by mortgage to repay existing mortgages and build the spire of the new St. Mary's; payments thereafter were to include £75 a year to each of the district parishes. When Stoke Newington became a municipal borough in 1900, the Palatine estate was handed over to the ecclesiastical vestries. In 1909 St. Mary's received £142 which it spent on the church.[27] By a Scheme of 1962 £100 a year each was to be paid to the parishes of St. Andrew and of St. Faith with St. Matthias and All Saints, any residue to go to St. Mary's. The £100 was raised to £500 by a Scheme of 1980. The income rose to £2,601 by 1966, of which £47 came from ground rents of five houses in Palatine Road and the rest from investments. The rents had shrunk to £37 by 1981, when the total income was £13,556.[28]

Sir William Terry (d. 1626), a London draper and the most highly assessed man in Stoke

[2] P.R.O., PROB 11/153 (P.C.C. 10 Barrington).
[3] Guildhall MS. 14233/2, s.v. 20 Nov. 1677; *Hist. Parl., Commons, 1660–90*, ii. 453–5.
[4] Guildhall MS. 14233/7, unpag. Para. based on Abstract of title, Albion Rd. 1837 (HA M 3894); Marcham, Digest, pt. 1; *Complete Peerage*, ii. 22–3, 27–8; iv. 82.
[5] Guildhall MS. 14233/18, 52 sqq.
[6] Ibid. 14233/1.
[7] Rocque, *Map. of Lond.* (1741–5).
[8] Abstract of title, Albion Rd.
[9] Para. based on Spratling, *Palatine Estate*.
[10] John Stow, *Survey of Lond.* ed. Strype (1720), ii, bk. 6, p. 132. Strype's source was a tombstone in the church.
[11] Guildhall MS. 9171/8, f. 225; Lysons, *Environs*, iii. 303; above, Pulteney est.
[12] *Lond. and Mdx. Chantry Certificates* (Lond. Rec. Soc. xvi), 72.
[13] Guildhall MS. 14233/1, s.v. 22 Oct. 1571.
[14] P.R.O., C 93/16/18.
[15] Vestry mins. 1681–1743, 15.   [16] Ibid. 19.

[17] Ibid. 129, 131–3; *Piety and Bounty of Queen toward Distressed Protestant Palatines* (1709) (copy in S.N.L. 41.1, LC 1629); above, Lond. rd.
[18] Vestry mins. 1681–1743, 141, 195.
[19] Robinson, *Stoke Newington*, 74.
[20] Vestry mins. 1784–1819, 393–4.
[21] For hos. on estate, above, Lond. rd.
[22] Robinson, *Stoke Newington*, 74.
[23] Marcham, Digest, pt. 1. When new trustees were last admitted in 1752, Eliz. Abney, lady of the manor, remitted the customary fine: *Table of Several Estates, Donations and Benefactions* (1793) (S.N.L. 41.1, LC 3113).
[24] *Palatine Estate Char. Scheme, 1859* (S.N.L. 41.1, LC 1289).
[25] *Rep. of Cttee. on Chars. 1873* (S.N.L. 41.1, LC 1295); Newspaper cutting Apr. 1888 (S.N.L. cuttings 41.106); above, Lond. rd.
[26] Newspaper cutting Apr. 1888 (S.N.L. cuttings 41.106).
[27] *Chwdns. accts. 1876–1910* (HA P/M/CW/3).
[28] Char. Com. reg. 250880.

Newington in 1611–12,[29] left his property to his son Thomas,[30] who had 65 a. there in 1639.[31] In 1648 Thomas sold some 60 a., mainly north of Church Street between the demesne and Stamford Hill, to Thomas Gower. Elizabeth Terry, spinster, and Judith, wife of Richard Lazenby, perhaps Thomas Terry's daughters and heirs, sold a house, barn, and two orchards in 1672 to Gower, who had acquired another tenement and appurtenances from Richard Gitters in 1667.[32] Gower, a London alderman who lived in Highgate, died in 1676 leaving a son Richard, also of Highgate,[33] who was succeeded in 1681 by his daughters Elizabeth, later wife of Edward Gold, a London merchant, and Anne, wife of William Rutland. In 1690 they sold the estate to Thomas Arnold and Thomas Gunston, a London merchant, who partitioned it between them in 1694.[34]

Gunston's portion, a house and 31 a., formed the core of the *ABNEY HOUSE* estate. He had bought a small estate in Stoke Newington in 1688[35] and acquired adjoining property in 1698 as part of an adjustment of boundaries with the neighbouring Fleetwood House estate,[36] and he purchased the lease of the manor in 1699.[37] He died in 1700, having settled all his copyholds on his sister Mary, wife of Thomas Abney.[38] Trustees sold some 8 a. to Nathaniel Gould in 1723 and 1726. After the death of the Abneys' daughter Elizabeth in 1782 the rest of the estate was sold with the lease of the manor to Jonathan Eade, whose trustees sold the Abney House estate separately in 1814 to James William Freshfield, a London banker.[39] In 1838 Freshfield enfranchised the estate and sold it to Abney Park Cemetery Co.[40]

Thomas Gunston's estate included two substantial houses. One acquired from John and Thomas Harris in 1688, had been occupied by John Gould or Gold, a mercer,[41] and was assessed for seven hearths in 1674.[42] The other, acquired from Richard Gower's daughters in 1690, once occupied by Thomas Wells, a victualler,[43] who in 1664 was assessed for six hearths[44] may have belonged to Thomas Terry before 1629.[45] Both houses were probably demolished when Thomas Gunston began to build a mansion house on his copyhold estate to replace the old manor house, demolished *c.* 1695. The house, which was unfinished at his death in 1700, took its name

from his successors. A red-brick building of seven bays and two storeys with basement and attics, set back from the road, it was described by Isaac Watts as 'solid and square'. A room contained panels with paintings of Ovid's *Metamorphoses* and Watts's paintings of flowers on the shutters and door.[46] Abney House remained the residence of the lessees of the manor until it was sold in 1814 to James William Freshfield, who lived there, when it was praised for the elegance of its interior.[47] It was rented by Wesleyans as the preparatory branch of their theological institute from 1839 to 1843[48] when the house was demolished[49] and the site added to the cemetery.

Thomas Arnold conveyed his share of the Terry estate, comprising a house and 27 a.,[50] to his son Thomas in 1696, and the younger Thomas (d. 1730) devised all his copyhold in Stoke Newington and Hornsey to his nephews Thomas King and David Lloyd.[51] King died in 1743 and his moiety passed to Edward King; King was succeeded in 1757 by his son John[52] who in 1789 sold his moiety of some 23 a. to Thomas Rigby.[53] In 1734 David Lloyd was succeeded in his moiety of Arnold's estate and in his moiety of Pride's (see below) by his sister Elizabeth Conway (d. 1768). On the death of Elizabeth's daughter Elizabeth in 1789[54] her interest in some houses in Church Street was sold to Jonathan Hoare[55] and in other houses and land to William Horton and the rest of her estate, houses and some 23 a., to Rawson Aislabie, who sold it to Thomas Rigby.[56] The combined moieties were sold by Rigby's devisees in 1817 to John Watson,[57] who secured the estate's enfranchisement in 1820.[58]

John Pride (d. 1678) and his wife Martha (d. 1679) had 5 a. of copyhold south of Church Street and west of the glebe, together with le Copthall or the church house. The estate passed to Gilbert Dean, who conveyed it in 1681 to William Hurst.[59] In 1693 Hurst conveyed one moiety of it to Susanna (d. 1721), wife of Thomas Arnold the elder, with remainder to her grandson David Lloyd (d. 1734), with whose moiety of Arnold's estate (see above) it descended. Hurst conveyed the other moiety in 1693 to Susanna's son-in-law David Lloyd (d. 1700);[60] Lloyd was succeeded by his widow Elizabeth (d. 1723) and she by their eldest son Thomas,[61] who in 1727 conveyed his

[29] P.R.O., E 179/142/284.
[30] Ibid. PROB 11/150 (P.C.C. 139 Hele).
[31] Robinson, *Stoke Newington*, 252–3.
[32] Guildhall MS. 14233/3, s.v. 1690; cf. abutments in Guildhall MS. 11816B, p. 129.
[33] P.R.O., C 6/275/53; C 10/115/55.
[34] Guildhall MSS. 14233/2, s.v. 1681; 3, s.v. 1690; 4, m. 1d.
[35] Ibid. 3.   [36] Ibid. 4, m. 4.   [37] Above, manor.
[38] Guildhall MSS. 14233/5, m. 1; 6, m. 1 and d.; P.R.O., PROB 11/458 (P.C.C. 179 Noel).
[39] Marcham, Digest, pt. 3; Guildhall MS. 14233/17, pp. 155, 158.
[40] Abstract of Ct. Rolls 1832–82, 345–6; below, pub. svces.
[41] Guildhall MSS. 14233/2, s.v. 1679; 3, s.v. 1688.
[42] P.R.O., E 179/143/370, m. 39.
[43] Guildhall MSS. 14233/3, s.v. 1690; 4, m. 1d.; Palmer, inventory 1695: *Hackney and Stoke Newington Recorder*, 1916 (S.N.L. 80, LC 1205); G.L.R.O., Cal. Mdx. Sess. Bks. ii. 42.
[44] G.L.R.O., MR/TH 1, m. 37d.
[45] P.R.O., C 3/416/128.
[46] Robinson, *Stoke Newington*, 56, 59; T. H. Shepherd's watercolours 1843: *Portrait of Lond. Suburb, 1844*, items 3, 4,

6, 7; HA WP 4453, 8563, 8578–9; above, plate 48; T. H. Shepherd's drawings 1843: S.N.L. illus. 57.2 ABN, LC 2, 411; engravings of ho. 1822, including staircase: S.N.L. illus. 57.2 ABN, LC 397–8.
[47] Robinson, *Stoke Newington*, 71.
[48] J. Vickers and B. Young, *Methodist Guide to Lond. and SE.*, 27.
[49] Auction poster for materials from ho. 26 July 1843 (S.N.L. cuttings 57.2 ABN).
[50] Guildhall MS. 14233/4, m. 1d.
[51] Marcham, Digest, pt. 3.
[52] Ibid.; Abstract of Ct. Rolls 1740–63, 110.
[53] Abstract of Ct. Rolls 1763–1801, 192.
[54] Ibid. 1740–63, 97; 1763–1801, 137, 188; Marcham, Digest, pt. 3.
[55] Abstract of Ct. Rolls 1763–1801, 188–9.
[56] Ibid. 189–92.
[57] Ibid. 1802–31, 268.   [58] Ibid. 1832–82, 337–8.
[59] Guildhall MS. 14233/2; Marcham, Digest, pt. 3.
[60] Guildhall MSS. 14233/3, s.v. 1693; 5, m. 1d.
[61] Abstract of Ct. Rolls 1675–1740, 96; Marcham, Digest, pt. 3.

moiety to John Nicholson.[62] Nicholson conveyed it in 1744 to George Green (d. 1764),[63] whose son George's mortgagee Duncan Davidson (or Davison) foreclosed in 1785.[64]

Jonathan Hoare, who as noted above bought part of the Conways' estate, also bought William Horton's share of that estate in 1790,[65] an interest in houses and land north of Church Street from John King in 1789,[66] and in the same year an interest in four houses which Henry Sanford had bought from Duncan Davidson in 1787.[67] In addition Hoare had by 1796 acquired of the demesne of Brownswood manor in Hornsey 28 a. which in 1577 had been held as Millfield by Richard Bowland of Newington[68] and 3 a. of copyhold of Brownswood, formerly the Conways'.[69] Hoare, in financial difficulties, mortgaged what was later called CLISSOLD PARK to Robert Pryor, who foreclosed and whose executors sold it in 1800 to Thomas Gudgeon.[70] Gudgeon, who from 1807 subleased some 10½ a. of Stoke Newington demesne on the north and east of his existing estate,[71] sold the estate to William Crawshay,[72] who in 1813 held 4 a. of Stoke Newington copyhold and 57 a. of leasehold, presumably in both Hornsey and Stoke Newington.[73] He held all Hoare's estate in Hornsey[74] in 1821 when he enfranchised the copyhold and purchased 19 a. of Stoke Newington demesne. In 1835 the estate passed to his daughter Eliza, who married the curate Augustus Clissold, whose courtship Crawshay had opposed. After Clissold's death in 1882 the estate reverted to the Crawshay family and George Crawshay sold it in 1886 to the Ecclesiastical Commissioners, who sold it in 1889 to the M.B.W. for a public park.[75]

The portion of the Terry estate allotted to Thomas Arnold in 1694 included a house, assessed for 7 hearths in 1674.[76] By the mid 18th century there were several houses on the north side of Church Street west of the church,[77] probably the four houses mentioned in 1723, which included one adjoining the churchyard and another lately built in an orchard.[78] It was probably one of these that Hoare was licensed to pull down in 1789,[79] the others being demolished by 1800 and in 1810.[80] On the site vacated by demolition

Jonathan Hoare's nephew Joseph Woods designed a seat for him, built by 1793[81] and part of the grounds was probably then converted into pleasure grounds.[82] A barn, stable, and farmyard survived on the Hornsey demesne in 1800 but had been converted to a coach house and stables by 1821, when the entire estate had been turned over to parkland.[83] The house was built with bricks made from clay dug at the northern end of the estate, forming hollows which were later made into lakes. Called Clissold House, it is of three storeys with five bays, flanked by one-bay wings, and has a Doric veranda on the main façade.[84] In 1983 the lower floors were in use as a cafeteria and for washing and changing facilities.[85]

FLEETWOOD HOUSE,[86] in Church Street, east of Abney House, was probably built c. 1634 by Sir Edward Hartopp, Bt. (d. 1658), an active Parliamentarian.[87] In 1664 his widow Mary (d. 1684) married Charles Fleetwood (d. 1692), the Cromwellian general and widower of Cromwell's daughter, Bridget (d. 1662). In 1695 Sir Edward's son, Sir John Hartopp, Bt. (d. 1722), settled the house on himself and his son-in-law Sir Nathaniel Gould (d. 1728), later governor of the Bank of England and M.P.[88] In 1711, when his daughter Frances Gould died, Hartopp settled 8 a. in the same way.[89] Gould enlarged the property with small purchases from his neighbours in 1712, 1723, and 1726, and in 1729 his daughter Elizabeth (d. 1763), wife of Thomas Cooke (d. 1752), a director of the Bank of England, was admitted to three houses and 18½ a.[90] Elizabeth was succeeded by her second cousin John Gould of Bloomsbury,[91] who sold the estate in 1763 to George Perrott (d. 1780), baron of the Exchequer. Perrott's sister Mary, wife of the Revd. John Terrett, as tenant for life under his will and his nephew George Perrott as reversioner sold the estate in 1797 to John Robley in trust for his father John the beneficial owner. By 1813[92] the elder John's widow Ann was in possession, the estate having been left in trust for his nine children. The younger John died in 1822 and George Robley, one of the trustees, was admitted in 1824. In 1827 he sold Fleetwood House and 10½ a. to the north and west to James William Freshfield and another 10½ a. farther

[62] Abstract of Ct. Rolls 1675–1740, 109.
[63] Ibid. 1740–63, 91.
[64] Ibid. 1763–1801, 123, 129, 171, 179.
[65] Ibid. 189, 196.
[66] Ibid. 192.   [67] Ibid. 183, 190.
[68] P.R.O., SP 12/113/17.
[69] Guildhall MS. CC. 184832, ff. 2v.–3v.
[70] Marcham, Digest, pt. 3; Memoirs of Sam. Hoare (1911), ed. F. R. Pryor, 25.
[71] Robinson, Stoke Newington, 291.
[72] Marcham, Digest, pt. 3.
[73] Ref. bk. to Wadmore map (1813).
[74] Guildhall MS. CC. 18432, ff. 2v.–3v.
[75] Marcham, Digest, pt. 3; F. W. Baxter, 'Rectors, lecturers, and asst. clergy of par. of St. Mary Stoke Newington' (MS. 1912, S.N.L. 14.013, LC 1902); J. J. Sexby, Municipal Parks (1898), 320–33; Ch. Com., Surveys S1, p. 613; below, churches; pub. svces.
[76] P.R.O., E 179/143/370, m. 39.
[77] Rocque, Map of Lond. (1741–5); Chatelain, NW. View of Newington, 1750 (S.N.L. illus. 80.5, LC 140); Hen. Overton, NW. View of Newington (above, plate 59).
[78] Marcham, Digest, pt. 3; Abstract of Ct. Rolls 1675–1740, 96.

[79] Abstract of Ct. Rolls 1763–1801, 190.
[80] Marcham, Digest, pt. 3.
[81] D.N.B. s.v. Jos. Woods; view by Wm. Ellis, 1793 (S.N.L. illus. 80 PAR, LC 3151).
[82] Marcham, Digest, pt. 3; Guildhall MS. CC. 184832, ff. 2v.–3v.
[83] M.L.R. 1800/5/103; 1821/7/147–8, quoted in Marcham, Digest, pt. 3.
[84] Sexby, Municipal Parks, 320–33; Pevsner, Lond. ii. 430.
[85] Inf. from head of parks and open spaces, Hackney L.B.
[86] Based on A. J. Shirren, Chronicles of Fleetwood Ho. (1951).
[87] The arms in the ho. included those of Hartopp and his wife whom he married in 1634: E. M. Thomas, 'Study of Church Street, Stoke Newington' (NW. Polytechnic Lond. thesis 1972, copy in S.N.L. 80).
[88] Guildhall MS. 14233/4, m. 2 and d.; Hist. Parl., Commons, 1715–54, ii. 74.
[89] Guildhall MS. 14233/7, m. 1.
[90] Marcham, Digest, pt. 3.
[91] Abstract of Ct. Rolls 1740–63, 118.
[92] Ibid. 1763–1801, 162, 212; ref. bk. to Wadmore map (1813).

north to Thomas Maughan. Both parts of the estate were enfranchised in 1838 and most of Freshfield's portion, east and west of his Abney House estate, was conveyed with it to the Abney Park Cemetery Co.[93] In 1848 John Freshfield possessed only the house and 1 a.[94]

Fleetwood House was occupied until 1766 by the numerous members of the Hartopp and Fleetwood families, who intermarried and formed two households by 1673.[95] Sir John Hartopp (d. 1722) spent much of his time there and in 1696 he engaged Isaac Watts as tutor to his son John, later the last baronet. In 1694 the house was described as formerly two, having been occupied by Smith Fleetwood and Nathaniel Gould respectively.[96] In the early 18th century Gould built an adjoining house to the west. The older house was mainly occupied by Sarah Hartopp (d. 1766) and her husband Joseph Hurlock and then let out. It was a girls' school from c. 1772 until the 1820s.[97] The Mercy family occupied it and about 1 a. of garden from the 1830s to 1872, first as a school and later as tenements for lodgers.[98] The western, newer part of the house was occupied, after Gould's death in 1728, by Elizabeth Cooke until 1763 and by George Perrott in 1770.[99] It was let in the 1780s[1] but one of the Robley family lived there in 1813 and 1824 and possibly in 1791.[2] A Quaker school opened there in 1824[3] but by 1838 the house was again in private occupation, by the St. Barbe family,[4] which was still there in 1871, when Mary St. Barbe ran a small school.[5]

Fleetwood House,[6] probably built c. 1634, of red brick, had extensive panelling, a fine staircase, large casement windows, and a ceiling ornamented with coats of arms. It was assessed for 15 hearths in 1664 and 25 in 1674,[7] probably after additions to accommodate the Fleetwood progeny. Shortly after 1766 the tenant Henry Guinard rebuilt the front of the older part in a Palladian style, which, together with the building erected by Gould early in the century, gave the whole house an 18th-century appearance, with three storeys, pediments, and some venetian windows,[8] although 17th-century features remained inside. By 1872 when it was demolished Fleetwood House contained about 60 rooms and was subdivided into tenements.[9] It made way for

Fleetwood Street and nos. 64–78 Church Street, built with its materials.[10] Some sections of plaster survived in 1983.[11]

STONEFIELDS[12] was a common field in 1460[13] but in 1638 and probably by 1617 was owned by Capt. Massey (d. 1649).[14] In 1682 George Hooper died holding the estate, then 30 a. of closes and parcels of pasture,[15] which were inherited by his son John (d. 1685) and then by his daughter Mary, who married William Twyford in 1686.[16] Twyford (d. 1729) was succeeded by his daughters Elizabeth (d. 1763) and Mary (d. 1769), wife of Robert Young. Elizabeth left her portion by will to her sister Mary, after whose death it was divided between Mary Young (d. 1778), spinster, and Martha (d. 1780), wife of James Davison, apparently daughters of Mary and Robert. Their son Robert (d. 1790), who succeeded to his mother's portion in 1769 and later to his sisters', left the estate to his daughters Martha (d. 1803) and Mary.[17] Mary succeeded to Martha's portion and in 1804 sold the whole estate to John Graham, auctioneer of Red Lion Square.[18] In 1808 Graham sold the south-western portion of the estate, 9 a. to James Kibblewhite and another 6 a. to John Hindle.[10] Graham (d. 1828) was succeeded by his son John Smith Graham (d. 1864), who was succeeded by his cousin Charles John Graham.[20] Kibblewhite's portion,[21] south of Graham's, descended on his death in 1853 to Robert Curling Cobb (d. 1866) and then to George Robert Green, Kibblewhite's great-nephew, who enfranchised it in 1881. Hindle, an auctioneer of Chancery Lane, whose portion lay between Cock and Castle Lane and Prospect Place, sold most of the land and houses facing Prospect Place to John Moore, chinaman of Holborn, in 1815 but still owned the rest in 1848.[22]

ECONOMIC HISTORY. AGRARIAN HISTORY. In 1086 Stoke Newington consisted of 2 hides of land, fully cultivated, for 2½ ploughs. There were 4 villeins, and 37 cottars on 10 a. The whole, belonging to St. Paul's cathedral, was worth 40s. T.R.E. and 41s. by 1086.[23] By 1329 the parish was apparently divided between the lord's demesne and the land of tenants.[24] The demesne,

[93] Marcham, Digest, pt. 3, including plans; Guildhall MS. CC. 212399; Abstract of Ct. Rolls, 1802–31, 278, 284, 296–8; 1832–82, 346–7.
[94] Tithe (1848), nos. 341–2.
[95] Guildhall MS. 9537/20, f. 16.
[96] Ibid. 14233/4.   [97] Below, educ., private.
[98] Pigot's Lond. & Com. Dir. (1834); P.R.O., HO 107/669/4, p. 25; ibid. RG 10/309/9/1A; Tithe (1848), no. 342; Marcham, Digest, pt. 3; T. H. Shepherd's drawing 1843 (S.N.L. illus. 57.2 FLE, LC 429).
[99] Cuttings of Stoke Newington 1722–1895, p. 4q.
[1] Guide for assessors of par. 1781–2; Marcham, Digest, pt. 3.
[2] Abstract of Ct. Rolls 1763–1801, 198–9; Ref. bk. to Wadmore map (1813); Marcham, Digest, pt. 3.
[3] Below, educ., private.
[4] Marcham, Digest, pt. 3.
[5] Tithe (1848), no. 341; P.R.O., HO 107/669/4, p. 25; ibid. RG 10/309/9/1A.
[6] Description based on Shirren, Chrons. of Fleetwood Ho.; N. & Q. 4th ser. ix. 296, 362–4; Robinson, Stoke Newington, 82.
[7] G.L.R.O., MR/TH 1, m. 37; P.R.O., E 179/143, m. 38d.

[8] Portrait of Lond. Suburb, 1844, items 10–12; HA WP 8027, WC 8567; T. H. Shepherd's drawings 1843 (S.N.L. illus. 57.2 FLE, LC 429, 1265–6); photos. (ibid. LC 385, 1295, 1654); above, plate 47.
[9] Beck, Church Street, 6–7.
[10] N. & Q. 4th ser. ix. 296, 362–4; O.S. Map 1/1,250, TQ 3386 NW. (1951 edn.).
[11] In HA.   [12] Based on Marcham, Digest, pt. 1.
[13] B.L. Add. Ch. 44737.
[14] P.R.O., C 93/16/18; Robinson, Stoke Newington, 252–3; portrait (S.N.L. illus. 78 Massey, LC 1066).
[15] Guildhall MS. 14233/2.   [16] Ibid. 3.
[17] Guide for assessors of par. 1781–2; Abstract of Ct. Rolls 1763–1801, 141, 159, 163, 195.
[18] Abstract of Ct. Rolls 1802–31, 232, 234.
[19] Cf. Ref. bk. to Wadmore map (1813).
[20] Graham's estate in 1848: Tithe (1848), nos. 864–84, 901–20, 1004–7, 1009–11, 1015, 1017–19, 1028–9.
[21] Tithe (1848), nos. 885–900, 921–32, 1023–5, 1030.
[22] Ibid. nos. 963–1003, 1012–14, 1016, 1020–3, 1026–7; Guildhall MS. 14233/17, 170, 195 sqq.
[23] V.C.H. Mdx. i. 122, no. 29.
[24] Guildhall MS. (formerly St. Paul's MS. B 103).

in the north part, was leased out by the 1460s,[25] and by the 1560s suffered from spoliation of the woods, lack of water, and dereliction of buildings.[26] William Patten, lessee of the manor, also acquired at least 40 a. of customary land, mostly bordering the demesne, which he conveyed to the Dudleys in 1570; most of it was subleased.[27] The demesne occupied 313 a. out of 536 a. (some 58 per cent) listed in 1617 and 1639. Of this, 77 a. was woodland, occupied by Sir Francis Popham himself, as was 45 a. of farmland in 1617. The rest of the demesne was divided among five tenants in 1617 and seven in 1639. The largest holdings were those of one Green (83 a.) in 1617 and H. Kempson (62 a.) in 1639. In 1649 Col. Alexander Popham had in hand 133 a. of the demesne, then said to total 323 a., the rest being divided among six other tenants, of whom one, Phillips, with 65 a., was the largest. The subleased demesne does not seem to have crystallized into farms, since acreages were constantly changing.[28]

From the late 17th century the demesne estate had been enlarged by copyhold land adjoining it on the south-east, which had been acquired by Thomas Gunston and on which Abney House was built. Subsequently the lords of the manor kept the copyhold (22 a.) in hand and created their park on it, while subleasing the demesne.[29] In 1715 some 286 a. of the demesne were leased to Thomas Arnold, who also held 24 a. of copyhold.[30] There is some controversy over a map of the demesne dated 1734 but omitting Church Row.[31] Buildings at the southern edge may represent the old manor house, which was demolished in 1695, and the map may have been copied from a much earlier one.[32] The map does, however, include the new course of the New River, dating from c. 1724, and the buildings may represent a home farm. By 1783 the demesne was divided into farms of 177 a. and 129 a., subleased to Thomas Porter and Henry Vernon respectively. Each was centred on a house on the north side of Church Street, presumably near Barn Street.[33] The division probably dated from the 1740s, and was in 1796 marked by The Old Cut, the original course of the New River.[34] In 1808 seven-year leases were made of holdings of 114 a., 60 a., and 45 a.[35] The largest holding, subleased to Thomas Jarman, was in 1813 subleased by him to Thomas Strong.[36]

The demesne was broken up after the Act of 1814 which permitted building subleases, although the expected building did not take place. By the 1830s the prebendary was complaining of a fall in the value of property, both as farmland and for housing. In 1835 there was some 265 a. of demesne.[37] By 1848 the largest subleases were of 55 a. to the New River Co. and of 50 a., but no farmhouse, to Edward Honeyball.[38]

Stoke Newington prebend was worth £3 9s. in 1254 and £28 in 1535.[39] The manor was valued at £487 a year above the reserved rent of £19 in 1649 and at £826 above the reserved rent of £28 in 1783. In 1814 the rack and ground rents of demesne land totalled £2,185.[40] Under the Act of 1814 the prebendary took a third of the manorial profits and the lessee two-thirds. In 1832 the prebendary's annual revenue was £1,450, of which £683 came from rack rents on demesne leases and £321 from ground rents on building leases, which were not as profitable as had been hoped.[41] From the 1840s and especially in the 1870s, however, they multiplied and in 1881 the Ecclesiastical Commissioners paid £180,000 to the Eade trustees for the leasehold interest.[42]

The rest of the parish, except for the glebe, was in 1814, and probably always, copyhold.[43] Cottagers, possibly descendants of the Domesday cottars, were mentioned in 1329[44] and rents of freeholders c. 1516,[45] although there is no other reference to freehold, except the rectorial glebe.[46]

Reliefs were paid on succession and entry fines on alienation in 1329.[47] In the 16th century the manorial customs included widows' dower right to a third of their husbands' property, admission fines at will, and the necessity to obtain permission to combine lands, cut down trees, or erect buildings; houses left in disrepair would be seized into the lord's hands.[48] By 1649 the fines at descent or alienation had become fixed at 1½ year's value and, together with other profits of courts, averaged £42 a year; the quitrents payable by copyholders at Michaelmas totalled £3 12s. 4½d.[49] In 1679 the lords were accused of demanding an entry fine of 3 years' value, contrary to manorial custom.[50] In 1783 some 64 copyholders paid £4 6s. 2d. a year in quitrents and fines and £174 6s. in fines and profits of courts. By 1814 some 90 copyholders paid £4 17s. 6½d. in quitrents and £766 in fines at death or alienation.[51] In 1805 and 1810 the lord agreed to building leases on some 30 a. of copyhold land[52] and the Act of 1814 allowed building leases of both copyhold and demesne

[25] P.R.O., C 1/46/73.
[26] Guildhall MS. (formerly St. Paul's MS. A 37/1114).
[27] Guildhall MS. 14233/1.
[28] Ibid. 11816B, pp. 127–32; P.R.O., C 54/3472, no. 17; Robinson, Stoke Newington, 250–3.
[29] Above, other est. (Abney Ho.).
[30] G.L.R.O., P94/MRY/81 (Statements on tithes, 1715).
[31] Robinson, Stoke Newington, map facing p. 37.
[32] F. W. Baxter, 'Old Man. Ho. of Stoke Newington' (MS., S.N.L. 57.2, LC 2839).
[33] Robinson, Stoke Newington, 39–40; draft index to par. ledger 1 (contemporary MS., S.N.L. 34.3, LC 2248).
[34] Letter from Wm. Greening 1796 (transcript of docs. in possession of New River Co., S.N.L. cuttings 46.2, LC 901).
[35] Robinson, Stoke Newington, 290–1.
[36] Ref. bk. to Wadmore map (1813), nos. 10–13, 15–17, 62, 81.
[37] Ch. Com. file 6438 (returns by prebendary 1832, 1835).
[38] Tithe (1848), 43–7, 78–9, 80, 85, 89, 104–5.

[39] Val. of Norw. ed. Lunt, 496; Valor Eccl. (Rec. Com.), i. 365.
[40] Guildhall MS. 11816B, p. 130; Robinson, Stoke Newington, 46, 295.
[41] Ch. Com. file 6438 (returns by prebendary 1832).
[42] Guildhall MS. CC. 212299. For leases of demesne after 1814, see Guildhall MSS. CC. passim, espec. 209277 (list of leases in 1873 but incomplete).
[43] Robinson, Stoke Newington, frontispiece map.
[44] Guildhall MS. (formerly St. Paul's MS. B 103).
[45] P.R.O., C 1/449/9.
[46] Below, churches.
[47] Guildhall MS. (formerly St. Paul's MS. B 103).
[48] Guildhall MS. 14233/1 (1579); Guildhall MS. (formerly St. Paul's MS. C (I Nowell), ff. 196v.–199).
[49] Ibid. 11816B, pp. 127, 132.
[50] P.R.O., C 6/275/53.
[51] Robinson, Stoke Newington, 39, 46–7.
[52] P.R.O., MAF 20/168, no. 2615; above, settlement and growth to 1870.

land. It also permitted enfranchisement, which took place throughout the 19th century, at least 140 a. being recorded in 1840.[53]

Thirty-three families were named on the single medieval court roll, for 1329.[54] Three, Pentecost, le Meyr, and Colyn, were also present in 1340[55] and there was still a Pentecost in Stoke Newington in 1449.[56] There were Salmans in 1329 and c. 1472.[57] One family may have been resident from the 1320s to the late 17th century: William atte Stoke was recorded in 1329 and the Stokkers, allied by marriage to the Jekylls, had property at least from the late 15th century to the 1570s[58] and may have included Thomas Stock (d. 1664), founder of the parish charity.[59] The Donnington family had connexions with Stoke Newington from the mid 15th to the late 16th century[60] and was one of several with interests in London. By the late 16th century, of 73 families mentioned in the court rolls, 10 were 'of London'. Some London merchants, like the draper William Parker, lived on their property in Stoke Newington, others, like Edward Tursett, subleased it.[61]

There seems to have been little continuity of either landowners or occupiers. Of 50 names in the late 17th-century court rolls, only three featured in those of the late 16th century.[62] Furthermore, only 20 of the 82 people assessed for hearth tax in 1674 were mentioned in the late 17th-century court rolls, suggesting a high proportion of leased property.[63]

Estates were small, the largest (outside the demesne) listed in 1617 and 1639 being those of Stephens (74 a.) and Thomas Terry, the elder and younger respectively (65 a.). Most were subleased, although Terry occupied 52 a. of his own land, some of it north of Church Street bordering the demesne lands, where he occupied 44 a. in 1649.[64] Among some 100 a. not listed in 1617 and 1639 was the estate held by the heirs of Richard Heard (d. 1579), who held some 87 a., including land in South Hornsey. After the Hornsey portion was sold probably soon after 1628, the 60-a. Pulteney estate was the largest in Stoke Newington; it was probably always subleased. Stephens's estate had broken up by the end of the 17th century and Terry's was divided in 1690.[65] Other estates were rarely more than 30 a. In 1813 the largest were those of Thomas Strong, lessee of all the farmland of the Pulteney estate and sublessee of most of 108 a. of demesne

leased to Thomas Jarman and part of 14 a. of the Abney estate. William Crawshay held some 60 a., which included the Hornsey part of Clissold Park. Edward and William Giles were lessees of 44 a. and 64 a. of demesne land. Thomas Rigby had 34 a. of copyhold, part of which he leased for market gardening, and William Rhodes held 31 a. from the Carr and Foy estates for brickmaking.[66] In 1848 the largest estate outside the demesne was the Abney Park Cemetery Co.'s 31 a. William Webb was lessee of 33 a. of brickfields from Martha Carr and Benjamin Massey. Augustus Clissold's 22 a., which he owned and occupied, were made up of copyhold and demesne land, which he had purchased.[67]

There were crofts and common fields, Onerefield and Goldbetesfield being named, in 1329.[68] Other common fields were Southfield, Northfield, Ikenfield, Stonefield, and Cukenfield(?) in 1460[69] and Conduitfield and Stirtlellfield in 1540.[70] The 'common fields of Newington', so called in 1571, included Northfield and Southfield.[71] Inclosure probably accompanied the conversion from arable to grass, Stonefield (later Stonefields) for example having been inclosed by 1682 and probably by 1617.[72] Closes belonging to Bartholomew Jekyll c. 1551 and to the Pulteney estate in 1678 included Winterfield.[73]

The lord's pasture was mentioned in 1329.[74] Cattle were common in the 16th century, on the demesne and on copyhold.[75] The lessee of the manor house in 1590 had two yoke of draught oxen, 14 kine and a bull, three yearlings, three sows and a boar and three small young pigs or 'shoattes'.[76] Presentments for converting tillage to pasture were made in the mid 16th century.[77] Wheat was grown in a close in Brownswood on Heard's estate in 1577[78] but in 1611 the estate was apparently entirely under grass for milk kine and horses.[79] A London butcher bought land at Newington Green in 1570[80] and in 1596 a grazier of Stoke Newington sold 57 sheep directly to a London butcher.[81] Hay and cattle were the main products of Thomas Terry's estate in 1629[82] and all of the 323-a. demesne, except 77 a. of woodland, was meadow or pasture in 1649.[83] In 1661 one London innholder leased land in Stoke Newington mainly for the hay, although he also kept cattle,[84] and in 1673 another bought the hay crop of a Newington estate.[85] Throughout the 12 years before 1715 no grain was grown on the

---

[53] Guildhall MSS. CC. 212398-9.
[54] Guildhall MS. (formerly St. Paul's MS. B 103).
[55] *Inq. Non.* (Rec. Com.), 199.
[56] Guildhall MS. 9171/4, ff. 258v.–259.
[57] P.R.O., C 1/64/410.
[58] Ibid. C 1/1200/4; 1237/47; ibid. E 179/141/131; Guildhall MS. 14233/1; G.L.R.O., M83/NB/1; *Cal. Pat.* 1558-60, 157.
[59] Below, charities.
[60] Guildhall MSS. 9171/4, ff. 258v.–259; 14233/1; above, other est. (Corbett).
[61] Guildhall MS. 14233/1.
[62] i.e. Stock (Stokker Jekyll), Johnson, and Wright: Guildhall MS. 14233/2.
[63] P.R.O., E 179/143/370, mm. 38d.–39.
[64] Ibid. C 54/3472, no. 17; Robinson, *Stoke Newington,* 250-3.
[65] Above, other est. (Pulteney, Abney Ho., Clissold Pk.); Robinson, *Stoke Newington,* 3-4.
[66] Ref. bk. to Wadmore map (1813).
[67] Tithe (1848), 338-40 (Cem. Co.); 504, 603, 622, 724

(Webb); 107-16 (Clissold, not including portion in Hornsey).
[68] Guildhall MS. (formerly St. Paul's MS. B 103).
[69] B.L. Add. Ch. 44737.
[70] P.R.O., C 1/1200/4.
[71] Guildhall MS. 14233/1.
[72] Ibid. 2; above, other est. (Stonefields).
[73] P.R.O., C 1/1372/25; Marcham, Digest, pt. 1.
[74] Guildhall MS. (formerly St. Paul's MS. B 103).
[75] Guildhall MS. 25626/1, ff. 23 and v., 40v., 123; P.R.O., C 1/1251/14.
[76] Inventory of contents of residences of Sir Rog. Towneshend (1590) (HA M 1528).
[77] At least 20 a.: Bodl. MS. Eng. Hist. c. 318, ff. 5–6.
[78] P.R.O., SP 12/113/7.
[79] Ibid. STAC 8/182/21.
[80] Guildhall MS. 14233/1.
[81] P.R.O., REQ 2/273/13.
[82] Ibid. C 3/416/128.
[83] Guildhall MS. 11816B, pp. 127-30.
[84] P.R.O., C 8/159/95.
[85] Ibid. C 6/58/1.

demesne. In 1707, of its 286 a., 186 a. were mown for hay. Twelve cows, with calves, were agisted, as were 12 horses for five weeks. The demesne also yielded 5 bushels of apples and 1 peck of pears, and supported a few hens and ducks.[86]

There was a grazier in the 1720s[87] and Stoke Newington was one of the places where butchers in the late 18th century selected cattle on their way to Smithfield.[88] The population was swollen in the summer during the 18th and 19th centuries by itinerant haymakers.[89] There was apparently no arable in the 1740s[90] and only a little, north of Newington Green, in 1800.[91] At the end of the 18th century, apart from 18 a. of market gardens, the whole of Stoke Newington was meadow and pasture supporting some 120 cows, whose dung helped to produce two or three crops of hay a year,[92] and in 1814 the 612 a. contained very little arable.[93] In 1848, excluding the demesne and glebe, there were some 270 a. in the parish, of which 40 a. were meadow and pasture; 36 a. of brickfield and 29 a. of cemetery had been grass-land from 1829 to 1835, 29 a. were under fruit and vegetables, and the rest was housing.[94] There were 8 a. of arable on the demesne and another 23½ a. may have been arable.[95] The brickfields, extending into the central detached part of South Hornsey, were exhausted by the middle of the century and for a short time the land supported a few cows kept by milkmen before it was built up as Albert Town.[96]

In 1831 four farmers employed labourers, of whom there were 40, and two employed none.[97] Part of the demesne was leased to a cowkeeper before 1837.[98] By 1851, when building was spreading over both demesne and copyhold, only two men were described as farmers' labourers; there were four cowkeepers, a cattle dealer, a cattle salesman, a drover, and a chaff cutter.[99] In 1861 there were cowkeepers in Barn Street, Meadow Street, and Green Lanes and a dairy-woman in Meadow Street.[1] In 1865 the driving of cattle through Church Street on Sundays caused great annoyance; it is not recorded whether they were local cattle or foreign cattle on their way to the market in Islington.[2] A cattle salesman lived in Green Lanes in 1871[3] and took leases of demesne land in 1878 and 1879.[4] By 1870 there were two farms of 20–50 a., one other agricultural

holding, and three people who kept stock but had no land. The farmland included 21 a. for hay and 36 a. of grazing, presumably supporting the parish's 32 milk cows, three other cattle, and four pigs.[5] In the 1870s cattle were grazed south of Burma Road, and Brooklands Farm had grazing rights in Clissold Park, where hay was also made.[6] By 1880 there were two agricultural holdings, 23½ a. of grass, 20 a. of other green crops, and four people keeping livestock, presumably the 37 milk cows, the only stock recorded.[7] No farming land was recorded in 1890, although six people kept 47 milk cows and five pigs.[8] In 1891 there were only three cowkeepers and 11 milk cows.[9] There were two cowsheds in 1903,[10] one of which closed in 1912[11] and the other between 1921 and 1925.[12]

NURSERIES AND MARKET GARDENS. The south-east corner of the parish, consisting of brickearth and gravel, more suitable than clay for horti-culture, was on the edge of the areas which, from the 16th century, supplied the capital with fruit and vegetables.[13] In 1597 a London fruiterer had by lease the apples, pears, cherries, plums, medlars, filberts, and barberries in an orchard in Stoke Newington, possibly belonging to the manor house, for 15 years.[14] In 1701 the orchard of Wentworth House had more than 36 fruit trees, including pears, apples, cherries, and wal-nuts.[15] In 1726 a house, probably in Church Street, had vines in the courtyard and a walled garden containing some 42 fruit trees, including apples, currants, and gooseberries.[16] A mer-chant's house in Paradise Row in 1755 had a large garden, with wall and other fruit trees, and a hothouse.[17] In 1722 Sir Nathaniel Gould's head gardener produced cucumbers at Fleetwood House two weeks before Christmas.[18] Less common was mustard seed, which was thrashed for Mr. Watkins in Newington in 1756.[19] In the early 19th century a show devoted entirely to gooseberries was held at Stoke Newington.[20]

Two gardeners of Stoke Newington were men-tioned in 1614[21] and the first Quaker meeting place in 1698 was the house of a gardener.[22] One living on the Palatine estate in 1724 built a house with a large garden nearby.[23] A gardener lived in Paradise Row in 1750[24] and in 1757 property near

[86] G.L.R.O., P94/MRY/81 (Statements on tithes, 1715).
[87] Thos. Lloyd: M.L.R. 1723/4/173, 193; 1726/5/319.
[88] P. E. Jones, *Butchers of Lond.* (1976), 103.
[89] Vestry mins. 1681–1743, 140; examinations before J.P.s. 1786–1806 (S.N.L., LC 2226).
[90] Rocque, *Map of Lond.* (1741–5).
[91] Milne, *Land Use Map of Lond.* (1800).
[92] Lysons, *Environs*, iii. 280; Middleton, *View*, 225, 560.
[93] Robinson, *Stoke Newington*, 3.
[94] P.R.O., IR 29/21/52.
[95] Tithe (1848), nos. 89–90. No. 80 was 'Gt. Footpath Field'. All other farmland was described as meadow.
[96] *Freeholder's Circular*, 1 Apr. 1852 (S.N.L. cuttings 41.8 ALB, LC 3573).
[97] *Census*, 1831.
[98] Guildhall MS. CC. 215114.
[99] P.R.O., HO 107/1503/11/2–6b.
[1] Ibid. RG 9/152/11/1–7.
[2] Vestry mins. 1862–89, 68.
[3] P.R.O., RG 10/309/9/1A.
[4] Guildhall MSS. CC. 212359, 212362.
[5] P.R.O., MAF 68/250.
[6] S.N.L. cuttings 32 Ormond, LC 2373.

[7] P.R.O., MAF 68/706.
[8] Ibid. MAF 68/1276.
[9] Ibid. MAF 68/1333.
[10] L.C.C. *Lond. Statistics*, xvi (1905–6), 94–5.
[11] Ibid. xxii (1911–12), 128–9; xxiii (1912–13), 162–3.
[12] Ibid. xxviii (1921–2), 76–7; Stoke Newington B.C. M.O.H. Rep. (1925), 602.
[13] F. J. Fisher, 'Development of Lond. food mkt'. *Ec. H. R.* 1st ser. v(2), 52 sqq.; L. G. Bennett, *Horticultural Ind. of Mdx.* (1952), 39.
[14] P.R.O., REQ 2/222/41.
[15] G.L.R.O., P94/MRY/83–4 (leases and schedule, 1701).
[16] Ibid. Acc. 212/3, 10.
[17] Cuttings of Stoke Newington 1722–1895, p. 3c (S.N.L. 80, LC 2411).
[18] Ibid. p. 1c.
[19] Ibid. p. 3n.
[20] H. Marsden-Smedley, *Chelsea Flower Show* (1972), 25.
[21] *Mdx. Sess. Rec.* ii. 31.
[22] W. Beck and T. F. Ball, *Lond. Friends' Mtgs.* (1869), 212.
[23] M.L.R. 1724/2/227.
[24] Ibid. 1750/3/750.

the White Lion in High Street passed from one gardener to another.[25] Market gardens occupied 18 a. in 1795[26] and 11 a. in 1848, when there were also 18 a. of orchards.[27] In 1851 there were 6 nurserymen, 2 seedsmen and florists, 1 market gardener, and presumably further market gardeners among the 49 gardeners most of whom were probably employed for the private gardens of large houses.[28] In 1851 there was a nurseryman and commercial gardener in the eastern part of South Hornsey.[29]

Thomas Rigby (d. 1816), who had property on either side of the eastern part of Church Street from 1775 and 16 a. of garden in 1813, which had been held since 1772 by another gardener, was the most important early market gardener.[30] Along the London road, particularly in the eastern part of South Hornsey, there were several nurseries in the early 19th century. The Ross family ran the Caledonian nursery in Stoke Newington Road from c. 1786, having some 25 a. of Hornsey land in 1796,[31] until c. 1840.[32] One of two other nurseries in the London road in 1830[33] belonged to William Watts and by 1855, as Brunswick nursery, was held by Thomas Watts in Middleton Place (no. 9 Stoke Newington High Street).[34] Thomas still had it in 1861[35] and, although the family connexion had been severed by 1876,[36] the nursery survived until the later 1890s.[37] Most of Watts's nursery ground was at the western end of Barrett's Grove and was built over after c. 1870.[38] Watercress beds near Barrett's Grove in the 1850s[39] were possibly still productive in 1871, when a watercress seller lived in Cock and Castle Lane.[40] Eden nursery, close to Watts's in Middleton, later Ross, Place, belonged to Robert Mackay from c. 1839 to c. 1860.[41]

John (Jackey) Milne leased land at the northeastern end of Albion Road from Thomas Cubitt, where he had a nursery by 1834.[42] It passed between 1842 and 1845 to John and Henry Brown,[43] who still had it in 1860, and survived in 1870.[44] In 1842 Milne also leased glebeland east of Church Path (Walk),[45] which by 1848 was described as 2 a. of garden ground, then leased by Henry Tyler.[46] In 1861 it was in the hands of Robert Oubridge,[47] who marketed geraniums[48] and founded a firm which survived until 1936, when the nursery was taken by Stroud Bros., who left in 1963.[49]

Other nurseries were those of Alfred Kendall, who leased 1¾ a. of demesne east of Queen Elizabeth's Walk from 1841 until his death in 1878 when the land was built over,[50] Charles Argent, with 2 a. on the west side of Park Street from c. 1845 to c. 1860,[51] and Robert Foot, with 6 a. of market garden on the east side bordering Abney Park cemetery from c. 1848 to c. 1859.[52] A nursery with watercress beds next to it, in Green Lanes north of Clissold Park, by 1848 was owned by Richard Bird.[53] Henry Bird had it in 1860[54] but by 1871 it had passed to Henry Stroud,[55] who renewed the lease in 1889.[56] Stroud Bros. remained at no. 182 Green Lanes until 1936 when the firm moved to Church Walk.[57] John West of Devonshire Cottages at the southern end of Green Lanes was a master florist employing two men in 1851[58] and still there in 1860.[59] Joseph Paxton, a gardener of Millfield Place, a little to the north, in 1851[60] was still in Green Lanes in 1876[61] and probably responsible for the large nursery north of the road near Newington Green from c. 1870 to c. 1894.[62] Manor Park nursery in St. Kilda's Road opened in 1889 and closed in the 1920s, although one greenhouse survived in 1936.[63] There were other nurseries at Grayling Road from c. 1895 to c. 1915[64] and Fairholt Road (Fernbank) from c. 1890 to c. 1894.[65]

Shirley Hibberd (1825-90), the horticultural writer, lived at no. 67 (later no. 12) Lordship Terrace, where he laid out the garden in 1858, and probably used Oubridge's nursery for his plant trials.[66]

MILLS. A watermill on Hackney brook near Green Lanes may be indicated by the name Millfield used of the land in Hornsey south of the brook in 1577.[67] In 1813 and possibly in 1735

[25] M.L.R. 1758/4/91. And cf. Stationers' Co. Apprentices 1701-1800 (1978), ed. D. F. McKenzie, 112.
[26] Lysons, Environs, iii. 280.
[27] P.R.O., IR 29/21/52.
[28] Ibid. HO 107/1503/11/1-6b.
[29] Ibid. HO 107/1702/1/4.
[30] Guide for assessors of par. 1781-2; M.L.R. 1775/7/320; ref. bk. to Wadmore map (1813).
[31] J. H. Harvey, 'Mid-Georgian Nurseries of Lond. region', T.L.M.A.S. xxvi. 298-9; Guildhall MS. CC. 184832, f. 6v.
[32] Pigot, Nat. Com. Dir. (1839); P.R.O., HO 107/663/4.
[33] Robson's Lond. Dir. (1830).
[34] Kelly's Dir. Mdx. (1855).   [35] P.R.O., RG 9/791/4.
[36] Ellis's Dir. Stoke Newington (1876-7).
[37] Kelly's Dir. Stoke Newington (1890, 1899-1900); O.S. Map 1/2,500, Lond. X (1870 edn.); XXX (1894-6 edn.).
[38] Tithe (1848), no. 930; O.S. Map 1/2,500, Lond. X (1870 edn.).
[39] Mary E. Shipley, Barbara Pelham [1906], 15.
[40] P.R.O., RG 10/309/9/1B.
[41] Pigot, Nat. Com. Dir. (1839); Kelly's Dir. Lond. Suburbs (1860).
[42] Robson's Lond. Dir. (1830); Cuttings of Stoke Newington 1722-1895, p. 7k (S.N.L. 80, LC 2411); Hobhouse, Thos. Cubitt, 47.
[43] Vestry mins. 1838-62, 120; tithe (1848), nos. 595, 600; P.O. Dir. Six Home Counties (1845).
[44] G.L.R.O., MBW 2120; O.S. Map 1/2,500, Lond. X (1870 edn.).   [45] Vestry mins. 1838-62, 120.

[46] Tithe (1848), nos. 663-4.   [47] P.R.O., RG 9/791/4.
[48] Country Life, clxvii, 13 Mar. 1980, 750-1.
[49] Kelly's Dir. Stoke Newington (1890-1929); Kelly's Dir. Lond. (1934-64).
[50] Ch. Com. file 6464; tithe (1848), no. 121; P.R.O., HO 107/1503/11/6, p. 97.
[51] Tithe (1848), nos. 262, 276; G.L.R.O., MBW 2120; P.O. Dir. Six Home Counties (1845).
[52] Tithe (1848), nos. 309, 313; Guildhall MS. CC. 121960.
[53] Tithe (1848), no. 105.
[54] Kelly's Dir. Lond. Suburbs (1860).
[55] Kelly's Dir. Mdx. (1871).
[56] G.L.R.O., MBW 1667, no. 21; Guildhall MS. CC. 245052.   [57] Above.
[58] P.R.O., HO 107/1503/11/2.
[59] Kelly's Dir. Lond. Suburbs (1860).
[60] P.R.O., HO 107/1503/11/2.
[61] Ellis's Dir. Stoke Newington (c. 1876-7).
[62] O.S. Map 1/2,500, Lond. X (1870 edn.); XXX (1894-6 edn.).
[63] Kelly's Dir. Stoke Newington (1890-1929); Sales parts. 1904 (HA M 3897); O.S. Map 1/2,500, Lond. II. 11 (1936 edn.).
[64] O.S. Maps 1/2,500, Lond. XXX (1894-6 edn.); II. 15 (1915 edn.).
[65] Ibid. XXI (1894-6 edn.); Kelly's Dir. Stoke Newington (1890).
[66] Country Life, clxvii, 13 Mar. 1980, 750-1; Evening News, 24 Apr. 1925 (S.N.L. cuttings 80, LC 113A); D.N.B.
[67] P.R.O., SP 12/113/17.

there was an old windmill on the Pulteney estate,[68] west of Green Lanes but within the Stoke Newington boundary.[69] It was in ruins by 1852.[70]

TRADE AND INDUSTRY.[71] There was a 'weye-maker' (?cheesemaker) in 1344[72] and hackneymen of Stoke Newington were mentioned in 1428, c. 1473, and c. 1540.[73] There were a tailor and a shoemaker in High Street in 1570,[74] an upholsterer and a needlemaker in the parish in 1612,[75] a tailor in 1614,[76] two carpenters in 1616, a coiner in 1617,[77] a joiner in 1665,[78] and a cordwainer in 1691.[79] In the 1690s 60–70 civet cats were farmed at Newington Green for the oil used for perfumery.[80] Gloves were washed and coloured in 1709 at a house in Church Street where lodgers were accommodated 'to encourage industry'.[81] Eighteenth-century inhabitants included a bricklayer and an armourer (1715),[82] a clockmaker (1746),[83] a staymaker (1758),[84] a carpenter (1775),[85] and several plumbers (before 1750, 1750, 1775).[86] In 1801 trade, manufacture, and crafts employed 53 people.[87] Shops in 1813 included those of 3 butchers, 3 carpenters, a baker, a smith, a plumber, and a stone mason.[88] In 1817 a building in Church Street had previously been a fruiterer's shop.[89]

There were some 140 shops and workshops in Stoke Newington in 1826, including the eastern, Hackney, side of High Street and Stoke Newington Road, of which 33 were in Church Street. They included a whitesmith, a builder, a bricklayer, and two painters but were mostly retailers, among whom were a fishmonger, a confectioner, a bookseller, a toy dealer, and a pawnbroker.[90] In 1831 retail trade and handicraft employed 290 people[91] and in 1834 the number of shops and workshops had risen to 211 including both sides of the London road. Among them were 3 hairdressers, 2 tobacconists, 4 pastrycooks, and an eating house in the London road and a hairdresser in Church Street.[92] In the mid 19th century tradesmen and small craftsmen still predominated over industry. They numbered 138 in 1849, of which 59 were in the Stoke Newington section of the London road and 55 in Church Street, and only a jeweller, a perfumer, and a hosier had been added to the categories of 1834.[93]

Shops remained important in the London road until well into the 20th century but industry, which apart from brickmaking had played a minor role until the later 19th century, grew with Stoke Newington's population. In 1826 there were a coachbuilder and a paper stainer in the London road[94] but in 1831 only three people in the parish were employed in manufacture[95] and in 1834 there was no distinguishing manufacture.[96] In 1841 there was a basketmaker and a coach painter in Diapason Row in the South Hornsey part of the London road.[97] Industry was still mostly concentrated in the London road in 1851. The Hornsey part, in addition to the coach painter, had 3 cabinet makers, a coach trimmer, a mechanic, a mason, and a printer's compositor.[98] The Stoke Newington frontage included 3 masons, a brewer, a coach painter, an envelope folder, a bedstead maker, and a staymaker. From the London road industry spread to Barrett's Grove, John's Place, and Back Lane (Boleyn Road), where there were several people employed in printing, a coachwright, and makers of cabinets, musical instruments, fishing rods, and dolls. In Church Street, where craft-based industry was beginning to grow, there was a whitesmith, an upholsterer, and makers of coaches, harness, cabinets, corsets, and straw bonnets. There were a few craftsmen in other parts of the parish, Lordship Road, Green Lanes, and Albion Road.[99]

From c. 1851 the skills of immigrants from the City and east end encouraged the establishment of a great number and variety of businesses. Among them were businesses in the clothing and furnishing industries, both associated with Jews, and printing, which moved out from Clerkenwell. Most firms were small and short lived, dependent initially on skilled craftsmen and later, with mass production, on cheap labour. In the 1850s and 1860s industry, in the guise of small craftsmen, proliferated especially in Albert Town and, to a lesser degree, in the eastern part of South Hornsey. In 1851 Victoria Grove had housed a timber worker and a printer's compositor[1] and by 1861 the area had a zinc worker, a cabinet maker and manufacturers of feathers and fancy brushes, and Albert Town a printer's compositor, a mason, a stone sawyer, a wire drawer, a whitesmith, makers of cabinets, mathematical and musical instruments, iron safes, chronometers, trousers, mantles, stays, water colours, and packing cases. Near Church Street were a surgical instrument

[68] Ref. bk. to Wadmore map (1813), no. 559; Nelson, *Islington*, plan (1735); below, ind.
[69] Tithe (1848), no. 727.
[70] G.L.R.O., MCS/498/703.
[71] Section on ind. from late 19th cent. based on dirs.: *Ellis's Dir. Stoke Newington* (1876–7); *Highbury, Stoke Newington Dir.* (1885); *Kelly's Dir. Stoke Newington* (1890–1929); *Kelly's Dir. Lond.* (1936–82).
[72] P.R.O., C 260/55, no. 47.
[73] Ibid. C 1/64/410; C 1/1039/22; *Cal. Close, 1422–9*, 404.
[74] Guildhall MS. 14233/1.
[75] G.L.R.O., Cal. Sess. Rec. x. 128.
[76] *Mdx. Sess. Rec.* ii. 118.
[77] Ibid. iii. 120, 310; iv. 99.
[78] *Mdx. County Rec.* iii. 376.
[79] E. Carpenter, 'St. Paul's Inventories' (cuttings from *Hackney & Stoke Newington Recorder*, 1916, S.N.L. 80, LC 1205).
[80] T. F. M. Newton, 'Civet Cats of Newington Green', *Rev. of Eng. Studies*, xiii. 10–19.

[81] P.R.O., C 7/644/5.
[82] M.L.R. 1751/1/470.
[83] Ibid. 1746/1/293.
[84] Ibid. 1758/4/343.
[85] Ibid. 1775/7/320.
[86] Ibid. 1750/2/546; 1750/3/750; 1775/7/320.
[87] *Census*, 1801.
[88] Ref. bk. to Wadmore map (1813).
[89] Abstract of Ct. Rolls 1802–31, 268.
[90] Pigot, *Com. Dir.* (1826), 492–3.
[91] *Census*, 1831.
[92] *Pigot's Lond. Dir.* (1834).
[93] *Hackney and NE. Lond. Dir.* (1849), which distinguishes E. and W. sides of Lond. rd.
[94] Pigot, *Com. Dir.* (1826), 492–3.
[95] *Census*, 1831.
[96] *Pigot's Lond. Dir.* (1834).
[97] P.R.O., HO 107/663/4.
[98] Ibid. HO 107/1702/1/4.
[99] Ibid. HO 107/1503/11/1–6.
[1] Ibid. HO 107/1702/1/4.

maker, a brassworker, and blind makers.[2] By 1871 Albert Town had a die sinker and makers of venetian blinds, umbrellas, and chandeliers.[3]

While most industry was carried on in workshops within private houses or gardens, factories began to appear, mainly in the south-eastern corner of Stoke Newington. A carriage factory was built behind Nelson Terrace off Castle Lane (Crossway) c. 1870[4] and workshops were built in the same road in 1874.[5] In 1878 'a building for engineering purposes' was erected in Barrett's Grove[6] and in 1880 John Studds, a builder and former carpenter, built a workshop there for himself.[7] He had a foundry in 1881[8] and by 1896 his premises housed other firms, including makers of electric plates and bicycles.

In 1876 in the eastern part of South Hornsey there was an ostrich feather manufacturer in Victoria Road, manufacturers of pianos, water colours, and opera glasses in Warwick Road, and a cabinet maker and printer in Nevill Road. The area lost most of its industry towards 1900 but Albert Town retained 17–18 firms throughout the period 1885–1914, although individual firms were short lived and small. Albion Road, hitherto an exclusive residential area, had 2 builders in 1880, 4 by 1885, and 6 by 1904. It housed a gas fitting manufacturer in 1881[9] and by 1890 Stock & Sons, coachbuilders, had replaced one of the builders. Clissold works were built at no. 151 in 1892 for a mantle maker,[10] 8 workshops were erected in the road in 1894,[11] and a factory was built for William Page, portmanteau maker, in 1895.[12] There were 11 firms by 1904, including a tennis racquet manufacturer and two cycle makers, and 14 by 1914, including a printer at no. 108. At the southern end Edward Hollands built a factory and outbuilding adjoining no. 42 Newington Green in 1909.[13] A factory was built behind nos. 15 and 17 Springdale Road in the south-west corner of the borough in 1911 for A. Chatterton & Co., embroiderers.[14]

The London road continued to house such varied craftsmen as a stonemason and makers of stays, umbrellas, spectacles, and blinds in High Street in 1871.[15] By 1876 there were 5 builders in Church Street, besides Whincop & Son, timber merchants, at no. 40, one of the few firms still in Stoke Newington in 1983, and Pinch & Whipple, staymakers, at no. 5. A piano maker's had opened by 1885 and workshops were erected in Clarence Terrace in the 1880s and 1890s,[16] especially for Yates & Co., dyers, who survived until the 1930s.

Prams and cycles were made by 1894 in Church Street, where there were some 22 manufacturers by 1914.

Industry began to spread north of Church Street at the end of the 19th century. In 1884 a chimney shaft was built at Hitchens Fire Proof Plastering Co.'s Grayling works at the back of Grayling Road.[17] Two factories were built beside Grayling works in 1902[18] and Albion works was built at no. 49 Grayling Road in 1908.[19] A drain-pipe manufacturer had opened alongside the railway in Manor Road by 1885. By 1914 Manor Road housed jam manufacturers, two clothing manufacturers, and makers of cycles and umbrellas. Carter, Paterson & Co. had van works in Lordship Road from 1908.

There were 76 factories and workshops registered in Stoke Newington parish in 1897 and 342, employing 1,709 people, in the borough, which included South Hornsey, by 1906.[20] Most factories were small, often in back gardens, while workshops were usually converted rooms. Outworking was widespread, especially in the clothing industry, and there were 274 outworkers in 1905.[21] By 1915 there were about 800 domestic workrooms in addition to the 286 registered factories and workshops.[22]

The number of registered factories and workshops varied little before the Second World War, being 284 in 1914, 330 in 1921,[23] and 329 in 1938, although the workforce increased to 6,030.[24] Despite conversions of rooms into workshops, noted in 1936, the main tendency was to build larger factories, usually on vacant land enclosed by streets. Since conversion of rooms was forbidden on the Church Commissioners' land, workshops in the north part were rare.[25]

One of the last undeveloped sites, the 10-a. Willows estate south and south-west of Paradise Row, was for sale in 1891. Carysfort Road was constructed, with houses in the 1890s[26] and a garage and the first factory to the north in 1912. Other factories were added in the 1920s, especially for Kemble & Co., piano manufacturers, and for Ever Ready Co.[27] About 1914 there was a 'Hygienic Steam Laundry' behind the east end of Paradise Row.[28] In 1931 and 1932 factories, called Shelford works, were built next to it in Shelford Place, adjoining the factories of Carysfort Road to the north-east.[29] In 1933 Shelford works housed two firms of dressing gown manufacturers. In 1934 additions were made to Warwick House, at the west end of Paradise

[2] P.R.O., RG 9/152/11/1–7; RG 9/791/5.
[3] Ibid. RG 10/309/9/1c; Kelly's Dir. Mdx. (1871).
[4] Abstract of Ct. Rolls 1832–82, 411.
[5] G.L.R.O., MBW 1643/119, no. 21.
[6] Ibid. 1675/151, no. 23.
[7] Ibid. 1692/168, no. 23.
[8] Ibid. 1701/177, no. 24.
[9] P.R.O., RG 11/281/10/1.
[10] G.L.R.O., AR/BA 4/30, no. 22.
[11] Ibid. 52, no. 50.
[12] Ibid. 60, no. 50.
[13] Ibid. 203, no. 44.
[14] Ibid. 233.
[15] P.R.O., RG 10/309/9/1A.
[16] G.L.R.O., MBW 1766/242, no. 24; AR/BA 4/30, no. 22; AR/BA 4/124.
[17] Ibid. MBW 1729/205, no. 24.
[18] Ibid. AR/BA 4/124.

[19] Ibid. 187.
[20] Stoke Newington vestry, Ann. Rep. (1896–7), 86; L.C.C. Lond. Statistics, xvii (1906–7), 55–7, 187. The 1906 figs. may have included the domestic workshops of outworkers.
[21] L.C.C. Lond. Statistics, xvi (1905–6), 182–3.
[22] Stoke Newington B.C. M.O.H. Rep. (1915).
[23] Ibid. (1914, 1921).
[24] J. H. Forshaw and P. Abercombie, County of Lond. Plan (1943), 88.
[25] N. Lond. Recorder, 17 Apr. 1936, quoted in Ch. Com. file 6439 pt. 2; New Lond. Life and Labour, ii. 231, 298.
[26] Sales parts. 1891 (S.N.L. cuttings 60.5); above, bldg. 1870–1914.
[27] G.L.R.O., AR/BA 4/403; below.
[28] W. Shepherd, 'Paradise Row c. 1914' (TS. 1976, S.N.L. cuttings 49.2, LC 3348).
[29] G.L.R.O., AR/BA 4/534, no. 36; 555.

Row,[30] which housed War Relief Toys, founded at no. 110 Church Street to give employment to disabled ex-servicemen.

In Albert Town, Wall Paper Manufacturing of High Holborn built a factory behind nos. 20-4 Spenser Road in 1913.[31] The same company owned the adjacent Howard works at no. 23 Howard Road, which were occupied by oil merchants by 1914 and Challenge Oil Co. by 1921, when the factory was rebuilt.[32] In 1919 A. Elmes & Co., exhibition stand fitters, a firm established in 1883,[33] built Elm Tree works at the southern end of Albion Road, behind the existing factory buildings of no. 42 Newington Green. Other purpose built factories by 1936[34] included a clothing factory north of Victoria Grove, probably built by H. W. Harrison & Co., who had been there since 1913, cabinet works built behind no. 193 High Street c. 1914, and several factories in Albion Road: a printing works built c. 1920 behind nos. 108 and 110, piano, later cabinet, works built behind nos. 180 and 182 c. 1922, and cabinet works of the early 1930s at no. 151A.

By 1939 there was no room for more industry. Four factories left between 1932 and 1938 and in 1943 further industrialization was undesirable.[35] The need for widespread rebuilding after 1945 provided the opportunity for resiting industry, which had grown up within residential areas. A proposal to concentrate industry south of Church Street between Clissold Crescent and Sandbrook Road[36] was strongly opposed in the 1950s by firms employing local labour.[37] In 1947 there were 297 factories employing 4,695 people and covering 2½ per cent of the total acreage of the borough; 177 factories each employed fewer than 10 people.[38] In 1952 there were 345 registered factories,[39] but the number had fallen to 292 by 1964, when there were 355 outworkers employed in the borough.[40] The contraction of industry, which accelerated during the 1970s and 1980s, was partly due to the policy of separating industry from housing and of building flats on every available space, but also to the general industrial decline. By the time that local authorities became aware of the resulting unemployment, firms had already closed or moved elsewhere.[41] In 1975 there were some 170 manufacturing firms; although there were 172 in 1983, they were smaller concerns, the floor space having been reduced from 65,289 sq. m. in 1975 to 59,463 sq. m.[42]

In 1983 industry was mainly in a large number of small premises, either former shops fronting main roads (particularly the London road and Church Street) or small workshops or old factories on cramped sites. The main purpose built industrial areas were at Carysfort Road and Shelford Place and, despite closures caused by redevelopment, around Albion Road and Church Walk.[43] Some of the larger factory buildings have been shared by several firms. In 1983 the firms with more than 1,400 sq. m. of floor space were H. Shawyer & Sons, manufacturers of veneered panels, with a purpose built factory at no. 43A Manor Road since 1938, Jack Rose (Shoes), which since 1966 had a factory built in 1914 for cabinet makers and used until 1955 as a furniture factory, Henry Serventi, shopfitters, in Barrett's Grove since 1961, a mouldings firm in Carysfort Road, and Howmedica (Dental Fillings) at Albion works, no. 49 Grayling Road, since c. 1953.

Brickearth covered the centre of the parish[44] and the name Tile Pits, given by 1649 to closes on the demesne approximately on the site of the later reservoirs,[45] shows that a still wider area was capable of being worked for bricks and tiles. There were tile kilns in Green Lanes in 1775[46] and brickpits for Clissold House c. 1790 were dug in the grounds.[47] At that time commercial brickmaking was concentrated just outside the parish, at Kingsland.[48] William Rhodes, of the Tilekilns, Hackney Road, in the 1830s, had a lease of land on the north side of Coach and Horses Lane in 1810.[49] In 1839 Thomas and William Rhodes (d. 1843) were described as brickmakers of Prospect Place (Boleyn Road).[50] William Rhodes's brickfields, which in 1832 had mainly been in South Hornsey bordering Cut Throat Lane, had probably passed to the Webbs by 1841.[51] The Rhodes family, however, retained a small piece of property in Coach and Horses Lane, which was enfranchised in 1859,[52] and had acquired a second brickfield in Stoke Newington in 1821 when Samuel Rhodes of Islington bought part of the Pulteney estate bordering Green Lanes near Newington Green.[53] It is not known whether the Rhodes family exploited the Green Lanes brickfield, which by 1834 had probably passed to Robert William Webb and George Webb, described as brickmakers of Newington Green.[54] They had apparently taken over the eastern brickfield by 1839 when they were described as brickmakers of Coach and Horses Lane.[55] In 1841 Webb's brickfield in South

[30] Ibid. 600, no. 36.
[31] Ibid. 266.
[32] Ibid. 373, no. 33.
[33] G.L.C. Photo. Libr. 7643.
[34] O.S. Map 1/2,500, Lond. II. 15 (1936 edn.).
[35] Forshaw and Abercrombie, *County of Lond. Plan*, 93, 166-7.
[36] G.L.R.O., AR/TP/2/157 (scheme 19).
[37] Ibid. 4/33.
[38] Stoke Newington, *Official Guide* [1955], 26.
[39] Stoke Newington M.B. *M.O.H. Rep.* (1952), 34.
[40] *Ann. Rep. on Health of Boros. of Hackney, Shoreditch, and Stoke Newington*, 1964 (S.N.L. 46, LC 3298).
[41] *Evening Standard*, 10 June 1976 (S.N.L. cuttings 41.8, LC 3206).
[42] Based on Land Use survey files 10/75 and 3/83 supplied by Hackney L.B., Planning & Dev. Dept.
[43] Hackney Boro. Plan, *Stoke Newington Planning Area*

(1982), SN 4-1, map 4.6; O.S. Map 1/1,250, TQ 3285 SE. (1954, 1970 edns.); TQ 3286 SE. (1952, 1970 edns.).
[44] Geol. Surv. Map 1″, drift, Mdx. XII. SW., SE. (1934 edn.).
[45] Guildhall MS. 11816B, p. 129; cf. map in Robinson, *Stoke Newington*, facing p. 37.
[46] *Six Well-Known Views nr. Lond.* no. 5 (copy in S.N.L. 85.1, LC 1323).
[47] Above, other est.
[48] Middleton, *View*, 24.
[49] Guildhall MS. 14233/19, p. 1; *Robson's Lond. Dir.* (1830); Marcham, Digest, pt. 1.
[50] Pigot, *Nat. Com. Dir.* (1839).
[51] Abstract of Ct. Rolls 1832-82, 315, 371.
[52] Ibid. 385; tithe (1848), nos. 838-9.
[53] Guildhall MS. 14233/18, 52 sqq., 64.
[54] *Pigot's Lond. Dir.* (1834).
[55] Pigot, *Nat. Com. Dir.* (1839).

Hornsey included cottages for the brickmakers.[56] It supplied bricks for arches and tunnels to the G.N.R. Co.[57] and left a pit some 14 ft. deep.[58] Between 1835 and 1847 36 a. of grassland were turned into brickfields,[59] most of it by the Webbs who were assessed in Stoke Newington in 1840 for 14 a. of brickfields and another 14 $\frac{1}{2}$ a. which they were probably not yet working.[60] In 1845 Robert William Webb was still in Coach and Horses Lane and George Webb was building on the western brickfield in Green Lanes.[61] Their successor William Webb of Albion Road in 1848 leased 14 a. on both sides of Cut Throat Lane from Martha Carr, probably the same as that held by the Webbs in 1840 (in addition, presumably, to the South Hornsey brickfield) and another 8 a. at Green Lanes from Benjamin Massey.[62] The Cut Throat Lane and the Hornsey fields were built over as Albert Town in the 1850s[63] and in 1855 William was operating at Green Lanes.[64] In 1860 he held the 8 a. at Green Lanes together with another 22 a. of brickfield at Newington Green.[65] By 1870 he was no longer a brickmaker,[66] and neither of his brickfields was listed in 1873.[67]

Henry Lee of Finsbury Square was licensed to dig for bricks on 18 a. in Stoke Newington in 1847.[68] Messrs. Lee's brickfield flourished during the 1850s, when their steam engine and furnace constituted a nuisance and permission to erect sheds was given.[69] The fields lay on either side of Pawnbroker's Lane, east of Webb's 14 a.[70] George Lee, probably Henry's son, took over c. 1860[71] and the field was taken for building in the 1870s.

Seven silkweavers of Stoke Newington were recorded between 1610 and 1617[72] and there was a silkman in the early 18th century.[73] In 1813 three tenements and outbuildings in Paradise Row were used as a weaver's factory,[74] which had gone by 1826.[75] In addition to dressmakers and shoemakers there were, throughout the first half of the 19th century, several staymakers, milliners, and straw hat makers, mostly in the London road and, to a lesser extent, in Church Street.[76] In 1851 a hat manufacturer in the Palatine houses and a button manufacturer in Barrett's Grove may have carried on business from their homes.[77] In 1861 there was a mantle maker in Cowper

Terrace and a trousers maker in Spenser Road, both in Albert Town,[78] and in 1871 a ladies' clothing manufacturer in Truman Place, in the south-east corner of the parish where larger-scale manufacture began.[79] By 1876 there was a hat manufacturer in High Street, a straw bonnet maker in Back (Boleyn) Road, and manufacturers of costumes and bags in Albert Town.[80] There were several mantle makers in 1885, mainly in the London road, Church Street, the south-east, and Albert Town, although there was also one shirt dresser in Albion Road, where by 1900 Clissold works housed a mantle maker. Manor Road was the home of the London Shirt and Collar Dressing Co. by 1908 and of four clothing firms by 1914.

In 1906 clothing employed 617 people, mostly women, 36 per cent of those employed in the borough's factories and workshops.[81] Some 3,325 inhabitants were employed in dress and another 544 in textile fabrics in 1911, although their workplaces were not all in the borough and many were outworkers.[82] During the 1920s and 1930s clothing firms opened in Albion Road, Crossway, Boleyn Road, and other areas previously occupied mainly by the metal working and furniture industries. Some larger factories were built, for example north of Victoria Grove for underclothing manufacturers probably in 1913,[83] and the number of outworkers declined. In 1938, 155 clothing factories employed 2,247 people, 35 per cent of those employed in factories in the borough, and there were 226 outworkers.[84] In 1947 there were 2,069 workers, 44 per cent of the factory population, in 141 clothing factories.[85] In 1951 making shirts, overalls, and underwear employed 440 people, women's outerwear 682, and tailoring 879.[86] The industry reached its peak in the 1960s, when there were some 150 clothing factories.[87] As always in the industry, firms opened and closed with great frequency,[88] for example increasing in Carysfort Road from none in 1959 to 9 in 1982 but contracting in Manor Road from 11 in 1959 to 4 in 1982. In the 1980s the industry was still dominated by Jews, although inroads were being made by more recent immigrants such as Greeks and Turks. A general decline left 87 firms occupying some 32,740 sq. m. in 1975 and 94

[56] P.R.O., HO 107/663/4.
[57] *Daily Chron.* 18 Sept. 1912; *Hackney & Kingsland Gaz.* 30 June 1913 (S.N.L. cuttings 36 Webb).
[58] *Freeholders' Circular*, 1 Apr. 1852 (S.N.L. cuttings 41.8 ALB, LC 3573).   [59] P.R.O., IR 29/21/52.
[60] The 14 a. was assessed at £8 an acre, the 14½ a. at £4 10s. an acre: Vestry mins. 1838–62, 57.
[61] *P.O. Dir. Six Home Counties* (1845); G.L.R.O., MBO/ DS/A 19.
[62] Tithe (1848), nos. 504, 603, 724; P.R.O., HO 107/1503/ 11/4, p. 22.   [63] Above, bldg. to 1870.
[64] *Kelly's Dir. Mdx.* (1855).
[65] G.L.R.O., MBW 2120 (Metropol. Bd. of Wks., Rate bk. vol. 142).
[66] *Green's Hackney Dir.* (1869–70).
[67] *O.S. Bk. of Ref. to Plan of Stoke Newington* (1873).
[68] Guildhall MS. CC. 212295. Described as nos. 391, 393–4 on Wadmore map.
[69] Vestry mins. 1838–62, 336, 360; Metropol. Bd. of Wks., *Mins. of Procs.* (1859), 363.
[70] O.S. Map 1/2,500, Lond. X (1870 edn.); *O.S. Bk. of Ref.* nos. 95, 101.
[71] G.L.R.O., MBW 2120, vol. 142; *Kelly's Dir. Lond. Suburbs* (1860); *Kelly's Dir. Mdx.* (1871).

[72] G.L.R.O., Cal. Mdx. Rec. v. 42; ix. 35; x. 128; *Mdx. Sess. Rec.* i. 457; iv. 99, 137.
[73] *Stationers' Co. Apprentices 1701–1800*, ed. D. F. McKenzie, 37.
[74] Ref. bk. to Wadmore map (1813), no. 125; Abstract of Ct. Rolls 1832–82, 357.
[75] Pigot, *Nat. Com. Dir.* (1826–7), 492–3.
[76] Ibid. (1826–7, 1839); *Pigot's Lond. Dir.* (1834); *P.O. Dir. Six Home Counties* (1845); P.R.O., HO 107/1503/11/1–6.
[77] P.R.O., HO 107/1503/11/1–6. Neither had factories in Lond.: *Kelly's Dir. Lond.* (1851).
[78] P.R.O., RG 9/791/5.
[79] Ibid. RG 10/309/9/1B.
[80] *Ellis's Dir. Stoke Newington* (1876–7).
[81] L.C.C. *Lond. Statistics*, xvii (1906–7), 55–7.
[82] Ibid. xxiv (1913–14), 72–7.
[83] O.S. Map 1/2,500, Lond. II. 15 (1936 edn.).
[84] Forshaw and Abercrombie, *County of Lond. Plan*, 88; Stoke Newington B.C. *M.O.H. Rep.* (1938), 39.
[85] Stoke Newington, *Official Guide* [1955], 26.
[86] P. G. Hall, *Inds. of Lond. since 1861* (1962), 40, 47, 49.
[87] M. G. Goss, 'Geography of Hackney and Stoke Newington' (TS. c. 1964, S.N.L. 80, LC 3689).
[88] Forshaw and Abercrombie, *County of Lond. Plan*, 87.

firms occupying 27,959 sq. m. in 1983, but clothing remained the most important of Stoke Newington's industries, occupying 50 per cent of industrial floor space in 1975 and 47 per cent in 1983.[89]

Until the 1830s the only workers in wood were carpenters. There was one cabinet maker, in High Street, in 1834 and 1845,[90] and there were three, all in the South Hornsey part of High Street, together with one in Church Street and one in Albion Road, in 1851. A cabinet maker of Woodberry Down, who employed 90 men and 12 women, and another at the northern end of Green Lanes probably carried on their businesses elsewhere. In 1851 there was also a timber worker in Victoria Grove and a bedstead maker in the Palatine houses.[91] There were cabinet makers in Devonshire Place, Green Lanes, by 1860[92] and in Prospect Place, Back Road, and Church Path in 1871.[93] By 1876 there were nine cabinet makers, mainly in the south-east, and 21 carpenters.[94]

From the 1870s the furniture industry expanded as skilled craftsmen, who in the earlier part of the century had left the City for Bethnal Green and Shoreditch, moved farther out to Stoke Newington. Cabinet makers remained the backbone of the industry into the 1920s. By 1871 there was a piano maker in Milton Road.[95] Other piano manufacturers were Agate & Co., at no. 183 Church Street from c. 1885 to 1957 (from c. 1934 a warehouse), Thomas Harrison, who built Grayling works in 1902 and Albion works in 1908,[96] and Kaiser's at no. 95 Carysfort Road from 1912 to 1915, when it was replaced by Kemble's, probably the same firm under another name. In 1906 wood and wooden products provided work for 169 people, 10 per cent of those employed in factories and workshops in the borough.[97] Kemble's expanded in Carysfort Road, building factories at no. 97B in 1923 and no. 97 in 1928, and taking over nos. 53B and 97A by 1929, to the last of which it made additions in 1939.[98] There were at least five other piano manufacturers by 1929 and cabinet factories were built on the site of the Edinburgh brewery by 1913 and on either side of Albion Road by 1936.[99] By 1938 there were 34 furniture factories employing 516 people, 8.5 per cent of those employed in the borough's factories.[1] The percentage had dropped to 6.2 by 1947, when there were 15 factories and 292 employees.[2]

As the number of craftsmen in cabinet making declined in the 1940s and that of piano manufacturers in the 1950s the mass-production of furniture, shop-fittings, and veneers increased. By 1975 there were 23 firms occupying 13,600 sq. m.,

21 per cent of the manufacturing floor area in Stoke Newington, and there were still 23 firms in 1983, occupying 12,436 sq. m.[3]

There was a printer in Stoke Newington Road in 1826[4] and one in Albion Road in 1851, by which date there were also eight print workers, mostly compositors and pressmen in the south-east corner of Stoke Newington, besides two in the eastern part of South Hornsey.[5] By 1860 there were three printers, in High Street, Back (Boleyn) Road, and Howard Road.[6] Printing firms, mostly small, spread from Clerkenwell in the second half of the century to south-eastern Stoke Newington and Hornsey detached, especially Albert Town. Spenser Road had a paper bag maker by 1890 and Victoria Road a tracing paper maker by 1904. In 1906 paper and printing employed 198 people, 11.6 per cent of those employed in factories and workshops in the borough.[7] There was a printer in Church Street by 1908 and one at no. 108 Albion Road by 1909. John Waddington, printers, was at no. 108 Albion Road from 1921 or earlier until 1966 and there was another printing company in Manor Road by 1929 and until 1959. Larger factories included Waddington's in Church Walk, built c. 1920 behind their works in Albion Road[8] but the smaller firms rarely lasted long. In 1938 there were 17 paper and printing factories employing 139 people, 2.3 per cent of the factory workforce in the borough.[9] By 1947 there were 13 factories and 645 employees, 13.7 per cent of those employed in the borough's factories.[10] In the early 1950s the centre of printing had shifted westward to Carysfort Road, Shelford Place, and the adjacent part of Church Street, where Kores Manufacturing Co. was making typewriter carbons and ribbons by 1951. By 1975 there were 14 firms occupying 4,770 sq. m., 7 per cent of the industrial floor space. Printing and paper was one of the few industries to have expanded by 1983, when there were 18 firms occupying 5,903 sq. m., 9 per cent of the floor area.[11]

There was a white lead mill on the western border in 1806.[12] Metal workers included workers in wire and zinc in High Street in 1855,[13] a tinplate worker in Lordship Road in 1860,[14] a wire drawer in Albert Town, and a brassworker in Red Lion Lane in 1861.[15] There was a Belgium iron foundry in Barrett's Grove by 1885 and electric plates were being manufactured in the same road by 1896. Grayling works in Grayling Road housed engineers in 1900 and there were electrical engineers in Castle Street, later Crossway, and Matthias Road by 1904. By 1906 metals and machinery employed 47 people,

[89] Hackney Planning Dept. Land Use survey files 10/75 and 3/83.
[90] Pigot's Lond. Dir. (1834); P.O. Dir. Six Home Counties (1845).
[91] P.R.O., HO 107/1503/11/1–6; HO 107/1702/1/4.
[92] Kelly's Dir. Lond. Suburbs (1860).
[93] P.R.O., RG 10/309/9/1C.
[94] Ellis's Dir. Stoke Newington (1876–7).
[95] Kelly's Dir. Mdx. (1871).
[96] G.L.R.O., AR/BA 4/124, 187.
[97] L.C.C. Lond. Statistics, xvii (1906–7), 55–7.
[98] G.L.R.O., AR/BA 4/403, 478, 710.
[99] O.S. Map 1/2,500, Lond. II. 15 (1936 edn.).
[1] Forshaw and Abercrombie, County of Lond. Plan, 88.
[2] Stoke Newington, Official Guide [1955], 26.

[3] Hackney Planning Dept. Land Use survey files 10/75 and 3/83.
[4] Pigot, Nat. Com. Dir. (1826–7).
[5] P.R.O., HO 107/1503/11/1–6; HO 107/1702/1/4.
[6] Kelly's Dir. Lond. Suburbs (1860).
[7] L.C.C. Lond. Statistics, xvii (1906–7), 55–7.
[8] O.S. Map 1/2,500, Lond. II. 15 (1936 edn.).
[9] Forshaw and Abercrombie, County of Lond. Plan, 88.
[10] Stoke Newington, Official Guide [1955], 26.
[11] Hackney Planning Dept. Land Use survey files 10/75 and 3/83.
[12] Islington libr., Dent's plan (1806).
[13] Kelly's Dir. Mdx. (1855).
[14] Kelly's Dir. Lond. Suburbs (1860).
[15] P.R.O., RG 9/152/11/1; RG 9/791/5.

2.75 per cent of those employed in factories and workshops in the borough.[16]

There were coachmakers in High Street and Victoria Place in 1839[17] and coach painters in Diapason Row, in the Hornsey section of High Street in 1841[18] and 1851, when there was another coach painter in the Palatine houses, a coach trimmer in the Hornsey section of High Street, a coach maker in Church Street, and a coachwright in Prospect Cottages, Back, later Boleyn, Road.[19] The last, William Shepherd, employed 10 men and 6 boys in 1871.[20] In 1869 John and William Rendall, wheelwrights of Stamford Hill, leased a new building on the site of nos. 41–9 Nelson Terrace, Stoke Newington Road, behind which in 1870 they built a carriage factory opening into Castle Lane.[21] The firm survived until 1938. Other coach and carriage builders had opened in Barrett's Grove by 1880, in Cowper Road by 1885, and in Albion Road by 1890. The latter, Stock & Sons, were building vans and carts by 1904, and motor bodies by 1935.

Cycles were made in Palatine Road by 1890, Church Street by 1894, Barrett's Grove by 1896, and Albion Road by 1904. There was a manufacturer of prams in Church Street by 1894. Cycles continued to be made, usually in short lived workshops, into the 1920s, and Mona Cycle Works Co. of Barrett's Grove survived until the 1930s.

Carter, Paterson & Co., carriers, at no. 35 (later no. 104) Church Street by 1880, opened a van works in Lordship Road in 1908, which passed to the Express Motor Co. by 1935. There were motor body builders in Dunsmure Road by 1925.[22]

There was a garage at no. 53A Carysfort Road by 1914. By 1929 it had become a motor engineers and by 1936 there were others in Boleyn Road, Manor Road, and Park Street. Electrical engineers and makers of electrical components, especially for radio, multiplied during the 1920s and 1930s. The Ever Ready Co. was making batteries at no. 95A Carysfort Road by 1921. There were 64 engineering factories by 1938, employing 2,502, 41.4 per cent of those employed in factories in the borough. The premises were larger than those for other industries, with an average of 39 employees each.[23] Although there were still 50 engineering firms in 1947, they employed only 852 people, 18 per cent of those employed in Stoke Newington's factories.[24] The larger firms, particularly in the motor industry, moved away to cheaper sites and the engineering firms that replaced them were small and specialist, occupying parts of factory buildings in areas like Carysfort or Grayling

roads. One of the few survivors in 1982 was Lewis Banks & Sons, an engineer's which opened in Barrett's Grove in the 1920s and had 40 employees in 1982.[25] Engineering firms had dwindled to 8, occupying 2,371 sq. m., 3 per cent of industrial capacity, by 1975 and to 7, occupying 965 sq. m., 1 per cent of floor space, by 1983. Ten metal working firms, occupying 1,728 sq. m., in 1975 were reduced to 6, with 1,424 sq. m., by 1983. There were 4 firms, occupying 1,086 sq. m. in motor manufacture in 1975 and 6, with 900 sq. m., in 1983; one electrical firm occupied 1,233 sq. m. in 1975 and two occupied 121 sq. m. in 1975. Floor space occupied by makers of plastics and synthetic resins declined from 3,105 sq. m. in 1975 to 2,853 sq. m. in 1983.[26]

A brewer, William Chase, was in Meadow Street (later Lordship Terrace) in 1834[27] and 1860.[28] There were other brewers in High Street and Stamford Hill by 1839[29] and Matthew Michell had opened the Edinburgh brewery in Gordon (later Beatty) Road, off the London road in South Hornsey, by 1851;[30] it closed in 1896.[31]

Some 13 per cent, 221 people, of those employed in Stoke Newington's factories and workshops in 1906 worked in food, drink, and tobacco.[32] Most were at Ridge's Royal Food Mill, which had opened in Boleyn Road by 1885, was replaced by a larger building in 1913,[33] and closed in 1957, at Osborn's, makers of anchovy paste, in Spenser Road by 1885, or at the manufacturing confectioners which opened in Barrett's Grove by 1904. In 1911 D. Politi, who had been making jam in Mountgrove Road, Brownswood, since 1870, built a factory in the garden of no. 10 Manor Road.[34] The family firm, which by 1921 made confectionery and was noted for its Turkish Delight, enlarged its premises which by 1982 comprised nos. 6–12 Manor Road and employed up to 100 people during busy seasons.[35] Most food firms were very small, in 1938 employing only 195 people, 3.2 per cent of the workforce in Stoke Newington's factories, in 29 factories[36] and in 1947 with 285, 6 per cent of the workforce, in 31 factories.[37] By 1975 there were only two firms, occupying 1,644 sq. m. After the opening of a factory to make Chinese noodles, by 1983 there were four firms in all occupying 2,561 sq. m.

LOCAL GOVERNMENT. MANORIAL GOVERNMENT. In 1294 the dean and chapter of St. Paul's successfully claimed view of frankpledge, the assize of bread and of ale, pillory, tumbril, infangthief, outfangthief, and fugitives' chattels in Stoke Newington.[38] Separate views and courts

16 L.C.C. *Lond. Statistics*, xvii (1906–7), 55–7.
17 Pigot, *Nat. Com. Dir.* (1839).
18 P.R.O., HO 107/663/4.
19 Ibid. HO 107/1503/11/1–6; HO 107/1702/1/4.
20 Ibid. RG 10/309/9/1c.
21 Abstract of Ct. Rolls 1832–82, 407, 411.
22 Stoke Newington, *Official Guide* [1928], pp. A46 sqq.
23 Forshaw and Abercrombie, *County of Lond. Plan*, 88.
24 Stoke Newington, *Official Guide* [1955], 26.
25 *Kompass*, ii, Company Inf. (20th edn. 1982).
26 Hackney Planning Dept. Land Use survey files 10/75 and 3/83.
27 Pigot, *Nat. Com. Dir.* (1834).

28 Tithe (1848), nos. 203, 205; G.L.R.O., MBW 2120, vol. 142. 29 Pigot, *Nat. Com. Dir.* (1839).
30 P.R.O., HO 107/1503/11/3, p. 1; *Kelly's Dir. Lond. Suburbs* (1860); *Cassell's Map of Lond.* (c. 1861–2).
31 *Kelly's Dir. Stoke Newington* (1895–6, 1896–7).
32 L.C.C. *Lond. Statistics*, xvii (1906–7), 55.
33 G.L.R.O., AR/BA 4/266; O.S. Maps 1/2,500, Lond. XXX (1894–6 edn.); Lond. II. 15 (1915 edn.).
34 G.L.R.O., AR/BA 4/233, no. 46.
35 Inf. from Mr. David Politi (1982).
36 Forshaw and Abercrombie, *County of Lond. Plan*, 88.
37 Stoke Newington, *Official Guide* [1955], 26.
38 *Plac de Quo Warr.* (Rec. Com.), 475–6.

were being held at Stoke Newington by 1329, for which there is a single extant court roll.[39] Felons' goods were taken by the bailiff of the lordship in the 1460s.[40] When the manor was leased in 1541, the lessee was to occupy the bailiwick and from 1545 leases included perquisites of court and felons' goods.[41] Court rolls and books survive for 1569–80 and 1675–1938.[42] In 1649 the lessee was to deliver copies of every court roll to the prebendary, who paid 8d. for the writing of each roll.[43] The appearance of the extant rolls, however, suggests that the steward who was presented in 1681 for great negligence in keeping the rolls was by no means untypical.[44]

View of frankpledge was held once a year, in June in 1329,[45] in November from 1569 to 1578, in January in 1579,[46] in July in 1679,[47] in May from 1681, and on Ascension day from the late 18th century. A general court baron followed the view. Special courts, entirely concerned with land transactions and frequent in the 19th century, could be held at any time, although admission fees were twice those at general courts.[48] The last view was held in 1841 and the last entry in the court books was made in 1938.[49]

In 1541 the prebendary undertook to pay for court dinners but by 1576 the lessee was paying at least £1 a year for them.[50] Courts were held at the old manor house[51] and the house, later Manor House school, built on its site.[52] By the late 18th century courts were being held at the Three Crowns[53] and from 1833 at the new Manor House tavern.[54]

There were six headboroughs and two ale-tasters in 1329[55] and a constable in 1377.[56] By 1569 the officers, a constable, 2 headboroughs, and 2 aleconners, were elected at the view of frankpledge. Two surveyors of the highways were presented in 1576 for performing their office badly and not rendering accounts.[57] During the 18th and early 19th centuries the aleconners also acted as common drivers[58] but by the 1820s a separate driver was appointed.[59] In 1841 the ale-conners' duties extended to examining the scales of grocers and cheesemongers.[60] The manorial pound, mentioned in 1571, adjoined demesne land and was on the north side of Church Street. In 1848 it was behind the Red Lion.[61]

PARISH GOVERNMENT. There was a parish clerk in 1365–6[62] and 1580.[63] The parish clerks, all of whose names are known from the early 17th century, were chosen by the rector.[64] In 1826 the vestry granted the parish clerk a gratuity to teach children psalmody.[65] There was a tendency for the office of vestry clerk, who was chosen at the Easter vestry, to become hereditary, the Yardley family holding it from c. 1817 to c. 1860.[66] Vestry minutes were presumably kept by the vestry clerk, who c. 1700 was barely literate.[67]

Two churchwardens held land for the parish in 1571.[68] In 1681 the parishioners successfully asserted against the rector, their ancient right to choose both wardens at the Easter vestry.[69] By the late 18th century wardens were elected according to the seniority of inhabitants, serving in successive years as under and upper warden. In 1784 the election as upper warden of a Jew, Solomon de Medina, who had already served as lower warden, was successfully opposed by a minority of the parishioners and by the commissary, who refused to administer the oath on the Old Testament.[70] There was probably a precedent for a Jewish churchwarden, Isaac Alvarez, in 1743.[71] A dissenter who was elected in 1792 nominated a deputy.[72]

Two overseers of the poor, first mentioned in 1577,[73] were elected at the Easter vestry[74] until 1811, when magistrates chose from a list submitted by the vestry.[75] They were said to be substantial householders in 1781[76] and usually a 'mercantile man and a tradesman' in 1834.[77] Two surveyors of the highways, in 1576 accountable to the manor court,[78] were by 1681 elected at the Christmas vestry.[79] By 1784 the vestry presented in September a list from which the magistrates chose surveyors[80] and by 1820 there was only one surveyor.[81] Elections at the Easter vestry also included those of the auditors of accounts, a small committee of four or six, which in 1701 included the rector 'for church affairs only'.[82]

All officers were chosen from the most important inhabitants. Sometimes one person combined two offices: a joint churchwarden and overseer was elected in 1687.[83] Many prominent residents, having business interests in London, paid a fine to be excused office. Among them were Sir John

[39] Guildhall MS. (formerly St. Paul's MS. B 103).
[40] P.R.O., C 1/46/73.
[41] Guildhall MS. (formerly St. Paul's MS. C (Sampson), ff. 212–14).
[42] Guildhall MSS. 14233/1–21. There are also draft, indexed ct. bks. for 1681–1823: ibid. 14234.
[43] Guildhall MS. 11816B, p. 132.
[44] Ibid. 14233/2.
[45] Guildhall MS. (formerly St. Paul's MS. B 103).
[46] Ibid. 14233/1. [47] Ibid. 2.
[48] Ibid. 2, 16, 19; Robinson, *Stoke Newington*, 48.
[49] Guildhall MSS. 14233/19, p. 132; 21, p. 179.
[50] Guildhall MSS. (formerly St. Paul's MS. C (Sampson), ff. 212–13); (formerly St. Paul's MS. A 37/1114).
[51] Guildhall MS. 11816B, p. 132.
[52] Robinson, *Stoke Newington*, 56.
[53] Guildhall MS. 14233/16, p. 32; tithe (1848), no. 378.
[54] Guildhall MSS. CC. 209373, 282581; tithe (1848), no. 20.
[55] Guildhall MS. (formerly St. Paul's MS. B 103).
[56] P.R.O., E 179/142/23, m. 26.
[57] Guildhall MS. 14233/1.
[58] Ibid. 2; 16, pp. 45–6.
[59] Guildhall MS. CC. 209372.

[60] Ibid. MS. 14233/19, pp. 132–3.
[61] Ibid. 1; 11816B, p. 133; tithe (1848), no. 242.
[62] *Sel. Cases from Coroners' Rolls* 1265–1413 (Selden Soc. ix), p. 54. [63] Robinson, *Stoke Newington*, 222.
[64] Ibid. 147–8. [65] Vestry mins. 1819–38, 193.
[66] Ibid. 10; 1784–1819, 32, 270; Robinson, *Stoke Newington*, 148; *Kelly's Dir. Mdx.* (1855); *Kelly's Dir. Lond. Suburbs* (1860). [67] Vestry mins. 1681–1743.
[68] Guildhall MS. 14233/1.
[69] Vestry mins. 1681–1743, 1–5.
[70] Ibid. 1784–1819, 34–7.
[71] Ibid. 1681–1743, 500.
[72] Ibid. 1784–1819, 161.
[73] Guildhall MS. 9537/4, f. 10v.
[74] Vestry mins. 1681–1743, 7.
[75] Ibid. 1784–1819, 414.
[76] Draft Index to par. ledger 1, s.v. overseers.
[77] *Rep. Com. Poor Laws*, H.C. 44, p. 178f (1834), xxxv.
[78] Guildhall MS. 14233/1.
[79] Vestry mins. 1681–1743, 6, 342.
[80] Ibid. 1784–1819, 47, 275.
[81] Robinson, *Stoke Newington*, 188.
[82] Vestry mins. 1681–1743, 7, 72; 1784–1819, 29.
[83] Ibid. 1681–1743, 20.

Hartopp in 1682, John Upton in 1684, Thomas Gunston in 1695, Daniel Defoe in 1721, and Jonathan Eade in 1786.[84] In 1743 the vestry, noting the reluctance to serve, insisted that those elected must serve or pay the fine,[85] which by 1786 was £20.[86]

Most other officers were salaried. A sexton, mentioned in 1701,[87] was appointed at the Easter vestry and in 1729 one was granted a salary because of his long service.[88] In 1800 and 1811 the sexton was a woman[89] and by 1819 the post was evidently regarded as a charity since the oldest of four candidates, all women, was chosen.[90] In 1835 there was a male sexton,[91] a member of the Foster family which continued to hold the office until 1901.[92] The expense from vagrants and disorderly people led to the appointment of a salaried and uniformed beadle in 1726.[93] For a few years after 1773 the beadle was a perpetual headborough.[94] Payment was made to an apothecary for the poor in 1727 and to a parish midwife in 1734,[95] and in 1824 the vestry decided to appoint a salaried surgeon and apothecary.[96] An organist was appointed for the new organ in 1807[97] but in 1824 a vestry committee was to ascertain his 'deficiency of performance' and he was instructed to take lessons.[98] As parish business increased, there was a sidesman to assist the churchwardens from 1772,[99] a deputy beadle fom 1810,[1] a salaried assistant overseer from 1822,[2] and a collector of the church and highway rates from 1825.[3]

The vestry existed by 1617[4] although extant minutes date only from 1681, with a gap for 1744–83.[5] In 1681 earlier vestry books were in the hands of a churchwarden who had been appointed by the rector and ejected by the vestry.[6] There are surveyors' accounts for 1823–48 and rate books for 1822–35,[7] poor rate books for 1838–40,[8] and churchwardens' accounts for 1840–1[9] and 1856–1910,[10] but other records, which in 1825 included accounts of the churchwardens, overseers, and surveyors, and poor and church rate books, have all been lost.[11]

Vestry meetings, in the vestry house in the late 17th century,[12] the church in 1700,[13] and the vestry room in the 19th century,[14] varied from 2–4 a year in the 1680s to 8 in 1731, 21 in 1784, 10 in 1800, and 9 in 1820. The average attendance remained remarkably constant: 13 in 1681, 11 in 1784, 12 in 1800, and 15 in 1820.[15] Very large attendances included more than 50 in 1808 and 126 in 1820, to nominate recipients for charity.[16] Meetings were usually chaired by the rector or one of the parish officers. *Ad hoc* committees were frequently used: they investigated such matters as the question of a workhouse in 1733,[17] turnpike roads in 1788,[18] and other roads in 1825,[19] the charity school in 1789,[20] the state of the church in 1790,[21] and the Palatine estate in 1809.[22] Sometimes committees assisted the parish officers, as in 1702 and 1820 when the overseers needed help in scrutinizing the distribution of parish relief.[23] Nevertheless the vestry declared in 1834 that all matters were managed in open vestry and not by boards and committees.[24]

Parish government was financed by rates, rent from parish property and church pews, burial fees, and such special subscriptions as a collection for refugees in 1699[25] or for defence in case of invasion in 1798.[26] Large expenses like repairs or extensions to the church were met by borrowing, as in 1716 when the parish field was mortgaged, 1806, and 1828.[27] All expenses were entered on the churchwardens' accounts and a single rate was levied until 1713, when separate poor and church rates were levied, each at 6d. in the £.[28] Church rates, 12d. in 1728[29] and 4d. in 1731 and 1784,[30] were usually 6d.[31] and levied once a year. Poor rates, ranging from 8d. in 1731 to 2s. 6d. in 1820, were often twice yearly.[32] In 1784 rates were fixed according to rack rents and were not to be increased for those who improved the houses in which they lived.[33] In 1823 rates on houses let at £6–20 a year were assessed on owners rather than occupiers.[34] The poor rate raised nearly £10 in 1620, £296 in 1776,[35] £1,365 in 1803, £1,401 in 1831 and £2,278 in 1835.[36] A highway rate was levied by 1698[37] and surveyors' accounts were presented for audit with those of the church-

[84] Vestry mins. 1681–1743, 7, 15, 44, 230–5; 1784–1819, 70.
[85] Ibid. 1681–1743, 501–2.
[86] Ibid. 1784–1819, 70.
[87] Ibid. 1681–1743, 79.
[88] Ibid. 1784–1819, 32, 270; Draft Index to par. ledger 1, s.v. sexton.
[89] Vestry mins. 1784–1819, 270, 414.
[90] Ibid. 1819–38, 4.
[91] Ibid. 492.
[92] Stoke Newington, *Official Guide* [1917], 26.
[93] Vestry mins. 1681–1743, 258.
[94] Draft Index to par. ledger 1, s.v. beadle.
[95] Ibid. s.v. apothecary, midwife.
[96] Vestry mins. 1819–38, 108.
[97] Ibid. 1784–1819, 414.
[98] Ibid. 1819–38, 108, 119.
[99] Draft Index to par. ledger 1, s.v. sidesmen.
[1] Vestry mins. 1784–1819, 407.
[2] Ibid. 1819–38, 58.
[3] Ibid. 139.
[4] Draft Index to par. ledger 1, s.v. bks. and writings.
[5] Vestry mins. 1681–1743, 1784–1895 (HA P/M/1, 3–7).
[6] Ibid. 1681–1743, 1.
[7] HA P/M/H/1.
[8] Ibid. P/M/P/1.
[9] Ibid. P/M/CW/1.
[10] Ibid. P/M/CW/3; P/M/8; G.L.R.O., P94/MRY/153.
[11] Vestry mins. 1819–38, 133.

[12] Ibid. 1681–1743, 1, 6.
[13] Ibid. 64.
[14] Ibid. 1819–38, 17.
[15] Ibid. 1681–1743, 1–25, 323–42; 1784–1819, 1–50, 270–81; 1819–38, 17–32.
[16] Ibid. 1784–1819, 371; 1819–38, 32.
[17] Ibid. 1681–1743, 365.
[18] Ibid. 1784–1819, 97.
[19] Ibid. 1819–38, 143–6.
[20] Ibid. 1784–1819, 125.
[21] Ibid. 136.
[22] Ibid. 393.
[23] Ibid. 1819–38, 19; Draft Index to par. ledger 1, s.v. committees.
[24] *Rep. Com. Poor Laws*, H.C. 44, p. 178f (1834), xxxv.
[25] Vestry mins. 1681–1743, 58.
[26] Ibid. 1784–1819, 239.
[27] Ibid. 1681–1743, 195; 1784–1819, 378; 1819–38, 220.
[28] Ibid. 1681–1743, 50, 60–1, 161.
[29] Ibid. 285.
[30] Ibid. 327; 1784–1819, 50.
[31] Ibid. 1819–38, 220.
[32] Ibid. 1681–1743, 327; 1784–1819, 50, 273, 276–7, 280; 1819–38, 22, 30.
[33] Ibid. 1784–1819, 42.
[34] Ibid. 1819–38, 78.
[35] Ibid. 186; *Abstract of Returns by Overseers, 1787*, H.C. 1st ser. ix, p. 628.
[36] *Rep. Com. Poor Laws*, H.C. 44, p. 178f (1834), xxxv; *2nd Ann. Rep. Poor Law Commrs*. H.C. 595-II, pp. 212–13 (1836), xxix; Robinson, *Stoke Newington*, 186.
[37] P.R.O., C 10/526/45.

wardens by 1798.[38] The highway rate, usually 6d., raised £173 12s. 6d. in 1781–2 and c. £230 in 1820.[39]

Poor relief to individuals was mostly in weekly payments to widows and orphans.[40] In February 1784 the weather was unusually severe and collections raised £120 for coal, bread, and large joints of beef to poor families.[41] There were proposals in 1795 to raise subscriptions to buy coal in bulk in summer to distribute at a cheap rate in winter.[42] In that year there were 29 claimants for relief and it was said that many were granted settlement because they had been servants in the parish.[43] About 300 people were given relief weekly or occasionally during 1834; a third were women over 50, many formerly servants, and 130 were children.[44]

In 1734 the vestry converted a leased house in Church Street into a workhouse. Casual poor were to be accommodated in the garrets and a widow's monthly payments were reduced because she refused to move there.[45] In 1739 a man from Waltham Holy Cross (Essex) agreed to provide food and lodging for some of the aged and infirm poor of Stoke Newington.[46] The poor were farmed for £100 a year from 1744 probably until 1773, when William Collier contracted to provide them with food, clothing, lodging, and medicine for 6d. a head a day. In 1777 there were said to be 20 paupers in the house, presumably the workhouse, another 3 probably in the parish houses at the east end of Church Street, where in 1779 4 widows were housed rent-free, and 23 out-pensioners.[47] After Collier's death in 1791 the poor were farmed to Messrs. Overton and Son of Mile End at 3s. 9d. a week each for three months. Overton had charge of the poor in 1800 and 19 paupers were still farmed out in Mile End at 6s. each a week in 1820. In addition the parish paid pensions of 2–10s. a week to 6 paupers in the parish houses and 60 out-pensioners.[48] The workhouse, said to house ten in 1795,[49] was evidently abandoned by 1819 when the vestry considered buying a workhouse. In 1820 a house was bought in Church Street,[50] which after 1825 housed the invalid asylum for women.[51] There was no workhouse in 1834, when 20 paupers were farmed at 4s. 6d.–5s. a week, a system said to have been successfully followed for many years. The parish then also supported three paupers at the county lunatic asylum and four children at Sewardstone (Essex) silk mill.[52] In 1826 the surveyors and overseers were to find work for the able-bodied[53] but by 1834 c. 15 able-bodied poor

were receiving regular relief, often on the instructions of magistrates after the overseers had refused payment.[54]

In the 1830s the poor occupied a very small part of the vestry minutes. Among other subjects the vestry had long been concerned with the church, charities, policing, the charity school, and apprenticing, including apprenticing girls to carpenters in 1735.[55] It regulated fees for christenings and burials in 1681 and 1696, when it charged double for strangers, and in 1702 was in conflict with the rector over several issues, including burial fees and letting pews to strangers.[56] It regulated fees for pews, of which it made a survey in 1792.[57] The vestry also disputed with turnpike trustees and trustees of watching and lighting. It administered parish property, the four houses left by Stock's charity and the parish field.[58]

LOCAL GOVERNMENT AFTER 1836. In 1836, under the Poor Law Amendment Act of 1834, Stoke Newington was united with Hackney in Hackney poor law union. Stoke Newington had still not elected its five members of the board of guardians in 1837[59] and there was some resentment in 1840 that payments to the union had been increased although the number of poor in the parish had diminished.[60] In 1844 the parish paid £1,300 for the poor[61] and in the 1850s it sent people to Australia.[62] Both Stoke Newington and Hackney maintained their own settled poor but costs of maintaining the union workhouse opened at Homerton in 1845 and the 'non settled or irremovable poor' were met from a common fund to which parochial contributions were fixed by the Poor Law Board. In 1857 Stoke Newington's contribution had been fixed at a tenth, based on the number of poor chargeable to the parish, which had 48 inmates in the workhouse in 1855.[63] By 1861 its contribution was still a tenth although it had only 28 indoor and 48 outdoor poor compared with Hackney's 559 and 1,401. Stoke Newington resented the recent change according to rateable value contributions, and felt that the settlement clerk at Homerton was remote.[64] Hackney union, to which the detached portions of Hornsey parish were added in 1900, remained the poor law authority until it was superseded by the L.C.C. in 1929.[65] Stoke Newington continued discontented, claiming in 1922 that 'it would be cheaper to send our paupers to the Hotel Cecil than to subscribe to Hackney union'.[66]

[38] Vestry mins. 1784–1819, 231.
[39] Robinson, *Stoke Newington*, 188.
[40] e.g. vestry mins. 1681–1743, 25–8, 61, 323; 1784–1819, 1.   [41] Ibid. 1784–1819, 8.
[42] *Proposals for supplying poor with coals*, 1795 (S.N.L. cuttings 41.1).
[43] Vestry mins. 1784–1819, 209–13.
[44] *Rep. Com. Poor Laws*, H.C. 44, p. 148f (1834), xxxv.
[45] Vestry mins. 1681–1743, 365, 370–2, 382–3.
[46] Ibid. 442.
[47] Robinson, *Stoke Newington*, 187; Draft Index to par. ledger 1, s.v. almshos.
[48] Robinson, *Stoke Newington*, 187; Draft Index to par. ledger 1, s.v. workhos.; vestry mins. 1784–1819, 15–29, 141, 270.   [49] Vestry mins. 1784–1819, 209–13.
[50] Ibid. 1819–38, 15, 23.   [51] Below, pub. svces.
[52] *Rep. Com. Poor Laws*, H.C. 44, p. 178h (1834), xxxv.

[53] Vestry mins. 1819–38, 182.
[54] *Rep. Com. Poor Laws*, H.C. 44, p. 178h (1834), xxxv.
[55] Vestry mins. 1681–1743, 385.
[56] Ibid. 1, 46, 85.   [57] Ibid. 6; 1784–1819, 165.
[58] Ibid. 1681–1743, 129; above, other est.
[59] Vestry mins. 1819–38, 543; *Hackney Official Guide* [1980], 24.   [60] Vestry mins. 1838–62, 50–2.
[61] *Parochial and Boro. Rates*, H.C. 635, p. 170 (1844), xlii.
[62] *3rd Ann. Rep. Poor Law Bd. 1850* [1340], H.C., p. 149 (1851), xxvi; *5th Ann. Rep. 1851* [1461], H.C., p. 133 (1852), xxiii; *6th Ann. Rep. 1853* [1797], H.C., p. 180 (1854), xxix.
[63] G.L.R.O., P94/MRY/282–4 (List of paupers 1855).
[64] Vestry mins. 1838–62, 198, 600–2.
[65] G.L.R.O., Ha B.G. (mins. of Hackney bd. of guardians); *Hackney Official Guide* [1980], 24.
[66] Royal Com. on Lond. Govt., *Mins. of Evidence* (1922), 971.

Until 1855 the open vestry, which met in the vestry room, dealt as before with business other than the poor. Attendances varied widely, fluctuating in 1840 between 9 and 68.[67] A great deal of time was occupied in controversy between the rector and High Church party on the one hand and the Low Church party and dissenters on the other: Quakers and other dissenters refused to pay church rates in 1838 and there were further clashes on the subject, in 1840, 1842 and 1853.[68] Salaries, the church fabric, the fire engine, charities, the Palatine estate, and the destruction of hedgehogs all figured in the churchwardens' accounts in 1840.[69]

The problem of drainage and sewerage was made urgent by the spread of building. In 1840 a committee recommended building leases on the Palatine estate with provision for sewers to be of a standard 'as if the parish were within the jurisdiction of the Building Act'.[70] The vestry in 1843 set up a committee to deal with the watercourse next to Queen Elizabeth's Walk[71] and in 1852 requested the Metropolitan Commission of Sewers, constituted in 1848,[72] to deal with Hackney brook.[73] In 1855 the Metropolis Local Management Act replaced the commission with the Metropolitan Board of Works and the parish vestries with new vestries and district boards. Stoke Newington became part of Hackney district, which sent one member to the M.B.W.

Stoke Newington parish formed one of the eight wards of Hackney district and was represented by six (twelve from 1892) of its vestrymen. Members of the new select vestry had to be resident householders rated at more than £40 a year.[74] Stoke Newington's ratepayers welcomed the transfer to metropolitan government of sanitary problems but deplored the introduction of a select vestry and the loss of control over rates.[75] In an attempt to involve those who were disqualified from membership under the 1855 Act, the vestry decided in 1857 that meetings should be open to all parishioners, although they presumably no longer had any say in decisions. The select vestry of 18 elected members, later increased by stages to 60, together with the incumbent and churchwardens, in theory had all the powers of the old vestry except those transferred to Hackney board of works.[76] The vestry still elected parish officers but in 1856 it decided to discontinue the church rate, 'that fruitful source of controversy'.[77] There were still disagreements over ritualism and the right of the rector to the chair.[78] Since the board dealt with drainage and sewerage, water supply, roads,

refuse disposal, lighting, building regulations, and health, there was little left for the vestry to do except make recommendations to their representatives on the board.[79]

The property qualification ensured that vestrymen were almost exclusively drawn from the wealthy and professional classes, mostly living in the northern part of the parish. The 24 members in 1880 came from Lordship Road and Park, Albion Road, Clissold Road, Church Row, and Paradise Row and included Joseph Beck of the Quaker family, Edward Paget Nunn the builder, John Runtz (d. 1891), and his son John Johnson Runtz, a City insurance broker.[80] The ratepayers' association, which existed by 1884, was the main group behind the selection of vestrymen and representatives on Hackney board of works and the board of guardians.[81] A committee of the association met once a month by 1891 and the policies of the association, which described itself as non-political, were mainly concerned with limiting expenditure and promoting the separation of Stoke Newington from Hackney.[82]

By the 1860s most vestry meetings were held in the parish schoolroom or the Manor rooms.[83] In 1874 no. 46 (in 1880 no. 126) Church Street was leased for vestry offices and as a meeting place[84] but by 1889 the premises were no longer large enough and the assembly rooms in Defoe Road were hired for meetings on the third Friday in each month.[85] In 1891 the parish was divided into wards: Lordship and Church wards, each with 15 vestrymen, Manor ward with 12, and Clissold and Palatine wards, with 9 each.[86]

Stoke Newington never accepted the union with Hackney and attempted in 1864, 1887, and 1890 to regain its independence.[87] It also opposed the increased centralization which it feared from the London Government Act of 1888, which replaced the M.B.W. by the L.C.C., although the L.C.C. was directly elected on the basis of parliamentary divisions.[88] Attendance of Stoke Newington's representatives at the district board's meetings during 1891–3 was consistently worse than that of Hackney's representatives.[89]

By mutual consent Stoke Newington and Hackney separated under the Metropolis Management (Plumstead and Hackney) Act, 1893,[90] which transferred the powers of the district board to the constituent parish vestries in 1894.[91] The Local Government Act of 1894 abolished the property qualification for vestrymen and the ex-officio chairmanship of the incumbent. Although the latter had long been in dispute, the first elected chairman was the rector.

[67] Vestry mins. 1838–62, 45, 65.
[68] Ibid. 1819–38, 573; 1838–62, 3–4, 46, 64, 117, 352–3.
[69] Chwdns. accts. 1840–1 (HA P/M/CW/1).
[70] Vestry mins. 1838–62, 68.   [71] Ibid. 122.
[72] 11 & 12 Vic. c. 112.
[73] Vestry mins. 1838–62, 323.
[74] Hackney dist. bd. of wks. List of Trustees, Guardians etc. (1859–60), 9; vestry mins. 1889–95, 146–7.
[75] Vestry mins. 1838–62, 410, 421.
[76] Ibid. 460, 507–8; 1862–89, 302.
[77] Ibid. 1838–62, 450.
[78] Ibid. 1862–89, 30, 62, 99, 100–4, 260, 396.
[79] e.g. in 1857 over lighting: vestry mins. 1838–62, 484.
[80] List of vestrymen 1880 (S.N.L. cuttings 34); S.N.L. illus. 78 Runtz, LC 1107; Reign of Geo. V, Repres. subjects of the King, 1912 (S.N.L. cuttings 32 Runtz, LC 2225).

[81] Cutting, May 1884 (S.N.L. cuttings 34).
[82] Letter, 1891, and brochure (S.N.L. cuttings 34, LC 1742, 1976).
[83] Vestry mins. 1838–62, 553, 560, 571, 573.
[84] Ibid. 1862–89, 268, 278; list of vestrymen 1880 (S.N.L. cuttings 34).
[85] Vestry mins. 1862–89, 664.
[86] Lond. Gaz. 14 Apr. 1891, p. 2063.
[87] Vestry mins. 1862–89, 29, 35–6, 605; 1889–95, 61; Hackney dist. bd. of wks. Ann. Rep. (1888), 20–3.
[88] Vestry mins. 1862–89, 494, 638; A. B. Hopkins, Boros. of the Metropolis (1900), 13.
[89] Hackney dist. bd. of wks. Attendances 1891–3 (HA J/ BW/3).
[90] 56 & 57 Vic. c. 55.
[91] Stoke Newington vestry, Ann. Rep. (1894–5), 5.

There continued to be 60 vestrymen, elected by the five wards[92] and meeting monthly in the assembly rooms.[93] The vestry retained the clerk, George Webb, who served as clerk of vestry and M.B. from 1862 to 1913,[94] and assistant clerk, and appointed a surveyor and chief sanitary inspector, two assistant sanitary inspectors, and a medical officer of health. It took over the whole of no. 126 Church Street, set up standing committees for general purposes and finance, and employed contractors for refuse disposal, sewerage, and drainage work.[95] It assumed responsibility for burials which had been exercised by a burial board since 1862.[96]

In 1900, under the London Government Act of 1899,[97] the old parish was united with South Hornsey in Stoke Newington M.B. There were 6 wards: South Hornsey with 9 councillors, Church and Lordship with 6 each, and Clissold, Manor, and Palatine with 3 each.[98] In 1953 the borough was divided into 10 wards with 3 councillors each: Brownswood, Church, Clissold, Defoe, Lordship, Manor, Milton, Palatine, Wilberforce, and Woodberry.[99] The council met once a month.[1]

BOROUGH OF STOKE NEWING-TON. *Gules, a cross lozengy ermine and sable, over all two crossed swords argent pommelled and hilted or; on a chief argent a lion rampant vert, its tail forked, between two oak trees eradicated proper fructed or*

[Granted 1934]

Until the Second World War Stoke Newington described itself as one of the very few metropolitan boroughs to conduct local government on non-party lines.[2] The ratepayers' association, which had lapsed, possibly after the widening of the franchise in 1894, was revived in 1900[3] and most councillors were its candidates and unopposed; they were described, if at all, as independent, although there were several municipal reformers in the years 1909–11.[4] Most had served on the old vestry, with professional or business interests in Stoke Newington or the City, and many were Conservative. John Johnson Runtz (d. 1922), the first mayor in 1900, was knighted in 1903, and had been an active Conservative since 1868.[5] Other Conservatives included William Eve (d. 1916), a surveyor in the City who had been a vestryman since 1871 and was mayor in 1901[6] and Herbert Ormond (d. 1934), mayor 1913–19 and 1929–34, head of a drapery firm in High Street, who lived in Lordship Road, and was knighted in 1920.[7] In 1922 the ratepayers' candidates included three manufacturers, three accountants, a barrister, a solicitor, a medical practitioner, a surveyor, an insurance manager, and an auctioneer.[8] George Alcock, a warehouse-man and former railwayman, who had been a vestryman and continued as a councillor, was a rare example of a 'working man' in local politics in the first decade of the 20th century. Although Alcock respected the local tradition of eschewing party labels, three candidates in 1900 stood as Progressives.[9] In 1918 Ormond caused bitter dissension by standing as an Independent parliamentary candidate and was accused of violating Stoke Newington's tradition that the council was not a political body.[10] Politics was said to have been forced upon the council in 1919 when the Socialist-Labour party 'invaded' the council chamber and 'pushed out men who had been there for years'.[11] In 1922 Labour, whose candidates included 3 carpenters, 2 bricklayers, a trades union organizer, a warehouseman, a plumber, and several industrial workers, mostly from the south part of the borough, contested 29 of the 30 seats[12] but lost heavily.[13] The first Labour councillor was elected in 1926[14] and by 1937 Labour had captured 13 of the 30 seats, the rest being taken by the United Ratepayers party. The Conservatives had contested, unsuccessfully, six seats.[15] In 1945 all 30 councillors were Labour and, except from 1949 to 1953, and 1968 to 1971 when the Conservatives dominated, Labour has remained in control of the borough until 1965 and of Hackney L.B. which succeeded it.[16] Women, who could serve on the old vestry, were excluded from the B.C. until 1917 when Miss Carrie Maud Eve, William's daughter, was co-opted.[17] She was a candidate for the ratepayers in 1922, when four women stood for Labour,[18] and in 1924 became mayor.[19] The percentage of the electorate voting averaged 47

[92] Ibid. 14; G. L. Gomme, *Lond. in reign of Victoria* (1898), 196, 198.
[93] Stoke Newington vestry, *Ann. Rep.* (1895–6), 145, 168.
[94] *Daily Chron.* 1 Sept. 1912; *Hackney & Kingsland Gaz.* 4 July 1913 (S.N.L. cuttings 36 Webb). Webb was a member of the brickmaking fam.: cf. above, trade and ind.
[95] Stoke Newington vestry, *Ann. Rep.* (1894–5), 6–9.
[96] Ibid. (1896–7), 8–9.
[97] 62 & 63 Vic. c. 14.
[98] Stoke Newington vestry, *Ann. Rep.* (1899–1900), 11–12; L.C.C. *Lond. Statistics*, xxvi (1915–20), 24.
[99] Lond. Cnty. *Stoke Newington (Councillors and Wards) Order*, 1952 (S.N.L. cuttings 80).
[1] *Kelly's Dir. Stoke Newington* (1909–10), 22; Stoke Newington B.C. *Mins.* 21 May 1958.
[2] e.g. Stoke Newington, *Official Guide* [1938], 23.
[3] Cuttings 1900; 26 Feb. 1917 (S.N.L. cuttings 34).
[4] *The Times*, 2 Nov. 1909, 12e; 3 Nov. 1909, 10b; 10 Nov. 1910, 8a; 10 Nov. 1911, 7c.
[5] *Reign of Geo. V, Repres. Subjects of the King*, 1912 (S.N.L. cuttings 32 Runtz, LC 2225); cutting 10 Nov. 1922 (S.N.L. cuttings 78 Runtz).

[6] *Hackney & Stoke Newington Recorder*, 18 Feb. 1916 (S.N.L. cuttings 33 Eve).
[7] *Stoke Newington Recorder*, 24 Aug. 1934; *Daily Mail*, 24 Aug. 1934; *Financial Times*, 24 Aug. 1934; cutting 9 Jan. 1920; *The Draper & Drapery Times*, 26 Aug. 1916 (all S.N.L. cuttings 32 Ormond).
[8] Cutting 23 Oct. 1922 (S.N.L. cuttings 35.3).
[9] *Stoke Newington Election Bills*, 1900–4 (HA SN/CEP/1).
[10] *Hackney & Stoke Newington Recorder*, 20 Dec. 1918 (S.N.L. cuttings 34.3).
[11] *Hackney & Kingsland Gaz.* 24 Nov. 1922 (S.N.L. cuttings 34.3).
[12] Cutting, 23 Oct. 1922 (S.N.L. cuttings 35.3).
[13] *Hackney Review & Stoke Newington Chron.* 4 Nov. 1922 (S.N.L. cuttings 35.3).   [14] *The Times*, 18 Sept. 1926, 19c.
[15] *Hornsey Jnl.* 5 Nov. 1937 (S.N.L. cuttings 35.3).
[16] *The Times*, 3 Nov. 1945, 2d; 14 May 1949, 2d; 11 May 1956, 5f; 8 May 1959, 8a; 17 May 1968, 5a; 18 May 1968, 3h.
[17] Hopkins, *Boros. of Metropolis*, 24; Stoke Newington, *Official Guide* [1921], 35.
[18] Cutting, 2 Dec. 1922 (S.N.L. cuttings 35.3).
[19] *The Times*, 2 Oct. 1924, 11g.

per cent before 1914, 36 per cent 1918–39, and only 33 per cent after 1945.[20]

The borough in 1900 had two departments, that of the town clerk with 3 clerks, and the sanitary department employing a medical officer of health, a borough engineer, 2 sanitary inspectors, 3 clerks, and 3 rate collectors, all housed in the two-storeyed, square, Italianate council offices built by South Hornsey district council in Milton Road in 1881; a new wing was added in 1915.[21] By 1919 the sanitary department had been divided into a surveyor's department, consisting of the surveyor and 2 assistants, and a public health department, consisting of the medical officer of health, 3 sanitary inspectors, and a clerk. There was also an electricity department with an electrical engineer and 3 assistants at the electricity station in Edward's Lane.[22] An assistant town clerk was appointed in 1923.[23] In 1924 no. 46 Milton Road was adapted for a finance department but in 1925 the council was censured for not having a chief financial officer.[24] There were 43 officials in 1930: 9 in the town clerk's department, 17 in the treasurer's, 9 in the surveyor's, and 8 in the medical officer of health's.[25] The M.B.'s standing committees had increased to 8 by 1930[26] and 12 by 1937, when a new town hall, designed by J. Reginald Truelove and including an assembly hall, was opened on the site of Church Row (nos. 166–80 Church Street).[27]

London Borough of Hackney. *Per fess in chief per fess sable and argent a maltese cross per fess argent and gules between two oak trees eradicated or fructed gules and in the base gules three bells or, the whole within a bordure barry wavy argent and azure*

[Granted 1969]

A survey of overcrowding was carried out in 1935 and a housing department was set up in 1948.[28] The council formed a direct labour force in 1941 to build shelters and undertake repairs,

and by 1949 it numbered 130 and was used to build council estates.[29] A closed shop for all council employees was instituted in 1946,[30] and by 1961 the council was indicted for wasting time and money with its direct labour force.[31]

In 1965, under the London Government Act, 1963, Stoke Newington was combined with Hackney and Shoreditch M.B.s in Hackney L.B., within which it formed four wards, Brownswood, New River, Defoe, and Clissold. Defoe was divided in 1978 into North and South Defoe. Stoke Newington town hall housed the directorate of finance.[32]

Stoke Newington formed part of North Hackney parliamentary and L.C.C. constituency until 1918 when it became a separate constituency.[33] Municipal reformers represented it on the L.C.C. from 1919 to 1937[34] and the Conservative Sir George Jones was the M.P. from 1918 to 1945, except from 1923 to 1924, when there was a Liberal.[35] In 1946 two Islington wards were combined with Stoke Newington constituency and from 1948 the borough was combined with Hackney North.[36] Labour has provided L.C.C. representatives since 1937[37] and the M.P. since 1945. David Weitzman was M.P. 1945–79.[38]

PUBLIC SERVICES. There was a common well on Newington Green *c.* 1541[39] and the main public source was the parish pond on the south side of Church Street near the old rectory, mentioned in 1569 as the pillory pond.[40] In 1828 it was filled in and a well and pump were fixed on the site.[41] In the 1560s William Patten spent considerable sums on supplying water to the manor house.[42] Permission to pipe or fetch water from neighbouring wells or pumps often featured in 18th-century leases.[43]

Some houses, particularly in Church Street, paid for piped water from the New River in the early 18th century.[44] From *c.* 1724 when the course was altered, the New River Co. was bound to supply Abney House and houses built on the demesne free of charge.[45] Six houses in Church Street were thus supplied in 1825.[46] By will dated 1664 Thomas Stock directed that the rent from

[20] L.C.C. *Lond. Statistics*, xxvi (1915–20), 24, 26; xxviii (1921–2), 25; xxx (1924–5), 23; xxxiv (1928–30), 18; xli (1936–8), 26; n.s. i (1945–54), 28; n.s. iv (1950–9), 24; n.s. vii (1955–64), 17.

[21] *Kelly's Dir. Stoke Newington* (1901–2), 36; Stoke Newington, *Official Guide* [1928], 20; photos. (S.N.L. illus. 31.31, LC 570).

[22] *Kelly's Dir. Stoke Newington* (1919–20), 22.

[23] *Hackney & Kingsland Gaz.* 5 Nov. 1923 (S.N.L. cuttings 36).

[24] *The Times*, 1 Oct. 1925, 16a; *Kelly's Dir. Stoke Newington* (1929), p. A 19.

[25] *Rep. on Town Hall Accn.* 11 Sept. 1930 (S.N.L. cuttings 31.3, LC 260).

[26] Ibid.

[27] Stoke Newington M.B. *Opening of New Municipal Bldgs.* 1937 (S.N.L.); *Architecture Illustrated*, Oct. 1937 (S.N.L. 31.3201, LC 2640); above, plate 52.

[28] Stoke Newington, *Official Guide* (1950), 83; [1955], 57.

[29] Ibid. [1955], 20.

[30] *The Times*, 25 Sept. 1946, 2g.

[31] Ibid. 21 Nov. 1961, 6d; 23 Nov. 1961, 8e.

[32] Royal Com. on Local Govt. in Gtr. Lond. *Mins. of Evidence* (1959), day 8, pp. 309–26; *Census*, 1971; START, *Interim Rep. on Social Trends in Hackney L.B.* (S.N.L. 40.4), map; *Hackney Official Guide* [1980], 39, 67; Hackney Boro.

Plan, *Stoke Newington Planning Area* (1982), map 1.1; Hackney L.B., *Council Mins.* May 1978.

[33] L.C.C. *Lond. Statistics*, xvi (1905–6), plate 1; xxv (1914–15), 24; xxvi (1915–20), 18; xxvii (1920–1), 14.

[34] W. E. Jackson, *Achievement: Short Hist. of L.C.C.* (1965), App. II, pp. 259, 264, 269.

[35] *The Times*, 30 Dec. 1918, Suppl. *id*; 9 Nov. 1922, 14a; 17 Nov. 1922, Suppl. *if*; 8 Dec. 1923, Suppl. *if*; 31 Oct. 1924, Suppl. *if*; 28 May 1929, 8e; 31 May 1929, 6c; 28 Oct. 1931, 6c; 16 Nov. 1935, 1g.

[36] Ibid. 30 Aug. 1946, 2c; L.C.C. *Statistical Abstract for Lond.* xxxi (1939–48), 24.

[37] Jackson, *Achievement*, 253–5, 266, 268, 275–7, 279.

[38] *Whitaker's Almanack* (1946 and later edns.).

[39] Consistory of Lond. Rec., Bks. of Depositions and Answers, vi (1541), f. 21 (copy in S.N.L. Letters 78 Arnold, LC 2123). [40] Guildhall MS. 14233/1.

[41] Abstract of Ct. Rolls 1802–32, 304; vestry mins. 1819–38, 249.

[42] Guildhall MS. (formerly St. Paul's MS. A 37/1114).

[43] e.g. M.L.R. 1718/4/241; 1765/3/7.

[44] P.R.O., C 10/526/45; G.L.R.O., Acc. 212/4.

[45] Memo. by official of New River Co. 1793 (transcript of docs. in possession of New River Co., S.N.L. cuttings 46.2, LC 901).

[46] Guildhall MS. CC. 212290.

one of his houses was to be applied to bringing the New River water along Church Street.[47] In 1897 the task was said to have been effected without any charge on Stock's property.[48] By 1856 nearly all houses within Hackney district had water laid on by the New River Co. or by the East London Water Works Co., which in that year provided service pipes in Paradise Row[49] but in 1867 only four houses in the district were on constant supply and houses in Cock and Castle Lane were supplied from two common cocks.[50] The water supply was still only intermittent until 1896 when the vestry's demand for a constant supply was met.[51] In 1904 the Metropolitan Water Board superseded all the metropolitan water companies[52] until itself superseded by the Thames Water Authority under the Water Act of 1973.[53]

Natural drainage was mostly by Hackney brook, north of Church Street.[54] In 1831, when cholera broke out, there was said to be a lot of bad drainage, Hackney (then called Manor) brook being particularly filthy.[55] In 1843 the vestry appointed a committee to deal with the drain next to Queen Elizabeth's Walk, a tributary of the brook.[56] In 1848 the brook, in the absence of a common sewer even in the main street and under the pressure of increased population, was said to be the receptacle of everything offensive. Drains were being laid from new houses directly to the brook.[57] In 1852 the vestry requested the Metropolitan Commissioners of Sewers to cover part of the brook, which carried 'the most obnoxious drainage from Highbury and Holloway',[58] and following further proposals in 1855[59] and 1856 the M.B.W., which had superseded the commissioners, agreed to replace the brook with a northern high level sewer,[60] and Hackney board undertook to provide sewers along the most populous roads, from Kingsland to Stamford Hill and along Church Street.[61] Most sewers had been constructed by 1860[62] and the whole system of main drainage was operating by 1868.[63] South Hornsey's sewage, previously discharged into the metropolitan sewers without payment,[64] was in 1874 officially admitted to the metropolitan system and the district charged sewerage rates.[65]

Watchmen were employed in the 16th century. Inhabitants were presented at the manor court in 1569 for the failure of the watch when summoned by the constable and in 1571 for failing to keep a watchman to guard a house within the demesne.[66] Payments were made for a watch in 1698[67] and the churchwardens' accounts in 1707 included disbursements to a private watch.[68] In 1750 the inhabitants of Stoke Newington raised subscriptions to provide a guard on the London road to protect coach and foot passengers.[69] In 1774, when Stoke Newington was said to be 'from its situation exposed to frequent robberies, burglaries, and other outrages', an Act was passed to light, watch, and water the parish: trustees who met each August and were empowered to make a rate of up to 1s. in the £, employed eight watchmen during the winter.[70] There were clashes between the trustees and the vestry in 1784 and 1786, when the vestry considered raising subscriptions to employ its own watchmen during the summer.[71] In 1828 there were nine night watchmen paid weekly by the trustees during winter and four patrols of private watchmen supported by voluntary contributions.[72] The vestry tried again in 1829, as it had in 1786, to gain control over the trustees.[73]

Stoke Newington was included in the metropolitan police area from 1829[74] and in 1830 the vestry declared that the new police were better than the watch, although there were complaints that parts of the parish, especially Cut Throat Lane, Lordship Road, Woodberry Down, and the northern part of Green Lanes, were insufficiently policed.[75] The lighting and watching trustees in 1854 were still concerned with lighting and watering the roads and employed a salaried clerk.[76] The London road and Green Lanes, which were lighted, watched, and watered under the turnpike Act of 1815,[77] were administered by a committee of the metropolitan turnpike roads commissioners from 1827 to 1836, who employed watchmen and a horse patrol. The numbers of the watchmen were steadily reduced from 25 in 1828 to 12 in 1834; in 1829 their swords were removed and in 1830 pistols were declared 'not necessary'.[78]

Punishments were presumably administered

[47] Vestry mins. 1681–1743, loose leaves at front [1674]; below, charities.

[48] *Endowed Chars. (County of Lond.)*, H.C. 128, pp. 723 sqq. (1897), lxvi(1).

[49] Hackney dist. bd. of wks. *M.O.H. Rep.* (1856), 6; Min. bk. (1855–7), 98. [50] Idem, *M.O.H. Rep.* (1867), 21.

[51] Ibid. (1893), 20, 22; Stoke Newington vestry, *Ann. Rep.* (1894–5), 14; *Hackney & Kingsland Gaz.*, *Jubilee Suppl.* 3 Apr. 1914 (S.N.L. cuttings 30, LC 3189).

[52] 2 Edw. VII, c. 41; L.C.C. *Lond. Statistics*, xvi (1905–6), 371.

[53] Robinson, *Stoke Newington*, frontispiece map.

[54] M. Cosh, *New River*, 7.

[55] Mins. of Cttee. of Health, 1831 (HA P/M/BH1).

[56] Vestry mins. 1838–62, 122.

[57] P.R.O., MH 13/261, no. 307/48.

[58] Vestry mins. 1838–62, 317, 323, 328; G.L.R.O., MCS 498/563; Hackney dist. bd. of wks. *Ann. Rep.* (1858), 5.

[59] Vestry mins. 1838–62, 421.

[60] G.L.R.O., MCS, MBW; 18 & 19 Vic. c. 120; Hackney dist. bd. of wks., Min. bk. (1855–7), 82; *Metropol. Drainage*, H.C. 233, pp. 270–5 (1857 Sess. 2), xxxvi.

[61] Hackney dist. bd. of wks. *Ann. Rep.* (1856–7), 3–4; (1858), 5.

[62] Ibid. (1860), 3.

[63] M.B.W. *Rep.* (1868–9), 10.

[64] Hackney dist. bd. of wks. *Surveyor's Rep.* (1872), 5.

[65] M.B.W. *Rep.* (1879), 15; 37 & 38 Vic. c. 97 (Local); *V.C.H. Mdx.* vi. 169.

[66] Guildhall MS. 14233/1.

[67] P.R.O., C 10/526/45.

[68] Vestry mins. 1681–1743, 122.

[69] Cuttings of Stoke Newington 1722–1895, p. 7a (S.N.L. 80, LC 2411).

[70] 14 Geo. III, c. 116 (Local and Personal); Robinson, *Stoke Newington*, 18–21.

[71] Vestry mins. 1784–1819, 48, 62, 66–7.

[72] *Rep. of Cttee. on Police of Metropolis*, H.C. 533, pp. 376–7 (1828), vi.

[73] Vestry mins. 1819–38, 272–4.

[74] 10 Geo. IV, c. 44.

[75] Vestry mins. 1819–38, 307, 320.

[76] Ibid. 419; *Returns on Paving, Cleansing and Lighting Metropol. Dists.* H.C. 127, pp. 5–6 (1854–5), liii.

[77] 55 Geo. III, c. 59 (Local and Personal); Robinson, *Stoke Newington*, 17.

[78] G.L.R.O., MRC 11 (Metropol. Rds. Com., mins. of cttees. 1827–36).

in and near the parish or pillory pond in Church Street in the 16th century. The constable was presented in 1572 for inadequate stocks and cucking stool and in 1576 the lord of the manor was to provide a tumbrel for scolds.[79] Control had presumably passed to the vestry by 1700 when the churchwardens' accounts included payments for repairing the stocks.[80] In 1716 the vestry ordered a cage to be built, and the next year someone pulled down both cage and stocks.[81] The culprit undertook to replace them in 1718 but in 1721 the vestry decided to move the cage, stocks, and whipping post to a place near the Green Dragon since their previous position, presumably also on the London road, was considered a nuisance by the road trustees.[82] The vestry decided to build a new cage on the south side of the brook in High Street, near the bridge at Stamford Hill, in 1803.[83] The cage was moved yet again in 1824, when it was built on land given by Joseph Eade in Red Lion Lane, near the pound and engine house.[84] The metropolitan police took over the cage and were presented in 1831 for erecting a chimney at the police station house in Red Lion Lane.[85] Although the police retained the station in 1870, by 1834 they were refusing to take charges there and Stoke Newington people had to go to Kingsland, presumably to the watchhouse on the Hackney side of High Street, south of Shacklewell Lane.[86] The police also had stables in Barrett's Grove by 1848[87] and in 1868 built a station at no. 33 High Street. A new section house was acquired in 1913 and rebuilding of the station was planned in 1959 and again for 1976; in 1982, however, the station was still essentially the Victorian one of 1868, although new offices had been built in Victorian Road. Stoke Newington formed part of the Kingsland and Hackney subdivision of N (Islington) division until 1878, when it became a subdivision in its own right with 104 police. Boundaries of the subdivision were revised in 1933 and in 1965, when Stoke Newington became a subdivisional station (GN) in Hackney L.B.[88]

Stoke Newington parish possessed by 1780 a fire engine which in 1805 was kept in an engine house probably at the church.[89] A new engine house was built probably in 1806 near the manorial pound on the north side of Church Street, near Barn Street.[90] In 1820 Joseph Eade granted a new site in Red Lion Lane, where an engine house was built at his expense shortly afterwards.[91] The vestry continued to maintain the engine until 1858, when Stoke Newington arranged to use the new engine and engine house built by Hackney on the east side of High Street.[92] The old engine was sold in 1860.[93] Under the Metropolitan Fire Brigade Act of 1865,[94] responsibility passed to the M.B.W., although Hackney board of works continued to use the High Street station until its replacement in 1886 by a new station called Stoke Newington station at the corner of Leswin and Brooke roads in Hackney.[95] Responsibility passed in 1889 to the L.C.C., which ran the fire brigade known after 1904 as London Fire Brigade,[96] and in 1965 to the G.L.C. In 1977 a new station opened in Stoke Newington Church Street, on the site of Fleetwood House.[97]

Lighting formed part of the provision of the turnpike roads Acts of 1774, 1789, and 1815. Under the Act of 1774 lamps were placed at intervals of 25 yards in the London road and of 30 yards in Church Street. The 1815 Act provided for lighting with gas.[98] The Imperial Gas Light Co. supplied gas lighting to the church in 1828[99] and by 1854 street lighting within the parish consisted of 92 gas and 44 naphtha lamps.[1] Hackney board of works approached the gas companies to replace naphtha and oil lamps with gas in 1856[2] and work was under way within the year although there were difficulties in Green Lanes and Stoke Newington Road because of boundaries with Hornsey and objections by residents of areas in Stoke Newington which paid lighting rates but had no lighting.[3] The number of gas lamps, supplied by the Imperial Gas Co. (which by 1887 had been amalgamated into the Gas Light & Coke Co.)[4] increased to 213 in 1868, 301 in 1877, 417 in 1884, and 540 in 1895.[5]

Hackney district board of works decided against supplying electricity in 1883 and again in 1890[6] but in 1893 it obtained a provisional order under the Electric Lighting Acts of 1882 and 1888. High Street and Woodberry Down were included in the area supplied by Hackney board and in 1902 Stoke Newington B.C. obtained an Act to supply the rest of the borough. In 1903 Hackney M.B. agreed to supply electricity in bulk to Stoke Newington, which did not generate its own

[79] Guildhall MS. 14233/1.
[80] Vestry mins. 1681–1743, 69.
[81] Ibid. 186, 204.
[82] Ibid. 208, 230. The Green Dragon was in High St., S. of Church St.: above, social.
[83] Vestry mins. 1784–1819, 305; Abstract of Ct. Rolls 1802–31, 293.
[84] Vestry mins. 1819–38, 15, 18, 101–2, 116; tithe (1848), no. 242.   [85] Abstract of Ct. Rolls 1802–31, 310.
[86] Vestry mins. 1819–38, 308, 321, 324, 472; Cassell's Map of Lond. (c. 1861–2); G.L.R.O., MBW 2499, map 9 (map of Metropol. pol. stas. 1870).
[87] Tithe (1848), no. 925.
[88] Inf. from Stoke Newington police sta. (1982).
[89] Draft Index to par. ledger 1, s.v. fire engine; vestry mins. 1784–1819, 328.
[90] Vestry mins. 1784–1819, 377; Ref. bk. to Wadmore map (1813), nos. 80, 89. The lease of the engine ho. ran from 1806: Robinson, Stoke Newington, 293.
[91] Vestry mins. 1819–38, 13, 15, 18, 101–2; tithe (1848), no. 242.

[92] Vestry mins. 1838–62, 55, 211, 488, 500, 516, 550.
[93] Churchwardens' accts. 1859–60 (HA P/M/CW/2).
[94] 28 & 29 Vic. c. 90.
[95] Hackney dist. bd. of wks. Ann. Rep. (1886), 9; Rep. of M.B.W., H.C. 157, p. 35 (1887), lxxi.
[96] G.L.R.O., F.B.
[97] Inf. from Stoke Newington fire sta. (1982).
[98] 14 Geo. III, c. 116 (Local Act); 29 Geo. III, c. 96 (Local Act); 55 Geo. III, c. 59 (Local Act); Robinson, Stoke Newington, 17–21.
[99] Vestry mins. 1819–38, 251.
[1] Returns on Paving, Cleansing and Lighting Metropol. Dists. H.C. 127, pp. 5–6 (1854–5), liii.
[2] Hackney dist. bd. of wks., Min. bk. (1855–7), 148.
[3] Ibid. Ann. Rep. (1856–7), 7, 11; vestry mins. 1838–62, 484.
[4] G.L.R.O., MBW 2499, maps 5, 7a–b.
[5] Hackney dist. bd. of wks. Ann. Rep. (1868), 3; Surveyor's Rep. (1877), 19; (1884), 20; Stoke Newington vestry, Surveyor's Rep. (1895), 128.
[6] Hackney dist. bd. of wks. Ann. Rep. (1883), 8; (1890), 7.

current.[7] An electricity substation was opened in Edward's Lane in 1906, which supplied all the area after the arrangement with Hackney terminated in 1907. It was extended in 1913, 1919, 1922, and 1924. A generating set was installed at the refuse destructor in Milton Road in 1909. Bulk supply was again taken from Hackney in 1928. Substations opened at Wordsworth Road in 1929, Lordship Road in 1933, and Victorian Road and Trumans Road by 1938.[8] Only 79 of 858 street lamps were electric in 1935 and they were confined to the main roads.[9]

Mary Lister founded an invalid asylum for 'respectable females' in 1825.[10] Intended to provide rest and medical care for domestic servants, it opened in the wooden house in Church Street previously used as a workhouse.[11] In 1830 it moved to no. 187 High Street, which housed 24 patients in 1851.[12] In 1909 alterations converted the asylum into a hospital, which by 1917 was called Stoke Newington home hospital for women.[13] The hospital had 31 beds in 1930. It moved to Stevenage during the Second World War and did not reopen after the war.[14]

In 1825 a group of gentlemen, which included Nathan Mayer de Rothschild and James William Freshfield of Abney House, opened Stamford Hill and Stoke Newington dispensary for the poor.[15] It opened on the Hackney side of High Street and moved in 1864 to no. 189 High Street, next to the female asylum, where an apothecary was resident.[16] By 1930 Stoke Newington borough, through its maternity and child welfare committee, was making a donation to the dispensary,[17] which treated 5,974 patients in 1946.[18] The dispensary closed in 1952 when, by a Charity Commission Scheme, its endowments were used to found the Stoke Newington and District Sick Poor Charity. The income, disbursed mostly in cash grants, was to be used for the sick poor of the area.[19]

A private lunatic asylum opened in Northumberland House, at the northern end of Green Lanes, in 1830.[20] It had 63 male and female inmates in 1851,[21] 80 in 1911, and 59 in 1951,[22] a few years before the house was demolished

to make way for Rowley Gardens.[23] In 1980 the institution reopened in Finchley as Northumberland nursing home.[24]

Bearstead Memorial hospital, a Jewish maternity hospital which had originated in the East End in 1895, opened with 32 beds in Lordship Road in 1947.[25] It had 60 beds by 1948 but only 24 in 1981, and had closed by 1983.[26]

In 1831 the vestry set up a committee to deal with cholera. Sub-committees for seven districts tried to remedy bad drainage and purchased blankets for the poor, but there was difficulty in obtaining a house as a cholera hospital. The committee, which had last met in December 1832, was briefly revived in 1849 to deal with another outbreak.[27] Hackney district board of works was the responsible authority in 1866 when cholera struck again, afflicting Hackney much more than Stoke Newington.[28]

Under the Metropolitan Poor Act, 1867,[29] which established the metropolitan asylum district for the relief of fever, smallpox, or insanity,[30] Stoke Newington continued to use hospitals outside the parish. Under the National Health Act of 1946 Stoke Newington fell within the area of the North East Metropolitan board, administered by Tottenham management committee. By 1981 it was part of Haringey Health District.[31]

In 1897 a parish nurse was appointed in commemoration of the queen's jubilee.[32] In 1914 Stoke Newington arranged to use a new tuberculosis clinic at the metropolitan hospital in Kingsland, Hackney.[33] The borough council had its own child welfare clinic at no. 44 Milton Road by 1915[34] and a maternity and child welfare centre at Barton House, no. 233 Albion Road, by 1927.[35] A third centre opened at Woodberry Hall in 1946, when foot, dental, physiotherapy, and toddlers' clinics were also introduced. Clinics as well as hospitals were by then under the care of the L.C.C.[36] The first comprehensive L.C.C. health centre opened at Woodberry Down in 1952.[37] The infant mortality rate, which averaged 118 per 1,000 in 1901–5 and 57 in 1921–5, was 18 in 1960.[38]

A municipal day nursery opened for the

[7] Ibid. (1893), 1 sqq.; 56 & 57 Vic. c. 40 (No. 3) (Local Act); 2 Ed. VII, c. 207 (Local Act); 3 Ed. VII, c. 7 (Local Act); L.C.C. *Lond. Statistics*, xvi (1905–6), 381.

[8] R. H. Rawll, 'Northern Dist. of Lond. Electricity Bd.' (TS. 1961, S.N.L. cuttings 46.93); G.L.R.O., AR/BA 4/149, 187; Stoke Newington, *Official Guide* [1917], 22; [1928], 24; [1931], 16; [1934], 16; [1938], 31.

[9] *Municipal Jnl.* xliv, 1 Mar. 1935 (S.N.L. cuttings 30, LC 2005); Stoke Newington B.C. *Ann. Rep.* (1936–7).

[10] P.R.O., C 54/16840, no. 14. Based on [I. P. Moline], *Short Hist. of Home Hosp. for Women 1825–1916* (S.N.L., LC 1280).

[11] Above, par. govt. The ho. was condemned as unsafe and demol. *c.* 1856: Ch. Com. file 6439.

[12] P.R.O., HO 107/1503/11/6.

[13] Stoke Newington, *Official Guide* [1917], 38.

[14] Stoke Newington B.C. *M.O.H. Rep.* (1930); *Kelly's Dir. Lond.* (1939); *Hospitals Year Bk.* (1940, 1945–6). For ho., see above, settlement and growth, the Lond. rd.

[15] Based on [G. A. Alexander], *Stoke Newington Dispensary 1825–75* (S.N.L., LC 1279).

[16] *Cassell's Map of Lond.* (*c.* 1861–2); P.R.O., C 54/16264, no. 8.

[17] Stoke Newington B.C. *M.O.H. Rep.* (1930).

[18] Ibid. (1946), 7.

[19] Char. Com. reg. 251231.

[20] *Prospectus of Northumberland Ho. Asylum*, 1835 (S.N.L. 47.3, LC 1211); above, settlement and bldg. to 1870.

[21] P.R.O., HO 107/1503/11/6, pp. 27–32.

[22] *Census*, 1911, 1951.

[23] Stoke Newington, *Official Guide* (1959); above, bldg. from 1940.

[24] S.N.L. 47.3.

[25] *Bearsted Memorial Hosp.* (pamphlet, S.N.L. LC 2344).

[26] *Hospitals Year Bk.* (1948, 1981, 1983).

[27] Mins. of Cttee. of Health, 1831 (HA P/M/BH1).

[28] Hackney dist. bd. of wks. *M.O.H. Rep.* (1867), 4; *M.O.H. Rep. on Cholera Epidemic of 1866*; *Sanitary Cttee. Rep.* (1866).

[29] 30 & 31 Vic. c. 6.   [30] G.L.R.O., MAB.

[31] Stoke Newington B.C. *M.O.H. Rep.* (1930); L.C.C. *Lond. Statistics*, N.S. i (1945–54), 65 and map; *Hospitals Year Bk.* (1948, 1981).

[32] Stoke Newington vestry, *M.O.H. Rep.* (1897–8), 21.

[33] Stoke Newington B.C. *M.O.H. Rep.* (1914), 132.

[34] Ibid. (1915).

[35] Ibid. (1927).   [36] Ibid. (1946), 3–5.

[37] *The Times*, 22 Jan. 1949, 6c; 15 Oct. 1952, 2g; L.C.C. *Woodberry Down Health Centre* (1952); L.C.C. *Lond. Statistics*, N.S. i (1945–54), 65–6.

[38] Stoke Newington B.C. *M.O.H. Quinquennial Health Survey* (1921–5), 8–9; *M.O.H. Rep.* (1960), 7.

children of women employed in war work after ratepayers noted the need in 1917.[39] The nursery, probably in Barton House in Albion Road, was closed in 1921 because of poor attendances.[40] Three day nurseries were opened in 1946.[41] In 1976 Defoe day care centre was opened at Hackney college in Ayrsome Road as a nursery for the children of girls who had not completed their education. The centre was threatened with closure in 1981.[42]

Stoke Newington churchyard and the burial ground of Abney chapel were closed under the Metropolis Burial Grounds Act of 1854.[43] The burial ground belonging to the Friends' meeting house in Park Street, which had opened in 1827 and was enlarged in 1849,[44] continued in use until 1957.[45] The main burial ground within Stoke Newington was at Abney Park, 32 a. between Church Street and Stamford Hill, where a cemetery designed by William Hosking was opened in 1840, mainly for dissenters.[46] Nearly 39,000 people had been buried there by 1867.[47] As Stoke Newington lay within the Metropolitan Burial District, Abney Park was among the burial grounds subject to the General Board of Health under an Act of 1850[48] and to the borough council after 1900,[49] but was owned by the Abney Park Cemetery Co.[50] until its liquidation in 1975. Hackney L.B. bought it in 1978 for £1 and partly restored it in 1980.[51] Hosking's Egyptian style lodges and entrance gates survive and his chapel, of stock brick with stone dressings in a 14th-century style and on the plan of a Greek cross, stands derelict.[52] The cemetery contains a monument by E. H. Baily to Isaac Watts, although not Watts's grave.[53]

In 1855, after the closure of the churchyard, a vestry committee concluded that as there were so few pauper burials a new cemetery was not necessary.[54] In 1862 the vestry set up a burial board which continued until 1896,[55] but no public cemetery opened within Stoke Newington. The duties of the burial board were confined to keeping the churchyard in order until 1881, when it applied for a faculty to build a mortuary there. The board maintained the mortuary until it was taken over in 1896 by the vestry, which was succeeded by the borough in 1900.[56] Stoke Newington arranged to use Hackney's

mortuary after its own had made way for municipal buildings in 1937.[57]

In 1886 the Ecclesiastical Commissioners purchased the Clissold or Crawshay estate for building but in 1887, after a local campaign led by Joseph Beck and John Runtz, they agreed to sell it to the M.B.W. as an open space. Clissold Park,[58] which consisted of 53 a. (25½ a. in Stoke Newington and 27½ a. in Hornsey) and a house,[59] was paid for by the commissioners, with substantial contributions by the M.B.W. and Stoke Newington vestry and smaller contributions from South Hornsey, Hackney, and Islington. In 1887 an Act authorized the purchase for a public park,[60] which opened in 1889.[61] The park, which was the responsibility of the M.B.W. and its successor, the L.C.C., was one of the first London municipal parks to provide animal and bird life: deer were introduced and the two lakes which had been filled were re-excavated. Neither the vestry nor the L.C.C., however, would finance the conversion of the house into a museum.[62]

Stoke Newington adopted the Libraries Acts in 1890, when the library commissioners agreed to make temporary use of the assembly rooms in Defoe Road.[63] In 1892 they opened a library in Church Street, built with contributions from J. Passmore Edwards.[64] Andrew Carnegie paid for an extension in 1904,[65] and the building was extended again in 1937, as part of the municipal buildings centred on the town hall. The borough council from 1900 administered the service through a public libraries committee. Branch libraries opened at Brownswood Road in 1948, Seven Sisters Road (Woodberry) in 1955, and Howard Road in 1957.[66]

The borough council opened slipper baths in Milton Road in 1909 and in Church Street in 1925[67] and swimming baths in Clissold Road in 1930.[68] Washhouses were opened next to the town hall in Milton Road in 1914.[69]

CHURCHES. A rector was appointed in 1314 to the church of Stoke Newington, which was a peculiar of the dean and chapter of St. Paul's, London.[70] Patronage was exercised by the Crown in 1404, because of the 'voidance of the bishopric', by the dean and chapter from 1414 to 1580,

[39] Cutting 26 Feb. 1917 (S.N.L. cuttings 34); Stoke Newington, *Official Guide* [1955], 56.
[40] Cutting 22 Apr. 1921 (S.N.L. cuttings 41.31).
[41] Stoke Newington B.C. *M.O.H. Rep.* (1946), 3–5.
[42] *Hackney Gaz.* 9 Jan. 1981 (S.N.L. cuttings 41.31, LC 3798).
[43] *Lond. Gaz.* 17 Nov. 1854, p. 3513.
[44] Mrs. Basil Holmes, *Lond. Burial Grounds* (1896), 294.
[45] 'Records of Friends' Burial Grd., Yoakley Rd.' (TS. 1957, S.N.L. cuttings 46.4).
[46] Beck, *Church Street*, 10; H. M. Colvin, *Dictionary of Brit. Architects* (1978 edn.), 437.
[47] *Return of Metropol. Burial Grds.* H.C. 477, p. 3 (1867), lviii.   [48] 13 & 14 Vic. c. 52.
[49] *Lond. (Adoptive Acts) Scheme*, 1900 (S.N.L. LC 1607).
[50] L.C.C. *Lond. Statistics*, xxxiv (1928–9), 108.
[51] *Hackney Gaz.* 19 Sept. 1978; 14 Mar. 1980 (S.N.L. cuttings 46.4, LC 3691, 3709).
[52] Pevsner, *Lond.* ii. 429; Colvin, *Brit. Architects*, 437; HA WP 8580.
[53] Gunnis, *Dictionary of Brit. Sculptors* (rev. edn.), 34; C. Bailey, *Harrap's Guide to Famous Lond. Graves* (1975), 135 is inaccurate.
[54] *Vestry mins.* 1838–62, 421, 424.
[55] Ibid. 605–7, 610; Stoke Newington burial bd., Min. bk. 1862–96 (HA P/M/B1).
[56] *Vestry mins.* 1862–89, 419; Stoke Newington vestry, *Ann. Rep.* (1894–5), 13; (1896–7), 8.
[57] Stoke Newington B.C. *M.O.H. Rep.* (1938).
[58] Based on J. J. Sexby, *Municipal Parks* (1898), 320–33.
[59] *Vestry mins.* 1862–89, 548, 556, 602; Ch. Com., Surveys S1, p. 613.
[60] 50 & 51 Vic. c. 137 (Local).
[61] *Vestry mins.* 1889–95, 2.
[62] Stoke Newington vestry, *Ann. Rep.* (1895–6), 9.
[63] *Vestry mins.* 1889–95, 48–9; *Hackney Official Guide* [1980], 29.
[64] *The Times*, 25 July 1892, 4e.
[65] Ibid. 14 June 1904, 3d.
[66] *Kelly's Dir. Stoke Newington* (1901–2), 36; Stoke Newington, *Official Guide* (1959).
[67] Stoke Newington, *Official Guide* (1959).
[68] *Opening of Publ. Swimming Bath*, 1930 (S.N.L. cuttings 46.26); *The Times*, 11 Apr. 1930, 17c.
[69] *Hackney & Stoke Newington Recorder*, 13 Nov. 1914.
[70] Hennessy, *Novum Rep.* 419.

and by the prebendary of Newington from 1585 to 1830. After the foundation of the Ecclesiastical Commissioners patronage passed to the bishop of London, who first exercised it in 1852.[71] During the Interregnum one rector, Thomas Manton (1644–56), was presented by the parliamentarian Col. Alexander Popham and another, Daniel Bull (1657–62), was elected by the vestry.[72] The church, whose dedication to St. Mary is not mentioned before 1522,[73] served the whole parish until the foundation of St. Matthias's in 1849.[74]

The annual value of Stoke Newington church was £6 13s. 4d. in 1366, £10 in 1535, £54 17s. in 1650, £420 in 1832, and £1,048 gross in 1896.[75]

In 1329 the rector held Churchfield of the lord of the manor by rent and suit of court and his executor refused to pay the heriot demanded by the bailiff.[76] In 1548 the rector received £20 a year, presumably from the lease of the parsonage, tithes, and glebe.[77] In the 1560s William Patten restored to the rector 18½ a. which had been described in Patten's lease of the manor as customary land belonging to the rectory, which was neither to be taken by the manorial lessee nor turned into freehold.[78] Great waste had been committed by the farmer of the rectory in 1572 but by 1649 the 18½ a. was worth £37 a year.[79] By the late 18th century it was treated as freehold and no payment was demanded by the lord at the rector's induction 'by an ancient agreement'.[80] The glebe, stretching south from the parsonage house,[81] was augmented by the bequest of a rector, Sidrach Simpson (d. 1704), of copyhold in Hackney and a copyhold house and 3 a. on the south side of Church Street (later called Wentworth House) on condition that the rector was resident and distributed £2 10s. a year to the poor. The next rector, John Millington (d. 1728), gave two thirds of the profits of land in Acton to the rector on condition that he read public prayers each day in church. In 1732 the parishioners associated with the rector in a suit to compel the chapter of St. Paul's to accept Millington's trust. By 1820 annual income from the two endowments was £60 and £46 respectively.[82] In 1832 the total income from land in Stoke Newington, Kingsland (Hackney), and Acton was £341 a year.[83] The land at Acton was

sold and ground rents in Penge (Kent) were purchased in 1865 and others in Herne Hill (Surr.) in 1905.[84] Most of the glebe was leased for building in 1850 and by 1923 the rector was said to have no land but £746 a year from ground rents.[85]

The rector received only tithes of 1s. 6d. an acre for copyhold land and the demesne was tithe free except for 6s. 8d. payable on the manor house, a payment which lapsed in the late 17th century when Church Row was built on the manor house site, the rector afterwards persuading each of the 9 tenants of Church Row to pay 1s.[86] Attempts to obtain tithes in kind in 1640 and to secure payment of tithe from demesne land in 1715 were unsuccessful and the same rate was paid in 1820.[87] By 1832 tithes were taken according to composition at 2s. 6d. a house, averaging £30 a year.[88] In 1846 the rector challenged the modus and in 1848 he obtained a rent charge of £100 a year in lieu of tithes.[89]

A 'mansion place' stood on the glebe in 1548 and had been repaired by Patten by 1565.[90] It needed repairs again in 1657 and in 1832 was very old and built of wood but habitable.[91] It was a weatherboarded building on the south side of Church Street opposite the church, with gables, casement windows, and tiled roofs.[92] When the old rectory house made way in 1855 for a second church, a house was built to the south in the garden.[93] It was described in 1917 as a 'commodious dwelling' with a delightful old garden,[94] but by the 1920s rectors found it far too large.[95] In the 1970s the top floor became a flat for the curate and the basement was converted into parish rooms and an office for Hackney deanery community relations.[96]

A bequest by Margaret Jekyll in 1545 for an annual obit probably never took effect, since her will was not proved until 1549.[97] In 1682 voluntary contributions were made for the maintenance of the minister's lecture,[98] and lecturers were appointed by the vestry from 1705 to 1853, when the office lapsed.[99] In 1742 a large vestry elected the rector, Ralph Thoresby, as lecturer and although he refused because his election 'gave offence to some', he was again elected in 1743.[1] In 1832 the rector, angered at the rejection of his

[71] Ibid. 419–20; *Cal. Pat.* 1399–1401, 437; 1401–5, 459.

[72] Robinson, *Stoke Newington*, 140–3; *Walker Revised*, ed. Matthews, 50.

[73] P.R.O., PROB 11/32 (P.C.C. 26 Populwell, will of John Stokker Jekyll).

[74] *Lond. Gaz.* 5 Jan. 1849, 33; below.

[75] *Reg. Sudbury* (Cant. & York Soc.), ii. 160; *Valor Eccl.* (Rec. Com.), i. 433; *Home Counties Mag.* i. 60; Ch. Com., NB 23/431 (inquiry 1832); *Crockford* (1896).

[76] Guildhall MS. (formerly St. Paul's MS. B 103).

[77] *Lond. and Mdx. Chantry Certificates* (Lond. Rec. Soc. xvi), 72; P.R.O., C 78/5/11, m.6.

[78] Guildhall MS. (formerly St. Paul's MS. A 37/1114); Guildhall MS. 11816B, p. 131.

[79] Guildhall MSS. 11816B, p. 132; 14233/1, unpag. (1572).

[80] Lysons, *Environs*, iii. 290; Robinson, *Stoke Newington*, 138–9.

[81] Tithe (1848), nos. 117, 662–72.

[82] Robinson, *Stoke Newington*, 144; vestry mins. 1681–1743, 352, 468.

[83] Ch. Com., NB 23/431 (inquiry 1832).

[84] Ibid. (return of benefices 1888); file 13971 pt. 1.

[85] Ibid. NB 23/431 (return of benefices 1923); G.L.R.O., P94/MRY/96 (deed 1850).

[86] *Cal. S.P. Dom.* 1637–8, 461; G.L.R.O., P94/MRY/81 (statements on tithes 1715).

[87] P.R.O., C 3/421/9; statements on tithes 1715; Robinson, *Stoke Newington*, 139.

[88] Ch. Com., NB 23/431 (inquiry 1832).

[89] P.R.O., IR 18/5544; IR 29/21/52.

[90] Ibid. C 78/5/11, m.6; Guildhall MS. (formerly St. Paul's MS. A 37/1114).

[91] Robinson, *Stoke Newington*, 141; Ch. Com., NB 23/431 (inquiry 1832).

[92] Robinson, *Stoke Newington*, facing p. 138; *Portrait of a Lond. Suburb*, 1844, item 21.

[93] I. G. Brooks, *Par. of St. Mary, Stoke Newington: Short Hist.* (booklet 1973, copy in S.N.L. 14.01, LC 3286); O.S. Map 1/2,500, Lond. X (1870 edn.).

[94] Stoke Newington, *Official Guide* [1917], 26. For illus., see [R. M. Panther], *Old North Lond.* (1928), 59.

[95] Ch. Com., NB 23/431 (return of benefices 1923).

[96] Brooks, *St. Mary*.

[97] P.R.O., PROB 11/32 (P.C.C. 26 Populwell).

[98] Vestry mins. 1681–1743, 9.

[99] Robinson, *Stoke Newington*, 147; Baxter, 'Rectors, lecturers and asst. clergy of par. of St. Mary Stoke Newington' (MS. 1912, S.N.L. 14.013, LC 1902).

[1] Vestry mins. 1681–1743, 497–8.

candidate, declared that he would perform the duties himself but had to give way.[2]

A rector was first recorded in 1314.[3] Dispensation to hold other benefices was granted in 1419 and 1461[4] and many early rectors were probably pluralists and absentees. From 1562 the list of rectors is complete.[5] Godfrey Becke (1566–8) lived in the parish before he became rector, possibly as curate, but Thomas Langley (1568–74), a minor canon of St. Paul's, was presented at the manor court in 1572 because he was not resident and did not exercise pastoral care 'to the great detriment of services'.[6] John Taverner (1629–38), although professor of music in Gresham college and secretary to the bishop of London, maintained a household at Stoke Newington. The parish was strongly parliamentarian during the Civil War and the rector William Heath (1639–44), who had been appointed by the royalist prebendary Thomas Turner,[7] was sequestered. His successor Thomas Manton, although mobile in his allegiances, was a leading Presbyterian writer and a 'godly and painful preacher'.[8] When he moved in 1656 the vestry chose Daniel Bull, who continued to preach in the church until 1662 in spite of being ejected at the Restoration and who then organized conventicles in the parish.[9]

There were frequent clashes between parishioners and Sidrach Simpson (1665–1704), master of Pembroke College, Cambridge, who was presented at St. Paul's peculiar court in 1673 and again in 1702 for encroaching on the body of the church with his pews, letting seats to outsiders, and neglecting to repair the chancel,[10] although he was also described as diligent and always resident.[11] John Millington (1705–28), an academic and pluralist, employed curates but, retaining one room in the parsonage, himself administered communion once a month.[12] William Cooke (1767–97), provost of Eton, was granted dispensation in 1767 to hold a fellowship at Eton together with Stoke Newington and another rectory; a classical scholar and later provost of King's College, Cambridge, and dean of Ely, he became deranged.[13] Cooke was succeeded by George Gaskin (1797–1829), one of his curates, who had been born at Newington Green and was first secretary of the S.P.C.K.

No vicarage was ordained although William, vicar of the church of Stoke in Middlesex, was mentioned in 1342.[14] There were assistant curates in 1540,[15] 1558,[16] and 1562, when it is uncertain whether the curate was William Apleforth, who in the course of accusations that he spoke against the queen was described as serving at Newington,[17] or John Apleforth.[18] There was an assistant curate in 1621 and from the late 17th century curates were usual though not invariable. There were two in the 1870s, three in 1881,[19] four in 1896, three in 1907, two in 1924, none from 1947 to 1955, and thereafter generally one. They included John Price (1706–18) and John Bransby (1814–25) who also ran schools, the scholar Henry Owen (1757–60),[20] Augustus Clissold (c. 1823–c.1840), the Swedenborgian enthusiast who married the heiress of Clissold Park,[21] and Richard Morris (1873–8), the philologist.

Archdale Wilson Tayler (1830–52) was appointed rector by the prebendary, his brother-in-law, and in 1832 held communion once a month, morning and afternoon prayers with sermons each Sunday, and prayers on Wednesdays and Fridays.[22] During the late 1830s the vestry became a battleground between the Low Church protestant reformism traditional to Stoke Newington and the new High Church Tractarianism of an influential group of laymen led by Robert Brett (d. 1874), who began practising as a local doctor in 1835 and moved to Newington Green in 1839.[23] The Low Church faction supported nonconformists who objected to church rates and to the vestry paying for organists and other exclusively church matters.[24] Brett started a Sunday school in 1837 and raised funds for an evening lectureship, maintaining that lack of an evening service drove people to the dissenting chapels. The first lecturer was John Jackson, headmaster of Islington proprietary school, a High Churchman who became incumbent of Muswell Hill in 1842 and bishop of London in 1868.[25] By 1838 accommodation, though increased by additions to the parish church in 1829, was again inadequate. The church held 900, less than half as many as attended nonconformist chapels.[26] The Tractarians, who found the rector 'amiable and inert', began to agitate for a chapel of ease but a large majority in the vestry in 1840 rejected the idea, on grounds of expense and because it would increase 'religious dissension'.[27] Tayler in 1845 attempted some Tractarian innovations but, after intervention by the dean of St. Paul's, agreed to restore the old services, to preach 'in the gown', and to omit the prayer for the Church Militant.[28]

[2] Vestry mins. 1819–38, 403–10; Baxter, 'Rectors'.
[3] Hennessy, *Novum Rep.* 419.
[4] *Cal. Papal Reg.* vii. 116; xi. 602.
[5] Inf. on rectors and asst. curates based on Hennessy, *Novum Rep.* 419–20; Baxter, 'Rectors'; Robinson, *Stoke Newington*, 145–6; Brooks, *St. Mary; Crockford* (1896 and later edns.).
[6] Guildhall MS. 14233/1, unpag.
[7] *D.N.B.* s.v. Turner.
[8] Lysons, *Environs*, iii. 291; *Home Counties Mag.* i. 60.
[9] *Calamy Revised*, ed. Matthews, 85; *Walker Revised*, ed. Matthews, 50; below, prot. nonconf.
[10] Guildhall MS. 9537/20, p. 16; vestry mins. 1681–1743, 85. There was also disagreement over the election of churchwardens: above, local govt.
[11] Statements on tithes 1715.
[12] Guildhall MS. 9550; G.L.R.O., P94/MRY/90 (lease 1727).
[13] *D.N.B.*; *Cal. H.O. Papers*, 1766–9, 245.

[14] *Year Bk.* 16 Edw. III (Rolls Ser.), (2), 265 n. 3.
[15] i.e. Ric. Nelson while Jas. Clyve was rector: Guildhall MS. 25626/1, f. 23 and v.
[16] Guildhall MS. 25626/1, f. 123.
[17] *Cal. S.P. Dom.* 1601–3 and Add. 525.
[18] Ibid. 1547–80, 192.
[19] *Mackeson's Guide* (1881), 95.
[20] *D.N.B.*
[21] Ibid.
[22] Brooks, *St. Mary*; Ch. Com., NB 23/431 (inquiry 1832).
[23] T. W. Belcher, *Rob. Brett* (1889), 2, 14; G.L.R.O., P94/MTS/35/1 (scrapbk. of St. Matthias, pp. 55 sqq.).
[24] Vestry mins. 1838–62, 3–4, 11, 64.
[25] Belcher, *Rob. Brett*, 45; *V.C.H. Mdx.* vi. 175, where Jackson's forename is wrongly given as Thos.
[26] *Lond. City Mission Mag.* iii (1838), 71.
[27] The 1829 repairs were still being paid for: vestry mins. 1838–62, 46 sqq.; scrapbk. of St. Matthias, pp. 55 sqq.
[28] Vestry mins. 1838–62, 176–7, 187.

In 1846 he acquired a Tractarian curate, Thomas A. Pope,[29] whose encouragement, coupled with the paying off of the church building debt, led to the foundation of the district church of St. Matthias in 1849.[30]

In 1851 the old church contained 150 free sittings and 545 for which pew rents were paid; it was attended on census Sunday by 700 in the morning, 120 in the afternoon, and 210 in the evening.[31] In 1853 the vestry set up a committee to consider increasing the accommodation, especially for the poor. It was argued that many 'highly respectable families' had joined other congregations solely because there was no room in the parish church. The Low Church faction objected to building on financial grounds, since the abeyance of church rates had brought peace 'with our numerous and highly respectable dissenting brethren' and only 150 more seats were necessary.[32] The congregation of St. Matthias's joined in a bizarre alliance with the Low Church faction to oppose rebuilding, especially a suggestion that money could be raised by mortgaging he Palatine estate.[33] Tayler's successor Thomas Jackson (1852–86), whose reputation for preaching may have been partly responsible for the overcrowding,[34] offered the site of the rectory house and garden for a new church. The committee accepted, while stressing that there should be no 'lavish expenditure in mere decoration or eccentricity in design rendering it ill-adapted for . . . the *Protestant* Church of England'.[35] The new church, with 1,100 sittings, was opened in 1858 and there were suspicions that the rector intended to pull down the old one or use it for schoolrooms. Congregations of more than 300 continued to attend the old church but evening services were discontinued and communion was administered only at long intervals. The bishop promised that, although the title and endowments of the parish church were being transferred to the new church, the old church was to continue as a chapel of ease.[36]

In 1860 the vestry agreed to pay £60 a year to the rector in compensation for the house and garden and undertook all repairs in return for the surrender of rectorial rights in the chancel. When raising money for the new church the rector also pledged that there would be no changes in services. In 1865 the election of vestrymen was fought on the issue of choral innovations made in 1864. After the Low Church faction's success, attributed by the rector's party to the votes of dissenters, the vestry discontinued the £60 payment in protest at the 'excess of music'. One churchwarden, F. J. Hamel, author of *Protestantism in Peril*, presented the rector to the bishop, who instructed Archdeacon Hale to attend the services. Hale supported the rector, who resisted the vestry, and scuffles took place in church over the appointment of an organist.[37] The rector eventually succeeded in establishing a reputation for music at St. Mary's.[38] By 1881 there were fully choral services.[39]

During the 1880s attention turned from battles over ritualism to social[40] and missionary work. St. Andrew's was founded in 1876, a soup kitchen was opened for the poor by 1882,[41] and mission services were held at no. 106 Church Street from 1883 to 1906.[42] Leonard Shelford, rector 1886–1904, had an especial interest in east London and promoted 'services for the people': mission services were held at the assembly rooms in Defoe Road from 1888, at the Good Shepherd mission from c. 1889 to c. 1903, at Holy Redeemer mission from 1892 to 1939, and at St. John the Baptist mission from 1894 to after 1913.[43] Shelford's curates included one associated with Socialism, besides a ritualist who built up a plainsong choir at the mission, another largely responsible for the formation of St. Olave's (1892), and another who introduced men's services and Lenten lectures by well known clergymen at St. Mary's old church.[44]

At the beginning of the 20th century St. Mary's was at its zenith with three or four curates, 40 district visitors, 120 Sunday school teachers, 100 choristers, and 100 mission workers.[45] On census Sunday 1903 attendances at the main church were 531 a.m. and 632 p.m. and at the old church 260 a.m. and 298 p.m.[46] Communicants in 1905 averaged 128 a week at the two services at the new and 35 at the one service at the old church.[47] The old church offered 'an old-fashioned service to old-fashioned worshippers', while the new was a 'highly ornate church of almost cathedral size' filled by large numbers 'who follow the fashion of the day'.[48] More sympathetically, it was said to have 'everything from an aesthetic and artistic point of view', to make services pleasing, and to have well maintained institutions.[49] In 1905 the assembly rooms were bought to become St. Mary's church

[29] G.L.R.O., P94/MRY/74 (curate's licence).
[30] For Pope and St. Matthias, below.
[31] P.R.O., HO 129/1/11/1/1/2.
[32] Vestry mins. 1838–62, 341–2; E. Taverner, *Few Observations on Proposed New Par. Ch. at Stoke Newington* (1854) (pamphlet, S.N.L. 14.012, LC 1267); *Remarks upon 'Few Observations'* (1854) (pamphlet, S.N.L. 14.0122, LC 1264).
[33] Vestry mins. 1838–62, 372.   [34] Brooks, *St. Mary*.
[35] Vestry mins. 1838–62, 352.
[36] Ch. Com. file 13970 (memorial by inhabitants to bp. 1858). Displeasure with the rector is reflected in the Easter offerings: £275 (1858), £5 (1859): St. Mary Stoke Newington offertory collections 1843–88 (S.N.L. 14.014, LC 2243).
[37] Vestry mins. 1838–62, 557–8; 1862–89, 62–3, 99–106, 203; T. Spinks, *St. Mary Stoke Newington. Case and Opinion on Rights of Rectors and Parishioners* (pamphlet 1869, S.N.L. 14.01, LC 1209); Baxter, 'Rectors'.
[38] Brooks, *St. Mary*.
[39] *Mackeson's Guide* (1881), 95.

[40] For clubs and socs. associated with St. Mary's, above, social.
[41] [St. Mary] *Par. Mag.* (1882) (S.N.L. 14.01, LC 1485).
[42] G.L.R.O., MBW 1721/197, no. 24; J. Dailey, 'St. Mary's mission room' (MS., 1976, S.N.L. cuttings 14.016, LC 3283).
[43] MS. notebk. by Sister Annie Jefferson, in charge of Mission Ho. (HA M 3898). For named missions, below. St. Thos.'s mission room, for which a fund was set up in 1890, apparently never materialized: *The Times*, 16 Apr. 1890, 9f.
[44] Brooks, *St. Mary*; Baxter, 'Rectors'; *St. Mary Ch. Monthly* (1900) (S.N.L. 14.01, LC 1503); H. S. Geikie, 'St. Mary's Old Ch. Stoke Newington: Men's Svce.' (TS. and cuttings c. 1920–7, S.N.L. 14.01, LC 2465).
[45] *Church Bells*, 22 Apr. 1898 (S.N.L. illus. 78 Shelford, LC 2013).   [46] Mudie-Smith, *Rel. Life*, 161.
[47] *St. Mary Ch. Monthly* (1900); Guildhall MS. 17885/6/27 (inquiry by bp. 1905).
[48] Booth, *Life and Labour*, 3rd ser. (i), 131.
[49] Mudie-Smith, *Rel. Life*, 130.

rooms.[50] The prosperity was due to the largely middle-class congregations[51] and, although the rector referred in 1903 to changes,[52] it was not until the 1920s that the influx of Jews and increasing local poverty much affected the church.[53]

When William Patten 'new builded'[54] the church of *ST. MARY*[55] in 1563, he virtually obliterated the medieval building. Built of stone, flint, and pebbles,[56] in 1500 it contained a chapel dedicated to St. Thomas and a rood in need of mending.[57] The medieval nave and south porch remained, encased in Patten's work which he described in 1565 as rebuilding the chancel, adding an aisle with, in addition to a chapel, a vestry at the east and a schoolhouse at the west end, 're-edifying' the whole body of the church, and repairing the rest of the fabric.[58] Above the 16th-century doorway is an 18th-century inscription, '1563 Ab alto'. The chapel, entered by a door above which are Patten's arms and the letters W.P. over 'Prospice', belonged, with its eight pews, to the lord of the manor.[59] The 16th-century building was of brick and included a west tower built within the medieval nave. A north aisle was added in 1716–17 and the chancel extended eastward in 1723.[60] In 1728 new windows were put in at the west end, the walls on the south side were raised and coped with stone, and all the church, except the new north aisle, was roughcast.[61] The church was repaired and 'beautified' in 1770, and the west end raised to the same height as the rest in 1785.[62] In 1791 the church was too small and its replacement was considered,[63] but in 1806 it was restored and the outside (except the north wall) covered with cement to imitate stone.[64]

A survey in 1827 revealed a rotten roof and bad drainage, with coffins floating under the floor. Restoration by Sir Charles Barry, completed by 1829, included extending the north aisle westward to a line with the tower, adding a second north aisle and a clerestory to the nave, raising the floor and ceiling, removing the 18th-century parapets, re-roofing, and replacing the wooden spire, which was already much decayed in 1791.[65] The church assumed a more conventional Gothic appearance and the accommodation increased from 499 to 700 sittings.[66] In 1853, when more space was needed, the vestry committee took the advice of George Gilbert Scott to replace the old building, a mere village church whose extensions had made it a 'heterogeneous mass'.[67] In 1928 the spire was again replaced and the cement was removed from the south aisle to reveal the Tudor brickwork. The old church was badly damaged by bombing in 1940 when the north aisle and 16th-century windows, given by Jonathan Eade in 1811, were destroyed. The church, but not Barry's north aisle, was restored by Charles M. O. Scott in 1953 with a new north-eastern vestry. The pews and Barry's pulpit and iron rails remain, as do the monuments, which include that of Elizabeth (d. 1602), wife of John Dudley (d. 1580) and Thomas Sutton (d. 1611), a marble wall monument with kneeling figures; there is a wall monument to Joseph Hurlock (d. 1793) and his wife by Thomas Banks.

In 1681 ringers were paid 4s. a day 'according to custom'.[68] In 1828 Thomas Mears of White-chapel recast the six bells,[69] one of which, the tenor, was recast by Mears in 1864.[70] Proposals to introduce an organ were rejected in 1791 but accepted in 1806.[71] The organist's performance was unsatisfactory in 1824 and the organ figured in the dispute between the High and Low Church factions in 1838.[72] John Herst, skinner, by will proved 1449, left a chalice to the church,[73] but the surviving plate all dates from the 17th and 18th centuries: a cup and paten (1634) and flagon (1638), the gifts of William Stephens, a cup and paten bought in 1657, and a large almsdish, given by the rector in 1711, all of silver gilt. There are two brass almsdishes dated 1713.[74] The plate was transferred to the new church in 1901 and a full set of communion plate was presented to the old church to replace it.[75] The parish registers begin in 1559.[76]

The new church of *ST. MARY*,[77] opposite the old one, was started in 1855 and consecrated in 1858. It was built to a design by Sir George Gilbert Scott in a 13th-century style of Kentish rag with Bath stone dressings and consists of apsidal chancel with aisles, aisled nave, north and

[50] Brooks, *St. Mary*.   [51] Mudie-Smith, *Rel. Life*, 129.
[52] Brooks, *St. Mary*.
[53] e.g. in 1911 the rector raised £600 a year to pay curates' salaries: Ch. Com. file 13971 pt. 1 (application for grant 1911). Cf. applications for grants 1920, 1924. By 1929 financial worry was said to have caused the breakdown of the rector: ibid. file 13971 file 2 (application for grant 1929).
[54] John Stow, *Survey of Lond.* ed. C. L. Kingsford (1908), i. 114.
[55] Based on Hist. Mon. Com. *W. Lond.* 91–2; Pevsner, *Lond.* ii. 428.   [56] Robinson, *Stoke Newington*, 149.
[57] Guildhall MS. 9171/8, f. 225.
[58] Ibid. (formerly St. Paul's MS. A 37/1114).
[59] Robinson, *Stoke Newington*, 150–1. Cf. plans in Hist. Mon. Com. *W. Lond.* and Spinks, *St. Mary Stoke Newington* (1869).
[60] Vestry mins. 1681–1743, 191–3, 204–5, 238.
[61] Ibid. 284; B.L. King's Maps, Topog. xxx. 10. a–c.
[62] Robinson, *Stoke Newington*, 150; J. R. Spratling, 'Old Ch. of St. Mary Stoke Newington' (S.N.L. 14.011, LC 1315).
[63] Vestry mins. 1784–1819, 136, 143–7. A survey in 1792 showed that there were 65 pews, 457 seats: ibid. 165–6. For view of ch. 1796, see Lysons, *Environs*, iii. 284 (grangerized copy in Guildhall Libr.).

[64] Robinson, *Stoke Newington*, 150.
[65] Vestry mins. 1784–1819, 146–7; 1819–38, 196–9, 217–20; G.L.R.O., P94/MRY/123 (faculty for ch. 1828); Brooks, *St. Mary*. And see view of ch. in 1836: B.L. Add. MS. 36370, f. 171; above, plate 54.
[66] P.R.O., HO 129/1/11/1/1/2; Ch. Com. file 13970 (memorial by inhabitants to bp. 1858).
[67] Vestry mins. 1838–62, 350.
[68] Draft Index to par. ledger 1.
[69] Vestry mins. 1819–38, 244.
[70] Geikie, 'St. Mary's Old Ch. Stoke Newington: Men's Svce.' (S.N.L. 14.01, LC 2465).
[71] Vestry mins. 1784–1819, 157, 357.
[72] Ibid. 1819–38, 108; 1838–62, 3–4.
[73] Guildhall MS. 9171/4, f. 256.
[74] Robinson, *Stoke Newington*, 156; vestry mins. 1681–1743, loose leaves at front; Hist. Mon. Com. *W. Lond.* 92.
[75] Spratling, 'Old ch. of St. Mary Stoke Newington'.
[76] G.L.R.O., P94/MRY/1–49. Those for 1559–1812 have been indexed: ibid. 42.
[77] Based on Brooks, *St. Mary*; B. F. L. Clarke, *Lond. Chs.* (1966), 170; A. Capes, *Old and New Chs. of Lond.* (1880), plate 32; above, plate 56. For plan see Spinks, *St Mary Stoke Newington* (1869); reopening of ch. 1923 (S.N.L. cuttings 14.01/N, LC 2446).

south transepts, and south-east vestry. A spire was completed on the western tower in 1890 by John Oldrid Scott. The church accommodated 1,300 people and had rich stained glass, a timbered roof, and an elaborate font. It was restored in 1923 but was badly damaged during the Second World War and again restored in 1957, when glass by Francis Skeat replaced the lost Victorian windows.

The first daughter church was St. Matthias,[78] which took its parish from the south-eastern part of Stoke Newington and the detached parts of South Hornsey. It was founded in 1849 largely through the efforts of Robert Brett and the assistant curate of St. Mary's, Thomas Pope. Pope married the rector's daughter and became perpetual curate of the new church, where he established a High Church tradition which survived his conversion to Roman Catholicism in 1854. Choral services at St. Matthias's were developed by the organist, William H. Monk (1852–89), musical editor of *Hymns Ancient and Modern*, composer of 'Abide with me', and plainsong enthusiast. Charles James Le Geyt, vicar 1858–77, a former curate of John Keble, introduced incense and vestments, a gift from some of the laity, in 1865 and Corpus Christi processions in 1867. The church, 'one of the most advanced churches in the kingdom', attracted enthusiastic congregations who had to be protected by police from protestant mobs.

Robert Brett, together with Richard Foster, another layman who had been involved in founding St. Matthias's, promoted other High Church foundations in the area, including St. Faith's mission chapel in 1868 and All Saints' in 1873, partly because they feared the appointment by the bishop, whose turn it was, of an antiritualist as vicar of St. Matthias's. In 1858 the vicar, who had tried to obey the bishop's instructions to extinguish altar lights, had resigned, mainly under pressure from Brett. When the new vicar, in obedience to the bishop who appointed him in 1878, tried to abandon ritual practices, he provoked a storm of protest: the whole choir resigned, offertories declined, and during the 1880s the controversial practices were reintroduced.[79]

In the 1850s St. Matthias's had been surrounded by a neighbourhood 'overrun with dissent', which it challenged with ritualism and where it succeeded in converting several Quakers.[80] As the social standing of the area

declined, elaborate ritual was defended as a means of attracting the poor, among whom St. Matthias's and St. Faith's undertook social and mission work from the late 1870s. In 1883 the Salvation Army was invited to St. Faith's to hear the bishop of London preach.[81] In 1905 the main problem of the southern churches was indifference, although the large numbers of Jews and nonconformists also caused difficulties. The vicar of St. Matthias's commented that the majority of the pious were dissenters.[82] In the north St. Andrew's, with its mainly middle-class congregation and some 'better working class', was praised for its church work and music in 1903.[83]

Declining numbers and wealth, together with severe bomb damage in the Second World War, led to reorganization of the parishes in the 1950s. In 1951 the boundaries of St. Mary's, St. Andrew's, St. Olave's, and St. John's, Brownswood Park,[84] were adjusted and St. Faith's was amalgamated with St. Matthias's. Initial opposition in St. Faith's was mollified when the patronage of the new benefice centred on St. Matthias's was vested in the City of London Corporation to secure the continuation of 'Catholic teaching and practice'. In 1956 the boundary of St. Mary's was again altered and All Saints' was amalgamated with the parish of St. Matthias and St. Faith.[85]

The daughter churches and missions of Stoke Newington were:[86]

ALL SAINTS, Aden Grove. Mission in iron ch. in Aden Grove in SW. Stoke Newington on site given by Ric. Foster 1872.[87] Dist. formed from St. Mary and St. Matthias 1873. Patron bp. of Lond., Corporation of Lond. by 1937.[88] Par. absorbed part of St. Matthias in reorganization 1951 but itself merged into new par. of St. Faith with St. Matthias and All Saints 1956, when ch. demol. and site sold. High Ch. but less ritualistic than St. Matthias and St. Faith. Fully choral svces., 4 each Sunday, one asst. curate 1881.[89] Well attended svces. and many social activities 1902.[90] Attendance 1903: 220 a.m.; 240 p.m. Bldg. seating 800 in Early Eng. style by F. Dollman and W. Allen 1876: chancel with vestries, aisled nave, narthex, NE. tower. Alabaster reredos; chancel and narthex screens.[91] Sch. and mission hall built next to ch. 1878.[92]

GOOD SHEPHERD. Mission svces. held by clergy of St. Mary's in room in Falcon Ct., Church Street, from c. 1889 until c. 1903.[93]

[78] G.L.R.O., P94/MTS/35/1 (Scrapbk. of St. Matthias, pp. 3, 23, 31, 33, 55 sqq.); ibid. 35/8 (*Musical Herald*, Apr. 1889); Brooks, *St. Mary*; Baxter, 'Rectors'; O. Chadwick, *Victorian Church* (1972), ii. 315–16.
[79] Scrapbk. of St. Matthias, pp. 55–65; T. F. Bumpus, *Historical Lond. Ch.* (booklet 1913, S.N.L. 14.04, LC 2207); Belcher, *Rob. Brett*, 74–5, 379.   [80] Belcher, *Rob. Brett*, 72.
[81] Chadwick, *Victorian Ch.* ii. 295, 317.
[82] Guildhall MS. 17885/6/29, 31, 32 (inquiry by bp. 1905).
[83] Mudie-Smith, *Rel. Life*, 129.
[84] For St. John's, see *V.C.H. Mdx.* vi. 176.
[85] Ch. Com. file 13971 pt. 4 (reorganization of pars. 1951); G.L.R.O., O/42/12; O/42/27/1, O/42/28/1–2; P94/FAI/19/2–7 (St. Faith, mins. of P.C.C. mtgs. 1948–51).
[86] Inf. about patrons and asst. curates from Hennessy, *Novum Rep.*; *Clergy List*; *Crockford*; *Lond. Dioc. Bk.* (various edns.); architectural descriptions based on Clarke, *Lond. Chs.*; Pevsner, *Lond.* ii; attendance figs. 1903 from Mudie-

Smith, *Rel. Life*, 161; reorganization of pars. 1951 and 1956 from Ch. Com. file 13971 pt. 4; G.L.R.O., O/42/12; O/42/27/1; O/42/28/1–2.
[87] Bumpus, *Historical Lond. Ch.*; G.L.R.O., MBW 1621/97, no. 21.
[88] *Lond. Gaz.* 21 Nov. 1873, p. 5133; *The Times*, 25 June 1937, 11e.   [89] *Mackeson's Guide* (1881), 13.
[90] Bumpus, *Historical Lond. Ch.*; Guildhall MS. 17885/6/29 (inquiry by bp. 1905); Booth, *Life and Labour*, 3rd ser. (1), 131.
[91] Bumpus, *Historical Lond. Ch.*; cutting, July 1876 (S.N.L. cuttings 14.07, LC 2476); architect's drawing (S.N.L. illus. 1407, LC 493); *Mackeson's Guide* (1881), 13; *Kelly's Dir. Stoke Newington* (1910–11).
[92] P.R.O., C 54/18115, m.23.
[93] MS. notebk. by Sister Annie Jefferson, in charge of Mission Ho. (HA M 3898); not listed in Mudie-Smith, *Rel. Life*.

HOLY REDEEMER. Chapel at no. 108 Church Street, briefly called St. Barnabas, dedicated 1892.[94] Mission svces. by clergy of St. Mary's until suspended 1939.[95] Attendance 1903: 181 p.m. 'Very successful' 1905.[96]

ST. ANDREW, Bethune and Fairholt rds. Originated in iron ch. on N. side of Manor Rd. 1876.[97] Dist. formed from St. Mary and St. Thos., Stamford Hill, 1883. Patron bp. of Lond.[98] Fully choral svces., 3 each Sunday by 1881 although V. 'of no. Ch. party' 1891.[99] High Ch. practices disclaimed 1905[1] but established by 1981. 3 asst. curates 1896, thereafter usually one. Attendance 1903: 696 a.m., 541 p.m., highest of any Anglican ch. in Stoke Newington. Endowment fund to enable V. to live without private means 1926–30.[2] Allotted £100 a year for repairs from Palatine estate char. 1962.[3] Bldg. of Bath stone and Kentish rag with Portland stone dressings in 13th-cent. style, seating 1,400, by A. W. Blomfield 1884, enlarged 1889: chancel, aisled nave, short transepts and spirelet.[4] Ch. repaired and side chapel built 1959.[5] Par. room in Fairholt Rd. 1885, replaced by large hall near ch. 1904.[6] Queen Anne style Vicarage by Blomfield. Hall and vicarage replaced by flats by 1982.[7]

ST. FAITH, Londesborough Road. Mission in small brick bldg. 1868, replaced by temp. iron ch. 1871.[8] Dist. formed from St. Mary and St. Matthias 1873.[9] Patron trustees, including V. and prominent laymen of St. Matthias, later Corporation of Lond.[10] Consecration an occasion of ritualist demonstration;[11] High Ch. from beginning. Fully choral svces., 5 each Sunday, altar lights by 1881.[12] Censer and confession by 1905.[13] Endowment for asst. curate 1874;[14] 2 asst. curates by 1881,[15] 3 by 1893, 2 by 1901, 1 by 1926, none by 1935. Attendance 1903: 181 a.m., 162 p.m. Bldg. in early French Gothic style by Wm. Burges and J. Martin Brooks 1873: basilica with 2 turrets on W. front; bellcot 1878, other additions 1879, 1881, 1883, 1889, 1891.[16] Ch. altered 1931 and badly damaged 1944.[17] Svces. continued in damaged bldg. but after 1949 V.

of St. Faith also in charge of St. Matthias; new benefice of St. Faith with St. Matthias centred on ch. of St. Matthias 1951. St. Faith's ch. demol.[18] Home for incurables in Milton Rd. 1876, mission ho. in Gordon Rd. 1881,[19] mission hall in Londesborough Rd. 1883.[20]

ST. JOHN THE BAPTIST. Weekly mission svces. by St. Mary's clergy at no. 2 Chapel Ct. or Pl. off High Street 1894.[21] Attendance 1903: 10 p.m. Licence renewed 1913.[22]

ST. JOHN OF BEVERLEY, Green Lanes. Institute for Deaf and Dumb, Ch. of Eng. char., built on site given by Ch. Com. 1913.[23] Chapel dedicated 1920. Additions 1921. Bldgs. destroyed by fire 1960 and smaller centre built on part of site 1963.[24]

ST. MATTHIAS,[25] Wordsworth Road. Svces. in sch. built 1849 when dist. formed from Stoke Newington and St. Mary, Hornsey.[26] Patron alternately Crown and bp. of Lond. Amalgamated in new benefice of St. Faith with St. Matthias, patron Corporation of Lond., 1951; absorbed All Saints par. 1956. Allotted £100 a year from Palatine estate 1962.[27] Endowment for one asst. curate 1869, two 1881.[28] Musical tradition and High Ch. practices cause of considerable controversy. Fully choral svces., 6 each Sunday by 1881.[29] Attendance 1851: 150 a.m., 145 aft., 200 evg.;[30] 1903: 250 a.m., 264 p.m. Bldg. of buff brick with Bath stone dressings in Dec. style, seating 756, by Wm. Butterfield 1851–3: short chancel, central saddleback tower, aisled and clerestoried nave with steeply pitched roof, N. and S. porches. Design approved by *Ecclesiologist* but attacked by historian E. A. Freeman.[31] Chancel screen, wall paintings, and windows added later. Vicarage 1863.[32] Ch. badly damaged 1941 and svces. held at institute.[33] Ch. restored but chancel cut off and interior whitened 'in a way that Butterfield would certainly not have approved' and reopened 1954.[34] Lively social life with increasing emphasis on mission and social work: iron ch. institute in Wordsworth Rd. 1894, replaced by new mission hall 1902,[35]

[94] Sister Annie's notebk.
[95] *St. Mary Ch. Monthly* (1939) (S.N.L. 14.01, LC 1526).
[96] Guildhall MS. 17885/6/27.
[97] Guildhall MS. CC. 212315; G.L.R.O., MBW 1659/135, no. 21.
[98] *Lond. Gaz.* 11 Sept. 1883, p. 4441.
[99] *Mackeson's Guide* (1881), 18; *Chs. and chapels of Lond. St. Andrew's Stoke Newington* (cutting 1891, S.N.L. cuttings 14.03, LC 2191).
[1] Guildhall MS. 17885/6/30 (inquiry by bp. 1905).
[2] *The Times*, 18 Jan. 1928, 15e; 24 Jan. 1930, 17d.
[3] Char. Com. reg. 250880.
[4] *Consecration of St. Andrew's Ch.* (S.N.L. 14.03, LC 1305); G.L.R.O., AR/BA 4/4, no. 24.
[5] Faculty among rec. in vestry (G.L.R.O., catalogue of par. rec.).
[6] G.L.R.O., MBW 1738/214, no. 24; *St. Andrew's Ch. Year Bk.* (1951) (S.N.L. 14.03, LC 3237).
[7] *Electoral Reg.* (1982) in S.N.L.
[8] Bumpus, *Historical Lond. Ch.*; G.L.R.O., MBW 1621/97, no. 21.
[9] *Lond. Gaz.* 27 June 1873, p. 3046; 8 Aug. 1873, p. 3724.
[10] G.L.R.O., O/42/27/1.
[11] Attended by 80 priests in surplices: Belcher, *Rob. Brett*, 381.   [12] *Mackeson's Guide* (1881), 45.
[13] Guildhall MS. 17885/6/31 (inquiry by bp. 1905).
[14] *Lond. Gaz.* 27 Mar. 1874, p. 1877.
[15] *Mackeson's Guide* (1881), 45.
[16] Bumpus, *Historical Lond. Ch.*; Belcher, *Rob. Brett*,

408–11; G.L.R.O., MBW 1628/104, no. 21; 1675/151, no. 23; 1684/160, no. 23; 1701/177, no. 24; AR/BA 4/4, no. 24; 22, no. 23; Pevsner, *Lond.* ii. 428; postcard (S.N.L. illus. 14.05, LC 1262).
[17] G.L.R.O., AR/BA 4/534, no. 36; J. Summerson, *Heavenly Mansions* (1949), 238.
[18] Ch. Com. file 13971 pt. 4 (reorganization of pars. 1951).
[19] P.R.O., ED 7/84.
[20] *Kelly's Dir. Lond. Suburbs* (1876); *Norris's Dir. Stoke Newington* (1882); Belcher, *Rob. Brett*, 410.
[21] *Monthly Notes* (1891 and later) (S.N.L. 14.6, LC 1243).
[22] G.L.R.O., AR/BA 4/266.
[23] Ibid.; Ch. Com. Estate maps, Stoke Newington Estate 1.
[24] Inf. from information officer (1981); G.L.R.O., AR/BA 4/373, no. 33.
[25] Based on G.L.R.O., P94/MTS/35/1 (scrapbk. of St. Matthias); Belcher, *Rob. Brett*, 49–92, 379.
[26] *Lond. Gaz.* 5 Jan. 1849, p. 33.
[27] Char. Com. reg. 250880.
[28] *Lond. Gaz.* 7 May 1869, p. 2686; 16 Dec. 1881, p. 6713.
[29] *Mackeson's Guide* (1881), 106.
[30] P.R.O., HO 129/1/11/1/1/1.
[31] Summerson, *Heavenly Mansions*, 163, 170; Clarke, *Lond. Chs.* 169.
[32] Photograph *c.* 1865: S.N.L. illus. 14. 043, LC 573.
[33] *St. Matthias Souvenir Brochure* (1946) (S.N.L. 14.04, LC 3041).
[34] *The Times*, 30 Apr. 1954, 10e; 10 May 1954, 8b.
[35] Vestry mins. 1889–95, 346; G.L.R.O., AR/BA 4/124.

mission rooms at no. 17 Spenser Rd. 1884, at no. 7 Watson Rd. 1890, and no. 72 Howard Rd. 1910.[36]

ST. OLAVE,[37] Woodberry Down. City ch. of St. Olave, Old Jewry, demol. 1888–9 and proceeds applied to new chs. in Lond. including Stoke Newington. Temp. iron ch. built on site given by Ch. Com.[38] at junction of Seven Sisters Rd. and Woodberry Down, and dist. formed from St. Mary and St. And., Stoke Newington, St. John, Stamford Hill, and St. Ann, Hangar Lane, 1892.[39] Par. enlarged 1951. Patron Ld. Chancellor. Usually one asst. curate. High Ch. practices introduced by second V. (1924–42). Some social activities 1905,[40] more during 1920s and 1930s. Attendance 1903: 476 a.m., 348 p.m. Bldg., next to iron ch., of red brick with Bath stone dressings in 13th-cent. style, seating 700, by Ewan Christian 1894: triple chancel and apse, wide nave with passage aisles, tower with small spire. 17th-cent. pulpit and font from St. Olave, Old Jewry. Iron ch. retained as par. room and extended 1896. Replaced by large new institute, seating 340, 1928.[41]

ROMAN CATHOLICISM.
There were several Elizabethan recusants in Stoke Newington, including two gentlemen, Francis Bastard and Ferdinand Bawde,[42] and in 1626 Jesuits took a house there where women connected with the queen brought up children 'of good sort'.[43] There were said to be no papists in the parish in 1640 and 1706[44] although in 1781–2 land at the southern end of High Street was called Papists land.[45]

Our Lady of Good Counsel originated in small iron church built in Bouverie Rd. 1888 and registered 1892.[46] Attendance 1903: 345 a.m.; 53 p.m. Roman Catholicism then said to have no influence in Stoke Newington.[47] Sanctuary, transepts, and chapels of new brick church by Thos. H. B. Scott built in Romanesque style next to iron church 1927. Completed 1936 with seating for 400.[48]

St. Thomas More's church registered at nos. 9–11 Henry Rd., Finsbury Park, Brownswood, 1975.[49]

Little Sisters of the Poor, previously in Queen's Road, Dalston, built St. Ann's House as convent and home for the aged at junction of Manor Rd. with Bouverie Rd. 1878.[50] Additions, including chapel, 1895 and new bldg. 1899.[51] By c. 1915 bldgs. covered extensive site.[52]

Sisters of Charity of St. Jeanne Antide from Ealing and Liverpool opened Bethany at no. 53 Bethune Rd. 1978, a private ho. containing chapel and housing four or five sisters who serve the neighbourhood.[53]

PROTESTANT NONCONFORMITY.
Daniel Bull (or Ball), rector of Stoke Newington 1657–60, remained in the parish after his ejection at the Restoration,[54] to become the Presbyterian minister of a community centred on Church Street and patronized by the Hartopps and Fleetwoods. Meetings were held at Sir John Hartopp's house[55] and, in 1672, at the houses of Thomas Stock's widow and of Daniel Bull.[56]

Among those indicted in 1686 for attending unlawful conventicles were the Hartopps, Fleetwoods, and John Gould or Gold, a London mercer. The conventicles were held at the houses of Thomas Spenser, a London tallow chandler, and of Elizabeth Bagby, both probably in Church Street.[57] The congregation described itself as one of protestant dissenters in the 18th century.[58] There was a tendency towards Unitarianism in the early 19th century but by 1846 the members called themselves Independents and in 1873 they joined the London Congregational Union.[59]

A second congregation of nonconformists grew up after the Restoration at Newington Green, where several dissenting academies opened[60] and where, in 1672, meetings were licensed at the houses of Samuel Lee, Mr. Barker, and George Thwing.[61] Charles Morton and James Ashurst, who had been ejected from his fellowship of Magdalen College, Oxford, in 1660, were first ministers[62] and early preachers included Samuel Lee in 1672 and Edward Terry, both ejected ministers, and William Wickens in 1690;[63] John Starkey was minister at Newington Green in 1690.[64] A permanent meeting house was built on the north side of the green in 1708.

[36] Kelly's Dir. Lond. Suburbs (1884); Kelly's Dir. Stoke Newington (1890, 1910–11).

[37] Based on B. Murray, 'Short hist. of St. Olave's' (TS. 1969, S.N.L. 14.02, LC 3220).

[38] Ch. Com., Estate maps, Stoke Newington Estate 1.

[39] Lond. Gaz. 9 Aug. 1892, pp. 4489–91.

[40] Guildhall MS. 17885/6/34 (inquiry by bp. 1905).

[41] G.L.R.O., AR/BA 4/69, no. 50; 478, no. 35; inf. from V. (1981).

[42] Miscellanea (Cath. Rec. Soc. ii), 237; Cath. Rec. Soc. xviii. 148; Mdx. County Rec. i. 198.

[43] Miscellanea, i (Cath. Rec. Soc. i), 96.

[44] B.L. Add. MS. 38856, f. 32; Guildhall MS. 9800/2.

[45] Guide for assessors of par. 1781–2.

[46] G.L.R.O., MBW 1756/232, no. 24; G.R.O. Worship Reg. no. 33555; inf. from the par. priest (1981).

[47] Mudie-Smith, Rel. Life, 130, 162.

[48] G.L.R.O., AR/BA 4/462, no. 34; G.R.O. Worship Reg. no. 50949; Stoke Newington Recorder, 25 Feb. 1927; Hackney Gaz. 5 Oct. 1927 (S.N.L. cuttings 17, LC 1885); inf. from the par. priest (1981).

[49] G.R.O. Worship Reg. no. 74082.

[50] G.L.R.O., MBW 1675/151, no. 23; Centenary booklet, 1876–1976; Cath. Dir. (1875–80).

[51] G.L.R.O., AR/BA 4/30, no. 22; 60, no. 50; 97, no. 58; 124, no. 52.

[52] O.S. Map 1/2,500, Lond. XXI (1894–6 edn.); Lond. II. 11 (1915 edn.).

[53] Inf. from Sister Letizia (1982).

[54] Calamy Revised, ed. Matthews, 85.

[55] Guildhall MS. 9537/20, p. 16.

[56] Orig. Rec. of Early Nonconf. ed. G. L. Turner, i. 235, 240, 282; ii. 958. Bull's ho. belonged to Stock and was at E. end of Church Street: Lysons, Environs, iii. 302.

[57] B.L. Add. MS. 38856, f. 98; Cal. Mdx. Sess. Bks. vii. 148, 156–7, 164; viii. 8, 16; Guildhall MS. 14233/2, unpag. (13 Feb. 1678); G.L.R.O., BRA 500/2; P.R.O., E 179/143/ 370, mm. 38d.–39.

[58] P.R.O., C 54/5975, no. 21.

[59] Ibid. 13881, no. 5; A. C. Upstill, 'Hist. Abney Cong. Ch.' (TS. 1962, S.N.L. 18.1, LC 3107).

[60] Below, educ.

[61] Orig. Rec. of Early Nonconf. i. 301; ii. 958; iii. 349; G.L.R.O., MR TH/1, m. 31d.; P.R.O., E 179/143/370, m. 39.

[62] Calamy Revised, 16; J. L. Tayler, Little Corner of Lond.: Newington Green (1925), 20–1, quoting Wilson MS. at Dr. Williams's Libr.

[63] Calamy Revised, 321, 480, 528.   [64] Ibid. 460.

Although three ministers between 1727 and 1757 conformed to the Church of England, the chapel remained Presbyterian. The intellectual tradition established by its connexion with the dissenting academies continued throughout the 18th century. Several ministers were also librarians of Dr. Williams's library and others kept schools. Richard Price, minister 1758–91, writer and friend of Joseph Priestley, Benjamin Franklin, and the Aikin family,[65] was a founder member of the Unitarian Society and the chapel thereafter became Unitarian.[66] Ministers included Anna Letitia Aikin's husband Rochemont Barbauld (d. 1808) and Thomas Cromwell, antiquarian author and minister 1839–64, and among the congregation were the poet Samuel Rogers (d. 1855) and the microscopist Andrew Pritchard (d. 1882), who was treasurer of the chapel 1850–72.[67]

In 1698 Quakers established a fortnightly meeting as a constituent of Peel monthly meeting in the house of Robert Walburton, gardener, in Stoke Newington. By 1716, however, attendance had declined to 8 or 10 and in 1734 the house where they met was taken over as a parish workhouse, although Quakers continued to pay rent until 1741.[68] There were five or six families of Quakers in 1782 and seven or eight by 1820.[69] Most lived in Paradise Row in Church Street and were wealthy City merchants.[70] In 1827, concerned that so many of its members had moved to Stoke Newington, Gracechurch Street monthly meeting held a joint meeting with Peel monthly meeting to consider establishing a new meeting house, and in 1828 a Quaker meeting house was built in Park Street, off Church Street.[71]

Other early nonconformists included dissenters meeting at the houses of William Spilsworth in 1706 and of Mary Hartopp in 1734.[72] Isaac Watts (d. 1748) spent the last 13 years of his life at Abney House,[73] where he was visited by protestants of all kinds, including John Wesley in 1738[74] and George Whitefield in 1739.[75] John Asty, the dissenting clergyman, spent the first years of his ministry in the early 18th century with the Fleetwood family,[76] and Whitefield also visited Fleetwood House in 1739. The crowds of about 20,000 in Newington, however, to whom Whitefield preached several times in 1739 were probably at Newington common in Hackney.[77] It was estimated in 1782 that nearly a quarter of the families in Stoke Newington were protestant

dissenters.[78] The proportion increased during the 19th century. A room over a coachhouse belonging to the Falcon in Church Street was used as a meeting house from c. 1796 to c. 1816.[79] Meeting places were licensed for worship by Independents at Stoke Newington in 1812 and 1813, by Calvinists in 1818, by Wesleyans in 1843,[80] and by unspecified dissenters in 1811 and 1816, although the last may have been in Hackney parish.[81] A meeting house for Calvinistic Methodists had opened recently in 1816.[82] Two of these early chapels were in courts off High Street, respectively north and south of its junction with Church Street.[83] Salem Baptist chapel, after 1858 in Bouverie Road, claimed to have been founded in 1838, and the Welsh Congregational chapel in Barrett's Grove dated its foundation to 1846 or 1848. The only places of worship recorded in 1851, however, were Abney (Congregational), Newington Green (Unitarian), and Park Street (Quaker) chapels, all long established, and the newer Salem (Baptist) and Primitive Methodist chapels. Nonconformists accounted for 59 per cent of the attendances at worship on census Sunday 1851.[84]

Rivalry with the established Church was sharpened during the later 19th century by Anglo-Catholic activity among the poor in the southern part of Stoke Newington and especially in the detached parts of South Hornsey.[85] The rapid increase in population was accompanied by a growth in all nonconformist denominations, some 10 chapels and missions opening and 1 closing during the period 1838–70 and 19 opening and 8 closing in 1871–1903, while other chapels were rebuilt or enlarged. By 1903 there were 16 chapels and 6 halls belonging to protestant nonconformists, who formed some 58 per cent of those attending worship on census day. Although numbers did not keep pace with the expanding population, nonconformity was 'vigorously in the ascendant'. The Methodists (32 per cent of nonconformist attendances) were the most numerous, followed by the Baptists (28 per cent), Congregationalists (13 per cent), Salvation Army (9 per cent), and Presbyterians (6 per cent).[86]

In the 20th century there was a decline, as middle-class supporters of the older denominations were displaced by working-class and Jewish populations from the East End. In the period 1904–39 only six places of worship,

---

[65] Tayler, *Newington Green*, 41; M. Thorncroft, *Trust in Freedom. Story of Newington Green Unitarian Ch. 1708–1958* (pamphlet, S.N.L. 18.4, LC 2889); *D.N.B.*

[66] Described as Socinian Independents: Robinson, *Stoke Newington*, 210.

[67] M. Pritchard, *Meeting Ho. at Newington Green, Bicentenary 1908* (S.N.L. 18.4, LC 3452); Tayler, *Newington Green*, 41 sqq.; *D.N.B.* s.vv. Barbauld, Cromwell, Pritchard, and Rogers; A. J. Shirren, *Sam. Rogers* (1963).

[68] W. Beck and T. F. Ball, *Lond. Friends' Mtgs.* (1869), 211–13; vestry mins. 1681–1743, 370–2.

[69] Robinson, *Stoke Newington*, 22.

[70] Above, Church Street.

[71] Beck and Ball, *Lond. Friends' Mtgs.* 157–8.

[72] G.L.R.O., MSP 1706 Jy/50; Cal. Sess. Bks. xvi (1732–5), sess bk. 917, p. 61.

[73] *D.N.B.*

[74] *Jnl. of John Wesley*, ed. N. Curnock (c. 1909), ii. 82.

[75] *Geo Whitefield's Jnls.* (1960), 201.

[76] *D.N.B.* s.v. Asty.

[77] The mtg. in May was specified as being on the common: *Geo. Whitefield's Jnls.* 276, 316, 317.

[78] Robinson, *Stoke Newington*, 22.

[79] Abstract of Ct. Rolls 1763–1801, 210, 215; 1802–31, 266.

[80] P.R.O., RG 31/3, nos. 840, 842, 1098, 2165.

[81] Ibid. nos. 793, 959, i.e. at Sandford's brewho.

[82] Brewer, *Beauties of Eng. & Wales*, iv (1816), 258.

[83] Cf. Chapel Yd. and Ct.: Miller, *Plan of Stoke Newington* (1855); Ref. bk. to Wadmore map (1813), no. 317; Abstract of Ct. Rolls 1832–82, 321.

[84] i.e. 2,222 out of a total of 3,747: P.R.O., HO 129/11/1. The total population was 4,840.

[85] Milton Rd. Cong. ch. owed its foundation to alarm at St. Matthias's: Raleigh Memorial Cong. ch. 'Hist. of our first Hundred Years' (TS. Booklet, 1981).

[86] Mudie-Smith, *Rel. Life*, 128, 131, 161–2. Total attendance at worship 16,822. Population 51,247: *Census*, 1901.

mostly mission halls, opened and at least six closed, several of them to become synagogues. Many chapels were damaged during the Second World War. Some did not reopen, and when others were rebuilt it was usually on a smaller scale. The decline of the old denominations was not accompanied by any great expansion of newer, pentecostalist sects, in spite of the growth of a West Indian population, many of whom were Rastafarians.

For abbreviations used in the accounts of protestant nonconformist churches, see above, p. 103. Attendance figures for 1903 are from Mudie-Smith, *Rel. Life*, 161–2.

CONGREGATIONALISTS. Abney chapel,[87] traditionally dating foundation to 1662, originated in mtgs. after Declaration of Indulgence, 1672. Mtg. ho. on N. side Church Street demol. *c.* 1700 to make way for Abney Ho.[88] Replaced by another *c.* 1706 farther W. near junction with Barn Street:[89] single-storeyed plain bldg. with tiled roof and wooden addition, seating 140 before gallery added.[90] Chapel supported by lds. of man., especially by Lady Abney and protégé Isaac Watts, who preached there. Controversy when Martin Tomkins (min. 1709–18) dismissed for Arianism. Decline in early 19th cent. and only 12 members 1814 but recovery by 1838 when new chapel opened S. side Church Street, opposite Abney Ho. Largest of all places of worship in par. 1838, with accommodation for 1,000.[91] Attendance 1851: 797 a.m.; 70 aft.; 541 evg.[92] Bldg. with pediment and twin pillared entrances with Ionic capitals before frontage altered by large Corinthian portico 1862;[93] further enlargements 1873, 1877, 1882.[94] Opened mission in Sandford Lane, Hackney, 1878. Membership increased from 174 (1839) to 250 (1850), 500 (1884), and 600 (1895). Attendance 1903: 489 a.m., 425 p.m., when described as strongest place in district, and especially active in social mission work in Hackney.[95] Decline to 375 members (1914), 100 (1930) when forced to sell mission hall, 43 (1943), and 24 (1951).[96] Extensive war damage. New brick ch. seating 250 built in shell of old bldg. 1957. Old lecture hall leased for factory use since end of war. Youth club in rebuilt vestry, 40 members (1962).[97]

Cong. Chapel Bldg. Soc. purchased extensive site in Milton Rd., S. Hornsey, 1851 and 1855, which sold to Harecourt chapel, Islington, 1859 under ministry of Dr. Alex. Raleigh (d. 1880).[98] Preaching sta. and Sunday sch. opened 1860 and reg. 1861.[99] Iron chapel seating 560 opened S. of sch. 1867. Membership increased from 14 (1861) to 114 (1867). Independent of Harecourt chapel 1872. Permanent ch. of red brick with stone dressings in Gothic style by John Sulman opened on new site at junction of Milton Rd. with Albion Grove 1880 and reg. as Raleigh Memorial chapel 1881. Chapel accommodated 1,000 and contained lecture hall seating 600, Sunday schs., and libr.[1] Attendance 1903: 190 a.m.; 167 p.m. Membership 78 (1939). Chapel damaged during Second World War, reopened 1954. Membership 69 (1951).[2]

Trinity Introductory Cong. ch. at corner of Walford and Nevill rds., S. Hornsey reg. 1866.[3] Ch. moved to Rectory Rd., Hackney, 1882 and bldg. became undenominational mission hall.[4]

Gohebydd Memorial chapel dated foundation to 1846 or 1848 but probably outside par.[5] Iron chapel built in Barrett's Grove 1873.[6] Permanent stone ch. seating 270 built in Gothic style for Welsh Congs. 1884.[7] Attendance 1903: 12 a.m.; 54 p.m. Membership 170 (1939). Disrupted by war and svces. suspended 1946. Demol. by 1952.[8]

UNITARIANS. Presb. mtg. ho. on N. side Newington Green built 1708 but originated in community of 17th-cent. dissenters.[9] Became Unitarian at end of 18th century. As area grew poorer, shifted emphasis from cultural interests to social and missionary work. Bldg. accommodated 200 in 1838.[10] Gallery built 1846.[11] Attendance 1851: 130 p.m.[12] Stuccoed chapel with round-headed windows; new roof and frontage, with large pediment and Tuscan pilasters, 1860.[13] In later 19th cent. chapel supported numerous societies and active in politics but in early 20th cent. weakened by controversy over min.'s social gospel. Attendance 1903: 166 a.m.; 80 p.m. Chapel damaged during Second World War and restored *c.* 1970.

SOCIETY OF FRIENDS.[14] Quakers in Stoke Newington from late 17th cent. but mostly met in City of Lond. Mtg. ho. by Wm. Alderson

[87] Para. based on Upstill, 'Abney Cong. Ch.'
[88] Robinson, *Stoke Newington*, 215; Spratling, *Extracts from Mins. of Stoke Newington Vestry and Chwdns.' Accts. 1681–1855* (publ. in *N. Lond. Guardian*, 1889–91, S.N.L. 34.3, LC 1605).
[89] Deed of 1756 refers to lease (1750) of ho. used as mtg. ho. for 44 years: P.R.O., C 54/5975, no. 21; cf. plan in Guildhall MS. CC. 212290.
[90] B.L. Add. MS. 36370, f. 173; *Portrait of Lond. Suburb, 1844,* item 1. [91] *Lond. City Mission Mag.* iii (1838), 71.
[92] P.R.O., HO 129/1/11/1.
[93] Illus. in *Handbk. and Souvenir of Exhibition at Abney Cong. Ch.* (1913) (S.N.L. 18.1, LC 2453); *Abney Ch. Mag.* n.s. x (1908) (S.N.L. 18.1, LC 1446).
[94] G.L.R.O., MBW 1711/187, no. 24; Stoke Newington, *Official Guide* [1921], 50.
[95] Mudie-Smith, *Rel. Life*, 130.
[96] *Cong. Year Bk.* (1951). [97] Inf. from ch. sec. 1981.
[98] Para. based on Raleigh Memorial Cong. ch. 'Hist. of our first Hundred Years'; *Raleigh Chron.* (diamond jubilee booklet, S.N.L. 18.1, LC 2454).
[99] G.R.O. Worship Reg. no. 14587.

[1] Ibid. 25380; *Bldg. News,* 11 June 1880 (S.N.L. illus. 18.1, LC 552, 3378). [2] *Cong. Year Bk.* (1939, 1951).
[3] P.R.O., C 54/16546, no. 8; G.R.O. Worship Reg. no. 17094.
[4] A. Mearns, *Guide to Cong. Chs. of Lond.* (1882), p. 38, no. 207; below. [5] *Cong. Year Bk.* (1898).
[6] G.L.R.O., MBW 1635/111, no. 21; below, Meths.
[7] G.L.R.O., MBW 1729/205, no. 24; photo. of chapel (S.N.L. illus. 19.21, LC 631).
[8] *Cong. Year Bk.* (1885, 1939, 1940, 1946); *Kelly's Dir. Lond.* (1952), s.v. Barrett's Grove.
[9] Para. based on Pritchard, *Mtg. Ho. at Newington Green*; Thorncroft, *Newington Green Unitarian Ch.*; Tayler, *Newington Green.* [10] *Lond. City Mission Mag.* iii (1838), 71.
[11] G.L.R.O., MBO/DS/B19/72.
[12] P.R.O., HO 129/1/11/1.
[13] Illus. of mtg. ho. before and after 1860: Janzon and Johnson, *Newington Green,* 4, 9; Pevsner, *Lond.* ii. 429; photos. and drawings (S.N.L. illus. 18.4, LC 577–81); above, plate 55.
[14] Para. based on material supplied by Friends' Ho. libr., Euston Rd., 1981.

in classical style of three bays with open portico in brick and plaster, seating 385, built 1828 in Park Street (later Yoakley Rd.) and opened 1829.[15] Surrounded by burial ground, enlarged 1850.[16] Attendance 1851: 231 a.m.; 127 p.m.;[17] 1903: 103 a.m.; 51 p.m. Early mtgs. supported by City businessmen but change in neighbourhood brought decline in numbers and wealth. Most of site sold to borough council 1955. Mtg. ho. demol. and replaced by small brick bldg., closed 1966 and sold to Seventh-day Adventists 1968. Char. founded 1707 by Mic. Yoakley for almshos. for Quakers in Margate (Kent) and Whitechapel. Whitechapel almshos. rebuilt N. of Stoke Newington mtg. ho. 1834.[18] Supported by John Kitching's trust. Demol. 1956 and inmates rehoused at Margate.[19]

BAPTISTS. Chapel Yard, just N. of junction of High Street with Church Street, took name from Bapt. chapel there 1838–45.[20] Replaced by Salem chapel in Church Street, 1849 and later housed Primitive Meth. chapel.

Salem chapel with 180 sittings reg. for Bapts. in converted bldg. in Church Street 1849.[21] Attendance 1851: 90 a.m.; 95 p.m.[22] Chapel, S. side of street between Abney chapel and High Street, still there 1860 but replaced soon afterwards by chapel in Bouverie Rd.[23]

Particular Bapts. built Salem chapel in Bouverie Rd. 1858.[24] Bldg. of stock brick with stone dressings, with pediment, pilasters, and two projecting entrances, seating 300.[25] Attendance 1903: 70 a.m.; 75 p.m. Closed 1922.[26] Used as Presb. mission hall 1925–52 and later as scout hall.[27]

Strict Bapt. chapel opened in Phillipp Street, Hoxton, 1848, moved to Zion chapel, seating 200, in Matthias Rd., S. Hornsey, 1858. Became Wes. mission room 1876.[28]

Proceeds of sale of Devonshire Sq., Bishopsgate Street Without, Bapt. chapel (founded 1638) were applied to chapel at junction of Stoke Newington and Walford rds., S. Hornsey, 1870, reg. by Particular Bapts. 1871.[29] Stone bldg. with plaster façade by Chatfeild Clarke, accommodating 1,050. Merged with Wellington Rd.

Hackney, chapel 1884; 821 members and 8 preachers 1890, when lecture and classrooms in Gothic style added.[30] Attendance 1903: 600 a.m.; 691 p.m.; largest Bapt. chapel in Stoke Newington, said to have the best attended svces. in N. Lond. and 'good evangelical preacher'. Had Christian Endeavour soc. and supported Walford hall.[31] Damaged in 1939–45 war. Rebuilt chapel seated 450 and had 85 members 1982.[32]

Mother ch. of Old Bapt. Union opened in Victoria Rd., S. Hornsey, 1880, moved to High Street and to Clonbrock hall, Clonbrock Rd. 1884.[33] Small stock- and red-brick chapel in Gothic style built 1894 in Wordsworth Rd., S. Hornsey, reg. 1898.[34] Attendance 1903: 70 a.m.; 102 p.m.

METHODISTS. In 1851 Primitive Meths. rented room in yard off High Street, which previously housed Bapt. chapel. Attendance 1851: 27 a.m.; 48 aft.; 66 evg.[35] Closed soon after 1871.[36]

Meth. New Connexion chapel, in Milton Rd., S. Hornsey, by 1859, reg. 1861. Primitive Meth. by 1885 and closed c. 1890.[37]

United Meth. Free chapel in Victoria Grove, S. Hornsey, by 1860, reg. 1861. Attendance 1903: 81 a.m.; 119 p.m. Closed 1910.[38]

There was a Primitive Meth. chapel at no. 3 Barrett's Grove in 1860.[39]

Wesleyans of Highbury circuit built chapel of flint and stone in Gothic style next New River in Green Lanes 1874. Apogee 1879 when sittings let to 474 people, including many of wealth. Attendance 1903: 283 a.m.; 285 p.m. Social character of area in decline by 1906 when sittings 260. Ch. spire damaged in storm before 1920 and removed.[40] Church burnt down 1968, and replaced by small brick chapel and youth and community centre in modern style, 1969.[41]

Primitive Meth. chapel and schs. built 1875 at corner of Castle Street (later Crossway) and Millard Rd.[42] and reg. 1882.[43] Attendance 1903: 129 a.m.; 142 p.m. Reg. cancelled 1951 although chapel listed until 1961.[44]

Green Lanes Wes. chapel opened mission in former Bapt. chapel in Matthias Rd. 1876.

[15] P.R.O., C 54/10543, no. 3; H. Lidbetter, *Friends' Mtg. Ho.* (1961), 17, 21, plates xli–xlii; Pevsner, *Lond.* ii. 429.
[16] P.R.O., C 54/14143, no. 12.
[17] Religious census (Friends' Ho. libr., Euston Rd. MS. vol. 227, f. 213).
[18] Beck, *Church Street*, 14; *Digest Endowed Chars.* H.C. 243, p. 301 (1875), lvii; *Jnl. Friends' Hist. Soc.* xiv. 149.
[19] Photo. (S.N.L. illus. 19.1, LC 3291).
[20] *P.O. Dir. Six Home Counties* (1845); Miller, *Plan of Stoke Newington* (1855); Whitley, *Bapts. of Lond.* 164.
[21] P.R.O., RG 31/3, no. 2314; G.L.R.O., MBO/DS/E19/228.
[22] P.R.O., HO 129/1/11/1.
[23] *Kelly's Dir. Lond. Suburbs* (1860).
[24] P.R.O., C 54/16734, no. 5.
[25] *Bapt. Handbk.* (1890), 199.
[26] Whitley, *Bapts. of Lond.* 164.
[27] Inf. from sec. of Presb. ch.
[28] Whitley, *Bapts. of Lond.* 173; *Cassell's Map of Lond.* (c. 1861–2); *Centenary Souvenir*, 6 (S.N.L. cuttings 18.3, LC 3800).
[29] Datestone on bldg.; G.R.O. Worship Reg. no. 20355.
[30] Whitley, *Bapts. of Lond.* 105–6; *Bapt. Handbk.* (1890), 199; Stoke Newington, *Official Guide* [1917], 38–9; *N. Lond. Recorder*, 13 May 1938 (S.N.L. cuttings 18.2, LC 3084).
[31] Mudie-Smith, *Rel. Life*, 130.
[32] O.S. Map 1/1,250, TQ 3385 NE. (1954, 1964 edns.);

[33] *Bapt. Union Dir.* (1981–2).
[33] Whitley, *Bapts. of Lond.* 226; G.R.O. Worship Reg. no. 27566; O.S. Map 1/2,500, Lond. XXX (1894–6 edn.).
[34] Datestone on bldg.; G.R.O. Worship Reg. no. 36472.
[35] Tithe (1848), nos. 379, 392; P.R.O., HO 129/1/11/1.
[36] *Kelly's Dir. Mdx.* (1871).
[37] G.R.O. Worship Reg. no. 11641; *Highbury, Stoke Newington Dir.* (1885); *Kelly's Dir. Stoke Newington* (1890); O.S. Map 1/2,500, Lond. X (1870 edn.); untitled TS. on chapels, 1979 (S.N.L. cuttings 18.3, LC 3802).
[38] G.R.O. Worship Reg. no. 11384; *Kelly's Dir. Lond. Suburbs* (1860); *Kelly's Dir. Stoke Newington* (1909–10, 1910–11).
[39] *Kelly's Dir. Lond. Suburbs* (1860), s.v. Barrett's Grove. No chapel listed in Barrett's Grove 1871 or 1876–8: *Kelly's Dir. Mdx.* (1871); *Ellis's Dir. Stoke Newington* (1876–7, 1878); but see above, Congs. (Gohebydd chapel).
[40] *Story of Green Lanes Wes. Ch.* (booklet 1920, S.N.L. 18.3, LC 1374); photo. (S.N.L. illus. 18.3, LC 225); P.R.O., C 54/17484, no. 36; G.L.R.O., MBW 1635/111, no. 21.
[41] Datestone on bldg.; G.R.O. Worship Reg. nos. 21803, 71239, 72334; *Hackney Gaz.* 26 Apr. 1968; 10 May 1974 (S.N.L. cuttings 18.3, LC 3650–1).
[42] G.L.R.O., MBW 1651/127, no. 21.
[43] G.R.O. Worship Reg. no. 26499.
[44] *Kelly's Dir. Lond.* (1961, 1963).

Attendance 1903: 136 a.m.; 341 p.m. Closed 1939.[45] Adjoining ho., no. 70, reg. as Wes. mission room 1922-52.[46]

Wes. Meths. built chapel seating 1,024 at Amhurst Pk. on N. border of Stoke Newington 1888.[47] Large bldg. of stock brick and stone in Gothic style. Attendance 1903: 269 a.m.; 251 p.m. Still Meth. 1952 but housed N. Lond. Progressive synagogue from 1956.[48]

PRESBYTERIANS. Presbs. acquired corner site between Manor and Lordship rds. from Ecclesiastical Com. 1880 and built ch. there 1884.[49] Bldg. in Gothic style seating 700. Membership 250 c. 1900.[50] Attendance 1903: 371 a.m.; 280 p.m. Licensed former Bapt. chapel in Bouverie Rd. as mission hall 1925-52. Ch. replaced by smaller brick bldg. in modern style accommodating 140, renamed Manor Rd. United Ref. ch., 1971.[51]

SALVATION ARMY. Barracks reg. between nos. 12 and 14 Milton Rd., S. Hornsey, 1882. Attendance 1903: 153 a.m.; 281 p.m. Reg. cancelled 1964.[52]

Barracks reg. at former gospel hall in High Street, opposite Tyssen Rd., 1887. Attendance 1903: 114 a.m.; 249 p.m. Closed by 1947 and reg. cancelled 1952.[53]

Salvation Army had training garrison at no. 8 Gordon Rd., S. Hornsey, 1892-4 and officers' quarters at no. 98 Hawkesley Rd. 1910.[54]

BRETHREN. Brethren met at assembly rooms in Defoe Rd. by 1894.[55] Attendance 1903: 56 a.m.; 52 p.m. Rooms sold to St. Mary's ch. 1905[56] and Brethren's mtgs. there presumably ceased.

Brethren met at Abney hall, no. 35A Church Street 1903.[57] Attendance 1903: 53 a.m.; 47 p.m.

Plymouth Brethren met at libr. hall in Church Street 1928 but ceased to do so after 1930.[58]

OTHER DENOMINATIONS AND UNSPECIFIED MISSIONS. Latter-day Saints had chapel in Church Street 1851 and 1855;[59] reg. hall at no. 59 Clissold Rd. 1937.[60] Hall used for Civil Defence

from 1940 and sold to borough council as hall of remembrance 1945.[61]

Spiritualists met at no. 99 Wiesbaden (later Belgrade) Rd. 1903.[62] Attendance 1903: 37 a.m.; 228 p.m. Housed synagogue after 1912.[63] Fourth Ch. of Christ Scientist met in libr. hall in Church Street 1919-29.[64] Hebrew Evangelization Soc. reg. mtg. hall at no. 94 Amhurst Park 1965.[65] Seventh-day Adventists from Holloway met in Friends' mtg. ho. in Yoakley Rd. 1966 and purchased bldg. 1968.[66] Mount Calvary Ch. of God reg. no. 2 Laura Terrace, Finsbury Pk. (formerly Brownswood in Hornsey), 1967.[67] The Nigerian Christ Apostolic Ch. held svces. at old St. Mary's ch. from 1980.[68]

Gospel hall at corner of Victoria and Stoke Newington rds., S. Hornsey, reg. by those 'who object to . . . any distinctive religious appellation' 1853-66.[69] Chapel for undesignated Christians built at rear of no. 6 Upper Prospect Pl. in SE. part of Stoke Newington 1871.[70] Mission rooms at rear of no. 77 High Street built by Revd. Wm. Booth of S. Hackney 1874 and used as Christian mission until reg. by Salvation Army 1887.[71] Walford mission hall in former Trinity Introductory Cong. ch. at corner of Walford and Nevill rds. from 1882;[72] supported by Devonshire Sq. Bapt. chapel 1903;[73] attendance 1903: 102 a.m.; 115 p.m.; United Meth. 1914,[74] synagogue from 1923.[75] Abney hall, no. 35A Church Street, reg. by undesignated Christians 1892-1952;[76] used as mission hall by Abney Cong. ch. 1902 and by Brethren 1903.[77] Gospel hall in Allen Rd., S. Hornsey, from c. 1894-c. 1902 but apparently closed by 1903.[78] Mission hall built in Howard Rd. 1923;[79] as Derwent hall, opposite Shakespeare Rd., reg. by undenominational Christians 1930-7.[80]

JUDAISM.[81] Two Sephardi Jewish London merchants had property in Stoke Newington in the mid 18th century and another was a churchwarden in 1743.[82] There was one Jewish family resident in 1782,[83] probably that of

[45] Green Lanes Wes. Ch.; Centenary Souvenir, 6 (S.N.L. cuttings 18.3, LC 3800).
[46] G.R.O. Worship Reg. no. 48552.
[47] Ibid. 30808; Guildhall MS. CC. 223827; P.R.O., C 54/19371, m. 17; untitled TS. on chapels, 1979 (S.N.L. cuttings 18.3, LC 3800).
[48] Kelly's Dir. Lond. (1952); below, Judaism.
[49] Stoke Newington Presb. Ch.: 'Our Work'; Guildhall MSS. CC. 212391, 216104.
[50] Presb. Ch. Rec. (1936-7) (S.N.L. 18.5, LC 1561); cuttings, 1925 (S.N.L. cuttings 18.5, LC 2454); Stoke Newington Presb. Ch.: 'Our Work'.
[51] G.R.O. Worship Reg. nos. 28682, 49946, 71779, 72377; inf. from ch. sec. (1981-2).
[52] G.R.O. Worship Reg. no. 26498.
[53] Ibid. 30445; sales partics. 1904 (HA M 3897); Kelly's Dir. Lond. (1947).
[54] Kelly's Dir. Stoke Newington (1892-4, 1910-11).
[55] Kelly's Dir. Lond. Suburbs (1894).
[56] Above, churches.
[57] Mudie-Smith, Rel. Life, 162; below.
[58] Stoke Newington, Official Guide [1928], 52; Stoke Newington B.C. Mins. (1930-1), 18 Nov. 1930.
[59] P.R.O., HO 107/1503/11/3, p. 28; Kelly's Dir. Mdx. (1855).   [60] G.R.O. Worship Reg. no. 57460.
[61] Ch. of Jesus Christ of Latter Day Saints (Hall of Remembrance), correspondence and council mins. (S.N.L. 19.9, LC 3701).

[62] Mudie-Smith, Rel. Life, 162.
[63] Below, Judaism.
[64] Kelly's Dir. Stoke Newington (1910-20); Stoke Newington, Official Guide [1928], 52.
[65] G.R.O. Worship Reg. no. 70324.
[66] Inf. from ch. clerk.
[67] G.R.O. Worship Reg. no. 71101.
[68] Inf. from rector.
[69] G.R.O. Worship Reg. no. 15557.
[70] G.L.R.O., MBW 1621/97, no. 21.
[71] Ibid. 119, no. 21; Norris's Stoke Newington Dir. (1883); Highbury, Stoke Newington Dir. (1885).
[72] Above, Congs.   [73] Mudie-Smith, Rel. Life, 130.
[74] Untitled TS. on chapels, 1979 (S.N.L. cuttings 18.3, LC 3803).
[75] Below, Judaism.
[76] G.R.O. Worship Reg. no. 33463.
[77] Booth, Life and Labour, 3rd ser. (i), 162; above.
[78] Ibid. p. 161; Kelly's Dir. Lond. Suburbs (1894, 1903).
[79] G.L.R.O., AR/BA 4/403, no. 33, where called Albion hall.
[80] G.R.O. Worship Reg. no. 52281; L.C.C. Municipal Map of Lond. (1930); Kelly's Dir. Stoke Newington (1925 and later edns.).
[81] Based on Jewish Year Bks.
[82] M.L.R. 1750/1/331; 1752/1/497; 1760/2/164; above, loc. govt.
[83] Robinson, Stoke Newington, 22.

Solomon de Medina, who married a Christian and had his children baptized but whose oath as churchwarden was refused by the commissary.[84] Isaac Furtado (d. 1801) had his children baptized in 1799 and was himself buried in the churchyard.[85] By 1820 there were seven or eight Jewish families in the parish,[86] all Sephardim who attended Bevis Marks synagogue in the City or whose children were baptized as Christians.[87] They included Benjamin D'Israeli (d. 1816), merchant and stockbroker and grandfather of the statesman, who lived at no. 7 Church Row (later no. 170 Church Street) from c. 1798.[88]

Ashkenazi immigrants began to arrive from the East End during the late 19th century and synagogues, later part of the United Synagogue, opened just outside the parish boundaries, in Hackney, though called Stoke Newington, in 1887 and at Finsbury Park in 1888.[89] Attendance at Jewish places of worship in Stoke Newington borough in 1903 totalled 343.[90] From the First World War the numbers of Jews leasing property in Stoke Newington multiplied, particularly north of Church Street.[91] Most of the 2,048 people classified as of foreign birth in the 1921 census were Jews from Europe, especially from Russia and Poland, and there were many others born in London of immigrant parents. More refugees, mostly from central Europe, arrived after 1933 and in 1939 many local shops and factories were said to be controlled by Jews. Another wave, mostly from eastern Europe, arrived after the Second World War,[92] accounting for many of the 3,883 classified in 1951 as born in foreign countries.[93]

A Liberal synagogue opened in 1921 but almost all the other synagogues which opened in the 20th century belonged to the Union of Orthodox Hebrew Congregations. Many of them belonged to the extremely orthodox Adath Yisroel and to the sects of Hassidim, which were often based on rabbis from Poland, Rumania, or the Ukraine and each synagogue or beth hamedrash tended to be small and to move from house to house. The first Adath Yisroel synagogue opened in Green Lanes in 1911 and another opened in Wiesbaden (later Belgrade) Road in the Palatine district in 1912. Most synagogues, however, dated from the late 1930s onwards: 14 opened after 1938. The influx of ultra-orthodox Hassidim, especially into the area of larger houses in northeast Stoke Newington, was accompanied in the 1960s and 1970s by the departure of the more prosperous and Anglicized United Synagogue members for north-west London.[94]

Finsbury Park synagogue was registered at no. 20 Portland Road, Brownswood (Hornsey), in 1888. It moved to Princess Road, a little to the north, in 1903 and was admitted as a district member of the United Synagogue in 1934. In 1961 it moved again, to a small brick building on the east side of Green Lanes, next to the reservoir.[95]

The ultra-orthodox Adath Yisroel Synagogue was founded in 1909 and in 1911 built a synagogue at the junction of Green Lanes and Burma Road, which in 1954 was replaced by a new synagogue seating 350 at no. 40 Queen Elizabeth's Walk.[96] As the headquarters of Adath Yisroel, no. 40 also housed the Central Mikvaoth board, the Adath Yisroel burial society, and the Association of Adath Yisroel synagogues in 1981.

In 1912 a house at no. 99 Wiesbaden Road was converted to use as New Dalston synagogue.[97] In 1923 the synagogue moved to the former Congregational Trinity chapel at the corner of Walford and Nevil roads.[98] It had joined the Union of Orthodox Hebrew Congregations by 1931 but had become independent by 1951.

North London Progressive synagogue was founded in 1921 by Liberal Jews meeting in the library hall in Church Street and, from 1922, in the Defoe assembly rooms. Attendances of 300 aroused local opposition. In 1926 a temporary building was erected in Belfast Road in Hackney but when the lease expired in 1936 the congregation returned to the library hall until 1941, when it moved to Montefiore House at no. 69 Stamford Hill in Hackney. A synagogue was consecrated in 1946 at no. 30 Amhurst Park in Hackney, which had been acquired a year earlier. In 1954 the council bought the site and the congregation bought the former Methodist church at no. 100 Amhurst Park, which was consecrated as a synagogue in 1956, when membership was 400. The main hall was reconstructed as a new synagogue in 1961, when membership was 900.[99]

The following were members of the Union of Orthodox Hebrew Congregations. Yeshuath Chaim synagogue was registered on the ground floor of no. 39 Bethune Road in 1941, moved to no. 61 Heathland Road in 1946, and to no. 45 in 1956.[1] Stanislowa beth hamedrash, registered in 1942 at no. 66 Allerton Road, moved to no. 55 Lordship Park in 1946, and to no. 93 in 1974.[2] Beth Chodosh moved from Dunsmure Road in Hackney, where it had opened by 1940, to no. 119 Lordship Road by 1945, and to no. 51 Queen Elizabeth's Walk by 1954. Beth Hacknesseth Schombre Hadass opened in 1949 at no. 93 Fairholt Road and moved in 1960 to no. 2 Heathland Road. In 1949 Zeire Yisroel beth

[84] Vestry mins. 1784–1819, 35–7; above, Church Street, loc. govt.
[85] Cuttings of Stoke Newington 1722–1895, p. 5m.
[86] Robinson, *Stoke Newington*, 22.
[87] e.g. Jacob Mocatto and Moses da Costa: vestry mins. 1819–38, 8, 32.   [88] Vestry mins. 1784–1819, 239; *D.N.B.*
[89] B. A. Kosmin and N. Grizzard, *Jews in an Inner Lond. Boro.* (*Hackney*) (booklet 1975, in S.N.L. and HA); *Highbury, Stoke Newington Dir.* (1885).
[90] Synagogues not distinguished: Mudie-Smith, *Rel. Life*, 162.
[91] Guildhall MSS. CC. 329010, 345106, 351036, 359861, 366028, 369055, 369059, 372471, 375726; *Kelly's Dir. Stoke Newington* (1900, 1910).

[92] Kosmin and Grizzard, op. cit.; *N. Lond. Recorder*, 21 Apr. 1939 (S.N.L. cuttings 19.8, LC 3120).
[93] *Census*, 1951.
[94] Kosmin and Grizzard, op. cit.; *Jewish Chron.* 27 May 1977.
[95] G.R.O. Worship Reg. 31012, 39847, 68319; A. Newman, *United Synagogue 1870–1970* (1977), 226.
[96] Inf. from sec. of Union of Orthodox Hebrew Congregations (1981); G.R.O. Worship Reg. 45149, 66114.
[97] G.L.R.O., AR/BA 4/249, no. 46.
[98] G.R.O. Worship Reg. 64453.
[99] Ibid. 61763, 64986, 65306; inf. from rabbi (1982).
[1] G.R.O. Worship Reg. 59948, 61437, 65563.
[2] Ibid. 60333, 61382, 73693.

hamedrash opened at no. 69 Lordship Road. It was enlarged in 1968, when it changed its name to Torah Etz Chayim, and seated 215 in 1981. A beth hamedrash of the Agudah Youth Movement opened on the first floor of no. 69 in 1959. Both were members of Adath Yisroel.[3] Moriah beth hamedrash was registered at no. 342 Seven Sisters Road from 1958 to 1971.[4] Yeshivah Horomoh beth hamedrash opened in 1958 in the synagogue in Green Lanes vacated by Adath Yisroel. It closed in 1972.[5] Beth hamedrash D'Chasidey Belz was registered in 1959 at no. 99 Bethune Road.[6] Beth Sholom, which opened in 1964 at no. 27 St. Kilda's Road, had existed as Brith Sholom society at no. 47 West Bank in Hackney in 1945.[7] Yeshiva Horomoh beth hamedrash was registered at the rear of no. 100 Fairholt Road in 1976.[8] Seven Sisters Road Hebrew congregation, which had been registered at no. 414 Seven Sisters Road in 1954,[9] moved in 1976 to no. 10A Woodberry Down.

The following did not belong to the Union: a beth hamedrash in two rooms at no. 83 Bethune Road from 1931 to 1952;[10] the Kol Jacob synagogue registered on the ground floor of no. 120 Manor Road from 1938 to 1952;[11] Holy Law synagogue, registered at no. 57 Lordship Park from 1952 to 1964;[12] a Sephardi Eastern Jewry synagogue at no. 7 Stamford Hill from 1956 to 1958.[13]

EDUCATION. William Patten built a schoolhouse on the western end of the church aisle which he built in 1563.[14] In 1664 Thomas Stock bequeathed the rent from one of his houses for educating five poor children.[15] From 1682 there were seats in the church reserved for schoolchildren, including those taught by the assistant curate John Price in 1712.[16] The vestry made payments to individuals for teaching parish children from 1707[17] and in 1728 agreed to establish a charity school to clothe and educate 6 boys and 6 girls.[18] By 1784 the vestry had appointed and paid a master and mistress to teach 10 boys and 8 girls.[19] The school was endowed by the charities of Thomas Thompson (1729), John Newman (1730), George Green (1764), Mary Hammond (1774), and Sarah Bowles (1788), although the income was not always applied according to the benefactors' wishes.[20]

In 1789 a vestry committee reported that the

school received £21 a year from the charities and £17 from the church rates. It considered that the school was ineffectual and it recommended the establishment of a school of 15 boys and 10 girls, funded by subscriptions and managed by a committee.[21] By 1795 endowment, voluntary contributions, and collections made at charity sermons provided for teaching 15 boys and 12 girls.[22] In 1819 there were 30 boys and 25 girls clothed and, with another 40 children, educated in a schoolhouse on the south side of Church Street, where the master and mistress lived.[23] In 1830 trustees leased a site north of Church Street, entered from Barn Street, where a National school, St. Mary's parochial school, opened in 1831.[24]

Dissenting ladies established a charity school c. 1790 where 14 girls were clothed and educated, supported by voluntary contributions and charity sermons at the meeting house.[25] The Sunday School society, which was founded in 1802, opened Sunday schools at Kingsland and Newington in that year and at Clapton in 1805. In 1808 they were replaced by a building at the southern tip of Stoke Newington, which opened in 1809 as a day school and developed into a British school using Lancasterian methods.[26] In 1820 both schools apparently survived, together with a Quaker school for girls, which was supported by the sale of their needlework.[27] In addition several (presumably private) day and boarding schools were mentioned in 1819, when the poor were said to have sufficient means of education.[28]

The Quaker girls' school of 1820 may have been the cottage school established by William Allen on his estate in Lordship Road, to which he alluded in 1823. Allen, interested in the Lancasterian system, supported the Quaker girls' boarding school founded in 1824 and also an infants' school in Stoke Newington,[29] although the latter may have been the school at Newington common in Hackney, which had moved to High Street by 1845.[30] Allen's school was mentioned in 1832[31] and was presumably one of the five day schools, which included the parish school and boarding schools, where 142 boys and 65 girls were taught in 1833. There was also a Sunday school supported by Independents, with 41 boys and 55 girls on the roll, in 1833. No mention was made of the British school then[32] or in 1846, when 195 children were educated at the parish

[3] Ibid. 68039; inf. from warden (1981) and sec. of Union of Orthodox Hebrew Congregations (1982).
[4] G.R.O. Worship Reg. 66618.
[5] Ibid. 66649, 69328.
[6] Ibid. 67385, 72424.
[7] Ibid. 70267.
[8] Ibid. 74453.
[9] Ibid. 64493.
[10] Ibid. 53277, 59320.
[11] Ibid. 58199.
[12] Ibid. 63523.
[13] Ibid. 65598.
[14] Guildhall MS. (formerly St. Paul's MS. A 37/1114); above, churches. A room near the S. door in the old church was still labelled 'the schoolroom' c. 1904: J. R. Spratling, 'Old Ch. of St. Mary Stoke Newington' (S.N.L. 14.011, LC 1315).
[15] Vestry mins. 1681-1743, loose leaves at front.
[16] Ibid. 152; below.
[17] Vestry mins. 1681-1743, 119, 140, 152.

[18] Ibid. 286.
[19] Ibid. 1784-1819, 23, 39.
[20] Ibid. 1681-1743, 467, 470; Draft Index to par. ledger 1, s.v. char. sch.; Lysons, Environs, iii. 302-3.
[21] Vestry mins. 1784-1819, 122-3, 125.
[22] Lysons, Environs, iii. 303.
[23] Digest of Returns to Sel. Cttee. on Educ. of Poor, H.C. 224, p. 551 (1819), ix(1); Robinson, Stoke Newington, 209.
[24] Educ. Enq. Abstract, 581-2; Guildhall MS. CC. 212343.
[25] i.e. presumably Abney Cong. chapel.
[26] British and Foreign Schs. Soc. Rep. (1837), 63.
[27] Robinson, Stoke Newington, 209.
[28] Digest of Returns to Sel. Cttee. on Educ. of Poor, 551.
[29] Life of Wm. Allen (1846), ii. 394; Shirren, 'Wilberforce and Anti-Slavery Campaign' (S.N.L. 41.6, LC 3391).
[30] Mins. of Cttee. of Health, 1831 (HA P/M/BH 1); Pigot's Lond. Dir. (1838), 471; P.O. Dir. Six Home Counties (1845).
[31] Mins. of Cttee. of Health, 1831.
[32] Educ. Enq. Abstract, 581-2. Although called Kingsland British sch., it lay within Stoke Newington.

day and Sunday schools, at two dames' day, and one boys' day school.[33]

Sunday schools attached to nonconformist chapels opened at Newington Green in 1840 and at Milton Road in South Hornsey in 1860, becoming day schools in 1860 and 1868 respectively.[34] St. Matthias Church of England school opened in 1849 but the Kingsland British school closed c. 1865.

Stoke Newington was included in the Finsbury division of the London school board, set up under the Public Education Act of 1870.[35] In 1871 there were two public schools (St. Mary and St. Matthias), two private schools run by committees (St. Faith and Newington Green), and 12 adventure schools. One was connected with St. Matthias's mission in Green Lanes while all the rest were dame schools. Together the schools accommodated 1,095 children, with 1,179 on the rolls and an average attendance of 894. Of those the public schools accommodated 649, had 798 enrolled, and an average attendance of 581.[36] Although most of the adventure schools were condemned as inefficient,[37] the board did not open its first temporary schools, in Church Street and Defoe Road, until 1878 and its first permanent school, in Oldfield Road, until 1882. Others opened in Church Street in 1892 and Princess May Road in 1899.

Milton Road Congregational school was the only public school in South Hornsey in 1871. The detached portions of South Hornsey were included in the area of Hornsey school board, which was formed in 1874[38] and opened a temporary school in 1875 in the Congregational school before moving to another chapel in Milton Road in 1876. The board opened a permanent school in 1878 in Wordsworth Road, which was transferred to the London school board when the detached parts of Hornsey were incorporated into Stoke Newington in 1900.

Newington Green Unitarian school closed in 1896 and in 1903 there were said to be eight efficient elementary schools: four board schools accommodating 6,312 children, with 5,207 on the roll and an average attendance of 4,538, and two Church of England and two private schools accommodating 926 children, with 943 on the roll and an average attendance of 803.[39] Raleigh Memorial school, which had replaced Milton Road Congregational school in 1880, was not included, presumably because it was not thought efficient, and it closed in 1925.

The L.C.C.'s education committee replaced the London school board in 1904. In 1913 it opened its first secondary school in Stoke Newington, Oldfield central, which was replaced by Stoke Newington central school in 1928. The existing schools were reorganized at about the same time, with Church Street and Princess May Road council schools and St. Mary and St. Matthias Church of England schools as primary and Oldfield Road and Wordsworth Road council schools as secondary schools. Both the last two also had infants' departments, although Wordsworth Road had lost its infants by 1936.

The Second World War saw schools evacuated, their buildings requisitioned and many badly damaged. In 1947 the London school plan proposed two new primary schools (Woodberry Down, opened c. 1951, and Sir Thomas Abney, opened c. 1954) and one new secondary school, besides reorganizing secondary education on comprehensive principles.[40] Woodberry Down was opened in 1955 as a comprehensive but other comprehensive schools, often renamed, were housed in existing premises: Clissold in those of Stoke Newington central, Daniel Defoe in Oldfield Road, and Wordsworth in the board school. Clissold and Wordsworth amalgamated in 1956 and the combined school, called Clissold Park in 1967, moved into new buildings in 1969, when Daniel Defoe closed. New primary schools opened at Grasmere (1965), Parkwood in Finsbury Park (1969), and Grazebrook (1970). In the voluntary sector the Jewish Avigdor primary and secondary schools opened after the Second World War but the latter closed in 1961. A declining birth rate and emigration from the area followed the expansion of the 1960s, and by 1979 there was a sharp fall in the numbers of children. Amalgamations followed, leaving only one secondary school in Stoke Newington after Clissold Park had merged with Woodberry Down in 1982.[41]

Public schools. The general sources are those indicated above, p. 119, with the addition of P.R.O., ED 3/5; ED 7/79, 84, 87; *Rep. from Sel. Cttee. on Educ. of Lower Orders in Metropolis*, H.C. 498, pp. 124–5 (1816), iv; *Educ. Enq. Abstract*, H.C. 62, pp. 581–2 (1835), xlii (2); *Rep. of Educ. Cttee. of Council, 1880* [C.2948-I], H.C. (1881), xxxii; *1885* [C.4849-I], H.C. (1886), xxiv; *1888* [C.5467-I], H.C. (1888), xxxvii; *1893* [C.7437-I], H.C. (1894), xxix; *Schs. in receipt of Parl. Grants, 1898* [C.9454], H.C. (1899), lxxiv; *Return of Schs. 1899* [Cd. 315], H.C. (1900), lxv(2); *Schs. under Admin. of Bd. 1901–2* [Cd. 1277], H.C. (1902), lxxix; *Public Elem. Schs. 1906* [Cd. 3510], H.C. (1907), lxiii; *1907* [Cd. 3901], H.C. (1908), lxxiv; G.L.R.O., SBL 1527 (Lond. sch. bd., lists of temporary schs. 1885, 1896; lists of schs. 1899, 1902).

ABNEY PARK PRIMARY, see Sir Thomas Abney primary.

ALBION RD. CENTRAL, see Stoke Newington Central.

AVIGDOR HIGH,[42] 65–9 Lordship Rd. Opened 1947 as Jewish grammar sch. for 300 SM. Maintained by L.C.C. from 1950. Controversy 1955 between L.C.C. and orthodox Jewish governors. SG 1960. L.C.C. withdrew support[43] and sch. closed 1961.

---

[33] *Nat. Soc. s. Inquiry, 1846–7*, Mdx. 10–11.
[34] Rest of section based on hist. of individual schs., below.
[35] 33 & 34 Vic. c. 75.
[36] G.L.R.O., SBL 1518, pp. 51–2.
[37] Ibid. 1329, pp. 104–5, 110–11; P.R.O., ED 3/5.
[38] *V.C.H. Mdx.* vi. 189–90.
[39] G.L.R.O., SBL 1527 (return of schs. 1903), p. 20.

[40] L.C.C. *Lond. Sch. Plan* (1947), 83 sqq.
[41] *Hackney Gaz.* 23 Feb., 14 Dec. 1979; 12 July 1981.
[42] Based on *Jewish Year Bk.* (1930 and later edns.).
[43] *The Times*, 29 Oct. 1955, 5b; 23 Feb. 1956, 12e; 24 Feb. 1956, 11d; 28 Feb. 1956, 1e; 29 Feb. 1956, 11c; 25 May 1961, 4e; 30 May 1961, 7e.

AVIGDOR PRIMARY, 67 Lordship Rd. Opened 1948 as Jewish JM sch. with boarding dept. at no. 63.[44] Vol. assisted JM, I by 1970. Roll 1981: 197 JM, I.

CHURCH STREET. Opened 1892 as bd. sch. N. of Dynevor Rd.[45] 1893 accn. 300 B, 300 G, 388 I, a.a. 592. Enlarged 1895.[46] 1898 accn. 1,242, a.a. 894; 1919 a.a. 391 B, 304 G, 264 I. JB, JG, I by 1932. 1938 a.a. 273 JB, 256 JG, 315 I. JM, I and renamed William Patten 1951.[47] Enlarged c. 1968. Roll 1981: 216 JM, 130 I, 50 nursery.

CHURCH STREET TEMP. Opened 1878 as bd. sch. in rented bldg. belonging to trustees of Abney Pk. chapel. 1880 accn. 331, a.a. 235. Closed and children transferred to Oldfield Rd. 1881. Reopened 1889 for GI. Sch. pence (2d.). Closed 1892 and replaced by Church Street.

CLISSOLD, see Stoke Newington Central.

CLISSOLD PARK. Comprehensive sch. formed 1967 by amalg. of Wordsworth and Daniel Defoe SM schs. New bldg. opened 1969 for 1,725 SM on extensive site in Clissold Rd.[48] Roll 1981: 850 SM. Amalg. 1982 with Woodberry Down in Stoke Newington comprehensive.[49]

DANIEL DEFOE, see Oldfield Rd.

DEFOE RD. TEMP. Opened 1878 as bd. sch. in rented assembly rooms in Defoe Rd. 1880 accn. 720, a.a. 173. Closed 1881 and children transferred to Oldfield Rd. Reopened 1889. Closed 1892 and replaced by Church Street.

GRASMERE PRIMARY, 92 Albion Rd. Opened 1965 for JM & I in former Stoke Newington Central sch. bldgs.[50] Roll 1981: 161 JM & I.

GRAZEBROOK PRIMARY, Lordship Rd. Opened 1970 for I. JM dept. added 1973. Enlarged 1976. Roll 1981: 209 JM & I, 48 nursery.

KINGSLAND BRITISH.[51] Built 1808 at corner of Cock and Castle Lane and Stoke Newington Rd. to replace 3 Sunday schs. Opened 1809 as day sch. for 30 B, 30 G. Joined British Soc. 1811. Accn. for 200 B added 1815 and rest of bldg. used for G. Roll 1817: 191 B, 119 G. Enlarged 1818. Supported by vol. subscriptions, sch. pence (2d.), and needlework of G. Clothing given to G. Roll 1834: 250 B, 130 G. Schoolroom for I built 1850.[52] Roll 1857: 170 BG; 1868: 90. Closed c. 1865.[53]

MILTON RD. CONG., S. Hornsey.[54] Sunday schs. built by Cong. ch. 1860 and 1864. Day sch. with accn. for 200 BG opened there 1868. Roll 1869: 209 B, 176 G. Supported by vol. contributions, sch. pence, and chapel funds. Parl. grant 1870, when a.a. 148 B, 141 G. Sch. offered to Hornsey sch. bd. 1875 but refused because insufficient accn. for I.[55] Sch. closed and site sold to S. Hornsey local bd. 1880. Sch. replaced by Raleigh Memorial.

MILTON RD. TEMP., S. Hornsey. Hornsey sch. bd. rented Milton Rd. Cong. sch. bldgs. for a year 1875, and Meth. New Connexion chapel in Milton Rd. for 1876–9. Accn. 352 BG, 100 I. Replaced by Wordsworth Rd.[56]

NEWINGTON GREEN. Unitarian chapel opened Sunday sch. 1840 and day sch. in rented cottage behind chapel 1860.[57] Teaching in 2 rooms, sch. pence (1–2d.). Roll 1871: 40 B, 33 G; a.a. 22 B, 21 G. Sch. rebuilt 1873; sch. ho. built 1887.[58] Licence to convert sch. into store 1896.[59]

OLDFIELD RD. Opened as bd. sch. for 240 B, 240 G, 320 I 1882 at junction of Oldfield Rd. and Ayrsome Rd.[60] Enlarged 1883, 1893, 1898.[61] Parl. grant and sch. pence (3d. 1882, ½d. 1893, nothing by 1899). 1885 accn. 1,598, a.a. 1,202; 1898 accn. 1,670, a.a. 1,395; 1919 accn. 498 M, 489 JM & I, a.a. 440 M, 384 JM & I. SB, SG, I by 1932. 1938 a.a. 270 SB, 275 SG, 261 I. SM, called Daniel Defoe, 1951.[62] Bldgs. became lower sch. of Clissold Pk. 1967, and were taken over by Hackney and Stoke Newington Coll. for Further Educ. 1969 when Clissold Pk. bldgs. opened.

OLDFIELD RD. CENTRAL. SM pupils from Oldfield Rd. transferred 1913 to sch. in Kynaston Rd. and Stoke Newington High Street. 1919 accn. 300 M, a.a. 249 M. Closed 1927 and premises absorbed by Oldfield Rd.

PARKWOOD PRIMARY, Queen's Drive. Opened 1969 just S. of Finsbury Pk. Roll 1981: 169 JM & I.

PRINCESS MAY RD. Opened 1892 as bd. sch. for 304 B, 304 G, 308 I between Princess May Rd. and Barrett's Grove.[63] 1906 accn. 304 B, 304 G, 353 I, a.a. 294 B, 283 G, 286 I. Enlarged 1913.[64] 1919 accn. 368 B, 368 G, 438 I, a.a. 302 B, 293 G, 288 I. JB, JG, I by 1932. 1938 a.a. 229 JB, 271 JG, 317 I. Renamed Princess May 1951.[65] JM, I by 1964. Roll 1981: 202 JM, 119 I.

RALEIGH MEMORIAL, Albion Rd.[66] Opened 1880 by Cong. chapel to replace Milton Rd. Cong. sch. Albion Rd. Also called Middle Class schs. Closed 1925.

ST. FAITH C.E., Londesborough Rd. Opened by 1871 as private sch. by St. Faith's ch. Roll 1871: 38 B, 32 G, a.a. 25 B, 30 G, Sch. pence (2d.). Considered 'not efficient' 1871. Probably used as Sunday sch. long after ceased to be day sch.[67]

ST. MARY C.E. PRIMARY, Barn Street. Opened 1831 as Nat. sch. but began as char. sch. much earlier. Roll 1833: 80 B, 45 G. Master and

[44] Jewish Year Bk. (1947 and later edns.).
[45] G.L.R.O., AR/BA 4/13, no. 24.
[46] Ibid. 60, no. 50.
[47] L.C.C. Educ. Cttee. Mins. (1951–2), 37.
[48] Secondary Schs. in Hackney (1969); Modern Bldgs. in Lond. ed. C. McKean and T. Jestico (1976), 51.
[49] Hackney Gaz. 12 July 1981 (S.N.L. cuttings 49.2, LC 3840); I.L.E.A., Div. Office 4, List of educ. establishments, Sept. 1982.
[50] I.L.E.A. Educ. Cttee. Mins. (1964–6), 177.
[51] Based on British and Foreign Schs. Soc. Rep. (1817), 78, 131; (1818), 105; (1834), 40; (1837), 63.
[52] G.L.R.O., MBO/DS/F19.
[53] British and Foreign Schs. Soc. Rep. (1857), 34, (1865–9). Roll no. of 90 repeated each year 1865–8. Cf. Stanford's Libr. Map of Lond. and Suburbs (1862 with additions to 1865); O.S. Map 1/2,500, Lond. XVIII (1870 edn.).

[54] Raleigh Memorial Cong. ch. 'Hist. of first Hundred Years'; V.C.H. Mdx. vi. 189.
[55] Hornsey sch. bd. mins. i. 23, 51, in Bruce Castle Mus., Tottenham.
[56] Ibid. i. 38, 65, 106; ii. 699.
[57] Pritchard, Meeting Ho. at Newington Green.
[58] G.L.R.O., MBW 1635/111, no. 21; 1756/232, no. 24.
[59] Ibid. AR/BA 4/69, no. 50.
[60] Ibid. MBW 1692/168, no. 23; 1701/177, no. 24.
[61] Ibid. 1721/197, no. 24; AR/BA 4/40, no. 22; 87, no. 57.
[62] L.C.C. Educ. Cttee. Mins. (1951–2), 73.
[63] G.L.R.O., AR/BA 4/97, no. 58.   [64] Ibid. 266.
[65] L.C.C. Educ. Cttee. Mins. (1951–2), 37.
[66] Raleigh Memorial Cong. ch. 'Hist. of first Hundred Years'.
[67] Stanford's Map of Lond. (c. 1904); O.S. Map 1/2,500, Lond. XXX (1894–6 edn.).

mistress, supported by char. endowment, subscriptions, and collections at par. ch. Leases of surrounding land 1848, 1866, and 1876, and bldgs. enlarged 1871, 1875, and 1913.[68] 1853 a.a. 92 B, 106 G, in 2 rooms; sch. pence (2d.). I sch. opened in old Rectory before 1855 and later in Rigby's bldgs. S. side Church Street, near High Street.[69] Parl. grants by 1866. 1871 accn. 315, a.a. 83 B, 69 G, 76 I, in three schoolrooms and one classroom. Endowment increased by £500 under will of Augustus Clissold (d. 1882)[70] and no fees charged by 1897.[71] 1887 accn. 445, a.a. 307; 1901 accn. 432, a.a. 230; 1919 accn. 120 B, 114 G, 112 I, a.a. 104 B, 210 G & I. JM & I by 1932. 1938 a.a. 286 JM & I. Vol. assisted status after 1944 Act. Enlarged 1980. Roll 1981: 81 JM, 45 I.

St. Matthias C.E. primary, Wordsworth Rd. Opened 1849 as Nat. sch. in bldgs. used as sch. during week and ch. on Sundays. Conveyed 1852 to trustees as sch. for children of labouring classes.[72] Roll 1871: 171 B, 156 G, 163 I. 3 classrooms in 2 bldgs. described as 'dark and disagreeable' 1871. Financed by vol. contributions and sch. pence (2d.) 1873. Chronic state of insolvency due to ch. troubles and refusal of managers to apply for parl. grant 1870s and to increasing poverty of district. Small parl. grant 1881. 1893 accn. 345, a.a. 364, sch. pence (2s. 9d.). Enlargement 1897 with large parl. grant.[73] 1901 a.a. 550. 1919 accn. 176 B, 158 G, 164 I, a.a. 157 B, 279 G & I. JB, JG & I by 1932. 1938 a.a. 128 JG & I. Bldgs. damaged during Second World War.[74] Reopened as vol. assisted JM & I 1951. New block opened 1971 for 150 JM.[75] Roll 1981: 300 JM & I.

Sir Thomas Abney primary. Opened by 1954 for JM, I at junction of Fairholt and Bethune rds. as Abney Pk. primary.[76] Renamed 1955. Roll 1981: 163 JM, 83 I.

Stoke Newington. Comprehensive SM sch. formed 1982 by amalg. of Clissold Pk. and Woodberry Down. Accn. for 1,080 in bldgs. of former schs.[77]

Stoke Newington central, 92 Albion Rd. Opened for 400 SM 1928.[78] 1932 a.a. 378. Renamed Clissold SM by 1951. Bldgs. taken over by Wordsworth SM 1956 and closed 1965. Grasmere primary built on site.

Stoke Newington parochial, see St. Mary C.E. primary.

William Patten, see Church Street.

Woodberry Down comprehensive. Opened 1955 for 1,250 SM in 3 four-storeyed blocks on 5 a. at junction of Woodberry Down and Woodberry Grove.[79] Roll 1977: 1,300 SM;[80] 1981: 1,040 SM. Amalg. 1982 with Clissold Pk. to create Stoke Newington comprehensive.

Woodberry Down primary, Woodberry Grove. Opened by 1951 for JM, I. Roll 1981: 196 JM, 100 I.

Wordsworth Rd. Opened 1878 for 566 B, 490 G, 528 I by Hornsey sch. bd. on site acquired 1876 at junction of Wordsworth and Palatine rds.[81] Altered 1882, enlarged 1889.[82] Transferred to Stoke Newington M.B. and L.C.C. 1900. 1901 accn. 1,602, a.a. 1,461; 1906 accn. 520 B, 473 G, 422 I, a.a. 469 B, 414 G, 383 I. SB, SG, I by 1932, when a.a. 376 SB, 380 SG, 146 I. SB, SG by 1936. 1938 a.a. 283 SB, 313 SG. JM, I by 1947,[83] SM, I by 1951. 1956 I dept. closed, SM moved to 92 Albion Rd., and Wordsworth Rd. bldgs. used as annexe and lower sch. of sch. named Clissold Pk. 1967.[84] Bldgs. closed 1969 when Clissold Pk. new bldgs. opened. Site used for Horizon special sch.[85]

Special schools. Crusoe House, Clissold Rd. Day sch. opened 1972 for maladjusted in new bldg. Roll 1981: 46 M. 1982 moved to Nile Street, Hoxton.[86]

Horizon, Wordsworth Rd. Moved 1974 from Wenlock Rd., Hoxton, to new bldg. on Wordsworth Rd. sch. site. Day sch. for educationally subnormal JM, SM.[87] Roll 1981: 151 M.

New River, Clissold Rd. Opened 1967 for visually handicapped in bldg. to replace schs. in Islington and Tower Hamlets. Enlarged 1975-7.[88] Roll 1981: 58 M.

Princess May, Princess May Rd. Accn. for 60 mentally deficient at Princess May sch. 1899. 1903 a.a. 49.[89]

Woodberry Down health centre, Green Lanes. Sch. for maladjusted 1956 and 1965.[90]

Evening and technical education. In 1816 106 men, averaging 50-70 a night, attended evening classes in Kingsland British school.[91] In 1871 evening classes were held at St. Matthias National school, for 47 girls, and at Newington Green Unitarian school, where 22 boys and 12 girls were taught in a school held for four hours a week during the winter.[92] In 1881 St. Faith's

[68] *Endowed Charities (County of Lond.)*, H.C. 128, pp. 723 sqq. (1897), lxvi, pt. 1; G.L.R.O., MBW 1621/97, no. 21; 1651/127, no. 21; AR/BA 4/266; Guildhall MS. CC. 17938l.
[69] *Kelly's Dir. Lond. Suburbs* (1860); G.L.R.O., MBW 2120 (Metropolitan Bd. of Works, rate bks. vol. 142); P.R.O. RG 9/152, f. 73; letter by dau. of Thos. Jackson, 1924 (S.N.L. letters 78 JACKSON).
[70] Vestry mins. 1862-89, 463.
[71] *Endowed Charities (County of Lond.)*, 723 sqq.
[72] P.R.O., HO 129/1/11/1/1/1; ibid. C 54/14385, no. 11; G.L.R.O., MBO/DS/E19; cf. S.N.L. illus. 49.1, LC 1506.
[73] G.L.R.O., AR/BA 4/78, no. 57; 187.
[74] *St. Matthias Souvenir Brochure* (1946) in S.N.L.
[75] *St. Matthias Centenary Appeal* (1953) in S.N.L; *Hackney Gaz.* 8 Oct. 1971.
[76] O.S. Maps 1/1,250, TQ 3387 NW. (1954 edn.).
[77] I.L.E.A. Div. Office 4, List of educ. establishments, Sept. 1982; *Hackney Gaz.* 12 July 1981.
[78] *The Times*, 15 Feb. 1928, 19d; *Stoke Newington Recorder*, 10, 17 Feb. 1928 (S.N.L. illus. and cuttings 49.2, LC 532).
[79] *The Times*, 31 Aug. 1955, 10c.

[80] *Secondary Schs. in Hackney* (1977).
[81] Hornsey sch. bd. mins. i. 160, in Bruce Castle Mus., Tottenham; G.L.R.O., MBW 1667/143, no. 21; *Architect*, 27 Apr. 1878. Sited within borders of Stoke Newington: *Surveyor's Plan of Par. of St. Mary Stoke Newington* (1896) (S.N.L. 85.2, LC 1631).
[82] G.L.R.O., MBW 1711/187, no. 24; AR/BA 4/4, no. 24.
[83] L.C.C. *Lond. Sch. Plan* (1947), 85.
[84] L.C.C. *Secondary Schs. in Hackney etc.* (1956); *Educ. Authorities Dir.* (1965, 1966); O.S. Map 1/1,250, TQ 3385 NW. (1954, 1970 edns.).
[85] I.L.E.A. *Educ. Cttee. Mins.* (1969-70), 11.
[86] I.L.E.A. Div. Office 4, List of educ. establishments, Sept. 1982.
[87] Ibid.; *Educ. Authorities Dir.* (1975), 896.
[88] *Educ. Authorities Dir.* (1975), 896.
[89] G.L.R.O., AR/BA 4/97, no. 58.
[90] *Educ. Authorities Dir.* (1956-7), 467; (1965), 660.
[91] *Rep. from Sel. Cttee. on Educ. of Lower Orders in Metropolis*, H.C. 498, p. 125 (1816), iv.
[92] P.R.O., ED 3/5.

church opened a school in its mission house in Gordon Road; it met three evenings a week during the winter and charged 3*d.* or 6*d.* a week.[93] An evening school, with an average attendance of 47, was held at Oldfield Road school in 1901.[94] North London College of Commerce, maintained by the L.C.C., was housed in Princess May school by 1955. It closed in 1964.[95]

Hackney and Stoke Newington junior commercial and technical college, which was founded in 1956, provided evening classes in local schools, including Woodberry Down. In 1969 the college, renamed Hackney and Stoke Newington college for further education, took over the former board school premises in Oldfield Road and in 1974 it was absorbed into Hackney college.[96]

Private schools. There were dissenting academies at Newington Green in the late 17th century[97] and private schools were numerous in Stoke Newington in the 18th and 19th centuries. Early schools included those of one Wyn *c.* 1682,[98] of Mrs. Elizabeth Tutchin, who had a nonconformist school at Newington Green before 1710,[99] and of John Price, the assistant curate, in 1712.[1] In the 1720s Erasmus Carter kept a boys' boarding school, probably on the site of Rigby's Buildings on the south side of Church Street, near High Street.[2] The King's Head society, founded in 1730, established its own institution at Newington Green *c.* 1732 under its first tutor, Abraham Tayler.[3] Dr. James Burgh (d. 1775), the moral and political writer, kept academies at Stoke Newington 1747–50 and the Islington part of Newington Green 1750–71, where Samuel Rogers was a pupil.[4] Thomas Day, author of *Sandford and Merton*, attended a school in Stoke Newington *c.* 1755[5] and Thomas Smith opened an academy, possibly on the south side of Church Street, in 1769.[6]

Elizabeth Crisp ran a girls' boarding school in the older part of Fleetwood House from 1772 or earlier to 1795.[7] Sarah Jefferies had a school there by 1813[8] and it may have been continued by the Graves or Greaves family.[9] In 1792 seats were assigned in the church for pupils of the boarding schools of Mrs. Crisp (8), of Jenkins (10), and of

Maddox, Wragg, and Williams (24 each).[10] John Barker had a school at no. 187 High Street in 1794.[11] Anthony Barbre, schoolmaster of Stoke Newington, occupied a cottage in High Street in 1799.[12]

Many schools, mostly small, short lived, girls' boarding schools, opened in Church Street during the 19th century.[13] There were 8 schools in Church Street in 1826, 12 in 1834, 11 in 1841, and 5 in 1851. Among the longer lived were those of Ann Giles and her sisters (1826–61), a girls' boarding school on the south side of Church Street, George Wallace or Wallis (1826–41), a boys' boarding school in Paradise Row, Mary Ann Sparshatt (1834–61), a day school, and Sarah Norville, who had a school in Albion Road in 1848,[14] and later in High Houses in Church Street (1851–72).

Notable among the Church Street schools was the Quaker boarding school for girls which opened in 1824 in the newer part of Fleetwood House with Susannah Corder as headmistress. In addition to the usual subjects, it offered astronomy, physics, and 'experimental philosophical chemistry', probably under William Allen, who supported and gave classes at the school. Ugo Foscolo, the poet, was engaged by Allen to give Italian lessons.[15] By 1838 Susannah Corder (d. 1864) had ceased to be headmistress and the school was no longer at Fleetwood House. It has been identified with the school of Sarah Sweetapple, on the south side of Church Street, which in 1841 housed 2 teachers and 12 girls;[16] it had closed by 1848.[17] The Quakers in their stiff cardboard bonnets 'were the sport of the young ladies of a rival non-Quaker establishment next door',[18] a school in the other half of Fleetwood House run by Mrs. Greaves and her daughters in 1826–7. By 1834 it had become a preparatory school under Mrs. Mercy. It had closed by 1838, probably, like the Quaker school, after the loss of its extensive garden to Abney Park cemetery.[19]

A house on the north side of Church Street, east of Edward's Lane and occupied by the Independent minister until 1801, was leased from 1806 by the Revd. John Bransby, lecturer at the parish church 1814–25,[20] who was running

[93] Ibid. ED 7/84.
[94] *Schs. under Admin. of Bd. 1901–2* [Cd. 1277], H.C. p. 399 (1902), lxxix.
[95] L.C.C. *Educ. Svce. Inf.* (1955), 83; *Educ. Authorities Dir.* (1956–7), 362; (1965).
[96] Inf. from Hackney college (1982).
[97] For details, see *V.C.H. Mdx.* i. 249.
[98] Vestry mins. 1681–1743, 8.
[99] *V.C.H. Mdx.* i. 252.
[1] Possibly the par. sch.: vestry mins. 1681–1743, 152; Robinson, *Stoke Newington*, 146.
[2] Vestry mins. 1681–1743, 275, 298; M.L.R. 1775/7/320.
[3] J.W. Ashley Smith, *Birth of Modern Educ.: Contribution of Dissenting Academies, 1660–1800* (1954), 193–4.
[4] *V.C.H. Mdx.* i. 248; cuttings of Stoke Newington 1722–1895, p. 40, newspaper cutting 1768 (S.N.L. 80, LC 2411); A.J. Shirren, *Sam. Rogers* (booklet 1963).
[5] *D.N.B.*
[6] A. Heal, *Eng. Writing Masters*, 102; cf. Guide for assessors of par. 1781–2.
[7] Shirren, *Chrons. of Fleetwood Ho.* 150–1; Lysons, *Environs*, iii. 299.
[8] Ref. bk. to Wadmore map (1813).
[9] Robinson, *Stoke Newington*, 82, gives Jos. Graves as the

occupier *c.* 1820. Mrs. Greaves occupied the house in 1827: Marcham, Digest, pt. 3. Mrs. and Miss Greaves ran a girls' boarding sch. in Church Street in 1828: *Boarding Sch. Lond. Masters' Dir.* (1828), 14.
[10] Vestry mins. 1784–1819, 165 sqq.
[11] Abstract of Ct. Rolls 1763–1801, 209; 1802–31, 309; 1832–82, 381.
[12] Marcham, Digest, pt. 1.
[13] Rest of section based on *Dirs.*; *Boarding Sch. Lond. Masters' Dir.* (1828); P.R.O., HO 107/669/4,5; HO 107/1503/11; ibid. RG 9/152; F. S. de Carteret-Bisson, *Our Schs. and Colls.* (1879, 1884).
[14] Tithe (1848), no. 633.
[15] Proposal to est. sch. 1824 (Friends' libr., Euston Rd., vol. K/6a); Shirren, *Chrons. of Fleetwood Ho.* 152, 157, 161, 164.
[16] P.R.O., HO 107/669/4, f. 16; Beck, *Church Street*, 18. There may have been a gap between the closure of Corder's sch. and the opening of Sweetapple's since neither was listed in 1838. [17] Tithe (1848).
[18] B. Marshall, *Emma Marshall* (1900), 12.
[19] Above, other est. (Fleetwood Ho.).
[20] Acct. of Bransby's sch. based on *Athenaeum*, May 1916, 221–2; June 1916, 294 (S.N.L. 78, LC 2958); Robinson, *Stoke Newington*, 216–17, 289.

Manor House boarding school there by 1813.[21] Edgar Allan Poe, a pupil from 1817 to 1820, described a school and master named Dr. Bransby in *William Wilson*, but with little resemblance to the Stoke Newington school or its master[22] who moved to Norfolk in 1825. The school was probably continued by Philip Theobald (? d. 1838),[23] who ran a gentlemen's boarding school in Church Street in 1826 and 1834. In 1841 Manor House school had 25 boarders under the Revd. G. Pike,[24] a dissenting minister, who was in charge by 1838. By 1845 John Dodd had taken over the school, which in 1851 housed 22 girls and was probably run by his wife Sarah, who had a boarding school with 21 girls in Church Row in 1841. Sarah and later her daughter Sarah Dodd continued the school until it was demolished in 1880.[25]

Schools were also numerous along the London road. George Hodgson (d. 1814), minister of Abney chapel, had a school in High Street after he moved from Church Street in 1801.[26] There were two girls' boarding schools in Nelson Terrace at the Kingsland end of the road in 1828 and Stoke Newington college in High Street in 1829.[27] Prospect House in Stoke Newington Road was a boys' school 1826–40,[28] initially under Benjamin Clements, and Minerva House on Stamford Hill a classical and commercial school under James Clements 1835–40. Among the longer lived were a girls' school on Stamford Hill kept by Mrs. and Miss Hornblower 1834–60 and a preparatory school kept by Jane Nias in Nelson Terrace 1834–51. There were 11 schools in 1834, 6 in 1841, and 5 in 1860, but most were very shortlived and, in spite of pretentious names like Nelson Terrace academy (1838–45) or Stamford Hill ladies' college (1860),[29] were probably mostly small dame schools.

There were a few schools at Newington Green, such as that kept by Thomas Rees, minister of the Unitarian chapel, for 20–30 boys, including foreigners, *c.* 1810[30] and College House (1821). A boys' school in Edward's Lane was kept by William Brown 1838–51 and one in Green Lanes by Richard Abbatt 1848–61 but very few of the schools listed in 1834 or 1851 were outside Church Street and the London road. As building spread from the 1870s, schools were dispersed, and even in Church Street, their main centre throughout the 19th century, the number declined. Only two of the 13 adventure schools listed in 1871 were in Church Street and they were held in rooms over shops. Most of those schools, which charged less than 9*d.* a week, were small dame schools founded in the 1860s and considered inadequate by the government inspectors.[31]

Schools in Church Street in the later part of the 19th century included a girls' school at no. 3 Church Row, later called Church House, run by the Misses Turner and Evans (1860) and by Amelia Oakshott 1872–84. In 1864 Stoke Newington Ladies college, which had been housed in no. 191 High Street, probably as Stamford Hill Ladies college, moved to Paradise Row but closed after a few years.[32] In 1864 Thomas Burgess Barker, chaplain of Abney Park cemetery, was lessee of Abney House[33] at no. 36 (later no. 106), on the north side of Church Street where with George Ingram he opened a boys' boarding school in 1869. Ingram (d. 1878) moved to no. 91 on the south side *c.* 1877, where in 1878 he built a schoolroom in the garden for 120 boys.[34] His widow continued the school, which survived in 1885 but had closed by 1890. Caroline Mess taught girls at no. 4 Church Row in 1872 and at Frankfort House, no. 176 Church Street, in 1884. Ivy House in Paradise Row housed a girls' school under Mrs. Soundy 1872–6 and St. John's college for girls under Miss M. Farmer 1900–1. Paradise House, also called Modern school, in Paradise Row 1879–1929, was a boys' day and boarding school which had opened in Redesdale House, Lordship Park, in 1876.[35]

In 1872 there were adjacent boys' schools at nos. 127 and 129 Stoke Newington Road. R. V. Chilcott had one and the other, Gordon House, housed a commercial college under Crawford Duncan, who had had a school at Oak Lodge in the same road in 1861. By 1876 Mrs. Anne Duncan's ladies' college had replaced Chilcott's school. The commercial college, a day and boarding school, was still there in 1879 and the girls' boarding school in 1884. Other schools included a girls' school at no. 4 Aden Grove 1872–88, a preparatory boys' school in South House in Albion Road 1877–88, run by E. Dean Jones,[36] whose Middle Class school was opened at Mildmay Park in Islington in 1870, and St. John's college, a primary and secondary day and boarding school for boys in Green Lanes, founded in 1881 and surviving in 1938.[37] Stoke Newington Grammar school was founded in 1886 to provide a mainly commercial education for 120 boys at nos. 6 and 8 Manor Road.[38] It closed in 1925. Servite Sisters ran a Roman Catholic High school at no. 114 Lordship Road 1900–10.

There were 25 private schools in Stoke Newington in 1872 and 22 in 1882 but by *c.* 1900 many of the larger houses, which had once

---

[21] Ref. bk. to Wadmore map (1813), no. 90.

[22] *Edgar Allan Poe Centenary 1849–1949*, 51, 53–8 and illus.; plan of sch. (S.N.L. illus. 49.1, LC 1247).

[23] Marcham, Digest, pt. 1.

[24] E. J. Greenberg, 'Contribution made by private academies in first half of 19th cent. to modern curriculums and methods' (Lond. Univ. M.A. thesis, 1953), 214.

[25] Newspaper cutting 1880 (S.N.L. cuttings 49.2).

[26] Robinson, *Stoke Newington*, 216–17.

[27] *Cruchley's New Plan* (1829).

[28] Cf. newspaper cutting 1829 in 'Cuttings of Stoke Newington 1722–1895', p. 6f. (S.N.L. 80, LC 2411).

[29] Probably ho. next dispensary, described in 1864 as 'lately used as a ladies' college': P.R.O., C 54/16264, no. 8.

[30] E. G. Geijer, *Impressions of Eng. 1809–10* (1932), 111, 114.

[31] P.R.O., ED 3/5.

[32] Abstract of Ct. Rolls 1832–82, 393; letter by dau. of Thos. Jackson, 1924 (S.N.L. letters 78 JACKSON).

[33] Not 'the' Abney Ho.

[34] F. B. Harvey, 'Abney Ho. sch.' (MS. 1939, S.N.L. 49.1, LC 3159; G.L.R.O., MBW 1675/151, no. 23; T. B. Barker, *Abney Pk. Cem.* (1869) (S.N.L. 80, LC 2351); Marcham, Digest, pt. 3.

[35] W. Shepherd, 'Paradise Row *c.* 1914' (TS. 1976, S.N.L. cuttings 49.2, LC 3348); *The Paradisian* (sch. mag. 1901–21, S.N.L. 49.2, LC 1297).

[36] G.L.R.O., MBW 1667/143, no. 21; Baxter, 'Rectors, lecturers etc.', s.v. Blackmore.

[37] Stoke Newington, *Official Guide* [1917], 44; [1931], 38; [1938], 63.

[38] *Prospectus* (S.N.L. cuttings 49.2, LC 2215).

housed schools, were being divided into flats, or industry was growing nearby. Throughout the 20th century the middle classes left the district and boarding schools moved farther out. In 1929 the Jewish Secondary School Movement opened a secondary school for boys in Alexandra Villas, Finsbury Park. By 1940 the headquarters of the movement was at no. 86 Amhurst Park and the school, called Avigdor House, was at no. 93, both just outside Stoke Newington. The school, evacuated during the war, reopened in 1947 in Stoke Newington.[39] By 1964 the only private schools were Jewish talmud torah schools, at no. 17 Stamford Hill and no. 114 Bethune Road respectively.

CHARITIES FOR THE POOR.[40] Margaret Jekyll of Newington Green, by will proved 1548, devised a rent charge of 10s. a year for the poor of Stoke Newington but there is no evidence that it was paid.[41] By will proved 1626 Sir William Terry devised the reversion of houses in Old Fish Street to the Drapers' Company of London to distribute £2 12s. a week in bread to the poor of several parishes, including Stoke Newington. Litigation by the company in 1634 and 1644 failed to secure the property and the charity was apparently never put into effect.[42]

Most charities were regulated by the vestry, which appointed a committee to examine them in 1740.[43] Other committees reported in 1764 and 1824.[44] The gross income from the parish charities, including the Palatine estate,[45] averaged £94 a year between 1818 and 1837.[46] In 1867 it totalled £507, of which £102 10s. 8d. was distributed in kind, £26 4s. 2d. in money, and the rest to the church and education. By 1893 it was £1,066. In 1896 the vestry unsuccessfully tried to take over the administration of the non-ecclesiastical charities from the churchwardens and rector, who declared that the charities were administered without inquiry as to the recipient's denomination.[47] In 1897 the eleemosynary charities were divided into two groups, those for bread or coal and the poor fund. By a Scheme of 1901 the right to nominate trustees for Stock's and Sanford's charities passed to Stoke Newington B.C.[48] and in 1904 the educational provisions of Green's, Bowles's and Stock's charities were separated from the eleemosynary provisions.[49] A Scheme of 1965 regulated most of the charities.

Distributive charities. By will proved 1639 William Stephens left £10 for stock for the poor and a rent charge of £5 on copyhold in South Hornsey, to be distributed by the rector and churchwardens at Christmas.[50] The £5 was distributed in payments to individuals in 1702[51] and as £3 in money and £2 in bread in 1775, when it was ordered that the clerk, sexton, and beadle should have no part of it.[52] The £5 was wholly distributed in bread by 1826 and until 1897 or later but was spent on coal in 1909. In 1965 it was represented by £200 stock.[53] In 1740 the vestry committee, finding that the £10 had not been applied, resolved that 10s. a year should be distributed in bread on St. Stephen's day. The 10s. was being paid in 1764 but had ceased by 1795 and in 1826 £10 was invested in consols.[54] By 1840 the dividend, together with that from John Stevens's charity, amounted to 14s., which was distributed in bread. The dividend fell to 13s. in 1897 and 12s. in 1909. In 1965 the charity was represented by £24 stock.

Thomas Stock, by will proved 1664, gave four houses in Church Street, next to the Three Crowns, to the churchwardens and four 'ancients' chosen by the vestry to apply the rents from two houses to the poor, from one to the school, and from one towards bringing water from the New River down the street.[55] In 1778 three of the houses were let for £20 a year[56] and in 1779 and 1793 one was occupied rent free by poor widows.[57] In 1799 the four houses were let together for £22 a year, of which £7 6s. 8d. was paid to the charity school and the rest to the churchwardens' general account. When the lease expired in 1820 the parish decided to pull the houses down. It purchased a fifth house that had been built by Stock as part of the group, enfranchised the land at a cost of £245, and leased four new houses on the site at £6 a year, paid into the churchwardens' account. In 1826, at the suggestion of the Charity Commissioners, the vestry decided to apply £1 1s. 4d. to the poor, 10s. 8d. to the school, and the balance as interest on the £245. From 1834 until the abolition of church rates in 1868 the balance was added to the church rates and from 1868 to 1887 it was used for church expenses. New leases in 1884 raised the income to £120, of which the parish took one fifth and the charity four fifths. A Scheme of 1901 transferred their nomination of the trustees to the borough council[58] and another in 1904 regulated the income. By that date the property had been sold

[39] *Jewish Year Bk.* (1930 and later edns.); above, list (Avigdor).

[40] Section based on *16th Rep. Com. Char.* H.C. 22, pp. 262 sqq. (1826–7), ix; *Digest Endowed Chars. Mdx.* H.C. 433, pp. 42 sqq. (1867–8), lii (1); *Endowed Chars. County of Lond.* H.C. 128, pp. 9 sqq. (1897), lxvi (1); *Rep. of Cttee. on Chars.* 1873 (S.N.L. 41.1, LC 1295); G.L.R.O., CL/LOC/1/70 (L.C.C. Local Govt. Cttee. adjustment of boundary of Stoke Newington and S. Hornsey). Figures for 1840 and 1909 from Stoke Newington chwdns. accts. 1840–1 (HA P/M/CW/1) and *Chwdns. accts. 1876–1910* (HA P/M/CW/3), for 1965 from Char. Com. reg. 251523.

[41] P.R.O., PROB 11/32 (P.C.C. 26 Populwell).

[42] Ibid. 150 (P.C.C. 139 Hele); C 8/71/14; *32nd Rep. Com. Char.* H.C. 140, p. 439 (1837–8), xxvi (2).

[43] Draft Index to par. ledger 1, s.v. benefactions.

[44] Vestry mins. 1819–38, 92–99.

[45] Above, other est.

[46] L.C.C. *Lond. Statistics,* xvi (1905–6), 63.

[47] *The Times,* 14 July 1896, 11c.

[48] Char. Com. reg. 251520.

[49] Ibid. 251523; *Char. Com. Scheme* (1904) (S.N.L. cuttings 41.106, LC 2257).

[50] Vestry mins. 1681–1743, loose leaves at front [1674].

[51] Ibid. 80.

[52] Draft Index to par. ledger 1, s.v. alms.

[53] Char. Com. reg. 251523.

[54] *Hist. of Parochial Chars. of Hackney and Stoke Newington,* 1856 (S.N.L. 41.1, LC 1313).

[55] If the New River had been completed within three years, the rent from the fourth ho. was to be used to keep all the hos. in repair: vestry mins. 1681–1743, loose leaves at front [1674].

[56] G.L.R.O., Acc. 213/4.

[57] Draft Index to par. ledger, s.v. almshos.; *Table of Several Estates, Donations and Benefactions* (1793) (S.N.L. 41.1, LC 3113).

[58] Char. Com. reg. 251520.

and the proceeds invested in £5,510 stock, of which one fifth was allocated to church purposes, a quarter of the residue (after payment for enfranchisement) to Stock's education foundation, and the rest to Stock's eleemosynary charity.[59] In 1909 the income for the latter was £97, of which £2 9s. 6d. was spent on meat, £1 19s. 1d. on bread, £10 13s. on coal, and the rest paid to the rector and churchwardens for the poor. In 1966 it was £113, distributed with Sanford's charity.[60]

By will proved 1704 the rector, Sidrach Simpson, left a rent charge of £2 10s. for bread for the poor. Bread was still being dispensed in 1909–10.

Elizabeth Baker, widow, by will proved 1716 bequeathed £50 to the churchwardens to apply the interest in weekly bread for six widows. The vestry decided to take the £50 for church building but undertook to distribute the bread.[61] No bread had been provided for some time before 1826 when the vestry, at the request of the Charity Commissioners, resolved that £2 10s. should be distributed each year according to the will. It was still being paid in 1909 from the church account. In 1965 the charity was represented by £102 stock.

By will proved 1740 John Stevens, a London stationer, left the interest on £10 to the churchwardens for bread for the poor at Christmas.[62] In 1740 the charities of William Stephens and John Stevens, each with £10 endowment, were confused and only one payment of 10s. in bread on St. Stephen's day was being made. By the late 18th century nothing was paid for either charity and in 1826 the vestry invested £10 for each charity in stock, creating a joint charity.[63]

By will proved 1764 George Green left a £1 rent charge to be distributed in bread besides £100 to produce £2 10s. a year for the charity school and the rest for the poor. Payment of the £1 was in dispute by 1779[64] and ceased after 1798. For most of the 19th century the dividend was £3, of which 10s. was distributed in bread. Green's education foundation was constituted in 1904[65] and in 1909 the whole dividend, then £2 10s., was paid to the school. In 1965 the £1 charity was revived as Green's eleemosynary charity, represented by £50 stock.

Sarah Bowles, widow, by will proved 1788 bequeathed £250 stock to the minister and churchwardens to distribute the dividend as follows: £4 4s. to the charity schools of Stoke Newington and Shoreditch, £2 12s. in bread to six people at church each Sunday, and 14s. to purchase yarn stockings for the poor at Christmas. The distribution of stockings had ceased by 1873 when £3 2s. 4d. was spent on bread. The total dividend had shrunk to £6 17s. by 1893 and to £6 5s. by 1910. Bowles's education foundation was constituted in 1904, leaving to Bowles's eleemosynary charity £110 of the £250 endowment in 1965.

By will dated 1802 Ann, widow of Henry Sanford of Stamford Hill, left part of the residue of her personal estate to be invested by the minister and churchwardens. From the dividends on £2,364 stock, £25 a year was to be given to five widows and the rest distributed to the industrious poor. In 1826 the dividends amounted to nearly £71 and the balance was distributed in blankets, flannel, and stockings. By 1873 it was spent on flannel, two thirds for St. Mary's, two ninths for St. Matthias's, and one ninth for St. Mark's, Dalston. Later it was spent on meat, £41 12s. being distributed in 3s. meat tickets in 1897, and £37 18s. 6d. in 1909. By a Scheme of 1901 the trustees were nominated by the borough council and in 1967 the £25 was still distributed to five widows and the income from £400 was used to purchase meat.[66]

John Field, collar maker of Stamford Hill, bequeathed £1,000 stock by will proved 1828 to the 'vicar' and churchwardens for bread and coal for the poor. The dividend, £30 in 1840 and 1867, was £25 in 1909 when £23 10s. was spent on coal and £1 10s. on bread. In 1965 the income was still £25 a year. John Field's son Henry, also a collar maker of Stamford Hill, by will proved 1836 left £250 stock for the same purpose. The dividend was £8 15s. in 1840, and £6 5s. in 1909 and 1965.

Mrs. Gantley's Gift was created by the will, proved 1881, of Mary Ann Gantley of no. 34 Park Street, who bequeathed the residue of her estate to provide widows' annuities. The residue amounted only to £8 10s.,[67] which produced 4s. 8d. in 1897, and 4s. in 1965.

By will proved 1882 the Revd. Augustus Clissold gave the income from £100 stock for the poor. In 1883 the vestry decided to use the dividend, £3 10s. in 1897 and 1909 and £3 in 1965, for four old women.[68]

In 1900, 1904, and 1912 William Eve and his wife founded a charity to apply a £20 rent charge in £5 annuities for four widows in Stoke Newington. As William and Caroline H. Eve's charity for aged persons, it was governed by a Scheme of 1964. The income was still £20 a year in 1968.[69]

The Sir Herbert Ormond Trust was founded in 1938 as a memorial to the former mayor. The dividends from £500 stock were applied in 10s. grocery and meat tickets for the aged poor. Under a Scheme of 1972, the income of approximately £15 was applied in gifts of money or kind to persons over 60.[70]

By will proved 1948 John Cooper left £1,000 for five poor of the borough. The income, £65 in 1967 and £50 in 1975, was distributed in lump sums.[71]

The Samuel Fisher Charitable Trust was set up in 1954 to help deserving cases in Stoke Newington. In 1962 there was £40 a year income from £1,140 stock.[72]

[59] *Char. Com. Scheme* (1904).
[60] Char. Com. reg. 251520.
[61] Vestry mins. 1681–1743, 196.
[62] Lysons, *Environs*, iii. 286, 304.   [63] Above.
[64] Draft Index to par. ledger 1, s.v. bread for poor, Green.
[65] Char. Com. reg. 251523.

[66] Ibid. 251519.
[67] Vestry mins. 1862–89, 416.   [68] Ibid. 463.
[69] Char. Com. reg. 256265–7; Stoke Newington, *Official Guide* (1950), 82.
[70] Char. Com. reg. 256264; Stoke Newington, *Official Guide* (1950), 82.
[71] Char. Com. reg. 251210.   [72] Ibid. 206382.

Stoke Newington Charities for the Poor. The eleemosynary portions of the charities of Stephens, Baker, Stevens, Green, Bowles, the Fields, Gantley and Clissold were regulated in 1965. The income from Baker's and Gantley's charities was to be for widows, and from the rest for bedding, clothing, food, fuel, furniture, weekly payments of up to 15s., gifts for the sick, assistance for those entering a trade, or subscriptions for almshouses or homes.[73]

[73] Ibid. 251523.

INDEX

NOTE. An italic page number denotes a map or coat of arms on that page. A page number preceded by the letters *pl.* refers to one of the plates between pages 124 and 125.

Some of the sub-entries (e.g. 'pub. hos.') under Islington and Stoke Newington relate to less than the whole of each ancient parish, and similar sub-entries under the names of parts of the parishes (e.g. Barnsbury) provide additional references.

CORRIGENDA

CORRIGENDA TO VOLUMES V, VI, AND VII

Earlier lists of corrigenda will be found in Volumes I and III–VII

Vol. V, page 85*a*, line 18, *delete* ', a master at Harrow school,'
85*a*, line 19, *for* 'curate' *read* 'vicar'
91*a*, line 2 from end, *for* 'took over the working of' *read* 'absorbed'
91*b*, line 4, *after* 'closed' *add* 'to passengers'
180*b*, line 8 from end, for 'Islington' *read* 'Westm.'
193*b*, line 14, *delete* '(Islington)'
347*b*, lines 20–1, *delete* 'the Bearsted . . . cases.'
396*a*, *insert* 'Glasshouse Yard, nonconf., 193'
401*b*, s.v. Islington, *delete* 'nonconf., 193' *and* 'Western Synagogue, 180'
420*b*, s.v. Westminster, *insert* 'Western Synagogue, 180'

Vol. VI, page 175*b*, line 13 from end, *for* 'Thomas' *read* 'John'
218*a*, s.v. Jackson, *insert* 'John, vicar of St. Jas., Muswell Hill, bp. of Lond., 175' *and delete final sub-entry*
226*b*, s.v. Wollaston, Sir John, *add* ', 203–4'

Vol. VII, page x, line 8, *for* 'Goldsmith's' *read* 'Goldsmiths''
2*a*, line 4, *for* 'District and Piccadilly railway lines' *read* 'L.S.W.R. line'
6*a*, line 25, *for* 'until' *read* 'from'
6*a*, line 18 from end, *for* 'the first' *read* 'first'
6*b*, line 26, *for* 'a joint' *read* 'an'
7*a*, line 18, *for* '1963' *read* '1933'
16*a*, line 23, *for* 'Bydone' *read* 'Brydone'
18*a*, line 2 from end, *for* 'Walter' *read* 'William'
38*b*, lines 1–5, *delete* 'sanctuary . . . Danish' *and substitute* 'apsidal sanctuary flanked by NE. vestry, SE. unfinished chapel; aisled and clerestoried nave; unfinished NW., SW. towers. 19th-cent. plaques, given by George V and Queen Mary, from Sandringham'
38*b*, line 6, *for* 'forty' *read* 'forty-five'
73*a*, line 22, *for* 'Westminister' *read* 'Westminster'
118*a*, line 5 from end, *for* '1905' *read* '1901'
139*b*, line 25, *for* 'Filbert' *read* 'Gilbert'
140*a*, line 10 from end, *for* 'Dickenson' *read* 'Dickinson'
181*a*, line 35, *for* '1965' *read* '1911'
181*a*, line 18 from end, *for* 'M. & S.W.J.' *read* 'N. & S.W.J.'
181*a*, lines 12–11 from end, *for* 'Hampstead' *read* 'Finchley Road'
187*b*, line 6 from end, *for* 'masked' *read* 'marked'
195, headline, *for* 'WILLESDON' *read* 'WILLESDEN'
197*a*, lines 8–9, *delete* 'and trams'
202*a*, line 10, *for* 'Metropolitan' *read* 'North London'
203*b*, line 27, *delete whole line*
257*a*, s.v. architects, *for* 'Wallis, Filbert' *read* 'Wallis, Gilbert'
262*b*, *for* 'Dickenson Rob' *read* 'Dickinson Rob'
269*a*, s.v. 'London Transport', *delete* '203,'
269*a*, *for* 'Lowe & Bydone' *read* 'Lowe & Brydone'
276*c*, s.v. Wallis, *for* 'Filbert' *read* 'Gilbert'
278*b*, s.v. Willett, *for* 'Wal.' *read* 'Wm.'
280, last line, *for* '221*a*' *read* '221*c*'